Francois Viljoen

The Torah in Matthew

Theology in Africa

edited by

Prof. Dr. Jan van der Watt
Facultaire Unie Filosofie, Theologie
en Religiewetenschappen,
Radboud Universiteit Nijmegen

Volume 9

LIT

Francois Viljoen

The Torah in Matthew

LIT

This book is printed on acid-free paper.

Bibliographic information published by the Deutsche Nationalbibliothek
The Deutsche Nationalbibliothek lists this publication in the Deutsche Nationalbibliografie; detailed bibliographic data are available on the Internet at http://dnb.d-nb.de.

ISBN 978-3-643-91019-6

A catalogue record for this book is available from the British Library

© LIT VERLAG GmbH & Co. KG Wien,
Zweigniederlassung Zürich 2018
Klosbachstr. 107
CH-8032 Zürich
Tel. +41 (0) 44-251 75 05
E-Mail: zuerich@lit-verlag.ch   http://www.lit-verlag.ch
Distribution:
In the UK: Global Book Marketing, e-mail: mo@centralbooks.com
In North America: International Specialized Book Services, e-mail: orders@isbs.com
In Germany: LIT Verlag Fresnostr. 2, D-48159 Münster
Tel. +49 (0) 2 51-620 32 22, Fax +49 (0) 2 51-922 60 99, e-mail: vertrieb@lit-verlag.de
e-books are available at www.litwebshop.de

TABLE OF CONTENTS

Acknowledgement vi

CHAPTER 1 INTRODUCTION 1

CHAPTER 2 THE TORAH IN THE RELIGIOUS WORLD OF MATTHEW 35

CHAPTER 3 THE FOUNDATIONAL STATEMENT IN MATTHEW 5:17-20 ON THE
CONTINUING VALIDITY OF THE *TORAH* 68

CHAPTER 4 ΔΙΚΑΙΟΣΎΝΗ AND IDENTITY FORMATION IN MATTHEW 93

CHAPTER 5 JESUS' *HALAKHIC* ARGUMENTATION ON THE TRUE INTENTION
OF THE LAW IN MATTHEW 5:21-48 132

CHAPTER 6 JESUS HEALING THE LEPER AND THE PURITY LAW IN THE
GOSPEL OF MATTHEW 170

CHAPTER 7 HOSEA 6:6 IN TWO SCENES OF CONFLICT AND IDENTITY
FORMATION IN MATTHEW 190

CHAPTER 8 THE LAW AND PURITY IN MATTHEW: JESUS TOUCHING A
BLEEDING WOMAN AND A DEAD GIRL 240

CHAPTER 9 EXTERNAL CULTIC TRADITION AND INTERNAL ETHICAL PURITY
IN MATTHEW 15 263

CHAPTER 10 THE DOUBLE LOVE COMMANDMENT 293

CHAPTER 11 TO OBEY THE WORDS OF TEACHERS OF THE LAW AND
PHARISEES, BUT NOT TO DO WHAT THEY DO (MATT. 23:3) 317

CHAPTER 12 CONCLUSION 348

LIST OF REFERENCES 372

FIGURES

Figure 1: Symbolic religious spaces ... 175

Figure 2: The interaction between the leper and Jesus in Matt. 8:2-3 ... 186

Figure 3: The intercalation of the stories of Jesus' healing the dead girl and the woman with blood flow in Matt. 9:18-26 ... 255

Figure 4: The interaction between the woman with blood flow and Jesus in Matt. 9:20-22 ... 257

Figure 5: The double love commandment for the Matthean community ... 312

TABLES

Table 1: Identity markers in Matthew 58

Table 2: Thematic connectedness of the statements in Matt. 5:17-20 76

Table 3: Parallels between Matt. 5:17-18 and Luk. 16:17 on the continuing validity of the Law. 77

Table 4: Parallelism of the opening statement in Matt. 5:17 77

Table 5: Structure of the statement in Matt. 5:18 81

Table 6: The antithetical parallelism of the statement in Matt. 5:19 85

Table 7: The emphatic pronouncement of Matt. 5:20 88

Table 8: The *inclusio* formed by the use of δικαιοσύνη in Matthew 94

Table 9: The parallel of the story in Matt. 3:13–17 with Mark 1:9 and Luk. 3:21a on the baptism of Jesus 106

Table 10: Composition of the Sermon on the Mount in terms of classical rhetorical speech 112

Table 11: The parallel of the beatitude on hunger in Matt. 5:6 and Luk. 6:21a 116

Table 12: The triadic composition of the introductory formulas of the antitheses in Matt. 5:21-47 139

Table 13: The antithetical argument in Matt. 5:21-26 143

Table 14: Anger and offences in Matt. 5:22 143

Table 15: The parallel between Matt. 5:25-26 and Luk. 12:58-59 145

Table 16: The antithetical argument on adultery in Matt. 5:27-30 146

Table 17: The antithetical statement on lust in Matt. 5:28 147

Table 18: Two proverbial solutions to avoid adultery in Matt. 5:29-30 148

Table 19: The parallel between the statements in Matt. 5:29-30 and Mark 9:43-48 149

Table 20: The antithetical argument on divorce in Matt. 5:31-32 150

Table 21: The antithetical argument on oaths in Matt. 5:33-37 153

Table 22: Three classes of valid and invalid oaths in Matt. 5:34b-35 156

Table 23: A fourth form of oath-taking rejected in Matt. 5:36 156

Table 24: The antithetical argument on retaliation in Matt. 5:38-42 158

Table 25: Three specific examples on how not to resist evil persons in Matt. 5:39b-41 159

Table 26: The parallel between Matt. 5:39b-42 and Luk. 6:29-30 on avoiding retaliation 160

Table 27: The antithetical argument on love for enemies in Matt. 5:43-47 162

Table 28: The parallel between Matt. 5:44 and Luk. 6:27-28 on loving one's enemies 163

Table 29: Two conditional clauses of the love that Jesus commands in Matt. 5:46-47 165

Table 30: The parallel between Matt. 5:46-47 and Luk.6:32-34 on Jesus' alternative command for love 166

Table 31: The parallel between Matt. 5:48 and Luk. 6:36 on being perfect and merciful 167

Table 32: The summaries and composition of miracle stories in Matthew 178

Table 33: Miracle and discipleship sections of Matthew's healing narrative 179

Table 34: The parallel of Matt 8:1-4 with Mark 1:40-45 and Luk. 5:12-16 on the story of the healing of the leper 182

Table 35: The comparison between Matthew, MTT and LXX on God's desire of mercy 193

Table 36: What God desires and what He despises in Hos. 6:6 195

Table 37: Miracle and discipleship sets in Matthew's miracle block 198

Table 38: The parallel of Matt. 9:9-12 with Mark 2:13-17 and Luk.5:27-32 on the story of Jesus eating with tax collectors and sinners 200

Table 39: Jesus' threefold response to the Pharisees' objection against Him eating with tax collectors and sinners in Matt. 9:12-13 205

Table 40: The parallel of Matt. 12:1-8 with Mark 2:23-28 and Luk. 6:1-5 on of the story of grain harvesting on the Sabbath 221

Table 41: The parallel of the story in Matt. 12:9-14 with Mark 3:1-6 and Luk. 6:6-11 on Jesus healing a man with a withered hand on the Sabbath 233

Table 42: The parallel of Matt. 9:18-26 with Mark 5:21-43 and Luk. 8:46-50 on the stories of Jesus' healing of the woman with blood flow and the dead girl 252

Table 43: The structure of the narrative of Jesus' healing of the dead girl in Matt. 9:18-25 261

Table 44: The composition of the narrative on the hand-washing dispute in Matt. 15:1-20 and its parallel Mark 7:1-23 269

Table 45: The structure of the narrative on hand-washing in Matt. 15:1-9 271

Table 46: The challenge of the Pharisees and the scribes in Matt. 15:1-2 273

Table 48: Two reasons for the Pharisees being called hypocrites in Matt. 15:7 281

Table 49: The basis of Jesus' argument in Matt. 15:10-11 283

Table 50: Jesus' response in Matt. 15:17-18 on the charge of the Pharisees' and teachers of the Law....287

Table 51: Composition of the narrative on the greatest commandment in Matt. 22:24-40 294

Table 52: The parallel between Matt. 22:34-40 and Mark 12:28-34 on the greatest commandment........296

Table 53: Synoptic comparison of the faculties involved when loving according God's commandment..........304

Table 54: The parallel between the love commandments in Matt. 22:37-38 309

Table 55: Broad outline of Matt. 21-25 320

Table 56: Matthew's elaboration on Mark's polemic..........328

Table 57: Jesus' twofold criticism of the religious leaders 330

Table 58: Jesus' indictment of the religious leaders illustrated with examples 333

Table 59: Contrast in community values of the Pharisees and teachers of the Law, and that of the followers of Jesus..........335

Table 60: Parallels between the seven "woe-sayings" of Luke and Matthew..........340

Table 61: Woes for wrong teaching and conduct 341

Acknowledgement

This book is the reworked and processed form of a study that I had undertaken at Radboud University, Nijmegen. I am particularly grateful towards Prof Dr Jan van der Watt who had created this opportunity and had encouraged me to undertake this research project. His incisive comments and gentle guidance as supervisor has made this study a pleasure and a very rewarding undertaking.

Francois P Viljoen
Professor in New Testament, North-West University, Republic of South Africa

CHAPTER 1

INTRODUCTION

1.1 BACKGROUND AND PROBLEM STATEMENT

1.1.1 Background to the research

Since many years Matthew's treatment of the *Torah* has remained a much debated issue. As early as in the sixteenth century Sebastian Münster labelled Matthew a "new *Torah*", and since then many scholars have reflected on this issue (cf. Lapide, 1984:55). It is apparent that Jesus' relation to the *Torah* forms a significant motif in Matthew's Gospel, much more than any of the other Synoptic Gospels (Loader, 1997:165). This relation is taken up as an important theme in the Sermon on the Mount with its strong Sinai typology (Allison, 1993:137; Floor, 1969:34; Loader, 1997:165), specifically in Matt. 5:17-48, and disputes about the *Torah* are repeated throughout the Gospel (e.g. Matt. 12:1-14; 15:1-9 and 22:34-40). It seems that when reading this Gospel, the central role of the *Torah* must be seriously considered. This role is even further heightened because of the new perspectives on Paul as debated by some scholars (Dunn, 1990; Sanders, 1983b; Wright, 2014). These scholars have challenged the traditional Lutheran and Reformed view that Paul considers Christians' good works not to factor into their salvation, but only their faith. The "new" perspective on Paul proposes that he was only questioning observances such as circumcision, ceremonial and dietary laws, and not good works in general. This heightens the question as to how the Law is treated in the first Gospel.

Furthermore, Matthew is read as a narrative text[1], which provides new insights regarding the characters and events in the narrative (cf. Fokkelman, 2000; Pennington, 2012:160). Jesus functions as the main character and protagonist in

---

[1] As narrative text the Gospel provides a written commentary to convey a story to an intended audience. This implies that the author holds a narrative point of view through which a story is communicated. As narrator the author delivers information to the audience by creating a plot. The plot of the narrative consists of significant events that make up the story, particularly as they relate to one another. In these events, characters are involved. The individual status of a character is defined in terms of its relation with the main and other characters (Prince, 2003:73).

the narrative and is portrayed in almost every scene. His teachings and actions form the focus of attention and the actions of other characters are directed towards Him (Weren, 1994:12). The narrator sides with Jesus without any reservations. In his commentary on the narrated story, he recommends Jesus' values to his readers and urges them to accept these values. Jesus is depicted as the last and greatest expositor of the *Torah*. Davies (1966:102) has written: "Matthew has draped his Lord in the mantle of a teacher of righteousness". The character of the Matthean Jesus is surrounded by other personages in whom readers can mirror themselves (Weren, 1994:12). Jesus is almost always surrounded by his disciples and the crowds. There are also individuals who suffer the pangs of sickness, disease and death. These personages frequently react positively to Jesus' teaching and ministry, and benefit accordingly. Besides these people, there are also the antagonists in the narrative. They are usually identified as the teachers of the Law and the Pharisees. They are opposed to Jesus' teachings and actions. Jesus reacts negatively towards them. The reader is urged to also regard these antagonists as negative characters. In this study this interaction with regard to Jesus and the *Torah* is in view.

This present study is furthermore relevant in the light of new insights that have developed in recent years on the diversity and dynamics within the Judaism that confronted Matthew (cf. Kraft & Nickelsburg, 1986; Neusner, 1972, 1979, 2007). This diversity within Judaism is usually related to Judaist attitudes towards the *Torah*. In current scholarship it is no longer acceptable to speak of clearly distinctive parties that are homogeneous within themselves, such as uniform Sadducees, Pharisees, Essenes or Zealots, nor is it acceptable to make a simple distinction between Palestinian and Diaspora Judaism (Loader, 1997:2). Though the Pentateuchal Law was central to Jewish thinking, different groups made distinctive interpretations of and additions to the *Torah*. However, the differences between their interpretations are not always clear cut. To complicate this, oral traditions were strong and lively. Questions arose about the status of the written Scriptures and oral traditions and the authority ascribed to these (Meier, 2009:32). It seems that the Matthean community developed within this turmoil of developing Judaism (Saldarini, 1994:111) and this seems to be reflected in the text.

1.1.2 Clarification of concepts related to the *Torah*

As this study focusses on the *Torah*, words used to refer to *Torah*-related concepts should be clarified. The intention in this section is to provide a broad overview of how these concepts are used in this study, and not to enter into a detailed scholarly debate about the use of these terms and concepts at this stage.

1.1.2.1 The Torah in the Hebrew Bible

The Hebrew word *Torah* is a term used to denote a wide range of meanings (Brown, 1975:70; Friedman, 1992:605-622; Meier, 2009:26-40). The broad semantic domain for *Torah* refers to the Law of Moses with its provisions as preserved in the Pentateuch (cf. Lindars, 1988). It includes instructions, teachings, directives and alike, transmitted in either oral or written form. This Law is presented as God's will and its demands should be obeyed by his people. The *Torah* forms the basis of Jewish identity. Each individual directive of *Yahweh* is qualified as a *torah* (in the singular) (e.g. Lev. 6:2), and thus He issues various *torot* (e.g. Exod. 18:16). In this sense individual *torot* were pronounced through mediators and eventually the written corpus of *torot* became known as the *Torah* (translated with a capital letter) (Meier, 2009:28). According to the story of Israel's origin, *Yahweh* revealed his *Torah* pre-eminently to Moses on Mount Sinai. The *Torah* of *Yahweh* is subsequently also known as the *Torah of Moses*. In the late Persian Period, perhaps in the fourth century B.C.E, the compilation of the Five Books of Moses, the Pentateuch (πεντάτευχος, "five scrolls"), came to be regarded as the *Torah par excellence* and the most important part of the Jewish Scripture (cf. Brown, 1975:65; Friedman, 1992:605; Koester, 1982:228).

The rabbis continued to reflect the broad spectrum of the *Torah* to include the narratives and legal sections (Meier, 2009:39). It may refer to the Pentateuch as such, but sometimes to the heart of the legal corpus, namely the Decalogue. In some contexts *Torah* is even used to refer to the Jewish Scriptures as a whole to include the Prophets and the Writings (Clines, 2011(8):612-613).

1.1.2.2   The Dual Torah

During the Talmudic era (c.a. 70 C.E. – 500 C.E.) the rabbis developed a doctrine of the *Dual Torah*. Though the doctrine of the *Dual Torah* does not occur in existing Judaic documents of the first centuries B.C.E and C.E, it is reasonable to assume that this concept already evolved in the rabbinic thought. According to this concept, Moses received the oral *Torah* on Mount Sinai alongside the written *Torah* (Porton, 1992a:26). This oral *Torah* was handed down until it was eventually written down in the rabbinic corpus (Meier, 2009:39). The Pharisees used the terms "traditions of the elders" or "traditions of the fathers" to refer to this oral Law. They considered these traditions as normative even though they were not contained in the Mosaic *Torah* as such (Meier, 2009:32).

1.1.2.3 Halakha

The term *halakha* should not be equated with the oral *Torah*. *Halakha* refers to legal opinions or rulings about human conduct by all sorts of Jewish teachers, such as Qumran's Teacher of Righteousness, Rabbi Hillel and Jesus (cf. Brown, 1975:59; Jaffee, 2001:43; Porton, 1992b:26). In rabbinic culture the *halakha*, with its legal discourse, were considered as binding, while the *haggadah* were more imaginative and free wheeling, yet this distinction is not always that clear (Porton, 1992a:19). While the *halakha* tend to enumerate rules and principles with strict adherence to intellectual processes, the *haggadah* expound them with stories and examples from imagination. Cohen (1975:25) has remarked that *halakha* "... stands for the rigid authority of the Law and theory which the *haggadah* illustrate by public opinion and the dicta of common-sense morality". Though the term *halakha* apparently was not used in a technical sense in the first century B.C.E and C.E, the *halakhic* way of argumentation developed prior to 70 C.E. Oral and written supplements to the Law emerged, with a great deal of competing interpretations amongst these rabbis. It is therefore common in scholarship to refer to these legal opinions from the first century as the *halakha* of these teachers (Meier, 2009:40).

1.1.2.4   Νόμος *in the LXX and the Second Testament*

In the LXX *Torah* is translated with νόμος, which in itself also carries a wide range of meanings where the precise denotation depends on its individual context. In the Synoptic Gospels, νόμος refers to the written Pentateuch (Meier, 2009:38). Placed alongside the Prophets (προφῆται) it forms the first of the two parts of the Jewish Scriptures[2]. The νόμος is not reduced to a merely legal or legalistic entity, but retains a breadth of meaning in the Gospels, as in the LXX and Hebrew Bible. In Mark the word νόμος is not used. Instead "Moses" (Μωσῆς) is used to refer to this corpus (Mark 1:44; 7:10; 10:3-4; 12:19, 26). In a similar way "Moses" is used in Matt. 8:4; 19:7-9; 22:24 and in Luke 5:14; 16:29, 31; 20:28, 37; 24:27. In Luke the combination "Moses and the Prophets" (Μωσῆς καὶ οἱ προφῆται) is used three times to refer to the two parts of the Jewish Scriptures (Luk. 16:29; 16:31; 24:27). Amongst the Gospels, only Luke speaks in terms of a tri-part of the Scriptures, "Moses, the Prophets and the Psalms" (Μωσῆς, οἱ προφῆται, αἱ γραφαὶ) (Luk. 24:27).

---

[2] This two part division of the Law and the Prophets occurs ten times in the New Testament: four times in Matthew (5:17; 7:12; 11:13; 22:40), once in Luke (16:16 // Matt. 11:13), once in John (1:45) three times in Acts (13:15; 14:14; 28:23) and once in Paul (Rom. 3:21).

In this study I alternate between the terms *Torah* and "Law", intending the wider sense of the Law that includes the guidance and teaching that God reveals to Israel.

1.1.3 Problem statement

While the Matthean Jesus, the protagonist in the narrative, makes a very strong statement on the continuing validity of the Law (Matt. 5:17-19), He comes into frequent conflict with the antagonists, the then preservers of the Law in the narrative, the Pharisees and teachers of the Law. The antagonists are upset by what they regard as Jesus' and his disciples' negligence and violation of the Law (e.g. Matt. 9:10; 12:2 and 15:2). These preservers of the Law are depicted as people who have strong convictions on how the Law should be preserved. However, the Matthean Jesus criticises their forms of righteousness and piety (e.g. Matt. 5:20; 6:1 and 15:3-9). He instructs them to go and learn the meaning of their Scriptures (Matt. 9:13) and He does not hesitate to call them hypocrites (e.g. Matt. 6:2, 16; 15:7; 23:13, 15, 25, 29). He severely questions their traditions related to the Law (Matt. 15:3-9). He defends his disciples when they pluck grain on the Sabbath and then continues to heal a man with a shrivelled hand (Matt. 12:2, 13). He even claims that someone greater than the temple is here (Matt. 12:6) and that the Son of Man is the Lord of the Sabbath (Matt. 12:8). The Pharisees are so upset about his claims and actions that they plot to kill Jesus (Matt. 12:13). In a *halakhic* argument, Jesus rejects the interpretations of six stipulations of the Law as offered by the rabbis of that time (Matt. 5:21-47) and poses alternatives. In his public ministry it seems as if He contravenes or at least is negligent of purity regulations in his contact with impure people (Matt. 8:3; 9:20, 25). In his final commandment He orders his disciples to teach new disciples to obey everything He has commanded them (Matt. 28:20). It seems as if the Matthean Jesus teaches an alternative interpretation of the *Torah*. The question is therefore how this alternative interpretation should be defined and how it should be interpreted in view of the foundational statement on the continuing validity of the Law (Matt. 5:17-19).

Besides the way the Law functions in the internal narrative world of the Gospel, the text also has a performative impact on its implied audience. Identity formation takes place. The question arises as to what kind of audience would justify such a polemic argument about the *Torah*. It seems that the audience experienced a similar kind of conflict about *Torah* observance. The question can be asked whether this conflict was internal (within their own group) or external (with other groups), or did it comprise elements of both.

Debates about the *Torah* form a significant and continuous thread throughout the plot of the first Gospel, and it seems as if this debate somehow reflects debates in the world external to the text. As such, the specific research question for this study is how the teaching on the *Torah* in the Gospel should be defined in its distinctiveness from the teachings of the opponents in the text, and how this narrative reflects *Torah*-related issues prevalent in the world external to the text.

1.2 AIM AND OBJECTIVES

1.2.1 Aim

In order to address the problem statement and research question, the aim of this research project is to define Matthew's distinctive teaching of the *Torah* as reflected in passages from the first Gospel that either directly or indirectly deal with Jesus and the *Torah*, and to create an understanding of how this teaching relates to the external world of his implied audience and the formation of their identity. The intention is to provide theological refection on Matthew's understanding of the *Torah* based on these investigations.

1.2.2 Objectives

In order to reach this aim, the following objectives are formulated for this research project:

1.2.2.1 The Torah in the religious world of Matthew

The first objective is to postulate broad outlines of the probable religious situation in which the first Gospel originated to create an understanding of the role of the *Torah* within this environment. This would provide a frame of reference for the interpretation of passages where Matthew (directly or indirectly) deals with the *Torah*. This is undertaken in Chapter 2, "The *Torah* in the religious world of Matthew".

This postulation is followed by the investigation of selected passages from the Matthean text where issues regarding the *Torah* are developed. These passages are prominent and seem to provide some insight into Matthew's overall teaching on the *Torah*, though the selection can not be regarded as comprehensive. The intention is to identify issues that might have been prevalent in the religious life of the intended audience by considering the internal world of the narrative.

1.2.2.2 The foundational statement in Matthew 5:17-20 on the continuing validity of the Torah

The first passage that is investigated is the densely formulated statement of Jesus in the Sermon on the Mount about the continuing validity of the *Torah* (Matt. 5:17-19). The objective with this investigation is to establish the significance of this passage within Matthew's overall teaching on the Law. This passage is presented in the form of a legal statement that forms the foundation for Jesus' teachings and actions related to the *Torah*, as well as *Streitgesprächen* He encounters about legal matters. This is done in Chapter 3, entitled "The foundational statement in Matthew 5:17-20 on the continuing validity of the Law".

1.2.2.3 ΔΙΚΑΙΟΣΥΝΗ in Matthew

Matthew's use of the term δικαιοσύνη (righteousness) is subsequently investigated. It seems that δικαιοσύνη is a central term in the Matthean Gospel to describe the behaviour required from the followers of Jesus. The term has a significant concentration in the Sermon on the Mount, but is also used beyond this Sermon to describe the behaviour of Jesus and John the Baptist. It is considered whether this term could be regarded as an identity marker for the Matthean community as a result of the performative function of the text. The issue of the identity formation of the implied audience by way of the text also receives attention. This study is presented in Chapter 4, "Δικαιοσύνη and identity formation in the Matthew".

1.2.2.4 Jesus' halakhic argumentation on the true intention of the Law in Matthew 5:21-48

The Sermon on the Mount includes Jesus' *halakhic* arguments in the form of six "antitheses" about the meaning of the *Torah* (Matt. 5:21-47), which signifies an alternative interpretation of the *Torah*. With an investigation of these antitheses the aim is to identify which understanding or traditions of the Law are denounced and to define Matthew's Jesus' distinctive teachings on each of the commandments at stake. Furthermore, the object is to elucidate the relation between these six antitheses and the foundational statement in Matt. 5:17-19. This investigation is reported in Chapter 5 under the title "Jesus' h*alakhic* argumentation on the true intention of the Law in Matt. 5:21-48".

1.2.2.5 Jesus healing the leper and the purity Law in the Gospel of Matthew

After the Sermon on the Mount, with its strong emphasis on the meaning of the *Torah*, Matthew continues by narrating Jesus' enactment of his teachings. Matthew narrates that just as Jesus had come down the mountain of this sermon, a leper approaches Jesus. Without any hesitation Jesus reaches out to the man and touches him (Matt. 8:1-3). No mention is made of Jesus undergoing purification rites afterwards. The objective is to investigate this interaction between Jesus and the leper in terms of Jewish purity regulations and the role of Jesus as healer. The implications of this narrative about healing and purity requirements for the probable intended audience are established. This study is contained in Chapter 6, entitled "Jesus healing the leper and the purity regulations in the gospel of Matthew".

1.2.2.6 Hosea 6:6 and identity formation in Matthew

It seems that the quoting of Hos. 6:6 ("Ἔλεος θέλω καὶ οὐ θυσίαν - I desire mercy, not sacrifice") plays a significant role in defining Jesus' teaching on the Law in two scenes of conflict with the Pharisees and in forming the identity of the Matthean community. This quotation is striking as it is unique amongst Synoptic parallels, and it is uttered twice in Matthean material (Matt. 9:13 and 12:7). The first time, this quotation is used within the context of Jesus being accused of eating with tax collectors and sinners (Matt. 9:9-12). Such an act demonstrated the crossing of societal barriers in those days. The second occurrence of this quotation appears in Jesus defending his disciples for plucking grain on the Sabbath, after which He continues to heal the man with a shrivelled hand (Matt. 12:1-13). The intention is to establish the significance of this double reference to Hos. 6:6 in the two contexts respectively, and to explore how it impacts on the Matthean Jesus' teaching and enactment of the *Torah*. In order to do this, the implication of table fellowship (Matt. 9:9-12) and the significance of the Sabbath in the Jewish society (Matt. 12:1-13) are investigated. In addition, the formative influence of these two narratives on the implied audience are defined. This is propounded in Chapter 7, which bears the title "Hosea 6:6 in two scenes of conflict and identity formation in Matthew".

1.2.2.7 The Law and purity in Matthew; Jesus touching a bleeding woman and a dead girl

Shortly after the short narrative of Jesus eating with tax collectors and sinners (Matt. 9:9-12), Matthew narrates the double story of Jesus touching a bleeding woman and a dead girl (Matt. 9:18-26). Once again these actions of Jesus have purity implications. Nevertheless, Jesus does not object when the bleeding woman touches Him, and does not hesitate to enter into the room of the dead girl and to touch her. Once again no mention is made of Jesus undergoing purification rites after doing so. The objective is to define the relation between purity regulations and Jesus' purifying power as depicted in these two scenes. For this reason Jewish purity regulations regarding death and menstrual bleeding are attended to, as well as the impact that Jesus as healer has on these regulations. Once again the formative function of this narrative for the implied audience is established to define the implication of this narrative for purity and healing in their community. This study is presented in Chapter 8, entitled "The Law and purity in Matthew; Jesus touching a bleeding woman and a dead girl".

1.2.2.8 External cultic tradition and internal ethical purity in Matthew 15

Matt. 15:1-20 is a narration of a controversy between the Pharisees and Jesus regarding the traditions of the elders and dietary regulations. This passage deals with the status of the oral and the written *Torah*. In this short narrative Jesus makes stark pronouncements about the tradition of the Pharisees when He addresses the Pharisees and the teachers of the Law, the crowds and his disciples respectively. The intention is to identify which aspects of the Law are challenged by Matthew's Jesus and what He regards as the true meaning of the Law. This issue is addressed in Chapter 9, "External cultic tradition and internal ethical purity in Matt. 15".

1.2.2.9 The double love commandment

Matt. 22:34-40 describes yet another scene where the Jewish leaders confront Jesus about the *Torah*, this time about what He considers to be the greatest commandment of the Law. Jesus' answer should provide a summary of the essence of his teaching on the *Torah*, and the aim is to determine both this essence and the performative function of these statements in the narrative. To do this, Jesus' answer is interpreted within the context of the Mediterranean perspective of the first century on group-orientated societies. This issue is explored in Chapter 10 under the title "The double love commandment".

1.2.2.10 "To obey the teachers of the law and Pharisees, but not to do what they do" (Matt. 23:3)

Jesus's instruction to the crowds in Matt. 23:3 to obey and do everything the teachers of the law and the Pharisees tell them, is the only case in Matthew where the teachings and conduct of the Jewish leaders are seemingly portrayed in a positive light. If this portrayal indeed is positive, it is clearly in tension with how Matthew construes these leaders and their teachings in the rest of the gospel. Jesus' positive remark furthermore stands in contrast with Matt. 28:20, where Jesus claims all authority to himself and instructs his disciples to teach all the nations to obey everything he has commanded them. The question therefore arises as to how this seemingly positive reference of Jesus should be interpreted. In answering this question, an intra-textual approach is followed in Chapter 11: "To obey the teachers of the law and Pharisees, but not to do what they do".

1.2.2.11 Conclusion

Chapter 12 forms the conclusion of the study. The objective in this chapter is to construct an overall picture of Jesus' teaching of the Law as depicted by Matthew based on the findings of the investigations undertaken in the respective chapters. In addition, the conclusion formulates a view of what Jesus' teaching holds for the identity of the implied audience of the Gospel. The chapter concludes with a summative theological reflection on Matthew's teaching on the *Torah*.

1.3   CENTRAL THEORETICAL ARGUMENT

The central theoretical argument propounded in this study is that the narrator of the first Gospel intentionally emphasises Jesus' teachings and enactment of the *Torah* to distinguish His interpretation of the Law from that of the Pharisees and teachers of the Law. Jesus takes the position of protagonist in the narrative, while the Pharisees and teachers of the Law act as the antagonists. The disciples and crowds function as supporting characters. This emphasis in the narrative probably reflects strenuous relations between groups external to the text on the topic of the *Torah*. The author probably uses this teaching on the Law in a performative way to form and establish the identity of his implied audience.

1.4   METHODOLOGY

1.4.1 The problem-orientated approach

The approach that underlies the different chapters is a problem-orientated approached, as this approach offers an effective way to answer the variety of questions explored in this study.

A text can be approached in a number of different ways. The discipline of Linguistics differentiates between synchronic and diachronic approaches

(Barton, 1999:14; Du Toit, 2009b:122). When reading the Gospel of Matthew, a reader can use it to investigate the historical events it describes, or to get insight in the Christian community that preserved the traditions incorporated in the text, or to shed light on the situation or ideas of the author, or investigate the manner in which the document originated. These investigations would all imply a diachronic reading of the text. On the other hand, a text can also be read synchronically, resulting in reading of the literary text in its self-contained world, abstracted from its historical context (cf. Barton, 1999:14; Foster, 2004:17; Lategan, 2009:84; Tuckett, 1987:1). Scholars proposing synchronic reading of the text often criticize diachronic readings as unliterary in character (Barton, 1999:14). At times it seems that practitioners of the different approaches tend to over-exaggerate the applicability of their own approaches, while negating the worth of other approaches. To my mind, it is undesirable to drive such a wedge between diachronic and synchronic approaches as they can be used to illuminate different aspects in the investigation of a text.

The interpretation of a text involves many aspects and this necessitates a multi-faceted process. It could be detrimental to stick to only one method. Depending on the questions asked, various methods can complement and reinforce one another (Brueggemann, 1997:58; Du Toit, 2009a; Kennedy, 2006:128; Perrin, 1972:5-18). For this reason a problem-oriented approach is followed in this study. In a problem-oriented approach, the challenges and issues presented by the text suggest which method should be used (Egger, 1996:8). While a set of methods are available, the researcher uses methods according to the requirements of the text and the questions to be answered. Each perspective on a text has its limitations, but with a plurality of methods the methods can strengthen each other to arrive at a richer and more integrated grasp of the meaning (Foster, 2004:6; Nel, 2014:270). The problem with such an approach, however, is that each approach requires some specialization. In a problem-orientated approach, it is therefore impossible to engage with the specialized detail of each method. Only those facets in each methodological approach that are relevant to answering the research question are utilized.

Furthermore, different approaches in their specialized forms sometimes discount principles of other approaches. Historical-critical approaches are often questioned in favour of synchronic approaches, but one cannot completely abandon a historical approach to a Biblical text (Barton, 1999:18; Catchpole, 1997:187) as these texts developed within historical contexts and were received and preserved in historical contexts. Historical-critical investigations therefore do provide useful insights for the interpretation of the Christian Bible. The ideal is that insights from both approaches are made available for mutual correction and enrichment in a complementary manner. In using problem-orientated approach to the text, the study employs both diachronic and synchronic perspectives as required to address certain problems.

A brief orientation within of the variety of approaches is therefore appropriate. The intention is not to give a detailed description of the various approaches, but to indicate which kind of questions require which kind of methods in this research.

1.4.2 Diachronic approaches - Historical criticism

Historical criticism (as classically developed by German scholars) entails diachronic approaches to a text[3]. Historical-critical exegetes are primarily interested in the process that resulted in the written document, the genetic question (Barton, 1999:9; Van Aarde, 2009:381). Historical criticism entails a variety of methods, some of which are employed in this research. It investigates the original sources that contained the words and deeds of Jesus (Source Criticism), the oral traditions preserving and developing these traditions (Form Criticism) and how the author reworked the material to present his ideas and perspectives (Redaction Criticism) (Catchpole, 1997:168; Matera, 1987:1). The assumption is that insight into the historical process of producing the document could offer answers as to cause and effect. The basis of this approach is that the Biblical texts are historical as they stem from a historical context. They are primarily referential, referring to entities beyond the texts themselves, and not purely "literary". In order to interpret these texts, one has to have some understanding of their historical contexts (Greidanus, 1988:299; Tuckett, 1987:186). Typical questions asked as part of Historical Criticism are: How did the document come into existence? Who wrote the document? To whom was it addressed? When and where was it written? What sources were used, and how were the sources adapted? (Barton, 1999:15; Blomberg & Markley, 2010:67).

---

[3] It is sometimes argued that Historical Criticism undermines the Biblical text as canonical Scripture (Ladd, 1971:51-52; Westermann, 1982:12). Depending on how Historical Criticism is applied, my assumption is that their methodologies do allow for a special position of the Biblical text. The Biblical text should still be approached with confidence of reliability (cf. Greidanus, 1988:37). A Historical Critical approach need not to reject that God acted in history as testified in the Biblical text or in the origin of the text. It should allow for a transcendant God to be acknowledged as the God of history. It also needs not to replace the Biblical text with a reconstructed earlier text.

1.4.2.1 Questions of introduction

Questions typically addressed in introductions to Biblical texts are related to historical-critical methodology (cf. Brown, 1997; Kümmel, 1975; Tuckett, 1987:41-67). In applying this approach to Matthew, one recognizes that this Gospel stems from a particular time in history. It was written by an author who found himself within a historical situation and addressed to an audience belonging to that history (Foster, 2004:9). To understand what the author is saying, the exegete has to place him/herself as responsibly as possible in the situation of the original audience. In this study I am interested in the concern that the author of the first Gospel had with the *Torah* and the related conflict with the Jewish religious leaders. For this reason I will endeavour to investigate the religious and social situation in which the Gospel originated.

However, such an enterprise raises some methodological problems. As the first Gospel itself serves as an important source to investigate its historical background, one may ask how far it is legitimate to use a text itself as evidence for its own background. Can one use the text as evidence to reconstruct its thought world and then use this reconstructed thought world to interpret the text? Such a procedure implies circular reasoning, yet it is almost unavoidable. For this reason it is beneficial to rather use sources other than the one under consideration when constructing the background of the document. It becomes more complicated where evidence apart from the Gospel is scarce (with the result that only one side of the conversation is represented), or when outside information appears to be in conflict with the Gospel evidence. Nevertheless, the Gospel is part of the religious world of the first century, which makes the Gospel indispensable to illuminate its contexts. Obviously, such an investigation has limits and it has to be done with necessary discretion and caution. Nel (2014:268) aptly warns that while the circumstances of a text are important in the hermeneutical process, these circumstances should never be taken as point of departure. The process of interpretation starts with the text and not with the circumstances of the author or the readers. Another issue one has to keep in mind is that the socio-historical context of the Gospel is not a uniform and unchanging entity. Questions may be asked as to how widespread the issues were with which the author was confronted, how uniform and large the community was that he addressed, and what kind of variety existed within the broader Jewish society. When dealing with Jewish sources, which often derive from later times, it remains a question whether the same issues were entertained in the time of Jesus or when the Gospel was written. Mechanical and positivistic answers to the questions of introduction should therefore be avoided. The assumption that scholarship can arrive at final objective truths is reminiscent of the Enlightenment. One should acknowledge that the answers to historical questions remain constructions that need constant revision and reformulation (Braaten, 1968:100). Scholars should be cautious of telling the readers what Biblical texts did or did not mean, but should rather show what they can or cannot mean (Barton, 1999:17).

1.4.2.2 Source criticism

Source criticism is also an indispensable part of my investigation of the Matthean text. This is particularly relevant because of the undeniable relationship between the different Synoptic Gospels. With regard to this literary relation between the Synoptic Gospels, the Two-Source Hypothesis is taken as point of departure. It is therefore assumed that Mark was written first and was used by Matthew and Luke. Furthermore, it is assumed that Matthew and Luke each had access to another source, the hypothetical Q. In addition to this Matthew and Luke presumably each made use of their own sprecial traditions as well – often referred to by the symbols "M" for Matthean material and "L" for Lukan material (De Silva, 2004:166)[4]. Matthew expanded considerably on Mark's text, especially adding teaching material. On the other hand, Matthew tends to shorten Mark's versions of parallel narratives. In my investigation of individual narratives in Matthew, I will consider omissions, additions or alterations by Matthew to Mark's text, and compare them with Lucan parallels. This may signify special interests of Matthew that may be relevant to my research questions. When studying the Gospel, one sometimes also comes across elements in the text that appear to be uncharacteristic of the author. This might also signify the use of sources or traditions of some kind. While scholars are sometimes tempted to split passages up into different sources and traditions, one should rather interpret the text as it stands. When an author uses sources, this presumably implies that he agrees with the sources. Therefore an exegete should not drive a wedge between the sources and the author. During the nineteenth century, scholars mainly used Source criticism to determine which traditions were the earliest as to discover the closest historical description of the life of Jesus. This is not my intention in this research. I regard Source criticism useful in terms of the contribution it makes towards Redaction criticism, and to illuminate the author's own ideas as he addresses issues in his situation (cf. Catchpole, 1997:169; Tuckett, 1987:89).

---

[4] These latter components make the label "Two-Source Hypothesis" something of a misnomer.

1.4.2.3 Form criticism

The assumption of Form criticism, which emerged shortly after the First World War, is that there is a correlation between the way in which a tradition is told, and the situation (*Sitz im Leben*) where it is used (Catchpole, 1997:169; Tuckett, 1987:95)[5]. This implies, for example, that controversy stories in Matthew about disputes between Jesus and the Jewish authorities somehow reflect conflicts that the early church experienced. In this study I compare certain narratives in Matthew's Gospel with their parallels in Mark and Luke. Using these comparisons, I will indicate how Matthew in some cases changed the form in which the narrative is presented. Assuming that Matthew used Mark, this difference in form might reflect a different situation. However, a form-critical approach is not without problems. There is no neat one-to-one correspondence between a form and a specific situation in the early church. The exegete should keep in mind that the form of a tradition does not necessarily provide a description of a particular community, but rather a typical situation within a community. Furthermore, there is often very little or no evidence for the alleged situation in the church apart from the Gospel itself. The text then implies a proposed situation, and the proposed situation provides the context against which the text should be interpreted. As pointed out earlier, such an argument is circular and asks for fine discernment in the interpreting process.

1.4.2.4 Redaction criticism

Form-critics tended to have a rather dismissive view of the activity of the evangelists themselves. The authors were mainly regarded as collectors who assembled individual traditions into a document[6]. This has changed with the development of modern Redaction criticism from the mid-twentieth century onwards (Catchpole 1997:169; Tuckett, 1987:117). Redaction criticism regards authors as more creative. According to this view, the way the authors adapted the traditions reveals something of their theological intentions (Foster, 2004:7). As far back as the nineteenth century, F.C. Baur (1847) already recognized that

---

[5] Form-criticism has attracted some opposition, probably due to Bultmann's skeptical views about the historicity of parts of the tradition (cf. Bultmann, 1963). However, such skepticism is not inherent to the method itself.

[6] It is often assumed that Form and Source critics merely regarded the evangelists as scissor and paste theologians or people who threaded beads of tradition into a string. Such assumption, however, is a serious oversimplification. The focus of the Form and Source critics were on the material the evangelists incorporated into their Gospels (cf. Foster, 2004:7).

all the Gospels were governed by individual *Tendenzen*. Lightfoot (1935) continued with this idea by demonstrating how Mark creatively shaped tradition in his Gospel. Nevertheless, modern Redaction criticism gained momentum with Marxsen's study on Mark (cf. Marxsen, 1969), Bornkamm's on Matthew (cf. Bornkamm, 1963a) and Conzelmann's on Luke (cf. Conzelmann, 1960)[7]. In this study, I discuss prominent passages where Matthew expresses his concern about the *Torah*. Where parallels with Mark and Luke exist, I will investigate the way in which Matthew has redacted this source in an attempt to recognize Matthews own intentions (cf. Weren, 1994:7).

Once again, this approach is not without its limitations. On the one hand we do not have access to all the sources Matthew used. On the other hand, in cases where we do have parallels with Mark, Matthew might not have changed Mark because he was probably content with the way Mark had formulated it (cf. Foster, 2004:8). If a Redaction-criticist only looks at the changes an author made to his sources, he/she will miss such instances, which would lead to a distorted picture of the evangelist's concerns. Furthermore, one should consider redactional activities of smaller passages within the work of the evangelist as a whole. The evangelist produced the whole text, and the whole text should be taken into account to discover something of the author's concerns and ideas. "Redaction criticism ... is often thought to have failed to see the whole text, concentrating more on the seams or changes in the text rather on what the text retains from its source ..." (Porter, 1995:82).

I therefore attempt to discover how individual passages concerning the *Torah* relate to other similar passages. Based on these relations I propose what I consider as important elements of Matthew's teaching on the Law and how that might have been applicable to his situation.

1.4.3 Synchronic and text-immanent approaches

Proponents of the synchronic approach argue that texts should not be used as windows onto their prehistory, but that they should be read as "self-contained worlds", regardless of the original authorial intent of the text (cf. Du Toit, 2009b:122; Foster, 2004:15). The benefit of this approach is that it endeavours to interpret the text that lies before us. Coupled with this is an appreciation of how a text works to communicate meaning and how it challenges and

---

[7] The German versions of these books of Marxsen, Bornkamm and Conzelmann were published in the mid 1950's.

transforms the values and convictions of the recipients of the text. But, as argued before, a text cannot be interpreted a-historically as if contained in a text-immanent capsule (Foster, 2004:16; Lategan, 2009:48). The text has an origin and an address. It is part of history and has referential points beyond itself. Certain historical questions still have to be asked as far as they serve to illuminate the text beforehand.

In a synchronic approach, emphasis is put on the text as structural entity (Lategan, 2009:45). Different components of a text are virtually in dialogue with one another and can therefore not be read in isolation (Weren, 1994:15). Pioneering work in this regard was done by the Swiss linguist, Ferdinand de Saussure (1857-1913)[8]. He viewed language as a synchronic system functioning according to a finite set of rules[9].

Later this developed into the text-immanent approach and literary criticism (Lategan, 2009:46). These approaches focus on the structure of the language and exclude the history of a text. An important benefit of these approaches is that close attention is paid to the text and the way it was constructed. Meaning is constituted in the first place by the language itself. The text-immanent reading of texts leads to a variety of specialized structural approaches (cf. Du Toit, 2009c:217-265; Foster, 2004:15), for instance Discourse analysis, with people like Louw (1982) and Nida (1983) as important proponents, Narrative analysis with Greimas (1970)[10] and Genette (1980)[11] as leading figures (cf. Van Aarde,

---

[8] De Saussure's pioneering work, *Cours de linguistique générale*, was published posthumous in 1916.

[9] De Saussure illustrates the synchronic structure of a text with the game of chess. Chess pieces are bound to a system. They have a conventional set of moves on a conventional board of 64 squares. The "value" of each piece is determined by rules applicable to that piece and its position on the board in relation to other pieces on the board (cf. Lategan, 2009:45). Witherington (2013:52) has remarked: "A text without a context is just a pretext for whatever you want it to mean".

[10] Greimas has identified actants in narrative texts who fulfil actantial roles, e.g.: the protagonist as the principle character or subject (like Jesus in the Gospels), the object(s) as the persons at whom the acts and values of the protagonist are directed (like the disciples, crowds or marginalized figures in the Gospels), the antagonists as those who oppose the efforts of the protagonist (like the Pharisees and scribes), the helpers who assists the protagonist (like the disciples in some cases) (Van Aarde, 2009:405).

[11] Genete (1980) has introduced the important difference between "plot" and "story" in *Discours du récit*. The "story" (histoire) refers to the chronological sequence of events, and "plot" to the way these events are presented in the narrative. When the events selected from the lives of people of certain times and places are combined into a series a plot develops and the story becomes a narrative

2009:381-418) and Rhetorical analysis[12] (Kennedy, 1966; Vorster, 2009:505-578).

Literary criticism encompasses a broad range of interests (Hayes & Holladay, 2007:91): literary structure (i.e., how a text is arranged or organised), literary style (i.e., techniques of language usage that distinguish an author or a text), literary purpose (i.e., what a writing achieves either as an expression of the author's intent or as a function of the text itself), literary mood (i.e., emotions associated with, or created by a writing), literary strategy (i.e., how various elements are developed within a single genre to achieve a certain purpose), and literary imagination (i.e., the world reflected in a text [or the author's mind] and the world a text creates in the reader's mind). Each of these approaches is specialized and encompasses considerable academic jargon and techniques. In a problem-orientated approach, it is not possible to engage with all these intricacies.

In the current study I apply insights from the text-immanent approach by reading the text as the literary product at hand. Such a text-immanent approach is useful to interpret components of the text in relation to one another. I approach the text as a network of interconnected components that together form causal relations within a semantic universum (cf. Weren, 1994:8-10). Individual words, phrases and scenes are engaged with one another and their meanings are dependent on their interplay. The first Gospel forms a well-structured unity characterised by a unique narratological arrangement. Different parts of the narrative are arranged in such a manner that the plot develops into a dramatic climax. The implied author acts as the narrator who guides the reader through the narrated world. His voice is constantly heard as he incorporates his commentary into the narrative. He determines what is told and how it is told.

However, I do not read the text as if in a self-contained autonomous world, as I wish to probe the meaning of the text within its original setting.

---

discourse (*récit*). The narrative discourse (*récit*) is directly available to the reader, while the story (*histoire*) should be abstracted from the narrative discourse (Van Aarde, 2009:384-385).

[12] Rhetorical analysis investigates the art of persuasive speech and the persuasive power of a text. The aim is to get a better understanding of what the author wanted to achieve and what proper responses could be expected of the readers by analysing the rhetorical structure of the text and strategies employed by the author.

1.4.4 Sociological approaches

Sociological methods to interpret the Biblical text bring a useful interaction between diachronic and synchronic approaches to the text (cf. Foster, 2004:10; Tuckett, 1987:136). Sociological studies explore the social needs, social conflicts, group interests, pressures and clashing ideologies as revealed in texts (Meeks, 1983:2; Theissen, 1983). This includes social descriptions and sociological explanations of the various aspects of the life depicted in the Biblical texts (Elliot, 1995; Tuckett, 1987:139). Sociological studies consider the text both as a reflection of and a response to the social and cultural settings in which it was produced. Elliot (1995:8) emphasises that the text and context is more closely intertwined than had been previously recognized.

The result is that scholars who follow sociological approaches have focused a great deal on discerning the situation behind various writings (e.g. Love, 2009; Malina, 2009:154-193). It is assumed that whoever produces or listens to a text, carries certain assumptions and expectations from his/her background into it. Sociological approaches reject radical a-historical approaches which neglect the significant relation to the world in which a text had been produced and read. Radical a-historical approaches therefore limit and can even skew the comprehension of a text. Stanton (1992:380) has remarked that if the horizons and expectations of the first readers of a text are ignored, "interpretation would be like a picnic – a picnic to which … we all bring our meanings".

The goal of discerning the situation behind a text is not without problems. While the text and the society are undoubtedly related, the correlation is not precise. There is a risk of referential fallacy. When reconstructing the social and religious setting of the text, one should keep in mind that this is based on the author's depiction of the world outside the text from his/her perspective, and not with the real world as such. The text at hand introduces an implied author, an implied setting and an implied audience. The reconstruction of the intended audience is therefore difficult. The document could have been intended to promote core values of the audience that already existed, but could also have been intended to change their values (cf. Foster, 2004:12).

Sociological approaches therefore investigate the implied community to better understand what the implied author of a text intended and how the implied readers would have appropriated the meaning. Where applicable I intend to apply such approaches when reading the Matthean Gospel.

1.4.5 Complementary use of methods

Looking at the three approaches of interpreting a text, namely the diachronic, synchronic and sociological (which provides a useful interaction between diachronic and synchronic approaches), it becomes apparent that each of these methods has its strengths and weaknesses. Such a multi-faceted approach underscores the remark of Weren (2014:4): "Meaning is the result of the interplay between a textual unit and such factors as language, literary context, and cultural setting. Within this interplay, a text usually acquires a multi-layered meaning while the text is still a unit". Meaning is therefore constituted by structure, discourse and intertextuality, as well as a socio-historical environment. Such an approach intends to "narrow the gap between the world within and the world outside the text by not merely concentrating on relations between texts but also on the texts' correlations with their socio-cultural contexts" (Weren, 2014:298).

I consequently use the methods in a restricted manner to complement each other. Obviously such an approach raises concerns of its own, for example how to discern between competing elements in each approach. I therefore prefer to make use of insights gained from each approach without entering into all the technicalities of the variety of methods. When using insights from diachronic methods to gain insight into the meaning of the text within its original setting, I consider insights from the synchronic methods to concentrate on the message of the text at hand, taking into consideration the interrelatedness of the different components of the text which determines the meaning of these components. This will be done with insights gained from the sociological approaches regarding the importance of the social setting of text in determining the meaning of this ancient text.

1.4.6 Reading Matthew in this study

My point of departure is that Matthew is an occasional writing. The author wrote to address specific concerns of his communities (cf. Foster, 2004:3; Luz, 2005:17). When reading Matthew, one soon realizes that the author has a specific interest in the meaning and interpretation of the *Torah* (Loader, 1997). Jesus is presented as the new and authoritative interpreter of the Law (e.g. the Sermon on the Mount, Matt. 5-7; 22:34-40), while the interpretation of the Pharisees and teachers of the Law is frequently denounced (e.g. Matt. 15:1-20; 23:13-39). The question therefore arises as to what in Matthew and his community's situation led to this emphasis.

To address these issues, the Matthean text is read as a transparent narrative[13] (cf. Catchpole, 1997:175; Foster, 2004:3; Luz, 2005:17) to identify by way of construction the issues that were probably prevalent in the community where the text was produced and read.

The recognition of the interconnectedness between text and context, as developed in sociological approaches, has made an important contribution towards Matthean scholarship. However, external evidence about the situation of this gospel is sparse. Scholars are forced to mostly rely on internal evidence. As discussed before, this immediately raises the problem of circular reasoning and the risk of referential fallacy. In order to read the text responsibly, one has to consider its circumstances, but to create a picture of these circumstances one mainly has to rely on internal evidence of the text itself. Unfortunately there is no sure way to avoid this dilemma. One can only read the text as cautiously and sensitively as possible and integrate the story witness with available external evidence. Furthermore, one must be willing to correct one's previous judgements.

Although one should be cautious to make a historical reconstruction of the gospel community based on the contents of the Gospel (as this requires a considerable amount of interpretation), one can regard the Matthean Jesus narrative as an "inclusive" narrative. Van Aarde (2011:49) has remarked: "Two 'worlds' are simultaneously included as a narrative entity". From the text a reader can recognize issues that were prevalent in the Gospel writer's community. The author retells the story of Jesus to address the contemporary needs of his audience. "A text is not an isolated phenomenon, but functions in a communicative context and has a pragmatical function" (Weren, 2014:9).

Gospels obviously are more "open texts" and are less likely to have specific information of local situations such as would be expected from letters (Bauckham, 1998:48)[14]. Yet the different Gospel writers filled communicative

---

[13] Though the terms "narrative" and "story" is often used interchangeable in literature, I use the term "narrative" to describe how the events are told, while "story" refers to what is told, namely the a sequence or set of events.

[14] In 1998 a collection of essays, edited by Richard Bauckham, was published that opposed the view that the Gospels had been addressed to specific and definable early Christian communities. The most important and trendsetting contribution to this volume, is probably the first essay by Bauckham himself, "For whom were Gospels written" (1998:9-49). Bauckham questions the distinctiveness of

needs by addressing particular situations and issues from the world in which they participated. Similarly, the author of the Matthean Gospel formed part of an early Christian community and he wrote his Gospel with his community and some of its issues in mind (cf. Love, 2009:1; Carter, 2000a:7; Klijn, 1968:45). Thus Matthew narrates the life of Jesus "*in illo tempore*, but the text is deeply influenced by the situation of the community within which it originated and for which it was originally meant" (Weren, 2014:251).

In Matthew's Gospel a considerable number of emphases are apparent from which one can recognize some of the issues of those days. To put it in other words; the *Sitz im Leben der alten Kirche* (the Matthean community) can indirectly be recognized in the *Sitz im Leben Jesu* as narrated in the Gospel material, the *Sitz im Leben der Evangelium*. This narrative about Jesus actually has three successive life-settings: its setting in the historical ministry of Jesus (*Sitz im Leben Jesu*), its setting in the restricted selection of Jesus' sayings in the Matthean community (*Sitz im Leben der alten Kirche*), and its setting in the Gospel of Matthew (*Sitz im Leben der Evangelium*). The last setting is immediately accessible in the written Gospel, while the other two settings are indirectly accessible through the Gospel.

---

the communities to which each of the Gospels was addressed. He rejects the extensive academic energy to construct the sociological profiles, the theological emphases and the tradition-critical strata of the communities to which they were written. He argues that all four Gospels were "open texts" (Bauckham, 1998:48) addressed very widely to most, if not all, Christians of those days.

He argues that close contacts among churches in the first-century Roman world existed so that the Christians formed a tightly knit community that transcended local churches (Bauckham, 1998:32-44). He assumes a high level of mobility and communication amongst Christians and their leaders, which would facilitate rapid circulation of significant documents such as the Gospels.

Bauckham's challenge, however, is not all that convincing (cf. Esler, 1998:235-238; Sim, 2001:3-27). Bauckham bases his argument on certain assumptions about the nature of the early Christian movement and some general observations of the Gospels, without internal evidence from the Gospels themselves. Evidence of a single and unified early Christian movement is lacking. Paul, for example, to the contrary refers to a major rift amongst followers of Jesus as he writes about his opponents who preach a different gospel and he curses them on account of it (Gal. 1:8-9). Furthermore, it is questionable to infer from the mobility of some Christians that the Evangelists also travelled extensively. The early Christians probably were less mobile and less communicative than what Bauckham suggests. Even if the Evangelists travelled periodically, each of them must have had a base in one location or another. Even if an author intended his document to be read by a wider than his primary readership, it remains different from implying that the document was written for all Christians of the day and age. The mere fact of the diversity of the Gospels, including the special sources they used, strongly indicate that they were written for specific churches that were geographically remote from one another and who experienced particular difficulties. It is more probable that the Evangelists first and foremost had the Christians in their immediate circles as their readership in mind. The concept of different niche for each of the Gospels therefore remains valid.

In the Gospel itself, a depiction is provided of the life setting of Jesus and his disciples on the one hand, while tendencies can be recognized that provide some idea of the community of the implied audience on the other.

Access to the life settings of Jesus with his disciples and that of the Matthean community are different. The Gospel contains a double meaning functioning on two levels (Keener, 2009:17; Luz, 2005:27; Weren, 2014:296). In the first place it tells the story of Jesus, but in such a way that the story of the Matthean community can indirectly be recognized in it (Saldarini, 1991:39). The past story of Jesus and his disciples includes the story of the community's experience on a secondary level. Matthew selected specific historical material and organised it in such a way to address the circumstances of the readers. The disciples subsequently serve as a "transparency" for the later Matthean community and symbolize some of their attitudes and behaviour.

On the first level of the narrative, the world directly depicted by the text, Matthew tells the story of Jesus' ministry and teaching in Israel. As a result of his ministry and teaching, Jesus was rejected and executed while He pronounced judgement on Israel's leaders and its people and commissioned his disciples to preach to the Gentiles. On the second level the world of Matthew's community is indirectly reflected. The evangelist tells the story of the church's commitment to Jesus and his teaching, which resulted in their alienation from the synagogue. Though many aspects of the Matthean community remain obscure, some stand out and make it possible to somehow characterize Matthew's group and its relation towards the non-Christian Jewish community (France, 1998:95; Stanton, 1993:99). It appears as if the Matthean community went through a dark period of feeling rejected by the synagogue and that they had to work through this traumatic experience (cf. Chapter 2). This grief is expressed in the Gospel. The Gospel speaks of persecution against missionaries on the part of Jews (Matt. 5:11-12; 10:23; 23:34), of martyrs' deaths (Matt. 10:21, 28; 22:5; 23:34, 37), of being handed over to Gentile courts (Matt. 10:17-18) and of divided families (Matt. 10:34-37). Thus the second level of the narrative gives a perspective on the Matthean church in a difficult period of reorientation because of this separation. The Gospel represents a (mainly) Jewish Christian community in conflict with non-Christian Jewish community(ies). It seems that the Matthean community had been expelled from the synagogues, or at least didn't feel welcome there (later on in Chapter 2 I discuss this issue in more depth). The Matthean community also lived within the Roman Empire, which caused tension in two directions. They felt themselves threatened by the Gentiles for being Jews, and by Jews for being followers of Jesus and accommodating non-Jews. This put them in a defensive position, and this can be recognized in the Matthean text.

When considering the Matthean community, however, one must be cautious not to view it as a single group of believers or a single house church (cf. Saldarini, 1994:87). As first century Christians met in houses, which would more than likely not have been able to accommodate more than fifty persons, the Matthean community should rather be regarded as a loose group or groups that interacted with one another in terms of shared beliefs, concerns and aspirations. It is even possible that the author had a circle of communities in mind and that the Gospel was already circulated at an early stage (Stanton, 1993:51; Van Aarde, 2011:46).

1.4.7 Reading on two levels

When reading the Gospel on two levels, the Gospel's teaching on the *Torah* should similarly be read on two levels[15] (Catchpole, 1997:175; Luz, 2005:17). It is plausible to assume that the interest in the *Torah* evident from the Gospel reflects at least some of interest in this topic in the implied audiences of the Gospel.

1.4.7.1 *The Torah in the narrative world of the first Gospel*

The *Torah* is the subject of a full-scale discussion in Matt. 5:17-48. In Matt. 5:17-19 Jesus emphatically denies that He opposes or neglects the Law. This statement can be considered as the Matthean Jesus' foundational statement on the continuing validity of the Law. Immediately following this foundational statement (Matt. 5:17-19), Matthew's Jesus pronounces that He requires from his disciples righteousness that surpasses that of the Pharisees and teachers of the Law (Matt. 5:20). Righteousness becomes a significant term in the Matthean gospel with a concentration in the Sermon on the Mount (Matt. 5:6, 10, 20, 6:1, 33) and beyond (Matt. 3:15 and 21:32). Righteousness plays a considerable role in how Matthew describes the function of the Law. Directly after Jesus' statement about greater righteousness (Matt. 5:20), Matthew's Jesus challenges prevailing interpretations of the Law in six so-called antitheses (Matt. 5:21-47), and motivates his alternative interpretation of the six commandments in dispute.

---

[15] The first level functions within the narrative world internal to the text. The second level reflects the external world in which the text came into existence.

Immediately following these "antitheses" (Matt. 5:21-47), Matthew's Jesus concludes "Be perfect, therefore, as your heavenly Father is perfect" (Matt. 5:48). With these strong statements on the validity of the Law and requirements of greater righteousness and perfection, and the antitheses about prevailing interpretations of the Law, the table is set for on-going debates in the Gospel between Jesus and the Pharisees along with the teachers of the Law. The Gospel continuously describes Jesus and the Pharisees as being in conflict about the true interpretation of the Law (cf. Moo, 1984:15).

In the Sermon on the Mount Jesus is depicted as the great teacher of the Law, followed by narratives in Matt. 8-9 describing how Jesus enacts what He regards as the true intention of the Law. He begins by healing a leper (Matt. 8:1-3). Purity, which formed an important part of *Torah*-observance, inter alia is at stake. As an impure person, the "leper" was not supposed to come close to Jesus, but he has the confidence that Jesus has the power to "purify/heal" him. The result is that Jesus sympathetically reaches out and touches him. Instead of Jesus being defiled by coming into contact with the leper, purity flows from Jesus to heal the leper.

Another intriguing passage about Jesus' stance on purity regulations appears in Matt. 9:18-26. Jesus touches a woman with blood flow and a dead girl. Jesus wears tassels (*tzitzit*), intended to remind the wearer to remain obedient to the Law. Instead of Jesus becoming impure by touching these persons, Jesus cleanses the impure woman and raises the dead girl to life. Apparently Jesus acts as the Holy One so that purity flows from Him to the impure persons, so that they could be cleansed instead of Him becoming unclean.

In Matt. 9:9-13 Pharisees blame Jesus for eating with tax collectors and sinners. "Tax collectors and sinners" represent a disgraceful formulaic pair in the Synoptic Gospels, and the Matthean Pharisees are of the opinion that association with them must be avoided. With an appeal to the will of God in Hos. 6:6, "I desire mercy, not sacrifice", Jesus shows mercy to these marginalized figures. Matthew's Jesus appeals to Hos. 6:6 again when the Pharisees confront Him for his disciples picking heads of grain on the Sabbath (Matt. 12:7). Sabbath played a key role in *Torah*-observance. The Sabbath issue is explicitly expressed in two consecutive passages. Pharisees object to the disciples of Jesus plucking grain on the Sabbath (Matt. 12:1-8) and that Jesus heals a man with a withered hand (Matt. 12:9-12). Within these controversies Jesus makes a strong and seemingly provocative claim: "Someone greater than the temple is here" (Matt. 12:6). Matthew's Jesus supersedes what was previously regarded as the role of the temple, which transferred to and was fulfilled in Him. Jesus apparently claims that new interpretations of Sabbath laws result from this.

The tradition of the elders related to dietary laws is challenged in Matt. 15:1-20. The oral Law, as observed and developed by the Pharisees, is in dispute. They intended to ensure purity with their traditions regarding hand washing. Jesus apposes their tradition with his view on purity: "What goes into someone's mouth does not defile them, but what comes out of their mouth, that is what defiles them" (Matt. 15:11).

Matt. 22:34-40 describes yet another scene where the Jewish leaders confront Jesus about the *Torah*. Jesus' answer to the expert of the Law about the greatest commandment is closely related to his teaching about the Law in the Sermon on the Mount. In both cases Jesus confirms that He upholds the Law and the Prophets and that He ensures their fulfilment. Jesus has no intention of abolishing the Law. Nevertheless, Jesus interpretation and application of the Law differs from that of the Pharisees. "In Matthew's mind the love command is the prism through which the others are to be understood" (Snodgrass, 1996:108). The verdict at the end judgement is based on whether one practiced love.

While the sentiment towards Pharisees and teachers of the Law is negative throughout the gospel, the conflict clearly intensifies during the week of the Passion, forming a crescendo of this conflict. Jesus battles and defeats his rivals. This culminates in Jesus's extensive criticism in Matt. 23. First, Jesus addresses the crowds, warning them of the insincerity of these Jewish leaders. Their conduct is hypocritical and their teachings are misleading. He pronounces a series of woes in which He accuses them of being hypocritical and spiritually blind. He bemoans the destiny of Jerusalem, which as in the days of Zechariah, will be desolate as this city has opposed and killed the true prophets of God.

From this brief overview it becomes clear that the *Torah* plays a significant role in the narrative world of the first Gospel.

1.4.7.2 *The Torah in the world of the intended audience*

The Gospel was written some forty years after the events in the narrative world in the text, and at a different location (cf. Hagner, 1993:lxxiii). Based on the prominence of the conflict about *Torah*-interpretation in the Gospel, it is fair to assume that this probably was an issue in the lives of the intended audience. It seems as if the intended audience probably experienced some conflict with non-Christian Jewish opponents about the meaning of the *Torah* (Foster, 2004:3;

Saldarini, 1994:12; Stanton, 1993:26). They presumably continued to have a firm commitment to the *Torah*, but developed a distinctive understanding of it based on the teaching of Jesus. Apparently this resulted in specific *Torah* observance, with different forms of piety and ethics.

1.5 RECENT RESEARCH ON THE *TORAH* IN MATTHEW

The question about Jesus and the *Torah* has been studied from various perspectives. It is not the intention to provide a comprehensive discussion of this research. I will start with a brief overview of the contributions, and then follow with a brief discussion of some of the most prominent research that has been done over the last 50 years on the *Torah* in Matthew as such. Based on this survey, an indication is provided of the contribution of this study to advance the argument.

1.5.1 The *Torah* in the Synoptic Gospels

There is a number of studies that consider the Law in the three Synoptic Gospels. These include the work of Berger (1972), Banks (1975), Hübner (1986), and Vouga (1988). More recently Loader (1997) has published a new study. His aim was not to even out the material into a single picture, but to consider the various ways the individual authors reflected on this issue. He includes the Gospels of Matthew, Mark, Luke and John, as well as the hypothetical Q and the Gospel of Thomas in his investigation.

1.5.2 The *Torah* in Mark, Luke and John

A number of studies have been published on the *Torah* in individual Gospels. On Mark there is the study of Sariola (1990). On Luke there were the studies of Wilson (1983), Klinghardt (1988) and Salo (1991). Pancaro (1975) and Kotila (1988) worked on John.

1.5.3 The *Torah* and the historical Jesus

The historical Jesus in relation to the Law has also been investigated. Here one can refer to the fourth volume of Meier's studies on the historical Jesus (2009). In his historical-critical approach, he has applied historical criteria to describe the historical Jesus. He approaches legal questions one by one to define the historical Jesus' relation to the *Torah* and its stipulations.

1.5.4 The *Torah* in Matthew

The studies on Matthew, which is directly relevant to this research, are the following:

1.5.4.1 Barth: Matthew's understanding of the Law

In his 1963-article on "Matthew's understanding of the Law", Barth has attended to the differentiation between what in the first Gospel belongs to tradition and what to editorial interpretation (cf. Barth, 1963:58). He has demonstrated how Matthew more firmly than the other Gospels warns of the judgement of God and exhorts his readers to do the will of God. He has argued that this emphasis is founded in the situation of the author or of his congregation (Barth, 1963:58-62).

Barth has discussed how important Matthew regards the abiding validity of the Law. Besides a number of other sayings in this regard found in the Christian tradition (e.g. Matt. 5:18-19; 10:5b; 23:2f, 23f, 25f), Barth pays attention to those statements which he has regarded as clearly demonstrating Matthew's unique interpretation on the continuing validity of the Law, viz. Matt. 5:17, 18c, 20; 7:12-27; 11:13 and 24:10-14. According to Barth (1963:75), Matthew's understanding of the Law is largely determined by his opposition to the antinomians.

Besides Matthew's opposition to the antinomians, he likewise opposes Pharisaism and the Rabbinate. This is demonstrated by the significance of the love commandment in Matthew. Barth has discussed Matt. 22:34-40; 7:12; 12:1-8 and 18:12-35 and draws the conclusion that to Matthew the whole Law and Prophets can be deduced from the command to love God and they neighbour (Barth, 1963:75-85). Barth has also discussed Matthew's view on the range of the valid law. Based on passages like Matt. 15:1-20 (other than Mark 7:1-13) and 23:2-3, he has reasoned that Matthew upheld the oral tradition, but opposed the Rabbinate's interpretation thereof (Barth, 1963:86-89). Matthew also has a conservative view of ceremonial law (Barth, 1963:89-92). He speaks of private sacrifice (Matt. 5:23), the paying of temple tax (Matt. 17:24-27) and that the Sabbath must still be observed (Matt. 24:40), but not in the strict sense of the Rabbinate (Matt. 12:1-4). With reference to Jesus' statement on the continuing validity of the Law (Matt. 5:17-19) followed by the antitheses (Matt. 5:21-47), Barth has argued that Matthew continued to observe the Law and the Prophets, but he opposed the interpretations of the Rabbinate.

With reference to Matt. 5:48 and 19:20, Barth (1963:95-105) derives that τέλειος (perfect) describes an attribute of disciples and the church. It denotes the ἡ δικαιοσύνη πλεῖον (more righteousness) (Matt. 5:20), which distinguishes the doers of the teaching of Jesus from the others. Perfection is the decisive characteristic of the new community. Only those who are τέλειος will enter the kingdom. However, it seems as if Matthew does not use the word τέλειος in the Greek ethical sense of being flawless, but in the sense of wholeness of consecration to God. Being τέλειος is contrasted with the superficial keeping of commandments. For Matthew the love commandment forms the central principle for the interpretation of the *Torah*. Barth (1963:105-125) investigates the depiction of the disciples in Matthew. Though they are required to be τέλειοι, their weaknesses and sin are described as well (e.g. Matt. 14:31; 16:8; 17:20; 28:17 and 21:20). From this it seems that Matthew's followers of Jesus are not led to rely on their own achievements. They should recognize their own shortcomings before God. They only live by the seeking love or the shepherd (Matt. 18:12-14).

To understand the Law in Matthew, one has to consider the Christology in Matthew as well (Barth, 1963:125-159). Matthew emphasises the lowliness of Jesus (Matt. 12:17-21), but this stands alongside a wealth of statements of his majesty (Matt. 21:4-11). Jesus is described as the Risen One ruling in the congregation (Matt. 28:16-20). When preaching about the Kingdom, one is also preaching the commandments of the Jesus of the Law. The preaching of the Law occasions the presence of the Risen One in the congregation. Jesus is also depicted as the Sinless One, the Righteous One who fulfils all righteousness and the One who does the will of God entirely (Matt. 3:14-17). In Matt. 12:20 the vocation of the servant of God is named, namely to bring judgement to victory. Completing and carrying out the judgement of God are considered to be his final comprehensive commission. This implies the complete establishment of the will of God. A further trait of Jesus is his voluntary act of obedience to suffer and die (Matt. 26:2, 18). Matthew teaches the atoning sacrifice of Christ and interprets this grace as actually establishing the judgement and righteousness of God. Jesus fulfils all righteousness in the place of sinners. Barth has opposed the view that Jesus was the giver of a *nova lex*[16] as proposed by scholars like for example Bacon (1930:223), Kilpatrick (1950:107) and

---

[16] The proposal the Jesus is the giver of a *nova lex* is based on the fivefold speeches of Jesus in the Gospel, the Moses and Sinai motives in the Sermon on the Mount and the emphasis on the Law in this first sermon.

Bornkamm (1963b:35). Jesus does not oppose the law of Sinai, but the Rabbinic interpretation of it.

Based on Matt. 5:17 and 11:13, Barth (1963:159-164) has constructed the antinomians in Matthew. He has disagreed with scholars like Schoeps (1949:120), who regarded them as Paulinists, or Holzmann (1911:509), who regarded them as ultra-Paulinists. He rather depicts them as Hellenistic libertines who rely on their spiritual gifts (χαρίσματα) rather than their faith (πίστις). Matthew's constant reminding to do God's will, to yield fruit and the threat of the judgement indicates the presence of such a group.

1.5.4.2 Meier: Law and history in the Gospel according to Matthew

In an earlier publication of Meier (1976) he did a Redactional-critical study of Matt. 5:17-20 in the light of the antitheses that follow (Matt. 5:21-48). He attends to the question of Matthew's redactional reworking of his source material and its congruency in the Matthean context. Meier's finding is that Matthew was not eclectic nor careless in his redaction of Matt. 5:17-20, but that Matthew had a clear theological intent in his teaching on the *Torah*, which he followed consistently. Matthew carefully redacted the passage according to his own interests: (1) theological, regarding the connection between salvation history, Christ and the Law, (2) pastoral, addressing exhortations to the church leaders and to all Christians, and (3) polemical, against the Pharisees. In his investigation of the antitheses, Meier has pointed out that the first (on murder, Matt. 5:21-26), second (on adultery, Matt. 5:27-30) and sixth antitheses (on neighbourly love, Matt. 5:43-47) do not revoke the letter of the Law, but in the third (on divorce, Matt. 5:31-32), fourth (on oaths, Matt. 5:33-37) and fifth (on retaliation, Matt. 5:38-42) the Law is indeed revoked. Meier's conclusion is therefore that the fulfilment of the Law and prophets that Jesus brings involves programmatic transcendence in a salvation-historical sense. As the eschatological Messiah, Jesus not only confirms or explains the Law, He fulfils it, which goes beyond some out-dated stipulations of the letter of the Law. With his death and resurrection the kingdom broke into this aeon in a powerful way. This would imply the abrogation of some of the elements in the Mosaic Law as demonstrated in the antitheses. "All things I have commanded you" (Matt. 28:20) are "*secundum, praeter* or *contra* the Mosaic Law" (Meier, 1976:168).

1.5.4.3   Foster: Community, law and mission in the Gospel according to Matthew

Foster (2004) has looked at issues within the social location of the Matthean community, the role that the Law presumable played in this community and the community's attitude towards Gentile mission. He has argued that although the Matthean group originated in Judaism, by the time the Gospel was composed, this community functioned outside the confines of its original setting. A breach had developed between the synagogue and evangelist's believers in Jesus. This group was recruiting new members from amongst the gentiles, which created some tension with the traditional *Torah* observers. Foster has focused on Matt. 5:17-48 as the central treatment of the Law in Matthew's Gospel. He has regarded Matt. 5:17-20 as "Matthew's programmatic statement of the Law" (Foster, 2004:18). Foster has compared Matt. 5:21-48 with the pre-destruction Judaism by ways of a close comparison with the *halakhic* letter in 4QMMT, which contains a series of antithetical statements. He has demonstrated how much of the debate in Matthew revolves around the issue of *Torah* observance and the fact that the mission amongst the gentiles marked a departure from various forms of Judaism as they emerged after the destruction of the temple. He has argued that the Matthean community was decisively rejected by other parties in Formative Judaism. The Gospel claims many of the prerogatives of Judaism as owned by the Matthean community. It is a pedagogical document in which the author instructs and encourages his community to continue and expand on an outwardly focussed Gentile mission.

1.5.4.4   Oliver: Torah praxis after 70 C.E.; reading Matthew and Luke-Acts as Jewish texts

The *Torah* praxis after 70 C.E. is investigated by Oliver (2013), who has considered the texts of Matthew and Luke-Acts. He has argued that both authors expected the Jewish followers of Jesus to continue observing the Jewish Law in full, though the Gentiles were expected to keep the ethical commandments and certain purity and dietary laws from the Mosaic *Torah*. This would enable fellowship between Jewish and Gentile worshippers within the Jesus movement. He investigates three markers of Jewish identity, namely the Sabbath, food laws (*kashrut*) and circumcision in Matthew and Luke-Acts. He has posited that both Matthew and Luke continued to observe the Sabbath. The issue was not *if* the Sabbath should be observed, but *how* it should be done. Matthew and Luke seek to justify the Sabbath praxis of Jesus and his disciples where it deviates from the "normative" conventions. Oliver has stated that the Sabbath controversies in the Synoptic Gospels actually deal with the authority of Jesus over the Sabbath, rather than with Sabbath praxis as such. Oliver has also discussed food laws and related purity regulations. According to him, many Jews of the Second Temple Period argued about how they should observe the purity system (e.g. the washing of hands before eating), but most of them agreed to observe *kashrut* (e.g. refraining from eating forbidden food like pork). He has argued that Matthew and Luke align themselves with the "mainstream" Jewish consensus about *kashrut*. When dealing with the Cornelius episode and the Apostolic Decree in Acts, he has argued that these passages deal with the moral purification of Gentile followers of Jesus, and not with the abrogation of *kashrut*. Regarding circumcision Oliver has argued that according to Luke, Jewish (male) followers of Jesus should continue to observe circumcision, while Gentile followers need not to observe this practice. Though Matthew mentions nothing about circumcision, Oliver has assumed that the same praxis would be applicable to Matthew. He has concluded that though Matthew and Luke represent different strands of Judaism (Matthew being in a bitter conflict with Pharisaic Judaism, and Luke reflecting a Hellenistic form of Judaism), they are both indebted to Jewish tradition and thought.

1.6 CONCLUSION

Though Matthew's treatment of the *Torah* has been debated for centuries, more recent studies have shown that one can no longer speak of a uniform understanding of the *Torah* by clearly distinctive groups within Judaism on the one hand, and of the interpretation of the *Torah* in the Second Testament on the other. It rather appears as if quite some turmoil developed amongst Judaist groups and that groups of followers of Jesus positioned themselves within this turmoil of localized Judaist societies. Trying to define the position of the Matthean community regarding the *Torah* within this unstable society seems to be important.

As different terms have been used in the Hebrew Bible, within the rabbinic movements and in the Second Testament to refer to the Law and other legal material, and since these terms have not always been used in a consistent and clearly distinctive manner, one should take caution when using these terms and interpreting the meaning of such terms in different materials and contexts.

This study aims to define the distinctive teaching on the *Torah* as reflected in passages of the first Gospel directly or indirectly deal with Jesus and the *Torah*. Jesus functions as the protagonist in these passages with different Jewish leaders as antagonists, while the disciples and crowds act as supporting characters. Though the identified passages provide a general picture of the understanding of the *Torah* in Matthew, this investigation cannot be regarded as comprehensive or including all aspects and perspectives on the *Torah* as found in this Gospel.

A problem-orientated approach seems to be useful to address the research questions as posed for this study. The problems that have to be addressed dictate the methodologies to be used. Diachronic, synchronic and sociological methodologies are used in a complementary way. Matthew is interpreted as an occasional writing in which the author addresses specific concerns of his community. It seems to be appropriate to read the Gospel as a transparent narrative in which the story of Jesus is told *in illo tempore*, but in such a way that the text is deeply influenced by the situation of the community within which it originated. The teaching of the *Torah* should therefore be interpreted in the narrative world of the Gospel, considering the fact that the way this narrative is composed also reflects aspects from the world of the implied audience.

The overview of more recent research on the *Torah* presents studies considering the *Torah* in the Synoptic Gospels (Berger, 1972; Banks, 1975; Hübner, 1986; Vouga, 1988 & Loader, 1997). Some work has been done on the *Torah* in Mark (Sariola, 1990), Luke (Wilson, 1983, Klinghardt, 1988 & Salo, 1991) and John (Pancaro, 1975 & Kotila, 1988). A comprehensive study in four volumes on the *Torah* and the historical Jesus has been done by Meier (2009). Barth (1963) was particularly influential in creating awareness of what the redactional activity of Matthew reveals of his understanding of the *Torah*. Meier (1976) has applied a redactional critical approach to investigate the fundamental statement on the validity of the *Torah* in Matt. 5:17-20. Foster (2004) has studied this statement along with the antitheses in Matt. 5:17-48 within the social location of the Matthean community. Oliver (2013) has investigated the *Torah* praxis in Matthew and Luke-Acts.

The current research aims to advance the understanding of the *Torah* in Matthew by investigating a wider spectrum of passages from the Gospel where teaching on the *Torah* appears to be obvious and prominent. Other than the studies done on the Synoptic Gospels in general, this study focusses on Matthew only to discover the unique teaching of this Gospel. While Meier has offered a comprehensive study on the Law and the historical Jesus with is 2009 study, the current study focusses the Law in the first Gospel and does not intend to be a historical study as such, but rather an investigation of the Law within the literary context of the Gospel. In his earlier study of 1976 Meier made a Redactional Critical study of Matt. 5:17-20 in light of the antitheses that follow in Matt. 5:21-48. The current study engages with Meier's study as part of the investigation of a larger scope of passages from Matthew. Barth (1963) has made a valuable contribution by arguing the importance of differentiating between what belongs to tradition and what to editorial interpretation in the first Gospel when attempting to define Matthew's theological intention with the Law. The current study builds on Barth's argument by investigating a variety of passages in the Gospel that may enhance our understanding of Matthew's view of the Law. Foster (2004) investigated the role that the Law presumably played within the social location of the Matthean community. The current study engages with Foster's study as the probable provenance of the Gospel, and continues to develop the argument as to how such a provenance is reflected in the text. Oliver (2013) has argued that Matthew and Luke expected the Jewish followers of Jesus to continue observing the Jewish Law in full, though the gentiles were expected to keep the ethical commandments and certain purity and dietary laws from the Mosaic *Torah*. The current study focusses on the first Gospel only. From the selected Matthean passages to be investigated, such a differentiation between Jewish and Gentile followers of Jesus seems to be improbable.

CHAPTER 2

THE TORAH IN THE RELIGIOUS WORLD OF MATTHEW

2.1 INTRODUCTION

Quite some research has been done on the Jewish society of the late second temple period (e.g. Brown, 1997; Cohen, 2006; Saldarini, 1994; Stanton, 1992; Wright, 2013), which provides a useful overview of the political, social, religious and philosophical worlds of the New Testament times. Obviously these depictions of the situation are constructed based on available sources from those times[17]. From these sources a general idea of this situation can be constructed, though the more localized situation of the first Gospel is more difficult to determine. Indeed, very little is directly known about the community in which the first Gospel was written[18], though, as argued in Chapter 1, most scholars have agreed that the story of Jesus and his disciples reflects, yet partly, the experience of the Matthean community.

My assumption in this study is that the debate about the *Torah* as described in the first Gospel partially reflects the unstable political and religious situation in which this document originated[19]. The interpretation of the *Torah* seemingly played a significant role religious turmoil of those times.

---

[17] When reading literature in which different groups are described, one has to realise that it is not clear to what extent these groups were constructed by the authors who promote their own groups or criticize their opponents and how much their description meets reality.

[18] Most commentaries on Matthew have brief sections about some aspects of the Matthean community such as the relationship between the community and Judaism, the nationality of its members (Jewish, gentile or both) and its geographical location. However, these constructions are mainly based on internal evidence of the text itself.

[19] To my view, the strict distinction between Judaism as a religion of the Law and Christianity as religion of love is inaccurate. The first Gospel deals extensively with the importance of adhering to the Law, but as interpreted by Jesus. The double-love commandment (Matt. 22:34-40) describes love as the essence of the Law.

In this chapter I intend to postulate broad outlines of the probable religious situation in which the first Gospel originated and what role the *Torah* played in it. This would provide a frame of reference for my interpretation of passages where Matthew (directly or indirectly) deals with the *Torah*.

To reach this aim, I will determine:

- the probable situation of the Matthean community within the broader Jewish religious society;
- the role that the *Torah* played in this society; and
- why Matthew shows special interest in the interpretation of the *Torah*.

When considering the setting or community involved in the Gospel, one should do this with great caution. The implied audience may not fully overlap with its historical audience. What is more, the internal evidence does not tell us whether we are dealing with the views of the author, the addressees, or both. Though it is usually assumed, we are not sure whether the author lived amongst the addressees.

2.2 THE MATTHEAN COMMUNITY WITHIN A JEWISH RELIGIOUS SOCIETY

This section presents an investigation of the developments within the broader Jewish society during the time of the New Testament and the first Gospel. This entails the investigation of developments within Judaism, and how the "Jesus movement" (church[20]) and eventually the Matthean community[21] were involved in these developments.

---

[20] The translation of ἐκκλησία as "church" somehow is problematic, as this translation is usually interpreted with anachronistic overtones of an institutionalized group, sharply differentiated from Judaism, with a technical Christian meaning as used by Paul and subsequent Christian literature. However, from the Gospel it seems that the Matthean "church" was less institutionalized. The group probably met for worship in house-based groups and Jesus would be present even when only two or three are gathered in his name (Matt. 18:20). Nevertheless this church was somewhat institutionalized: it exercised discipline God's name by handling the keys of heaven (Matt. 16:19 and 18:15-18), it claimed permanence as Jesus built it and promised that the gates of Hades would not overcome it (Matt. 16:18).

[21] Most studies on Matthew refer to the "Matthean community". However, this designation needs closer clarification. A community usually implies a sense of identity and a common set of values and perceptions, which result in a supportive group. As is argued in this study, the Matthean group was still in a process of establishing its own identity as deviant Judaistic group. When using the term

2.2.1 Developments within Judaism

It seems that a variety of Judaist groups existed in New Testament times, but a movement towards formative Judaism developed specifically after the destruction of the temple.

In this part I firstly describe what I assume this fragmentation looked like, and secondly the dynamics that the movement towards formative Judaism introduced.

2.2.1.1 Fragmentation of Judaism

From the post-exilic period onwards Israel was encroached on by Seleucid and Roman leaders respectively and often mistreated by Hasmonean rulers. Revolts and the eventual destruction of the temple in Jerusalem left the people of Israel volatile, which led to fragmentation of the society into competing rabbinic, apocalyptic, revolutionary and Christian-Jewish movements (Saldarini, 1994:111).

While the Jerusalem temple was still standing, it functioned as the main institution of the society (Wright, 2013:310). Those in control of the temple established policies for the daily practices of Jews, but not all Jews accepted them willingly (Brown, 1997:75). During the latter part of the Second Temple period the broader society increasingly mistrusted persons in powerful religious and political positions (Wright, 2013:310). Though our knowledge is limited, it seems that several deviant groups[22] such as Zealots and various quietist-pietistic apocalyptic groups formed, separating themselves from the temple leadership (Blenkinsopp, 1981:25; Cohen, 2006:5; Stanton, 1992:386). As is typical of deviant groups, they sectioned themselves off from the influence and hostility of the temple leadership as dominant group (Saldarini, 1994:112). These groups regarded the religious leaders as fraudulent, as they betrayed their people and

---

"community" for the Matthean group, one should keep in mind that its identity probably was still in a forming process (cf. Saldarini, 1994:85-87).

[22] Most of these "deviant groups" were "sectarian" in nature. Scholars usually refer to these groups as Jewish sects, including the "Jesus movement" as one of these sects. Sects are religious groups that reject the social environment in which they exist (Saldarini, 1994:109). Wilson (1973:21) has described the typical trait of deviant sects as "concern with transcendence over evil and the search for salvation and consequent rejection of prevailing cultural values, goals, and norms, and whatever facilities are culturally provided for man's salvation".

turned from God. This was believed to have caused the hardship the people were experiencing.

Disputes developed over different interpretations of the Law, and deviant groups sought to establish their own rules to govern their practices (Wright, 2013:310). This resulted in a reinterpretation or even rejection of temple rules. The Essenes, the rabbis and the church left behind literature in which these reinterpretations were noted.

The Jewish historian, Josephus, depicted the Jewish society during the Maccabean struggle under Jonathan (c.a. 145 B.C.E): "At that time there were three parties [heresies] (αἵρεσεις) among the Jews which held different opinions about human affairs: the first of them were called the Pharisees, the second the Sadducees and the third Essenes" (Jewish War, 2.8.2). In a setting of 6 C.E. Josephus reported: "From most ancient times there were among the Jews three philosophies pertaining to ancestral tradition, that of the Essenes, that of the Sadducees, and the third system called the Pharisees" (Ant. 18.1.2). Josephus mentions only three groups, probably the most prominent of those times. However, more groups existed.

The Essenes is a clear example of such a deviant group with sectarian sentiments. During the second century B.C.E. this community developed from an opposition against developments in the Temple. They despised the temple as they regarded the presiding priests as wicked (Brown, 1997:76). Awaiting an immanent messianic coming during which God would destroy all iniquity, they withdrew themselves from the established community because they regarded the temple and Jewish establishment as foul and unrighteous. They formed a new remote community in the desert where the ancient Israelites were purified in the time of Moses. Based on the ranking of holiness, they organized themselves under the leadership of the "Teacher of Righteousness". In their documents they justify their separation and strongly denounce the apostasy of the majority of Israel and its religious leadership in particular (cf. the Community Rule, 1QS 9, 11) (Vermes, 1975:88-93).

The Pharisees became critical of and eventually split from the Hasmonean descendants of the Maccabees, as the Hasmoneans became increasingly secularized (Brown, 1997:77). The Pharisees were less strict and more innovative than the Essenes in their interpretation of the Law. Besides the written Law of Moses, they also adhered to an oral Law, which they claimed also derived from Moses. This resulted in them being labelled as the Judaism of the Dual *Torah*. Furthermore, they believed in the resurrection of the body and angels – a belief also reflected in the Jesus movement.

At times the relations between the different Judaist groups turned vicious (Brown, 1997:78). 1QpHab 11:2-8 describes how an unnamed high priest in the late second century B.C.E sought to kill the Essene Teacher of Righteousness on the Day of Atonement according to the Essene calendar[23]. Josephus described how Alexander Jannaeus early in the first century B.C.E massacred 6000 Jews at the Feast of Tabernacles because they (probably Pharisees) challenged his qualifications to hold the priestly office (War, 1.4.3; Ant. 13.13.5). Between 135 and 67 B.C.E. the Pharisees incited hatred amongst the masses against the high priests John Hycranus (Ant. 13.10.5-6) and Alexander Jannaeus (Ant. 13.5.5). Bickerman (1947:103) has remarked: "Early Pharisaism was a belligerent movement that knew how to hate". Sanders (1990:87-88) lists several accounts of even strong intra-Pharisee disputes. Writers of the Dead Sea Scrolls (4QpNah 3-4.1.6-7) criticize "the furious young lion [the high priest Alexander Janneaus] ... who carries out revenge on seekers of smooth things [Pharisees] and who hangs people alive". All these incidents took place before the Roman prefecture in Judea. Roman rulers would later supress such internal religious violence, which in its turn enticed political tension between the Jews and the Romans (Brown, 1997:78).

The Pharisees were probably the most influential during the time of Jesus' public ministry. Josephus (War. 2.8.14; Ant. 18.1.3) described the Pharisees as the leading "heresy" and extremely influential in the towns and villages. This explains the many confrontations between Jesus and the Pharisees in the Gospels[24]. The picture that the Gospel presents was probably influenced by the post-70 C.E. conflicts between Christians[25] and the emerging rabbinic teachers

---

[23] Difference between the Temple and Essene calendars caused considerable tension (Wright, 2013:317).

[24] Mark records many references to Pharisees and confrontations between Jesus and the Pharisees (e.g. Mark 2:15-17; 2:18-21; 2:23-28; 3:1-6; 7:1-23; 8:11-15; 10:2 and 12:13), but only one with the Sadducees (Mark 12:18). Essenes are never mentioned in the New Testament.

[25] The use of the word "Christian" for the believers of the first Gospel needs specification. During the first century the believers in Jesus should not be seen as a group completely separated from Judaism. Complex overlapping relationships between varieties of Jewish groups, including the Jesus-followers, existed.

(who were closely related to the Pharisees), but it most probably also does reflect a historical conflict in Jesus' lifetime (Brown, 1997:79).

As the deviant groups felt themselves subjected and exploited by groups in power, they established identities of their own, while criticizing the establishments that controlled their lives. They competed amongst each other to claim the best positions. They developed systems to justify their own existence and to define and protect inner group values. As minority groups they usually regarded themselves as the righteous remnants of Israel being endangered by others. They used "the righteous" as a technical designation to set their group apart from their opponents (Saldarini, 1994:26). The "normative" Judaism was thus largely replaced by "sectarian" Judaisms (Harlow, 2012:392; Van Aarde, 2011:48).

In this process these groups would frequently oppose outsiders openly. The author of 1 Enoch writes that those in power are corrupt and will be punished, while he regards his own community as righteous (cf. 1 En. 94-104). Similarly, the Psalms of Solomon denounces the hypocrisy of lawless people in powerful positions, while his own community will eventually receive the power to pass judgement on those sinners (cf. Ps. of Sol. 1:3-8). 2 Baruch and 4 Ezra, reflect the same sentiments and convictions. 2 Baruch describes the many that did not follow the *Torah* and the few, Baruch's community, who did (2 Bar. 15-18). 4 Ezra contrasts the wicked many with the few of its own community who truly kept the Law. These few are called the righteous who will inherit the world to come (4 Ezra 3-8).

Deviant groups repeatedly used stereotypical terms as "buzzwords" to justify themselves (e.g. "the righteous ones") and to denounce outsider groups (e.g. "the lawless ones"). Such terms were often used in a polemical sense to distinguish the insiders as a minority group from the outsiders who controlled or competed with them (Overman, 1990:17):

> "The righteous should inherit these things, but that the ungodly should perish" (4 Ezra 7:17);
>
> "The ungodly shall be punished, and ... the righteous shall be saved" (4 Ezra 9:13-15);
>
> " ... the works of those who wrought unrighteousness ..." (2 Bar. 14-15);
>
> "The paths of righteousness are worthy of acceptation, But the paths of unrighteousness shall suddenly be destroyed and vanish" (1 Enoch 94:1);

"I am full of righteousness" (Ps. Sol. 1:1-2);
"You have rendered to the sinners according to their deeds, Yes according to their sins, which were very wicked" (Ps. Sol. 2:16).

These documents reflect sentiments that existed in the time of Matthew. 4 Ezra dates back to the late first century C.E., 2 Baruch to the early second century C.E., 1 Enoch to the late first century C.E., while the Psalms of Solomon dates back to the late second or early first century B.C.E (Vriezen & Van der Woude, 2005:596, 611). Similar denouncing terms are found in Matthew too. Matthew frequently refers to the righteousness[26] of his group (e.g. Matt. 1:19; 3:15; 5:6, 10, 20; 6:1, 33; and 10:41), while denouncing this lawless wicked generation (e.g. Matt. 7:23; 12:39-45; 13:41; 16:4; 17:17 and 24:12) and the Pharisees and teachers of the Law as hypocrites (e.g. Matt. 23). The use of such terms obviously led to much tension between communities.

According to Josephus, the Pharisees "seem to interpret the laws more accurately" (Ant. 13.5.9). Matthew, however, presents Jesus as the true interpreter of the Law. For Matthew's argument it was important to defend his conviction that Jesus gives the correct interpretation of the *Torah*. Jesus' relation to the *Torah* forms a central motif in his Gospel. Thus Jesus is seen as the last and greatest expositor of the Law (Davies, 1966:102). Jesus' relation to the *Torah* is taken up in the Sermon on the Mount, specifically in Matt. 5:17-48. In Chapters 3, 4 and 5 I shall further discuss Jesus' teaching on the *Torah* as presented in the Sermon on the Mount.

The keys of the temple became a symbol to indicate whether leaders were reliable to execute their religious duties (Viljoen, 2009b:658). 4 Baruch 4:4 expresses this sentiment: "Take the keys of the temple … because we were not worthy of keeping them, for we were false stewards" (cf. also 2 Baruch 10:18 and 'Avot de-Rabbi Nathan[27]). Other persons who are able to perform those duties properly, including the correct interpretation of the Law, would emerge to handle the keys. The Testament of Levi reached its final form in the second

---

[26] Unlike the authors of the many Jewish writings, Matthew does not use the substantive "the righteous" as technical designation for his group.

[27] It should be considered that 'Avot de-Rabbi Nathan is a Jewish *haggadic* work probably only compiled in the Geonic era (c.a. 700–900 C.E.). One should be very cautious when using Jewish material in New Testament research, as they were written thereafter. However, some traditions in these works probably reflect earlier Jewish though and practices.

century C.E. (Vriezen & Van der Woude, 2005:652), and Test. Levi 10:3 describes the tearing of the temple veil in order to expose the shameful behaviour of the priests behind the veil. The priests broke the Law and set the words of the Prophets aside (Test. Levi 14:4-6). The Testament of Levi continues to describe the wickedness of the priests who did not understand or follow God's laws, defiled the altars, persecuted just men and took innocent blood on their heads (Test. Levi 16:2-4). Matthew describes how the priests and the elders persuaded the crowd to take responsibility for the innocent blood of Jesus (Matt. 27:25) and that the keys of the Kingdom of Heaven (Matt. 16:19[28]) will be handed over to the church. This implies that authority is taken away from the Jewish religious leaders and that a tremendous degree of authority is assigned to Peter and the church instead (Saldarini, 1994:1).

Blenkinsopp (1981:1) has discussed the dynamics between the group that possessed the authority and those who split off from it by using the image of a parent body and offspring or siblings. While the siblings often criticized the parent body, rivalry amongst siblings became severe. It is very often the case that the closer the relationship between groups, the more intense the conflict between them (Coser, 1998:67). In their self-definition, one group competed with other related groups and drew lines between them.

From this brief discussion, it is plausible to assume that normative Judaism did not exist in the time of Jesus, as several deviant groups developed that competed with one another for self-affirmation.

2.2.1.2   Development towards Formative Judaism

The Jewish revolt of 66-70 C.E. and the destruction of the temple changed the dynamics of the religious groups (Brown, 1997:81). Revolutionary groups such as the Zealots and Sicarii were eliminated and the Essene settlement destroyed. The termination of temple sacrifices weakened the influence of the Sadducees. A need for a new religio-cultural formation evolved (Van Aarde, 2011:48; Saldarini, 1994:13). This led to a process of self-definition and consolidation of the fragmented society towards Formative Judaism. This implies a process of social construction and self-definition in Jewish communities. In this

---

[28] Matt. 16:19: "I will give you the keys of the Kingdom of Heaven; whatever you bind on earth will (but rather: have been) be bound in heaven, and whatever you loose on earth will (but rather: have been) be loosed in heaven".

development several movements competed to claim their position and to gain influence.

Groups claimed that their beliefs and behaviour are based on ancient and established traditions to legitimate themselves. Adherence to the traditions of the fathers lent credence and pedigree to their views, as they claimed to be heirs of a great movement (Baumgarten, 1987:77; Overman, 1990:160; Van Aarde, 2011:41).

The rabbinic movement[29] gradually won recognition as a guide for the people (Brown, 1997:81). Rabbis were emerging as leaders of this formative movement, which developed to fuller expression in the later rabbinic Judaism (Cohen, 2006:207; Shanks, 1963:344). Christian writings in the post-70 period increasingly referred to the emerging rabbinic Judaism when they spoke of Judaism.

According to tradition a council took place in Jamnia (Yavneh)[30] on the Palestinian coast around 90 C.E. with rabbi Gamaliel II[31] presiding. The aim of this council was to consolidate the different Jewish factions and to reconstruct their social, religious and communal life (Overman, 1990:38). Synagogues[32] became identifiable places for the gathering and worship of the rabbinic movement (Kee, 1990:20).

---

[29] Much of the Pharisees fed into the rabbinic movement, though it is not clear how it has happened (Brown, 1997:83). While the Pharisees were in confrontation with other Jewish groups, the rabbinic movement was more inclusive. Though legal disputes occurred amongst them, it did not lead to violence.

[30] I intentionally mention that the council of Jamnia in 90 C.E. took place "according to tradition", as no conclusive evidence exists to prove this (Saldarini, 1994:14). The tradition suggests that after the Romans crushed the First Jewish Revolt, an academy of scholars gathered at Jamnia on the Palestinian coast. They were close to Pharisaic thought and were honoured as rabbis. This group would emerge as an influential force (Brown, 1997:214). According to Saldarini (1994:14) the meetings of rabbis in Jamnia were probably informal and sporadic, while their decisions were applied to voluntary association.

[31] Gamaliel II was the son of Gamaliel, the famous interpreter of the Law (Brown, 1997:82).

[32] Jewish assemblies in villages and towns probably took place in large houses, or multi-purpose buildings or public squares. According to Saldarini (1994:101) buildings that were dedicated synagogues only emerged in the third of fourth century C.E.

A significant part of the communal self-definition of the rabbinic movement was the adaption of procedures to expel those who did not conform to their value system. Such a procedure is pronounced in the *Birkat ha-Minim,* a "Blessing on the heretics" (actually a curse), which went through a process of development to be finalised probably only by the beginning of the second century[33]:

> For apostates let there be no hope. The dominion of arrogance do thou speedily root out in our days. And let the *Nazareans* and the *Minim* perish in a moment. Let them be blotted out of the book of the living. And let them not be written with the righteous.

Reference to the *Minim* (heretics) testifies to a variety in Judaism. This "blessing" denounced all kinds of movements that the rabbinic movement considered to be heretic. This included Christians. It seems that in later years this "blessing" was specifically aimed at Christians (Brown, 1997:82). It sparked tension between Judaism and Christianity.

One should, however, keep in mind that in the time of Matthew, Judaism was still not a fixed coherent community. A variety of traditions and developments still existed. A comprehensive, unified and stable Talmudic system would only develop over time (Saldarini, 1994:15). Jewish communities spread over the Roman Empire varied from one another and adapted to different local conditions.

2.2.2 The church amongst rivalling groups

The "Jesus movement" (church)[34] developed within these complex group relations (cf. Davies, 1966:286; Wright, 2013:311) and was caught up in this rivalry amongst Jewish religious groups for self-definition. The Matthean community formed part of this greater "Jesus movement".

---

[33] Scholars traditionally dated the *Birkath ha Minim* c.a. 85 C.E (e.g. France, 1998:85; Horbury, 1982:19-61): This date, however, is dubious. The *Birkath ha Minim* developed over a period of time while synagogues at different locations and times increasingly did not tolerate the presence of other deviant groups and Christians (Saldarini, 1994:14, 19). It is also not clear how widespread the *Birkath ha Minim* has been used.

[34] It is improbable the "Jesus movement" initially formed as a cohesive entity. As Christians were scattered over the Roman Empire, their identity developed over time in a variety of ways at different situations and at different locations.

In this section I firstly describe how I assume the church developed amongst these Jewish movements, and secondly where the Matthean community fits into this picture.

2.2.2.1 The church amongst Judaism

Hummel (1966:55) has described the relationship of the church with Judaism as part of a larger "family conflict" or a rival amongst *feindliche Brüder*. It was not so much a conflict with the Christian community as an outsider group, but strife within Judaism. The church was not the rebellious child of a stable normative Jewish parent religion. As is evident from the fragmentation of the Jewish society in those days, a stable parent group no longer existed. The church can rather be considered as one of the many Judaist deviant groups. The conflict between the church and Judaism should therefore not be defined as a mother-daughter conflict, but rather as a rivalry between siblings, such as the Pharisees, Sadducees, Essenes, Zealots, Sicarii, Samaritans, Therapeutae, and others (cf. Cohen, 2006:216).

The *Birkat ha-Minim*, though later formalized as mentioned before, reflects a tension that was building up between opposing religious views. Initially this "blessing" was addressed to all "heretic" movements and "sects" that would not form part if the rabbinic movement. This included the Christian community. The Christian community found itself in a process of increasing hostility and alienation from its Judaist (especially as in the rabbinic movement) roots.

This conflict within Judaism was associated with "rival claims to exclusive truth within the same religious symbol system" (Radford Ruether, 1974:30). Charges of heresy and sectarianism were used to establish own groups and to discredit opponents.

As a marginalized group, the Jewish Christians defined themselves as Jesus-followers distinct from the other Judaist movements of the time (Saldarini, 1991:49). Their self-definition is expressed in various writings collected in the Christian Bible. At the beginning of the second century the demarcation between Jews and Christians were clearly drawn, although that demarcation developed over a period of several decades. Just as non-Christian Judaism was not yet a cohesive community in the time of Matthew, the same applies to different Christian communities. The "Jesus movement" probably had not yet formed a clear cut identity separate from Judaism either. While some Christian communities separated themselves totally from Judaism, others were still strongly attached to their Jewish roots (Saldarini, 1994:25).

2.2.2.2 The Matthean church and the Judaism of the broader society

The Matthean community originated in this unstable and transitional period in Israel's political and religious history[35]. As a partially transparent document, Matthew's Gospel reflects specific tensions, underlying conflicts and concerns (Foster, 2004:3; Saldarini, 1994:12; Stanton, 1993:26) that fit into the history of the complex Jewish-Christian relations of the first century (Harlow, 2012:391).

Tension is quite foregrounded in the Matthean Gospel. Sim (1999:186) has remarked that the tension of the Matthean community with other Jewish groups was born from proximity rather than distance:

> Polemical and stereotypical language such as we find in Matthew does not reflect distance between the parties. On the contrary, it reflects both physical and ideological proximity between the disputing groups, since its very purpose is to distance one party from the other.

The first Gospel reflects a struggle to come to terms with this estrangement. Matthew's response to this estrangement can be seen in the Gospel's apologetics and polemics[36].

Bornkamm (1963a:55) has argued that this unstable environment is reflected in the Matthean narrative of the stilling of the storm (Matt. 8:23-27). According to his view the little boat in the stormy sea represents the church in Matthew's redaction. With this narrative Matthew expresses his sentiments that his community was endangered and struggled to survive, but by putting their trust

---

[35] Though it is difficult and arguments on the dating of the Gospels are not precise (cf. Hagner, 1993:lxxiii-lxxv), I concur with the majority view that Matthew was written sometime after the destruction of the temple in 70 C.E. The reference in Matt. 22:7 to the king burning the city probably reflects the destruction of Jerusalem. The triadic formula in Matt. 28:19 and the abiding presence of Jesus in Matt. 28:20 reveals a theological development related to the late New Testament period. The controversies with the Pharisees and the condemnation of the free use of the title "rabbi" (Matt. 23:7-8), which is unique to Matthew, fit well into the early rabbinic period after 70 C.E. If one further considers the dependence of Matthew on Mark – a Gospel commonly dated between 68 and 73 C.E., it is quite plausible that Matthew was written between 80 and 90 C.E. (Brown, 1997:217; Van Aarde, 2011:46).

[36] Several passages in the Gospel reflect Matthean polemics and apologetics, e.g. the charge that followers of Jesus are breaking the Law, is rejected in Matt. 5, the legitimacy of the Jewish leadership is attacked in Matt. 23, and the charge that the disciples stole Jesus' body (Matt. 27:62-66) is answered in Matt. 28:11-15.

in Jesus, they were able to survive and establish their own identity. Bornkamm (1963b:22) has argued that the conflict was mainly inner-Jewish.

This inner-Jewish conflict is related to the rivalry between parties within this movement towards Formative Judaism (Ascough, 2001:102; Keener, 1999:45, Overman, 1990:2). As the Matthean community had a specific locality, the question remains with which parties they competed.

Bornkamm (1963b:22) has been of the opinion that the Matthean community struggled within the synagogue/rabbinic environment (*intra muros*). His viewpoint has been shared by several scholars (cf. Barth, 1963:65; Hummel, 1966:159; Davies, 1966:276; Saldarini, 1994:3). Saldarini (1994:21) has remarked: "The author of Matthew ... is most probably a Jew who, though expelled from the assembly in his city, still identifies himself as a member of the Jewish community". Saldarini (1994:20-25) has described the Matthean community as a *Torah*-obedient deviant group within first century Judaism. They were dislodged from their local synagogues in Syria. They defended and justified their way of life against opposition from rabbinic Judaism. They sought to establish a firm identity of their own.

However, some scholars have adopted an *extra muros* perspective (e.g. Stendahl, 1968:xiii; Schweizer, 1963:405; Stanton, 1993:102). They argue that the Matthean community no longer formed part of the synagogue, as they withdrew or had been expelled from it. This distance between Matthew and the synagogue is reflected in Matthew's references to the synagogue. Matthew uses the phrase "their synagogue" five times (Matt. 4:23, 9:35; 10:17; 12:9; 13:54) and "your synagogue" once (Matt. 23:34) to underline the distance between Jesus and the synagogue community (Carter, 2000a:31).

Weren (2014:251-265) distinguishes three phases in the development of the Matthean community. During the first phase (prior to 70 C.E.) this Christian group regarded themselves to be full members of the Jewish community (Weren, 2014:254-255). During the second phase (70-80 C.E.) they became a minority within the Jewish community (Weren, 2014:255-259). This was a time of growing conflict with the Pharisees, who were trying to redefine Judaism. During the last phase (80-90 C.E.) the Jewish Christians gradually detached them from the Jewish community (Weren, 2014:260-264).

Hare (1967:125) has spoken of "social ostracism and mutual hostility" between these two groups. Within this "family conflict" the "parent group[37]" felt betrayed and thought their values were being undermined, while the dissenting group struggled to come to terms with their new separate status. According to Hare, the struggle of the Matthean community is reflected in the intensity of conflict in the Gospel with the "parent body". Boundaries were established to exclude opposing outsiders[38], but also to define the convictions of those within the community[39].

However, as has previously been argued, Matthew's polemics are not aimed against Jewish people as an established group, but against other "siblings" who rejected the Matthean community for their understanding of God's will. The break between the Jewish and Christian groups was not a clean break, as the conflicts between them varied according to time and place.

The identity and nature of these "siblings" ask for further consideration. After 70 C.E. deviant groups such as the Zealots, Sicarii and Essenes were eliminated and the influence of the Sadducees weakened. Minor groups were marginalized and later on faded away. The Pharisees emerged as the dominant group (Brown, 1997:78).

From the Matthean Gospel it seems that the Pharisees were regarded as their main opponents. It is significant that Matthew's polemic with the Pharisees is particularly harsh. Anti-Pharisaic arguments played an important role in the self-definition of the Matthean community in the crises of separation and

---

[37] As I argued before it is inappropriate to consider Matthew's opponents as a stable "parent group" as much diversity existed within Judaism.

[38] Matthew has a twofold view of the outsider-group. One part consists of the opponents, who are the scribes, Pharisees and Jewish religious leaders. The other part consists of those who are open to the gospel of Jesus. The author of Matthew uses the word λαός (people) in its ordinary sense to refer to a social and political entity of the land of Israel, but also as people who need salvation: "you are to give Him the name Jesus, because He will save his people from their sins" (Matt. 1:21). Matthew uses the term ὄχλος (crowd) most frequently to refer to people who gathered around Jesus. For the most part the crowds are depicted as friendly and good-willed, but are easily misled by Jewish leaders. The chief priests and the elders persuade the crowds to ask for Jesus' death and Barabbas' release (Matt.27:20) (cf. Saldarini, 1994:27-43). The fact that Matthew use these terms to identify different groups, suggests that the Matthean groups was forming a new subgroup, which were in conflict with the majority.

[39] The formulation of group convictions provided means to discipline insincere and unfaithful insiders.

transition (Carter, 2000a:6). Carter (2000a:1) labels the first Gospel a "counter-narrative" against synagogual control[40] by the Pharisees. This heightened conflict against the Pharisees is strongly reflected in Matthew's controversy stories. Repschinski (2000:329) comments on Matthew's attack on the Pharisees in these stories: "Matthew intends the audience of the controversy stories to reflect a group that turns from the fraudulent leadership of the opponents of Jesus towards an acknowledgement of the Matthean community as the rightful leaders of Israel". Especially the discourse of the woes (Matt. 23) and the parables on the tenants and the wedding banquet (Matt. 21:33-22:14) express this conflict (cf. Saldarini, 1994:46). It is also expressed as Matthew intensifies the conflict in the narratives he took over from Mark (Repschinski, 2000:63ff). Mark's sympathetic scribe (Mark 12:38) asking about the greatest commandment is portrayed as a hostile Pharisee in Matt. 22:35. Whereas Mark refers to the Pharisees as hypocrites once (Mark 7:6) and Luke not at all, Matthew has fourteen such references, six of which are in the Woe Discourse of Matt. 23 (Matt. 6:2, 5, 16; 15:7; 16:3; 22:18; 23:13, 14, 15, 23, 25, 27, 29: 24:51). Unlike Mark, the synagogue became an almost foreign institution to Matthew. At the climax of Matthew's narrative he addresses his readers directly by telling them of a rival account of the resurrection of Jesus which holds that his disciples stole his body from the tomb, and adds "and this story has been widely circulated among the Jews to this very day" (Matt. 28:15). In adding this Matthew makes it clear that those who accept the alternative story are miserably misled.

Van Aarde (2011:41-49) has suggested that the conflict in the first Gospel should be credited to a local scenario. He has proposed that Matthew should be regarded as a scribe who was in conflict with other scribes (teachers of the Law) in a village community[41]. The village scribes were in the process of establishing

---

[40] Though to a lesser extent, the tension with the Roman Imperial power is also reflected in the characters of Herod (Matt. 2) and Antipas (Matt. 14) as Roman allies, Vespasian (Matt. 17) and Caesar (Matt. 22) are indirectly mentioned in relation to Roman taxes, and Pilate directly in person (Matt. 27) (Carter, 2001:35).

[41] A plausible construction is that the Matthean community originated after 70 C.E. in northern Galilee and southeren Syria, probably in the vicinity of Antioch (Van Aarde, 2011:46). Syria is added in Matt. 4:24 to Mark's description of the spread of Jesus' activity. While Van Aarde has suggested a village setting, an urban setting seems more plausible (cf. Brown, 1997:212; Foster, 2004:9). Matthew uses "city" (πόλις) twenty-six times compared to four of "village" (κώμη). The dominant influence of Matthew in later years, suggests that it was addressed to a major Christian church in an important city. Based on these arguments, Antioch seems to be a strong possibility, though it cannot be proven with certainty.

the first phase of a Pharisaic rabbinate. However, it is also possible that the Gospel of Matthew was written as a Christian response to the Judaism that was emerging after 70 C.E. at Jamnia where the rabbis were honoured as the interpreters of the *Torah* (Davies & Allison, 2004a:xxi*)*. It rather seems that the Matthean community lived in the shadow of a large Jewish community that resented them (Brown, 1997:215). As they shared the same Scriptures, their differences[42] were the subject of dispute.

Since the temple no longer existed, the rabbis sought to find God in their own communities. A similar activity was found amongst the Jesus-followers who tried to find God amongst them. This resulted in two sets of teachers of the Law: those like Matthew who followed Jesus and others who upheld the traditional view of the messiah.

I mention a few significant references in the first Gospel which support this viewpoint.

2.2.2.2.1 God with us

Finding God within the Matthean community is an important motif in the Gospel. At the beginning of his Gospel Matthew writes about the name of Jesus: "'The virgin will conceive and give birth to a son, and they will call him Immanuel', which means 'God with us' (Μεθ' ἡμῶν ὁ Θεός)" (Matt. 1:26). He likewise ends his Gospel with the promise of Jesus: "And surely I am with you always (ἐγὼ μεθ' ὑμῶν εἰμι πάσας τὰς ἡμέρας), to the very end of the age". (Matt. 28:20). Matthew describes the presence of Jesus in the church by saying "For where two or three gather in my name, there am I with them (οὗ γάρ εἰσιν δύο ἢ τρεῖς συνηγμένοι εἰς τὸ ἐμὸν ὄνομα, ἐκεῖ εἰμι ἐν μέσῳ αὐτῶν" (Matt. 18:20). These announcements equal Roman claims that the Caesar was the agent of Jupiter and the present deity (*deus praesens*) (Statius, *Silvae* 5.2.170). Jesus is the beloved Son of God (Matt. 3:17 and 17:5). He teaches his disciples to speak of and pray for the "Kingdom" of God (e.g. Matt. 6:10).

2.2.2.2.2 Scriptures are fulfilled

Like the movement towards Formative Judaism, the Matthean community was also in a process of establishing their identity. As Formative Judaism attempted

---

[42] While both communities tried to create clear identities and boundaries, they overlapped one another.

to assure credence by claiming that their procedures were based on that of the traditions of their ancestors[43], Matthew presented the life of Jesus in terms of the fulfilment of Scriptures[44]. While other New Testament writers quoted a few obvious texts as fulfilled in Jesus, Matthew explored this motif extensively (Davies & Allison, 2004a:211; Menken, 2004:3; Versteeg, 1992:23). France (1998:167) labels fulfilment as "the special trademark" of this Gospel. Matthew thus claims his community to be heir to a great movement.

2.2.2.2.3 Church and synagogue

While the synagogues became gathering places in Judaism, Matthew distances his group from the synagogues and establishes a separate structure that stands independent from the synagogues. Matthew's Jesus refers to this new community as the ἐκκλησία (church) (Matt. 16:18 and 18:17). Being a general LXX translation for *qahal* the congregation of the people of God (e.g. Deut. 31:30), Jesus uses the term to describe the group of restored Israelites that He was gathering around Himself. However, συναγωγή (synagogue) was also commonly used as translation of *qahal* (Keener, 1999:428). By using this emotive concept from the Jewish Bible and translating it distinctively as ἐκκλησία (church), Matthew obviously intends to indicate that his group – as part of a greater church community- took over the role of the congregation of the people of God and he distinguishes them from the synagogues and its leaders. Matt. 8:11-15[45] even speaks of transference of the kingdom of God to a new people. While the Jewish leaders claimed to lead the synagogue, the church was lead by leaders who confess Jesus as the Christ, the Son of the living God (Matt. 16:16).

---

[43] Josephus wrote that the Pharisees prided themselves on the accuracy of their adherence to ancestral tradition (Ant. 17.2.4).

[44] Cf. Viljoen, 2007:314-320 where I discuss the significance of fulfilment quotations in Matthew.

[45] Matt. 8:11-15: "I say to you that many will come from the east and the west, and will take their places at the feast with Abraham, Isaac and Jacob in the Kingdom of Heaven. But the subjects of the kingdom will be thrown outside, into the darkness, where there will be weeping and gnashing of teeth."

2.2.2.2.4 Keys of the Kingdom of Heaven

The church disciplined those who were unfaithful to the values of this community based on the authority of Jesus (Matt. 18:15-17[46]). The formula "I will give you the keys of the Kingdom of Heaven; whatever you bind on earth will (but rather: have been, since δεδεμένον is a perfect participle) be bound in heaven, and whatever you loose on earth will (but rather: have been, since λελυμένον is a perfect participle) be loosed in heaven" (Matt. 16:19) and "I tell you the truth, whatever you bind on earth will be (but rather: have been, since δεδεμένα is a perfect participle) bound in heaven, and whatever you loose on earthy will be (rather: have been, since λελυμένα is a perfect participle) loosed in heaven" (Matt. 18:18) propose a tremendous degree of authority for Peter and the community. The first pronouncement refers to Peter himself, while the second indicates the corporate responsibility of the church. The authority is exercised by Peter on behalf of the church (Matt. 16), as well as by the church corporately (Matt. 18).

2.3. THE *TORAH* IN THE JEWISH SOCIETY

It seems that the newly formed groups used the *Torah* to justify their parting from other groups and to define their norms of existence. Their rivalry very much centred on the correct interpretation of the *Torah*. My argument is that the *Torah* became a feature of division between different groups and that it was used as boundary marker.

2.3.1 The *Torah* as feature of division

In reaction to the Jewish revolt, Rome destroyed Jerusalem, the temple and the temple service in 70 C.E. This left the Jewish community bewildered. The Jews struggled with to come to terms with their loss and probably with the question of whether this destruction was the punishment of God for their sins. If the destruction was God's punishment for sin, they had to consider how to know God's will with certainty in order to avert similar disasters in future. This resulted in many significant reformulations of important theological ideas and religious practices. Various Jewish groups debated questions about the meaning

---

[46] Matt. 18:15-17: "If your brother sins against you, go and show him his fault, just between the two of you. If he listens to you, you have won your brother over. But if he will not listen, take one or two others along, so that 'every matter may be established by the testimony of two or three witnesses.' If he refuses to listen to them, tell it to the church; and if he refuses to listen even to the church, treat him as you would a pagan or a tax collector.

and practice of the *Torah* and about the authority to interpret it (Carter 2000, 140; Cohen, 2006:123; Foster, 2004:2; Saldarini, 1994:5). Temple-based worship was replaced by small localized groupings with a mutual emphasis on *Torah* conservation and interpretation (Neusner, 1979:42; Van Aarde, 2011:46). The Law emerged as a central symbol in Jewish religion. Overman (1990:69) has written:

> The law now emerged as the central symbol for post-70 Judaism. Who was recognized as the authoritative interpreters had a great deal to do with who emerged as the accepted and established movement.

The group that would be recognized as the most authoritative and accurate interpreters of the Law, would become the dominant force. Josephus described the Pharisees as the most accurate interpreters of the Law (Jewish Wars, 1.5.1; 2.8.14).

The importance of the Law was obviously nothing new. Since the time of the Deuteronomistic historian there had been a continuous urge to arrive at a more exact observance of the Law (Foster, 2004:49). Yet in the fragmented Jewish society of the first century C.E., this observance became more intense. Competing groups who each regarded themselves as the righteous few used the Law to legitimate their own position against their adversaries.

The Essenes believed they understood the Law correctly and that others in Israel, especially in the temple, failed to understand it. According to 1QS9 God has "concealed the teaching of the Law from the men of falsehood, but shall impart true knowledge and righteous judgement to those who chose the Way". The true meaning of the Law was explicated by the Teacher of Righteousness. The Essene community used his interpretation of the Law to validate their own beliefs and practices and to denounce those of other groups, specifically of the Jerusalem leaders.

Other Jewish documents from the late second temple period until the first century C.E. reveal similar sentiments. Like the Essenes, 1 Enoch claims that the enemies of its community do not follow the Law correctly and lead people astray with false versions of the Scriptures (1 En. 99:12), while its own community understands their mysteries and makes them available to the chosen community (1 En. 92:1; 93:1). The Psalms of Solomon also attacks the Jewish leaders as people who violated and corrupted the Law (Ps. Sol. 4:1, 8, 22), while the community of the text is regarded as the faithful people who remain true to God's Law (Ps. Sol. 14:10). In 2 Baruch, Baruch himself emerges as God's agent who truly instructs the righteous community (2 Bar. 38:1-4). Baruch is paralleled with Moses as he left his people and ascended Mount Zion to receive God's instructions. Like Moses, Baruch is portrayed as God's lawgiver. In 4 Ezra 14, Ezra appears as Moses *redivivus*: "I revealed myself in the bush, and spoke to Moses ... So too I now give this order to you" (4 Ezra 14: 3-7).

Because of the importance of the *Torah* for the people of God, the interpretation of the *Torah* became a feature of the division in Judaism. The different groups studied the Law in minute detail. They identified 613 commandments in the *Torah* (248 positive and 365 negative) (Morris, 1992:107; Neusner, 2007:77). It was their desire to meet the specific obligations of these commandments, which resulted in competitive disputes as to what they meant in practice. With a legalistic turn of mind, each group claimed to be living according to the principles of the *Torah*. Obviously this implied that other groups were not doing so. "In such polemic the need for a group to find in the *Torah* its own self-affirmation had the inevitable corollary of making the *Torah* an instrument by means of which one group condemned another" (Dunn 2003, 292). In many cases a study of what a group rejects, reveals what that group is in itself.

In Pharisaic Judaism the *Torah* was not limited to the written version. Pharisaic Judaism entertained the concept of a dual *Torah*, which refers to the written and oral law (Neusner, 1994:5-7; 2007:111; Schiffman, 2012:424). The Pharisaic Dual *Torah* implies an oral supplement to the written *Torah* which provides guidelines how to apply the written *Torah* in daily life. This approach earned them the title and identity of "Judaism of the Dual *Torah*". The oral law was preserved through the oral tradition and the rabbis. According to the Babylonian Talmud[47] a rabbi was considered equivalent to a scroll of the *Torah* (Neusner, 1994:6). This Talmud states: "He who sees a disciple of a sage who has died is as if he sees a scroll of the *Torah* that has burned" (Y. Moed Qatan 3:7.X) and "An elder who forgot his learning because of some accident which happened to him – they treat him with the sanctity owed to an ark [of the *Torah*]" (Y. Moed Qatan 3:1.XI). The Essene community, however, distinguished between the "revealed law" (the written *Torah*) and the "hidden law" derived from their own exegesis of the written law and only known by their community. Both of these

---

[47] Though the Babylonean Talmud only formalized in written form in late antiquity (third to fifth century C.E) (Cohen, 2006:5), it probably reflects sentiments of earliers rabinnic sages.

groups believed that this second *Torah* was divinely inspired (Schiffman, 2012:424).

The social location of Matthew is linked to the evangelist's view of the Law. Barth (1963:159) has remarked:

> Matthew does not share the understanding of the law in the Rabbinate but rather opposes the Rabbinate face to face. But it will still not be correct to speak of a *lex nova* because the identity with the law of Sinai is not strongly emphasised.

With regard to Matthew's discussion of the Law, the evangelist developed a subtle dialectic with his opponents, presumably some village teachers of the Law (scribes) in the process of establishing a Pharisaic rabbinate. Matthew's Jesus strongly criticizes the Pharisees' oral traditions (e.g. Matt. 15:1-9) (cf. Chapter 9) and questions their interpretations of the *Torah* (e.g. Matt. 5:21-47) (cf. Chapter 4). He denounces their righteousness with an emphasis on personal integrity (e.g. Matt. 5:20, and 6:1) (cf. Chapter 5). These traditional teachers of the Law presumably felt that their core values were undermined by Jesus' followers. This probably led to Matthew's community being accused of abrogating the Law. The Matthean Jesus rejects such accusations in texts such as Matt. 5:17-19 (cf. Chapter 3). The Matthean community, as sibling of the local Pharisaic Judaism, strived to establish its claims of following the true interpretation of the Law (Foster, 2004:28). Matthew presents Jesus as a unique and authoritative teacher of Law (cf. Matt. 7:28-29) who was in continuous dispute with Pharisees and teachers of the Law who concentrated on the minute interpretation of the commandments of the *Torah*, but missed the true intention of the Law.

Matthew describes Jesus as the one who brought the definitive interpretation of God's will. Matthew claimed that Jesus provided the answer. Jesus superseded current understandings of the Law with his reinterpretation. In the Sermon on the Mount Jesus is presented as a Moses type. In the beginning of the Sermon (Matt. 5:1-2) the Sinai typology is significant (Loader, 1997:165). This leads to an anticipation of a new revelation to be delivered by a new Moses. He had come to fulfil the Law (Matt. 5:17). Matthew claims that "He taught as one who had authority, and not as their teachers of the Law" (Matt. 7:29) (Viljoen, 2012a:5). Therefore Matthew reports the words of Jesus: "All authority in heaven and on earth has been given to me" (Ἐδόθη μοι πᾶσα ἐξουσία ἐν οὐρανῷ καὶ ἐπὶ τῆς γῆς). Therefore go and make disciples … teaching them to obey everything I have commanded you (διδάσκοντες αὐτοὺς τηρεῖν πάντα ὅσα ἐνετειλάμην ὑμῖν)" (Matt. 28:18-20). Matthew claims that Jesus has the authority to interpret the Scriptures. His interpretation provides the answer to the correct way of understanding the Scriptures. As followers of Jesus, Matthew sees himself and his community as the guardians of the correct understanding of the Law and the Prophets (Overman, 1996:50). Jesus' interpretation of the *Torah* marked the identity of the Matthean community.

2.3.2 The *Torah* as it was used as a boundary marker

The tension amongst the Jews was intensified by the fact that they struggled to maintain their identity within the Hellenistic culture and under the Roman Empire. The Hasmonean dynasty also showed a particular affinity to Greek culture (Wright, 2013:311). This resulted in a strong tendency towards Jewish exclusiveness. The Jews fended off foreign influences in their struggle to maintain their identity (Saldarini, 1994:13). They realized that purity was their means to protect their lifestyle from gentiles and unfaithful Jews (Wright, 2013:311). After the destruction of the temple, holiness in relation to God had to be maintained and they did this with purity practices and separation from the nations. The synagogue activities played an important role in this self-affirmation (Knight, 2004:11). It was at this point that the distinction between Judaism in its diversity and Israelite religion became evident[48]. Specific interpretation of the *Torah* was used to assure Jewish exclusivity and to create group identity. Such emphases gave "Judaism" its nationalistic, anti-Gentile and exclusive character (Dunn, 2003:292).

Laws regarding the Sabbath, circumcision, diet and purity were foremost to form the behaviour and thought of the Jewish society (cf. Wright, 2013:310). Observance of these laws was considered as normal and formed identity markers of the society. Jewish religious leaders defended and enforced these identity markers, which resulted in boundary markers between Jews and gentiles.

In Matthew's Gospel these laws/identity markers are recognizable, indicating the Matthean community's closeness to the Jewish society. However, it seems

---

[48] While the Israelite religion had a temple, Judaism had synagogues. Israelite religion had priests, while Judaism had sages or rabbis. Israelite religion had animal sacrifices, while Judaism had prayers. Israelite religion was located primarily in the homeland of Israel, while Judaism was found spread over the Roman Empire. However, the transition from the one to the other happened over a period of time, though the destruction of the temple in 70 C.E. could be regarded as a decisive event (cf. Cohen, 2006:8-12).

that the Matthean community challenged the way the rabbinic movement in their society interpreted these laws. They based their understanding on the teaching and activity of Jesus. The following table indicates the most prominent passages where the first Gospel refers to or implies such laws:

Identity marker	Matthean reference
Sabbath	Matt. 12:1-14
(Circumcision) / baptism	Matt. 28:19
Dietary laws	Matt. 15:1-20 and (9:10-13)
Purity	Matt. 8:1-4; 9:18-26

Table 1: Identity markers in Matthew

2.3.2.1 Sabbath

The observance of the Sabbath was the clearest marker of identity in the Jewish community (Wright, 2013:315-318). According to Biblical evidence it was a well-established feast by the early Second Temple Period (cf. Isa. 56:2; Neh. 13:15-22). It was regarded as sign of the covenant (Exod. 31:14-17) with mention of its origins in the creation narrative (Gen. 2:2-3). Even the Elephantine papyri records concerns for the Sabbath amongst the Jews in Egypt during the fifth century B.C.E. Nevertheless, the way the Jews observed the Sabbath varies, as questions were raised about what was permitted on the Sabbath. Practices concerning issues like marital sex, saving human and animal lives, conducting warfare, fasting and travelling varied. The Sabbath controversies in Matt. 12:1-14 signify a reinterpretation of the Sabbath Law by the Matthean community, serving as an identity marker of this community. Matthew's Jesus does not reject the Sabbath *per se*, but the Matthean Pharisees' *halakha* on the Sabbath (cf. Chapter 7 were I attend to these Sabbath controversies in more detail).

2.3.2.2 Circumcision

Circumcision is another important Jewish identity marker[49]. Circumcision has its roots in Gen. 17 and was demanded in order for a male to be part of the covenant community. By performing this ritual with one's son, an individual passed the privileges and ethical responsibilities over to the next generation.

---

[49] The practice of circumcision, however, was not unique to the Israelites. According to Jer. 9:25-26 other Semitic groups were also practicing circumcision, the Edomites, Ammonites and Moabites, but the Philistines are called the uncircumcised in a derogatory manner (Wright, 2013:312).

Additionally, individuals who were not biologically related to Abraham could also be assimilated into the nation by way of circumcision (Wright, 2013:311-314). Antiochus IV Epiphanes outlawed circumcision along with other identifiable Jewish customs. This resulted in the Maccabean revolt in die mid-second century B.C. (1 Macc. 1:44-49, 60-63). The faithful in Palestine condemned the Jews who rejected circumcision (1 Macc. 1:13-15; Josephus, Ant. 12.241). When the Maccabeans defeated Seluecides and the Hasmonean Kingdom was established in Palestine, a ruling was imposed that all Jews had to be circumcised (1 Macc. 2:46; Josephus, *Ant.* 12.278; 13.257-258, 318-319). This illustrates how important Jews regarded circumcision in Second Temple Judaism. The importance of this ritual is also reflected in the Dead Sea Scrolls. According to 1 QH 14.20 the uncircumcised may not walk on God's holy path and 4Q458 declares that the uncircumcised will be destroyed in the last days. In Matthew a shift can be recognized. Matthew doesn't mention circumcision at all. One could argue (e.g. Saldarini, 1994:157) that the reason why Matthew does not mention circumcision is that he accepted its importance. This, however, is unlikely. Unlike Luke (Luk. 2:21), Matthew does not mention Jesus' circumcision. New gentile believers were not required to be circumcised, but to be baptized (Matt. 28:19). They were not regarded as "God fearers" as the uncircumcised, but as full members of the community. It seems that baptism replaced circumcision to allow both males and females into their community.

2.3.2.3   *Dietary laws*

The number of Biblical texts devoted to food laws (e.g. Lev. 11:1-47; Deut. 14:2-20) makes it clear that the Israelite diet was extremely important as another identity marker. Food laws were not simply related to dietary health, but also to covenantal purity. Though some Jews in the Greco-Roman period discarded some dietary laws in an effort to adapt to the surrounding cultures, Philo (Migr. 89-93) confirms that the general population remained diligent in keeping the food laws. In Matt. 15:1-20 Jesus states that what enters a person's mouth, does not defile him/her, but what comes out of the mouth, signifying a reinterpretation of food laws (cf. Chapter 9).

In the Jewish society eating with others was also strictly regulated. Sharing meals was a way of bounding the community together by confirming identity. Eating with gentiles was taboo, though some Jews found it acceptable if a Jew hosted the dinner or brought his own food to the gentile's house (Judith 12:1-4, 19; Add Esth. 14:17; Josephus, Life 14; Rom. 14:1-2). Gentiles found the Jewish adherence to food laws anti-social and reclusive. Philostratus (Vit. Apol. 33) described how the Jews set up walls between themselves and the gentiles with their food laws. 3 Macc. 3:4 states: "they [the Jews] kept their separateness with respect to foods. For this reason they appeared hateful to some". Matthew reveals a different attitude. In Matt. 9:9-13 the Pharisees blame Jesus for eating with tax collectors and sinners, but Jesus justifies Himself with the words "It is not the healthy who need a doctor, but the sick" and "go and learn what this means: 'I desire mercy, not sacrifice.' For I have not come to call the righteous, but sinners." This story in Matthew signifies a reinterpretation of the custom of table sharing (cf. Chapter 7).

2.3.2.4 Purity

The fourth Jewish identity marker is purity (Wright, 2013:318-321). Jews developed distinct strategies to define, achieve and maintain purity as described in Leviticus, Deuteronomy and Ezekiel. Nevertheless, purity laws varied amongst Jewish groups in the Second Temple Period. A strict degree of purity was imposed in the Essene community as they maintained a lifestyle similar to the priesthood of the Zadokite temple. The Essene community regarded themselves as the temple. To form part of the community one had to maintain the purity of the priestly code. They treated their meals as holy food eaten outside the temple by the priests, they abstained from wine because it was prohibited to drink wine in the temple and they avoided sexual intercourse due to the impurity caused by semen (CD 12.1). The first Gospel reflects issues regarding purity. Jesus touches a leper (Matt. 8:3), a woman with blood flow touches Him (Matt. 8:20), Jesus enters the room of a dead girl and takes her by the hand (Matt. 8:25), yet no mention is made of Jesus undergoing purification rites afterwards (cf. Chapters 6 and 8). The Pharisees and scribes charge Jesus as his disciples don't wash their hands before eating (Matt. 15:2), but Jesus counter-charges the Pharisees that they break the command for the sake of their tradition (Matt. 15:3) and asserts that eating with unwashed hands do not defile a person (Matt. 15:20) (cf. Chapter 9). Jesus assures his followers that those who are pure at heart will see God (Matt. 5:7-8). Jesus accuses the teachers of the Law and Pharisees of "straining out a gnat, but then swallowing a camel" (Matt. 23:24) and of cleaning the outside of their cups and dishes, but not their insides (Matt. 23:25-26) (cf. Chapter 10). From these accounts it seems that Matthew's Jesus also reinterprets purity regulations for his followers.

From this preliminary overview of these four identity markers and references to them in the first Gospel, it seems that Matthew's Jesus reinterpreted these markers. It seems that the Matthean community was still closely related to the Jewish society, though their deviance is apparent. While the identity markers normally served to separate Jews from gentiles, the different interpretation of these laws resulted in a separation between the Matthean group and the rest of the Jewish society. The character of the boundary marker between insiders and outsiders changed. The Matthean community differentiated them from the Pharisaic/rabbinic movement they encountered.

Changes that the Matthean community introduced into their interpretation of the identity markers are typical of deviant groups (Saldarini, 1994:111). Matthew narrates the story of Jesus and his disciples to defend and establish the respectability of their "deviant" behaviour. The Gospel challenges the conventional standards and delegitimizes the religious leaders who controlled the definitions of what was considered to be normal and deviant. This issue will be developed in the following chapters of this study to provide a clearer profile of the Matthean identity in contrast to that of their opponents.

The shift in the identity of the Matthean community can also be recognized in their accommodation of gentiles in their midst[50]. In contrast to the exclusivity of Jews, the first Gospel offers gentiles an open door. The Gospel concludes with the responsibility of the community to spread the teaching of Jesus to all nations[51]. The Matthean inclination towards Gentile mission in contrast to the exclusivity of the Jewish community is further evident from aspects that are highlighted in the Gospel (cf. Versteeg 1992, 21-27):

- The Gospel begins the genealogy of Jesus with the unusual inclusion of the names of gentile women (Matt. 1); the veneration of the baby Jesus by the magi from the East in contrast to the animosity of Herod and the Jewish religious leaders (Matt. 2); and the child murder and flight from Bethlehem to a safe haven in Egypt (Matt. 2).
- The narrative develops around the theme that Jesus came to his people, but was rejected by them (Matt. 1:21).
- The privileged position of Israel is emphasized when Jesus sends out the twelve exclusively to the people of Israel, telling them that if they are not

---

[50] The opposition of the synagogue could have been a contributing factor in the community's outreach to gentiles (Brown, 1997:215. Though it seems that gentile mission rejected in Matt. 10:5-6 and 15:24, Jesus in his farewell words commands mission to the gentiles (Matt. 28:19).

[51] It has often been suggested that Matthew's Gospel was written in Antioch, though conclusive evidence are lacking. According to Acts this was the city in which the followers of Jesus were first called "Christians" (Acts 11:26). They were mission-minded as it was this community who sent Paul and Barnabas out on their first missionary journey (Acts 13).

welcomed, they have to leave that house or town and wipe the dust from their feet (Matt. 10).
- While the animosity of the Jews against Jesus increases, the Canaanite woman recognizes Jesus as the Lord (Matt. 15).
- The scribes and Pharisees reject Jesus and Jesus delivers the terrible accusation of the scribes, Pharisees and Jerusalem, namely "Therefore I tell you that the kingdom of God will be taken away from you and given to a people who will produce its fruit" (Matt. 21:43) within the wider context of Matt. 21 and 23.
- The Roman officer and soldiers confess: "Surely he was the Son of God" (Matt. 27:54).
- The Roman guards report that Jesus rose from death, while the chief priests and the heads of families offered them a large amount of money to pretend that Jesus' disciples stole his corpse (Matt. 28:11-15).
- The Gospel ends climactically with the commissioning: "Therefore go and make disciples of all nations ..." (Matt. 28:19-20).

In the verses directly preceding the discussion of Jesus' teaching on the *Torah* Matthew reports the following words of Jesus: "You are the salt of the earth ... you are the light of the world ..." (Matt. 5:13-16). It appears that Matthew drew a direct link between the interpretation of the *Torah* and the faithful people's responsibility to witness to the world. The Matthean community's decision to carry the proclamation of Jesus to the Gentiles must have created much tension with the synagogue, which used the *Torah* as means to maintain Jewish exclusivity (Repschinski, 2000:27). Luz (1990:84) has proposed that Matthew elected himself as advocate to defend his community's decision for the Gentile mission. An alternative interpretation of the *Torah* is proposed to combat Judaist exclusivism. In the light of the Great Commission (Matt. 28:20), the basic entrance requirement to the Matthean community was belief in Jesus and acceptance of his teaching with the accompanying baptism (Gnilka, 1988:501; Saldarini, 1994:79). The traditional Jewish boundary markers, Sabbath observance, circumcision, food laws and purity are not mentioned in this context.

2.4 MATTHEW'S ISSUE WITH THE *TORAH*

Within this Jewish environment, the Matthean group struggled on two fronts. On the one hand they defended themselves against non-Christian Jews who rejected them for accepting Jesus as the Messiah. On the other hand the Matthean community defined themselves against libertine antinomian Christians who set aside the Law in their doctrine and mission.

When reading the first Gospel against this background, it becomes clear that the Matthean community was caught up in this unstable situation. The evangelist defines the position of his community in terms of specific *Torah* observance. While countering some form of Christian libertinism and allegations against the *Torah* observance of his community, he encourages his community to remain loyal to Jesus and his teaching of the *Torah*.

2.4.1 Contra non-Christian Jewish allegations

A convincing possibility for Matthew's insistence that Jesus did not come to abolish the Law is that Matthew reacted to counter Jewish suspicion[52] of Jesus' teaching as accepted in their community (Loader, 1997:167). Matthew responds to Jewish charges that Christians abolished[53] the Law, and therefore emphatically denies this charge in Matt. 5:17-20 (Carter, 2000a:140; Davies & Allison 2004a:482; Keener, 1999:50), verses that are unique to Matthew (Matthew *Sondergut*)[54]:

Moule (1982:69) has commented that Matt. 5:17-20 "which sounds like extreme legalism is better interpreted as a defence against anti-Christian Pharisaic allegations that Christianity lowered moral standards". Scholars have connected this accusation with the devastating circumstances resulting from Rome's destruction of Jerusalem, the temple, and the priesthood in 70 C.E. (cf. Matt. 22:7; 23:38; 24:2; 26:61) (Neusner, 1972:313-327). Jews probably accused Christians of lowering their moral standards and thus bringing God's wrath over his people.

---

[52] Following Jesus' interpretation of the *Torah* resulted in the alienation between the Matthean community and the synagogue. To be in tension with the synagogue was not only a religious matter. It meant estrangement from one's people and community.

[53] Abolish means "destroy" as in the destruction of the temple in 24:2, 26:61; 27:49, Matthew's only other uses of this verb (Carter, 2000a:140), probably indicating some link between the interpretation of the Law and the destruction of the temple.

[54] "Do not think that I have come to abolish the Law and the Prophets; I have not come to abolish them but to fulfil them. I tell you the truth, until heaven and earth disappear, not the smallest letter, not the least stroke of a pen, will by any means disappear from the Law until everything is accomplished. Anyone who breaks one of the least of these commandments and teaches others to do the same will be called least in the Kingdom of Heaven, but whoever practices and teaches these commands will be called great in the Kingdom of Heaven. For I tell you that unless your righteousness surpasses that of the Pharisees and the teachers of the Law, you will certainly not enter the Kingdom of Heaven."

2.4.2 Contra antinomian or libertine Christians

Bornkamm (1963b:24) has identified another dimension in Matthew's attention to the Law. Based on Matt. 5:17-19 Bornkamm assumes that Matthew is reacting against a tendency amongst some Christians who misunderstood Christian freedom and therefore abandoned the Law. This confirms that Matthew was fighting on two fronts, namely the assertion of his community's stance on the Law against Jews who were not believers in Jesus, and against Christian antinomians or libertines on the other side (cf. Brown, 1997:215). These antinomians could either have been part of Matthew's community or of another Christian branch. Barth (1963:75) has argued along similar lines by stating that Matthew's understanding of the law was determined by his opposition on two battle fronts, on the one side against the antinomians (with pericopes such as Matt. 5:17-20) and on the other against the Pharisaism and Rabbinate (*inter alia* with his use of the double-love command in Matt. 22:34-40). Barth has developed the identity of such a group with lax attitudes to the Law based on three pericopes (the antitheses in Matt. 5:17-20; the passage on false prophets, the negligence of doing God's will and building on wrong foundations in Matt. 7:15-48 and the warning against false prophets in Matt. 24:11). He has rejected the possibility of them being a group of Paulinists because no πίστις (faith) terminology is used in these pericopes, and has suggested that they must have been Hellenistic Christians (Barth, 1963:162). While Paul emphasized the Christian freedom from the bondage of the Law, Barth has been of the opinion that Matthew directed his attack against Hellenistic elements in the church that went much further than Paul[55]. According to Barth they were libertines who were of the opinion that Christ had abolished the Law.

Mohrlang (1984:42-47) has also suggested that Matthew was engaged in fending off a more lax view of the Law supposedly deriving from Pauline Christians, while not totally condemning the Pauline perspective. He concludes that Matthew remains closer to traditional Judaism than Paul. Along the same line of thinking, many scholars assume that Paul's conception of the Law differs radically from the teaching in this Gospel. Bruce (1983:43) has indicated that in earlier scholarship the statement that "anyone who breaks one of the least of these commandments and teaches others to do the same will be called least in

---

[55] The relation of Matthew's church to Pauline Christianity has much been debated (see Davies 1966, 316-366; Hagner, 1997:20-31).

the Kingdom of Heaven" (Matt. 5:19) was directed against Paul. This implies that these words did not come from Jesus, but from a group that did not like Paul.

Some scholars regard Matthew's Gospel to reflect the preference of a group of early Christians who felt strongly about the maintenance of the full authority of the Law for Christians without their view specific referring to Paul's teaching. Bultmann (1963:138) has suggested that Matthew "records the attitude of the conservative Palestinian community in contrast with that of the Hellenists". It is often assumed that Matthew uses the interpretations preferred by stricter Jewish Christians, often labelled M as it was only used in Matthew's Gospel[56]. This would depict the outlook of Matthew and his community (Bruce, 1983:43).

One should, however, remain cautious of identifying such a group too specifically, as very little clear evidence is available (cf. Hagner, 1993:182). These supposed antinomian adversaries are never explicitly mentioned "but rather must be 'discovered' beneath obscure texts and allusions" (Foster, 2004:154). To assume for example that Matthew reacts against Paul, is nothing less than speculation. It is possible that there were people who aimed to abolish the Law. Yet this *per se* does not mean that they were Hellenistic antinomians (France 1998:110). Matt. 5:17-19 might just as well have been directed to people within the community whose behaviour was incompatible with Christian discipleship (cf. Van Aarde, 2011:41). These possibilities are further examined in Chapter 3 of this study.

2.4.3 Addressed to his own community

The implied audience of the first Gospel is Matthew's own community who had probably been unsettled about their faith because of the accusations by non-Christian Jews who accused them of abolishing the Law. The author was writing to address the painful situation of a Jew who followed Jesus' teachings and therefore experienced increasing rejection from fellow Jews. This tension is in all likelihood the reason of some of the emphasis Matthew puts on the Beatitudes at the opening of the Sermon on the Mount, for example "… Blessed are those who hunger and thirst for righteousness … who are persecuted because of righteousness, … blessed are you when people insult you, persecute

---

[56] Another, more comprehensive selection on which both Matthew and Luke are considered to have drawn from is commonly labelled Q.

you and falsely say all kinds of evil against you because of me ..."[57] (Matt. 5:3-12). The Gospel was meant to provide a context for making sense of the past and a directive to shape the presence and the future of the community that found itself on the margins of the rest of the Jewish community (Carter, 2000a:33). It could also be that there was some confusion within his community about the understanding and application of the *Torah* in the new faith environment. If one takes this to be the case, he addressed his community to clarify their uncertainties about the status of the *Torah*.

It is important for Matthew's argument to defend his conviction that Jesus has given the correct interpretation of the *Torah*. Jesus is seen as the last and greatest expositor of the Law. Matthew argues that Jesus has the authority to redefine the *halakhic* stipulations (Matt. 5:21-47) (cf. Chapter 4). The evangelist reassures his community that their way of observance of the *Torah* does not abrogate it, but is actually the fulfilment of the Law through a higher standard of righteousness (cf. Chapter 5).

2.5 CONCLUSION

Reading the Gospel of Matthew as a transparent narrative shows that the story of Jesus provides a window through which modern readers can picture the community in which the Gospel was created and for whom it was intended. As this picture is a construct mainly based on the internal witness of the first Gospel, which is in turn intended as an internal document to its own community, opponents are presented from a specific perspective.

It seems that the crisis of 70 C.E. led to a reconsideration of the correct interpretation of the *Torah*. The *Torah* was an important issue for all Jewish movements. Rivalling deviant factions frequently defended their position based on their group's form of adherence to the *Torah*, while denouncing their opponents in the same instance. While Judaism in the villages constructed new societies in the synagogues based on their *Torah* interpretation, the Matthean community was structured as church and based their *Torah* observance on what Jesus had taught them. The Sabbath observance, circumcision, dietary and purity laws functioned as identity markers to separate Jews from Gentiles. Matthew's Jesus reinterprets these cultic practices to set alternative boundaries.

---

[57] Some scholars might argue that Matthew put these words in the mouth of Jesus to suit his argument. It can also be argued that the tension that Matthew and his community were experiencing, reminded him of these words of Jesus.

While Judaism(s) started to use the *Torah* as a means to fend off foreign influences, the Matthean community propagated Gentile mission. This decision intensified their conflict with the synagogue, who accused them of not adhering to the *Torah*. Matthew defended the position of his community by claiming that Jesus, who brought the authoritative interpretation of the *Torah*, ordered them to do so. Jesus is presented as the new Lawgiver (Moses). Matthew thus comforted his community, who felt insecure as a result of the rejection they experienced from the Judaistic sibling they encountered in their villages.

A more detailed treatment of Matthew's teaching about the Law and the important role Jesus played in his understanding of the Law follow in the subsequent chapters.

CHAPTER 3

THE FOUNDATIONAL STATEMENT IN MATTHEW 5:17-20 ON THE CONTINUING VALIDITY OF THE *TORAH*

3.1 INTRODUCTION

Matt. 5:17-20 is pivotal to Matthew's[58] teaching of the Law, not only in the Sermon on the Mount, but within the whole framework of his Gospel. This passage is densely formulated, forms the first explicit statement[59] of Jesus concerning the Law, and precedes the *Streitgespräche*[60] (controversy stories or debates) about the Law and related legal material in the Gospel (e.g. Matt. 9:9-13; 12:1-4; 15:1-9 and 22:34-40, passages that will be discussed in chapters to follow) (cf. Repschinski, 2000:62).

Very few passages in the New Testament have enticed so much scholarly debate as the interpretation of these verses. Part of the problem is that this highly concentrated statement is made up of a series of -sayings that speak in an unexpected, paradoxical and absolute manner (Van der Walt, 2006:172). Each of these proverbial sayings "accentuates a particular side of the truth without considering the possible exceptions to the rule ... the hearer then has to ponder the matter himself" (Ridderbos, 1987:112). Though such statements can be confusing, Morris (1992:91) has remarked that to add qualifications to these sayings would have caused the words to lose their impact.

---

[58] As discussed before, I use the name "Matthew" to refer to the implied author of the Frist Gospel, without entering the academic discussion into the historical person of the author.

[59] This statement actually consists of a series of statements combined to form a structural and thematic unit.

[60] Bultmann (1963:11-61) identified four elements in *Streitgespräche*: (1) they provide an action or attitude; (2) which is used by opponents; (3) in an attack in the form of a question or accusation; and (4) the attack is followed by a reply, often including a counter-question or a quotation from Scripture.

It has been argued that Matt. 5:17-20 portrays an understanding of the Law with a strong Jewish character, which does not cohere with Matthew's overall teaching. Scholars like Descamps (1995:173) and Luz (2005:186) have been of the opinion that Matthew (by including these words) did not think through the whole problem of the Law and that he was eclectic and even sloppy in his treatment of the issue. Kümmel (1934:121-127) has felt that Matthew in this passage even intensifies the demands of the Law as *Torahverschärfung*, based on his immediate awareness of the will of God. But then it seems as if Matthew contradicts himself by his description of the teaching and life of Jesus that follows (e.g. the in the so-called "antitheses" in Matt. 5:21-48, his attitude towards Sabbath-observance in Matt. 12:1-14 and purity regulations in Matt. 15:1-20). With the arrival of form-critical methodology, this problem was easily solved by relegating Matt. 5:17-20 as (a) piece(s) of text coming from a conservative Jewish-Christian milieu, which does not concur with the rest of Matthew's report on the life and teaching of Jesus (cf. Tuckett, 1987:95). This would confirm the form-critical idea of cracks in the text. Since the advent of the redaction-critical analysis, however, more emphasis has been placed on the role of the evangelist in reworking the tradition to form a logical flow of argument (Banks, 1974b:226; Hagner, 1993:102; Tuckett, 1987:95). Matthew's argumentative flow should therefore be considered.

In this chapter, I argue that the author of the first Gospel presents Jesus' foundational statement about the continuing validity of the *Torah* (Matt. 5:17-20) in a cohesive manner, though making use of tradition statements, in such a way as to address concerns about the continuing validity of the Law. In doing this, I will attend to the literary context of the saying, its origin and redaction, and then follow with the interpretation of the respective parts of the statement. From this investigation conclusions will be drawn regarding Matthew's interpretation of the Law and his message to his implied audience.

3.2   THE LITERARY CONTEXT OF THE FOUNDATIONAL STATEMENT

3.2.1 First of five discourses

The foundational statement on the Law (Matt. 5:17-20) forms a pivotal part of Matthew's prominent theme about the meaning of the Law in relation to the teaching and life of Jesus. This statement is situated within the Sermon on the Mount, the first of five great discourses in the Gospel (Riesner, 1978:177-178): the Sermon on the Mount (Matt. 5-7), the missionary charge (Matt. 10:5-42), the parables discourse (Matt. 13:3-52), instructions to the community (Matt.

18:3-35), and the woes and eschatological discourse (Matt. 23-25)[61] each followed by a narrative on the actions or sayings of Jesus which are related to the preceding discourses (cf. Davies & Allison, 2004a:60). These five discourses serve as main building blocks or architectonical structure of the first Gospel. Some scholars have seen in this structure an allusion to the five books of the Pentateuch (cf. Bacon, 1930:48), an idea that fits into Matthew's overall emphasis on the Law, yet it cannot be confirmed with all certainty that this really was the intention of Matthew.

In the Sermon on the Mount, Matthew presents Jesus' teaching on the Law in a rather lengthy discourse. Many scholars do not regard this as one sermon delivered by the historical Jesus during one occasion. One suggestion is that Matthew gathered and adapted traditions on sayings of Jesus that He uttered during several occasions during his earthly ministry (cf. Domeris, 1990:67). Johnson (1951:240) has remarked:

> Jesus would not have given all this teaching on a single occasion. The sermon is made up of aphorisms, maxims and illustrations which were remembered and treasured out of many discourses.

Obviously the sermon in the Gospel cannot be a verbatim report, as much of the material is found scattered in varied forms in other contexts in Luke's Gospel (Van der Walt, 2006:173). It is possible that some of the material found in the sermons was delivered in varied forms on other occasions. Morris (1992:92) has remarked: "An itinerant preacher normally makes repeated use of his material, often with minor or even major changes". It is obvious that Matthew has made use of inherited material, which he edited to fit into his overall argument and offers it as an address of Jesus. He offers this text as a sermon of Jesus as, in the introductory (Matt. 5:1-2) and the concluding verses (Matt. 7:28-29)[62], Matthew refers to at the beginning and the end of Jesus' address.

---

[61] Combrink (1983:61-90) has identified a chiastic structure between the discourses:

The Sermon on the Mount (Matt. 5-7) parallels the Woes and the eschatological discourse (Matt. 23-25). The Missionary charge (Matt. 10) parallels the Community discourse (Matt. 18). The Parables discourse (Matt. 13) is framed by the above-mentioned parallels.

[62] The concluding formula, ὅτε ἐτέλεσεν ὁ Ἰησοῦς τοὺς λόγους τούτους (when Jesus had finished these words) occurs at the end of each of the major teaching discourses in Matthew (Matt. 7:28; 11:1; 13:53; 19:1 and 26:1).

In this discourse, Matthew alludes to Moses when presenting Jesus. Some scholars even refer to Jesus as being presented as the new Moses (cf. Allison, 1993:137-270; Floor, 1969:34). Already at the beginning of the Sermon where Jesus went up the mountain to teach (Matt. 5:1-2), the Sinai typology is significant (Loader, 1997:165). This opening leads to an anticipation of a new revelation to be delivered by a new Lawgiver. This expectation is met where Jesus repeatedly refers to the meaning and intention of the Law and elaborates on the Decalogue as such (Matt. 5:21-47) (cf. Chapter 4). In Judaism it was a well-known concept that the Mosaic character could transmigrate to later legislators and teachers (e.g. Ezekiel). According to 4 Ezra chapter 14 the scribe received the old revelation of Sinai plus additional, new revelations (Allison, 1993:185). Within this convention, Jesus is portrayed as teacher and revealer comparable to Moses. His authority is emphasised, as Matthew concludes the Sermon with a postscript: "the crowds were amazed at his teaching, because He taught as one who had authority (ἦν γὰρ διδάσκων αὐτοὺς ὡς ἐξουσίαν ἔχων), and not as their teachers of the law" (Matt. 7:28-29).

Some scholars find a polarisation between the Sermon on the Mount and the rest of the Matthean Gospel. It is assumed that the broader Matthean kerugma of the saving death and resurrection of Christ has been replaced by the doctrine of reward in the Sermon on the Mount. Betz (1985:17 ff.) has suggested that the Sermon on the Mount is an epitome of the teaching of Jesus, as compiled by conservative Jewish Christians in Jerusalem around the middle of the first century. For them, Jesus was only an authoritative teacher of the Law. The saving death of Jesus was not part of their religion. Betz has suggested that Matthew has incorporated their work into his Gospel despite the fact that it differs significantly from his own viewpoint.

However, the view that the Sermon on the Mount is lacking a Christology, beyond Jesus as the respected teacher of the Law, is rejected by most scholars (cf. France, 1998:163).[63] The Sermon on the Mount should not be viewed only as a general discourse on ethics, but actually as the description of the distinctive life of those who are under the rule of the Kingdom of Heaven. As throughout Matthew's Gospel, it is those who respond to Jesus who come under the rule of God. Theirs is the Kingdom of Heaven (Matt. 5:3, 10), they are blessed (Matt.

---

[63] The Reformers and Puritans used to summarise the relation between Jesus (as Christ) and the Law. The Law sends us to Christ to be justified, and Christ sends us back to the Law to be sanctified (cf. Stott, 1978:36). Lloyd-Jones (1976:18) wrote: "There is nothing that so leads to the gospel and its grace as the Sermon on the Mount."

5:3-10). They are persecuted and insulted for Jesus' sake (Matt. 5:11). Based on these considerations it seems that the Sermon on the Mount does fit into the development of Matthew's plot, the revelation of Jesus as the Messiah, and peoples' response to his message.

Following the Sermon on the Mount, where Jesus is presented as the impressive and authoritative teacher of the Law, Jesus is subsequently presented in the following narrative in demonstrating how the Law should be practiced (Grundmann, 1971:111, 245). In Chapter 6 I discuss the relation between the teaching and actions of Jesus in more detail. The investigation of this relation, will throw further light on the how the Sermon on the Mount fits into Matthew's overall teaching about the Law.

3.2.2 Beatitudes

The Sermon on the Mount begins with a set of statements, which describe the way of life of faithful disciples of Jesus. "As a musical masterpiece begins with an introitus, the Sermon on the Mount opens with an extraordinary sequence of statements, the so-called beatitudes" (Betz, 1995:92). Taken together, the set of beatitudes in Matt. 5:3-12[64] constitutes the exordium of the Sermon on the Mount. The Beatitudes are pastorally-orientated promises, which Matthew employs to encourage his community, even when being ostracised because of their discipleship and way of living: "Blessed are you when people insult you, persecute you and falsely say all kinds of evil against you because of me ..." (Matt. 5:11-12). While the Sermon begins with a series of blessings (Matt. 5:1-12) it ends with a series of warnings (Matt. 7:1, 15, 21 & 26-27). This pattern is similar to the Book of the Law (Deuteronomy), which suggests a parallel between Jesus and Moses, both as mediators of the commandments of God (Domeris, 1990:67).

---

[64] The set of beatitudes with which Matthew begins the Sermon on the Mount, differs quite significantly from those recorded by Luke. Luke only gives four beatitudes and balances them with four woe sayings. The Matthean beatitudes probably form a collection of sayings by Jesus (not necessarily as the *ipsissima verba Jesu*) from the broader Jesus-tradition (Betz, 1985:42). Jesus might have pronounced blessings combined with curses as found in Old Testament parallels (Gen. 27:27-29, 39-40; Deut. 28). In an attempt to explain the difference between the Matthean and Lukan versions of the beatitudes, Van Bruggen (1990:85) has made the rather unconvincing suggestion that "[b]eide evangelisten hebben echter uit de stellig langere bergrede hun eigen keuze gemaakt", as now evidence is available of such and extended list and because of the significant correspondence between the beatitudes that Luke en Matthew share.

3.2.3 Essence of discipleship: salt and light

The statement in Matt. 5:17-20 is preceded by a section of metaphoric exhortations. The parallel metaphors of salt for the earth (Matt. 5:13) and light for the world (Matt. 5:14-16) depict the life that should be characteristic of Jesus' disciples. Some scholars find a definite break between verses 16 and 17 (e.g. Meier, 1976:42). However, the break is not that abrupt. It seems that Matthew's implied audience tended to remove themselves from society presumably because they were persecuted for their loyalty to Jesus and their understanding and practise of righteousness as Jesus commanded. Matthew apparently exhorts them not to retract, but to continue witnessing with their style of living, as they were indeed following the authoritative teachings of Jesus. With the statements that follow, Matthew confirms that they are indeed adhering to the Law as taught by Jesus, their foundational leader. Matthew's Jesus presents the model for this distinctive discipleship in Matt. 5:13-16, and then continues to address the basic criticism of the opponents, who seemingly regard the life of discipleship required by the Matthean community, as an abrogation of the *Torah*. Matthew uses these exhortations in a pastoral manner to encourage his audience to continue with their way of living, even when experiencing persecution. They should not keep silent or hide from the world (Foster, 2004:164).

3.2.4 Concluding link and preceeding antitheses

The foundational statement on the Law is concluded in Matt. 5:20: λέγω γὰρ ὑμῖν ὅτι ἐὰν μὴ περισσεύσῃ ὑμῶν ἡ δικαιοσύνη πλεῖον τῶν γραμματέων καὶ Φαρισαίων, οὐ μὴ εἰσέλθητε εἰς τὴν βασιλείαν τῶν οὐρανῶν (For I tell you that unless your righteousness surpasses that of the Pharisees and the teachers of the Law, you will certainly not enter the Kingdom of Heaven). Structurally and thematically this verse forms a link between the previous statement (Matt. 5:17-19) and the *halakhic* argumentation with six antitheses that follow (Matt. 5:21-47). The structural link is visible as the formulaic opening words λέγω γὰρ ὑμῖν are repeated in each of the six antitheses that follow (Matt. 5:22, 28, 32, 34, 39, & 44). Thematically, the δικαιοσύνη (righteousness) required to enter the Kingdom of Heaven, is illustrated by the following set of antitheses. Allison (1993:183) has remarked: "Structurally, 5:21-48 consists of six paragraphs, each illustrating the truth of 5:17-20". Furthermore the use of the term δικαιοσύνη (righteousness) forms a literary foundational statement to form a janus-like link between the preceding and following passages.

This brief overview of the literary context of Matt. 5:17-20 shows that the foundational statement on the Law does fit into the overall structure of the Sermon on the Mount. In turn, the Sermon on the Mount has a functional position within the architectonical structure of the Gospel with its emphasis on the meaning of the *Torah*. My assumption is therefore that the statement cannot be correctly understood in isolation of the wider narrative.

3.3   ORIGIN AND REDACTION OF MATTHEW 5:17-20

The study of Matt. 5:17-20 is complicated by the complex and debated tradition history of the verses. On Source- and Form critical grounds some scholars, each of the verses has to be assigned to different strata of the early community, as they present differing views of the Law (cf. Moo 1984:24). In dealing with the saying that appears to promote strict observance of the *Torah*, scholars have suggested that Matthew took over pre-Matthean material that does not smoothly fit into his overall argument (Luz, 2005:6). Streeter (1924:512) has suggested:

> This tradition, corresponding to that element in Matthew which we have styled M, includes sayings of a strongly Judaistic character ... It cannot be too emphatically insisted that this element in Matthew reflects, not primitive Jewish Christianity, but a later Judaistic reaction against the Petro-Pauline liberalism in the matter of the Gentile Mission and the observance of the Law.

Brooks has attempted to identify M material and has suggested that contradictions or paradoxes in the text (*aporiae*) may reveal source material. He has spoken of "a disjunction in the text that would not be expected from an author" (Brooks, 1987:18). Following the same argument, scholars have suggested that the content of Matt. 5:17-20 do not cohere with the evangelist's overall theology, and should therefore be regarded as a clumsy use of inherited material by the author. Many interpreters "dislike the thought of attributing such a legalistic logion to the evangelist" (Luz, 1990:258). With regard to Matt. 5:19, Meier (1976:165) has remarked: "In many ways, 5:19 is the most difficult verse to explain within the present Matthean context. It seems like an undigested morsel next to the carefully redacted 5:18." Meier (1976:165) has further suggested that

> 5:18-19 in the tradition may show successive stages of Jewish-Christian attitudes on the Law. Vs. 5:18bc may reflect the severe view of stringent Jewish Christians, while 5:19 may be the corrective of more moderate Jewish Christians. This attempt at

moderation has produced a curious piece ..., a kind of literary fossil now embedded in 5:19.

Related to this, the question arose which of this material can be traced back to the historical Jesus, and to make Him the anchor of interpretation of the Law. Guelich (1982:152) has remarked:

> Whereas 5:17, 18 may have distant roots in Jesus' ministry, 5:19 reflects the nomistic nuance of a strict Jewish-Christian community who may well have shaped the tradition of 5:17, 18 and added 5:19 as a commentary.

In discussing the redaction of Matt. 5:17-19, Foster (2004:178) has argued that "it seems foolhardy to assert that these Matthean verses find their origin in the ministry and teaching of Jesus in anything more than the faintest of echoes".

It is very likely that more persons, other than the four evangelists and the author of the assumed Q, wrote about the life of Jesus. Besides the "Two Document" (as proposed by C.H Weisse and H.J. Holtzman) and "Four Document" (as proposed by B. H. Streeter) Synoptic hypotheses it is very difficult to decide how the evangelists made use of existing material. Many scholars spend a lot of effort trying to identify the sources of Matthew and what he has done with them. In fact, none of the other material has survived. However, Matt. 5:17-20 has no parallel in Mark, and probably also not in Q. Matt. 5:18 however is paralleled in Luk. 16:17, εὐκοπώτερον δέ ἐστιν τὸν οὐρανὸν καὶ τὴν γῆν παρελθεῖν ἢ τοῦ νόμου μίαν κεραίαν πεσεῖν (It is easier for heaven and earth to disappear than for the least stroke of a pen to drop out of the Law), which probably is a rewriting of Matt. 5:18 (Davies & Allison, 2004a:482).

As discussed in the previous section on the literary context of Matt. 5:17-20, it rather seems that when Matthew incorporated a source, it was because he made it his own and appropriated it to fit into his discourse. It is therefore more important to understand what the words mean in their new situation. Childs (1984:62) has aptly remarked on this.

> The assumption that the many tensions within the Gospel are to be resolved by sharply distinguishing between tradition and redaction ... renders impossible a canonical reading of the Gospel as a whole. Thus the judgment that portions of ch. 5 are 'traditional ballasts' which distort Matthew's real intention, is a highly tendentious approach.

In the following interpretation of Matt. 5:17-20, I argue that this foundational statement does fit into the argument of Matthew. Obviously Matthew made use of sources, but he has used them in such a way that they fit into his understanding of the validity of the Law in his context. He explicitly anchors his perspective of the Law on the authoritative teaching of Jesus.

3.4 INTERPRETATION IN CONTEXT

Matt. 5:17-20 consists of an opening statement followed by three closely connected verses (cf. Davies & Allison, 2004a:481). They are structurally similar as they consist of parallel phrases (see the underlining in the table below) and are thematically connected as all of them defend the continuing validity of the *Torah* (see the words in bold in the table).

Matt. 5:17: Opening statement	
Μὴ νομίσητε ὅτι <u>ἦλθον καταλῦσαι</u> **τὸν νόμον** ἢ τοὺς προφήτας· (notion rejected) οὐκ <u>ἦλθον καταλῦσαι</u> ἀλλὰ πληρῶσαι· (notion confirmed)	Do not think that <u>I have come to abolish</u> **the Law** or the Prophets; I have not come to abolish them but to fulfil them.
Matt. 5:18: Supporting statement	
ἀμὴν γὰρ λέγω ὑμῖν, <u>ἕως ἂν</u> παρέλθῃ ὁ οὐρανὸς καὶ ἡ γῆ, (qualification) ἰῶτα ἓν ἢ μία κεραία οὐ μὴ παρέλθῃ ἀπὸ **τοῦ νόμου**, <u>ἕως ἂν</u> πάντα γένηται (qualification).	For truly I tell you, <u>until</u> heaven and earth disappear, not one jota one tittle will by any means disappear from **the Law** <u>until</u> everything is accomplished.
Matt. 5:19: Implication	
<u>ὃς ἐὰν</u> οὖν λύσῃ μίαν **τῶν ἐντολῶν** τούτων τῶν ἐλαχίστων καὶ διδάξῃ οὕτως τοὺς ἀνθρώπους, ἐλάχιστος κληθήσεται ἐν τῇ βασιλείᾳ τῶν οὐρανῶν· (negative implication) <u>ὃς δ᾽ ἂν</u> ποιήσῃ καὶ διδάξῃ, οὗτος μέγας κληθήσεται ἐν τῇ βασιλείᾳ τῶν οὐρανῶν (positive implication).	Therefore <u>anyone</u> who sets aside one of the least of these **commands** and teaches others accordingly will be called least in the Kingdom of Heaven, but <u>whoever</u> practices and teaches these commands will be called great in the Kingdom of Heaven.
Matt. 5:20: Second statement	
λέγω γὰρ ὑμῖν τι ἐὰν μὴ περισσεύσῃ ὑμῶν **ἡ δικαιοσύνη** πλεῖον τῶν γραμματέων καὶ Φαρισαίων, οὐ μὴ εἰσέλθητε εἰς τὴν βασιλείαν τῶν οὐρανῶν.	For I tell you that unless your **righteousness** surpasses that of the Pharisees and the teachers of the law, you will certainly not enter the Kingdom of Heaven.

Table 2: Thematic connectedness of the statements in Matt. 5:17-20

Matt. 5:17-18 has indirect parallels in Luk. 16:17 as indicated in bold in the text below.

Matt. 5:17: Opening statement	Luk. 16:16
Μὴ νομίσητε ὅτι ἦλθον καταλῦσαι **τὸν νόμον ἢ τοὺς προφήτας** οὐκ ἦλθον καταλῦσαι ἀλλὰ πληρῶσαι	Ὁ **νόμος καὶ οἱ προφῆται** μέχρι Ἰωάννου· ἀπὸ τότε ἡ βασιλεία τοῦ θεοῦ εὐαγγελίζεται καὶ πᾶς εἰς αὐτὴν βιάζεται.
Do not think that I have come to abolish the Law or the Prophets; I have not come to abolish them but to fulfil them.	The Law and the Prophets were proclaimed until John. Since that time, the good news of the kingdom of God is being preached, and everyone is forcing their way into it.
Matt. 5:18: Supporting statement	**Luk. 16:17**
ἀμὴν γὰρ λέγω ὑμῖν, **ἕως ἂν παρέλθῃ ὁ οὐρανὸς καὶ ἡ γῆ, ἰῶτα ἓν ἢ μία κεραία οὐ μὴ παρέλθῃ** ἀπὸ τοῦ νόμου, ἕως ἂν πάντα γένηται.	Εὐκοπώτερον δέ ἐστιν τὸν οὐρανὸν καὶ τὴν γῆν παρελθεῖν ἢ τοῦ νόμου μίαν κεραίαν πεσεῖν.
For truly I tell you, until heaven and earth disappear, not one jota one tittle will by any means disappear from the Law until everything is accomplished.	It is easier for heaven and earth to disappear than for the least stroke of a pen to drop out of the Law.

Table 3: Parallels between Matt. 5:17-18 and Luk. 16:17 on the continuing validity of the Law.

Both Matthew and Luke refer to the Law and the Prophets and that the Law remains valid into the finest detail until heaven and earth disappear.

3.4.1 Opening statement: Matthew 5:17

The opening statement comes in the form of an antithetical parallelism. In the first leg of the parallelism a wrong notion is rejected, and in the second a correct one is confirmed. The words ἦλθον καταλῦσαι (I have come to abolish) is repeated (indicated with underlining), linking the two legs of the parallelism. In the second leg of the parallelism a contrast is stated, καταλῦσαι (to abolish) and πληρῶσαι (to fulfil) (indicated in bold):

Μὴ νομίσητε ὅτι ἦλθον καταλῦσαι τὸν νόμον ἢ τοὺς προφήτας (notion rejected)

οὐκ ἦλθον **καταλῦσαι** ἀλλὰ **πληρῶσαι**· (notion confirmed)

Table 4: Parallelism of the opening statement in Matt. 5:17

3.4.1.1 Notion rejected

The statement opens with Jesus' declaration rejecting a notion that He came to abolish the Law and the Prophets: μὴ νομίσητε ὅτι ἦλθον καταλῦσαι τὸν νόμον ἢ τοὺς προφήτας (do not think that I have come to abolish the Law or the Prophets) (Matt. 5:17a). The aorist in "μὴ νομίσητε" (do not think) prohibits any such thinking at all and forms a common lead in in disarming potential objections (cf. Matt. 10:34) (Osborne, 2010:181). These words are probably both polemically and apologetically intended (Betz, 1985:40). It seems that the message of Jesus became a matter of dispute. Bornkamm (1963b:51) and Barth (1963:160) have proposed that these words are addressed at two opposing fronts: on the one side the Jews who do not believe in Jesus, and on the other side antinomians within Matthew's community. It seems that Matthew (with these words) anticipates charges against his community's understanding of the Law. Davies and Allison (2004a:481) have described these verses as a *prokatalepsis* in anticipation of possible objections. According to Guelich (1982:136) the purpose of μὴ νομίσητε (do not think) is "to counter false assumptions or misunderstandings about Jesus' coming"). However, Matthew's implied audience probably consists of his own community, rather than of the outsiders who do not believe in Jesus, or antinomians. Matthew's Jesus begins with the second person plural in Matt. 5:11 and carries it through Matt. 5:13, and repeats it in Matt. 5:17 and Matt. 5:20, and keeps the pattern in the "antitheses" (Matt. 5:21-47). One can therefore assume that these words are not directly a defence against Pharisees and teachers of the Law, but an explanation of the meaning of the Law to an insider community (Meier, 1976:66). Indirectly, Matthew addresses the opponents who brought these charges, but his main concern is his own community, as they probably were being ostracised for their way of living (Luz, 1990:260).

Matthew introduces the apparent charge, ὅτι ἦλθον καταλῦσαι τὸν νόμον ἢ τοὺς προφήτας (that I have come to abolish the Law or the Prophets), possibly a slogan used by the opponents. To be accused of propagating the abolishment of the Law and the Prophets was an extremely serious issue within Judaism, as it would result in being branded as an apostate and heretic (Betz, 1985:43)[65]. Matthew immediately refutes the charge with a pastoral encouragement to his unsettled audience, who seemingly have been accused and persecuted by *Torah*

---

[65] A characteristic description of an apostate is found in Abot 3.15: R. Eleazer the Modiite said: He who profanes holy things ... and gives interpretations of *Torah* which are not according to *Halachah*, even though he possess *Torah* and good deeds he has no portion in the world to come"

observant opponents (Foster, 2004:212). At this point, it becomes important to decide on the meaning of the word νόμος (law). Taking into account that the word is used in conjunction with προφήται (prophets) and with the parallel of ἰῶτα and κεραία (jota and tittle) in the next verse, it most likely refers to the written law, and not the oral traditions which Pharisees also regarded as being part of the *Torah* (Neusner, 1994:5-7; 2007:11)[66]. The presence of the term ἦλθον, has led some scholars to argue that this saying belongs to *logia* and *Reflexionszitate* known as ἦλθον-words ("I have come"-words). On Form critical grounds Von Harnack (1912:1-30) has identified such a *Gattung* in the synoptic tradition with "die ausdrücklichen Selbstzeugnisse Jesu über den Zweck seiner Sendung und seines Kommes". With the "I have come"-statements, Jesus was conscious of his divine mission as redeemer and Law-giver (Guelich, 1982:134-135). Matthew's Jesus denies that He has come to καταλῦσαι (abolish) the Law and the prophets. Within this context, the verb means "to end the effect of validity of something" (Foster, 2004:184).

Very strategically Matthew uses this ἦλθον-word to put the Law and the prophets in context of the mission of Jesus. Matthew puts the Law and the prophets, the centre of the Jewish faith, in direct relation to Jesus, who is the centre of Christian faith (Meier, 1976:123). He affirms Jesus' loyalty to the Jewish Scriptures by proposing a prophetic reading and understanding of the Law. Four of the eight occurrences of ὁ νόμος (the Law) in the Gospel are presented as part of the expression ὁ νόμος καὶ οἱ προφῆται (the Law and the Prophets) (Matt. 5:17; 7:12; 11:13 (in reverse order) and 22:40). Two more are in the contexts where the Law is being discussed in relation with the prophets[67] (Matt. 5:18 & 22:36). Yet, another is referred to in context of the prophetic source where Hos. 6:6 is quoted to validate Jesus' comments on the Sabbath (Matt. 12:5), and lastly an allusion to Mic. 6:8 can be recognised in Matt. 23:23. Also, when the eating with unwashed hands becomes an issue (Matt. 15:1 ff.), a word from the prophets (Isa. 29:13) provides an answer to the "hypocritical" objections of the opponents. Even the regulations about the temple activities (Matt. 21:13) are determined by words from the prophets (Isa. 56:7 and Jer. 7:11). The implication of Matthew's argument is that the Pharisaic application of the Law is not in line with the prophetic view and it is therefore wrong (Matt.

---

[66] Cf. Chapter 10 where I pay attention to the so-called Dual *Torah* of the Pharisees.

[67] According to Meier (1976:71) only the Law and Prophets were read during synagogue worship, which indicates their importance for the Jews. Though the Psalms were sung in worship, none of the writings were read.

23:28). In Judaism, the *Torah* was regarded as the direct expression of God's will. The prophets were the custodians and interpreters of the Torah[68] (Meier, 1976:72). Ultimately, Jesus Himself is presented as a prophet who gives the authoritative interpretation of the Law. In his preaching and action Jesus stands in line with great prophets of the Jewish Bible who warned against religious hypocrisy and loveless formalism.

3.4.1.2 Notion confirmed

After repeating the negative accusation οὐκ ἦλθον καταλῦσαι (I did not come to abolish), to emphasise the contrast with the previous statement, the evangelist counterbalances the charge with a positive affirmation: ἀλλὰ πληρῶσαι (but to fulfil) (Matt. 5:17b). The operative word is πληρῶσαι (to fulfil). The dismissal of the accusation that Jesus came to καταλῦσαι (abolish) the Law and the prophets, can only be appreciated when read parallel with πληρῶσαι (to fulfil) (Luz, 1990:260).

It is important to notice that the word used as contrary to "abolish", is not to "confirm" or to "enforce" the Law, but to "fulfil" it. The proper way to keep any commandment was to fulfil the purpose for which it was given. This implies that the interpretation of the Law as done by Jesus, differs from what the opponents traditionally thought its meaning to be. The debate therefore is not about the recognition or obedience of the Law, but about the understanding of God's intention with the Law (Hill, 1972:117). The fulfilment of the Jewish Scriptures in Jesus is the basic orientation of Matthew's Gospel (France, 1998:196; Moule, 1967/1968:293-320), and thus also forms the crux of Jesus' argument on the Law (Menken, 2003:181; Moo, 1984:24). "Fulfil" in this context has the meaning of bringing to full intent and expression. Jesus brings out the intended meaning of the Law through his definite re-interpretation (Hagner, 1993:105). Jesus' own coming represents the fulfilment of the requirements of the Law (Ladd, 1993:123). Patte (1987:73) has described this fulfilment as the "vocation" of Jesus. He did not oppose the *Torah*, but brought it to fruition (Carson, 1982:77). Jesus came to affirm the Scriptures and to bring them to new actuality in people's lives. The Law is even lifted to a higher plane. As seen in the antitheses to follow in Matt. 5:21-28 the Law has a deeper meaning than before (Osborne, 2010:182). For Matthew, the Law and the prophets continue to be authoritative – but as they are re-interpreted by Jesus

---

[68] The prophets were therefore regarded as less important than the Torah.

(Stanton, 1993:49). The Law finds its valid continuity in Jesus, the one towards whom it has pointed. With such an interpretation of Matt. 5:17 in mind, Banks (1974a:226) has remarked:

> It is not so much Jesus' stance towards the Law that he (Matthew) is concerned to depict: it is how the Law stand with regard to him, as the one who brings it to fulfilment and to whom all attention must now be directed.

3.4.2 Supporting statement: Matthew 5:18

The opening words in Matt. 5:17 are followed by a statement in Matt. 5:18)[69] that comprises of four separate clauses:

- an announcement of solemn speech (ἀμὴν γὰρ λέγω ὑμῖν - For truly I tell you);
- a temporal qualification concerning the ending of the created world (ἕως ἂν παρέλθῃ ὁ οὐρανὸς καὶ ἡ γῆ - until heaven and earth disappear);
- a declaration of ensuring the validity of the smallest detail of the Law within the created order (ἰῶτα ἓν ἢ μία κεραία οὐ μὴ παρέλθῃ ἀπὸ τοῦ νόμου - not one jota nor one tittle, will by any means disappear from the Law); and
- another temporal qualification (similarly introduces with ἕως ἂν – until) that reinforces the lasting validity of the Law while the created order remains (ἕως ἂν πάντα γένηται - until everything is accomplished).

The structure of statement can be presented as follows:

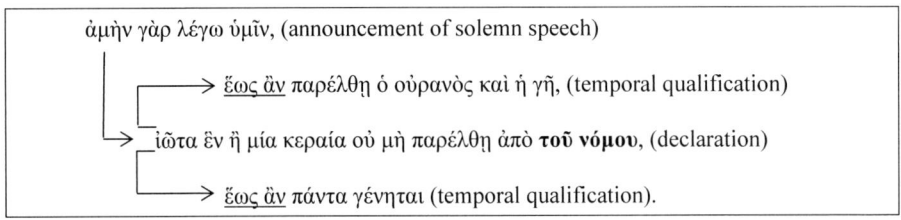

Table 5: Structure of the statement in Matt. 5:18

---

[69] Most scholars recognise this fourfold division (cf. Davies & Allison, 2004a:487).

The principle declaration is located in the middle and is bracketed by two temporal qualifications.

3.4.2.1   Announcement of solemn speech

The first clause (ἀμὴν γὰρ λέγω ὑμῖν - For truly I tell you) "stresses the gravity of what follows" (Hagner, 1993:106). The solemnity is created by the use of the term ἀμὴν (amen). The introductory position of this word is distinctively Christian, as it is not found in the Jewish Bible or rabbinic literature. Of the 51 times ἀμὴν is used in the Christian Bible as a declaration of solemn speech, 31 of these instances are in Matthew (Foster, 2004:188; Osborne, 2010:182). This is the first time Matthew uses the amen-formula, with the result that the impact would have been strongly felt by the first readers.

3.4.2.2   First temporal qualification

Having announced that a significant statement that deserves the full attention follows, the permanence of the Law is secondly stated (ἕως ἂν παρέλθῃ ὁ οὐρανὸς καὶ ἡ γῆ - until heaven and earth disappear). This clause is similar to various Jewish passages (e.g. Ps. 148:6 (LXX); 2 Bar. 19:2) where the same theme is developed (Banks, 1975:214). Matthew's Jesus uses a popular Jewish saying about the eternal validity of the Law, and applies it to his teaching on the fulfilling of the Law in order to demonstrate his essential continuity with it. Meier (1976:41-65), however, has argued that this statement does not imply the continuing validity of the Law, but is marking the *terminus ad quem*. He has proposed a *Heilsgeschichte*-scheme, where the death and resurrection of Jesus function as the turning of the ages, which would close the era of *Torah* obedience. This argument will be taken up again in the discussion of the second temporal statement in the fourth clause, which forms a parallelism to this first temporal clause.

3.4.2.3   Declaration ensuring the continuing validity of the Law

Thirdly, a declaration is made about the validity of even the smallest part of the Law (ἰῶτα ἓν ἢ μία κεραία οὐ μὴ παρέλθῃ ἀπὸ τοῦ νόμου - not one jota nor one tittle, will by any means disappear from the Law). The Semitic origin of Jesus' words is illustrated by the inclusion of Hebrew words ἰῶτα and κεραία (jota and tittle) in the text. Beyond providing some local colour to the narrative, it also demonstrates Jesus' respect for the written Hebrew script of the *Torah* (Betz,

1985:44). Out of respect for the *Torah* only Hebrew was used in that period in discussions on the Jewish law (cf. Fitzmyer, 1970:501; Joosten, 2004:89).[70] It might be that this *logion* somehow existed originally in Hebrew, and it might have been used to accuse the Matthew's community of wrong doing. The ἰῶτα (jota) was the smallest letter of the Hebrew alphabet. The idea of the ἰῶτα (jota) representing the whole law, is reflected in a rabbinic story about Deuteronomy 17:17. According to this story, the Book of Deuteronomy complained before the Lord that Solomon had abolished a yot in it, and therefore in principle had abolished all of the book. The Lord replied: "Solomon and a thousand like him will pass, but not one word of you shall pass." (Strack & Billerbeck, 1965:247). The κεραία (tittle) denotes the accents and breathings in the Hebrew text, thus referring to something seemingly insignificant. The meaning of the statement is qualified by the two temporal qualifications that respectively precede and follow this saying (Banks, 1975:214). It seems that Matthew had the objections of the opponents of the Matthean community in mind, who probably questioned the way Jesus and the community observed the Law. Matthew argues that fulfilling the Law does not imply the punctilious observance of the Pharisees, but an observance as defined by Jesus. The authoritative teaching of Jesus would reveal the whole meaning of the *Torah* (Hagner, 1993:106).

3.4.2.4 Second temporal qualification

The fourth part of the statement (ἕως ἂν πάντα γένηται - until everything is accomplished) should be read parallel to the second (ἕως ἂν παρέλθῃ ὁ οὐρανὸς καὶ ἡ γῆ - until heaven and earth disappear), as it reiterates the time until which the Law will be valid[71]. Jewish and Rabbinic sources (1 Macc. 4:46; b. Sabb. 151b; Lev. Rab. on 7:11-12 and 11:2; Midr. Ps. 146:7) witness to a variety of beliefs about the fate of the *Torah* in the messianic age to come (Davies, 1966:156-190): that it would stay the same; be inviolate forever; that obscure parts would become clear; that certain sacrifices and festivals would cease; that purity laws would be revised; or that a new *Torah* would come into place (Davies & Allison, 2004a:493). Scholars do not agree when that age will come.

---

[70]Kooyman (1992:79 ff.) has argued that the distinction between Aramaic and Hebrew layers in the tradition cannot be distinguished that clearly. Beyond arguments around "die Muttersprache Jesu" one should not only distinguish Jesus' language in his ministry, but also the *mother tongue* of Matthew (the author).

[71] This part is strongly reminiscent of the introduction of *Reflexionszitate* in the text (Meier, 1976:53).

Some scholars argue that "until everything is accomplished" (Matt. 5:18), does not as such point to the end of the world, but to the fulfilment of all that God has planned. Therefore all is accomplished not so much by the faithful observance of the Law, but rather in that its preparatory function has been successfully achieved. In this sense Meier (1976:65) has proposed that the age had already arrived.

> The Mosaic Law as a whole and *qua* Mosaic lasts only until the apocalyptic event of the death-resurrection of Jesus. After this *Wende der Zeit*, the norm for the disciple is 'all whatsoever I commanded you'.

Referring to the events that took place with the death and resurrection of Jesus, Meier has argued that the earthquake was a well-known theophanic and apocalyptic motif from Jewish literature. He has argued that Jesus' demands move in a sphere above the Law, which continuing validity exists only in and through Him (Meier, 1976:88). Meier's thesis is opposed by Davies and Allison (2004a:474), who have argued that "until heaven and earth pass away" most naturally implies that there is still a period of time before the Law passes away. While Sim (1999:125) has agreed that the coming of the eschatological ages will bring an end to the *Torah*, he proposes that this event would take place with the *parousia*. A discussion on the apocalyptic timetable, however, is not really useful to understand Matthew's argument. The antitheses that follow do not in any way refer to eschatological events, but rather to Jesus' authority to teach the correct interpretation of the Law for his disciples in their time (Foster, 2004:211).

It is therefore more convincing that the author wants to assure his readers that charges probably brought against them of not adhering to the *Torah*, are unfounded. In a pastoral manner, he affirms continuity with the Law, but in a nuanced way as taught by Jesus. He claims that "the life of discipleship, that he portrays as being taught by Jesus, is not the abolition of the Law, but is in fact the consummative fulfilment of *Torah* values" (Foster, 2004:183).

Taking these considerations into account, the following interpretation of Matthew's argument can be proposed. Matthew argues that Jesus expressed the full intended meaning of the Law. In this regard, France (1998:196) has suggested that one should distinguish between the authority and the function of the *Torah*. To affirm that the Law remains authoritative with no jot or tittle lost, does not necessarily imply that it will continue to function in the same way. When read along with the focus on the fulfilment as the key to understanding

Jesus' relation to the Law, it is probable that the practical functioning of the Law would not remain the same as it was before his coming. Even though the Law remains permanently important, it should function differently in a pre- and post-fulfilment situation. The argument is that Jesus completed the Law by extending its demands and bringing it to which it pointed. Jesus' teaching and ministry would demonstrate this fulfilment. Matthew is therefore saying to his adversaries, the Law is fulfilled, but not in the manner you expected it (Foster, 2004:186). The "antitheses" that follow in Matt. 5:21-47, demonstrate this interpretation of the meaning of the Law (in Chapter 5 I attend to these "antitheses" in more detail).

3.4.3 Implication: Matthew 5:19

The foundational statement on the validity of the Law continues[72] with the binding force and practical implication of the continuing validity of the Law in a neatly formed antithetical parallel statement. The two parts of the parallel are each introduced with (who ever - ὃς ἐὰν and ὃς δ' ἂν) (indicated with underlining) (protases). The parallel actions are either "loosing and teaching" (negative) or "doing and teaching" (positive) (indicated in bold). The negative and positive results (apodoses) are indicated with italics ("will be called the least in the Kingdom of Heaven" or "will be called great in the Kingdom of Heaven"). Reference is not made to the Law (ὁ νόμος) as in the previous verses, but to the commandments or ordinances (αἱ ἐντολαὶ) of the *Torah.*

<u>ὃς ἐὰν</u> οὖν **λύσῃ** μίαν τῶν ἐντολῶν τούτων τῶν ἐλαχίστων καὶ **διδάξῃ** οὕτως τοὺς ἀνθρώπους,
    ἐλάχιστος κληθήσεται ἐν τῇ βασιλείᾳ τῶν οὐρανῶν·
<u>ὃς δ' ἂν</u>   **ποιήσῃ** καὶ **διδάξῃ**,
    οὗτος μέγας κληθήσεται ἐν τῇ βασιλείᾳ τῶν οὐρανῶν.

Table 6: The antithetical parallelism of the statement in Matt. 5:19

The statement exhibits the basic form of a *Satz heiligen Rechtes* (usually translated as sentence of holy Law). *Satz heiligen Rechtes* is a term coined by Käsemann (1955:248 and 1969:17) to refer to *Talionisformel* (reciprocity formulas) that dealt with the eschatological activity of God (Van Aarde, 2011:41). Käsemann has argued that the primary *Sitz im Leben* in the early church of these pronouncements was in the Christian prophesy. The

---

[72] The connection with the previous statement is established with οὖν (therefore).

Talionisformel coupled the ethical behaviour with the corresponding reward or punishment.

The protasis and apodosis of each part of the parallelism correspond in the relationship of guilt and punishment (Matt. 5:19ab), or fulfilment of duty and reward (Matt. 5:19cd).

3.4.3.1 Prohibited negative behaviour of annulling the commandments (first protasis)

The question arises whether the action of annulling (λύω) (Matt. 5:19a) implies teaching or doing. As the word stands parallel to ποιέω (Matt. 5:19c), the idea of breaking by action is better suited in this context (Meier, 1976:90). The object of annulment is called μίαν τῶν ἐντολῶν τούτων (one of these commandments). An ἐντολή refers to an individual ordinance of the Law as a whole. Difference of opinion exists of what these ordinances refer to. Strack and Billerbeck (1965:90) have suggested that this statement refers to the pharisaic debate on the scale of importance of the counted 613 *miswot* in the *Torah*.[73] With reference to the implied ranking of *miswot* in this verse, Sim (1999:126) has argued that Matthew was a Jewish Christian who believed that even the least of the Mosaic commandments had to be observed and taught to others. Opposing this proposal, scholars such as Schweizer (1976:108), Lohmeyer (1967:110), Banks (1975:223) and Betz (1985:49) have suggested that μίαν τῶν ἐντολῶν τούτων (one of these commandments) do not refer to the ordinances of the *Torah*, but to Jesus' own commandments. This would imply and contrast between the Pharisaic theology based on the *Torah* and the commands of Jesus is described in the Sermon on the Mount. However, their argument is not convincing as this statement forms part of a cluster of sayings dealing with the validity of the "law and the prophets" by which the author probably responds to accusations of breaking the Law. France (1998:195) has convincingly responded to Bank's proposal by remarking that his proposal "is to destroy the clear sequence of thought from verse 18 to verse 19, and to ignore the regular use of ἐντολη to refer to Old Testament laws". It is more convincing to assume that Matthew is still referring the Mosaic *Torah* with his reference to the ἰῶτα ἓν ἢ μία κεραία (jota of title) in Matt. 5:17.

---

[73] According to the popular view one never knew what reward to expect for obeying which precept. As a result a light precept should be esteemed as a heavy one and all should be regarded as of equal importance (Strack & Billerbeck, 1965:90).

3.4.3.2 Required positive behaviour of keeping the commandments (second protasis)

The combination between doing and teaching in Matt. 5:19b is significant. Strack and Billerbeck (1965:84) have remarked that the older rabbinic view had been that the practical observance of the Law was more important than the study of it. Only after Hadrian's edict that forbade the study of the *Torah*, did rabbis under Akiba decide that the study of the Law is more important – as study led to practice[74]. Matthew's Jesus mentions the importance of both. Osborne (2010:183) has felt that the emphasis on "teaching" along with "doing" the Law stems from the responsibility of the disciples to teach one another. The content of the teaching should be lived out by the teacher (Betz, 1985:47). The Sermon on the Mount not only prepares disciples, but also the teachers of the disciples.

The difference between ποιέω (do) (Matt. 5:19) and πληρόω (fulfil) (Matt. 5:17) is noteworthy. Lohmeyer (1967:111) has explained the difference between Jesus who fulfils the Law to its full meaning (Matt. 5:17), and the disciples who are subjects of the Law and who obey and do them (Matt. 5:19).

3.4.3.3 Eschatological reciprocitive punishment or reward (apodoses)

Considering the eschatological punishment and reward side of this legal statement (ἐλάχιστος κληθήσεται ἐν τῇ βασιλείᾳ τῶν οὐρανῶν· - he will be called the least in the Kingdom of Heaven, and οὗτος μέγας κληθήσεται ἐν τῇ βασιλείᾳ τῶν οὐρανῶν, he will be called great in the Kingdom of Heaven), it is interesting to note that the exclusion from the kingdom is not envisaged as a result of not observing of the least of the commandments, but a ranking of persons, by being the smallest of great. This is related to rewards as motivation for the correct conduct (Hagner, 1993:109). The idea of gradations of honour and dishonour in the Kingdom of Heaven[75] was common in Jewish tradition (cf.

---

[74] The Hillelites placed studying above doing, while the Shammaites placed doing above studying the Law (cf. mish. 'Abot 1.15, 17; 3:10; Sipre on Deut. 11:13; y. Ber. 1.5.3b) (Davies & Allison, 2004a:498).

[75] The concept of the βασιλεία τῶν οὐρανῶν (kingdom of the heavens) is quite complex in Matthew and frequently uses (e.g. Matt. 3:2; 4:17, 24; 5:3, 10, 19, 20; 6:10, 23; etc.). The past, present and future are all involved in various stages of the coming of the kingdom. In Matt. 5:19 the future reference is most probable, read in context of the reward and punishment scheme of the Jews, and because of the close proximity of the same word in Matt. 5:20 where it clearly has a future meaning.

Assump. Mos. 12:10-13; Test. Levi 13:9[76]). These Jews noted that one could not be certain in this world who is great and who is small. That would become clear in the world to come. Those who were prepared to make themselves small for the sake of the *Torah* would become great in the future world. Once one's status in the next world has been attained, it could not be changed (Strack & Billerbeck, 1965:249). The place one will occupy in the Kingdom of heaven will be determined by the degree one has been loyal to the commandments of the written *Torah*. However, according to the interpretation of Schweizer (1976:108), Lohmeyer (1967:110), Banks (1975:223) and Betz (1985:49) who have suggested that μίαν τῶν ἐντολῶν τούτων (one of these commandments) refer to Jesus' own commandments in contrast to that of the written *Torah* (which I regard as an less convincing, as discussed above) this statement would imply that one's position in the Kingdom will be determined by the degree of his/her loyalty to the teaching of Jesus. Such an interpretation would imply a differentiation between the written *Torah* and the commandments of Jesus, a differentiation which I consider to be less.

3.4.4 Second statement: Matthew 5:20

As a Janus-like hinge, Matt. 5:20 serves as logical conclusion to the preceding statement on the continuing validity of the Law (Matt. 5:17-19) and as link to the "antitheses" that follow (Matt. 5:21-47).

It starts off with the introductory formula, λέγω γὰρ ὑμῖν (for I tell you), thereby making this statement an emphatic summary of the previous statements and of the antitheses that follow. Then, as in the previous verse, that pronouncement is given in the form of a *Satz heiligen Rechtes,* which consists of a protasis (ethical behaviour) and an apodosis (eschatological reciprocity):

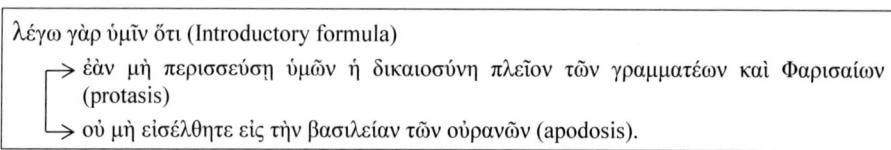

Table 7: The emphatic pronouncement of Matt. 5:20

---

[76] The Assumption of Moses probably dates back to the beginning of the first century C.E. of even earlier (Vriezen & Van der Woude, 2005:608) and the Testament of Levi to the beginning of the second century C.E. (Vriezen & Van der Woude, 2005:567).

3.4.4.1 Introductory formula

Matt. 5:20 repeats the emphatic formula of verse 18, λέγω γὰρ ὑμῖν (for I say to you), hinting to the independent, authoritative teaching of Jesus. This verse once again responds to the implied accusation in Matt. 5:17a of μὴ νομίσητε ὅτι ἦλθον καταλῦσαι τὸν νόμον ἢ τοὺς προφήτας (do not think that I have come to abolish the Law). Matthew probably had his audience in mind, who possibly experienced accusations regarding their understanding and practice of the Law. Thus they could identify with the disciples in this narrative (Carter, 1994:32; Overman, 1996:80).

3.4.4.2 Ethical behaviour (protasis)

According to the *Satz heiligen Rechtes* (ὅτι ἐὰν μὴ περισσεύσῃ ὑμῶν ἡ δικαιοσύνη πλεῖον τῶν γραμματέων καὶ Φαρισαίων, that unless your righteousness surpasses that of the Pharisees and the teachers of the Law), Matthew's Jesus wants his disciples, and Matthew seemingly wants his readers to surpass their opponents in righteousness. The popular rabbinic view was that one had to fulfil the legal prescriptions of the Law punctiliously to gain eschatological merit. It was important to gain enough merit to outweigh one's guilt at the final judgement (Meier, 1976:109).

The question arises whether Matthew likewise required the δικαιοσύνη (righteousness) of his community to surpass that of the opponents in quantity or rather in quality. Though some scholars such as Segal (1991:21) regard the surpassing as quantitative, it should rather be interpreted as qualitative. Matthew does not require a bigger and better pharisaism, or a more punctilious observance of the minute parts of the Law. The "more abundant righteousness" is explained by the six antitheses that follow in Matt. 5:21-48 and the charge of hypocrisy in Matt. 6:1-6. According to Matthew, the wrong conduct of the scribes and the Pharisees is not the result of the quantity of their deeds, but because of their wrong understanding of the Law and of a false attitude behind their deeds (Betz, 1985:53). The opponents are denounced for parading their pious acts in public to gain praise, while members of Matthew's audience are encouraged to perform their acts of piety in private where only God can see (Sim, 1999:122).

Matthew predominantly uses the term δικαιοσύνη (righteousness) in an ethical sense and not a righteousness as result of Jesus' redemptive act (cf. Chapter 4 where I attend to Matthew's use of this term in more detail). It refers to the conduct of a person in accordance to the will of God. In Matt. 5:20, Matthew uses δικαιοσύνη (righteousness) in terms of teaching and doing the will of God (in correlation with Matt. 5:19). This phrase gives expression to Matthew's understanding of true discipleship. Matthew assures his addressees that the righteousness is the outcome of living according to the interpretation of the Law, as taught by Jesus. According to Matt. 5:10, it seems as if Matthew's audience were persecuted because of their "righteousness", but were comforted with the promise of sharing in the Kingdom of Heaven (Matt. 5:10b). Similarly in Matt. 5:20 the readers are urged to practice greater righteousness than that of the teachers of the Law and the Pharisees, so that they can enter the Kingdom of Heaven.

The stereotypical opponents in the first Gospel οἱ γραμματεῖς (the scribes) and οἱ Φαρισαῖοι (the Pharisees) are referred to. As discussed in Chapter 2, these groups are both the opponents of Jesus during his ministry, and probably of the Matthean community (cf. Betz, 1985:53). According to Meier (1976:112) the scribes in particular were the interpreters and teachers of the Law, and devoted themselves to studying and teaching it. The Pharisees were a group of pious Jews who devoted themselves to strict observance of the Law, both oral and written. As one of the Jewish religious groups they often included teachers of the Law. The Pharisees were especially known for their zeal to keep the Law (Meier, 1976:112). Guelich (1982:159) distinguishes between the scribes as teachers of the Law, and Pharisees as the doers of the Law, which correlates with "teaching" and "doing" in Matt. 5:19. The scribes[77] originally were the official recorders or the Law and became experts in interpreting the *Torah*, while the Pharisees were lay leaders of religious observance (Osborne, 2010:183). In Matthew's text the teachers of the Law and the Pharisees banded together as representative group of Jewish theology and piety, and act as continuous opponents of Jesus.

3.4.4.3   *Eschatological reciprocity (apodosis)*

In the apodosis of the *Satz heiligen Rechtes*, οὐ μὴ εἰσέλθητε εἰς τὴν βασιλείαν τῶν οὐρανῶν (you will certainly not enter the Kingdom of Heaven), Matthew discusses the reward or punishment in terms of entering the Kingdom of Heaven[78]. Meier (1976:113) has suggested that two images lie behind

---

[77] For an extensive discussion of the scribes consult Orton (1989:39-133).

[78] Matthew uses the image of "entering the kingdom" as equivalent to conversion and eternal life (Matt. 7:21; 18:3, 8-9; 19:17, 23, 24; 23:14).

Matthew's use of the expression "to enter the Kingdom of Heaven", i.e. the entrance of Israel into the Promised Land (Deut. 4:1), and the requirements of cultic purity and ethical righteousness to enter through the temple gates (Ps. 15, 24 & 118:19). In Matt. 5:20 this image is projected onto eschatological events. These final words of the pericope tie up with the last words of Matt. 5:3, 10, 19b and 19d, ἡ βασιλεία τῶν οὐρανῶν (the Kingdom of Heaven) – thus providing a unity to the first part of Matt. 5. The expression is only taken up again at the end of the Sermon in Matt. 7:21 to conclude the extended argument.

3.5 CONCLUSION

With the fundamental statement of the Law in Matt. 5:17-20, Matthew seemingly electively made use of inherited materials. However, to argue that the statement is a careless compilation of clashing elements and that the statement as a whole does not smoothly fit into Matthew's overall teaching of the Law, is unfair. Matthew thematically links the material quite well and presents the subsequent statements with stylistic eloquence.

The study of the different parts of this statement proved that Matthew carefully composed this statement. The interrelatedness of the different components is significant. It starts off by denouncing false assumptions about Jesus and the Law. In Matt. 5:17 he uses ἦλθον – sayings that are in parallel to describe how Jesus brought and taught the intended meaning of the Law. This is followed in verse 18, with a carefully structured four part solemn declaration about Jesus' respect for even the seemingly insignificant parts of the Law. Verse 19 presents a double *Satz heiligen Rechtes* to affirm the results of "loosing and teaching" or "doing and teaching" the commandments or ordinances of the *Torah*. The statement concludes with yet another solemn declaration with a *Satz heiligen Rechtes*, explaining the kind of righteousness required from disciples of Jesus. It is therefore reasonable not to read the different parts in an atomistic manner with clashing layers of tradition, but in its redacted and cohesive form.

It is also necessary to recognise the place of this statement as a whole within the logical flow of discourse within the Sermon of the Mount as a whole. The Sermon opens with a set of beatitudes *inter alia* describing true righteousness, the appropriate way of living by faithful disciples of Jesus (Matt. 5:1-12). This is followed by encouraging words to continue with such righteous living, even amidst intolerance and false accusations from opponents (Matt. 5:13-16). The accusation of breaking the Law is then proved to be false by a solemn declaration of Jesus (Matt. 5:17-20). The final verse of this declaration functions as a Janus-like hinge to the following antitheses (Matt. 5:21-48) where Jesus' teaching of the precepts of the Law is presented.

This densely formulated statement of Jesus about the Law is polemical and apologetical, laying the foundation for the *Streitgespräche* and legal material that follows in the Gospel.

Yet, it seems that Matthew directs these words primarily towards his own community. In such case Matt. 5:17-20 can be regarded as a pastorally-orientated assurance to his community, who probably were unsettled because of accusations by *Torah*-abiding Jewish opponents that they were breaking the Law. Matthew's argument is that the issue is not about the recognition or obedience of the Law, but about the understanding of the intention of God with the Law. Matthew encourages his audience to continue with righteousness that surpasses that of the scribes and Pharisees. Jesus is regarded as their foundational Leader. He defined the true meaning of the Law and spoke with ultimate authority.

Matthew poses two strongly divergent options to his readers: Either you continue with the traditional way of law observance, thereby ignoring the fulfilment of the Law and the prophets, or you accept the authority of Jesus who divinely interpreted the true intention of the Law.

CHAPTER 4

ΔΙΚΑΙΟΣΥΝΗ AND IDENTITY FORMATION IN MATTHEW

4.1 INTRODUCTION

It seems that δικαιοσύνη (righteousness) forms a fundamental term in the Matthean Gospel, as it plays a significant role in how Matthew describes the function of the Law and the position of his community. It looks as if the author uses this term in an attempt to correct and reinforce some issues in the social setting of his community (Carter, 2000a:13-14; Przybylski, 1980:105-116; Tagawa, 1970:149).

The noun δικαιοσύνη (righteousness) occurs seven times in Matthew's Gospel (Matt. 3:15; 5:6; 5:10; 5:20; 6:1; 6:33; 21:32). This is more than in any other writing of the New Testament, except for Romans and 2 Corinthians (cf. Talbert, 1992:747 for the occurrence of this word in the New Testament). Matthew uses this noun to refer to Jesus, John the Baptist and the disciples, with a remarkable concentration in the Sermon on the Mount. Δικαιοσύνη only occurs in sayings of Jesus. Most of these sayings are unique to Matthew, e.g. in Matt. 3:15; 5:10. 20, 6:1; 21:32. In cases where Jesus' sayings are shared by Luke[79] (Q), the word δικαιοσύνη (righteousness) only appears in the Matthean version (Matt. 5:6 and 6:33) of the sayings. He repetitively uses this word in the Sermon on the Mount (Matt. 5:6; 5:10; 5:20; 6:1; 6:33). The argument in this chapter is that Matthew intentionally utilizes the term δικαιοσύνη to define the identity of his community in contrast to outsider groups. My contention is that δικαιοσύνη is used to describe the proper behavioural norms of his community to distinguish them from outsiders. By doing this the Gospel not only reflects their norms, but also impacts on their distinctive identity as followers of Jesus.

While in two cases (Matt. 5:20 and 6:1) the Matthean Jesus contrasts the δικαιοσύνη of the disciples with that of the Pharisees and the teachers of the

---

[79] Luk. 6:21 and 12:31.

Law, all seven cases seemingly reveal remarkable significance and meaning related to Matthew's teaching of the Law:[80]

- John had to baptise Jesus for it was proper for them both to fulfil all δικαιοσύνη (Matt. 3:15).
- Those who hunger and thirst for δικαιοσύνη are blessed (Matt. 5:6).
- Those who are persecuted because of δικαιοσύνη are blessed (Matt. 5:10).
- Unless the disciples' δικαιοσύνη surpass that of the Pharisees and the teachers of the Law, they will not enter into the Kingdom of Heaven (Matt. 5:20).
- The disciples should not commit acts of δικαιοσύνη before men to be seen by them (Matt. 6:1).
- The disciples have to seek the kingdom of God and his δικαιοσύνη (Matt. 6:33).
- John came to show the way of δικαιοσύνη (Matt. 21:32).

The first of these occurrences refer to both Jesus and John (Matt. 3:15) and the last to John (Matt. 21:32). It seems that these two occurrences form a wide *inclusio* around the concentration of five occurrences of the word in the Sermon on the Mount, where it refers to the life of the disciples.

```
⎡   Δικαιοσύνη of Jesus and John
⎢      Δικαιοσύνη of Jesus' disciples (Sermon on the Mount)
⎣   Δικαιοσύνη of John
```

Table 8: The *inclusio* formed by the use of δικαιοσύνη in Matthew

This *inclusio* impacts on how the δικαιοσύνη of the disciples in the Sermon on the Mount should be interpreted.

---

[80] Whilst this chapter focuses the use of the noun, δικαιοσύνη, it should be mentioned that the corresponding adjective, 'righteous' (δίκαιος), occurs seventeen times in this gospel. In Mark and Luke there are only two and eleven occurrences respectively. Of the seventeen cases there is only one instance where the usage is parallel to Mark and Luke, namely in Matt. 9:13: 'For I have not come to call the righteous, but sinners' (parallel to Mark 2:17 and Luk. 5:32). Six other cases occur in pericopes or passages with synoptic parallels, but where 'righteous' is not used in the parallel passages. These additions in Matthew's versions signify some redactional trend in Matthew's use of the adjective too, but the study of the adjective falls outside focus of this chapter.

The argument in this chapter is that Matthew intentionally utilises δικαιοσύνη to define the identity of his community in contrast to outsider groups. Δικαιοσύνη is used to describe the proper behavioural norms of his community, which distinguish them from outsiders. The Gospel not only reflects their norms, but also impacts on their identity as followers of Jesus. Therefore the concept of identity formation in the Gospels is briefly explained. Thereafter the history of interpretation of the meaning of δικαιοσύνη is discussed. To gain a better understanding of the possible meanings of this word, its Jewish and Greco-Roman environments are considered. With these considerations in mind, the seven occurrences of δικαιοσύνη in Matthew are investigated. From this investigation some conclusions follow regarding how Matthew uses δικαιοσύνη in these two cases to form the identity of his community and to shape their lifestyle.

4.2 IDENTITY FORMATION IN THE GOSPELS

The seminal study of Kilpatrick (1950:59−100) draws attention to the fact that the biblical gospels seek to shape a community of disciples. The gospels have a formational function in addition to its informational function (Carter, 2000a:8). The study of Burridge (1992) on the genre of the gospels illustrates how gospels shape communities of disciples. His argument is plausible that the gospels belong to the genre of ancient Greco-Roman biographies (βιοι). Such biographies originated amongst groups of people who were formed around charismatic leaders and teachers (Burridge, 1992:80). Typical of this genre, the gospels focus their attention on Jesus of Nazareth. Like the ancient βιοι (biographies), the gospels not only instruct and express the adoration of Jesus, but also set models for the audience to follow[81] (Burridge, 1992:214). Thus the gospels have a community-building function. They present Jesus as the expression of the communities' values (Talbert, 1992:749). Accordingly, the

---

[81] Keener (1999:25) comments on categorizing the Gospels as biographies: "Although the historical accuracy of biographies varied from one biographer to another, biographies were always primarily historical works. Historians wanted to make their accounts interesting and hade specific emphasis in writing, but such practices do not keep one from writing good history". Keener (2003:11-53) has discussed ancient biographies and has argued that Matthew's approach relates to the better historians such as Polibius who not only included praise and blame of individuals, but also that they should pursue fairness and truth. The attribution of praise and blame must be based on truth. Aune (1988:125) has similarly written: "... while biography tended to emphasize encomium, or one-sided praise of subject, it was still firmly rooted in historical fact rather than literary fiction. Thus while the Evangelists clearly had an important theological agenda, the very fact that they chose to adapt Greco-Roman biographical conventions to tell the story of Jesus indicates that they were centrally concerned to communicate what they thought really happened'.

gospels are identity-forming and lifestyle-shaping narratives (Carter, 2000a:8). "Identity" is considered here to refer to that which defines the central commitment of the members of the community. It shapes the appropriate way of life, set of practices and behaviours[82].

Scholars (Sanders *et al.*, 1980–1982; Neusner & Frerichs, 1985; Saldarini, 1994) have identified a variety of devices that groups in the Greco-Roman world employed to define themselves and outsiders. Many of these devices can be recognised in Matthew too, as Carter (2000a:9–11) has argued:

- Naming: Names such as μαθηταὶς (disciples) (e.g. Matt. 5:1, 10:24, cf. Matt. 4:18–20), μακάριοι (blessed) (Matt. 5:3–11), ἐκκλησία (church) (Matt. 16:18; 18:17), etc. are used to reinforce group identity and to warn the group not to be like the other groups.
- Central focus: Commitment to Jesus forms the central focus of the community's identity (Matt. 4:19–22; 9:9; 10:1–4; 19:21).
- Claims of exclusive revelation: The Gospel presents Jesus as the revealer of God's presence (Matt. 1:23; 28:20), will (Matt. 5–7; 10; 13; 18; 24–25), reign (Matt. 4:17) and forgiveness (Matt. 1:21; 9:1–8; 26:28).
- Rituals and association: Worship (Matt. 2:1–12; 5:23–24), teaching (Matt. 7:24–27), baptism (Matt. 28:19), appropriate interaction with other members (Matt. 6:14–15; 22:38–39; 18:15–20) and so forth are features that strengthen the identity of the community.
- Social organisation: The community makes decisions about appropriate behaviour and has its own disciplinary structures (Matt. 18:15–18).

---

[82] This argument can also be demonstrated by the social sciences, as they express the relation between identity formation and behavioural norms. Theissen (2007:15–17) has explained how psychology and the social sciences can be used as hermeneutical or heuristic tools to understand historical texts. He has explored internal mental processes to discover how people perceive, remember, think, speak and solve problems (cf. Neisser, 1967) in order to understand the texts from the past. Roitto (2011) relates to Theissen by demonstrating how cognitive sciences provide a framework to understand the relationship between identity and behavioural norms in the letter to the Ephesians.

- Critical of opponents: Matthew criticizes Jesus' opponents by naming them the ἐχθροὶ (enemies, e.g. Matt. 22:44), ὑποκριταὶ (hypocrites, e.g. Matt. 6:2), τυφλοί ὁδηγοί (blind guides, e.g. Matt. 15:14), ὄφεις, γεννήματα ἐχιδνῶν (serpents, brood of vipers, Matt. 23:33).
- Apocalyptic eschatology: The righteous and the wicked have two distinct destinies. God will punish the wicked and vindicate the oppressed righteous (Matt. 13:24–25; 25:31–46).
- Community definition by origin: The Gospel begins with Jesus' genealogy, miraculous conception and early childhood (Matt. 1–2). Jesus brings the community into existence (Matt. 1:21; 4:18–22; 9:9; 10:1–4).
- Community definition by teaching and actions: The five teaching sections (Matt. 5–7; 10; 13; 18; 24–25) outline the appropriate actions for the community.

My argument is that when considering Matthew's use of the word δικαιοσύνη, this word describes the primary actions or virtues required from the community.

The objective of this chapter is to demonstrate how Matthew uses δικαιοσύνη as identity marker. As argued in Chapter 2 of this study, Matthew was writing to his own community, who were mainly Jewish and estranged from the synagogue (Carter, 2000a:30; Saldarini, 1994:54; Tagawa, 1979:149). It seems that Matthew used the Gospel to counter Jewish suspicion against his community for following Jesus and for accepting his teaching as normative for their religious behaviour (France 1998:99). The evangelist probably seeks to assure his community that when they follow the commands of Jesus, they are not abrogating the *Torah*, but fulfilling it by bringing it to a higher standard of righteousness.

4.3 A BRIEF OVERVIEW OF RECENT INTERPRETATIONS OF ΔΙΚΑΙΟΣΎΝΗ IN MATTHEW

BDAG (2000:247-249) provides the following lexicographical definitions of δικαιοσύνη based on its use in the New Testament and other early Christian literature:

- the quality, state, or practice of judicial responsibility with a focus on fairness, justice, equitableness, fairness of human

beings and transcendent figures (cf. Heb. 7:2; 22:33; Rev. 19:11);
- the quality or state of juridical correctness with a focus on redemptive action (e.g. Rom. 1:17; 3:21f; 5:21; 9:30; Gal. 2:21; 3:21); and
- the quality or characteristic of upright behaviour of uprighteousness in general or by fulfilling divine expectations and standards (e.g. Matt. 5:6, 10, 20; Jam. 1:20).

Louw and Nida (1989) have discussed the possible meanings of δικαιοσύνη in the New Testament within the several semantic subdomains:

- moral and ethical qualities and behaviour, by doing what God requires (e.g. Matt. 5:10) (1989:744);
- association causing one to be in a proper or right relation with someone else and forensic righteousness (e.g. Rom. 1:17[83]; 3:24; 4:25) (1989:452-453);
- religious activities by observing requirements set by one's religion (e.g. Matt. 6:1) (1989:532); and
- transfer of possessions by giving to those in need as an act of mercy, such as almsgiving, charity and giving to the needy (e.g. Matt. 6:1; Acts 10:4) (1989:570).

In the light of the lexicographical definitions of BDAG (2000:247-249) and Louw and Nida (1989:452-453; 532; 570 & 744), it is clear that δικαιοσύνη potentially has different meanings. However, scholars have often defined the meaning of δικαιοσύνη in the New Testament without distinguishing between Paul and Matthew's use of the word (e.g. Fiedler 1977). In his often-quoted monograph, Przybylski (1980) warns against "Paulinizing" Matthew's use of δικαιοσύνη. This would imply that one transposes Paul's meaning(s) of δικαιοσύνη to Matthew's use of the word (Reumann, 1992:737). Such a transposition does not do justice to Matthew, as it is an established principle that a document should be understood in its own terms. According to basic semantic principles, the meaning of a word cannot be established without its context. A

---

[83] Louw and Nida (1989:452) recognise that some scholars understand δικαιοσύνη in Rom. 1:17 as referring to God's faithfulness to his promises made to Abraham. However, they find it difficult to relate such an interpretations with the statement about faith in Rom. 1:17b).

word's meaning is dependent on its relation with its immediate and wider context (De Saussure, 1966:82; Cruse 1986; Thiselton, 1979:79; Nida & Taber, 1974:15). Since Przybylski more scholars have attended to the distinction between Matthew's use of δικαιοσύνη and that of Paul (cf. Hagner, 1997).

During the first half of the 20th century, reformed scholars often read Paul's use of δικαιοσύνη [84] mainly in soteriological terms[85] (cf. Ridderbos, 1971:171–191; Schrenk, 1978:202; Stuhlmacher 1966). With reference to the semantic subdomains as defined by Louw and Nida (1989:452-453), the meaning of δικαιοσύνη is limited to the second definition as indicated above. However, this often had the effect that New Testament texts were read through the eyes of the Reformation controversies about righteousness and justification. The result is that Matthew's use of this word is "Paulinized" with a mainly soteriological meaning. Such an approach fitted very well with a simplified hermeneutical approach where Romans 1:17[86] is used as lens to interpret all references to δικαιοσύνη in the New Testament. A soteriological reading of δικαιοσύνη in Matthew would temper the strong emphasis on demands in the Sermon on the Mount which, with a shallow reading of Matthew, looks as if Jesus requires humans to be perfect before they can enter the Kingdom of Heaven.

The debate surrounding the meaning of δικαιοσύνη in Matthew has primarily revolved around the question of whether the word should be interpreted soteriologically (second sematic sub-domain as identified by Louw & Nida, 1989:452-453) or ethically (the other three semantic subdomains as suggested

---

[84] The word δικαιοσύνη is prominent in Paul's writings, as it occurs 57 times in his letters. Much scholarly discussion, without consensus, is currently taking place about Paul's use of this word. Paul uses the term mostly as part of the phrase δικαιοσύνη του θεου, this phrase has traditionally been interpreted to denote God's gracious saving action in forensic and soteriological terms (e.g. Rom. 1:17; 3:5, 21; 10:3) (Schrenk, 1978:202-210). Within the same tradition, the word δικαιοσύνη by itself refers to righteousness as a gift accounting to salvation (e.g. Rom. 4:5; 1 Cor. 1:30; 2 Cor. 3:9; Gal. 3:6). In a smaller number of cases Paul probably also uses the word in an ethical sense (Rom. 6:13, 16, 18; 2 Cor. 6:14; 9:10).

[85] Scholars from the so-called 'New perspective on Paul' also question such a reading of Paul. The 'new perspective on Paul' is an attempt to lift Paul's letters out of the Lutheran-Reformed framework and to interpret them based on what is said to be an understanding of first-century Judaism. It is argued that in the 'old perspective' Paul was understood to be arguing that Christians' good works do not contribute to salvation, only faith. According to the new perspective, Paul was questioning only observances such as circumcision and dietary laws, but not good works in general (Dunn, 2008).

[86] Rom. 1:17: 'For in the gospel a righteousness from God is revealed, a righteousness that is by faith from first to last, just as it is written: "The righteous will live by faith"'.

by Louw & Nida, 1989:532, 570 & 744), or on a continuum with elements of both (Betz, 1995:130). Does δικαιοσύνη refer to a gift of salvation from God on the one extreme, or to an ethical demand on humans on the other extreme? Other questions are whether Matthew uses the term for one single meaning only, or does he incorporate elements of both meanings into the term.

Some earlier scholars (e.g. Dupont, 1973:305; Hill 1967:124; Strecker, 1971:157–187) interpreted the occurrences of δικαιοσύνη as *Rechtschaffenheit* in adherence to ethical demands on humans and not as a gift from God. The acceptance of this interpretation has increased since the publication of Przybylski (1980) and has been adopted in commentaries by Luz (1990:177), and Davies and Allison (2004a:327). However, Fiedler (1977) and Giesen (1982:237–241) have proposed an opposite interpretation by arguing that all occurrences should be interpreted in a soteriological sense as an *Heilsgabe*. In contrast to the viewpoint that Matthew always uses δικαιοσύνη in the same sense, some scholars (e.g. Guelich, 1982:84–87; Meier 1976:77–80; Reumann, 1982:127–135; Schweizer, 1976:53–56; Ziesler, 1972:144) have come to argue that Matthew uses it with different meanings: sometimes as a soteriological gift, and at other times as an ethical demand, or even as both simultaneously. Ziesler (1972:144), for example, has argued that δικαιοσύνη in Matt. 5:6 refers to God's gift, whilst in Matt. 5:20 it refers to God's demand on man. He (Ziesler, 1972:144) has concluded:

> It is probably no accident that 5:6 precedes 5:20: human righteousness is inadequate, and what is needed is not only a more thorough kind, but one which comes as God's gift to those who long for it.

Similarly, Schweizer (1976:55) has remarked that δικαιοσύνη in Matt. 5:20 "undoubtedly refers to human actions according to the norm of what God's righteousness requires", whilst in Matt. 6:33 it is "probably to be understood as a gracious gift, given by God in mercy". The assumption would then be that Matthew does not use δικαιοσύνη consistently. It is therefore often argued that δικαιοσύνη as demand is subordinate to δικαιοσύνη as gift (cf. Kertelge, 1971:47).

Though there is scholarly disagreement about the meaning of δικαιοσύνη in Matthew, many scholars (cf. Banks, 1974:242b; Betz, 1995:130; Deines, 2004:122; Frankemölle, 1997:71) have agreed that it should be regarded as an important term in Matthew's gospel. Tagawa (1970:149) has remarked: "It is well known, for example, that δικαιοσύνη is one of the fundamental concepts in

Matthew". My argument is that if Matthew uses δικαιοσύνη as such a key term, it is an implausible conclusion to regard Matthew's use of the term as loose and inconsistent. He would most probably have used such a key term in a rather defined and consistent manner.

It is helpful to next consider the wider context in which Matthew used the term in order to illuminate the different meanings of δικαιοσύνη. Therefore the meaning of δικαιοσύνη is investigated in its Jewish and Greco-Roman settings. In view of Matthew's undoubted indebtedness to Judaism, the Jewish setting would have played a major role in the way Matthew used the word. However, the word's use in the Greco-Roman context of the first century should also be taken into consideration, since that also (perhaps indirectly) formed part of the setting of Matthew.

4.4 ΔΙΚΑΙΟΣΎΝΗ WITHIN ITS JEWISH AND GRECO-ROMAN SETTINGS

In an attempt to determine the distinctive meaning(s) Matthew attached to the word δικαιοσύνη, the sections below presents an investigation of the possible meanings of the word in its Jewish and Greco-Roman contexts.

4.4.1 Δικαιοσύνη within its Jewish setting

Matthew wrote his gospel within a religious context with conceptual ideas. His use of δικαιοσύνη most probably reflects the Jewish understanding of the term in Greek translation or in some Semitic language (Betz, 1995:30; Hill, 1967:139). The Jewish scriptures must have made a significant contribution to Matthew's conceptual heritage (Menken, 2004:1-10). Matthew used this heritage as he frequently (sometimes freely) quoted from the LXX, applied some of the quotations in fulfilment formulae, and built many of his arguments on motifs from the Jewish scriptures (Menken, 2004). However, because of the considerable time difference between the Jewish scriptures and the Gospel, later terminology developments in the meaning of "righteousness" should also be considered. Documents from the Dead Sea Scrolls and Tannaitic literature might be helpful to discover these developments. The Jewish scriptures should provide the point of departure from which the meaning of the term developed as found in these later Jewish writings.

4.4.1.1 "Righteousness" in the Hebrew Bible

"Righteousness" in the Hebrew Bible derives from the root *ts-d-q*. The meaning of this root cannot be determined *a priori*. Words deriving from this root occur

523 times in the Hebrew Bible within a wide variety of genres and settings (Schrenk, 1978:195; Scullion 1992:725). Ziesler (1972:20–35) analysed righteousness terminology of *tsedeq*, *tsedaqah* and the adjective (*tsaddiq*) in the Jewish scriptures. According to his account, there are 115 occurrences of *tsedeq* (masculine), 158 of *tsedaqah* (feminine) and 208 of *tsaddiq* in the Kittel edition of the Hebrew Bible. Quell (1964:175) discovered no discernible difference in meaning between the masculine and feminine forms of the noun *tsedeq* and *tsedaqah* in the Hebrew Bible. In quite a number of cases where *tsedeq* and *tsedaqah* are used, it carries the meaning of God's saving activity, especially in Deutero-Isaiah, for example, Isa. 46:13: "I am bringing my *tsedeq* near, it is not far away; and my salvation will not be delayed" (cf. Talbert, 1992:748; Hill, 1967:86–98; Ziesler, 1972:22–32). However, there are also a number of cases where it refers to good moral conduct concerning how one stands before the *Torah*, or God (Spicq, 2012:8; Talbert, 1992:748). Significantly, righteous acts and almsgiving can be described using any one of the three terms, as *tsedeq* (Isa. 58:8),[87] *tsedaqah* (Prov. 21:21)[88] and *tsaddiq* (Ps. 112:6).[89] Out of the 208 occurrences of *tsaddiq*, 186 probably refer to proper religious human conduct that is right before God and in line with the keeping of the covenant. In 22 cases it refers to the person of God in terms of either a salvific or punitive aspect, which is particularly prominent in the Prophets.

4.4.1.2 *"Righteousness" in early Judaism*

4.1.2.1 Δικαιοσύνη *(righteousness) in the LXX*

Reumann (1992:737–738) has discussed the problems encountered with the translation of the Hebrew Bible into Greek for use in diaspora synagogues. The range of translators did not always fully understand the Hebrew texts and it seems that they were not always able to translate all the nuances of the original version. The translation of the *ts-d-q* words with the Greek δικαιοσύνη narrowed the broader sense of the Hebrew term. The Greek word was mostly restricted to justice, which could result in a distortion of the understanding of the meaning of the original version (e.g. Jer. 23:5; 32:15). However, in the sense

---

[87] Isa. 58:8: "… your *tsedeq* will go before you".

[88] Prov. 21:20–21: "In the house of the wise are stores of choice food and oil, but a foolish man devours all he has. He who pursues *tsedaqah* and love finds life, prosperity and honour".

[89] Ps. 112:5–6: "Good will come to him who is generous and lends freely, who conducts his affairs with justice. Surely he will never be shaken; a *tsaddiq* will be remembered forever".

that δικαιοσύνη was used in the LXX, it was connected with faith and faithfulness and was thus abetted in Hellenistic-Jewish literature. Δικαιοσύνη implies a relationship (Schrenk, 1978:195). A person is righteous when he/she meets certain expectations in virtue of the relationship. According to Isa. 5:7, the Lord Almighty looked for human δικαιοσύνη in his the house of Israel, but was disappointed to only find ἀνομία (iniquity). The prophets constantly appeal to God's people to practice δικαιοσύνη, as that is what Yahweh expects from them (Hos. 10:12; Jer. 22:3; Ezek.45:9) (Spicq, 2012:330)

4.1.2.2   "Righteousness" in the Damascus document

The texts of the Dead Sea Scrolls are of great religious and historical significance as they preserve evidence of religious developments of late Second Temple Judaism[90] (cf. VanderKam 2009). Though these documents were specifically located at Qumran, they are actually a collection of 972 texts from the Hebrew Bible and extra-biblical documents that come from a wider area. These manuscripts generally date from between 150 BCE and 70 CE[91] and demonstrate Jewish conceptual developments in the times leading up to the writing of the Matthean text. Przybylski (1980:13–38) investigates the meaning of words connected to the root *ts-d-q* in the Dead Sea Scrolls. He finds that the concept of righteousness is specifically significant in the Cairo Damascus (CD) document, which was a product of the Qumran community as such. The Damascus document comprises two separate sections: the Admonition and the Laws. The Admonition consists of moral instruction, exhortation, and warnings addressed to members of the community, together with polemic against its opponents. The Laws describe the arrangements of the new community as expressed by the Teacher of Righteousness (cf. Davies, 1983). In the Damascus document, Przybylski (1980:17–19) recognises a difference in meaning between *tsedeq* (masculine) and *tsedaqah* (feminine) that is different from the Hebrew Bible. The term *tsedeq* developed into a technical term, symbolising everything

---

[90] Second Temple Judaism refers to the religion of Judaism in the era between the construction of the second temple in Jerusalem in 515 BCE and its destruction by the Romans in 70 CE. As discussed in Chapter 2 of this study, significant religious developments took place during this period, such as growing interest in the authority of scriptures, the centrality of law and morality, and of apocalyptic expectations.

[91] There is no unanimity of opinion about the time span of the development of the Dead Sea Scrolls. The *terminus ad quem* is quite certain, as most scholars agree that the scrolls found in the caves of Qumran were stored there no later than 70 CE – the date of the destruction of the temple in Jerusalem (Dupont-Sommer 1961:340; VanderKam 2009:7).

that is right in the sight of God. Members of the Qumran community knew the concept of righteousness through the teaching of the Teacher of Righteousness. Those "who know *tsedeq*" (CD 1:1)[92], know what was communicated to them by the Teacher of *tsedeq* (CD 1:11). They do not walk in "waters of falsehood" (CD 1:15), but "in the ways of *tsedeq*" (CD 1:16). The Teacher of Righteousness teaches the "precepts of *tsedeq*" (CD 20:32). *Tsedeq* thus implies the ideal conduct in adherence to God's ordinances. A person who strives to live according to this ideal is regarded as righteous (*tsaddiq*). In contrast, *tsedaqah* is used for God's saving gracious activity and gift of salvation (CD 20:20). By doing *tsedeq*, one shows that one appreciates God's gift of *tsedaqah*.

4.1.2.3   Ts-d-q in the Tannaitic literature

It is also helpful to consider the concept of righteousness in the Tannaitic literature (cf. Reumann 1992:739). The Tannaitic period begins with the disciples of Shammai and Hillel, and ends with the contemporaries of Rabbi Judah ha-Nasi, a time span from approximately 10 CE until 200 CE.[93] The Tannaitic literature demonstrates the development of Jewish thoughts during the time of the New Testament and approximately a century thereafter. Matthew's gospel fits into this time frame of development of Jewish thoughts. In contrast to the Hebrew Bible where there is no discernible difference in meaning between the masculine noun *tsedeq* and feminine *tsedaqah*, the Tannaitic literature follows the development of a differentiation of meaning as seen in the Damascus document (Przybylski 1980:39). The noun *tsedeq* is primarily used for all aspects of teaching that is normative for human conduct. The Lord is *tsaddiq*, and a person who lives according to the norm of *tsedeq* is also considered to be *tsaddiq*. "For the Lord is *tsaddiq*, he loves our righteous deeds *tsedqotenu*, so you are righteous *tsaddiq*" (Sifre[94] Deut. 49, 11:22). *Tsedaqah* developed a very specific meaning as almsgiving (Tosefta Peah[95] 4:19):

> *Tsedaqah* and deeds of loving kindness are equal to all the commandments of the Law ... *tsedaqah* is done with a man's money, deeds of loving kindness either with money or personally.

---

[92] CD refers to the Cairo Damascus document of the Qumran community.

[93] The rabbis who lived during this period are known as the Tannaim.

[94] Sifre refers to classical Jewish legal Biblical exegesis, based on the biblical books of Numbers and Deuteronomy.

[95] The Tosefta is a compilation of the Jewish oral law from the period of the *Mishna*.

tsedaqah thus became an important part of the *tsedeq* of a *tsaddiq*. By living according to the norm of *tsedeq*, the *tsaddiq* demonstrates that he appreciates his relationship with God.

From this investigation of the Jewish context it seems that there was a development in the meaning of "righteousness" words from the time of the writing of the Hebrew Bible to the time that Matthew wrote as reflected in the writings of the Qumran community and of the Tannaim. *Tsedeq* implied the ideal conduct in adherence to God's ordinances. In contrast, *tsedaqah* developed the meaning of God's saving gracious activity and a gift of salvation. When considering the meaning of δικαιοσύνη in Matthew, this development and differentiation of meaning should be taken into consideration.

4.4.2 Δικαιοσύνη in its Greco-Roman setting

To gain an understanding of the Greco-Roman meaning of δικαιοσύνη, it is useful to consider the influential ancient analysis of this word as offered by Aristotle in his *Nicomachean Ethics* (Eth. Nic.), book 5 (cf. Rackham, 1934; Thom, 2009:319). In the post-epic period the term developed an ethical meaning in addition to its legal meaning (Schrenk, 1978:192-193). Civil virtue is based on justice and the observance of law and judicial procedure. Aristotle made a distinction between δικαιοσύνη as a general and as a more specific virtue (Eth. Nic. 6.1). This distinction became the norm for later authors. Plato applied δικαιοσύνη to virtuous conduct in general (Pakaluk, 2005:182–186; Spicq, 2012:327). Aristotle qualified this general virtue as a relational concept indicating the appropriate relationship between two parties (Eth. Nic. 5.1.1129b26−27). After Aristotle, philosophers of the Stoa described the general social virtue of δικαιοσύνη to include other virtues, such as χρηστότης (goodness), εὐκοινωνησία (good fellowship), εὐσυναλλαξία (fair dealing), and εὐσέβεια (piety) (Schrenk, 1978:193). Furthermore, Aristotle described a particular meaning of δικαιοσύνη as justice (Eth. Nic. 5.2.1130a14−b29). Such justice is concerned with the equal distribution of goods. He furthermore distinguishes between distributive and corrective justice (Eth. Nic. 5.2.1130b30−1131a1; 5.4.1132a18). Aristotle further remarked that law is always a general statement intended to cover a wide variety of situations (Eth. Nic. 5.10.1137b11−19). To apply the law to specific cases, δικαιοσύνη is required from a person to recognise the purpose of the law or the intention of the lawgiver (Eth. Nic. 5.10.1137b19−27). A combination of these definitions is found in the philosophical syncretism of the Greco-Roman period from the first century BCE onwards (Thom, 2009:334).

4.5 ΔΙΚΑΙΟΣΥΝΗ IN MATTHEW

With this background of the potential meanings of δικαιοσύνη in mind, the attention now shifts to δικαιοσύνη in Matthew. It is plausible to assume that Matthew used δικαιοσύνη within this Jewish and Greco-Roman context with an emphasis on the Jewish nuances. As previously argued in Chapter 2 of this study, Matthew's implied audience mostly consisted of people of Jewish background.

4.5.1 Jesus was baptised to fulfil all δικαιοσύνη (Matt. 3:15)

In Matt. 3:13–17 the author describes the baptism of Jesus. While all three of the Synoptic Gospels narrates this baptism, Matthew elaborates on the story.

Mark 1:9	Matt. 3:13-16a	Luk. 3:21a
Καὶ ἐγένετο ἐν ἐκείναις ταῖς ἡμέραις ἦλθεν Ἰησοῦς ἀπὸ Ναζαρὲτ τῆς Γαλιλαίας καὶ ἐβαπτίσθη εἰς τὸν Ἰορδάνην ὑπὸ Ἰωάνου. At that time Jesus came from Nazareth in Galilee and was baptized by John in the Jordan.	Τότε παραγίνεται ὁ Ἰησοῦς ἀπὸ τῆς Γαλιλαίας ἐπὶ τὸν Ἰορδάνην πρὸς τὸν Ἰωάνην τοῦ βαπτισθῆναι ὑπ' αὐτοῦ. ὁ δὲ διεκώλυεν αὐτὸν λέγων Ἐγὼ χρείαν ἔχω ὑπὸ σοῦ βαπτισθῆναι, καὶ σὺ ἔρχῃ πρός με; ἀποκριθεὶς δὲ ὁ Ἰησοῦς εἶπεν αὐτῷ Ἄφες ἄρτι· **οὕτως γὰρ πρέπον ἐστὶν ἡμῖν πληρῶσαι πᾶσαν δικαιοσύνην.** τότε ἀφίησιν αὐτόν. βαπτισθεὶς δὲ ὁ Ἰησοῦς ... Then Jesus came from Galilee to the Jordan to be baptized by John. But John tried to deter him, saying, "I need to be baptized by you, and do you come to me?" Jesus replied, "Let it be so now; it is proper for us to do this to fulfil all righteousness." Then John consented. As soon as Jesus was baptized ...	Ἐγένετο δὲ ἐν τῷ βαπτισθῆναι ἅπαντα τὸν λαὸν καὶ Ἰησοῦ βαπτισθέντος, When all the people were being baptized, Jesus was baptized too.

Table 9: The parallel of the story in Matt. 3:13–17 with Mark 1:9 and Luk. 3:21a on the baptism of Jesus

Only Matthew describes how John tried to dissuade Jesus from baptising Him and of how Jesus responded (indicated by the underlining in the table above) indicating specific redactional interest. Jesus responds that He had to be baptised by John so that all righteousness could be fulfilled for them: "οὕτως γὰρ πρέπον ἐστὶν ἡμῖν πληρῶσαι πᾶσαν δικαιοσύνην" (it is proper for us to do this to fulfil all righteousness) (indicated in bold and underlining) (Matt. 3:15).

It is significant that this Matthean addition offers two key Matthean themes, namely "fulfilment" (πληρῶσαι) (cf. Menken, 2004) and "righteousness" (δικαιοσύνη) (Davies & Allison, 2004a:325; Turner, 2008:118). Matthew frequently uses the verb "fulfil" to introduce a citation from the Jewish Bible (Matt. 1:22; 2:15, 17, 23; 4:14; 5:17; 8:17; 12:17; 13:35; 21:4; 26:54, 56; 27:9). This confirms that the respective events described occurred according to what was previously declared in the Jewish Scriptures.

What δικαιοσύνη means in this context is not easy to decide. One option is to interpret δικαιοσύνη here as God's salvific activity, as *tsedaqah* is used in the Jewish Damascus document and Tannaitic literature. Accordingly, Jesus' baptism represents the inauguration of Jesus' ministry, which would eventually lead to his redemptive death on the cross. This would imply that the baptism typifies his death by which justice is effected (Cullmann, 1950:15–17). Cullmann refers to Isa. 53:11[96] in saying that Jesus' baptism prefigured his death through which forgiveness and righteousness are accomplished for believers. Along similar lines, Barth (1963:140) has argued that Jesus, by his baptism, entered the path of the passion and resurrection to save his people. Morris (1992:65) has been of the opinion that Matthew here pictures Jesus as dedicating himself to the task of making sinners righteous. As Messiah, He would pave the way so that his followers could eventually enjoy eschatological "righteousness" as a gift from God. Meier (1976:79) and Hagner (1992:116; 1993:56) have also argued in favour of such a *heilsgeschichtliche* interpretation. An objection against such an interpretation is the use of the plural ἡμῖν (for us). Unless it is a royal "we", the fulfilment is not by Jesus only. The most likely other candidate to form part of "us" is John. Consequently, not only Jesus, but also John should fulfil all righteousness (Hagner, 1993:56; Talbert, 2010:55; Turner, 2008:118). This makes it improbable to limit the δικαιοσύνη in Matt.

---

[96] Isa. 53:11: "... by his knowledge my righteous servant will justify many, and he will bear their iniquities".

3:15 only to Jesus' salvific activity. When John baptises Jesus it allows both to fulfil all δικαιοσύνη.

It is also possible to understand δικαιοσύνη in an ethical sense as *tsedeq* in later Jewish writings and in the Greco-Roman literature. In New Testament times, δικαιοσύνη had already established itself in the moral vocabulary of the Greco-Roman world (Davies & Allison, 2004a:325; Schrenk, 1978:198; Spicq, 2012:331). Such an interpretation fits very well with the prominent role assigned to adherence to the Law in Matthew. As Matthew requires righteousness from his community, he would find it important to demonstrate that Jesus himself was committed to total righteousness, as He forms the central focus of the identity community (Carter, 2009:10). Jesus, knowing the messianic prophecies, obediently fulfilled all righteousness. The baptism of Jesus recalls the honourable act of Joseph, who was a righteous man (δίκαιος ὤν) (Matt. 1:19). According to this interpretation, Jesus and John would be pictured as being committed to fulfil righteousness by behaving as expected from them. Jesus is depicted as the righteous one (τῷ δικαίῳ ἐκείνῳ) (cf. Matt. 27:19). He fulfilled all righteousness. John came to perform a specific task in preparing the way for Jesus. By doing this, John also fulfilled righteousness. Both Jesus and John had to act in a way that is faithful to their covenant relationship with God. Jesus and John needed to do what God wanted in an eschatological context (Carter, 2000a:11), and thus fulfilled God's plans set forth for each of them respectively in the predictions of the Jewish scriptures (Eissfeldt, 1970:213; Foster, 2004:200; Loader, 1997:159; Meier, 1976:79; Spicq, 2012:331). Their righteousness "characterizes proper human response to God, implying faithfulness, obedience, and ethical integrity" (Senior, 1998:55). However, this act that fulfilled all righteousness is not meant to be exhaustive, as the aorist of the verb πληρῶσαι (an ingressive aorist) indicates (Jordaan, 2014:67). This act is rather the beginning of more to follow (Talbert, 2010:53). Such an interpretation resonates with the opening words of Matt. 3:1–3,[97] which refers to the fulfilment of Isaiah's prophecy on the one who will come to prepare the way for the Lord. The impeccable Jesus and John, his messenger, are obedient to God's will. The themes of righteousness and fulfilment furthermore find their echo in Jesus' statement on the continuing validity of the

---

[97] Matt. 3:1–3: 'In those days John the Baptist came, preaching in the Desert of Judea and saying, "Repent, for the Kingdom of Heaven is near". This is he who was spoken of through the prophet Isaiah: A voice of one calling in the desert, "Prepare the way for the Lord, make straight paths for him."'

Law in Matt. 5:17.[98] Righteousness similar to that of Jesus and John is what is demanded form Jesus' disciples in the Sermon on the Mount. This righteousness entails fidelity to the commandments of God as Jesus would interpret them (Beare, 1981:99). These considerations make an ethical interpretation of δικαιοσύνη in Matt. 3:15 very plausible. The δικαιοσύνη of Jesus and John thus sets the norm for proper conduct for his disciples. Jesus' messianic life of δικαιοσύνη, with that of John added to this, provides the extent and direction for his community's life (Stuhlmacher, 1986:30). The disciples were expected to follow in their footsteps and to also fulfil all δικαιοσύνη. Jesus' and John's righteous act would later be balanced in the passage about John who came "in the way of righteousness" (ἦλθεν γὰρ Ἰωάνης πρὸς ὑμᾶς ἐν ὁδῷ δικαιοσύνης) (Matt. 21:32) to do what was expected of him, presumably forming a wide *inclusio* around the theme of δικαιοσύνη in the Sermon on the Mount (Talbert 1992:745).

Whilst this interpretation seems likely, it also poses some difficulty. The obvious objection against such an interpretation would be that there is no command in the Hebrew Bible that might hint at the necessity of Jesus being baptised. Baptism is a sign of repentance, whilst the Son of God actually needs no repentance (Hagner, 1992:116; Talbert, 2010:54). However, it can also be argued that with the baptism Jesus humbly identifies himself with God's repentant people as the servant of the Lord (France, 2008:100; Van der Walt, 2006:152). The Messiah is a representative person and thus embodies Israel. As such, He identifies Himself with his people fully and obediently acts out this role (Hagner, 1993:57; Mounce, 1991:25). Furthermore, read in connection with Matt. 3:1-3, the baptism implies the culmination of the preparation work of John the Baptist. It can therefore be argued that John and Jesus as such carried out the total will of God: John as preparer and Jesus as humble servant of the Lord.

It should be considered that righteousness in Hebrew and Greco-Roman thought refers to actions that are faithful to relationships and commitments (Carter, 2000a:102; Reumann, 1982:12–135). Read in terms of the patronage system of reciprocity in Roman Palestine (cf. Malina & Rohrbauch, 2003:388), this requires a more nuanced reading of Matt. 3:15. In the Hebrew Bible, God (as "patron") demonstrates his goodwill and righteousness by being faithful to his covenantal commitments to deliver his people (Ps. 51:14; 65:5; Isa. 46:13;

---

[98] Matt. 5:17: 'Do not think that I have come to abolish the Law or the Prophets; I have not come to abolish them but to fulfil them'.

51:5–8). God's people (as "clients") accordingly, in response to his goodwill, act righteous when they are faithful to covenantal requirements (Ps. 72:1, 2, 7). Furthermore, God's righteousness is related to human righteousness. God gives righteousness, which humans perform (Guelich, 1982:371–372). The righteousness described in Matt. 3:15 fits this tradition. Jesus and John enact God's saving will. Matthew portrays Jesus and John the Baptist as prototypes who were fully committed to enacting God's righteousness. Taking into consideration the group-orientated society of the first-century Mediterranean world[99], it makes sense that righteousness would refer to actions fitting within this covenantal group. Righteous actions could be considered as positive reciprocity within this group.

4.5.2 Δικαιοσύνη in the Sermon on the Mount

The Sermon on the Mount presents a unique arrangement of Jesus' teaching. Within this unique presentation Matthew offers his distinctive understanding of the Law and righteousness. Five of the seven occurrences of the word δικαιοσύνη in Matthew are found in the Sermon on the Mount. This concentration indicates that the term represents an important theme in the Sermon on the Mount. Betz (1995:130) has accordingly remarked: "Within the SM, the term δικαιοσύνη occupies a place of central importance" and Davies and Allison (2004a:499) has written: "The word 'righteousness' ... expresses the essence of the sermon on the mount".

The Sermon on the Mount forms one of the five teaching blocks in the Gospel (Matt. 5-7; 10, 13, 18 and 24−25), each closed by a similar refrain "Καὶ ἐγένετο ὅτε ἐτέλεσεν ὁ Ἰησοῦς τοὺς λόγους τούτους" (and when Jesus had finished these words) (Talbert, 2010:6). In these teachings, Matthew's Jesus instructs his disciples about attitudes and practices that distinguish them from other people and exhorts them to persevere faithfully (Carter, 2000a:8).

The Sermon on the Mount is also referred to as the Constitution of the Kingdom of Heaven (Van der Walt, 2006:185). Those who are included in the Kingdom of Heaven must live in an appropriate manner. In their daily lives and interaction with other people, the citizens of the Kingdom are called upon to live according to the will of God. "Die Bergpredigt enthält also eine missionarische Jünger-Ethik" (Deines, 2004:446). This in itself signifies that

---

[99] See Malina & Rohrbaugh (1992:56) for a discussion of group orientated societies of the ancient Mediterranean world.

δικαιοσύνη in the Sermon probably refers to the fulfilment of the *Torah* by enacting the will of God. The Sinai typology is seemingly already implied at the beginning of the Sermon when Jesus goes up the mountain to teach (Matt. 5:1–2;[100] Floor, 1969:34; Loader, 1997:165). This opening leads to an anticipation of a revelation to be delivered by a new Lawgiver. The expectation is met as Jesus teaches the Law in the Sermon. Jesus states that He did not come to abolish the Law, but to bring it to fulfilment (Matt. 5:17–19) and He repeatedly refers to the meaning and intention of the Law in the *halakhic* argument of Matt. 5:21–48 (cf. Chapter 5 of this study). He calls his followers to do the will of God in a way that supersedes that of the scribes and Pharisees[101] (Matt. 5:20, 48; 6:1–18). Besides the Sinai typology, an allusion to Mount Zion[102] might also have been implied (Carter, 2000a:130). At Mount Zion, nations would come to learn of God's ways (cf. Isa. 2:3; Mic. 4:2; Ps. 24:3).

When Jesus sat down to teach, his disciples came to Him. This is the first instance where the word μαθηταὶ (disciples) is used to identify the followers of Jesus. As Carter (2000a:9) has indicated, such naming forms a typical feature in identity formation of a group. In the Greco-Roman and Jewish worlds, this word was used for adherents of a recognized master (Wilkins, 1988). Jesus continues to teach his followers the requirements of the Law.

The Sermon on the Mount sketches a society of justice in contrast to the values, commitments and practices of the majority who do not form part of the Kingdom of Heaven (Carter, 2000a:128; Gnilka, 1986:112; Thom, 2009:338). In the narrative world it seems that the sermon is intended to shape and strengthen the disciple's identity and lifestyle, which differs from that of the scribes and the Pharisees, and a similar intention is implied for the Matthean community as implied audience of the text. The community is reminded of the importance of their interaction with God, one another and the surrounding society, which is distinctive from that of the non-Christian Jewish community.

---

[100] The phrase 'went up the mountain' was frequently used to describe Moses going up Sinai to receive the Decalogue (Exod. 19:3; 24:12, 13, 28; 34:2, 4; Deut. 9:9; 10:1, 3).

[101] The scribes and the Pharisees are the stereotypical opponents in the first Gospel.

[102] The phrase 'went up the mountain' in several instances refers to Mount Zion (Isa. 2:3; Mic. 4:2; Ps 24:3; 1 Macc 5:54; 7:33).

Δικαιοσύνη forms a key theme in the Sermon on the Mount, extending from Matt. 5:6 where it first appears in the Beatitudes through to the conclusion of his argument in Matt. 6:33. Δικαιοσύνη in Matt. 5:20 and 6:1 furthermore forms an *inclusio* around the *halakhic* antitheses of Matt. 5:21–47. By way of the antitheses, Matthew illustrates the new δικαιοσύνη that is called for. After these positive statements about appropriate conduct, Matt. 6:1 forms a hinge to introduce critique of inappropriate behaviour (Matt. 6:1–18).

Kennedy (1980:39–63) and Mack (1990:82–85) have suggested that the Sermon on the Mount be analysed in terms of the parts of classical rhetorical speech. By referring to these suggestions and with some variations to details, Thom (2009:315–316) has plausibly proposed the following outline of the composition[103]:

Exordium (Introduction): Defining the righteous disciple (Matt. 5:3–16) Beatitudes (Matt. 5:3–12) Metaphors of salt and light (Matt. 5:13–16)
Propositio (Statement of the theme): Exceeding righteousness (Matt. 5:17–20) True fulfilment of the Law (Matt. 5:17–18) Exceeding righteousness (Matt. 5:19–20)
Probatio (Argument): Understanding and practicing the righteous life (Matt. 5:21–7:21) Righteousness and the interpretation of the Law (Matt. 5:21–48) Righteousness and piety (Matt. 6:1–18) Righteousness and priorities (Matt. 6:19–34) Judgement and discrimination, actions and consequences (Matt. 7:1–11)
Peroratio (Conclusion): Warnings regarding words and actions of the religious life (Matt. 7:13–27)

Table 10: Composition of the Sermon on the Mount in terms of classical rhetorical speech

From this proposed view of the composition of the Sermon on the Mount, it becomes clear that the term δικαιοσύνη appears at important positions in the Sermon. It is found at the beginning of the *exordium* (Matt. 5:6 and 10) and within this *exordium* at important central (fourth beatitude) and closing positions (eighth) in the Beatitudes. In the *propositio,* the term is used to

---

[103] Weren (1994:64-65) has identified similar components of the Sermon, with variants on the division: (1) Exordium – Matt. 5:3-16; Corpus – Matt. 5:17-21; Peroratio – Matt. 7:13-26.

broaden the theme by demanding of the disciples a δικαιοσύνη that exceeds that of the Pharisees and teachers of the Law (Matt. 5:20). In Matt. 6:1, δικαιοσύνη is used in the introduction to the second part of the *probatio* to warn that δικαιοσύνη should not be practiced to be applauded by people. In Matt. 6:33, δικαιοσύνη is used in the conclusion of the third part of the *probatio* to urge the disciples to seek δικαιοσύνη as their first priority.

4.5.2.1 *Δικαιοσύνη in the exordium to the Sermon on the Mount*

The Beatitudes (Matt. 5:3−12) form the first part of the *exordium* to the Sermon on the Mount. Various scholars have indicated that the Beatitudes were common pronouncements in the Greek language and formed a specific genre (cf. Van Aarde 1994:163). Some *formgeschichtlichen* and *gattungsgeschichtlichen* studies have been done on the Beatitudes as such. Koch (1974:21−23) is a prominent exponent arguing for a *gattungsgeschichtlice* past behind the series of beatitudes. The Beatitudes refer to a religious prophecy of salvation regarding joy or blessing of some nature that implies eschatological participation. It conveys the meaning that it will ultimately be well with those who first seek God's kingdom (e.g. Matt. 6:33).This style of blessing can be called "an indirect exhortation", which induces a particular pattern of ethical behaviour (Domeris, 1990:68). God will comfort these people at the final restoration (Keener, 1999:166). The Beatitudes do not only concern emotions or personal qualities, but God's preference for certain attitudes and actions (Carter, 2000a:130).

As declarative statements, the Beatitudes in Matthew pose theological dogma[104] with regard to the eschatological distinctive religious joy of the righteous, who share in the salvation of the Kingdom of God (Lioy, 2004:120). The Beatitudes also imply the judgement of God as supreme Judge, anticipating his eschatological verdicts. The ultimate mercy of God will be revealed on the day of the judgement (Keener, 1999:166). Principles of eschatological divine justice are pronounced, and these impact on the present. "Divine justice not only is above time and space but also reaches into time and space" (Betz, 1995:96). These principles lay claim on the recipient to respond with an appropriate conduct of life. By revealing this new way of life, the Beatitudes effect moral behaviour. The addressees have to respond with adequate attitudes, actions and thoughts that are different to conventional ways of behaviour (Luz, 1990:221).

---

[104] In this way, the Beatitudes stand in the tradition of the Jewish wisdom literature. In the Jewish wisdom literature, wisdom is based on the divine justice as revealed in the *Torah* (Betz, 1995:94).

Therefore the set of beatitudes describes the way of life of faithful disciples of Jesus. Ethical exhortations are embedded in promises and encouragements of gracious blessings. Matthew's Jesus uses a standard literary form of the Hebrew Bible as found in Ps. 1:1–2: "Blessed is the man who does not walk in the counsel of the wicked ... But his delight is in the Law of the Lord" (Keener, 1999:165). For Matthew, the Beatitudes describe the life of Jesus' disciples in the narrative world, and presumably also the parameters of conduct for his community. "The Beatitudes sketch the attitudes that the Matthean Christians should manifest and allude to the suffering that they endured" (Harrington, 1991:82).

Hanson (1994:100–101) indicates the relationship between the Beatitudes and the values of honour and shame. The Beatitudes present behaviour and attitudes that God as "Patron" considers honourable and which the community should also value (Carter, 2000a:576; Malina & Rohrbaugh, 2003:41). While they are declarations of favour, they also encourage what is regarded as favoured behaviour.

It appears that Matthew *inter alia* employs these beatitudes to reinforce the identity of his group. They define features of a faithful, favoured, blessed and honourable group (Carter, 2000a:130; Malina & Rohrbaugh, 2003:41). However, the honour comes from God and not from the usual social sources. By calling them the blessed ones[105], Matthew's Jesus separates his disciples from other groups, and Matthew presumably does the same with his community. Their commitment to Jesus must be strong enough to withstand persecution for his sake (Matt. 5:11–12)[106]. Though oppressed in the present, they will be rewarded in heaven (Matt. 5:12). In this way, the Beatitudes constitute and affirm the community's unique identity and practices.

The Beatitudes reveal numerical arrangements of sayings that are common in gnomonological literature. Green (2001:176ff) examined the relationship between the beatitudes and discovered a complex web of relationships between the individual beatitudes.[107] The first beatitude of the Sermon on the Mount (as

---

[105] He thus names his followers, which is a typical feature of identity formation as discussed before (cf. Carter, 2000a:9-11).

[106] The ostracism described here, was the usual fate of the poor in agrarian societies, but this would become the fate of all who join Jesus groups (Malina & Rohrbauch, 2003:41).

[107] The poor in spirit and the meek are variations on the theme of the '*anawim*'. Less directly, also those persecuted for righteousness form part of this group. The merciful converse with the poor in

in the Sermon on the Plain) heads the list and forms the basis. Those that follow are climactic developments to reach the ultimate climax in Matt. 5:12. In addition to this, the same phrase in 3b and 10b (ὅτι αὐτῶν ἐστιν ἡ βασιλεία τῶν οὐρανῶν) forms an *inclusio* around 5:4–9[108], emphasising the reference to δικαιοσύνη in Matt. 5:10.

The sequence of eight beatitudes is divided into two sections of four, each ending with δικαιοσύνη. Accordingly, the fourth and eighth beatitudes form a parallel construction. These two beatitudes are the longest in the series of eight in Matt. 5:3–10, indicating their relative importance[109]. The first group of beatitudes probably alludes to Isa. 61 where oppressive situations are described, but these will be reversed because the oppressed are honoured by God. The next four beatitudes describe human actions honoured by God as they express God's transforming reign until its completion (Carter, 2000a:131; Deines, 2004:138). After the set of eight descriptive beatitudes in which the audience is addressed indirectly (in the third person), the ninth beatitude follows as conclusion, addressing the recipients directly (in the second person). In this direct address, the audience is encouraged to persist in its loyalty to Jesus even when they are persecuted for his sake.

With these preliminary observations in mind, one can now consider the use of δικαιοσύνη as it occurs in two of the beatitudes.

4.5.2.1.1   Hunger and thirst for δικαιοσύνη (Matt. 5:6)

Matthew's Jesus speaks metaphorically of an intense longing for δικαιοσύνη in terms of hunger and thirst. This beatitude is the equivalent of Luk. 6:21a.

Matt. 5:6	Luk. 6:21a
μακάριοι οἱ πεινῶντες **καὶ διψῶντες τὴν δικαιοσύνην**, ὅτι αὐτοὶ χορτασθήσονται.	μακάριοι οἱ πεινῶντες νῦν, ὅτι χορτασθήσεσθε.

---

spirit and the peacemakers with the meek. The mourners humbling themselves before God express their humility in awareness of their sinfulness. The fasting conveys the negative aspect of the longing for God. The pure in heart forms the climax of the composition.

[108] Within the context of the Sermon on the Mount, Jesus is clearly portrayed as the King of this Kingdom.

[109] The relative importance of a statement is often emphasized by an increase in length (Thom, 2009:325).

| (Blessed are those who hunger and thirst for righteousness, for they will be filled). | (Blessed are those who hunger now, for you shall be satisfied.) |

Table 11: The parallel of the beatitude on hunger in Matt. 5:6 and Luk. 6:21a

From this comparison, it appears that Matthew redactionally added καὶ διψῶντες τὴν δικαιοσύνην (and thirst after righteousness) (Davis & Allison, 2004a:451) as is evident from the following considerations: The Greek grammar in this addition is somewhat awkward with the accusative after πεινῶντες καὶ διψῶντες and the lopsided correspondence of χορτασθήσονται with πεινῶντες and not διψῶντες. Furthermore, καὶ διψῶντες breaks the π-alliteration in the first four beatitudes: πτωχοί, πενθοῦντες, πραεῖς and πεινῶντες[110].

Two opposite interpretations of δικαιοσύνη can be considered. The first option would be to interpret it as God's eschatological gift of justice that would come during the eschatological era (Deines, 2004:148–154). Bratcher (1989:234) has suggested a corresponding paraphrase of the text: "... whose greatest desire is that God's purpose prevails". As the Beatitudes are intended to encourage the downtrodden, an eschatological interpretation would fit the context well (Hagner, 1992:112). Δικαιοσύνη could refer to God's exercise of justice, leading to the eschatological vindication of the poor, meek and persecuted disciples (Bultmann, 1951:273; Deines, 2004:154; Gundry, 1982:70). With such an interpretation, δικαιοσύνη would involve the realization of prophecies of the Hebrew Bible, such as those found in Isa. 61:2[111] and Ps. 37:11.[112] Furthermore, such an interpretation is closer to the corresponding beatitude in Luk. 6:21: "Blessed are you who hunger now, for you will be satisfied". Matthew would then have expanded the blessing to include δικαιοσύνη in the sense of eschatological justice. With the probable allusion to Isa. 61 in mind, δικαιοσύνη would refer to God's righteous punishment of a society that deprives the downtrodden of life and resources for living (Carter, 2000a:134). In a literal sense, the verb χορτασθήσονται (will be satisfied) in the motivating clause obviously fits this meaning of δικαιοσύνη better than the sense of ethical

---

[110] However, the break in the alliteration is not complete. In Matt. 5:6 there is a parallel alliteration of the π- and δ-sound: πεινῶντες καὶ διψῶντες τὴν δικαιοσύνην, resulting in π ... δ ... ψ ... δ (the ψ qualifies as a semi-alleteration of the π-sound). This phenomenon softens the harsh break in the π-alliteration.

[111] Isa. 61:2: '... to proclaim the year of the Lord's favour and the day of vengeance of our God'.

[112] Ps. 37:1: 'But the meek will inherit the land and enjoy great peace'.

δικαιοσύνη, though in Jewish literature the combination between 'hunger' and 'thirst' is quite often used in a metaphorical sense (cf. Ps. 42:2).

The opposite interpretation would be to interpret δικαιοσύνη here in an ethical sense as a virtue required from the disciples. In such a case, this beatitude refers to δικαιοσύνη as desire and aim to live in full accordance with the will of God (Davies & Allison, 2004a:452; Strecker, 1971:156; Spicq, 2012:332; Turner, 2008:151). This meaning relates to the Jewish sense of the word that implies the ideal conduct in adherence to God's ordinances (Przybylski, 1980:17–19)[113]. One cannot have this strong desire to live according God's will without, at the same time, strongly desiring to do what is right (Morris, 1992:99). Plummer (1982:65) has explained these metaphors strikingly:

> To believe oneself to be in possession of righteousness, like the Pharisee in the parable is fatal … One must feel the want of it, and have a passionate and persistent longing for it.

The use of the present participles πεινῶντες καὶ διψῶντες (hungering and thirsting) should be noted. It implies that δικαιοσύνη is something that should be desired continuously. "Righteousness should ever be sought, must always be a goal which lies ahead: it is never in the grasp" (Davies & Allison, 2004a:453). Such ethical conduct designates the highest form of true discipleship. This beatitude functions as an encouragement to the community to strive towards living according to the standards that Jesus has set. God's will should be done on earth as it is done in heaven (Matt. 6:10).

The second interpretation fits well with Matthew's nuance and broader context. Matthew frequently emphasises the correct lifestyle for the followers of Jesus in contrast to that of the scribes and the Pharisees. Stott (1978:10) has spoken of a "counter culture" of the followers of Jesus. Matthew criticizes hypocrites for boasting about their righteous accomplishments (cf. Matt. 6:1–2). His community should rather realize their lack of attaining the right behaviour before God, and then they will receive what they are longing for as a gift. "A humble person who acknowledges sin – not a smug one who congratulates himself on his goodness – receives God's endorsement" (Turner, 2008:152). The first three beatitudes would then express the need to admit one's spiritual

---

[113] In the Greco-Roman world, δικαιοσύνη refers to justice as a relational concept. It includes other virtues such as goodness, good fellowship, fair dealing and piety (Thom, 2009:324). This meaning also fits the context of this beatitude well.

poverty, to mourn over sin and oppression and to rest in God's care amidst oppression (Matt. 6:3−5). The fourth beatitude would fit this set by expressing the need to hunger for living according to God's will. One should furthermore ask why Matthew, in comparison to Luk. 6:21, has expanded the *Vorlage* to add the term δικαιοσύνη. It could be that Matthew thus made this beatitude part of the main argument in the Sermon on the Mount about the righteous living of the followers of Jesus. This confirms the argument that Matthew used δικαιοσύνη as a significant term.

The objection that such an ethical interpretation of δικαιοσύνη would contradict Matthew's teaching on salvation need not be compelling. Ethical conduct, living in keeping with the will of the Father, does not exclude grace (Morris, 1992:99). Matthew's argument is not that righteous behaviour earns salvation, but that it is the fruit of insight into God's ways[114] (Guelich, 1982:371; Luz, 1990:221). Righteousness does not create a relationship with Jesus, but is the result thereof. It is a given righteousness, not an achieved one. The blessed one does not achieve it, but hungers and thirsts for it. "They will be filled" surely means that God will fill them. The fact that humans cannot produce such righteousness demonstrates how rich this concept is. Humans cannot rely on their own power to achieve righteousness, but they can rely on God.

The Hebrew and Greco-Roman notions of righteousness should be considered the two extemes of a continuum of interpretations of δικαιοσύνη (Betz, 1995:130).[115] Righteousness is a social value that refers to commitments and relationships. Accordingly, God's and human righteousness are not independent of each other. God is righteous in that He acts faithful to his covenantal commitments to deliver his needy and oppressed people from an unjust society. For their part, his people are committed to act faithful to covenantal requirements (Guelich, 1982:372). With such a reading, the fourth beatitude provides a vision of a society where God's empire is already at work. This vision shapes a community who lives in this "now-and-not-yet"-state. They

---

[114] These attitudes are comparable with what Paul labels the 'fruit of the Spirit' (Gal. 5:22) but should be distinguished from the 'works of the law'. Stott (1978:31) has remarked: 'Just as the nine fold fruit of the Spirit which Paul lists is to ripen in every Christian character, so the eight beatitudes which Christ speaks describe his ideal for every citizen of God's Kingdom'. These attitudes, actions and thoughts are different from what the Greeks call 'virtues', being approximations towards the divine absolute..

[115] Betz (1995:130) has considered the Greco-Roman background of δικαιοσύνη and emphasizes the Jewish sense of the term.

expect God's final vindication, while living a righteous life under God's current transforming reign.

4.5.2.1.2 Persecuted for the sake of δικαιοσύνη (Matt. 5:10)

With the eighth beatitude Matthew's Jesus warns his disciples that their behaviour will be met with resistance:

μακάριοι οἱ δεδιωγμένοι **ἕνεκεν δικαιοσύνης**, ὅτι αὐτῶν ἐστιν ἡ βασιλεία τῶν οὐρανῶν (Blessed are those who are persecuted because of righteousness for theirs is the Kingdom of Heaven).

There is no counterpart to this beatitude in Luke.[116] With addition Matthew thus once again emphasises the important motif of δικαιοσύνη in his argument.

According to this beatitude, δικαιοσύνη is the cause of persecution (Davies & Allison, 2004a:459; Spicq, 2012:23). As argued in Chapter 2, Matthew's audience probably had some experience of persecution and would not be surprised at this beatitude. Matthew uses the verb persecute (διώκω) four times in this chapter (Matt. 5:10, 11, 12, 44) and twice elsewhere (Matt. 10:23; 23:34), each time referring to the persecution of Jesus' followers. In the New Testament as a whole, this verb is also mostly used for the infliction of suffering on people who believe and act in a manner that the establishment finds strange (Morris, 1992:101). The just way of living (Matt. 5:3−9) challenges the broader society, its power structures and its beneficiaries. Society certainly would strike back (Carter, 2000a:136). Matthew's Jesus speaks of those who are committed to conduct that is appropriate for people under the rule of God.[117] Δικαιοσύνη demonstrates this highest value of discipleship that marks the life of those who live under God's rule as King. Disciples respond to persecution not by giving up, nor by retaliation. Clearly there is no reason why δικαιοσύνη in this beatitude should not be understood in an ethical sense. While salvation is grace, a certain kind of conduct is expected from those who received God's gift. Based on their relationship with Jesus, they enact the righteousness of God's saving reign.

---

[116] Beare (1981:133) and Guelich (1982:93) have suggested that this evidences a redactional genesis.

[117] The rule of God most probably has some intertextuality with the most visible kingdom of its time, namely Rome's empire and its righteousness. Followers of Jesus recognize God's empire instead.

Just as the first four beatitudes form a set that is concluded with the first statement on δικαιοσύνη, the fifth to eighth beatitudes also form a set. The beatitudes in the second set all refer to right attitudes and good deeds, challenging the norms of an unjust society by showing mercy, being pure at heart and making peace (Matt. 5:7–9). This series is concluded with the second reference to δικαιοσύνη in the eighth beatitude.

Matt. 5:10 is very similar to a phrase found in 1 Pet. 3:14: ἀλλ' εἰ καὶ πάσχοιτε διὰ δικαιοσύνην, μακάριοι. τὸν δὲ φόβον αὐτῶν μὴ φοβηθῆτε μηδὲ ταραχθῆτε (but even if you should suffer for what is right, you are blessed). This is probably a reflection of the same logion contained in oral tradition (Hagner, 1992:114). In 1 Peter, an ethical context is supposed as a question is posed in the previous verse, καὶ τίς ὁ κακώσων ὑμᾶς ἐὰν τοῦ ἀγαθοῦ ζηλωταὶ γένησθε; (who is going to harm you if you are eager to do good?' (1 Pet. 3:13). This strengthens the possibility of an ethical use of the logion in Matt. 5:10. It seems that Matthew uses this beatitude to explain to his community why they suffer persecution. He probably intends to affirm that their beliefs and conduct are correct and to encourage them to remain loyal to Jesus.

This beatitude is immediately expanded in Matt. 5:11–12 where suffering ἕνεκεν ἐμοῦ (for my sake) is explained. Because of their commitment to Jesus, his disciples could expect persecution for their righteous behaviour. This commitment demands more than what was usually expected of people. Although Jewish teachers would expect students to suffer for God's sake, they would not have called students to suffer for their (the teachers') own sake (Keener, 2009:171).

The eighth beatitude therefore strongly reinforces commitment to Jesus as the central feature of the identity of followers of Jesus. Jesus is more than an ordinary Jewish teacher. His disciples should act on his behalf before oppressive powers. While this beatitude encourages the ostracized followers of Jesus, it is also invective to the opponents who fail to recognize and accept God's agents.

4.5.2.2 Δικαιοσύνη in the propositio to the Sermon on the Mount

The *propositio* to the Sermon of the Mount is given in Matt. 5:17–20. These verses state the theme of the Sermon in general. The *propositio* is concluded with the summary statement about the δικαιοσύνη of the disciples that should surpass that of the scribes and the Pharisees (Matt. 5:20). Such critique of opponents is typical of identity formation (Carter, 2000a:10). This verse also functions as immediate introduction to the antitheses in Matt. 5:21–48 with

Jesus' interpretations on what δικαιοσύνη means in practice (see Chapter 5). In such a case, Matt. 5:20 is paralleled by Matt. 6:1, which is also followed by a series of practical examples (on doing charity (Matt. 6:2−4), prayer (Matt. 6:5−15) and fasting (Matt. 6:16−18).

Matt. 5:20, ἐὰν μὴ περισσεύσῃ ὑμῶν ἡ **δικαιοσύνη** πλεῖον τῶν γραμματέων καὶ Φαρισαίων, οὐ μὴ εἰσέλθητε εἰς τὴν βασιλείαν τῶν οὐρανῶν (unless your righteousness surpasses that of the teachers of the Law and the Pharisees, you will certainly not enter the Kingdom of Heaven) functions like a hinge between the preceding statement on the continuing validity of the Law (Matt. 5:17−19) and the antitheses with their *halakhic* arguments that follow in the first part of the *probatio* (Matt. 5:21−47; Davies & Allison, 2004a:498). This statement does not have a parallel in Mark or Luke, which indicates the redactional interest of the author. The concluding words of Matt. 5:48[118], Ἔσεσθε οὖν ὑμεῖς τέλειοι ὡς ὁ Πατὴρ ὑμῶν ὁ οὐράνιος τέλειός ἐστιν. (be perfect, therefore, as your heavenly Father is perfect) appears to be a restatement of the message in Matt. 5:20. Matt. 5:48 forms the culmination to the argument started in Matt. 5:20. Being "righteous" is paralleled with "being perfect". By greater δικαιοσύνη, Matthew points towards perfection.

Δικαιοσύνη and perfection are described in the six *halakhic* examples of this exceeding righteousness in Matt. 5:21−47, between the introductory and concluding statements. The argument on the validity of the Law emphasises conduct that corresponds to God's will, while the antithetical examples are "instructions about the practice of eschatological righteousness" (Barth, 1963:139). This δικαιοσύνη refers to the life of justice that God's empire requires (Carter, 2000a:143; Deines, 2008:81; Spicq, 2012:332). Each of the antitheses is obviously intended to illustrate what exceeding righteousness means in practice. Within a polemical context, the antitheses offer exemplary illustrations of the requirements of true righteousness according to the model of God's own perfection. The introductory statement in Matt. 5:20 creates an expectation that the following series of sayings would provide an explanation and exegetical guide to what such righteousness implies. This righteousness refers to the practical side of one's religion. All six antitheses appear to deal with examples of conflict and broken relationships and instructions on how such relationships should be restored (Betz, 1995:201−205; Thom, 2009:328).

---

[118] The Lukan parallel reads: Γίνεσθε οἰκτίρμονες, καθὼς ὁ Πατὴρ ὑμῶν οἰκτίρμων ἐστίν. (Be merciful, just as your Father is merciful) (Luk. 6:36). While in Matthew "beig perfect" parallels being "righteous", being merciful fits into the redactional interest of Luke (cf. Viljoen, 2003: 199-209).

There can be very little doubt that δικαιοσύνη in Matt. 5:20 refers to ethical conduct, and for the following reasons. Matthew's Jesus uses δικαιοσύνη in a polemical context because the righteousness that Jesus required far transcends what the scribes and Pharisees considered as righteous. This distinction of righteousness is qualitative and not quantitative. In the Sermon on the Mount, true δικαιοσύνη is contrasted with the elaborate but superficial type of righteousness of the Matthean scribes and Pharisees, which is criticized in Matt. 6:1. Betz (1995:193) has suggested that this criticism includes hypocrisy (Matt. 6:1−18) as the attitude of mere formal compliance with the written Law, as well as the interpretation of the Law through the lenses of tradition (Matt. 5:20−48). According to Matthew, discipleship draws a distinction between true righteousness and merely strict legal correctness, for Christology is the foundation of ethics (Turner, 2008:164). Stott (1978:75) has remarked on Matthew's argument by saying: "Pharisees were content with an external and formal obedience, a rigid conformity to the letter of the Law; Jesus teaches us that God's demands are far more radical than this". By referring to these words of Jesus, it seems that the author of the Gospel wants to make the identity of his community distinct with a strong dichotomy by comparing their righteousness with that of the scribes and the Pharisees in the narrative world, but probably also in the world of his community. He shapes the identity and lifestyle of his community within a dominant culture that does not share their convictions, or criticizes them for that.

Matthew assures his addressees that righteousness is the outcome of living according to the meaning and intention of the Law, as interpreted in the Sermon on the Mount. He advocates a righteousness that is based on his group's values, which surpass those of their opponents (Matt. 5:20). The similarity with the hortatory epilogue of the *halakhic* letter from Qumran (4 QMMATT.) is striking.[119] In a form of antithetical debate, the Qumran apologist assures his community that walking according to the interpretation presented in his legal antitheses will be reckoned as righteousness (Foster, 2004:83). In Matthew, the disciples are instructed to observe everything Jesus has commanded them.

---

[119] 4QMMT (*Miqsat Ma'ase ha-Torah* or *'Some Precepts of the Law'*) was discovered at Qumran. Qimron & Strugnell (1994:25) dated this *halakhic* letter between the early 1st century BCE and the early 1st century CE. 4QMMT directly and indirectly makes use of the antithetical form of contrasting two opposing viewpoints in its *halakhot* to promote the viewpoint of the Qumran community.

4.5.2.3 Righteousness and piety in the probatio of the Sermon on the Mount

5.2.3.1 Acts of δικαιοσύνη not with the intention to be seen by people (Matt. 6:1)

In Matt. 5:17–48, Matthew makes it very clear that Jesus is committed to and expects the keeping of the true intention of the Law. Δικαιοσύνη in God's kingdom (Matt. 5:20) requires more than the formal obedience to the letter of the Law. Matthew's Jesus in Matt. 6:1 continues to describe another aspect by warning against hypocritical δικαιοσύνη in Matt. 6:1–18.

Δικαιοσύνη is once again used in a polemical context, προσέχετε [δὲ] τὴν δικαιοσύνην ὑμῶν μὴ ποιεῖν ἔμπροσθεν τῶν ἀνθρώπων πρὸς τὸ θεαθῆναι αὐτοῖς (be careful not to practice your righteousness in front of others to be seen by them)[120]. The expression τὴν δικαιοσύνην ὑμῶν in Matt. 6:1 is very similar to ὑμῶν ἡ δικαιοσύνη in Matt. 5:20. The δικαιοσύνη of Matt. 6:1 evidently refers back to the δικαιοσύνη of Matt. 5:20 (Deines, 2004:437). While Matt. 5:20 deals with the nature of true δικαιοσύνη in general, Matt. 6:1 warns against the pitfalls of practising insincere δικαιοσύνη (Strack & Billerbeck, 1965:386). Jesus contrasts the outward religious performances of the hypocrites to impress people with that of the disciples who aim to please their Father in heaven. Members of the Matthean community are encouraged to perform their acts of piety without pretence and in private where only God can see, not like the hypocrites who parade their pious acts in public to gain praise (Betz, 1995:351; Davies & Allison, 2004a:579; Sim, 1999:122). In an honour and shame society, one's good reputation is sustained by the esteem of others who benefit from one's public actions (Carter, 2000a:158; Malina & Rohrbauch, 2003:370; Witherington, 2013:49). Jesus therefore opposes a fundamental societal pattern.

There is very little reason to doubt that the ethical conduct of the disciples is pertinent in this verse (*contra* Deines, 2004:421).

Three specific activities follow to describe such δικαιοσύνη (cf. Weren, 1994:73):

- doing charity (ὅταν οὖν ποιῇς ἐλεημοσύνην, Matt. 6:2–4);
- praying (καὶ ὅταν προσεύχησθε, Matt. 6:5–15); and

---

[120] Matt. 6:1 has no parallel in Mark or Luke.

- fasting (ὅταν δὲ νηστεύητε, Matt. 6:16-18).

These three examples were central to Jewish piety during the Second Temple period[121] (Betz, 1995:338; Morris, 1992:135). Tobit[122] 12:8-9 links these three deeds and prioritizes giving alms.[123] The problem with the hypocrites in Matthew was not that they did not perform these acts, but that they performed them insincerely. The hypocrites (ὑποκριταὶ) made people into spectators by impressing them to sustain their own status.

The first example of true or false δικαιοσύνη refers to offerings of mercy (Matt. 6:2-4). Giving to the needy was a crucial duty for pious Jews (cf. Deut. 15:7-11)[124]. The mercy of God requires that people would show mercy to each other, as is stated in the fifth beatitude (Matt. 5:7). In Matthew, Jesus interprets the holiness code in terms of the mercy code (Snodgrass, 1996:111). Everybody would have accepted that it was a religious duty to help the poor, but Jesus points out that it can be done in an objectionable manner. When almsgiving is no longer what it purports to be, in other words service to God, it can no longer be regarded as an act of mercy (Morris, 1992:136). To be regarded as a righteous deed, such offering must be done for the benefit of the needy and not to seek public recognition or honour for it. Hands (1968:26) points out that when the wealthy helped the poor in an honour and shame culture, it was often self-regarding in that the giver anticipated more honour for himself. Almsgiving was an important means in patron-client relationships to maintain social stratification. The wealthy would look down on the poor with ridicule.[125] A striking example of this is Seneca's wise man who would provide relief, but not for pity or sorrow (Clem. 2.6.6). In such a case, almsgiving is misused for the sake of self-esteem. Jesus teaches that it is important to give without being

---

[121] The Second Temple period in Jewish history is the period between 530 BCE and 70 CE.

[122] It is generally believed that the book was written in the second century BCE on the basis of the scrupulous attention to ritual details and the stress laid upon giving alms.

[123] Tobit 12:8: Prayer is good with fasting and alms and righteousness. A little with righteousness is better than much with unrighteousness. It is better to give alms than to lay up gold: For alms doth deliver from death, and shall purge away all sin. Those that exercise alms and righteousness shall be filled with life.

[124] Poverty was very common in those days and the lot of the poor very hard.

[125] 'Poverty ... makes people the target of ridicule, not of assistance' (Juvenal, Sat 3.147-154).

known to give. Unrighteous acts of almsgiving are performed by hypocrites. The word ὑποκριτής (hypocrite) was mostly used for actors who consciously performed in a play. Batey (1971:563) indicates that Matthew consciously alludes to a ὑποκριτής as an actor and speculates whether Jesus' use of the term comes from his contact with the theatre in Sepphoris. Performing acts of righteousness in a hypocritical manner implies that worship is turned into a spectacle. Hypocrites act with ethical pretence. The identity of the disciples does not lie in seeking public admiration but in enacting God's saving mercy. It is assumed that disciples would share resources with the needy. Such acts would denote the presence of God's empire.

The second example of true or false δικαιοσύνη refers to praying (Matt. 6:5-15). It seems that, as with almsgiving, there was a tendency amongst those who prayed to use their prayers as a means of impressing others with their piety. Jesus' teaching on praying in a righteous manner consists of two warnings on how not to pray (Matt. 6:5 and 7), each balanced by positive teaching (Matt. 6:6 and 5:8) followed by the model prayer (Matt. 6:9-15). The first warning contrasts the disciples' lifestyle with the piety of the Jews in the synagogue (Carter, 2000a:161). Matthew's Jesus warns against the public pretence of hypocrites when praying. Righteous praying should be done in private and not for show.[126] Seeking public approval for praying implies that prayer ceases to express love for God but serves the one praying. Instead, prayer is intended as communication with God and not as means to build one's reputation in front of people (Morris, 1992:139).The second warning is against verbosity when praying. This warning defines the disciples' prayer probably over against that of the Gentiles. Jesus compares such praying with the long-winded babbling[127] of the pagans to get the attention of the gods or even the repetition of magical formulas (Betz, 1995:365). The Greek Magical Papyri evidence the use of meaningless sounds believed to be the language of gods (Betz, 1992:161-162). Righteous praying is done in simplicity. The model prayer then provides a positive illustration in contrast to the hypocritical performance of the Jews in the synagogue and the babbling of the heathen prayers. This prayer expresses a worldview and shapes the community that prays it (Carter, 2000a:169). It depicts the heaven, the place where God's will is done, and the earth, the location of the prayers and the place of disobedience. Evil confronts God's

---

[126] Jesus forbids hypocritical prayers in public, not sincere prayer in public.

[127] The word used of babbling (βατταλογέω) describes an intentionally repetitive speech pattern similar to the involuntary repetitions of a person who stutters (Turner, 2008:185).

order on earth while the prayer seeks the manifestation of God's kingdom on earth. Those who pray form a community of children on earth. They know God as their Father and yearn to do his will on earth amidst evil and temptation. They depend on God's grace to sustain their existence. They pray for a transformation of life to be in accordance with God's will.

The third religious activity related to δικαιοσύνη refers to fasting (Matt. 6:16–18).[128] The same pattern is found as in the previous teaching on giving and praying. The warning once again is against hypocrisy. Turner (2008:191) has aptly remarked:

> Jesus was not impressed ... with a theatrically altered appearance. Such behaviour may have been the norm for actors who sought the crowd's applause, but it is singularly inappropriate for disciples who seek the Father's approval.

Fasting is supposed to express the opposite to greed, injustice and the unequal accumulation of means. This deprivation is intended to humble the one who fasts. This is what is expected of disciples of Jesus. However, done in a hypocritical manner as the Pharisees and the teachers of the Law are accused of doing, it is misused for personal gain and reputation, instead of as an act of humbling oneself.

One can therefore conclude that the δικαιοσύνη of the deeds in Matt. 6:1 does not lie in what is done, but in how it is done. The opponents also gave alms, prayed and fasted, but they did it hypocritically to gain personal reputation. These deeds are only regarded as righteous if they are done with sincerity, to honour God and to establish his reign in an evil and unequal society.

The two sections, namely Matt. 5:20–48 and 6:1–18, show similarities. Both begin with a general statement about true righteousness (Matt. 5:20 and 6:1). Both of these statements are followed by a number of practical examples that exhibit repetition, symmetry and contrast amongst them. Higher righteousness is described as honest internal intentions that lead to external actions. Δικαιοσύνη encompasses both the theoretical and practical aspects of religious conduct that is acceptable to God.

---

[128] This link between fasting and righteousness probably echoes the warning of Isa. 58:3ff: 'Yet on the day of fasting, you do as you please and exploit your workers ...'.

4.5.2.3.2 The disciples should seek the Kingdom of Heaven and its δικαιοσύνη (Matt. 6:33)

The fifth and last occurrence of righteousness in the Sermon on the Mount is found in Matthew 6:33[129]:

ζητεῖτε δὲ πρῶτον τὴν βασιλείαν [τοῦ θεοῦ] καὶ τὴν δικαιοσύνην αὐτοῦ (but seek first his kingdom [of God] and his righteousness).

From Matt. 5:21 onwards, Jesus explains the δικαιοσύνη of his disciples that should surpass that of the Pharisees and teachers of the Law. He describes the distinct lifestyle of the community of disciples. Along with the Beatitudes (Matt. 5:3−12) and the encouragement to be the light of the world and the salt for the earth (Matt. 5:13−16), God's rule shapes this way of life. The examples continue in Matt. 6:19−34, with a focus on materialism and daily necessities. Jesus recognizes the necessity of material provision but warns against not trusting God for his provision and a desire for material goods while depriving others of their means. In the Greco-Roman world, one's wealth or lack of it reflected one's social status (Carter, 2000a:172). In Matt. 6:33, the disciples are exhorted to seek God's kingdom and his δικαιοσύνη as their first priority. The use of the present imperative, ζητεῖτε, is significant (Thom, 2009:335). Δικαιοσύνη should be sought continuously. This would be regarded as the highest value of discipleship. This positive command balances the prohibition of anxiety in Matt. 6:31, μὴ οὖν μεριμνήσητε λέγοντες· Τί φάγωμεν; ἤ· Τί πίωμεν; ἤ· Τί περιβαλώμεθα; (so do not worry, saying, 'What shall we eat?' or 'What shall we drink?' or 'What shall we wear?'). A selfish quest for material goods defines the identity and goals of people who seek personal benefit. The community of disciples is defined by a different goal. They want God's kingdom to be established.[130] Betz (1995:481) has fittingly regarded this sentence as the *telos* formula and culmination of the argument on δικαιοσύνη. Similarly, Deines (2004:441) has viewed this sentence as the summary of the message of the Sermon on the Mount.

---

[129] This statement in Matt. 6:33 also has not parallel in Mark or Luke, demonstrating redactional interest of Matthew.

[130] This implicitly might have been intended as contrast to the Roman empire of that time.

Matthew is a prolific user of the word Kingdom.[131] The kingdom has both present and future significance (Morris, 1992:161). It indicates God's rule, now and in the eschatological age. Kingdom should be understood as rule rather than a realm (Marcus, 1988:663-675; Van der Walt, 2006:39). It refers to the fact that God is ruling rather than to an area over which He is sovereign. God's reign has already been established amongst disciples through the ministry of Jesus (Matt. 4:17; 12:28). However, the final goal has not yet been reached. The disciples should strive for the completion of God's purposes by praying for it (Matt. 6:10), living the distinctive lifestyle as required by God's rule and anticipating the completion of God's purposes.

The δικαιοσύνη in Matt. 6:33 occurs in the same context as the statements about δικαιοσύνη in Matt. 5:20 and 6:1, which refers to the practice of δικαιοσύνη. The command in Matt. 6:33 is therefore that people under God's rule should constantly be seeking to do his will. In line with such an interpretation, Lloyd-Jones (1976:143) has remarked: "[*Jesus*] is not telling his hearers how to make themselves Christian; but He is telling them how to behave because they are Christian". Seeking δικαιοσύνη implies "thoroughgoing and determined obedience to the deepest intent of the Law" (Mohrlang, 1984:113). These actions seek to establish a society where justice is served and God's rule is manifested. One could interpret the καὶ between kingdom and righteousness epexegetically (Hagner, 1992:114). This would exemplify the lifestyle of disciples in anticipation of God's final rule and eschatological delivery.

It therefore seems that the meaning of δικαιοσύνη in Matt. 6:33 corresponds with those in Matt. 5:20 and 6:1. Matt. 6:33 makes the implication of δικαιοσύνη more explicit by linking it to a warning against greed and anxiety for material needs. The norm for the disciples' conduct is based on a specific interpretation of the *Torah*. By following Jesus and his interpretation of the *Torah*, people find their identity as citizens of the kingdom of God. They should exercise their identity as citizens of this kingdom by acting righteously according to the precepts given by Jesus. Δικαιοσύνη implies observing all that Jesus commanded (Matt. 28:20).

---

[131] βασιλεία occurs 55 times in Matthew, 20 times in Mark and 46 times in Luke.

4.5.3 John has come in the way of δικαιοσύνη (Matt. 21:32)

Later in his text Matthew again writes about the δικαιοσύνη of John, a reference that is unique to the first Gospel. It once again appears that Matthew regards δικαιοσύνη as an important attribute for people loyal to Jesus.

Matthew writes that the chief priests and elders, motivated by animosity and a desire to trap Jesus, questioned the source of Jesus' authority (Matt. 21:23). Jesus returns the question by asking them about the source of John's authority (Matt. 21:25). Jesus then tells the story of the two sons to clarify the priests' and elders' failure to obey God and to warn his disciples not to repeat those same mistakes. The elite's non-responsiveness is further emphasised by Jesus' reference to John the Baptist. Jesus affirms John's authority by stating that John has come in the way of righteousness: 'ἦλθεν γὰρ Ἰωάννης πρὸς ὑμᾶς ἐν ὁδῷ δικαιοσύνης' (Matt. 21:32). The metaphor "way of righteousness" comes from the Hebrew Bible and refers to living according to God's just will, for example Prov. 2:20,[132] 21:16[133] and 21:21[134] (Hagner, 1995:614; Przybylski, 1980:94–96; Strecker, 1971:187; Turner, 2008:509). It includes the full spectrum of proper response to God, including repentance and good deeds (Senior, 1998:238). The same phrase is also found in 2 Pet. 2:21,[135] where it clearly refers to righteous conduct. John both preached and exemplified righteousness (France, 2008:310). As in Matt. 3:15, δικαιοσύνη is again used in relation to the coming and performance of John the Baptist. Jesus recalls John's role in proclaiming the "way of the Lord" (τὴν ὁδὸν κυρίου) (Matt. 3:3). Δικαιοσύνη indicates that John acted faithfully in accordance with God's previously declared purposes (Carter, 2000a:426; Spicq, 2012:32). Betz (1995:131) has fittingly remarked that "the way of righteousness" in Matt. 21:32 "could just as well describe the teaching of the Sermon on the Mount as a whole".

Matthew once again portrays John the Baptist as righteous. It is noteworthy that, besides the righteousness of Jesus in Matt. 3:15, only John's actions are regarded as righteous. He is portrayed as the prototype of a follower of Jesus

---

[132] Prov. 2:20: 'Thus you will walk in the ways of good men and keep to the paths of the righteous'.

[133] Prov. 21:16: 'A man who strays from the path of righeousness comes to rest in the company of the dead'.

[134] Prov. 21:21: 'He who pursues righteousness and love finds life, prosperity and honor'.

[135] 2 Pet. 2:21: 'It would have been better for them not to have known the way of righteousness'.

who is fully committed to acting righteous. In the Sermon on the Mount, the disciples are exhorted to similar acts of righteousness.

4.6 CONCLUSION

The author uses δικαιοσύνη as a key element to describe the proper behavioural norms for his community. Matthew portrays Jesus and John the Baptist as prototypes of those who perfectly fulfilled all δικαιοσύνη in their ministry (Matt. 3:15; 21:31). Those who obey their calls to discipleship must strive towards such δικαιοσύνη. An individual who wants to be part of the Matthean community should be loyal to Jesus. True discipleship is demonstrated by doing the will of God as enacted by Jesus and taught and practiced by his loyal follower, John. They were able to recognise the will of God in specific circumstances.

References to the δικαιοσύνη of Jesus and John in Matt. 3:15 and of John in Matt. 21:31 form an *inclusio* around the discussion of δικαιοσύνη in the Sermon on the Mount. Δικαιοσύνη is the goal that Jesus' disciples should pursue as demonstrated by Jesus and John.

Δικαιοσύνη forms an important theme in the Sermon on the Mount. It starts off in the beatitudes on those who hunger and thirst for δικαιοσύνη (Matt. 5:6) and are persecuted for the sake of δικαιοσύνη (Matt. 5:10). The theme continues with the call for greater δικαιοσύνη (Matt. 5:20), which confirms the fundamental statement on the continuing validity of the Law (Matt. 5:17–19) and is illustrated by six antithetical examples (Matt. 5:21–47). This δικαιοσύνη is described in terms of being perfect (Matt. 5:48). The disciples are called to aim for better δικαιοσύνη in their attitudes and actions than that of the scribes and the Pharisees. The theme is continued with a general statement about δικαιοσύνη in Matt. 6:1 to introduce warnings and teachings on religious practices that cannot be regarded as righteous because they are done in a theatrical manner. The pretentious "piety" of the hypocrites as described in Matt. 6:2–18 is unacceptable for Jesus' disciples, and per implication also within Matthew's community. This theme is concluded with the disciples being called first to seek God's kingdom and his δικαιοσύνη (Matt. 6:33), thus making explicit the meaning of δικαιοσύνη as doing the will of God.

Δικαιοσύνη is a goal for Jesus' disciples to pursue. In the Sermon on the Mount, δικαιοσύνη is related to Matthew's emphasis on "doing the will of God" (cf. Matt. 7:21; 12:46–50). Δικαιοσύνη gives expression to Matthew's understanding of the practice of true discipleship.

The identity of disciples is thus defined by their distinctive δικαιοσύνη. As a distinctive group, they act distinctively. Separated from those who oppress and persecute them, they are the blessed ones. They should continuously strive towards δικαιοσύνη. Their δικαιοσύνη should outweigh that of the Pharisees and teachers of the Law as they should reveal the true intention of God's will. This δικαιοσύνη is not captured in legal principles but must exceed what is commonly expected. Their acts of piety should not be pretentious like those of the outsiders and should not be intended to enhance their social status. Disciples should share their means of living and trust God to provide in their needs. In anticipation of God's final rule, they should strive towards establishing God's rule in their society.

An individual who wants to be part of the Matthean community should be loyal to the teaching of Jesus about the *Torah* and earnestly and continuously yearn for what is regarded as true δικαιοσύνη (Matt. 5:6). Matthew explains in terms of the δικαιοσύνη of his community why they suffer rejection by those who do not follow Jesus' teaching (Matt. 5:10). He distinguishes the identity of his community by comparing their δικαιοσύνη with that of the scribes and Pharisees (Matt. 5:20). He regards the outsider groups' δικαιοσύνη as superficial and labels it as hypocritical (Matt. 6:1). Followers of Jesus are regarded as citizens of the kingdom of God. Matthew encourages his recipients to act as citizens of the kingdom of God by exercising δικαιοσύνη, as defined by Jesus (Matt. 6:33). With the coming of the kingdom, its citizens are called to a new standard of δικαιοσύνη. For Matthew, δικαιοσύνη is a matter of inward motivation and of outward performance directly related to the following of Jesus.

The call to δικαιοσύνη is based on the existing relationship between Jesus and his disciples. Righteousness is required as part of this relationship, but it does not help to create it. True discipleship is demonstrated by doing the will of God as defined and interpreted by Jesus. Doing the will of God is what Matthew regards as the distinguishing mark of the disciple community. In this way they would surpass the δικαιοσύνη of the scribes and Pharisees.

CHAPTER 5

JESUS' *HALAKHIC* ARGUMENTATION ON THE TRUE INTENTION OF THE LAW IN MATTHEW 5:21-48

5.1 INTRODUCTION

As argued in Chapter 3, the central claim in the Sermon on the Mount is that Jesus did not come to abolish the Law and the Prophets, but to reveal their true intension and meaning in contrast with the interpretations of the Matthean scribes and Pharisees. Matthew's Jesus makes a fundamental statement about the continuing validity and fulfilment of the Law in Matt. 5:17-19, followed by his demand for "better righteousness" in Matt. 5:20. Matthew's Jesus then continues with six "antitheses" in Matt. 5:21-48. My argument in this chapter is that Matthew's Jesus uses these "antitheses" to explain how He came to fulfil the Law (as claimed in Matt. 5:17-19) and exemplifies the "better righteousness" He refers to in Matt. 5:20.

Matt. 5:21-48 represents a *halakhic*[136] form of debate to urge norms of conduct with a series of six theses each introduced by variant forms of ἠκούσατε ὅτι ἐρρέθη τοῖς ἀρχαίοις (you have heard that it was said to/by the people long ago) (Matt. 5:21, 27, 31, 33, 38, 43), followed by variant forms of ἐγὼ δὲ λέγω ὑμῖν (but I say to you)-statements by Matthew's Jesus (Matt. 5:22, 28, 32, 34, 39, 44) (Weren, 1994:70). Though it is quite common to label the ἐγὼ δὲ λέγω ὑμῖν-statements as "antitheses", this term in itself already represents an assumption (Moo, 1992:455) and I therefore refer to the six "antitheses" within quotation marks in this chapter. The grammar allows for more nuances in translation: "you have heard, but I (in contrast to that / in addition to that / in agreement

---

[136] *Halakha* guides aspects of day-to-day life. A literal translation yields "the way to go". *Halakha* constitutes the practical application of the 613 *mitzvot* ("commandments") in the Torah as developed through discussion and debate. *Halakha* has been developed since before 500 BCE. It forms a body of intricate judicial opinions, legislation, customs, and recommendations, many of them passed down over the centuries, and an assortment of ingrained behaviors. It became the subject of intense study and debate (Sigal, 2007:3-60) (cf. the clarification of this and other concepts in Chapter 1).

132

with that) say to you" over and against the usual interpretation of the Law in the narrative world of the Matthean text (Davies & Allison, 2004a:504). The nature of the contrast between the theses and the "antitheses" can therefore be interpreted in more than one way. In a mild sense it could mean that Jesus sharpened and internalized the *Torah*. He would go beyond the literal interpretation of the *Torah* and thus break with the casuistry of the Matthean scribes and the Pharisees, but not revoke the stipulations of the *Torah* itself. Understanding the contrasts as such quite easily fits the first (Matt. 5:21-26), second (Matt. 5:27-30) and sixth (Matt. 5:43-47) "antitheses". Yet the other way of understanding the nature of the contrasts is to assume that the "antitheses" indeed involve the abrogation of the *Torah* itself. This kind of contrast apparently more easily fits the third (Matt. 5:31-32), fourth (Matt. 5:33-37) and fifth (Matt. 5:38-42) "antitheses".

In an attempt to explain these contrasts, Pryzybylski (1980:81) has suggested that the new interpretation of the Law should be understood in the sense that Matthew's Jesus is applying the Rabbinic principle of making a fence around the *Torah*. The third Talmudic claim is that the oral law forms a fence around the written *Torah*: "Moses received the *Torah* at Sinai and transmitted it to Joshua, Joshua to the elders, and the elders to the prophets, and the prophets to the men of the Great Synagogue. The latter used to say ... make a fence round the *Torah*" (Aboth 1.1). This Jewish hermeneutical principle was used to protect the Law "by surrounding it with cautionary rules to halt a man like a danger signal before he gets within breaking distance of the divine statute itself" (Moore, 1970:259). Accordingly, Jesus would have applied this rabbinic hermeneutical principle in the Sermon on the Mount to state his argument of upholding the *Torah* up to its finest details. This brings Pryzybylski to the conclusion that "the logical antidote to the practice of the relaxing of the commandments would be to make a fence around the *Torah*" (Pryzybylski, 1980:82). This suggestion sounds convincing when applied to some of the "antitheses" (the first, second and sixth), but does not adequately answer all the issues.

Other scholars explain the apparent contradiction between Jesus' claim that He did not come to abolish the *Torah* in Matt. 5:17-19 and the six "antitheses" in Matt. 5:21-47 by arguing that Jesus in the "antitheses" does not refer to the written Mosaic Law as such, but merely to the oral traditions of the scribes and Pharisees (cf. Weren, 1979:70). Barth (1963:93) has remarked: "It is plain that the antitheses are not directed primarily against the Old Testament itself, but against the interpretation of it in the Rabbinate". Patte (1987:78) has regarded the difference as an antithesis between a literal, narrow interpretation of the

Law as done by the rabbinate and a broad interpretation as done by Matthew's Jesus. However, when applied to each "antithesis" respectively, the issue still remains quite complicated.

Another scholarly argument is that the "antitheses" intensify the demands by calling for a higher standard of righteousness (δικαιοσύνη) based on Jesus' statement in Matt. 5:20. Davies (1966:102) has argued that "we cannot speak of the Law being annulled in the antitheses, but only of its being intensified in its demand, or reinterpreted in a higher key". Allison (1993:184) has argued that Jesus transcends the traditional commandments by replacing some and making additional commands:

> Jesus uses the Scriptures as a point of departure to demand more from his disciples. In most cases he extends the Scripture by interpreting its ethical and societal implications for human living ... but in the fourth (vv. 33-37) and fifth (vv. 38-42) examples he allows part of the Scripture to pass away (vv. 18-19).

Scholars such as Overman (1996:82) and Ridderbos (1987:299) have argued that the "antitheses" do not revoke the *Torah*. They have regarded the "antitheses" merely as more detailed expositions of the Law. Such an argument fits the "antitheses" on murder (Matt. 5:21-26), adultery (Matt. 5:27-30) and love of enemies (Matt. 5:43-47) fairly well. However, the "antitheses" dealing with divorce (Matt. 5:31-32) and the *lex talionis* (Matt. 5:38-42) do not fit this assumption that easily. In more than one case Jesus' interpretation in the "antitheses" points to a more demanding challenge than the mere literal application of the Law. The principle of love for the neighbour in the Hebrew Bible is extended to include enemies (Matt. 5:43-47). The apparent permission for divorce in Deut. 24:1-4 is withdrawn (Matt. 5:31-32). The elaborate system of oaths and vows is simplified by the principle μὴ ὀμόσαι ὅλως (do not swear at all) with the implication that this system comes from the evil one (Matt. 5:33-37)! The *lex talionis*, ὀφθαλμὸν ἀντὶ ὀφθαλμοῦ καὶ ὀδόντα ἀντὶ ὀδόντος (an eye for an eye and a tooth for a tooth), is replaced by a radical principle, μὴ ἀντιστῆναι τῷ πονηρῷ (do not resist one that is evil) (Matt. 5:38-42). On the surface it is clear that in Matthew's narrative world Jesus is opposed to the literal interpretation of the Laws by the scribes and Pharisees.

Therefore, other scholars hold that Jesus clearly abrogated the commandments of the Hebrew Bible in some instances. Carter (2000a:144) has made a remark regarding the fifth and sixth "antitheses", stating: "oaths and revenge are not part of the life in God's kingdom". Meier (1976:157) has claimed that Jesus' teaching with regard to the *lex talionis* in Matt. 5:38-42) is

> ... perhaps the clearest and least disputable case of annulment in the antitheses. Probably one cannot even speak of a *permission* being annulled. Such introductory phrases as Deut. 19:21a ("and your eye shall show no pity") indicate an obligatory command rather than a permission.

Bornkamm has argued that the third (Matt. 5:31-32), fifth (Matt. 5:38-42) and sixth (Matt. 5:43-47) "antitheses" not only show a sharpening of the Law as is the case in the first (Matt. 5:21-26), second (Matt. 5:27-30) and fourth (Matt. 5:33-37), but the abolition of the Law. Consequently, according to Bornkamm (2009:16), the "better righteousness" of Matt. 5:20 is at least partly concerned with a new Law. Strecker (1971:146) has supported the view that the "antitheses" largely replace the demands of the Hebrew Bible by way of new regulations.

If this is the case Matthew's treatment of the *Torah* seems to be inconsistent. In Matt. 5:17-19 he portrays Jesus as being adherent to the Law, but then, under the pretence of being true to the traditions, he actually initiates a new Law!

In this chapter I argue that the author of the first Gospel presents Jesus' antithetical arguments about the meaning of the *Torah* (Matt. 5:21-48) to demonstrate how Jesus revealed its true intention. Thus Matthew's Jesus did not abolish the Law and the Prophets, but fulfilled them (Matt. 5:17-20). He exemplifies "better righteousness" (Matt. 5:20). In doing this, I will attend to the literary context of the antithetical arguments, the form of Jesus' debate, and then follow with interpretation of the respective "antitheses". Conclusions about Matthew's teaching of the Law follow from this investigation.

5.2 LITERARY CONTEXT OF THE *HALAKHIC* ARGUMENTS

As will be discussed in more detail in Chapter 5, the *halakhic* argument in Matt. 5:21-47 (in terms of classical rhetorical speech) forms part of the *probatio* of the Sermon of the Mount. Matthew presents the Sermon on the Mount as a literary unit to form a logical argument about the meaning and practice of the *Torah*. When investigating the *halakhic* argument in Matt. 5:21-47, it is therefore necessary to consider its literary context.

Matthew frequently presents Jesus as being in debate with the Pharisees and scribes on their interpretation of the *Torah* (e.g. Matt. 9:10-12; 12:1-13; 22:34-

40). The interpretation of several stipulations of the Law became flash points and make-or-break issues on which differences and divisions in Judaism developed (Dunn, 2003:292). Within this environment Jesus' views and practice are presented as part of the legal debate and even as contrast to the legal norms of the day as described in the Gospel (Moo, 1984:15). Matthew tells that this resulted in an increasing rejection of Jesus by the Jewish religious leaders and people. It seems that the Matthean community in later years could identify with the rejection Jesus and the disciples experienced (cf. Chapter 2). The community regarded Jesus as their authoritative leader and interpreter of the *Torah* (Weren, 1979:73).

The Sermon on the Mount forms a significant component of Matthew's argument about the true intention of the *Torah* in contrast to the teachings and praxis in the narrative world of the Gospel. Matthew presents Jesus as a new Moses (Allison, 1993:137-270; Floor, 1969:34). At the beginning of the Sermon on the Mount (Matt. 5:1-2) the Sinai typology is significant (Davies & Allsion, 2004a:423; Loader, 1997:165). As Moses went up the mountain to receive the Law, Jesus goes up the mountainside and sits down to teach the Law. Anticipation is created of a new revelation to be delivered by a Moses-like figure. In the Sermon Jesus elaborates on certain stipulations of the Law as such. This correlates with the well-known concept in Judaism that the Mosaic character could transmigrate to later legislators and teachers (e.g. Ezekiel, cf. Ezek. 8:1). According to 4 Ezra the scribe receives the old revelation of Sinai plus an additional, new revelation (Allison, 1993:185). Matthew's Jesus describes the nature of the Kingdom of Heaven. He elaborates on how a citizen of that Kingdom is supposed to act in the present (Lioy, 2004:117; Van der Walt, 2006:186).

5.2.1 *Exordium* of the Sermon on the Mount (Matt. 5:3-16)

The set of beatitudes (*macarisms*) in Matt. 5:3-12 functions as the opening of what could be regarded as the *exordium* to the Sermon on the Mount. The Beatitudes contain blessings with implied commands for the followers of Jesus. These beatitudes therefore introduce the moral instructions that follow in the rest of the Sermon (Luz, 1990:215; Viljoen, 2008:207). The Beatitudes imply that when followers of Jesus adhere to the moral law as He teaches it, their lives will be filled with joy, purpose and eternal hope. Several elements that later occur in the "antitheses" are anticipated in the Beatitudes, such as peacemakers (first and fifth "antitheses") that will be called sons of God (Matt. 5:9), being persecuted (fifth and sixth antitheses) for the sake of righteousness (Matt. 5:10), suffering insults and false accusations (first, fifth and sixth "antitheses") for the sake of Jesus (Matt. 5:11) and receiving a reward for perseverance (fifth and sixth "antitheses") (Matt. 5:12).

As second part of the *exordium*, the Beatitudes are followed by an exhortation using the metaphors of τὸ ἅλας τῆς γῆς (the salt of the earth – probably referring to their influence within their community) and τὸ φῶς τοῦ κόσμου (the light of the world – probably referring to their influence outside their own community) to depict the distinctive life of the followers of Jesus (Matt. 5:17-20). It seems that people become salt and light when they practice the teaching of Jesus on righteous living. The salt and light refer to their good deeds that are based on Jesus' interpretation of the *Torah* (Matt. 5:21-47).

5.2.2 *Propositio* of the Sermon on the Mount (Matt. 5:17-20)

The legal statement in Matt. 5:17-19 (cf. Chapter 3) introduces Jesus' teaching as such with catch words such as Law (νόμος) and Prophets (προφῆται). This statement could be considered as the preamble to the six *halakhic* arguments in Matt. 5:21-47. In the former (Matt. 5:17-19) Matthew provides the fundamental and somewhat abstract statement about the continuing validity of the Law, and then continues to provide practical examples of how the Law should be interpreted (Matt. 5:21-47). Obviously Matthew intended his audience to recognize the logical link between these two sections. Although the antithetical debate does not provide an explicit commentary on the foregoing fundamental statement, they do illustrate the intention of this statement in practice (Osborne, 2010:186).

As a Janus-like (facing in two directions) hinge, Matt. 5:20, which deals with greater δικαιοσύνη (righteousness), functions as a transitional statement between two sections. The debate about the Law introduced in Matt. 5:17-19 is concluded with different forms of δικαιοσύνη, announcing that the δικαιοσύνη of the followers of Jesus should exceed that of the scribes and the Pharisees. It simultaneously creates an expectation that the following series of sayings would provide an explanation and exegetical guide of what such righteousness should imply (Osborne, 2010:186). The antithetical argumentation is framed by δικαιοσύνη, as it occurs again in Matt. 6:1 where the "righteous" acts of οἱ ὑποκριταὶ (the hypocrites) are denounced. As δικαιοσύνη forms a literary *inclusio* to circumscribe the "antitheses", δικαιοσύνη forms an important hermeneutical key to the interpretation of the "antitheses". Müller (1999:170) has remarked that "the realisation of such righteousness as conforms with God's will ... is a manifestation of the Law's true significance".

5.2.3 *Probatio* of the Sermon on the Mount (Matt. 5:21-7:21)

The *halakhic* arguments with the six "antitheses" form the first part of the *probatio* of the Sermon. These six "antitheses" are drawn to an end with ἔσεσθε οὖν ὑμεῖς τέλειοι ὡς ὁ πατὴρ ὑμῶν ὁ οὐράνιος τέλειός ἐστιν (be perfect, therefore, as your heavenly Father is perfect) (Matt. 5:48). This concluding statement apparently summarizes the intention of the "antitheses" in terms of a τέλειός-requirement. The future indicative of the verb ἔσεσθε is usually interpreted as a command. Schweizer (1976:135), however, made the noteworthy comment that this formulation includes a promise, which is grammatically plausible (Jordaan, 2014:72). Jesus formulates the statement in such a manner that his disciples may expect divine assistance in striving towards the set goal. The ὑμεῖς (you) in this statement is emphatic. Jesus does not require the Jews who do not follow Him or the Gentiles to be perfect, but his disciples. Being τέλειοι (perfect) implies that they should attain the aim for which God had created them.

As the antitheses function as explanations of the fundamental statement in Matt. 5:17-20, are drawn to conclusion with the τέλειός (perfect)-requirement, and are set within the framework of δικαιοσύνη (righteousness) terminology, these structural markers play an important role in interpreting Jesus' antithetical argumentation.

5.3 THE FORM OF THE DEBATE

The nature of the series of theses and "antitheses" differs considerably, but Matthew presents them as a unit. The series has a legal tone as a result of the basic structure, which consists of six paragraphs (unique to Matthew), each stating a thesis followed by Jesus' interpretation of that thesis in contrast to the popular understanding of his day.

Jesus' antithetical debate on the *Torah* is presented in a highly ordered sixfold scheme. The six theses (or examples) are all introduced by variations of a repetitive formula, which is unparalleled in the Gospels. Either the full formula ἠκούσατε ὅτι ἐρρέθη τοῖς ἀρχαίοις (you have heard that it was said to/by the people long ago) (Matt. 5:21 and 33), or the medium formula ἠκούσατε ὅτι ἐρρέθη (you have heard that it was said) (Matt. 5:27, 38 and 43) or the short formula ἐρρέθη δέ (it was said) (only in Matt. 5:31) is used. Matthew constructed the introductory formula with significant parallelisms to form two triads. As a result, parallelisms are formed between the first and the fourth, the second and the fifth, and the third and the sixth in a well-organised pattern:

Triad 1:	Triad 2:
First: Ἠκούσατε ὅτι ἐρρέθη τοῖς ἀρχαίοις ⟷	Fourth: **Πάλιν** ἠκούσατε ὅτι ἐρρέθη τοῖς ἀρχαίοις
Second: Ἠκούσατε ὅτι ἐρρέθη ⟷	Fifth: Ἠκούσατε ὅτι ἐρρέθη
Third: Ἐρρέθη δέ ⟷	Sixth: **Ἠκούσατε** ὅτι ἐρρέθη

Table 12: The triadic composition of the introductory formulas of the antitheses in Matt. 5:21-47

The second triad is introduced with πάλιν (again), while ἠκούσατε (you have heard) is repeated in the last thesis to form a conclusion to the series.

The second person plural in ἠκούσατε (you have heard) refers to the disciples of Jesus. Matthew probably implies the Matthean community too. The hearing probably refers to the Scriptures as read in the synagogue along with the explanations of Jewish teachers. The reference to the passive form in ἐρρέθη (it is said) is not decided easily. If it refers only to the teaching of the scribes, the problem of interpreting the "antitheses" is easier solved. However, elsewhere Matthew always uses this passive form of the verb for the words of God or the prophets (e.g. Matt. 1:22; 2:15, 17, 23). Furthermore, most of the theses refer to passages or paraphrases from the written *Torah*, and not from the oral tradition. Obviously the traditional and assumed distorted scribal interpretation of the *Torah* is included when one considers the preceding words ἐὰν μὴ περισσεύσῃ ὑμῶν ἡ δικαιοσύνη πλεῖον τῶν γραμματέων καὶ Φαρισαίων, οὐ μὴ εἰσέλθητε εἰς τὴν βασιλείαν τῶν οὐρανῶν (for I tell you that unless your righteousness surpasses that of the Pharisees and the teachers of the Law, you will certainly not enter the Kingdom of Heaven) in Matt. 5:20. Davies and Allison (2004a:510) have remarked: "In both Jewish and Christian writings, 'it (was) said (by God)' is common for introducing Old Testament quotations". The uncertainty of how to interpret this passive form of the verb influences the understanding of the dative τοῖς ἀρχαίοις of the phrase. If ἐρρέθη (it was said) refers to the speaking of the scribes, the dative can be interpreted as a dative of agency with the verb ἐρρέθη. The King James Bible translates these references as such: "Ye have heard that it was said by them of old time". However, Matthew has no other example of using the dative in such a way. The dative rather indicates the audience to whom the words had been directed. With these words, Matthew's Jesus most probably refers to the traditional understanding of the commandments (Osborne, 2010:189).

The "antithetical" statements display similar patterns. After the introductory formula has been given, a passage or paraphrase from the written *Torah* follows. In Matt. 5:21 an interpretative addition is given as well (and anyone who murders will be subject to judgement). The formula used by Jesus suggests that He is quoting the *Torah* as it was usually heard by his audience.

Each of these statements is then followed by an antithetical response with the definite interpretation by Jesus. Jesus time and again declares ἐγὼ δὲ λέγω ὑμῖν (but I say to you) implying that there are deeper principles to the Law than what is commonly assumed. Jesus refers to the inner attitude behind the external act (Osborne, 2010:187). The dominant note, hinted by the emphatic "but I tell you", is the independent, authoritative teaching of Jesus. Osborne (2010:187) labels this alternative teaching the "*Torah* of the Messiah". The goal of this teaching is nothing but perfection (cf. Matt. 5:48), which demanded and received reaction from the crowds (Matt. 7:28-29) (Viljoen, 2012a). Matthew's Jesus argues that He will pose revisions in *halakhah* in order to better fulfil the Law (Sigal, 2007:70).

There is no analogy to the "antitheses" of the Sermon on the Mount elsewhere in early Christian literature (the only parallel is between Matt. 5:25-26 and Luke 12:57-59 [Q-material]) (Osborne, 2010:189), and they consequently form one of the most intriguing parts of the New Testament. However, this antithetical debate can be located against the wider background of Judaism (as discussed in Chapter 2), where dissenting groups interacted with their opponents. Daube (1956:55-62) has drawn attention to a rabbinic method of teaching, found in the *Midrash halakhah*, which may lie behind this pattern. He points out that the rabbi might say "I hear" and then refer to a passage from Scripture. The rabbi then would continue to a give literal, but wrong interpretation of that passage, followed by what he regarded as the true meaning. Daube cites such an exposition of the fifth commandment: "Honour thy father and thy mother. I might understand ... honour them with words only" (*Mekhilta* on Exod. 20:12). The rabbi then explains how the *Midrash* refutes such an interpretation and that it goes beyond speech. The expression "he who hears" is used in the sense of "he who sticks to the superficial, literal meaning of Scripture". In Matthew, however, there is no rabbinical argumentation of the progressive interpretation of the passage, but the statements of Jesus, who speaks with supreme authority (cf. Matt. 7:29). Taking this rabbinical method as model for Matt. 5:21-47, the latter objects against a strictly limited obedience of the Law on the surface level that leaves scope for a good deal of ungodly attitude and behaviour (Morris, 1992:113).

Foster (2004:80) has compared Matt. 5:21-48 with the antithetical debate in the *halakhic* letter of Qumran (4QMMT). 4QMMT directly and indirectly makes use of the antithetical form of contrasting two opposing viewpoints in its *halakhot* to promote the viewpoint of the Qumran community. Similarly, Matthew's Jesus also uses the antithetical *halakhic* arguments to describe the higher form of δικαιοσύνη (righteousness) required from his followers. Jesus does not merely pose an alternative *halakhic* position, but the authoritative interpretation of the *Torah*. The Qumran community regarded the right interpretation of the *Torah* as fundamental to their decision to part from their mother group, as they strove to a higher state of righteousness. In Matthew a similar tendency surfaces as the correct interpretation of the Law and true righteousness were probably key issues in the Matthean community's parting from Judaistic movements, as argued in Chapter 2.

Loader (1997:173) has observed: "The status of his [Jesus'] antithetical statement is, however, not a second opinion, but an authoritative declaration made on his own God given authority". Jesus' self-referential announcements are regarded as the highest source of authority for the correct understanding of the Law. Matthew makes the exclusive claim that Jesus is the legitimate interpreter of the *Torah*.

> This is not simply a claim that the group has the right interpretation of the *Torah*, but this constitutes a higher claim, namely the right to re-interpret the law thereby making its authority subservient to that of Jesus (Foster, 2004:92).

> Volgens Mattëus hoeven zijn lezers zich niet langer te verlaten op de halachische leer van de joodse leiders. Het is noodzakelijk en voldoende wanneer zij zich in woord en daad oriënteren op wa Jezus hun heeft opgedragen (Weren, 1979:73).

The "antitheses" therefore explain the issues that led to the Matthean community's schism from Judaism.

5.4　JESUS' ANTITHETICAL ARGUMENTS ABOUT THE *TORAH*

The antithetical arguments[137] function as explanations of the fundamental statement in Matt. 5:17-20 and the call for a higher righteousness (Matt. 5:20)

---

[137] Some parts of four of the arguments in Matthew have parallels in the other Synoptic Gospels, though in varied contexts and not as part of halakhic arguments: On murder, Matt. 5:21-26 // Luk. 12:57-59; on adultery, Matt. 5:27:27-30 // Mark 9:43-48 // Luk. 16:18; on retaliation, Matt. 5:38-42 // Luk. 6:29-30; and on love of enemies, Matt. 5:43-47 // Luk. 6:27-28, 32-36.

for Jesus' followers. As discussed before, there is no easy answer to the question whether Jesus merely interpreted the Law or abrogated it. Jesus' six varied "antithetical" arguments are investigated respectively in the sections that follow to seek an answer to the issue and to evaluate the assumption that these statements do form part of a coherent argument to describe the ethical requirements for the followers of Jesus and per implication of the Matthean community.

5.4.1 The antithetical argument on murder (Matt. 5:21-26)

The first "antithetical" argument is the longest of the six statements and exhibits the following form.

5:21: Thesis	
Introductory formula: Ἠκούσατε ὅτι ἐρρέθη τοῖς ἀρχαίοις	You have heard that it was said to the people long ago,
First ruling: Οὐ φονεύσεις·	'You shall not murder,
Second ruling: ὃς δ' ἂν φονεύσῃ, ἔνοχος ἔσται τῇ κρίσει.	and anyone who murders will be subject to judgement.'
5:22: Three-fold "Antithesis"	
Introductory formula: ἐγὼ δὲ λέγω ὑμῖν	But I tell you
Three antithetical statements:	
ὅτι πᾶς ὁ ὀργιζόμενος τῷ ἀδελφῷ αὐτοῦ ἔνοχος ἔσται τῇ κρίσει·	that anyone who is angry with a brother will be subject to judgement.
ὃς δ' ἂν εἴπῃ τῷ ἀδελφῷ αὐτοῦ Ῥακά, ἔνοχος ἔσται τῷ συνεδρίῳ·	Again, anyone who says to a brother or sister, 'Raca,' is answerable to the court.
ὃς δ' ἂν εἴπῃ Μωρέ, ἔνοχος ἔσται εἰς τὴν γέενναν τοῦ πυρός.	And anyone who says, 'You fool!' will be in danger of the fire of hell.
5:23-24: First example (internal)	
ἐὰν οὖν προσφέρῃς τὸ δῶρόν σου ἐπὶ τὸ θυσιαστήριον κἀκεῖ μνησθῇς ὅτι ὁ ἀδελφός σου ἔχει τι κατὰ σοῦ, ἄφες ἐκεῖ τὸ δῶρόν σου ἔμπροσθεν τοῦ θυσιαστηρίου καὶ ὕπαγε πρῶτον διαλλάγηθι τῷ ἀδελφῷ σου, καὶ τότε ἐλθὼν πρόσφερε τὸ δῶρόν σου.	"Therefore, if you are offering your gift at the altar and there remember that your brother or sister has something against you, leave your gift there in front of the altar. First go and be reconciled to them; then come and offer your gift.
5:25-26: Second example (external)	
ἴσθι εὐνοῶν τῷ ἀντιδίκῳ σου ταχὺ ἕως ὅτου εἶ μετ' αὐτοῦ ἐν τῇ ὁδῷ· μή ποτέ σε παραδῷ ὁ ἀντίδικος τῷ κριτῇ, καὶ ὁ κριτὴς τῷ ὑπηρέτῃ, καὶ εἰς φυλακὴν βληθήσῃ· ἀμὴν λέγω σοι, οὐ μὴ ἐξέλθῃς ἐκεῖθεν ἕως ἂν	"Settle matters quickly with your adversary who is taking you to court. Do it while you are still together on the way, or your adversary may hand you over to the judge, and the judge may hand you over to the

ἀποδῷς τὸν ἔσχατον κοδράντην.	officer, and you may be thrown into prison. Truly I tell you, you will not get out until you have paid the last penny.

Table 13: The antithetical argument in Matt. 5:21-26

5.4.1.1   Thesis (Matt. 5:21)

The argument starts with the fullest form of the introductory formula ἠκούσατε ὅτι ἐρρέθη τοῖς ἀρχαίοις (you have heard that it was said to the people long ago) (Matt. 5:21a). This is followed by a thesis that consists of two elements, the apodictic ruling of οὐ φονεύσεις ('you shall not murder), which refers to passages from the written *Torah* – the Decalogue (Exod. 20:13 and Deut. 5:17 LXX) and the additional casuistic ruling of ὃς δ' ἂν φονεύσῃ, ἔνοχος ἔσται τῇ κρίσει (and anyone who murders will be subject to judgement) (Matt. 5:21b).

5.4.1.2   Threefold "antithesis" (Matt. 5:22)

The antithetical response to the thesis is given in Matt. 5:22. It opens with the introductory formula ἐγὼ δὲ λέγω ὑμῖν (but I tell you) emphatically marking the definite and authoritative interpretation of Jesus. France (1985:125) comments: "This is not a new contribution to the exegetical debate, but a definite declaration of the will of God". Matthew's Jesus indicates that the commandment goes further than was commonly assumed. For the people of the day it was seemingly enough not to physically put a person to death. Jesus argues that this is just the beginning of the understanding of this command. Anger is murder in mind (cf. 1 Joh. 3:15) (Osborne, 2010:190). In contrast to the single thesis in Matt. 5:21, Jesus makes three antithetical statements in Matt. 5:22, demonstrating Matthew's preference for using triadic structures.

The statements develop from a general act of anger into two specific offences in parallel form:

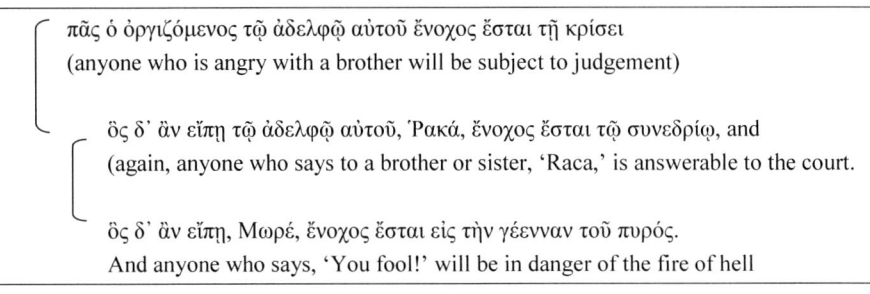

Table 14: Anger and offences in Matt. 5:22

It is likely that Matthew's community would recognize their own experience of being insulted by those who taunt them these two specific offences are mentioned. In the eyes of God all these offences are liable for justice. As indicated before, Pryzybylski (1980:82) has applied the hermeneutical principle of a fence around the commandment to Matt. 5:21-26. Accordingly, the fence consists of the recommendation that one should not even be angry with one's brother (presumably including sister), for in this way one will definitely obey the commandment not to kill. This hermeneutical principle might fit this context, but becomes less obvious in some of the "antitheses" that follow. It is clear, however, that Jesus goes beyond the act of murder as such. He warns against anger and hatred that gives rise to murder. Though these thoughts cannot be examined in a human court, they are no less culpable in the sight of God. Jesus urges his followers to also submit their thoughts to God (France, 1985:125).

5.4.1.3 Two examples (Matt. 5:23-26)

After this threefold "antithesis", two examples are given to illustrate Jesus' interpretation in practice. The first example relates to internal relations, and the second to external relations (Osborne, 2010:189).

5.4.1.3.1 Internal relations

The first example provides an internal illustration that depicts how a person can avoid hostilities amongst brothers (presumably including sisters): ἐὰν οὖν προσφέρῃς τὸ δῶρόν σου ἐπὶ τὸ θυσιαστήριον κἀκεῖ μνησθῇς ὅτι ὁ ἀδελφός σου ἔχει τι κατὰ σοῦ, ἄφες ἐκεῖ τὸ δῶρόν σου ἔμπροσθεν τοῦ θυσιαστηρίου καὶ ὕπαγε πρῶτον διαλλάγηθι τῷ ἀδελφῷ σου, καὶ τότε ἐλθὼν πρόσφερε τὸ δῶρόν σου (therefore, if you are offering your gift at the altar and there remember that your brother or sister has something against you, leave your gift there in front of the altar. First go and be reconciled to them; then come and offer your gift) (Matt. 5:23-24) (Osborne, 2010:190). In this example a shift in the use of pronouns takes place from the third person to the second. Though this might reflect a seam in the tradition (cf. Forster, 2004:100), it rather sharpens the personal application of the example to Jesus' (and Matthew's) audience (Hagner, 1993:117; Morris, 1992:115). This example illustrates the incongruence that can occur between cultic accuracy and unforgiving attitudes. The importance of brotherly/sisterly reconciliation above punctilious sacrifice correlates with Jesus' consistent emphasis of love for one's neighbour and with the fifth clause of the Lord's Prayer (Matt. 6:12), which links the forgiveness of others with the forgiveness of God (Davies & Allison, 2004a:516). The words ὕπαγε πρῶτον διαλλάγηθι τῷ ἀδελφῷ (first go and be reconciled to them) are significant. The worth of a sacrifice is annihilated when it is done in bad spirit. Worship is compromised as long as there is disunity within the religious community (Osborne, 2010:191). The negative prohibition of the command is interpreted beyond the letters of this stipulation to the ultimate intention of the *Torah*. Jesus goes beyond the basic meaning of the Law as stated in Matt. 5:21 by urging for reconciliation and the restoration of relationships (Guelich, 1967:190). The worshiper should get his/her priorities right. Before he/she can worship, he/she must reconcile (Morris, 1992:116). This example probably reflects internal relations amongst followers of Jesus. It seems that Matthew's intention is not only polemical, but also pastoral. It is not possible to entertain strenuous relations with one's brother/sister and continue with superficial cultic punctuality.

4.1.3.2   External relations

The second example returns to the judicial setting, with a probable external illustration. This part of the antithesis has a parallel in Luk. 12:58-59, though in a different contexts and not as part of a *halakhic* argument on a stipulation from the Law. In Luke Jesus addresses the crowds to interpret the times and urges them: "Why don't you judge for yourselves what is right? (Luk. 12:57).

Matt. 5:25-26	Luk. 12:58-59
ἴσθι εὐνοῶν τῷ ἀντιδίκῳ σου ταχύ, ἕως ὅτου εἶ μετ' αὐτοῦ ἐν τῇ ὁδῷ, μήποτέ σε παραδῷ ὁ ἀντίδικος τῷ κριτῇ καὶ ὁ κριτὴς τῷ ὑπηρέτῃ καὶ εἰς φυλακὴν βληθήσῃ· ἀμὴν λέγω σοι, οὐ μὴ ἐξέλθῃς ἐκεῖθεν, ἕως ἂν ἀποδῷς τὸν ἔσχατον κοδράντην.	ὡς γὰρ ὑπάγεις μετὰ τοῦ ἀντιδίκου σου ἐπ' ἄρχοντα, ἐν τῇ ὁδῷ δὸς ἐργασίαν ἀπηλλάχθαι ἀπ' αὐτοῦ, μή ποτε κατασύρῃ σε πρὸς τὸν κριτήν, καὶ ὁ κριτὴς σε παραδώσει τῷ πράκτορι, καὶ ὁ πράκτωρ σε βαλεῖ εἰς φυλακήν. λέγω σοι, οὐ μὴ ἐξέλθῃς ἐκεῖθεν ἕως καὶ τὸ ἔσχατον λεπτὸν ἀποδῷς.
Settle matters quickly with your adversary who is taking you to court. Do it while you are still together on the way, or your adversary may hand you over to the judge, and the judge may hand you over to the officer, and you may be thrown into prison. Truly I tell you, you will not get out until you have paid the last penny.	As you are going with your adversary to the magistrate, try hard to be reconciled on the way, or your adversary may drag you off to the judge, and the judge turn you over to the officer, and the officer throw you into prison. I tell you, you will not get out until you have paid the last penny.

Table 15: The parallel between Matt. 5:25-26 and Luk. 12:58-59

It appears that these words in Matthew, however, reflect on the stipulation about murder. It seems that in the Matthean context the statement reflects the strenuous relation between the Matthean community and its adversaries that taunt them. Jesus' counter-argument is that legal hostilities must be avoided.

Thus the negative and minimal meaning of the command "not to murder" is expanded to include a positive call for reconciliation, both within the community and beyond. For Matthew's Jesus, relationships are very important. While the first example mainly refers to relations within the religious community, the second example probably refers to external relations, even with unbelievers.

With this extended antithetical statement Matthew's Jesus argues that keeping the commandment of οὐ φονεύσεις (you shall not murder) implies much more than was generally assumed. The deeper implications of God's commandment should be recognized and put into practice.

5.4.2 The antithetical argument on adultery (Matt. 5:27-30)

The second argument is also taken from the Decalogue, οὐ μοιχεύσεις (you shall not commit adultery), the seventh commandment (Exod. 20:14 and Deut. 5:18).

Matt. 5:27: Thesis	
Introductory formula: Ἠκούσατε ὅτι ἐρρέθη	"You have heard that it was said,
Ruling: Οὐ μοιχεύσεις.	'You shall not commit adultery.'
Matt. 5:28: "Antithesis"	
Introductory formula: ἐγὼ δὲ λέγω ὑμῖν	But I tell you
Antithetical statement: ὅτι πᾶς ὁ βλέπων γυναῖκα πρὸς τὸ ἐπιθυμῆσαι αὐτὴν ἤδη ἐμοίχευσεν αὐτὴν ἐν τῇ καρδίᾳ αὐτοῦ.	That anyone who looks at a woman lustfully has already committed adultery with her in his heart.
Matt. 5:29: First proverbial solution	
εἰ δὲ ὁ ὀφθαλμός σου ὁ δεξιὸς σκανδαλίζει σε, ἔξελε αὐτὸν καὶ βάλε ἀπὸ σοῦ· συμφέρει γάρ σοι ἵνα ἀπόληται ἓν τῶν μελῶν σου καὶ μὴ ὅλον τὸ σῶμά σου βληθῇ εἰς γέενναν.	If your right eye causes you to stumble, gouge it out and throw it away. It is better for you to lose one part of your body than for your whole body to be thrown into hell.
Matt. 5:30: Second proverbial solution	
καὶ εἰ ἡ δεξιά σου χεὶρ σκανδαλίζει σε, ἔκκοψον αὐτὴν καὶ βάλε ἀπὸ σοῦ· συμφέρει γάρ σοι ἵνα ἀπόληται ἓν τῶν μελῶν σου καὶ μὴ ὅλον τὸ σῶμά σου εἰς γέενναν ἀπέλθῃ.	And if your right hand causes you to stumble, cut it off and throw it away. It is better for you to lose one part of your body than for your whole body to go into hell

Table 16: The antithetical argument on adultery in Matt. 5:27-30

5.4.2.1 Thesis (Matt. 5:27)

The introductory formula ἠκούσατε ὅτι ἐρρέθη (you have heard that it was said) (Matt. 5:27a) and the reference to the *Torah* οὐ μοιχεύσεις (you shall not commit adultery) (Matt. 5:27b), are more abbreviated than in the first argument. The formulaic opening drops the τοῖς ἀρχαίοις (to the people long ago), but this audience is obviously assumed. Then a two-word commandment is quoted from Exod. 20:14 // Deut. 5:18 (LXX) and in this case no corresponding penalty is mentioned for breaking the commandment.

5.4.2.2 Antithetical statement (Matt. 5:28)

The antithetical statement follows in Matt. 5:28. This statement has a distant parallel in Luk. 16:18.

Matt. 5:28	Luk. 16:18
ἐγὼ δὲ λέγω ὑμῖν ὅτι πᾶς ὁ βλέπων γυναῖκα πρὸς τὸ ἐπιθυμῆσαι αὐτὴν ἤδη ἐμοίχευσεν αὐτὴν ἐν τῇ καρδίᾳ αὐτοῦ	Πᾶς ὁ ἀπολύων τὴν γυναῖκα αὐτοῦ καὶ γαμῶν ἑτέραν μοιχεύει, καὶ ὁ ἀπολελυμένην ἀπὸ ἀνδρὸς γαμῶν μοιχεύει.
but I tell you that anyone who looks at a woman lustfully has already committed adultery with her in his heart.	Anyone who divorces his wife and marries another woman commits adultery, and the man who marries a divorced woman commits adultery.

Table 17: The antithetical statement on lust in Matt. 5:28

In Luke this statement does not form part of an antithetical argument and the reason for adultery is specified differently. In Luke it forms part of a warning directed to the Pharisees who are supposed to justify themselves. The Lukan Jesus warns them: "You are the ones who justify yourselves in the eyes of others, but God knows your hearts. What people value highly is detestable in God's sight" (Luk.6:15). In Matthew the context is different.

With the statement in Matthew, Jesus argues that He does not revoke the Law on adultery, but states that a lustful heart is just as bad. Jesus states that the original intent of this prohibition calls for more than literal compliance. It calls for the removal of the cause of the sin and focuses the intent of the heart (Betz, 1995:231; Meier, 1976:136). Jesus warns even against "thought-adultery" (Foster, 2004:105).

In many societies of the ancient world it was acceptable for a man to have sexual relations with another woman as long as it did not involve another marriage, as it would then violate the rights of her husband. The key to determination of whether a sexual act was adultery or not depended on the woman's marital status. The offence was regarded as an offence against the marital partner or fiancé of the woman (Shields, 2006:57) since it was theft of his property (Osborne, 2010:196). Therefore a man was generally not regarded as an adulterer when engaging in sexual activity outside the marriage, unless the partner herself was a married or engaged woman (Morris, 1992:122; Sigal, 2007:116). The common understanding was that adultery was not so much seen as moral depravity, but as the violation of a husband's right to have sole sexual possession of his wife and thus to assure that her children were his (Schields, 2006:57). Jesus, however, makes no distinction between male and female in the application of this commandment. Both men and women had to be faithful. As a matter of fact, Jesus specifically warns men against adultery. A man commits adultery when he has relations with a woman not his wife, whether or not she is anyone else's wife (Sigal, 2007:117). Jesus elevates the status of women and forbids men to abuse them. Banks (1975:190) and Luz (1990:296) draw attention to close parallels of this warning in rabbinic literature. The *Mekhilta* of Rabbi Shimon III states: "He is not to commit adultery ... either by the eye of by the heart". In *Pesiqta Rabbati* 24.2 a similar ruling occurs: "Even he who visualises himself in the act of adultery is called an adulterer". The Book of Jubilees 20:3-4 urges: "Let them not fornicate with her after their eyes and hearts". Yet these Jewish teachers did not parallel the severity of the proverbial elaborations that follow.

5.4.2.3 Two proverbial solutions (Matt. 5:29-30)

Twin proverbial applications follow, demanding drastic action to avoid the temptation of adultery.

The first concerns the right eye and the second the right hand:

> εἰ δὲ ὁ **ὀφθαλμός σου ὁ δεξιὸς** σκανδαλίζει σε (if your right eye causes you to stumble),
> <u>ἔξελε αὐτὸν καὶ βάλε ἀπὸ σοῦ</u> (gouge it out and throw it away)
>> *συμφέρει γάρ σοι* ἵνα ἀπόληται ἓν τῶν μελῶν σου καὶ μὴ ὅλον τὸ σῶμά σου βληθῇ εἰς γέενναν (for it is better for you to lose one part of your body than for your whole body to be thrown into hell (Matt. 5:29).
>
> καὶ εἰ **ἡ δεξιά σου χεὶρ** σκανδαλίζει σε (and if your right hand causes you to stumble)
> <u>ἔκκοψον αὐτὴν καὶ βάλε ἀπὸ σοῦ</u> (cut it off and throw it away)
>> *συμφέρει γάρ σοι* ἵνα ἀπόληται ἓν τῶν μελῶν σου καὶ μὴ ὅλον τὸ σῶμά σου εἰς γέενναν ἀπέλθῃ (for it is better for you to lose one part of your body than for your whole body to go into hell) (Matt. 5:30).

Table 18: Two proverbial solutions to avoid adultery in Matt. 5:29-30

The twin statement in Matt. 5:29-30 has a parallel in Mark 9:43-48, though in a different context with a trifold proverbial statement.

Matt. 5:29-30	Mark 9:43-48
²⁹ εἰ δὲ **ὁ ὀφθαλμός σου ὁ δεξιὸς** σκανδαλίζει σε ἔξελε αὐτὸν καὶ βάλε ἀπὸ σοῦ· *συμφέρει γάρ σοι ἵνα ἀπόληται ἓν τῶν μελῶν σου καὶ μὴ ὅλον τὸ σῶμά σου βληθῇ εἰς γέενναν* ³⁰ καὶ εἰ **ἡ δεξιά σου χεὶρ** σκανδαλίζει ἔκκοψον αὐτὴν καὶ βάλε ἀπὸ σοῦ· *συμφέρει γάρ σοι ἵνα ἀπόληται ἓν τῶν μελῶν σου καὶ μὴ ὅλον τὸ σῶμά σου εἰς γέενναν ἀπέλθῃ* ²⁹ If your right eye causes you to stumble, gouge it out and throw it away. It is better for you to lose one part of your body than for your whole body to be thrown into hell. ³⁰ And if your right hand causes you to stumble, cut it off and throw it away. It is better for you to lose one part of your body than for your whole body to go into hell.	⁴³ Καὶ ἐὰν **σκανδαλίσῃ σε ἡ χείρ σου**, ἀπόκοψον αὐτήν· καλόν ἐστίν σε κυλλὸν εἰσελθεῖν εἰς τὴν ζωήν, ἢ τὰς δύο χεῖρας ἔχοντα ἀπελθεῖν εἰς τὴν γέενναν, εἰς τὸ πῦρ τὸ ἄσβεστον. ⁴⁵ καὶ ἐὰν **ὁ πούς σου σκανδαλίζῃ σε**, ἀπόκοψον αὐτόν· καλόν ἐστίν σε εἰσελθεῖν εἰς τὴν ζωὴν χωλόν, ἢ τοὺς δύο πόδας ἔχοντα βληθῆναι εἰς τὴν γέενναν. ⁴⁷ καὶ ἐὰν **ὁ ὀφθαλμός σου σκανδαλίζῃ σε**, ἔκβαλε αὐτόν· καλόν σέ ἐστιν μονόφθαλμον εἰσελθεῖν εἰς τὴν βασιλείαν τοῦ Θεοῦ, ἢ δύο ὀφθαλμοὺς ἔχοντα βληθῆναι εἰς τὴν γέενναν, ⁴⁸ ὅπου ὁ σκώληξ αὐτῶν οὐ τελευτᾷ καὶ τὸ πῦρ οὐ σβέννυται. ⁴³ If your hand causes you to stumble, cut it off. It is better for you to enter life maimed than with two hands to go into hell, where the fire never goes out[138]. ⁴⁵ And if your foot causes you to stumble, cut it off. It is better for you to enter life crippled than to have two feet and be thrown into hell. ⁴⁷ And if your eye causes you to stumble, pluck it out. It is better for you to enter the kingdom of God with one eye than to have two eyes and be thrown into hell, ⁴⁸ where " 'the worms that eat them do not die, and the fire is not quenched.'

Table 19: The parallel between the statements in Matt. 5:29-30 and Mark 9:43-48

In Mark Jesus warns the twelve not to cause little ones to stumble: "If anyone causes one of these little ones—those who believe in me—to stumble, it would be better for them if a large millstone were hung around their neck and they were thrown into the sea" (Mark 9:42) and then continues with a threefold proverbial warning directed at one's hand, foot and eye.

---

[138] Some manuscripts add the wording of verse 48 as verses 44 and 46.

In carefully constructed parallel statements in Matthew Jesus also warns against temptations, but then within the context of adultery. He does not advocate self-mutilation, but uses a hyperbole to emphasize the seriousness with which his followers should prevent lustful thoughts. With this strong imagery Jesus emphasises that serious measures must be taken to defeat wrong sexual urges (Osborne, 2010:197). So, the right eye which, ironically, should keep one from stumbling into a trap, can cause one to stumble. If a valuable member such as a right eye causes one to sin, it is better to get rid of it. Parallel to the right eye, the right hand's activity could cause stumbling. The hand puts into action what the eye has stimulated. One should be willing to even renounce ones' favourite activities if they cause stumbling.

Once again the principle of Matt. 5:20 is explained with this antithetical argument on adultery by showing that the δικαιοσύνη (righteousness) as required from the followers of Jesus should exceed that of the scribes and the Pharisees. Jesus is depicted as the authoritative interpreter of the *Torah* and is concerned with the inner state that leads to action, rather than the simple outward deed. Jesus does not abolish the commandment, but reveals its true intention.

5.4.3 The antithetical argument on divorce (Matt. 5:31-32)

The antithetical argument on divorce is the shortest of the series of six. It has no parabolic appendix or pedagogical applications. With this argument Jesus departs from thought life (as in the first two arguments) and turns to ethical actions (Osborne, 2010:198).

Matt. 5:31: Thesis	
Introductory formula: Ἐρρέθη δέ	"It has been said,
Ruling: Ὃς ἂν ἀπολύσῃ τὴν γυναῖκα αὐτοῦ, δότω αὐτῇ ἀποστάσιον.	'Anyone who divorces his wife must give her a certificate of divorce.'
Matt. 5:32: "'Antithesis"	
Introductory formula: ἐγὼ δὲ λέγω ὑμῖν	But I tell you
Twofold statement:	
ὅτι πᾶς ὁ ἀπολύων τὴν γυναῖκα αὐτοῦ παρεκτὸς λόγου πορνείας ποιεῖ αὐτὴν μοιχευθῆναι,	that anyone who divorces his wife, except for sexual immorality, makes her the victim of adultery,
καὶ ὃς ἐὰν ἀπολελυμένην γαμήσῃ μοιχᾶται.	and anyone who marries a divorced woman commits adultery.

Table 20: The antithetical argument on divorce in Matt. 5:31-32

5.4.3.1 Thesis (Matt. 5:31)

Matt. 5:31 comprises the formulaic opening in its shortest form ἐρρέθη δέ (it has been said) and the *Torah* reference ὃς ἂν ἀπολύσῃ τὴν γυναῖκα αὐτοῦ, δότω αὐτῇ ἀποστάσιον (anyone who divorces his wife must give her a certificate of divorce). The *Torah* reference differs from those in the previous statements in that it does not come from the Decalogue and is not a direct citation from Scripture. The citation alludes to Deut. 24:1. It is important to recognize that in Deut. 24:1 divorce is assumed and not approved (France, 1985:127). The implication is then that if a man indeed divorced his wife, he was commanded to give her a certificate of the divorce. However, in due time, it seems that not only the certificate as such, but also the divorce itself was regarded as demanded by Moses (cf. Matt. 19:7).

5.4.3.2 "Antithesis" (Matt. 5:32)

It is against this presumed common assumption that Jesus again responds with the introductory formula ἐγὼ δὲ λέγω ὑμῖν (but I tell you) followed by a twofold antithetical statement. In the first part He states ὅτι πᾶς ὁ ἀπολύων τὴν γυναῖκα αὐτοῦ παρεκτὸς λόγου πορνείας ποιεῖ αὐτὴν μοιχευθῆναι (that anyone who divorces his wife, except for sexual immorality, makes her the victim of adultery). Scholars such as Meier (1976:140) have been of the opinion that this "antithesis" is a clear example that Jesus indeed did revoke the Mosaic Law that allows divorce. Luz (1990:301) has on the other hand argued that Jesus did not revoke this stipulation as such, but limits the circumstances under which divorce can be permitted to πορνεία (sexual immorality). Furthermore, according to this statement, the man is assigned a role in the act of adultery by causing the wife's adultery. The focus is once more on the role of the man in the second part of the statement καὶ ὃς ἐὰν ἀπολελυμένην γαμήσῃ, μοιχᾶται (and anyone who marries a divorced woman commits adultery). This final clause of the divorce statement prohibits another man to marry a divorced woman.

The conditions under which divorce can be permitted are based on an interpretation of the ruling of Deut. 24:1 (NIV translation): "If a man marries a woman who becomes displeasing to him because he finds something indecent about her, and he writes her a certificate of divorce, gives it to her and sends her from his house...". The ruling is based on the *'erwat dabar* (something indecent) of Deut. 24:1 (Sigal, 2007:111-117). The LXX translation reflects the meaning not as a sexual misdeed as such, but in a more general legal reason for divorce as ἄσχημον πρᾶγμα (something indecent). However, the translation could also be interpreted as an euphemistical reference to adultery or sexual immorality.

The Vulgate translates *erwat dabar* with *aliquam foeditatem* (something indecent), also not referring to sexual indecency as such, but to any reason of indecency. In rabbinic literature different interpretations of Deut. 24:1 appear. Rabbi Hillel (born approximately 110 BCE and died 10 CE) took the phrase in a broader sense to include actions such as a woman speaking disrespectfully of her husband or burning his food (Str-B 1.314-317). Rabbi Shammai (50 BCE – 30 CE) interpreted the indecency more narrowly to include adultery, and according to the moral customs of the day, as a woman appearing on the street with her hair down, with uncovered arms or a slit on the side of her skirt (Str-B 1.315) (Guelich, 1982:203; Weren, 1979:72). The Shammaite school of thought, however, took Deut. 24:1 to refer to adultery as such (Betz, 1995:247). The Qumran community did not allow divorce for any reason (11QTemple 57:17-19) (Mueller, 1980:247-256). From these materials it is clear that Deut. 24:1 was interpreted differently. In the third "antithesis" Jesus argues (similar to the Shammaite school of thought) that πορνεία (adultery) can be the only ground for divorce, as such an act *de facto* annuls a marriage by creating a new sexual relation in its place (Janzen, 2000:66-80).

Matthew claims that Jesus calls on his followers to appreciate the true intention of marriage. Marriage was intended as a lifelong union between man and woman, and should not be dissolved lightly. Moses did not command divorce, but a certificate from a man if he indeed divorced his wife. This bill of divorce was intended to protect women against the harshness of men. "The aim of the legislation is not to condone divorce as such, but to mitigate its evil consequences" (Stonehouse, 1944:204). A man could not simply chase his wife away and afterwards claim that she is still his wife. The bill of divorce implied that the husband gave up his claim to a wife (Morris, 1992:121) as if she were his "possession".

The antithetical argument in Matt. 5:31-32 therefore does not negate the commandment of Deut. 24:1 on divorce. The sorrowful possibility of divorce is accepted, but the grounds on which divorce can be permitted are strictly limited. The Law is still in place, but elevated to a level according to the quest for greater δικαιοσύνη (righteousness) as stated in Matt. 5:20. Matthew presents Jesus not as abrogating the Law, but as revealing its true intention (Matt. 5:17).

5.4.4 The antithetical argument on oaths (Matt. 5:33-37)

The fourth antithetical argument opens the second triad of *halakhic* arguments.

Matt. 5:33: Thesis Introductory formula: Πάλιν ἠκούσατε ὅτι ἐρρέθη τοῖς ἀρχαίοις Two-part ruling: Οὐκ ἐπιορκήσεις (negative), ἀποδώσεις δὲ τῷ Κυρίῳ τοὺς ὅρκους σου (positive).	Again, you have heard that it was said to the people long ago, 'Do not break your oath, but fulfil to the Lord the vows you have made.'
Matt. 5:34a: Antithesis Introductory formula: ἐγὼ δὲ λέγω ὑμῖν μὴ ὀμόσαι ὅλως·	But I tell you, do not swear an oath at all:
Matt. 5:34b-36: Four-fold reason μήτε ἐν τῷ οὐρανῷ, ὅτι θρόνος ἐστὶν τοῦ Θεοῦ· μήτε ἐν τῇ γῇ, ὅτι ὑποπόδιόν ἐστιν τῶν ποδῶν αὐτοῦ· μήτε εἰς Ἱεροσόλυμα, ὅτι πόλις ἐστὶν τοῦ μεγάλου Βασιλέως· μήτε ἐν τῇ κεφαλῇ σου ὀμόσῃς, ὅτι οὐ δύνασαι μίαν τρίχα λευκὴν ποιῆσαι ἢ μέλαιναν.	either by heaven, for it is God's throne; or by the earth, for it is his footstool; or by Jerusalem, for it is the city of the Great King. And do not swear by your head, for you cannot make even one hair white or black.
Matt. 5:37: Simple alternative ἔστω δὲ ὁ λόγος ὑμῶν ναὶ ναί, οὒ οὔ· τὸ δὲ περισσὸν τούτων ἐκ τοῦ πονηροῦ ἐστιν.	All you need to say is simply 'Yes' or 'No'; anything beyond this comes from the evil one.

Table 21: The antithetical argument on oaths in Matt. 5:33-37

5.4.4.1 Thesis (Matt. 5:33)

Matthew's Jesus opens the fourth antithetical statement with πάλιν (again), which marks a new beginning, thus linking the first three statements to the last three in the series of six. This is fittingly followed by the full introductory formula ἠκούσατε ὅτι ἐρρέθη τοῖς ἀρχαίοις (you have heard that it was said to the people long ago) (Matt. 5:33a), demonstrating a parallel in the triadic structure.

After the introductory formula the thesis is not given in the exact words of the Hebrew Bible, but in a two-part compressed compilation of the teaching on taking oaths (Matt. 5:33b). Matthew's Jesus uses both the negative and the positive to emphasise the importance of a sworn testimony.

The first part of the composite citation comes as a negative, οὐκ ἐπιορκήσεις (do not brake your oath) and is closely related to Lev. 19:12, "do not swear falsely by my name". It is significant that the LXX version of the text added a reference to unrighteousness: καὶ οὐκ ὀμεῖσθε τῷ ὀνόματί μου ἐπ᾽ ἀδίκῳ (and do not swear unrighteously by my name). Swearing in God's name is prohibited when it is linked with unrighteousness, and oath-taking was necessary for this reason. The LXX version fits well with the plea in Matt. 5:20 for δικαιοσύνη (righteousness) that exceeds those of the scribes and the Pharisees. Matthew usually referred to the LXX version[139] in his quotations. As the necessity of taking oaths was associated with the problem of unrighteousness, it explains Jesus' total rejection of oaths for his followers (Foster, 2004:116).

The second part of the thesis comes as a positive ἀποδώσεις τῷ κυρίῳ τοὺς ὅρκους σου (but fulfil to the Lord the vows you have made) and relates to Num. 30:2, Deut. 23:21-23 and Ps. 50:14. It states that vows should be honoured as they have been made to the Lord. Such an oath is true before the Lord. Gundry (1994:92) points out how Matthew substitutes oaths for vows as in Ps. 50:14. This shift in terminology demonstrates that the distinction between oaths and vows was generally not clear (Davies, 1966:129). Matthew's Jesus uses a summative and composite citation from Jewish Scriptures of the topic without making use of lengthy verbatim quotations. This enables him to focus on his authoritative counter-proposal.

5.4.4.2   *"Antithesis" (Matt. 5:34a)*

As with the previous three cases, Jesus' antithetical proposal opens with ἐγὼ δὲ λέγω ὑμῖν (but I tell you), but it does not continue with the phrase ὅτι πᾶς ὁ ... (that anyone who ...) as they do. Instead a new fixed form is introduced for the fourth to the sixth antithetical phrases with a direct appeal, not to a hypothetical third party, but to the direct audience who are instructed to conform to the imperative of the "antitheses". This second person group are in the historical setting the disciples of Jesus, but in the narrative world the auditors of Matthew's Gospel (Foster, 2004:120).

The fourth antithesis reads μὴ ὀμόσαι ὅλως (do not swear an oath at all) (Matt. 5:34a). Apparently the system of oaths is undercut with a simple contrasting prohibition to swear at all. Some scholars view this prohibition as a clear cut revocation of this legislation of the Law in the Hebrew Bible (e.g. Meier,

---

[139] At that stage, however, there was no standardized version of the LXX.

1976:150). This assumption is strengthened with the words τὸ δὲ περισσὸν τούτων ἐκ τοῦ πονηροῦ ἐστιν (anything beyond this comes from the evil one) (Matt. 5:37). This issue indeed becomes problematic, as the Hebrew Bible commanded the taking of an oath in specific cases, e.g. the when goods of a neighbour were lost or stolen while a man was supposed to safeguard it (Exod. 22:6-7, 10) or when a woman was suspected of adultery (Num. 5:19-22). Furthermore Deut. 6:13 and 10:20 regulate the taking of oaths in general. The impression is that Matthew's Jesus intentionally presents this issue in the form in which the Jews commonly understood the issue. However, underlying this, it seems that people thought that a lie between people did not concern God, but when the divine Name has been evoked, one could expect to be punished as the Lord's honour was at stake (Morris, 1992:123). Swearing implied self-cursing should one not speak the truth when making an appeal to God. The implication is that only when an oath was sworn did it have to be truthful.

5.4.4.3 Fourfold reason (Matt. 5:34b-36)

Matthew's Jesus continues his counter-proposal with a motivation for this imperative not to swear at all. He does this in two sections. The first section consists of three parallel ways to avoid the divine name when taking oaths (Matt. 5:34b-35) and then by swearing by the head of a human (Matt. 5:36).

With the triadic parallelism (Matt. 5:34b-35) Matthew's Jesus probably refers to established circumlocutions for the divine name in taking oaths. It seems as if people easily took oaths. Oaths played an important role in Judaism. The *Mishnah* has a complete tractate (the sixth treatise of the order *Nezikin*, and is divided into eight chapters, containing sixty-two paragraphs) on oaths (*Shebu'ot*). Three classes are identified with examples of valid and invalid oaths (Morris, 1992:122).

With the three examples (Matt. 5:34b-35) Matthew's Jesus rules out three possible oath referents, namely heaven, earth and Jerusalem[140], which primarily reflects the Jewish notion of avoiding the use of the Tetragrammaton[141]:

---

[140] Without necessarily indicating a direct textual relation, Jas. 5:12 also states a threefold form when taking oaths: "Above all, my brothers, do not swear – not by heaven or by earth or by anything else".

[141] According to Deut. 6:13 and 10:20 oaths were to be made in God's name. By the first century, however, the Jews would no longer pronounce his name, and therefore substitutes for God's name were used (Davies & Allison, 2004a:536).

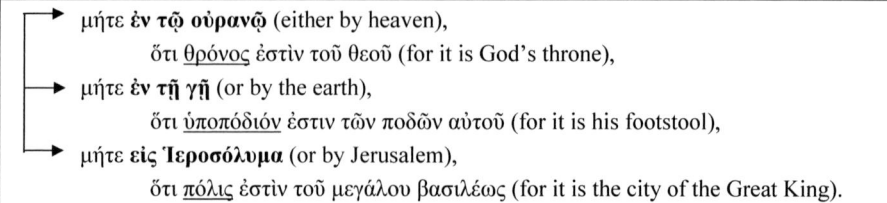

Table 22: Three classes of valid and invalid oaths in Matt. 5:34b-35

Morris has argued that Jews had lengthy discussions on when an oath should be considered binding and when not. "People would swear by heaven or earth or a similar oath and later claim that they were not bound by that oath because God was not mentioned" (Morris, 1992:124)[142]. Jesus, however, links to each referent a ὅτι-(for) statement to indicate how that oath imposes upon the divine realm anyway. These statements are probably reminiscent of Isa. 66:1[143]. Jesus therefore ridicules such a circumlocution of the binding of oaths.

Matt. 5:36 then rejects another form of taking an oath:

> μήτε ἐν τῇ κεφαλῇ σου ὀμόσῃς (and do not swear by your head),
> ὅτι οὐ δύνασαι μίαν τρίχα λευκὴν ποιῆσαι ἢ μέλαιναν (for you cannot make even one hair white or black).

Table 23: A fourth form of oath-taking rejected in Matt. 5:36

This fourth statement differs in style and content from the previous three. The reason is no longer a positive statement about the realm of God, but a negative one concerning human powerlessness (Osborne, 2010:20). The reason for not swearing moves from the greatness of God to the littleness of humans. The reason now is not the fear of the Lord, but the impotence of humans (Morris, 1992:125).

With these four reasons the oath taking of the opponents of Jesus and the Matthean community is clearly parodied.

---

[142] According to *Shebu'ot* 4:13 oaths "by heaven or by earth" are regarded as not binding.

[143] Swearing "by the earth" does not avoid the link with God, for God says: "Heaven is my throne, and the earth is my footstool" (Isa. 66:1).

5.4.4.4 Simple alternative (Matt. 5:37)

In the final verse of the fourth antithetical statement the alternative of taking an oath is given: ἔστω δὲ ὁ λόγος ὑμῶν ναὶ ναί, οὒ οὔ·(all you need to say is simply 'Yes' or 'No') (Matt. 5:37a)[144]. Matthew's Jesus concludes the antithesis with a remark that every alternative to this proposition is bad; τὸ δὲ περισσὸν τούτων ἐκ τοῦ πονηροῦ ἐστιν (anything beyond this comes from the evil one) (Matt. 5:37b). As mentioned before, these concluding words compel some scholars to assert that this clearly implies an abrogation of the stipulations of the taking of oaths.

In an attempt to unravel the issue, Betz (1995:271) has suggested that with ἐκ τοῦ πονηροῦ (from the evil one) Jesus alludes to magical formulations from the demonic realm: "Overtones of demonic evil cannot be denied, because 'oath' was understood since Hesiod[145] to be a demonic being". The use of the definite article before πονηροῦ (evil) is likely to refer to the personification of evil (Foster, 2004:121). However, there is no necessity to link these words to Hesiod to understand Jesus' negative pronouncement about oaths. Jesus simply argues that it should never be necessary for his followers to swear an oath before people should believe them. Their words should always be reliable, so that nothing more than straightforward statements should be needed from them. The righteousness of the followers of Jesus should be such that their statements should be thoroughly reliable so that the taking of an oath would be unnecessary[146]. Their "greater δικαιοσύνη (righteousness)" (Matt. 5:20) will be demonstrated in such a way[147].

---

[144] This conclusion is also closely related to the concluding words of Jas. 5:12: "Let your 'Yes' be yes, and your 'No,' no, or you will be condemned".

[145] The Greek poet Hesiod is generally thought by scholars to have been active between 750 and 650 BC.

[146] Matthew's negative critique of oaths surfaces at several incidents: Matthew's Jesus rejects the misuse of the *Korban* vow (Matt. 15:3-6) and the hypocritical use of vows by the scribes and the Pharisees (Matt. 23:16-22). False testimonies are brought in against Jesus during his trial (Matt. 26:59-62), but when Jesus is instructed to speak under oath, He replies without an oath (Matt. 26:63-64). Peter denies Jesus, the second and third time under oath (Matt. 26:74-74).

[147] Such a prohibition of the swearing of oaths also occurs in the Damascus Document of Qumran (Vermes, 1975:108). Josephus wrote about the Essenes: "any word of theirs has more force than an oath; swearing they avoid, regarding it as worse than perjury, for they say that one who is not believed without an appeal to God stands condemned already" (War. 2:135).

As with the previous antithetical statements, Jesus argues that returning to the ideal of a truthful and righteous society, the taking of oaths becomes unnecessary. The taking of oaths is actually an admission that the society has failed to be truthful.

5.4.5 The antithetical argument on retaliation (Matt. 5:38-42)

With the fifth argument Jesus continues with the theme of a higher form of ethics and righteousness. Jesus not only instructs his followers not to retaliate, but even to do more than their enemies would ask for.

Matt. 5:38: Thesis	
Introductory formula: Ἠκούσατε ὅτι ἐρρέθη	"You have heard that it was said,
Ruling: Ὀφθαλμὸν ἀντὶ ὀφθαλμοῦ καὶ ὀδόντα ἀντὶ ὀδόντος.	'Eye for eye, and tooth for tooth.'
Matt. 5:39a: Antithesis	
Introductory formula: ἐγὼ δὲ λέγω ὑμῖν	But I tell you,
Antithetical statement: μὴ ἀντιστῆναι τῷ πονηρῷ· ·	do not resist an evil person.
Matt. 5:39b-42: Four examples	
ἀλλ' ὅστις σε ῥαπίζει εἰς τὴν δεξιὰν σιαγόνα σου, στρέψον αὐτῷ καὶ τὴν ἄλλην	If anyone slaps you on the right cheek, turn to them the other cheek also.
καὶ τῷ θέλοντί σοι κριθῆναι καὶ τὸν χιτῶνά σου λαβεῖν, ἄφες αὐτῷ καὶ τὸ ἱμάτιον·	And if anyone wants to sue you and take your shirt, hand over your coat as well.
καὶ ὅστις σε ἀγγαρεύσει μίλιον ἕν, ὕπαγε μετ' αὐτοῦ δύο.	If anyone forces you to go one mile, go with them two miles.
τῷ αἰτοῦντί σε δός, καὶ τὸν θέλοντα ἀπὸ σοῦ δανίσασθαι μὴ ἀποστραφῇς.	Give to the one who asks you, and do not turn away from the one who wants to borrow from you.

Table 24: The antithetical argument on retaliation in Matt. 5:38-42

5.4.5.1 Thesis (Matt. 5:38)

The introductory formula of the second argument of the second group of three parallels has the exact form of the second argument of the first group: ἐκούσατε ὅτι ἐρρέθη (you have heard that it was said) (Matt. 5:38a). This once again demonstrates an aspect of the careful structuring of the entire argumentative sequence. As in the third and fourth argument, this formula is followed by a summary of *Torah* legislation, rather than a verbatim quotation. The compressed citation ὀφθαλμὸν ἀντὶ ὀφθαλμοῦ καὶ ὀδόντα ἀντὶ ὀδόντος (eye for eye and tooth for tooth) (Matt. 5:38b) refers to three passages from the

Pentateuch, Exod. 21:24, Lev. 24:20 and Deut. 19:21. It is important to realize that the *lex talionis* was not intended to sanction revenge as such, but to prevent excesses of punishment. The Law regulated equivalent compensation without respect to person[148].

5.4.5.2   *"Antithesis" (Matt. 5:39a)*

With a slightly modified version, the emphatic introduction of Jesus' counterproposal is similar to that of the previous antithesis ἐγὼ δὲ λέγω ὑμῖν μὴ ... (but I tell you do not ...). The imperative that follows, then denounces any form of retaliation ἀντιστῆναι τῷ πονηρῷ (do not resist an evil person) (Matt. 5:39a). The fact that Matthew intentionally portrays the *lex talionis* as the Jewish norm probably signifies the strenuous relation between his community and the Jewish community from which it has separated (Broer, 1994:20). The "bad one" possibly refers to religious opponents of the Matthean community which they experienced as oppressive and unjust (Hare, 1967:122). Matthew's Jesus demands from his followers not to retaliate, specifically not under these circumstances. The thought is not that evil should remain unopposed, but that evil should be answered with good (Osborne, 2010:208). Followers of Jesus must refuse to drop to the level of the aggressor by returning evil for evil.

5.4.5.3   *Four examples (Matt. 5:39b-42)*

Matthew follows the imperative of how the evil person should not be resisted with three specific examples (Matt. 5:39b-41) and a general principle (Matt. 5:42).

The three specific examples are:

ἀλλ' ὅστις σε ῥαπίζει εἰς τὴν δεξιὰν σιαγόνα [σου] (if anyone slaps you on the right cheek)
    στρέψον αὐτῷ καὶ τὴν ἄλλην·(turn to them the other cheek also).
καὶ τῷ θέλοντί σοι κριθῆναι καὶ τὸν χιτῶνά σου λαβεῖν (and if anyone wants to sue you and take your shirt),
    ἄφες αὐτῷ καὶ τὸ ἱμάτιον·(hand over your coat as well).
καὶ ὅστις σε ἀγγαρεύσει μίλιον ἕν (and if anyone forces you to go one mile),
    ὕπαγε μετ' αὐτοῦ δύο (go with them two miles)

Table 25: Three specific examples on how not to resist evil persons in Matt. 5:39b-41

---

[148] The *lex talionis* has already been expressed in the Code of *Hammurabi* (dd. c. 18th century BC) (Morris, 1992:126).

Matt. 5:39b-42 has a parallel in Luk. 6:29-30 in a variant form. In Luke Jesus addresses the crowds and his disciples with the Sermon on the Plain. The Lukan version does not form part of a *halakhic* argument.

Matt. 5:39b-42	Luk. 6:29-30
ἀλλ' ὅστις σε ῥαπίζει εἰς τὴν δεξιὰν σιαγόνα [σου] στρέψον αὐτῷ καὶ τὴν ἄλλην καὶ τῷ θέλοντί σοι κριθῆναι καὶ τὸν χιτῶνά σου λαβεῖν ἄφες αὐτῷ καὶ τὸ ἱμάτιον καὶ ὅστις σε ἀγγαρεύσει μίλιον ἕν ὕπαγε μετ' αὐτοῦ δύο 39b If anyone slaps you on the right cheek, turn to them the other cheek also. 40 And if anyone wants to sue you and take your shirt, hand over your coat as well. 41 If anyone forces you to go one mile, go with them two miles. 42 Give to the one who asks you, and do not turn away from the one who wants to borrow from you.	29 τῷ τύπτοντί σε ἐπὶ τὴν σιαγόνα πάρεχε καὶ τὴν ἄλλην, καὶ ἀπὸ τοῦ αἴροντός σου τὸ ἱμάτιον καὶ τὸν χιτῶνα μὴ κωλύσῃς. 30 παντὶ αἰτοῦντί σε δίδου, καὶ ἀπὸ τοῦ αἴροντος τὰ σὰ μὴ ἀπαίτει. 29 If someone slaps you on one cheek, turn to them the other also. If someone takes your coat, do not withhold your shirt from them. 30 Give to everyone who asks you, and if anyone takes what belongs to you, do not demand it back.

Table 26: The parallel between Matt. 5:39b-42 and Luk. 6:29-30 on avoiding retaliation

The first illustrative example (Matt. 5:39b) presents a slightly fuller form of the saying also found in Luk. 6:29a. Jeremias (1963:29) has suggested that this example refers to insults the audience had to suffer on behalf of Jesus. A slap on the right cheek by a right-handed person probably refers hitting with the back of the hand. Jews regarded such a slap as extra insulting. According the *Mishnah*, such an action carried a double fine (*Baba Qammah*. 8:6).

The second example (Matt. 5:40) is also paralleled by Luk. 6:29b, though in a variant form. Once again followers of Jesus are urged to avoid any confrontation with their opponents and oppressors. The proper response to an opponent, who deprives a disciple of his inner garment, is not to resist, but even to give the outer garment as well. The outer garment was more expensive and one that even the poorest had the right to keep (as it was used for their bedding as well), and it could not be taken away permanently (Exod. 22:26-27 and Deut. 24:12-13) (Osborne, 2010:209). This example possibly reveals an aspect of the social situation of the Matthean community, who suffered a form of quasi-legal prosecution by its opponents (Foster, 2004:128).

The third example (Matt. 5:41) is unique to Matthew. This saying resembles the Roman practice of requisitioning transportation of goods. This example probably anticipates the story of the Roman soldiers who requisitioned Simon of Cyrene to carry the cross of Jesus (Gundry, 1994:94). It seems that the evangelist thus indicates some link between Jesus' suffering and the experience of his followers.

These three examples possibly reflect something of the turmoil that the Matthean community had experienced because of their faith. In all three cases provocative and even subversive contrasts are proposed against the misuse of power that often rules the world (Luz, 1990:328). "The aggression enacted by the adversaries of the community is to be overcome by the non-violent reaction of group members" (Foster, 2004:125).

After the three specific examples, Matt. 5:42 concludes the fifth "antithesis" with a general and summative principle τῷ αἰτοῦντί σε δός, καὶ τὸν θέλοντα ἀπὸ σοῦ δανίσασθαι μὴ ἀποστραφῇς (give to the one who asks you, and do not turn away from the one who wants to borrow from you). Jesus demands of his followers not only to refuse retaliation, but to actively seek generosity by helping the very same people who demanded things from them (Osborne, 2010:206). Hagner (1993:132) has remarked: "It is the unworthy who experienced the surprise of unexpected grace, so they act in similar manner toward the undeserving among them".

Some scholars (Foster, 2004:122; Guelich, 1982:224; Meier, 1976:157) see the denouncement in this "antithesis" as another example of the annulment of judicial stipulations of the *Torah*. However, when reading this argument of Jesus along with his urging of his community to a greater righteousness, a different scenario appears. Jesus requires an unselfish attitude regarding one's own rights and a positive concern for others. With this argument Jesus once again wishes to demonstrate a higher form of δικαιοσύνη (righteousness) that should distinguish his followers from their opponents.

5.4.6 The antithetical argument on love for enemies (Matt. 5:43-47)

The theme of higher δικαιοσύνη (righteousness) amidst persecution is continued in the final "antithesis" of the series. The extended treatment of the topic of persecution in the final beatitude (Matt. 5:11-12) is picked up again in this final argument. The threat of persecution presumably felt very real for Matthew's audience because of their parting with the synagogue, which resulted in a strenuous relationship with their familiar religious and social environment, as argued in Chapter 2 of this study.

Matt. 5:43: Thesis Introductory formula: Ἠκούσατε ὅτι ἐρρέθη Double ruling: Ἀγαπήσεις τὸν πλησίον σου καὶ μισήσεις τὸν ἐχθρόν σου.	"You have heard that it was said, 'Love your neighbour and hate your enemy.'
Matt. 5:44: Antithesis Introductory formula: ἐγὼ δὲ λέγω ὑμῖν, Twofold antithetical statement: ἀγαπᾶτε τοὺς ἐχθροὺς ὑμῶν καὶ προσεύχεσθε ὑπὲρ τῶν διωκόντων ὑμᾶς·	 But I tell you, love your enemies and pray for those who persecute you,
Matt. 5:45: First Reason ὅπως γένησθε υἱοὶ τοῦ Πατρὸς ὑμῶν τοῦ ἐν οὐρανοῖς, ὅτι τὸν ἥλιον αὐτοῦ ἀνατέλλει ἐπὶ πονηροὺς καὶ ἀγαθοὺς καὶ βρέχει ἐπὶ δικαίους καὶ ἀδίκους.	 that you may be children of your Father in heaven. He causes his sun to rise on the evil and the good, and sends rain on the righteous and the unrighteous.
Matt. 5:46-47: Second reason ἐὰν γὰρ ἀγαπήσητε τοὺς ἀγαπῶντας ὑμᾶς, τίνα μισθὸν ἔχετε; οὐχὶ καὶ οἱ τελῶναι τὸ αὐτὸ ποιοῦσιν; καὶ ἐὰν ἀσπάσησθε τοὺς ἀδελφοὺς ὑμῶν μόνον, τί περισσὸν ποιεῖτε; οὐχὶ καὶ οἱ ἐθνικοὶ τὸ αὐτὸ ποιοῦσιν;	 If you love those who love you, what reward will you get? Are not even the tax collectors doing that? And if you greet only your own people, what are you doing more than others? Do not even pagans do that?

Table 27: The antithetical argument on love for enemies in Matt. 5:43-47

5.4.6.1 Thesis (Matt. 5:43)

As expected, the introductory formula corresponds with that of the fourth argument, but in a fuller form: ἐκούσατε ὅτι ἐρρέθη (you have heard that it was said) (Matt. 5:43a), also found in the second (Matt. 5:27) and fifth (Matt. 5:38) statements. This extended version forms a climactic ending, but also refers to the role of hearing in the context of persecution.

The thesis to which Jesus responds consists of two rulings: ἀγαπήσεις τὸν πλησίον σου (love your neighbour) and μισήσεις τὸν ἐχθρόν σου (hate your enemy) (Matt. 5:43). The first ruling refers to Lev. 19:18 in which the final element of "as yourself" is dropped. Morris (1992:129) has suggested that this omission can be assigned to the Matthean scribes lowering this standard of Leviticus. Jesus here refers to their derived attitude regarding this command. However, in previous theses, Matthew also offered references to the Law in abbreviated form. It rather seems that Matthew used the abbreviated forms to focus on the "antithesis" that follows, while the full reference is assumed. This abbreviated form also allows him to form a parallelism with the second ruling.

The second ruling on the hating of enemies does not have a direct parallel in the Hebrew Bible. The teaching in the Hebrew Bible with regard to enemies is complex. Elements of hating enemies can be found in several texts, such as Exod. 34:12 and Deut. 7:2; 20:16; 23:4, 7. The Psalmist also speaks of hating those who hate God (e.g. Ps. 139:21-22). On the other hand, the Hebrew Bible also commands believers to love resident aliens (Lev. 19:34) and help enemies (Exod. 23:4-5 and Prov. 25:21-22). Matthew probably responds to the popular understanding of the love of neighbours, which in practice leads to a negative attitude towards enemies. This attitude appears strongly in the Qumran Manual: "They may love all the sons of light … and hate all the sons of darkness" (1 QS 1:3-4, 9-10).

5.4.6.2 "Antithesis" (Matt. 5:44)

Similar to the previous five "antitheses", the emphatic contrasting alternative thesis then follows; ἐγὼ δὲ λέγω ὑμῖν (but I tell you) (Matt. 5:44a). Two imperatives are given: ἀγαπᾶτε τοὺς ἐχθροὺς ὑμῶν (love your enemies) and προσεύχεσθε ὑπὲρ τῶν διωκόντων ὑμᾶς (pray for those who persecute you) (Matt. 5:44bc), which oppose the second imperative of verse 43, καὶ μισήσεις τὸν ἐχθρόν σου (and hate your enemies).

The Sermon on the Plain has a similar imperative, which according to the Q-theory, derives from Q-material.

Matt. 5:44	Luk. 6:27-28
ἀγαπᾶτε τοὺς ἐχθροὺς ὑμῶν καὶ προσεύχεσθε ὑπὲρ τῶν διωκόντων ὑμᾶς love your enemies and pray for those who persecute you	[27] Ἀγαπᾶτε τοὺς ἐχθροὺς ὑμῶν, καλῶς ποιεῖτε τοῖς μισοῦσιν ὑμᾶς, [28] εὐλογεῖτε τοὺς καταρωμένους ὑμᾶς, προσεύχεσθε περὶ τῶν ἐπηρεαζόντων ὑμᾶς. [27]: Love your enemies, do good to those who hate you, [28] bless those who curse you, pray for those who mistreat you.

Table 28: The parallel between Matt. 5:44 and Luk. 6:27-28 on loving one's enemies

Matthew's version of the imperatives is shortened and unlike Luke, forms an antithesis in a halakhic argument.

Piper (1979:174) has proposed that the command of enemy love in Matthew is determined by the eschatological situation that Jesus brought. The *lex talionis* forms part of the old aeon (age) of sin and strife. Yet, those that have been transferred to the Kingdom of Heaven are already taking part in the new aeon. Followers of Jesus experienced the tension between these two ages. The counter-proposal exhibits parallels with Luk. 6:27-28[149], though Matthew's variant draws elements from the final beatitude in Matt. 5:11-12[150]. Matt. 5:44 seemingly refers to persecution as in Matt. 5:11, 12, which probably reflects the persecution the Matthean community feared and somehow experienced. This could have caused bitterness towards members of the society who blamed them for being followers of Jesus. Therefore Matthew reminds his readers that Jesus urges them to love their enemies and to pray for those who persecute them. Love is combined with prayer for persecutors. It is more than a sentimental feeling, and should be an honest desire for their good. With this counter-proposal Matthew's Jesus upholds and intensifies the command to love one's neighbour (Matt. 5:43b), but counters emerging attitudes to hate one's enemy (Matt. 5:43c). This counter-proposal should therefore not be seen as a revocation of the *Torah* as such, but as a deviation to some understanding which limits the love commandment. Matthew's Jesus rejects a negative attitude towards outsiders that presumably developed from *Torah* tradition.

5.4.6.3   Reasons (Matt. 5:45-47)

Matthew's provides two reasons for his command.

---

[149] Luk. 6:27-28: Ἀγαπᾶτε τοὺς ἐχθροὺς ὑμῶν, καλῶς ποιεῖτε τοῖς μισοῦσιν ὑμᾶς, εὐλογεῖτε τοὺς καταρωμένους ὑμᾶς, προσεύχεσθε περὶ τῶν ἐπηρεαζόντων ὑμᾶς (Love your enemies, do good to those who hate you, bless those who curse you, pray for those who mistreat you).

[150] Matt. 5:11-12: μακάριοί ἐστε ὅταν ὀνειδίσωσιν ὑμᾶς καὶ διώξωσιν καὶ εἴπωσιν πᾶν πονηρὸν καθ' ὑμῶν [ψευδόμενοι] ἕνεκεν ἐμοῦ. χαίρετε καὶ ἀγαλλιᾶσθε, ὅτι ὁ μισθὸς ὑμῶν πολὺς ἐν τοῖς οὐρανοῖς· οὕτως γὰρ ἐδίωξαν τοὺς προφήτας τοὺς πρὸ ὑμῶν ("Blessed are you when people insult you, persecute you and falsely say all kinds of evil against you because of me. Rejoice and be glad, because great is your reward in heaven, for in the same way they persecuted the prophets who were before you).

4.6.3.1   To become sons of God

He starts off with the promise that those who follow Him will be sons of God, ὅπως γένησθε υἱοὶ τοῦ πατρὸς ὑμῶν τοῦ ἐν οὐρανοῖς (that you may be sons of your Father in heaven). One's eschatological blessing is related to one's obedience to the command of enemy love (Piper, 1979:173). The command of enemy love has to be obeyed if one is to enjoy the blessings of God's kingdom. McNeile (1980:71) has remarked: "Sons are those who partake of their Father's character". Verse 45 continues the theme that there should be no distinction between those to be loved, ὅτι τὸν ἥλιον αὐτοῦ ἀνατέλλει ἐπὶ πονηροὺς καὶ ἀγαθοὺς καὶ βρέχει ἐπὶ δικαίους καὶ ἀδίκους (because He causes his sun to rise on the evil and the good, and sends rain on the righteous and the unrighteous). The fundamental motivation for Jesus' command for enemy love is the mercy of God (Piper, 1979:173). Plummer (1982:89) has remarked: "To return evil for good is devilish; to return good for good is human; to return good for evil is divine". This promise of becoming sons and daughters of the heavenly Father, thematically links up with the seventh beatitude that peacemakers will be called sons of God (Matt. 5:9) and reference to evil (Matt. 6:11) and heavens (Matt. 5:12) in the extended last beatitude. The love of the followers of Jesus is based on the love of God. God's good gifts, the sunshine and the rain, are given to all, bad as well as good. Jesus' followers must show the same generosity.

4.6.3.2   Different to tax collectors and pagans

Matt. 5:46-47 presents the second reason for the alternative command of Jesus in a carefully constructed isocolon. Each part consists of a conditional clause followed by two double rhetorical questions:

First conditional clause (Matt. 5:46)
ἐὰν γὰρ ἀγαπήσητε τοὺς ἀγαπῶντας ὑμᾶς (If you love those who love you,
τίνα μισθὸν ἔχετε (what reward will you get?);
οὐχὶ καὶ οἱ τελῶναι τὸ αὐτὸ ποιοῦσιν (are not even the tax collectors doing that?)
Second conditional clause (Matt. 5:47)
καὶ ἐὰν ἀσπάσησθε τοὺς ἀδελφοὺς ὑμῶν μόνον (and if you greet only your own people),
τί περισσὸν ποιεῖτε (what are you doing more than others?);
οὐχὶ καὶ οἱ ἐθνικοὶ τὸ αὐτὸ ποιοῦσιν (do not even pagans do that?);

Table 29: Two conditional clauses of the love that Jesus commands in Matt. 5:46-47

This second reason also has a parallel in the Sermon on the Plain. Once again Matthew's version is shortened and forms part of *halakhic* argument.

Matt. 5:46-47	Luk. 6:32-34
⁴⁶ ἐὰν γὰρ ἀγαπήσητε τοὺς ἀγαπῶντας ὑμᾶς τίνα μισθὸν ἔχετε; οὐχὶ καὶ οἱ τελῶναι τὸ αὐτὸ ποιοῦσιν ⁴⁷ καὶ ἐὰν ἀσπάσησθε τοὺς ἀδελφοὺς ὑμῶν μόνον, τί περισσὸν ποιεῖτε; οὐχὶ καὶ οἱ ἐθνικοὶ τὸ αὐτὸ; ⁴⁶ If you love those who love you, what reward will you get? Are not even the tax collectors doing that? ⁴⁷ And if you greet only your own people, what are you doing more than others? Do not even pagans do that?	³² καὶ εἰ ἀγαπᾶτε τοὺς ἀγαπῶντας ὑμᾶς, ποία ὑμῖν χάρις ἐστίν; καὶ γὰρ οἱ ἁμαρτωλοὶ τοὺς ἀγαπῶντας αὐτοὺς ἀγαπῶσιν. ³³ **καὶ γὰρ ἐὰν ἀγαθοποιῆτε τοὺς ἀγαθοποιοῦντας ὑμᾶς, ποία ὑμῖν χάρις ἐστίν; καὶ οἱ ἁμαρτωλοὶ τὸ αὐτὸ ποιοῦσιν.** ³⁴ καὶ ἐὰν δανίσητε παρ' ὧν ἐλπίζετε λαβεῖν, ποία ὑμῖν χάρις ἐστίν; καὶ ἁμαρτωλοὶ ἁμαρτωλοῖς δανίζουσιν ἵνα ἀπολάβωσιν τὰ ἴσα. ³² If you love those who love you, what credit is that to you? Even sinners love those who love them. ³³ And if you do good to those who are good to you, what credit is that to you? Even sinners do that. ³⁴ And if you lend to those from whom you expect repayment, what credit is that to you? Even sinners lend to sinners, expecting to be repaid in full.

Table 30: The parallel between Matt. 5:46-47 and Luk.6:32-34 on Jesus' alternative command for love

In Matt. 5:46-37 earlier themes in Matt. 5 are taken up with the mentioning of reward (cf. Matt. 5:12) and righteousness (cf. Matt. 5:20). Both these questions urge the followers of Jesus to greater righteousness, as stated in Matt. 5:20. They are called to more than an internally focussed love (Foster, 2004:137).

The isocolon illustrates the implications of the love command. The verb ἀσπάσησθε (you greet) stands parallel with ἀγαπήσητε (you love). Greeting goes along with loving, with the implication that one should show favour (Hagner, 1993:135). The Jewish greeting was "peace", which implied a prayer. In the ancient Mediterranean society, the type of greeting a person received, demonstrated their social status in society (Osborne, 2010:213). According to Matt. 23:7, the scribes and the Pharisee elite loved demonstrative greetings. It might be that the Matthean community, because of their alienation from the synagogue, refused to continue recognizing the social status the social elite and preferred not to greet them (Betz, 1995:959).

The love that Matthew's Jesus requires extends outside the "in-group" to include outsiders and opponents. Such an attitude depicts the higher form of ethics required of followers of Jesus.

5.4.7 Being perfect as conclusion to the series of antithetical arguments (Matt. 5:48)

Matt. 5:48 is directly linked with the last antithetical statement, but also forms the conclusion of the series of six: Ἔσεσθε οὖν ὑμεῖς τέλειοι ὡς ὁ πατὴρ ὑμῶν ὁ οὐράνιος τέλειός ἐστιν (be perfect, therefore, as your heavenly Father is perfect) (Osborne, 2010:214).

The parallel in Luke replaces being perfect (τέλειοι) with being merciful (οἰκτίρμονες), which is a redactional tendency with Luke (cf. Viljoen, 2003:199-209).

Matt. 5:48	Luk. 6:36
Ἔσεσθε οὖν ὑμεῖς **τέλειοι** ὡς ὁ πατὴρ ὑμῶν ὁ οὐράνιος **τέλειός** ἐστιν Be perfect, therefore, as your heavenly Father is perfect	Γίνεσθε **οἰκτίρμονες**, καθὼς ὁ Πατὴρ ὑμῶν **οἰκτίρμων** ἐστίν. Be merciful, just as your Father is merciful.

Table 31: The parallel between Matt. 5:48 and Luk. 6:36 on being perfect and merciful

The Matthean version strongly echoes Lev. 19:2: "Be holy because I, the Lord your God, am holy" and Deut. 18:13: "You must be blameless (LXX: τέλειός) before the Lord your God". These texts imply perfect adherence to the *Torah* (cf. Ps. 15:2; 84:11). Matthews's Jesus thus states that his explication of the *Torah* in the previous six *halakhic* arguments, illustrates perfect adherence to the *Torah*.

This imperative links up with the call for greater righteousness in Matt. 5:20. The opening δικαιοσύνη (righteousness) (Matt. 5:20) and the closing τέλειός (perfect) (Matt. 5:48) form an *inclusio* of the series emphasising Matthew's calling for a higher ethic for his community. This standard is set by the authoritative interpretation of the Law by Jesus (cf. Weren, 1979:72). The command is set as a future indicative form of the verb. Grammatically such a form implies a command, though Morris (1992:133) has proposed that Jesus here probably suggests a promise as well, which is grammatically possible (cf. Jordaan, 2014:72). His followers can count on divine assistance.

5.5 CONCLUSION

Based on the arguments in this chapter, it can be concluded that Matthew presents Jesus' teaching on the Law in a congruent manner. Jesus' antithetical arguments explain the higher form of righteousness that is required of his followers (Matt. 5:20), people who are regarded as citizens of the Kingdom of Heaven (Matt. 5:3, 10, 20). This would distinguish them from other Jewish movements. Matthew's Jesus quoted and abbreviated certain commandments from the Law while alluding to a common understanding of those commandments.

With ἐκούσατε ὅτι ἐρρέθη-theses Matthew's Jesus introduces a literal but misleading understanding of the *Torah*. He then follows with opposing ἐγὼ δὲ λέγω ὑμῖν-"antitheses". Matthew presents Jesus' antithetical statements not as second opinion, but as the authoritative declaration (Matt. 7:28-29) made by the Son of God to reveal the true intention of that stipulation.

- Matt. 5:21: Moses forbade murder (Exod. 20:13; Deut. 5:17).

    Matt. 5:22: Matthew's Jesus argues that this commandment implies more than physical murder to include a hateful attitude. The commandment actually requires a spirit of reconciliation.

- Matt. 5:27: Moses condemned adultery (Exod. 20:14; Deut. 5:18).

    Matt. 5:28: Matthew's Jesus argues that this commandment also includes adulterous thought, even of men who commonly were not thought to be adulterers.

- Matt. 5:31: Moses ordered a formal certificate in case of divorce (Deut. 24:1-4), which was understood as permission to divorce.

    Matt. 5:32: Matthew's Jesus argues that the certificate was intended to protect women from harsh realities and was not meant to be a means to easily dissolve a marriage. He restricts the permission for this formal certificate to cases where divorce *de facto* has already occurred because of adultery.

- Matt. 5:33: Moses gave rules for taking oaths (Lev. 19:12).

Matt. 5:34: Matthew's Jesus argues that the taking of oaths is only necessary in an unjust society. In a truthful society oaths should not be taken at all.

- Matt. 5:38: Moses recommended the precept: "eye for eye, tooth for tooth" (Exod. 21:24; Lev. 24:20; Deut. 19:21).

Matt. 5:39: Matthew's Jesus argues that retaliation should be completely avoided and that the sufferer is required to be benevolent towards the oppressor.

- Matt. 5:43: Moses required love for one's neighbour (Lev. 19:18), which was understood as permission to hate enemies.

Matt. 5:44: Matthew's Jesus argues that the love commandment does not exclude enemies. Love of the enemy, in effect love of all, is required.

These antithetical arguments left the crowds with amazement (Matt. 7:28-29).

Matthew argues that for Jesus the *Torah* functions differently than for the Pharisees and the teachers of the Law. Matthew's Jesus surpasses the mere literal meaning of the Law, but proceeds to unveil the true intention of its commandments. Jesus poses six theses, which He does not abrogate or even confirm, but transcends. Matthew's Jesus argues that the keeping of the *Torah* implies more than outward actions, as it starts with an inner heartfelt attitude that is reflected in outward actions. This reflects a change in anthropology. Human actions are controlled by persons' affective centres, their hearts. Women are more highly valued, so that they become more than objects of lust or possession of husbands. Persons outside the own group are also considered as objects of love.

CHAPTER 6

JESUS HEALING THE LEPER AND THE PURITY LAW IN THE GOSPEL OF MATTHEW

6.1 INTRODUCTION

It seems that Matthew's Jesus is not concerned with becoming impure or pure again after contracting impurity (Deines, 2008:65). Matthew does not mention any purification rites in connection with Jesus and the disciples, not even before entering the temple. He only describes Jesus taking actions that seemingly contravene purity regulations found in the Hebrew Bible. These include regulations such as refraining from contact with persons with skin diseases (Lev. 13-14 and Num. 5:2), but Jesus touches a leper (Matt. 8:3); or avoiding contact with woman with abnormal menstrual discharge (Lev. 25-30), but Jesus does not object when such a woman touches Him (Matt. 9:20-22); and avoiding contact with a dead body (Num 5:2; 19:11-13) or entering the room of a dead person (Num. 19:14), but Jesus enters the room with the dead girl and touches her (Matt. 9:25). In cases where such contact occurs accidentally or is necessary, the Hebrew Bible prescribes that the defiled person has to undergo specific purification rites (Num. 19). The neglect of such purification rites was reckoned as prohibited impurity and reason to be cut off from the community (Num. 19:13, 20). Matthew, however, makes no mention of Jesus undergoing such purification rites. Considering that Matthew's readers were mostly Jewish Christians, hearing of Jesus' apparent negligence probably would have been reason for concern. Matthew also tells the story where Jesus criticizes the tradition of the Pharisees about hand washing before meals (Matt. 15:10, 16-20). Furthermore, in the woe-sayings of Matt. 23, Jesus criticizes the practice of cleaning utensils for eating, while the people who eat, are dirty within (Matt. 23:25-27), referring to the condition of their hearts. Israelites, particularly during the first[151] and second[152] temple period, normally observed the laws of

---

[151] The First Temple was constructed by Solomon in c.a. 832 BCE and destroyed by the Babylonians under Nebuchadnezzar II in c.a. 485 BCE (Grintz, 2007:601-608; Eisen, 2004:54).

purity (*taharah*) and impurity (*tum'a*), as their identity was strongly defined by these laws (Hayes, 2007:750; Westerholm, 1992:127-131). The Jews most probably would have found Jesus' attitude towards purity regulations disturbing.

In this chapter one of Jesus' apparent provocative actions against the Jewish purity regulations is investigated, namely Jesus touching a leper (Matt. 8:3)[153]. Though Jesus emphasises that He did not come to abolish the Law (Matt. 5:17-19), it seems as if He demonstrates an alternative interpretation of the purity Law. The intention of this chapter is to establish what light the narrative of Jesus healing the leper could cast on Jesus' relation to and on the interpretation of the Law. To do this, this chapter first investigates Jewish purity regulations with regard to leprosy and purification rites, followed by the textual context in Matthew of Jesus as teacher of the Law. Jesus' healing of the leper will then be evaluated in the light of the Jewish purity laws and social values of those times. This comparison finally culminates in certain conclusions related to the identity of Matthew's community.

6.2 PURITY AND LEPROSY IN THE HEBREW BIBLE

Purity can be described as the condition that God requires of his people. Only those who are pure may come in contact with Him. In the Hebrew Bible purity is linked with the requirement of righteousness (Chilton, 2000:877). The Psalms explicitly state this association[154]. Only the one who has clean hands and a pure heart may ascend the mountain of the Lord and stand in his holy place (Ps 24:3-4) (cf. Pss. 18:21; 26:4-7; 51:4, 8, 9, 12; 119:9).

Impurity results from coming into contact with anything that assumingly should not exist, for example a corpse, or what was considered a monstrous beast (Chilton, 2000:874). The Priestly writings of the Hebrew Bible, especially the

---

[152] The Second Temple period lasted between c.a. 530 BCE and 70 CE, when the Second Temple existed. The Second Temple period ended with the First Jewish-Roman War and the Roman destruction of Jerusalem and the temple (Avi-Yonah, 2007:608-611).

[153] I discuss other cases in which purity and impurity is concerned, viz. where Jesus does not resist when a woman with blood flow touches Him (Matt. 9:20-22) and where Jesus enters a room with a dead girl and touches her (Matt. 9:25) in Chapter 8. Jesus' argument on purity and dietary laws in Matt. 15 is also significant, and I attend to this argument in Chapter 10.

[154] This link between purity and morality is significant as it seemingly becomes a hermeneutical key to Jesus' interpretation of purity regulations.

Holiness Code (Lev. 17-26), present a systematic legislation on the topic of purity and impurity. A person or object can become *tama'* (ritually impure) in several ways, ranging from sexual immorality (Lev. 18, 20), rules of diet (Lev. 11) or touching unclean object or beings (e.g. Num. 19:22) (Westerholm, 1992:125-127; Wright, 1992b:730-736). In the Jewish communities in the second temple period the concept of purity functioned as an identity marker and was regarded as an absolute binding inheritance from early Judaism. This issue was directly related to the authority of the Mosaic Law (Hübner, 1992:741). Biblical laws on purity have been extended in rabbinic *halakhah*, as at least one third of the *Mishnah*[155] deals with ritual purity (Hayes, 2007:750). The importance of purity regulations is particularly evident in the writings of Qumran with their strong emphasis on purity in their Purity Texts (4Q274-279, 281-284 and 512-514). In these texts laws are recorded that were promulgated to clarify and supplement the Mosaic code (cf. Bowley, 2000:873-874). The identity of their community was based on purity laws (Hübner, 1992:742).

Lev. 17-26 describes a broad spectrum of impurities, from those which are harmless and last for one day only up to those that are extremely severe (Hayes, 2007:746; Wright, 1992b:736-738). In this essay I limit my focus to the issue of leprosy and the purification rites related to it.

6.2.1 Leprosy and impurity

Leprosy, *tsara'at*, was regarded as an impurity (Lev. 13–14; Num. 5:2). Modern discussions on leprosy focus on the distinction between the disease caused by Hansen's Bacillus and superficially similar diseases. In the Bible "leprosy" is used to describe a variety of skin diseases of varying severity (Hayes, 2007:747; Wright & Jones, 1992b:277), so that the translation of *tsara'at* as "leprosy" for today's context might not always be accurate. "Leprosy" was used to describe all kinds of repulsive scaly and flaky conditions that affected people, clothing and houses (Pilch, 1981:108-113).

Leprosy was highly dreaded in the ancient world. It was regarded a terrible and defiling disease as those who were infected were physically and ceremonially regarded as unclean (Hagner, 1993:198; Morris, 1992:189; Talbert, 2010:112;

---

[155] The *Mishnah* consists of six orders (*sedarim*), each containing 7–12 tractates (*masechtot*). The sixth order is the longest of the orders, comprising 12 tractates. These tractates deal with purities (*tehorot*), pertaining to the laws of purity and impurity, including the impurity of the dead, the laws of food purity and bodily purity.

Wright & Jones, 1992b:281). In the Hebrew Bible leprosy was usually viewed as God's punishment for sinful behaviour (cf. 2 Kgs 5; 2 Cr. 26:16-21; Num. 12:10-15). It was associated with death and people perceived it as a living death (Num. 12:12; Job 18:13). The notion that lepers were living dead is reflected in several texts (e.g. Num. 12:12; 2 Kgs. 5:7 and Job 18:13) (Davies & Allison, 2004b:11). There are even texts that regard leprosy as the activity of demons (*b. Hor.* 10a). According to rabbis it was so difficult to heal leprosy that they compared such healing with raising a person from the dead (Luz, 2001a:5; Marshall, 1978:208; Witherington, 2006:178).

Leprosy was associated with uncleanness and a great social stigma was attached to it (Ellingworth, 1992:463; Pilch, 1981:108-113). It was a socially devalued condition with serious social consequences. People diagnosed with or suspected of leprosy were excluded from the community (Lev. 13:45-46, Num. 5:2-3). Contact with lepers had to be avoided and lepers had to warn others not to come close to them (Lev. 13:45).

Pharisees were equally concerned about avoiding lepers as an entire tractate of the *Mishnah,* the "Blemishes" *(Nega'im)*[156], is devoted to this issue (Chilton, 2000:877). Lepers were regarded as impure and unholy. This unholy condition was seen to violate God's will: "You shall be holy because I am holy" (Lev. 11:44-45). The community was concerned about pollution, rather than contagion, when coming into contact with lepers (Pilch & Malina, 1998:104). Leprosy was regarded as highly symbolic within the sphere of death (Senior, 1998:97). As living dead they were regarded as being under God's judgement (Hagner, 1993:198). Josephus confirms in his writings (37 – c 100AD) that this was still the situation that lepers had to endure in the time of Jesus. Josephus wrote: "Anyone who touches or lives under the same roof (with a leper) is regarded unclean" (*Contra Apionem*, 1.281) and that such people were kept away from the normal society (*Antiquitates Judaicae*, 9:74). "As an attack on the skin ... leprosy threatens or attacks ... integrity, wholeness and completeness of the community and its members" (Carter, 2000a:199; cf. Pilch, 1981:130). Roth (1994:108-109) points out that no command existed to take care of lepers. Lepers had to form their own colonies separate from the healthy communities and survive on their own (Lev. 13:45) (Davies & Allison, 2004b:11; Morris, 1992:188).

---

[156] The *Nega'im* consists of fourteen chapters. This tractate describes the various forms of leprosy which affected people, clothing and homes. It describes the different symptoms of the disease, and the various rituals involved in purifying someone who has been affected.

The Hebrew Bible reports two occasions where lepers are healed, that of Miriam's seven day leprosy (Num. 12) and Elisha's healing of Naaman (2 Kgs. 5:1-15). This second story is of particular interest as it describes the ability to heal a leper as the sign of a prophet (2 Kgs. 5:8). As rabbis regarded the cure of a leper as difficult as raising a person from the dead, the supernatural healing of lepers was expected as one of the signs of the messianic age[157] (Ellingworth, 1992:463; Hagner, 1993:198). At the beginning of the series of healing narratives in Matt. 8-9[158], the narrative of the healing of the leper thus presents Jesus as the messianic prophet (Davies & Allison, 2004b:11). This is confirmed with the statement of Jesus in Matt. 11:5 ("go back and report to John ... those who have leprosy are cured") that the healing of lepers formed part of eschatological expectations.

6.2.2 Purification rites

Extensive purification rites were prescribed for persons who recovered from "leprosy". It consisted of three phases (Wright & Jones, 1992b:280-281). For the first phase bird blood and water had to be sprinkled on such a person and a live bird sent away to remove the impurity from the person (Lev. 14:2-7). During the second phase the person had to bath, launder and shave at the beginning and end of a seven day quarantine period (Lev. 14:8-9). During the third phase the person had to bring sacrifices (Lev. 14:10-32), and blood and oil were placed on the ear, thumb and toe of the healed person (Lev. 8:22-30). Once this had been done, the person could be assimilated into the community again.

The impurity resulting from contact with a contaminated person also had to be dealt with (Wright, 1992b:737-738). A person who helped to purify a person or house that has recovered from "leprosy" was regarded as polluted and had to launder and bath (Lev. 14:2-7, 49-53). However, if pollution could have been avoided or purification was delayed, such action was considered as sinful and required additional ablution (Lev. 5:2-3). Persons who advertently did not purify themselves would suffer being כָּרֵת *karat* (being cut off), or expelled and

---

[157] It is to this expectation that Jesus inter alia replied to the enquiry of John the Baptist: "Are you the one who was to come, or should we expect someone else?" that "those who have leprosy are cured" (Matt. 11:3-4).

[158] Matthew sets out a distinctive arrangement of the series of miracle stories parallel to those reported in Mark. He makes the dramatic healing of the leper the first miracle, while Mark (Mark 1:40-45) describes it as the last miracle of the first day of healing in Capernaum (Senior, 1998:95).

extirpated (Lev. 18:24-30; Num. 19:13, 20) (Chilton, 2000:874; Hayes, 2007:749).

6.2.3 The impurity of leprosy and the religious space

As leprosy was associated with death (Num. 12:12; Job 18:13), it was considered impure. Impurity threatens what is holy (Wright, 1992a:237). Purity is related to holiness and impurity to profaneness (Lev. 10:10). God, the "Holy One of Israel" (Isa. 1:4; 5:19, 24), is the ideal manifestation and source of holiness. As God is holy, He requires of his people to be holy too, as is echoed with the refrain: "You are to be holy to me because I, the Lord, am holy" (Lev. 11:44-45; 19:2; 20:7-8, 24-26; 22:32-33).

The spaces in which God's people operate should reflect their holiness. The symbolic space for the religious community can be demonstrated with the following figure.

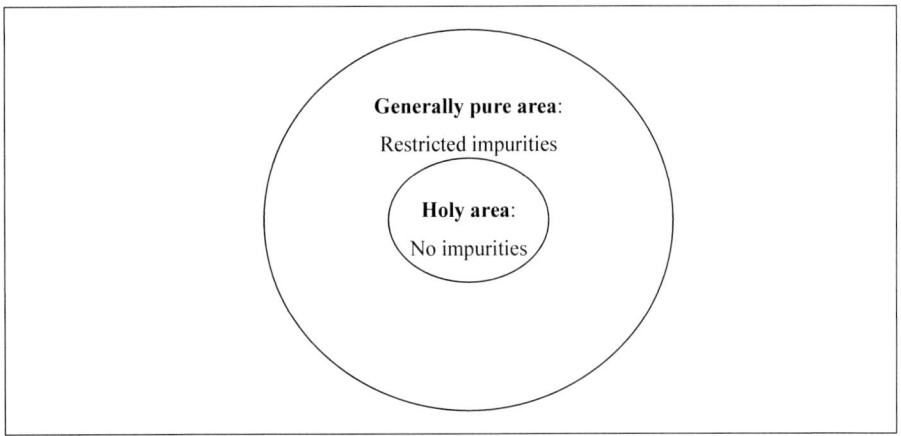

Figure 1: **Symbolic religious spaces**

The religious community has two spheres, the generally pure area and the holy area. Within the holy area, no impurity is permitted. The religious community lives within the generally pure area. Some impurities can be rectified within this sphere by way of proper adherence to specified purification rituals. Otherwise such impurity must be cut out of the community (referring to the practice of *karat* (cutting off)) and be expelled to the impure area. If impurity threatens to pollute the generally pure community, such as leprosy, it should be removed from the community (Wright & Jones, 1992b:281). Lepers therefore had to abide outside the borders of the generally pure area.

6.2.4 Jesus and purity in Matthew

In the Matthean Gospel it seems as if Jesus on several occasions[159] does not observe these laws of purity. In Matt. 15 the Jewish religious leaders found such conduct by Jesus offensive and objectionable. This led to Jesus' dispute with Pharisees and scribes on purity regulation (Matt. 15:20) and his very harsh woe saying against the scribes and the Pharisees on their cleaning rites (Matt. 23:25-26).

The question therefore arises of how this described behaviour of Jesus correlates with His explicit statement that his mission was not to abolish the Law or Prophets, but to fulfil them (Matt. 5:17-19). A secondary question arises as to what the Matthean Jesus then regards as pure and impure. With his description of these actions and arguments of Jesus, Matthew seemingly intends to inform his readers of an alternative interpretation and application of purity regulations as demonstrated by Jesus. Jesus values purity highly as He pronounces in the Beatitudes: "Blessed are the pure in heart, for they will see God" (Matt. 5:8), but He clearly means something different from what was observed by the Jews in the narrative. According to this beatitude, a pure heart seems to be a marker of the identity of a follower of Jesus.

When Jesus touches the leper (Matt. 8:3), He apparently provokes purity regulations. This incident is investigated in order to offer a proposal of how Jesus' interpretation of purity should be understood.

6.3 THE TEACHER OF THE LAW ENACTS THE LAW

When observing the narrative of Jesus' touching of the leper, it is important to consider the textual context of the Law in which this narrative is set.

Matthew ends his account of the Sermon on the Mount by telling that Jesus came down from the mountain as Moses once did from Mount Sinai (Exod. 19:14; 32:1; 34:29). He thus draws a parallel between Jesus and Moses, and the Mount of Jesus' sermon and Mount Sinai (Carter, 2000a:198; Davies & Allison, 2004a:9; Luz, 2001a:5). The impressive and authoritative teacher of the Law found in the discourse is subsequently presented in the narrative as going into

---

[159] When approached by a leper, Jesus does not scare away, He even touches him (Matt. 8:3); He does not object when a woman with blood flow touches Him (Matt. 9:20); and He enters the room of a dead girl and even takes her by the hand to heal her (Matt. 9:25).

action to demonstrate how the Law should be practiced. Jesus confirms his authority by performing ten miracles. Grundmann has fittingly described the Sermon on the Mount as "das Wirken des Christus Jesus durch das Wort" (the work of Christ Jesus through the word) (Grundmann, 1971:111) and the miracles that follow as "das Wirken des Christus Jesus durch die Tat" (the work of Christ Jesus through the deed) (Grundmann, 1971:245).

The discourse (Sermon on the Mount) and the narrative (ten miracle stories) are linked by two summaries of the miracles Jesus performed (Matt. 4:23-25[160] and Matt. 9:35[161]) to form some sort of compositional frame around them (Morris, 1992:186; Senior, 1998:94; Talbert, 2010:109).

---

[160] "Jesus went throughout Galilee, teaching in their synagogues, proclaiming the good news of the kingdom, and healing every disease and sickness among the people ... and people brought to him all who were ill with various diseases, those suffering severe pain, the demon-possessed, those having seizures, and the paralyzed; and he healed them".

[161] "Jesus went through all the towns and villages, teaching in their synagogues, proclaiming the good news of the kingdom and healing every disease and sickness".

> "Jesus went throughout Galilee, teaching in their synagogues, proclaiming the good news of the kingdom, and healing every disease and sickness among the people ... and people brought to him all who were ill with various diseases, those suffering severe pain, the demon-possessed, those having seizures, and the paralyzed; and he healed them" (Matt. 4:23-25).
>
> > Sermon on the Mount (Matt. 5-7).
> > Healing narrative (Matt. 8-9)[162].
>
> "Jesus went throughout Galilee, teaching in their synagogues, proclaiming the good news of the kingdom, and healing every disease and sickness among the people ... and people brought to him all who were ill with various diseases, those suffering severe pain, the demon-possessed, those having seizures, and the paralyzed; and he healed them" (Matt. 9:35).

Table 32: The summaries and composition of miracle stories in Matthew

Both these summaries refer to the Kingdom of God. With his inaugural proclamation "Repent, for the Kingdom of Heaven is at hand" (Matt. 4:17)[163], Jesus states that the future Kingdom of God is breaking into the present already (Duling, 1992:57). The Kingdom does not only signify the territory where God rules, but also his activity as ruler as envisioned in Deutero-Isaiah (Davies & Allison, 2004a:389). For Jesus the coming of the Kingdom did not comprise of one moment, but realizes through a series of events over a period of time. A similar process is described in Jubilees 23 (ca. 200 B.C, Vriezen & van der

---

[162] It is significant that the series of healing miracles includes one nature miracle, namely the stilling of the storm (Matt. 8:23-27). Matthew moves this nature miracle from the context as in Mark, and places it within a series of healing miracles (Matt. 8-9). After presenting Jesus as the Messiah of the Word in the Sermon on the Mount, Matthew continues to describe Jesus as the Messiah of the deed in the miracle narrative. The evangelist brings out a new motive by the context in which he places the miracle of the stilling of the storm. Before this miracle he places Jesus' teaching on the cost of following Jesus (Matt. 8:18-22) and afterwards Jesus' calling of Matthew to follow Him (Matt. 9:9-12) and the question why Jesus' disciples do not fast (Matt. 9: 14-17). Matthew interprets the journey of the disciples with Jesus in the storm and the stilling of the storm with reference to discipleship. The scope of the miracle is widened to become a description of discipleship and the church. When following Jesus, one can expect tribulation and rescue, and storm and security (Bornkamm, 1963a:52-57). With the story of the stilling of the storm Matthew describes the challenges the church is confronted with. At the same time he uses the story to explain how Jesus subdues demonic powers and brings the βασιλεία (Kingdom) of God. By placing this miracle amongst the healing miracles, the healing miracles similarly become descriptions of the coming of God's Kingdom in a broken world.

[163] "Kingdom of Heaven" is seemingly used as equivalent of "kingdom of God". This periphrasis for God is probably a result of rabbinic influence to avoid the divine name. Moreover, Matthew does not only use "Kingdom of Heaven" (e.g. Matt. 4:17; 18:1; 20:1; 25:1), but also "kingdom of God" (e.g. Matt. 6:33; 12:28), "kingdom of my Father" (Matt. 26:29), "kingdom of the Son of man" (Matt. 16:28) and the absolute, "the kingdom" (Matt. 4:23; 9:25).

Woude, 2005:577) according to which the age of blessedness enters history step-by-step. Similarly, the eschatological transition of the so-called "Apocalypse of the Weeks" is a prolonged process (1 Enoch 93 and 91:12-17) (c.a. end of first century B.C, Vriezen & Van der Woude, 2005:396). When Jesus announces that the Kingdom of Heaven has come and is coming, He indicates that the process of the realisation of God's rule has started, but the completion lies in the future, when the last things will come. The coming of the Kingdom is being established by Jesus. His teaching (Sermon on the Mount) and activity (healing miracles) step-by-step realize the blessings associated with the coming of the Kingdom.

The healing narrative describes a series of ten miracle stories. Matthew tells a series of nine healing miracles stories (Matt. 8-9)[164] and a nature miracle of Jesus stilling the storm (Matt. 8:23-27), making a total of ten (cf. Weren, 1994:83).). This block of nine/ten miracles, in sets of three, are separated by two discipleship sections (Matt. 8:18-22; 9:9-17) (Davies & Allison, 2004b:6; Kingsbury, 1988:59; Osborne, 2010:332; Overman, 1996:112).

Miracles 1-2-3	Discipleship	Miracles 4-5-6	Discipleship	Miracles 7/8 - 9-10
Matt. 8:1-17	Matt. 8:18-22	Matt. 8:23-9:8	Matt. 9:9-17	Matt. 9:18-34

Table 33: Miracle and discipleship sections of Matthew's healing narrative

As early as 1927, Klostermann (1927:72) has argued that Jesus' ten miracle stories allude to the ten miracles of the exodus from Egypt (Exod. 7-12) and can be interpreted as a new Moses typology. Some arguments can be identified in favour of Klostermann's argument. Micah prophesied that Israel and Judah would experience a new exodus from exile: "As in the days when you came out of Egypt, I will show them my wonders" (Mic. 7:15). Some early Christians applied this prophesy to the ministry of Jesus: "As Moses did signs and miracles, so also did Jesus. And there is no doubt but that the likeness of the signs proves him (Jesus) to be that prophet of whom he (Moses) said that he should come 'like myself'" (Pseudo-Clementine, *Recognitiones*, 1.57)[165]. Jesus

---

[164] The nine healings are that of the leper, the centurion's servant, Peter's mother in law, the Gaderene demoniacs, the paralyzed man, the ruler's daughter, the woman with blood flow, the blind men and the dumb man.

[165] Scholarly opinion differs about the date of the *Recognitiones*, but it seems that it was written in the third or fourth century C.E.

is regarded as the new Moses. One could criticize this stance as Jesus' acts of mercy are not directly comparable with the plagues in Egypt (Hagner, 1993:195; Morris, 1992:186), but one should also take into consideration that the contexts of these miracles are different. Further criticism of such correlation can be offered as Matthew's miracle stories are presented in triads of three each (Matt. 8:2-17; 8:18-9:17 and 9:18-34) (Garland, 2001:92; Osborn, 2010:280; Talbert, 2010:111). However, the narrative of the bleeding woman is sandwiched in between that of the healing of the dead girl, so that there are indeed ten miracle stories. Interesting enough, Philo (c.a. 25 B.C.E – 50 C.E., Vriezen & van der Woude, 2005:660) also presents the plagues of Exod. 7-12 in terms of three triads (*De Vita Mosis*, 1.97-139). Drawing a link between Moses and Jesus therefore seems to be plausible. As Moses in Exodus did ten miracles and gave the Law, Jesus authoritatively interprets the Law (in the Sermon on the Mount, cf. Matt. 7:29) and then authoritatively performs his interpretation of the Law (in the miracle narratives). The miracle narratives depict the authority (ἐξουσία[166]) of Jesus over illness, nature, demons, paralysis, disabilities and death (Osborne, 2010:280).

6.4 JESUS TOUCHING A LEPER (MATT. 8:3)[167]

Matthew begins the healing miracles, which exemplifies Jesus' authority, with his first triad by telling how Jesus healed people in Israel:

- the man with leprosy (Mat. 8:1-4);
- the servant of the centurion (Matt. 8:5-13); and
- Peter's mother-in-law (Matt. 8:14-16).

These three healing stories are concluded with the remark that Jesus healed many demon-possessed people (Matt. 8:16) and a reference to Isa. 53:4: "He took up our infirmities and carried our diseases" (Matt. 8:17) (Senior, 1998:96; Talbert, 2010:111). Matthew alludes to the fact that Jesus should be identified with the servant of the Isaiah songs and recognized as the promised Messiah (Hagner, 1993:210).

---

[166] Of the nine verses where ἐξουσία (authority) is found in Matthew, four occur in the miracle narratives (Matt. 8:9; 9:6, 8 and 19:1).

[167] Matt. 26:6 describes Jesus staying in the house of Simon, who was affected by leprosy. He was probable a leper that has been cured (by Jesus?). It is highly unlikely that a leper who was still ill would act as a host for a meal (Davies & Allison, 20014b:443; Hagner, 1995:757). Nevertheless, it indicates that Jesus yet again befriended a (previously) social outcast.

With the first of these healings Jesus is approached by a leper with the request to be cleansed (Matt. 8:2). Matthew is the only gospel that puts this story first in the series, which seems to be deliberate. It appears that Matthew intends to illustrate the teaching of the Sermon on the Mount about the *Torah* (Davies & Allison, 2004a:10). Jesus did not abolish the *Torah* as given by Moses, but interprets it differently than the scribes and the Pharisees of the narrative.

The story is paralleled in Mark 1:40-45 and Luk. 5:12-16.

Matt. 8:1-4	**Mark 1:40-45**	**Luk. 5:12-16**
Setting: 1. **Καταβάντος δὲ αὐτοῦ ἀπὸ τοῦ ὄρους** ἠκολούθησαν αὐτῷ ὄχλοι πολλοί. When Jesus came down from the mountainside, large crowds followed him.		12a. Καὶ ἐγένετο ἐν τῷ εἶναι αὐτὸν ἐν μιᾷ τῶν πόλεων. While Jesus was in one of the towns,
Entreating approach of the leper: 2. καὶ ἰδοὺ λεπρὸς **προσελθὼν προσεκύνει** αὐτῷ λέγων· **Κύριε**, ἐὰν θέλῃς δύνασαί με καθαρίσαι. A man with leprosy came and knelt before him and said, "Lord, if you are willing, you can make me clean."	40. Καὶ ἔρχεται πρὸς αὐτὸν λεπρὸς παρακαλῶν αὐτὸν καὶ γονυπετῶν λέγων αὐτῷ ὅτι Ἐὰν θέλῃς δύνασαί με καθαρίσαι. A man with leprosy came to him and begged him on his knees, "If you are willing, you can make me clean."	12b. καὶ ἰδοὺ ἀνὴρ πλήρης λέπρας· καὶ ἰδὼν τὸν Ἰησοῦν πεσὼν ἐπὶ πρόσωπον ἐδεήθη αὐτοῦ λέγων· **Κύριε**, ἐὰν θέλῃς δύνασαί με καθαρίσαι. a man came along who was covered with leprosy. When he saw Jesus, he fell with his face to the ground and begged him, "Lord, if you are willing, you can make me clean."
Healing response of Jesus: 3. καὶ <u>ἐκτείνας τὴν χεῖρα ἥψατο αὐτοῦ</u> λέγων· Θέλω, καθαρίσθητι· καὶ εὐθέως ἐκαθαρίσθη αὐτοῦ ἡ λέπρα. Jesus reached out his hand and touched the man. "I am willing," he said. "Be clean!" Immediately he was cleansed of his leprosy.	41. καὶ <u>σπλαγχνισθεὶς ἐκτείνας τὴν χεῖρα αὐτοῦ ἥψατο</u> καὶ λέγει αὐτῷ Θέλω, καθαρίσθητι. Jesus was indignant. He reached out his hand and touched the man. "I am willing," he said. "Be clean!" 42. καὶ εὐθὺς ἀπῆλθεν ἀπ᾽ αὐτοῦ ἡ λέπρα, καὶ ἐκαθερίσθη.	13. καὶ <u>ἐκτείνας τὴν χεῖρα ἥψατο αὐτοῦ</u> εἰπών· Θέλω, καθαρίσθητι· καὶ εὐθέως ἡ λέπρα ἀπῆλθεν ἀπ᾽ αὐτοῦ. Jesus reached out his hand and touched the man. "I am willing," he said. "Be clean!" And immediately the leprosy left him.

	Immediately the leprosy left him and he was cleansed.	
Jesus' dismissal command: 4. καὶ λέγει αὐτῷ ὁ Ἰησοῦς· Ὅρα μηδενὶ εἴπῃς, ἀλλὰ ὕπαγε σεαυτὸν δεῖξον τῷ ἱερεῖ, καὶ προσένεγκον τὸ δῶρον ὃ **προσέταξεν Μωϋσῆς** εἰς μαρτύριον αὐτοῖς. Then Jesus said to him, "See that you don't tell anyone. But go, show yourself to the priest and offer the gift Moses commanded, as a testimony to them."	43. καὶ ἐμβριμησάμενος αὐτῷ εὐθὺς ἐξέβαλεν αὐτόν, Jesus sent him away at once with a strong warning: 44. καὶ λέγει αὐτῷ Ὅρα μηδενὶ μηδὲν εἴπῃς, ἀλλὰ ὕπαγε σεαυτὸν δεῖξον τῷ ἱερεῖ καὶ προσένεγκε περὶ τοῦ καθαρισμοῦ σου ἃ **προσέταξεν Μωϋσῆς** εἰς μαρτύριον αὐτοῖς. See that you don't tell this to anyone. But go, show yourself to the priest and offer the sacrifices that Moses commanded for your cleansing, as a testimony to them." 45. ὁ δὲ ἐξελθὼν ἤρξατο κηρύσσειν πολλὰ καὶ διαφημίζειν τὸν λόγον, ὥστε μηκέτι αὐτὸν δύνασθαι φανερῶς εἰς πόλιν εἰσελθεῖν, ἀλλ' ἔξω ἐπ' ἐρήμοις τόποις ἦν· καὶ ἤρχοντο πρὸς αὐτὸν πάντοθεν. Instead he went out and began to talk freely, spreading the news. As a result, Jesus could no longer enter a town openly but stayed outside in lonely places. Yet the people still came to him from everywhere.	14. καὶ αὐτὸς παρήγγειλεν αὐτῷ μηδενὶ εἰπεῖν, ἀλλὰ ἀπελθὼν δεῖξον σεαυτὸν τῷ ἱερεῖ, καὶ προσένεγκε περὶ τοῦ καθαρισμοῦ σου **καθὼς προσέταξεν Μωϋσῆς** εἰς μαρτύριον αὐτοῖς. Then Jesus ordered him, "Don't tell anyone, but go, show yourself to the priest and offer the sacrifices that Moses commanded for your cleansing, as a testimony to them." 15. διήρχετο δὲ μᾶλλον ὁ λόγος περὶ αὐτοῦ, καὶ συνήρχοντο ὄχλοι πολλοὶ ἀκούειν καὶ θεραπεύεσθαι ἀπὸ τῶν ἀσθενειῶν αὐτῶν· Yet the news about him spread all the more, so that crowds of people came to hear him and to be healed of their sicknesses. 16. αὐτὸς δὲ ἦν ὑποχωρῶν ἐν ταῖς ἐρήμοις καὶ προσευχόμενος. But Jesus often withdrew to lonely places and prayed.

Table 34: The parallel of Matt 8:1-4 with Mark 1:40-45 and Luk. 5:12-16 on the story of the healing of the leper

Typical of Matthew, he shortens his version of the story[168] to give it an apophthegmatic character. Matthew omits Jesus' compassion (σπλαγχνισθεὶς, Mark 1:41a), his strong warning (ἐμβριμησάμενος αὐτῷ, Mark 1:43) and the man's disobedience (ὁ δὲ ἐξελθὼν ἤρξατο κηρύσσειν πολλὰ καὶ διαφημίζειν τὸν λόγον, Mark 1:45). This brief pericope lacks the first and last elements of a full version of such a healing pericope (Hagner, 1993:197)[169] as no mention is made of the condition of the leper (first element) and no reaction of the onlookers (last element) is reported. The effect is a stronger emphasis on the interaction between the leper and Jesus.

The narrative begins with a transitional verse (Matt. 8:1) followed by the rest of the story consisting of three parts (paralleled in Mark and Luke), but without a narrative conclusion:

- The approach of the leper (Matt. 8:2a) followed by his entreaty (Matt. 8:2b);
- The response of Jesus (Matt. 8:3a) followed by Jesus' healing words (Matt. 8:3b); and
- The command of Jesus (Matt. 8:4).

6.4.1 Setting of the scene (Matt. 8:1)

Matthew's setting is unique. He adds the transition from the Sermon on the Mount to the miracle story (καταβάντος δὲ αὐτοῦ ἀπὸ τοῦ ὄρους, Matt. 8:1), which almost identically parallels the LXX version of Moses' descent from Sinai (καταβαίνοντος δὲ αὐτοῦ ἀπὸ τοῦ ὄρους) (Exod. 34:29). This suggests a Moses typology (Davies & Allison, 2004a:9; Hagner, 1993:198). Jesus as Messiah has just given the *Torah*, and the impression is created that He now proceeds to execute the *Torah*. The large crowd that follows Jesus provides the audience for the healing miracle[170] to follow.

---

[168] Carson (1984:197) points out that Matthew on average shortens the stories on Jesus as Messiah by 10 percent, controversy stories by 20 percent and miracle stories by 50 percent.

[169] Theissen (1983:72-80) has identified the various elements in miracles stories.

[170] Significantly Matthew does not use the word τέρας (miracle) to describe the miracles of Jesus (Weren, 1979:86). The only time this term occurs in the first Gospel is where Jesus warns his disciples against false Messiahs and false prophets (Matt. 24:24). Matthew uses the word δύναμις (mighty deed) for the miracles of Jesus (Matt. 11:20-23; 13:54, 58 and 14:2). Jesus is not depicted as one doing the spectacular. Full emphasis is put on his power.

6.4.2 Entreating approach of the leper (Matt. 8:2)

In Matt. 8:2 the author turns to Mark 1:40-45 (paralleled in Luk. 5:12-16). The leper in the story acted contrary to the instructions stipulated in Lev. 13-14 of how persons with such skin diseases should act. Being contagious and unclean persons, lepers were supposed to isolate themselves from others, demonstrate their impurity and warn people of their illness. They had to wear torn clothes, let their hair be unkept, cover the lower part of their faces and shout "Unclean! Unclean!" (*tame' we-tame'*) (Lev. 13:45). The LXX version is "ἀκάθαρτος κεκλήσεται" (he must shout: "unclean"!). Instead of shouting "Unclean! Unclean!", which implies "be warned, I am unclean and will make you unclean too", the leper in the story begs, "make me clean", which implies "You are clean and you have the power to make me clean too". This contrast highlights the social and religious implication of his illness on the one hand, but also his trust that he can find healing from Jesus.

To understand the impact of this desired healing, one has to consider what healing implied in the ancient Mediterranean world. Healing involved (and even today) more than physical healing from a disease. Healing implies the restoration of the total well-being of a person (Pilch, 1988:60-66). This includes the restoration of meaning of life and honour. A healed person can again fully participate in societal activities. Healing, therefore, is culturally constructed. In this regard, one has to consider the difference between disease and illness. A disease causes sickness and is a pathological issue. Sickness exists irrespective of whether a culture recognizes it or not. Sickness is caused by viruses and germs. Illness, on the other hand, refers to misfortunes in well-being beyond a pathological state. An ill person is a socially devalued person. Restoring meaning of life for an ill person implies healing. The leper, who approached Jesus, had a disease that resulted in illness. He suffered a condition that was socially unacceptable. He was devalued and unwelcome in society (cf. Weren, 1979:86). He was regarded as unclean and unholy. He had to live outside the community as he could pollute the people of the community. The threat he posed for the community needed to be demonstrated and declared by his appearance and shouting (Lev. 13:45). When Jesus healed him, He restored the leper's social stance and gave him new meaning in life.

It is significant that in Matt. 8:2 (as in Luk. 5:12b), other than in Mark 1:40, the leper addresses Jesus as κύριε (Lord)[171]. In Matthew's version the leper προσελθὼν προσεκύνει αὐτῷ (approached and knelt before Him). The movement of the leper (προσελθὼν) is probably symbolic (Davies & Allison, 2004b:10). Combined with his kneeling before Jesus (προσεκύνει αὐτῷ[172]) it appears that the leper comes to worship Jesus with praying faith (cf. Edwards, 1987:65-74; Weren, 1979:87). Grundmann (1971:248) has proposed that Matthew describes Jesus as the new cultic centre. Jesus becomes the functional equivalent of the temple, a sentiment that is repeated in Matt. 12:6. The leper acknowledges Jesus' authority to heal (Osborne, 2010:283). Other than Elijah who had to pray by calling the name of the Lord to heal a leper (2 Kgs. 5:11), the leper calls Jesus Lord and asks Him to heal him.

6.4.3 Healing response of Jesus (Matt. 8:3)

Matthew's healing story is all the more striking as it is offered in the form of a striking parallelism. Verses 2 and 3 are similarly constructed: Participle + finite verb + saying + direct speech, which emphasises the close link between these two verses (Davies & Allison, 2004b:13). This link accentuates the interaction between the leper and Jesus. The interaction can be visually illustrated:

---

[171] The centurion who pleaded for his servant (Matt. 8:6, 8) and the blind man (Matt. 9:28) also called Jesus "κύριε (Lord) when they pleaded for healing.

[172] The leader of the synagogue also kneeled before Jesus pleading that Jesus would heal his dying daughter (Matt. 9:18) (cf. Chapter 8).

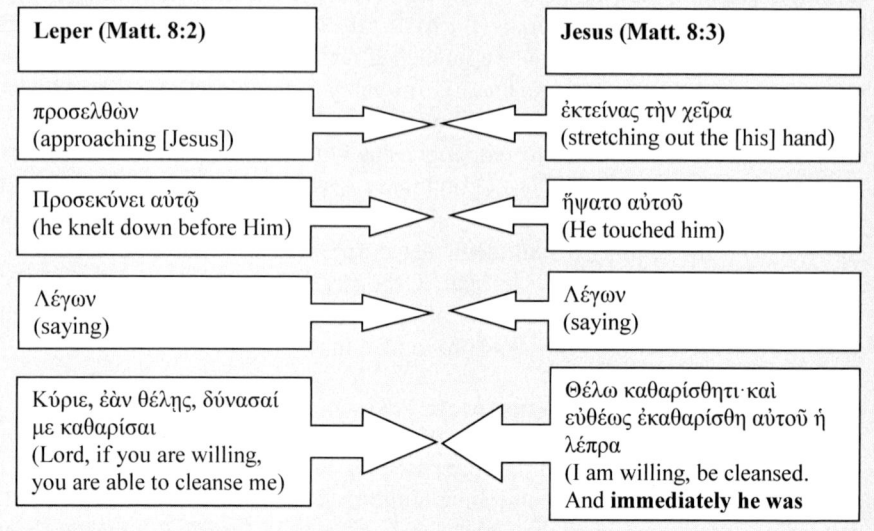

Figure 2: The interaction between the leper and Jesus in Matt. 8:2-3

Jesus responds (Matt. 8:3) to the approaching leper (Matt. 8:2), not by resenting him or scaring away, but by stretching out his hand towards him. As the leper kneels before Him, Jesus responds by touching him. Instead of warning Jesus of his uncleanness, the leper makes a statement of faith and begs for healing. In response to the leper Jesus answers that He is willing to heal the man, orders him to be healed and the man is healed.

Jesus' touching of the leper has special significance. As leprosy was regarded as an unclean disease, Jesus was not supposed to come close to this man, let alone to touch him. Neither Moses (Num. 12:9-15) nor Elisha (2 Kgs. 5:1-14) touched the leper they healed. Nevertheless, Jesus reaches out and touches this man to heal him and thereby seemingly violates the Levitical law stated in Lev. 5:3[173], but even more, He demonstrates no fear of being infected by the disease. Jesus approaches the man without fear. This depicts Jesus' power over illness. The act of Jesus to touch the leper is all the more significant as the Greek phrase (ἐκτείνας τὴν χεῖρα) emphasises that Jesus reaches out to him. Furthermore,

---

[173] Chrysostom in his homily on this passage proposes that by this acts Jesus shows that He is set over the Law, and that to the clean, henceforth, nothing is unclean.

Jesus did not have to touch this man, as in some other healing stories Jesus healed people by speaking only. Osborne (2010:285, 351) has called this act the "love hermeneutic", meaning the willingness to break Jewish social and religious taboos to help the suffering (Weren, 1979:87). Jesus is pictured as one whose concern for people apparently outweighs legal prescriptions.

A significant element of the act of touching should be considered. In the LXX, the more than 80 occurrences of touching establishes it as a common gesture of a miracle healer (Luz, 2001a:6; Theissen, 1983:62-63). Touching formed an important part of ancient healing stories. It was assumed that power and energy would flow from the holy person or healer to the ill one. When Jesus touched the leper, the leprosy and impurity did not spread to Jesus. Jesus is the holy one and healer. The power to heal and cleanse flows from Jesus to the leper to conquer the disease. Leprosy is unable to affect Jesus (Davies & Allison, 2004b:13). To the healing touch, the powerful command is added: καθαρίσθητι (be healed / clean). The word used for "to heal" (καθαρίσαι) proves the point. Illness with its devastating effects is cured, including uncleanness. Jesus is depicted as the mighty conqueror of illness (Weren, 1979:85). He does not use a magical formula, but simply gives an order. The power resides in Jesus, not in what He says. Jesus, the holy one, is the Saviour who has the authority to heal and to cleanse (Osborne, 2010:284).

6.4.4 Jesus' dismissal command (Matt. 8:4)

This miracle narrative is concluded with a reference to a Mosaic regulation (Lev. 13:49). Jesus commands (as paralleled in Mark 1:44 and Luk. 5:14) the healed man to go and show himself to the priest and to offer the gift Moses commanded (ὃ προσέταξεν Μωϋσῆς, Matt. 1:4). This reference to the Mosaic regulation provides yet another link between this miracle narrative and the foregoing Sermon on the Mount. Jesus, the teacher of the Law, demonstrates how He enacts the Law.

Significantly, the narrative concludes with Jesus instructing the man to take his sacrifice and to show himself to the priests. It should be noted that the first and the second phases of the purification rituals as prescribed in Lev. 14:2-9 are left out. Jesus has already removed the impurity from the man (first phase of cleansing), and has already declared the man clean (second phase). What remains is the sacrifice of the third phase so that the priest would allow him to be readmitted to the full communal and spiritual life. Jesus proves to have special power and authority. As Emmanuel, He is the holy one. Purity flows from Him to heal the infected person and He has the authority to declare the purity of the cleansed person. Jesus did not see any need to undergo any purification action for Himself. The Gospels do not record that Jesus ever personally underwent any form or ritual purification. As the holy One He could not be defiled by touching the leper. Evans (2012:183) has remarked that instead of Jesus being defiled by the leper, "purity flows from Jesus to the leper, healing the disease and restoring the man to a state of purity".

The prescribed purification rites have been fulfilled. They pointed to Jesus. With his healing power He assured that the true intention of the purity laws could be realized (Gundry, 1982:138). The messianic times have arrived, times of health and the absence of all illness (Talbert, 2010:112).

6.5 THE PURITY REQUIRED OF THE FOLLOWERS OF JESUS

This healing narrative probably reveals the understanding of purity laws within the Matthean community. The community regarded Jesus as Emmanuel, the holy God amongst them. As Healer, He has come to save his people from their sins (Matt. 1:21)[174]. He purifies and thus hallows his followers. As cleansed people they have to live as holy people. It seems as if the concept of purity has been transposed from a cultic to an ethical level. In the Sermon on the Mount Jesus demands from his disciples pure hearts: μακάριοι οἱ καθαροὶ τῇ καρδίᾳ, ὅτι αὐτοὶ τὸν θεὸν ὄψονται (blessed are the pure in heart, for they will see God) (Matt. 5:8). The phrase "pure in heart" echoes the obligation described in Ps. 24:3-4: "Who may ascend the mountain of the Lord? Who may stand in his holy place? The one who has clean hands and a pure heart ...". A pure heart counters mere external ceremonial cleaning (cf. Matt. 23:25-26). Pure hearts should mark the identity of Jesus' disciples. Their external behaviour should be based on an internal ethical conviction.

6.6 CONCLUSION

This short narrative about Jesus who heals a leper describes another step in the coming of the Kingdom of God towards the paradisiac state pictured in

---

[174] The angel's prophesy from the opening of the Gospel (καλέσεις τὸ ὄνομα αὐτοῦ Ἰησοῦν, αὐτὸς γὰρ σώσει τὸν λαὸν αὐτοῦ ἀπὸ τῶν ἁμαρτιῶν αὐτῶν, Matt. 1:21) provides a significant theme to the developement of the narrative of the Gospel (Repschinski, 2004:7), which alerts the reader to be observant to it in the narrative. The name of the Son to be born, is related to his saving ministry that would follow. By word play the verb σώζειν is connected with the name Ἰησοῦς. By this the reader is guided to understanding Jesus' life of saving activity. This statement presents the reader with the challenge of tracing the actual ways of how this salvation is realized by the ministry of Jesus.

Deutero-Isaiah. Jesus is in the process of establishing God's rule. He is described as a compassionate healer and amazing miracle worker. Though it seems as if Jesus is violating the Law by touching the leper, the narrative actually demonstrates Jesus' authority and healing power. Meaning of life is being restored for ill people. While Jesus does not become impure when touching the leper, purity flows from Him towards the leper. The purity laws find their fulfilment in Him.

As the leper was purified, all Jesus' followers are purified. Boundaries of purity laws to categorize and isolate others are no longer applicable to them. Ritual purity becomes a moral category. Their inner beings, their hearts, must be pure. Purity involves integrity of the whole person.

CHAPTER 7

HOSEA 6:6 IN TWO SCENES OF CONFLICT AND IDENTITY FORMATION IN MATTHEW

7.1 INTRODUCTION

The quotation of Hos. 6:6, ἔλεος θέλω καὶ οὐ θυσίαν (I desire mercy, not sacrifice) in Matthew's Gospel plays an important role in Jesus' arguments to defend his and his disciples' actions against the accusations of the Pharisees[175]. This reference forms the central argument in two scenes of conflict between the Pharisees and Jesus. The first scene describes Jesus defending his table fellowship with tax collectors and sinners after the calling of Matthew (Matt. 9:9-13). The other describes Jesus defending his interpretation of the Sabbath law (Matt. 12:1-14).

The appearance of this quotation is striking for at least two reasons. Firstly, this citation in Matthew is unique amongst the parallel Synoptic narratives, but is uttered twice in Matthean material. This reference is even absent from the entirety of the rest of the New Testament. This suggests that this quotation is of particular importance to the first evangelist. Secondly, in both of these scenes Jesus is in dispute with the Pharisees and is accusing their conduct. The accusation of bad conduct is a theme of Hosea 6 too[176].

When reading Matthew, one soon discovers that resistance plays a prominent role in this narrative (Repschinski, 2000). Jesus is continually engaged in some conflict with religious leaders, especially with the Pharisees (Kingsbury,

---

[175] As discussed in Chapter 2, the way Matthew describes the Pharisees is polemic. The issue about the correspondences between the Pharisees in the text and the Pharisees in history (in the time of Jesus and in the time of Matthew) should be recognized, though this issue does not form part of the investigation of this study.

[176] In Hos. 6:6 Yahweh speaks of his frustration with the fleeting devotion of Israel. He declares the reason of issuing judgement against them. He asserts that He wants true piety and not mere outward pretention of religious zeal (Garrett, 1997:160; Limburg, 1988:27).

1988:4-8). The central issue involves their contrasting views on society and religious practises and Jesus' authority (Carter, 2000a:2). Similarly, the scenes in Matt. 9:9-13 and 12:1-14 with their significant references to Hos. 6:6 describe such conflicts.

The Gospel writer addressed particular situations and issues of his own time and this is most probably what is reflected in the text (Carter, 2000a:7; 2004:74-77). As discussed in Chapter 2, the author of the Matthean gospel formed part of (an) early Christian congregation(s) and he wrote his gospel with this/these congregation(s) and its/their issues in mind (Luz, 2005:17; Saldarini, 1991:39; Van Aarde, 2011:41-49). The two episodes discussed in the current chapter probably reflect issues of conflict with the Pharisees in the *Sitz im Leben* of Matthew and his community. In the manner in which Matthew tells the story, he apparently draws the religious and social issues of his original readers into the discourse[177] (Kingsbury, 1988:3) and integrates applicable arguments into his narrative (Osborne, 2010:25).

Evidently Hos. 6:6 was important for Matthew and his community in order for them to define their identity and maintain their identity against the new post-70 C.E. Jewish establishment[178]. It seems as if the community suffered some kind of conflict with a Pharisaic component of their society (Carter, 2000a:32; Keener, 1999:46; Luz, 2005:244; Repschinski, 2000:329; Saldarini, 1991:49). Matthew clearly identifies the Jewish leaders as Jesus' opponents. He describes Jesus as the undisputed victor in all these confrontations. Hinkle Edin (1998:355) has fittingly remarked: "For Matthew the difference between Jesus and his adversaries is based on Hosea 6:6". A similar observation was made by Schlatter (1959:308): "Der Spruch (Hos. vi.6) hat sicher in der Wirksamkeit Jesu und weiter im Verkehr der ersten Christenheit mit der Judenschaft eine grosse Bedeutung gehabt, da er den Gegensatz zwischen Jesus und dem Pharisäismus bis in die letzten Gründe hinein beleuchtete". Matthew and his community are involved in an ongoing *Auseinandersetzung* with Judaism (Hill, 1978:117). Like the Pharisees, Matthew's community recognized the Law,

---

[177] Chatman (1978:19-27) designates two parts to a narrative as the "story" and the "discourse" The "story" is about "what" is told, and the "discourse" is "how" it is told.

[178] As discussed in Chapter 2, most scholars today opt for the origin of the Gospel somewhere in Syria. This view can be traced back to the classic proposal of Streeter for the case of an origin in Antioch (Streeter, 1924:500-527). Although not all Streeter's arguments are compelling, the general suitability of a church in Syria may be accepted, though it cannot be fully decided (Davies & Allison, 2004a:143-147; Hagner, 1993:lxxv; Kilpatrick, 1950:131-134).

though they differed on how they interpreted what the Law meant in practice (Carter, 2004:75-76; Hill, 1972:117). Ἔλεος (mercy) as expressed in the double quotation seemingly formed their key to the true *Erkenntnis* of the will of God and of the Law (Bornkamm, 1963b:26; Trilling, 1964:83)[179].

Kilpatrick (1950:59-100) draws attention to the educational role and communal orientation of the first Gospel. The Gospel does not merely have an informational, but also a formational function. It intends to shape its community by telling them about how Jesus instructed his disciples to live a distinctive way of life (Combrink, 2006:26-27). This insight about the formational function of the Gospel is confirmed by Burridge (1992:109-190), who demonstrates that the Gospels belong to the genre of ancient biographies (βίοι). Thus the Gospels not only instruct the audience about their praise of Jesus, but also offer a model to follow. They set Jesus forth as expression and norm for a community's values (Carter, 2000a:8; 2004:231; Talbert, 1992:749). It can therefore be assumed that Matthew also tells the stories about Jesus' interpretation of Hos. 6:6 and related behaviour to constitute a lifestyle that embodies their identity as disciples of Jesus.

The aim of this chapter is to establish the significance of the double reference to Hos. 6:6 in the mentioned two scenes of conflict in Matthew's gospel, as the interpretation of the *Torah* by the Pharisees and Jesus respectively is at stake. Several issues will receive attention in an attempt to reach this aim. Firstly, the chapter will consider how the original setting of the quotation in Hosea contributes to the reading of the text in its Matthean contexts. Then the meaning of the quotation in its Matthean settings will be established. The meaning is sought not only to understand what the Matthean Jesus intended with these references, but also how these stories reflect the situation of the Matthean community. The way Matthew used these stories to form the communal identity[180] of his community is subsequently considered.

---

[179] The third occurrence of ἔλεος in the first Gospel is in Matt. 23:23: "You give a tenth of your spices – mint, dill and cumin. But you have neglected the more important matters of the law – justice, mercy (ἔλεος) and faithfulness". It is once again unique to Matthew and appears in context of criticism of the Pharisees (and teachers of the law). This triad recalls Mic. 6:8. Within this context ἔλεος denotes loyal love towards God that manifests in loving-kindness and mercy (Hill, 1977:110).

[180] As discussed before, scholars have identified a variety of devices that groups in the Greco-Roman world employed to define themselves and outsiders, such as naming of groups, having a central focus, claiming exclusive revelation, upholding unique rituals and association, organizing socially, criticizing opponents, upholding apocalyptic vision, defining origins and defining appropriate actions

7.2 THE FORM AND SETTING OF THE QUOTATION

As illustrated below, the Matthean form of the quotation offers a word-for-word translation of the Hebrew of the Masoretic text, though it differs slightly from the most common LXX (Rahlfs) version.

Matthew	ἔλεος θέλω καὶ οὐ θυσίαν	I desire mercy and not sacrifice
Masoretic text	חֶסֶד חָפַצְתִּי וְלֹא־זָבַח	I desire mercy and not sacrifice
LXX	ἔλεος θέλω ἢ θυσίαν[181]	I desire mercy rather than sacrifice

Table 35: The comparison between Matthew, MTT and LXX on God's desire of mercy

The text form of most of Matthew's quotations shows inconsistency from source texts, which raises questions about the sources he might have used. Some of his quotations are closer to the Masoretic text than to the LXX[182], while some seem to have been influenced other Greek translations and Targums (Luz, 1990:159). When sharing material with the other Synoptics Matthew usually presents the LXX version of the quotations of the Jewish Bible. It seems that when Matthew uses Mark, the LXX is used in the quotations. The LXX versions of the quotations in Matthew were therefore not Matthew using the LXX, but rather him using Mark. With Matthew's own quotations the rendering is closer to the Masoretic text. It could be that Matthew used another (unknown) Greek translation used in Christian circles (Plummer, 1982:47; Soares Prabhu, 1976:83-84). It could also be that Matthew used an existing revised form of the LXX (Menken 2003:280). It is even possible that Matthew independently rendered the Masoretic or another Hebrew text.

Matthew uses the Jewish Scriptures quite extensively. Several studies have been devoted to this matter (e.g. Menken, 2004; McConnell, 1969). Matthew often does not wholly stick to the precise wording or plain sense of the text he cites. Prophetic words are often newly rendered and interpreted within the context of

---

for the community (Sanders, Baumgarten, Mendelsohn & Meyer, 1980-82; Neusner & Frerich, 1985; Saldarini, 1994).

[181] In some versions of the Vulgate this variation of the LXX is rendered as "plus quam" rather than "et non".

[182] It should be borne in mind that the LXX, though a translation, predates the Masoretic textual tradition. Though the Masoretic text mostly reflect ancient readings, in the beginning of the first century C.E. it emerged as the one and only consonantal text, but actually preserved only one of more textual traditions (Aejmelaeus, 2007:194).

Jesus-events (Müller, 2001:321, Weren, 1994:16). Stendahl (1968) has pointed out that the use of Scripture in Matthew shows remarkable similarities to the *Pesher*-commentaries amongst the Dead Sea Scrolls, especially the Habakkuk commentary (1QpHab). Gundry (1967:155-159) has named Matthew the "Targumist"[183]. The Aramaic *Targums* that have survived show that there was a living tradition of biblical translation and interpretation to bring out the perceived applications of quotations within new contexts.

Moule has blamed Matthew of ignoring the original meaning of words and taking them out of context. He regards Matthew's appeals to the Jewish Scriptures "manifestly forced and artificial and unconvincing" (Moule, 1977:129). Menken (2003:195) has remarked that in New Testament times "all sorts of textual manipulations were ... used in early Jewish and Christian circles to reduce the distance between the scriptural word and its alleged fulfilment". He has also written that perfect correspondence between the old text and the new reality is very rare (Menken, 2003:198). France (1998:182), however, has pointed out that Matthew's method of using the Jewish Scriptures should be understood within Matthew's understanding of its fulfilment in Jesus. Matthew should rather be seen as an innovative theologian whose thoughts are controlled by his conviction of the climactic place of Jesus in the development of God's purpose in history. Matthew recognized a further dimension of continued divine purpose of text, a *sensus plenior* that comes to light in ongoing revelation. Thus Matthew does not set the meaning of the original text aside, but places it in the wider context of divine actions. While he continues to refer to the textual units from where the texts originate, he interweaves the quotation into a new literary setting (Weren, 1994:16). Yet in the two citations of Hos. 6:6 by Jesus in Matthew, the Masoretic text was precisely rendered and it seems that the original context indeed contributed significantly to the understanding of Matthew's text. The LXX variant rather seems to be a careful reinterpretation of the text to avoid reading the text as if Hosea radically repudiates the whole sacrificial cult with its impious feastings.

In the original prophetic context of Hosea, the theme of covenantal loyalty is dominant (Garret, 1997:160; Limburg, 1988:28-30; Repschinski, 2000:79). It refers to the proper behaviour of partners in a covenantal relation. It suggests loyalty and constancy, as well as indicating love (Morris, 1981:71). Yahweh

---

[183] The Targum consists of paraphrases, explanations, and expansions of the Jewish scriptures that rabbis gave in the common language of the listeners.

remains true to his covenant with his people. This should also be the attitude of people who are in a covenantal relationship with God. They should show constant loyalty and love towards God and his people.

The names of Hosea's three children, Jezreel (signifying that Yahweh would soon punish the house of Jehu for the massacre at Jezreel)[184], Lo-Ruhamah (meaning "not loved"[185]) and Lo-Ammi (meaning "not my people")[186] form the theological framework of Hosea's message (Garret, 1997:55; Van Leeuwen, 1978:37). The text provides a series of accusations and predictions of woe related to Israel and Judah. Yahweh laments Israel's incapacity to repent and their lack of true devotion (Dearman, 2010:99). It expresses the estrangement between Israel and Yahweh and Yahweh's intention to leave Israel to its own fate (Harper, 1979:213).

In a proverb-like parallel form, Hos. 6:6 כִּי חֶסֶד חָפַצְתִּי וְלֹא־זָבַח וְדַעַת אֱלֹהִים מֵעֹלוֹת (for I desire mercy, and not sacrifice, and the knowledge of God rather than burnt-offerings) identifies the two great desiderata of Yahweh, mercy and knowledge of God. He contrasts this with sacrifice and burnt-offerings, which Yahweh despises:

כִּי חֶסֶד חָפַצְתִּי
וְלֹא־זָבַח
וְדַעַת אֱלֹהִים
מֵעֹלוֹת

Table 36: What God desires and what He despises in Hos. 6:6

---

[184] The naming of the child as Jezreel (Hos. 1:4-5) is similar to announcing that the nation of Israel will come to an end (Dearman, 2010:94).

[185] The reason of the shocking name Lo-Ruhamah (Hos. 1:6-7) is given in the seconds half of verse 6. God will no longer have mercy on Israel. The name symbolizes God's judgement to come on Israel (Dearman, 2010:96).

[186] The name of the third child, Lo-Ammi, is yet another way to portray the judgement over Israel (Hos. 1:9) (Dearman, 2010:99; Harper, 1979:213; Van Leeuwen, 1978:42).

Mercy (חֶסֶד) and knowledge (דַעַת) are frequently used as a pair in the Hebrew Bible, either as attributes of the Yahweh or as human virtues[187] (Keil, 1980:74). In Hos. 6:6 they are used in the latter sense (as in Hos. 4:1 and Prov. 3:3).

Mercy (חֶסֶד) involves goodness and kindness in moral behaviour, a loving and compassionate heart that is associated with dedication and covenantal loyalty to God (Brown, Driver & Briggs, 1952:338-339; Clines, 2011:277-281; Van Leeuwen, 1978:141). It does not refer to love in a general sense, but love towards inferiors and people in need (Keil 1980:74). Keil (1980:99) provides a fitting definition: "*Chesed* is love to one's neighbour, manifesting itself in righteousness, love which has its roots in the knowledge of God". This means that "mercy" is directly paired with knowledge (דַעַת) of God, which implies true recognition of Yahweh's nature and will (Brown, Driver & Briggs, 1952:395; Clines, 2011:457) and a living relationship with Him, experiencing his love and compassion (Van Leeuwen, 1978:141). Mercy thus forms the fruit of the knowledge of God, for such knowledge does not only mean acquaintance with his nature and will, but knowledge of his love, compassion and faithfulness, which the believer heartily experiences (Keil. 1980:74).

These two desires of Yahweh (mercy (חֶסֶד) and knowledge (דַעַת)) stand in contrast with the cultic feasting and burnt offering that He despises (Macintosh, 1997:234). These two values resonate in several instances in the prophetic book: mercy (חֶסֶד) in Hos. 2:19 (MT 2:21); 6:4; 10:12; 12:6 (MT 12:7) and knowledge (דַעַת) in Hos. 4:6. They form the pillars of the covenantal ethos that Yahweh desires from his people (Dearman, 2010:197). In Hosea Yahweh mourns the lack of such an ethos: "Hear the word of the Lord, you Israelites, because the Lord has a charge to bring against you who live in the land: 'There is no faithfulness, no love (חֶסֶד), no acknowledgment (דַעַת) of God in the land'" (Hos. 4:1).

The question arises whether the Hebrew idiom conveys a negation of the sacrificial system as such. Macintosh (1997:234) chooses for this interpretation. However, an alternative interpretation is possible where Hosea does not condemn sacrificial worship as such, but the faulty reliance upon it amidst moral corruption. Such rituals are meaningless without covenantal ethos by the worshippers (Beare, 1981:227; Garret, 1997:161; Harper, 1979:287; Van

---

[187] Mercy without knowledge makes one negligent, and knowledge cannot be sustained without mercy (Keil, 1980:74).

Leeuwen, 1978:142)[188]. "Sacrificial practice ... is neither magic nor coercive of its divine author, but is rather a gift to the covenant community intended a means to greater ends" (Dearman, 2010:197). In Hosea Israel formally upholds the motions of sacrificial rituals, but they lack true understanding and devotion. In such a case the rituals actually had become obstacles to true devotion (Garret, 1997:161). Israel's covenant with Yahweh requires devotion that goes far beyond the mere adherence to rituals (Stuart, 1987:110). In this sense Hosea therefore expresses the divine demand for חֶסֶד (mercy) rather than sacrifice. All six the occurrences of חֶסֶד in Hosea (2:19[21]; 4:1; 6:4, 6; 10:12; 12:6[12:7]) appear in a covenant context and in close association with other covenantal terms (Dearman, 2010:197). Hosea speaks against religious acts without inner piety (Turner, 2008:153). Steadfast love, devotion and fidelity to Yahweh are required (Zimmeli, 1985:382). According to Hosea Israel's love is not steadfast. Israel's love is short-lived, like fleeting dew or cloud cover that disappears with sunrise. Furthermore, their devotion is not characterized by any expression of mercy. They keep to the letter of the Law in observing sacrifice, but not to the heart of it, as they lack mercy and love (Osborne, 2010:337). They are neither loyal to God nor to their fellow Israelites (Hos. 4:1-2).

It should be considered whether the Matthean Jesus cites this verse in Matt. 9:13 and 12:7 in line with the intention of Hosea, and this is subsequently discussed. In both cases it seems as if He uses Hos. 6:6 to condemn what He considered the rigid and inhumane attitudes of the Pharisees of the narrative. He accuses them of a lack of mercy towards people and knowledge of the will of God.

7.3 THE CITATION OF HOSEA 6:6 IN MATTHEW 9:13: JESUS EATING WITH TAX COLLECTORS AND SINNERS

The first scene in which Hos. 6:6 is quoted falls in the second discipleship section within a block of ten miracles (if the healing of the woman with haemorrhage and raising of the ruler's daughter, Matt. 9:18-26, is read as two miracles, otherwise it could be counted as 9, which equals a neatly structured 3 times 3). Matt. 8-9 forms this block of nine/ten miracles in sets of three, separated by two discipleship sections (Matt. 8:18-22; 9:9-17) (Davies & Allison, 2004b:6; Kingsbury, 1988:59; Osborne, 2010:332; Overman, 1996:112).

---

[188] Hosea joins other prophets (cf. 1 Sam. 15:22; Am. 5:21-27; Isa. 1:11-17; Micha 6:6-8; Jer. 7:21) that describe public cultic activity as divinely given gifts to be used with gratitude and not as means of magical coercion (Dearman, 2010:197).

Miracles 1-2-3	Discipleship	Miracles 4-5-6	Discipleship	Miracles 7/8 - 9-10
Matt. 8:1-17	Matt. 8:18-22	Matt. 8:23-9:8	**Matt. 9:9-17**	Matt. 9:18-34

Table 37: Miracle and discipleship sets in Matthew's miracle block

Encounters of conflict between Jesus and the religious leaders surface on several occasions in this block, for example when Jesus forgives a paralytic his sins (Matt. 9:3), when He sits at a table with tax collectors and sinners (Matt. 9:10-11), when Jesus' disciples do not fast (Matt. 9:14) and when He exorcises a demon (Matt. 9:32-34).

While the first discipleship section (Matt. 8:18-22) expresses the radical demand of Jesus and the cost of discipleship, the second (Matt. 9:9-17) expresses the meaning of the coming of the Kingdom of Heaven. A new social paradigm is established (Osborne, 2010:332) as Jesus came for the despised (who positively respond to his calling) and not for the superficially religious elite (who reject Jesus).

In Matt. 9:9-13 Jesus' ministry to sinners, the downtrodden and despised, is described. Jesus forgives sins and heals the "sick" (Matt. 9:9-13). Matthew contrasts inadequate responses to Jesus' ministry (of the Pharisees) with what should be the proper response (of the tax collectors and sinners) (Blomberg, 1992:154; Osborne, 2010:332).

Matt. 9:9-12 describes the scene where Jesus calls Matthew and has a meal with marginalized people of the Jewish society. It expresses God's mercy for outsiders of the community and the constitution of a new community. In the meantime the conflict with the religious leaders grows. On form-critical grounds this scene can be described as an objective story or controversy dialogue. Such stories usually consist of a word or deed of Jesus, followed by objections by opponents and Jesus' pronouncement that silence his critics (Davies & Allison, 2004b:96). These elements are presented as:

- Words and deeds of Jesus that provoke the attention of his opponents: Jesus' calling of the tax collector (Matt. 9:9) and his table fellowship with sinners (Matt. 9:10);
- Objection by the Pharisees (Matt. 9:11); and
- Jesus' response that silences his opponents (Matt. 9:12-13)

This story is paralleled in Mark 2:13-17 and Luk.5:27-32.

Matt. 9:9-12	Mark 2:13-17	Luk. 5:27-32
I Deeds and words of Jesus The call of the tax collector to become a disciple (Matt. 9:9) Setting of the scene 9a. Καὶ παράγων ὁ Ἰησοῦς ἐκεῖθεν εἶδεν ἄνθρωπον καθήμενον ἐπὶ τὸ τελώνιον, **Μαθθαῖον** λεγόμενον, As Jesus went on from there, he saw a man named Matthew sitting at the tax collector's booth.	13. **Καὶ ἐξῆλθεν πάλιν παρὰ τὴν θάλασσαν· καὶ πᾶς ὁ ὄχλος ἤρχετο πρὸς αὐτόν, καὶ ἐδίδασκεν αὐτούς.** 14a. καὶ παράγων εἶδεν **Λευεὶν τὸν τοῦ Ἀλφαίου** καθήμενον ἐπὶ τὸ τελώνιον, 13. Once again Jesus went out beside the lake. A large crowd came to him, and he began to teach them. 14a. As he walked along, he saw Levi son of Alphaeus sitting at the tax collector's booth.	27a. Καὶ μετὰ ταῦτα ἐξῆλθεν, καὶ ἐθεάσατο τελώνην ὀνόματι **Λευεὶν** καθήμενον ἐπὶ τὸ τελώνιον, After this, Jesus went out and saw a tax collector by the name of Levi sitting at his tax booth.
Calling of the tax collector 9b. καὶ λέγει αὐτῷ, Ἀκολούθει μοι. καὶ ἀναστὰς ἠκολούθησεν αὐτῷ. "Follow me," he told him, and he got up and followed him.	14b. καὶ λέγει αὐτῷ Ἀκολούθει μοι. καὶ ἀναστὰς ἠκολούθησεν αὐτῷ. "Follow me," Jesus told him, and he got up and followed him.	27b. καὶ εἶπεν αὐτῷ Ἀκολούθει μοι. 28. **καὶ καταλιπὼν πάντα ἀναστὰς ἠκολούθει αὐτῷ.** 27b. "Follow me," Jesus said to him, 28. and he got up, left everything and followed him.
Table fellowship with sinners (Matt. 9:10) Development of the scene 10. Καὶ ἐγένετο αὐτοῦ ἀνακειμένου ἐν τῇ οἰκίᾳ, καὶ ἰδοὺ πολλοὶ τελῶναι καὶ ἁμαρτωλοὶ ἐλθόντες συνανέκειντο τῷ Ἰησοῦ καὶ τοῖς μαθηταῖς αὐτοῦ. While Jesus was having dinner at the house, many tax collectors and sinners came and ate with him and his disciples.	15. Καὶ γίνεται κατακεῖσθαι αὐτὸν ἐν τῇ οἰκίᾳ αὐτοῦ, καὶ πολλοὶ τελῶναι καὶ ἁμαρτωλοὶ συνανέκειντο τῷ Ἰησοῦ καὶ τοῖς μαθηταῖς αὐτοῦ, ἦσαν γὰρ πολλοὶ καὶ ἠκολούθουν αὐτῷ. While Jesus was having dinner at Levi's house, many tax collectors and sinners were eating with him and his	29. Καὶ ἐποίησεν δοχὴν μεγάλην Λευεὶς αὐτῷ ἐν τῇ οἰκίᾳ αὐτοῦ· καὶ ἦν ὄχλος πολὺς τελωνῶν καὶ ἄλλων οἳ ἦσαν μετ' αὐτῶν κατακείμενοι. 29. Then Levi held a great banquet for Jesus at his house, and a large crowd of tax collectors and others were eating with them.

	disciples, for there were many who followed him.	
Objection by the Pharisees		
11. καὶ ἰδόντες **οἱ Φαρισαῖοι** ἔλεγον τοῖς μαθηταῖς αὐτοῦ, Διὰ τί μετὰ τῶν τελωνῶν καὶ ἁμαρτωλῶν ἐσθίει ὁ διδάσκαλος ὑμῶν; When the Pharisees saw this, they asked his disciples, "Why does your teacher eat with tax collectors and sinners?"	16. καὶ **οἱ γραμματεῖς τῶν Φαρισαίων** ἰδόντες ὅτι ἐσθίει μετὰ τῶν ἁμαρτωλῶν καὶ τελωνῶν, ἔλεγον τοῖς μαθηταῖς αὐτοῦ Ὅτι μετὰ τῶν τελωνῶν καὶ ἁμαρτωλῶν ἐσθίει; When the teachers of the Law who were Pharisees saw him eating with the sinners and tax collectors, they asked his disciples: "Why does he eat with tax collectors and sinners?"	30. καὶ ἐγόγγυζον οἱ **Φαρισαῖοι καὶ οἱ γραμματεῖς** αὐτῶν πρὸς τοὺς μαθητὰς αὐτοῦ λέγοντες Διὰ τί μετὰ τῶν τελωνῶν καὶ ἁμαρτωλῶν ἐσθίετε καὶ πίνετε; 30. But the Pharisees and the teachers of the Law who belonged to their sect complained to his disciples, "Why do you eat and drink with tax collectors and sinners?"
Jesus' response 12. ὁ δὲ ἀκούσας εἶπεν, Οὐ χρείαν ἔχουσιν οἱ ἰσχύοντες ἰατροῦ ἀλλ' οἱ κακῶς ἔχοντες. 13. **πορευθέντες δὲ μάθετε τί ἐστιν, Ἔλεος θέλω καὶ οὐ θυσίαν:** οὐ γὰρ ἦλθον καλέσαι δικαίους ἀλλὰ ἁμαρτωλούς. 12. On hearing this, Jesus said, "It is not the healthy who need a doctor, but the sick. 13. But go and learn what this means: 'I desire mercy, not sacrifice.' For I have not come to call the righteous, but sinners."	17. καὶ ἀκούσας ὁ Ἰησοῦς λέγει αὐτοῖς Οὐ χρείαν ἔχουσιν οἱ ἰσχύοντες ἰατροῦ ἀλλ' οἱ κακῶς ἔχοντες· οὐκ ἦλθον καλέσαι δικαίους ἀλλὰ ἁμαρτωλούς. On hearing this, Jesus said to them, "It is not the healthy who need a doctor, but the sick. I have not come to call the righteous, but sinners."	31. καὶ ἀποκριθεὶς ὁ Ἰησοῦς εἶπεν πρὸς αὐτούς Οὐ χρείαν ἔχουσιν οἱ ὑγιαίνοντες ἰατροῦ ἀλλὰ οἱ κακῶς ἔχοντες· 32. οὐκ ἐλήλυθα καλέσαι δικαίους ἀλλὰ ἁμαρτωλοὺς εἰς μετάνοιαν. 31. Jesus answered them, "It is not the healthy who need a doctor, but the sick. 32. I have not come to call the righteous, but sinners to repentance."

Table 38: The parallel of Matt. 9:9-12 with Mark 2:13-17 and Luk.5:27-32 on the story of Jesus eating with tax collectors and sinners

Matthew follows Mark fairly closely. As in Mark, Jesus calls a tax collector to become his disciple and the tax collector follows instantaneously (Matt. 9:9), followed by Jesus' table fellowship with outcasts (Matt. 9:10), the Pharisees' objection (Matt. 9:11) and Jesus' response (Matt. 9:12-13). The difference is that Matthew, as Luke does, drops the reference to the large crowd that followed Him and whom He taught. Furthermore, he uses the name "Matthew" instead of "Levi son of Alphaeus" and significantly adds the pronouncement in Matt. 9:13 while quoting from Hos. 6:6.

7.3.1 Jesus' attention-provoking words and deeds

7.3.1.1   *Setting of the scene (Matt. 9:9a)*

In setting the scene, Matthew omits Mark 2:13, with no reference to the sea or Jesus teaching the crowds and substitutes Λευεὶν τὸν τοῦ Ἀλφαίου (Levi son of Alphaeus) with Μαθθαῖον (Matthew). This change of name has been explained in different ways (Davies & Allison, 2004b:98; Gnilka, 1986:330-331). One suggested explanation is that the author knew that Levi was also called Matthew. He either knew this from tradition or he himself was this person. Another explanation is that the author of the first Gospel realized that Levi was not one of the twelve (cf. Matt. 10:2-5), and therefore felt compelled to identify Mark's Levi with Matthew. A third suggested explanation is that Matthew is called a tax collector in Matt. 10:3 (in contrast to Mark and Luke), and he therefore identified Levi the tax collector with Matthew. Yet another proposed explanation is that the name Μαθθαῖον (Matthew) is chosen because of assonance with μαθηταῖς (disciples), helping to emphasise the theme of discipleship. A fifth, but quite improbable suggestion is that this Gospel is a pseudepigraphon with the title "According to Matthew" and Matt. 9:9 could therefore be an attempt by the author to recognize this fictitious author. A sixth suggestion is that Levi was of no interest to the community of the first Gospel, while Matthew was closely connected to their community and its tradition. Though all of these suggestions are possible, the third suggestion seems to be quite probable; the tax collector in Matt. 10:3 is identified with Levi, the tax-collector of Matt. 9.

As in Mark and Luke, Matthew/Levi is a tax collector sitting at his booth. According the Gospels, tax collectors[189] were deeply despised and were

---

[189] Though the tax collectors had some political and economic power, they had little social status because of their greed and exploitation of the community. From the Second Testament it seems that they were despised as agents of Roman oppression and regarded as greedy and self-serving for extorting from them more than was required by their superiors in order to enrich themselves (Osborne, 2010:335). They often compromised regulations for purity in their dealing with Gentiles and their money (France, 2008:171; Hagner, 1993:238; Senior, 1998:105). Others in the empire shared this negative view of tax collectors. Cicero (De office. 15-51), Diogenes Cynicus (Ep. 36.2) and Dio Chrysostom (Orat, 14.14) lump them together with beggars, thieves and robbers. According to *Misha Tohorot* 7.6 "of tax-gatherers enter a house, the house becomes unclean". Tax collectors

regarded as unpatriotic. They were associated with shameful characters such as beggars, thieves and adulterers (cf. Matt. 5:46. Luk. 3:12-13; 5:29-30; 7:34, etc.). Τελῶναι καὶ ἁμαρτωλοὶ (tax collectors and sinners) represent a disgraceful formulaic pair in the Synoptic Gospels (Malina & Rohrbaugh, 2003:415-416; Overman, 1996:126).

7.3.1.2 Calling of the tax collector, Matthew (Matt. 9:9b)

By calling the tax collector, Jesus in the parlance shows mercy to this marginalized figure. He breaks a social and religious convention not to associate with tax collectors as they were regarded as shameful and impure figures. He calls him into a new relationship with Him that is merciful (Carter, 2000a:219). Matthew obeys and follows Jesus. He picks up this theme of discipleship from Matt. 4:19-20 and 8:18-22. In the Synoptic Gospels the word 'to follow' (ἀκολούθει) functions almost as a technical term for discipleship by people who put their trust in Jesus (Senior, 1998:104). The present imperative indicates a continuing following, which describes a lifelong call of discipleship (Morris, 1992:219; Osborne, 2010:335). While those disciples who were fishermen could go back to their fishing from time to time, the tax collector could not do so. Luk. 5:28 underlines this fact as he writes that this tax collector left behind everything he had. Matthew's immediate obedience is amazing. Jesus' calling is powerful and effective (Davies & Allison, 2004b:99).

7.3.1.3 Table fellowship with the tax collector and sinners (Matt. 9:10)

The narrative then continues with Jesus having dinner with "tax collectors and sinners" in Matthew's[190] house (Matt. 9:10). Jeremias (1966:48-49) notes the significance that Jesus reclined (αὐτοῦ ἀνακειμένου) and that many tax collectors came and reclined (συνανέκειντο) with Him. Presumably it was custom for the Jews to sit for meals, while reclining was done at feasts and

---

were regarded among the very low level of imperial society (Overman, 1996:127). Malina & Rohrbaugh (2003:415-416) however warn that the understanding of the position of tax collectors should be nuanced. A distinction should be made between "chief" tax collectors such as Zaccheus mentioned in Luk. 19:2 and their employees, such as referred to in Matt. 5:46; 9:10; 10:3 etc. The chief tax collectors enriched themselves, but their employees were usually rootless people unable to find other work. This contributed to the low moral opinion towards these people. Furthermore, paying taxes and tolls had a very strong negative association for the Jews as burden of their subjugation by the Romans (Witherington, 2013:51)

[190] While Luk. 5:29 tells that Levi held a great banquet for Jesus in his house, Mark 2:15 and Matt. 9:10 do not qualify who's house it was.

parties. The festive character of the event is thus emphasised. Table fellowship and feasting in particular were regarded as important social events and symbols of closeness of those participating (Blomberg, 2005:15; Hagner, 1993:238). Illustrating the closeness as symbolized by this meal, Smith (1980) has proposed that Jesus' meals as depicted in the Gospels must also be understood in terms of Greek symposia. Symposia formed key Hellenic practice by aristocrats to celebrate special occasions and to introduce new members to their selected group. Persons with whom one would participate in festive meals and symposia were defined by peer groups and social status (Osborne, 2010:335). Malina and Rohrbaugh (2003:381) have remarked with regard to meals in antiquity: "the microcosm of the meal is parallel to the macrocosm of every day social relations". Eating together usually implied the same social position, ideas and values. Roman sources described meals where guests of different social ranks are seated in different rooms and are served with different wines and food, depending on their social status (Martial, Epigrams, 1.20; 3.60; Juvenal, Satires; Pliny, Letters 2.6). In the group-orientated society of the Ancient Mediterranean world, one's identity was mainly formed by which social group one belonged to[191] (Witherington, 2013:49). With this meal Jesus declares that the tax collectors and sinners are accepted as part of his group.

Jesus eating with these sinners recalls the previous pericope where Jesus forgives sinners (Matt. 9:2-6). The first Gospel emphasises that Jesus' forgiveness implies more than words. Jesus demonstrates that the opportunity to receive God's mercy is opened to all, also to the despised. Jesus acts as God's representative. For those who respond to his calling, He gives new opportunities and He redefines those who are regarded as righteous (Davies & Allison, 2004b:101). Jesus' action seems to be intentionally provocative, like a prophet performing a parable or setting out a prophetic symbol. Jesus forms a new social community based on his enactment of mercy. It is likely that Jesus intended this festive meal as proleptic to the coming of the kingdom of God. Jesus often spoke of the kingdom in terms of a great banquet (Matt. 8:11; 22:1-14; 25:1-13; 26:29). "God's mercy was being opened to all in Israel, including – perhaps especially? – those who ... were despised by most pious Jews" (Davies & Allison, 2004b:101).

---

[191] Sociologist refer this this convention as collectivist or dyadic personalities (Witherington, 2013:49).

Jesus relativizes a soteriological scheme based on the Law in terms of a relationship with Him (Davies & Allison, 2004b:101). He acts as the eschatological envoy of God. Those who respond to his calling receive the opportunity to form part of his community and thus to enter into the kingdom of God. Jesus thus cut the old religious understanding of who should be regarded as righteous. All Jews, whether pious or impious, where faced with the same decision, namely how to respond to the calling by Jesus.

7.3.2 Objection by the Pharisees (Matt. 9:11)

The Pharisees[192] in the narrative severely questioned Jesus' disciples as a result of this deed.[193] The Pharisees refer to Jesus as ὁ διδάσκαλος ὑμῶν (your teacher), apparently in a sarcastic manner. In the first Gospel Jesus' opponents call Him "teacher", often in what seems to be in a derogative manner (e.g. Matt. 12:38; 22:16, 24, 36). The Matthean Pharisees use the typical Matthean "our" and "your/their" language indicating their dislike of Jesus, his teaching and his disciples (Matt. 9:11). Through his actions Jesus expresses full acceptance of tax collectors and sinners. Table fellowship with tax collectors and sinners is described as objectionable to Pharisaic practice[194]. Socially such association was regarded as unfitting and eating with sinners would make a person unclean and therefore unsuitable to participate in sacrifice (Turner, 2008:252). Yet Jesus follows an inclusive approach and eats with people excluded and disapproved of by Pharisees. In conflict with the Pharisees' religious and social pre-occupations, Jesus eats with people whom they judge fit only for the judgement of God. As agent of God's mercy He demonstrates the meaning of mercy (Carter, 2000a:219).

---

[192] In Matthew's narrative it is the Pharisees alone who reproach Jesus, while Mark mentions "the scribes and the Pharisees" and Luke "the Pharisees and the scribes".

[193] Eating with such people would imply that Jesus identifies with them. This would characterize Jesus' ministry, as He often shared meals with such people. He therefore was accused of being a "glutton and drunkard" and a "friend of tax collectors and sinners" (Matt. 11:9 // Luk. 7:34) (Sanders, 1983a:5-36).

[194] Pharisees were scrupulous regarding what they ate and with whom they shared their meals. For the sake of righteousness they were guardians of separation from sinners (Hagner, 1993:238; Morris, 1992:221; Osborne, 2010:336; Overman, 1996:129). They were careful to keep themselves unspotted by association with whom they regarded as sinners (Beare, 1981:227). "Keep thee far from an evil neighbour and consort not with the wicked" ('Abot 1:7) was the rabbinic dictum.

7.3.3 Jesus' response (Matt. 9:12-13)

Jesus himself responds in three parts:

(1) Matt. 9:12: ὁ δὲ ἀκούσας εἶπεν, Οὐ χρείαν ἔχουσιν οἱ ἰσχύοντες ἰατροῦ ἀλλ' οἱ κακῶς ἔχοντες (on hearing this, Jesus said, "It is not the healthy who need a doctor, but the sick); (2) Matt. 9:13a: πορευθέντες δὲ μάθετε τί ἐστιν, Ἔλεος θέλω καὶ οὐ θυσίαν (but go and learn what this means: 'I desire mercy, not sacrifice.') and (3) Matt. 9:13b: οὐ γὰρ ἦλθον καλέσαι δικαίους ἀλλὰ ἁμαρτωλούς (for I have not come to call the righteous, but sinners).

Table 39: Jesus' threefold response to the Pharisees' objection against Him eating with tax collectors and sinners in Matt. 9:12-13

In his response Jesus asserts his authority. Mark and Luke include the first and third parts of Jesus' response, but Matthew alone mentions Jesus' citation from Hos. 6:6, which forms the second part of the response. In so doing, Matthew's version validates Jesus' mission by a scriptural reference to God's will. This addition emphasises the controversy between the participants (Repshinski, 2000:78). While the Pharisees regarded Jesus' action as socially and religiously unacceptable, Jesus validates his action with reference to the Prophet as acts of mercy (Mounce, 1991:84). By implication the Pharisaic attitude is presented as unmerciful and contrary to Scripture. According to the Pharisees, one should keep a distance from people who could make one cultically impure and therefore unfit for sacrifice. Jesus, however, defends his stance with reference to "sacrifice" in the Hosean text (Weren, 1994:91).

7.3.3.1   First part of Jesus' response (Matt. 9:12)

In the first part of his response, Jesus uses a proverb that has several parallels in the ancient world[195]: Οὐ χρείαν ἔχουσιν οἱ ἰσχύοντες ἰατροῦ ἀλλ' οἱ κακῶς ἔχοντες[196] (it is not the healthy who need the doctor, but the sick) (Matt. 9:12). Obviously Jesus implies spiritual sickness. With "the sick" Jesus refers to Matthew and the tax collectors and sinners with whom He eats. In our current

---

[195] Davies & Allison (2004b:103) lists "For the one whose body is ill needs a physician" (Menanander, Fragment 591); "Physicians are not among the healthy but spend their time among the sick" (Plutarch, Apophthegmata laconic, 230F); "Physicians are commonly with the sick but they do not catch the fever" (Diogenes, Laertius 6.1.1).

[196] οἱ κακῶς ἔχοντες can be translated more directly: "Those who have/experience misery".

context, we associate sickness with physical aspects. However, in Matthew it relates to vulnerability that goes much further and includes social and religious facets (Weren, 1979:86). With "those who are well" He refers to the Pharisees. However, this does not mean that they are actually (socially and religiously) healthy, but that they regard themselves as healthy. Jesus is the doctor enacting God's mercy towards those who realise their need to be healed, the tax collectors and sinners (Osborne, 2010:336). He breaks the tragic effect of sin. In the biblical text the images of sin and disease are closely related[197]. Death is regarded as the ultimate consequence of sin. Sickness lies on the continuum between sin and death. Sickness is the sequel to sin and the predecessor of death. Underlying this connection is the social implication of both illness and healing (Senior, 1998:106; Weren, 1994:86), as discussed in Chapter 6. Οἱ κακῶς ἔχοντες (the sick people – those who experience misery beyond physical ailment) Jesus talks about, are the socially disvalued and isolated people excluded from society. However, Jesus came to restore their value in life by reconnecting them with the community. Jesus facilitates such reconnection by eating (feasting) with them. Jesus crosses the boundaries of religious and social taboos by which vulnerable and people need are isolated.

7.3.3.2 Second part of Jesus' response (Matt. 9:13a)

Jesus then continues by referring to Hos. 6:6 and suggests that the Pharisees, who pride themselves on their knowledge of Scripture, should go and learn what it means that God desires mercy and not sacrifice (Matt. 9:13a)[198]. With this reference, Hos. 6:6 is used as source of *halakha*, thus arguing the practical application of this prophetic saying. It is appropriate, but also ironic that Jesus answers the Pharisees with a citation from the Scriptures, as they prided themselves on their knowledge of and faithfulness to God's revelation (Davies & Allison, 2004b:104). The introductory words πορευθέντες δὲ μάθετε τί ἐστιν (but go and learn what it means) represents a rabbinic formula to encourage pupils for *Torah* study[199], which means "go and discern the sense of Scripture"

---

[197] It is noteworthy that Hos. 6:6 appears in context of the sickness of the Lord's people as result of their sins (Hos. 5:12-14; 6:1, 5) and their call for repentance so that they can be healed (Hos. 6:2-3) (Van Bruggen, 1990:159).

[198] This is a powerful comeback. Since they called Him teacher (Matt. 9:11), Jesus gives them a teaching assignment (Osborne, 2010:227).

[199] Rabbinic parallels to this phrase are found in Seder Eliyahu Rabbah 18 and m. 'Abot 2.9 (Turner, 2008:253).

or "go and make a valid inference from the scriptural statement" (Davies & Allison, 2004b:104; Gnilka, 1986:332; Hill, 1978:111; Osborne, 2010:337). The implicit accusation by the Pharisees that Jesus does not observe purity requirements by eating with tax collector and sinners, is put into context with sacrifice (Weren, 1979:92). According to Jesus, the observance of cultic requirements is meaningless if it is not accompanied by mercy towards others. When compared to Mark's and Luke's versions of the story, Matthew significantly adds this citation in between Jesus' statement of the sick who are in need of a doctor (Matt. 9:12) and that He came to heal the sinners (as the metaphorical sick people) (Matt. 9:13b). Furthermore, Jesus argues that the fact that the Pharisees accuse Him of eating with the marginalized proves that they do not understand the true meaning of being merciful. Thus the Pharisees become ironic and tragic figures in the narrative (Repschinski, 2000:80). The Pharisees are regarded as people who are unable to interpret Scripture correctly. They are unable to realise that Hos. 6:6 is applicable to Jesus' outreach to tax collectors and sinners (Davies & Allison, 2004b:104). Jesus' association with tax collectors and sinners are regarded as an expression of indiscriminate and steadfast love as referred to by Hosea. Matthew describes Jesus as exercising the true intention of this prophetic word.

The implications of Matthew's understanding of "I desire mercy, not sacrifice" should be considered. Meier (1980:94) has argued that this verse implies a complete rejection of temple sacrifice. However, this seems improbable as Matthew says nothing else about temple cult[200] (Mounce, 1991:113). Matthew rather relates to the prophet Hosea, who did not intend to abolish the temple, but to reform it by stressing inner purity and not mere ritual purity (Turner, 2008:253). Another option would be that Matthew portrays Jesus as exalting compassion above strict adherence to the Law (Cope, 1976:67). Carson (1984:225) has proposed a similar interpretation, arguing that this antithesis should not be understood as an absolute negation of sacrifice. It is cast in a Semitic antithesis, where "not A, but B" means "B is of more basic importance than A". Such an interpretation makes the understanding of Matt. 5:17 about the continuing validity of the Law problematic. Jesus does not downplay the Law and sacrifices, but has argued that adherence to the Law starts with a

---

[200] It should be noted that 'Aboth R. Nat. 4 cites Hos. 6:6 in a lament by Rabbi Johanan ben Zakkai over the destruction of the temple: "My son, be not grieved; we have another atonement as effective as this. And what is it? It is acts of loving kindness, for it is said: 'For I desire mercy and not sacrifice'". Davies (1966:306) connects this reinterpretation with the fall of Jerusalem He teaches that sacrifice will be continued by compassionate deeds after the destruction of the temple.

compassionate heart (Turner, 2008:254). It seems more probable that Matthew's understanding of ἔλεος (mercy) carries the same connotation of חֶסֶד as in the Hosean context. Cultic observance without covenant loyalty is worthless. In Hosea the deserters still followed the letter of the Law by offering sacrifices, but forgot the heart of the Law, which entailed mercy and love (Osborne, 2010:337). Mercy and love should present the covenant in action. God is gracious and merciful and therefore requires his people to show mercy too (Davies & Allison, 2004b:105). The Matthean Jesus demonstrates that covenant loyalty implies the acceptance of repentant outsiders such as the tax collectors and sinners into the covenant community rather than to exclude them.

Jesus warns the Pharisees that they are repeating the same error as Israel in Hosea[201]. By their very desire to maintain the Law, they actually turn away from the covenant and their professed love for the Law become like a morning cloud, like the dew that evaporates quickly (Hos. 6:4) (Repschinski, 2000:80). With this reference Matthew's Jesus affirms that God requires faithful adherence and love for God and merciful actions, and not heartless sacrifice or mere formal religious piety, as was the case with Israel in the Hosean text (Turner, 2008:253). Jesus argues that the way the Pharisees treat others demonstrates their failing relation to God (Osborne, 2010:337). By not having a heart of mercy towards the sinners, the Pharisees show their inappropriate relationship with God (Hill 1978:109).

The showing of mercy signifies more than mere pity and compassion. Lohmeyer (1967:173) has made a noteworthy remark about Matthew's reference to Hos. 6:6: "Hier liegt der Gegensatz zwischen Erbarmen und Opfer, zwischen christliche Caritas und jüdischen Gottesdienst". This quote signifies the separation between the community that follows Him and the Judaists. The quotation indicates a removal of boundaries between Jesus and the outcasts. In contrast with Pharisean convictions, Jesus welcomes these religious outcasts and grants them fellowship. The identity of Matthew's community is moulded on the person of Jesus. His followers should do the same.

---

[201] In Matt. 23 the Pharisees are accused of a lack of steadfast love.

7.3.3.3 Third part of Jesus' response (Matt. 9:13b)

In conclusion, Jesus describes his own mission with an ἦλθον (I have come)-saying[202] that states the character of his mission: οὐ γὰρ ἦλθον καλέσαι δικαίους ἀλλὰ ἁμαρτωλούς (for I have not come to call the righteous, but the sinners) (Matt. 9:13b). The δίκαιοι (righteous) is contrasted with the ἁμαρτωλοι (sinners), the supposed δίκαιοι being the Pharisees and the supposed ἁμαρτωλοι being the tax collectors and sinners (righteous). The δίκαιοι do not refer to the objective fact, but to the assumed subjective opinion of self-righteousness by the Pharisees. Jesus' saying thus contains irony (Davies & Allison, 2004b:107). The call is for salvation for those who admit their sin, and the goal of their salvation is discipleship (Osborne, 2010:337). Once again the relation between sickness and sins is demonstrated. Jesus' care and cure reach into the deepest levels of one's person (Weren, 1979:87). Calling the despised and eating (feasting to demonstrate a social relation) with the marginalized are the ways in which Jesus carries out his mission.

Matt. 8:17 interprets Jesus' healings in terms of Isa. 53:4: ὅπως πληρωθῇ τὸ ῥηθὲν διὰ Ἡσαΐου τοῦ προφήτου λέγοντος Αὐτὸς τὰς ἀσθενείας ἡμῶν ἔλαβεν καὶ τὰς νόσους ἐβάστασεν (This was to fulfil what was spoken through the prophet Isaiah: "He took up our infirmities and bore our diseases"). This version closely relates to the Hebrew text: "Surely he took up our pain and bore our suffering" (Isa. 53:4). In the LXX version the diseases are interpreted metaphorically to refer to sins: (He bears our sins, and is pained for us) (cf. Weren, 1979:88). In the story of Jesus eating with the tax collectors and sinners (Matt. 9:9-13), this metaphoric interpretation applies. Jesus, the doctor, came to heal the sick, namely the sinners.

This healing activity defines the meaning of mercy (Matt. 9:13a). It implies the healing of disturbed relations within a society, which is the result of a separation between people claiming to be righteous and the people who they regard as sinners.

7.3.4 Implications for the Matthean community

My suggested scenario is that Matt. 9:9-13 reflects the experience and mission of the Matthean community. Following the example of Jesus to accommodate

---

[202] This is the third of the seven "I have come"-statements in Matthew: Matt. 5:17 (2x); 9:13; 10:34 (2x); 35; 20:28) which explains Jesus' God given mission.

outsiders in their community, the Matthean community most likely experienced similar opposition as that of Jesus. As argued in Chapter 2, the Matthean community was struggling to establish its identity within a post-70 C.E. Jewish society (Saldarini, 1991:49). Jewish Christians welcomed Gentile Christians into their community, but were blamed for doing so (Luz, 1990:84; Repschinski, 2000:27), similar to the blame Jesus received for eating with sinners and tax collectors.

Elements of identity formation can be recognized in this narrative. The tax collectors and sinners, who were welcomed by Jesus, can be associated with the Gentile Christians in Matthew's community. Matt. 21:31 ("tax collectors and prostitutes are entering the kingdom of God ahead of you") probably relates to the same dispute. The evangelist in Matt. 9:9-12 probably has the fellowship of his Jewish-Christian community with Gentile Christians in the church in mind. He defends their stance by appealing to the example of their Master and the conception of his mission on earth, which they have inherited. His community does not regard themselves as the healthy who have no need of a doctor, but as sinners who have been healed by Jesus, and thus experienced God's mercy and love. Accordingly, they welcome those into their fellowship whom Jesus calls, though they might not meet the standards of legal purity that were set by their contemporary Pharisees. By implication Matthew suggests that those who accuse his community for this action must also go and learn what Hos. 6:6 means. Hummel (1966:40) has remarked accordingly: "Die Aufnahme der Heiden in die Gemeinde geschieht im Gehorsam gegenüber dem Gebot des Erbarmen ... über den kultisch-rituellen Vorschriften". Obedience to God would result in the removal of social and religious barriers between Christians from the Jews, and Christians from the Gentiles. The ultimate opposers of such an inclusive community are the Pharisees.

Matthew's Jesus in Matt. 9:13 uses the quotation of Hos. 6:6 effectively to illustrate the religious short-sightedness of the Pharisees. Thus Matthew legitimizes the approach of his community towards people who are regarded as outsiders. This passage provides an interpretative frame and theological perspective for the Matthean narrative on the attitude of Jesus and his followers amidst their antagonists.

7.4 THE CITATION OF HOSEA 6:6 IN MATTHEW 12:7: SABBATH CONTROVERSY

In Matt. 12:1-14 Jesus is involved in a debate about the Sabbath praxis, an issue that was central in Jewish religious life in New Testament times. In the time of

Jesus the Sabbath was well established as one of the central characteristics of the Jewish religion (Oliver, 2013:46). Sabbath observance was regarded as of great importance in Judaism (Beare, 1981:269). The *Mishnah* recognizes that the written law was far less comprehensive than the traditional rules of application. It devotes the whole of *Shabbat* 7 to what is considered as work on the Sabbath. These rules treated the plucking of a bit of grain as reaping and the rubbing of them in the hands as threshing. In the *Mishnah*, Tractate *Hagigah*[203] 1.8 states: "The rules about the Sabbath ... are like mountains hanging on a hair, for Scripture is scanty and the rules many". The Jews had at least three stipulated lists of categories of prohibited works on the Sabbath (Jb. 50.6-13; CD 10.14-11.18; m. Sab. 7.2). Through the centuries up to 100 C.E., the rules regarding works prohibited on the Sabbath increasingly became more specific and meticulous. Yang (1997:97-99), however, has argued that the emphasis on the covenantal significance of the Sabbath was significantly weak.

This probably reflects something about the situation of the original audience of the Gospel. There is little reason to doubt that there were frequent debates between Christian and non-Christian Jews in society about Sabbath observance, especially as long as the synagogue was still a matter of concern for the Christians of the Matthean community (Beare, 1981:269; Hill, 1978:116; Yang, 1997:99). It might be that members of this community were accused by Pharisaic Judaism for what they regarded as Christian laxity in Sabbath observance. If the Sabbath played such a key role in the Judaism in the time of Jesus and of the Matthean community, it is obvious that Jesus' attitude towards the Sabbath was an important part of Matthew's argument on Jesus and the Law.

The Sabbath issue is explicitly expressed in two consecutive passages, Matt. 12:1-8 (paralleled in Mark 2:23-28 and Luk. 6:1-5) and Matt. 12:9-14 (paralleled in Mark 3:1-6 and Luk. 6:6-11). The two consecutive passages in Matt. 12 describe two separate stories, but are jointly presented in the narrative. All the Synoptic Gospels link them together, thus demonstrating the interconnectedness of the argument. Matthew, however, places the Sabbath stories later in his document after firmly stating Jesus' view on the Law in the Sermon on the Mount. A cursory reading of the Sabbath material could lead to the assumption that Jesus is there presented as abrogating the Law. Yet

---

[203] Tractate Hagigah deals with Pilgrimage Festivals and the pilgrimage offering that men were supposed to bring in Jerusalem as well as topics of ritual purity.

Matthew places the Sabbath controversies after the statement of Jesus in Matt. 5:17-19: μὴ νομίσητε ὅτι ἦλθον καταλῦσαι τὸν νόμον ἢ τοὺς προφήτας· οὐκ ἦλθον καταλῦσαι ἀλλὰ πληρῶσαι (do not think that I have come to abolish the Law or the Prophets; I have not come to abolish them but to fulfil them) (cf. Chapter 3) on the continuing validity of the *Torah*. Furthermore, Matthew's Jesus in Matt. 5:20 refers to "better righteousness" that is needed to enter the kingdom of God: ἐὰν μὴ περισσεύσῃ ὑμῶν ἡ δικαιοσύνη πλεῖον τῶν γραμματέων καὶ Φαρισαίων, οὐ μὴ εἰσέλθητε εἰς τὴν βασιλείαν τῶν οὐρανῶν (unless your righteousness surpasses that of the Pharisees and the teachers of the Law, you will certainly not enter the Kingdom of Heaven). As argued in Chapter 4, this righteousness is not a stricter adherence to the Law, but adherence of a different kind. The debate is not about the recognition or obedience of the Law, but about the understanding of the intention of God with the Law (Hill, 1978:117). Therefore it seems that Matthew argues not *if* the Sabbath should be observed, but *how* it should be done (cf. Carson, 1982:98; Weiss, 1990:25).

However, not all scholars agree. Rordorf (1968) has specifically denied that Matt. 5:17-18 is an authentic saying of Jesus. He has argued that Jesus' actions amount to deliberate provocative breaking of the Law. His attitude is inter alia shown by what Rordrof has called "the offensive incident" of the disciples plucking grain, and Jesus' reply that the Son of Man is Lord also of the Sabbath. "The Sabbath commandment was not merely pushed into the background by the healing activity of Jesus: it was simply annulled" (Rordorf, 1968:70). According to Rordorf Jesus' attitude must have been "something monstrous" (Rordorf 1968:65) to the early church. Brown (1966:210) has made a more nuanced remark by saying "that Jesus violated the rules of the scribes for the observance of the Sabbath is one of the most certain historical facts about his ministry". According to Brown Jesus challenged the way the scribes observed the Sabbath by demonstrating and teaching an alternative interpretation of the meaning of this day.

For this study on the Law in Matthew, it is therefore necessary to also take a closer look at what Matthew regards as the actual intention of the Sabbath and how he describes Jesus' attitude towards the Sabbath.

7.4.1 Intention with the Sabbath

7.4.1.1 Three-dimensional scope

Bacchiocchi (1986:154-176) has identified the following three-dimensional scope of the Sabbath in the First Testament:

7.4.1.1.1 Aetiology of the Sabbath

The first dimension is found in the aetiology of the Sabbath (Bacchiocchi, 1986:154). The Sabbath resonates God's rest (*nuah*) and blessings of the seventh day of creation (Gen. 2:2-3; Exod. 20:8-11; 31:17). In the First Testament the notion of rest (*menuhah*) expresses aspirations for a peaceful life in a land of rest (Deut. 12:9; 25:19; Isa. 14:3; 32:18) and God will find his "resting place" amongst his people and especially in his sanctuary at Zion (1 Chron. 23:25; 2 Chron. 6:41; Ps. 132:8, 13, 14; Isa. 66:1).

7.4.1.1.2 Messianic perspective

The messianic interpretation of the Sabbath provides the second dimensional scope (Bacchiocchi, 1986:158). The Sabbath served to symbolise the future peace and rest of the Messianic age. *Mishnah Tamid* 7:4[204] views the time of redemption as: "all Sabbath and rest in the life everlasting". The divine blessing of the seventh day (Gen. 2:3) in prophetic and rabbinic minds offered the basis of a messianic age. The peace and harmony that once existed between Adam and the animals would be restored in the messianic age when "the wolf will live with the lamb, the leopard will lie down with the goat, the calf and the lion and the yearling together; and a little child will lead them …" (Isa. 11:6). In those days "the earth will be full of the knowledge of the Lord as the waters cover the sea" (Isa. 11:9). Therefore one should behave on the Sabbath as if the peace and harmony of the Messianic age had already come. The availability and abundance in the Garden of Eden of "trees that were pleasing for the eye and good for food" (Gen. 2:9) inspired a prophetic vision of extraordinary abundance during the Messianic age. Amos declares: "The days are coming … when the reaper will be overtaken by the ploughman and the planter by the one treading grapes. New wine will drip from the mountains and flow from all the

---

[204] The Mishnah contains the oral traditions of the Pharisees from the Second Temple period and was redacted by Rabbi Yehudah haNasi between 180 and 220 C.E. Though the Mishnah was only redacted after the Matthean text, it is plausible that many of the oral traditions already were in circulation.

hills." (Amos 9:13.) Similar descriptions are found in Isa. 4:2, 7:22; 30:23-25; Syriac Baruch 29:4-6 (late first or early second century C.E.) and Enoch 10:17-19 (last part dated circa the end of first century B.C.E.). Papias, one of the earliest church fathers (*c.* 60-130 C.E.), applied this vision almost verbally to an envisioned 1000 year reign (millennium) as the cosmic Sabbath when Christ and the resurrected saints would enjoy peace and prosperity on the earth (as recorded by Irenaeus, against Heresies 5:33, 3-4). A fitting description of the rabbinic expectation of the Sabbath is provided in an imaginative and dramatic *Midrash* from c. 100 C.E.: "Israel said before the Holy One, Blessed be He: 'Master of the World, if we observe the commandments, what will we have?' He said to them: 'the world-to-come.' They said to Him: 'Show us its likeness.' He showed them the Sabbath" (Otiot de-Rabbi Akiba).

7.4.1.1.3   God's deliverance

Thirdly, the Sabbath commemorates God's deliverance (Bacchiocchi, 1986:162). The creation story somehow is a deliverance story: deliverance from disorder to order, from chaos into cosmos. The repetition of the phrase "it was good" (Gen. 1:4, 10, 12, 18, 21, 24, 31) portrays the picture of perfection and satisfaction. It also commemorates Israel's deliverance from Egypt (Deut. 5:12-15), thus symbolising messianic redemption. The release from the pressure of work and social inequalities is experienced on and through the Sabbath. This is pronounced in the prologue to both the Exodus and Deuteronomic versions of the Decalogue: "I am the Lord your God, who brought you out of Egypt, out of the land of slavery." (Exod. 20:2 and Deut. 5:6.) The Sabbath served not only to provide personal rest and liberation from social injustices, but also to epitomise and nourish the hope for future messianic peace, harmony, prosperity, joy, rest and redemption from sin (Bacchiocchi, 1986:176). The ultimate purpose of the Sabbath has eschatological significance as it soteriologically signifies the eternal rest for the people of God as pronounced in Hebr. 4:1-13.

7.4.1.2   *Sign of covenantal relationship between the God of mercy and his people*

Besides this three-dimensional scope of the Sabbath that Bacchiocchi has identified, one should recognize God's Lordship of the Sabbath. His Lordship is frequently asserted, as can be seen in the phrases "my Sabbath" (Exod. 31:12-17; Lev. 19:3, 30 and 26:2). This day should be understood as a sign of the covenantal relationship between Yahweh and his people (Ezek. 20:12). In the observance of the Sabbath the people should take delight in Yahweh (Isa. 58:13-14). The Edenic Sabbath offered the concept of "Sabbath of delight": a day of joy, light, harmony and peace (Ps. 92). Prophets warn that a legalistic or hollow observance of the Sabbath without observing its true covenantal character, is rejected by Yahweh (Isa. 1:13; Amos 8:5). The Sabbath is not intended as a burden, but as an expression of God's mercy. That is why the Sabbath should be called a "delight". Yahweh detests formalistic Sabbath activities if it is accompanied by unmerciful behaviour (Isa. 1:15-17).

From this brief overview it seems that the First Testament gives a different perspective of the Sabbath command than the later preoccupation with detailed casuistic regulations imposed by the Pharisees and rabbis. In Jewish literature there were at least three stipulated lists of prohibited works on the Sabbath: Jubilees 50.6-13 (c. 160-150 B.C.E); Qumran, CD 10.14-11.8 and Mishnah Sabbath 7.2 (Second temple period). These lists developed specific and meticulous regulations. It seems that this growing number of more specific regulations made the Sabbath inconvenient and burdensome. It directed the concern of the people away from why they should keep the Sabbath to how they should keep it (Yang, 1997:98). This seems to have been the issue with the Sabbath in Matthew's narrative.

7.4.2 "Prologue" to the Sabbath controversy stories: Rest for the weary (Matt. 11:25-30)

Reading the Gospel as a literary unit, it is important to consider the wider contexts in which a specific pericope appears. The Sabbath controversy pericopes are preceded by Jesus' invitation and promise of rest (Matt. 11:25-30). The opening words of the Sabbath narrative, ἐν ἐκείνῳ τῷ καιρῷ (at that time) (Matt. 12:1) ties this text to the previous pericope (Matt. 11:25-30), which opens with the same words (Oliver 2013:82). The thematic correspondence can be recognised in several aspects.

Matthew 11:25 refers to the σοφοί and συνετοί (wise and learned), which naturally refer to the opponents of Jesus, and the Pharisees and scribes in particular who regard themselves as the wise and the learned. They are represented as being well versed in the *Torah*, but unreceptive to God's revelation in Jesus (Carter, 2000a:257). Obsessive in protecting their own interest and control, they became severe opponents of Jesus – throughout the Gospel and again with regard to the Sabbath.

Davies and Allison (2004b:296) have described Matt. 11:25-30 as a "capsule summary of the message of the entire gospel". These highly Christological verses have a poetic form and consists of three strophes (Hagner, 1993:316; Weren, 1994:108):

- The first strophe (Matt. 11:25b-26a // Luk. 10:21a) comes in the form of a prayer and deals with God's revelation, not for the wise and the learned, but for the little ones;
- the second strophe (Matt. 11:26b-27 // Luk. 10:21b-22) describes Jesus' role in God's plan of salvation; and
- the third strophe (Matt. 11:28-30), which is unique to Matthew, consists of an invitation to all who are wearied to find rest with Jesus.

In the first strophe, which is prayer-like, Jesus contrasts the σοφοὶ and συνετοὶ (wise and learned) with the νήπιοι (little children) (Matt. 11:25) who are privileged to receive the special revelation (Matt. 11:27). The metaphor νήπιοι (little children) indicates the receptiveness and humbleness of these people (Oliver 2013:83). Jesus seemingly includes his disciples in this category – the small community of disciples who have responded to Jesus' call (Weren, 2014:51). Matthew most likely also has the Christian community of his days in view (Luz, 2001a:181).

The special revelation entails the intimate relationship between the Father and Jesus (expressed in the second strophe), which Jesus' opponents did not realise. The irony in the narrative is striking. In contrast to the "wise and the learned", Jesus alone is in the position to exactly declare what God is like (Keener, 1997:222). Jesus describes Himself in the language of divine Wisdom (e.g. Sir. 1:6-9; 24:19; 51:23-27; Wis. 8-9) (Davies & Allison, 2004b:296-297; Hagner, 1993:323). Speaking of God's law as his own, Jesus implicitly claims even more authority than Moses. The repeated use of γινώσκειν (know) in derivative forms in the first eight verses of Matthew 12 refers back to ταῦτα (these things) that are hidden from the wise, but revealed to children. To those to whom it is revealed it is also given to recognise the Father in his Son (Lybaek, 1997:493; Weren, 2014:56).

The third strophe is unique to Matthew. Jesus invites people by saying δεῦτε πρός με (come to me) (Matt. 11:28), which echoes Wisdom's call (Prov. 8:1-7; 9:4-5; Sir. 24:19; 51:23-27). The ultimate wisdom is to be found with Him (Davies & Allison, 2004b:185). He extends a welcome to πάντες οἱ κοπιῶντες καὶ πεφορτισμένοι (all those who are wearied and burdened), presumably implying the result of a legalistic interpretation of the *Torah* by the Pharisees and the scribes. Jesus claims that his interpretation of the *Torah* has a different effect. The ζυγός (yoke) of Jesus (Matt. 11:29-30)[205] is easy in comparison with that of his opponents. In the First Testament "yoke" is a symbol for foreign and harsh rule (e.g. Gen. 27:40; 1 Kings. 12:4-14). The release of the foreign yoke implies freedom and forgiveness (Isa. 9:3; 10:27). During the Second Temple period the term yoke was commonly used for the instruction of the *Torah* (e.g. 2 En. 34:1-2; 2 Apoc. Bar. 4:13; cf. Acts 15:10 and Gal. 5:1; cf. Deines, 2008:67; Hagner, 1993:324; Oliver, 2013:85). In Sir. 6:18-31 and 51:23-27 the terms "wisdom", "law" and "yoke" are linked together. The yoke of wisdom is the instruction of the Law. Jesus' interpretation would be the easy yoke He offers to the burdened. Matt. 11:27 mentions the words πάντα μοι παρεδόθη ὑπὸ τοῦ Πατρός μου, (all things have been committed to me by the Father) by which Jesus affirms his authority as Son of God to interpret the Torah.

Jesus is πραΰς and ταπεινὸς τῇ καρδίᾳ (gentle and humble in heart) (Matt. 11:29). Jesus' gentleness stands in contrast to the implied approach of the Pharisees. The gentle Jesus grants this grace to those who are like little ones and who are meek (cf. Matt. 5:3, 5). The ἀνάπαυσις ταῖς ψυχαῖς ὑμῶν (rest for your souls) that is promised (Matt. 11:29) anticipates the following Sabbath story. The Sabbath was often translated in the LXX with ἀνάπαυσις (Exod. 23:23; Deut. 5:14). This rest consists of peace of mind in the presence of God. Here Jesus invites his audience to enjoy that kind of ἀνάπαυσις with Him. "Jesus is the true Sabbath" (Davies & Allison, 2004b:187).

It appears that the eschatological understanding of rest, especially in relation to the Sabbath, was well established in the early Christian period (cf. Heb. 4:1-13). Eschatological visions anticipated a return to the complete state of God's creation to what it was before the fall. According to Heb. 4 the eschatological Sabbath rest that has been expected through Israel's history is fulfilled in Jesus. In the Gospels the ministry of Jesus as giver of rest is described in terms that announce the eschatological hope of redemption in the Hebrew Scriptures: τυφλοὶ ἀναβλέπουσιν καὶ χωλοὶ περιπατοῦσιν, λεπροὶ καθαρίζονται καὶ κωφοὶ ἀκούουσιν, καὶ νεκροὶ ἐγείρονται καὶ πτωχοὶ εὐαγγελίζονται (the blind receive sight, the lame walk, those who have leprosy are cured, the deaf hear, the dead are raised, and the good news is preached to the poor" (Matt. 11:5 // Luk 7:22.)

---

[205] The words of Ben Sira shows close resemblance to this logion: "Put your neck under her (Wisdom's) yoke." (Sir. 51:26.)

The association between Jesus, Sabbath rest and the eschatological hope adds force to the Christological argument of the Sabbath controversies. In his ministry of mercy and healing, the true meaning of the Sabbath has realised (Lybaek, 1997:495).

Matthew's Jesus repeats his invitation with a parallel imperative: ἄρατε τὸν ζυγόν μου ἐφ' ὑμᾶς καὶ μάθετε ἀπ' ἐμοῦ (take my yoke upon you and learn from me). By learning from Jesus εὑρήσετε ἀνάπαυσιν ταῖς ψυχαῖς ὑμῶν (you will find rest for your souls) (Matt. 11:29-30). With these words Jesus probably invites people to be liberated from ways in which the Torah is enforced, inter alia by 613 legalistic commands that the Pharisees stipulated.

It is obvious that the controversy stories about the Sabbath should be read in context with this preceding pericope. The Sabbath should have a new form in the presence of the κύριος τοῦ σαββάτου (Lord of the Sabbath) (Matt. 12:8). Matthew's argument is that Jesus brings true rest to those being burdened by the legalistic understanding of the Sabbath. The prologue provides Christological affirmation of the Person of Jesus and provides an invitation to see, hear and understand true wisdom, which He teaches and demonstrates.

7.4.3 Harvesting grain on the Sabbath (Matt. 12:1-8)

In this narrative Jesus responds to the objection of the Pharisees to Jesus' disciples plucking grain on the Sabbath with several arguments. In one of his arguments He appeals to Hos. 6:6 again (Matt. 12:7). The Sabbath controversy appears in all three the Synoptic Gospels, but Matthew is the only who includes this citation. It is significant that the author inserts this reference in between two very strong statements, this first on something greater than the temple, (Matt. 12:6) and the second on the Son of Man being the Lord of the Sabbath (Matt. 12:8). The temple and the Sabbath were both extremely important symbols for the Jews. While the temple had already been destroyed when the Gospel was written and its function somehow replaced by synagogue activities, Sabbath-observance remained a stronghold in Judaism. This citation emphasises a basic hermeneutical difference between Jesus and the Pharisees regarding the Sabbath observance (Overman, 1996:176; Turner, 2008:309). Matthew seemingly includes this citation as it expresses Matthew's main argument that the Pharisees are assiduous about legal observance while they neglect the crucial matter of mercy and loving kindness (ἔλεος). Comparing the story in the Synoptic Gospels brings to light some more significant emphases by Matthew that stresses this argument:

Matt. 12:1-8	Mark 2:23-28	Luk. 6:1-5
Setting of the scene (Matt. 12:1) Ἐν ἐκείνῳ τῷ καιρῷ ἐπορεύθη ὁ Ἰησοῦς τοῖς σάββασιν διὰ τῶν σπορίμων· οἱ δὲ μαθηταὶ αὐτοῦ **ἐπείνασαν** καὶ **ἤρξαντο τίλλειν στάχυας** καὶ ἐσθίειν. At that time Jesus went through the grainfields on the Sabbath. His disciples were hungry and began to pick some heads of grain and eat them.	Setting of the scene (Mark 2:23) Καὶ ἐγένετο αὐτὸν ἐν τοῖς σάββασιν παραπορεύεσθαι διὰ τῶν σπορίμων, καὶ οἱ μαθηταὶ αὐτοῦ ἤρξαντο ὁδὸν ποιεῖν τίλλοντες τοὺς στάχυας. One Sabbath He was going through the grainfields, and as his disciples walked along, they began to pick some heads of grain.	Setting of the scene (Luk. 6:1) Ἐγένετο δὲ ἐν σαββάτῳ διαπορεύεσθαι αὐτὸν διὰ σπορίμων, καὶ ἔτιλλον οἱ μαθηταὶ αὐτοῦ καὶ ἤσθιον τοὺς στάχυας ψώχοντες ταῖς χερσίν. One Sabbath He was going through the grainfields, and his disciples began to pick some heads of grain, rub them in their hands and eat the kernels.
Objection by the Pharisees (Matt. 12:2) οἱ δὲ Φαρισαῖοι ἰδόντες εἶπαν αὐτῷ, Ἰδοὺ οἱ μαθηταί σου ποιοῦσιν ὃ οὐκ ἔξεστιν ποιεῖν ἐν σαββάτῳ When the Pharisees saw this, they said to him, "Look! Your disciples are doing what is unlawful on the Sabbath."	Objection by the Pharisees (Mark 2:24) καὶ οἱ Φαρισαῖοι ἔλεγον αὐτῷ Ἴδε τί ποιοῦσιν τοῖς σάββασιν ὃ οὐκ ἔξεστιν; The Pharisees said to him, "Look, why are they doing what is unlawful on the Sabbath?"	Objection by the Pharisees (Luk. 6:2) τινὲς δὲ τῶν Φαρισαίων εἶπαν Τί ποιεῖτε ὃ οὐκ ἔξεστιν τοῖς σάββασιν; Some of the Pharisees asked, "Why are you doing what is unlawful on the Sabbath?"
Jesus' response with questions and statements (Matt. 12:3-8) 3a. ὁ δὲ εἶπεν αὐτοῖς, He answered, Rhetorical Question 1: Haven't you read (Matt. 12:3b-4) Οὐκ ἀνέγνωτε 3b. τί ἐποίησεν Δαυὶδ ὅτε ἐπείνασεν καὶ οἱ μετ' αὐτοῦ; 4. πῶς εἰσῆλθεν εἰς τὸν οἶκον τοῦ θεοῦ καὶ τοὺς ἄρτους τῆς προθέσεως	Jesus' response (Mark 2:25-26): 25a. καὶ λέγει αὐτοῖς· He answered, Rhetorical Question: Haven't you read (Mark 2:25b-26) 25b Οὐδέποτε ἀνέγνωτε τί ἐποίησεν Δαυείδ, ὅτε χρείαν ἔσχεν καὶ ἐπείνασεν αὐτὸς καὶ οἱ μετ' αὐτοῦ; 26. πῶς εἰσῆλθεν εἰς τὸν οἶκον τοῦ Θεοῦ ἐπὶ Ἀβιαθὰρ ἀρχιερέως καὶ τοὺς ἄρτους	Jesus' response (Luk. 6:3-5): 3a. καὶ ἀποκριθεὶς πρὸς αὐτοὺς εἶπεν ὁ Ἰησοῦς Jesus answered them, Rhetorical Question: Haven't you read (Luk. 6:3b-4) 3b. Οὐδὲ τοῦτο ἀνέγνωτε ὃ ἐποίησεν Δαυεὶδ ὁπότε ἐπείνασεν αὐτὸς καὶ οἱ μετ' αὐτοῦ ὄντες; 4. ὡς εἰσῆλθεν εἰς τὸν οἶκον τοῦ Θεοῦ καὶ τοὺς ἄρτους τῆς προθέσεως λαβὼν

ἔφαγον, ὃ οὐκ ἐξὸν ἦν αὐτῷ φαγεῖν οὐδὲ τοῖς μετ' αὐτοῦ, εἰ μὴ τοῖς ἱερεῦσιν μόνοις; 3b. "Haven't you read what David did when he and his companions were hungry? 4. He entered the house of God, and he and his companions ate the consecrated bread—which was not lawful for them to do, but only for the priests.	τῆς προθέσεως ἔφαγεν, οὓς οὐκ ἔξεστιν φαγεῖν εἰ μὴ τοὺς ἱερεῖς, καὶ ἔδωκεν καὶ τοῖς σὺν αὐτῷ οὖσιν; 25b "Have you never read what David did when he and his companions were hungry and in need? 26. In the days of Abiathar the high priest, he entered the house of God and ate the consecrated bread, which is lawful only for priests to eat. And he also gave some to his companions."	ἔφαγεν καὶ ἔδωκεν τοῖς μετ' αὐτοῦ, οὓς οὐκ ἔξεστιν φαγεῖν εἰ μὴ μόνους τοὺς ἱερεῖς; 3b. "Have you never read what David did when he and his companions were hungry? 4. He entered the house of God, and taking the consecrated bread, he ate what is lawful only for priests to eat. And he also gave some to his companions."
Rhetorical question 2: Or haven't you read (Matt. 12:5): ἢ οὐκ ἀνέγνωτε ἐν τῷ νόμῳ ὅτι τοῖς σάββασιν οἱ ἱερεῖς ἐν τῷ ἱερῷ τὸ σάββατον βεβηλοῦσιν καὶ ἀναίτιοί εἰσιν; Or haven't you read in the Law that the priests on Sabbath duty in the temple desecrate the Sabbath and yet are innocent?		
Statements (Matt. 12:6-7) Jesus greater than the Temple (Matt. 12:6) λέγω δὲ ὑμῖν ὅτι τοῦ ἱεροῦ μεῖζόν ἐστιν ὧδε. I tell you that something greater than the temple is here. God's demand for mercy rather than sacrifice (Matt. 12:7):	Statement (Mark 2:27) The Sabbath is made for man καὶ ἔλεγεν αὐτοῖς Τὸ σάββατον διὰ τὸν ἄνθρωπον ἐγένετο, καὶ οὐχ ὁ ἄνθρωπος διὰ τὸ σάββατον· Then he said to them, "The Sabbath was made for man, not man for the Sabbath.	

εἰ δὲ ἐγνώκειτε τί ἐστιν, Ἔλεος θέλω καὶ οὐ θυσίαν, οὐκ ἂν κατεδικάσατε τοὺς ἀναιτίους. If you had known what these words mean, 'I desire mercy, not sacrifice,' you would not have condemned the innocent.		
Concluding pronouncement (Matt. 12:8): κύριος γάρ ἐστιν τοῦ σαββάτου ὁ υἱὸς τοῦ ἀνθρώπου. For the Son of Man is Lord of the Sabbath."	Concluding pronouncement (Mark 2:28): ὥστε κύριός ἐστιν ὁ Υἱὸς τοῦ ἀνθρώπου καὶ τοῦ σαββάτου. So the Son of Man is Lord even of the Sabbath."	Concluding pronouncement (Luk. 6:5): καὶ ἔλεγεν αὐτοῖς Κύριός ἐστιν τοῦ σαββάτου ὁ Υἱὸς τοῦ ἀνθρώπου. Then Jesus said to them, "The Son of Man is Lord of the Sabbath."

Table 40: The parallel of Matt. 12:1-8 with Mark 2:23-28 and Luk. 6:1-5 on of the story of grain harvesting on the Sabbath

7.4.3.1 *Setting of the scene (Matt. 12:1)*

Only Matthew mentions the time of the event. He writes ἐν ἐκείνῳ τῷ καιρῷ (at that time) and thus links this story about the Sabbath with Jesus' character as described at the end of the previous chapter. In Matt. 11:28-30 Jesus invites all who are weary and burdened to find their rest with Him (δεῦτε πρός με πάντες οἱ κοπιῶντες καὶ πεφορτισμένοι, κἀγὼ ἀναπαύσω ὑμᾶς ...). Matthew depicts the liberating yoke of Jesus in the Sabbath praxis. He compares the easy yoke of Jesus with the heavy burden of the Pharisees (Carson, 1982:66). Furthermore, this link is preceded by Jesus' remark about the lack of understanding amongst the σοφοὶ and συνετοὶ (wise and learned) (Matt. 11:25), which probably refers to the Pharisees who, with all their regulations about legal righteousness, were laying burdens on others instead of giving them rest.

Other than in Mark and Luke, Matthew puts Jesus at the forefront of the story by mentioning Jesus by the name ἐπορεύθη ὁ Ἰησοῦς (Jesus went) (Matt. 12:1). This is significant when it is read along with the concluding pronouncement (for the Son of Man is Lord of the Sabbath) (Matt. 12:8). Matthew thus makes use of an *inclusio* to identify Jesus as the Son of Man and Lord of the Sabbath. It is also remarkable that the Pharisees accused Jesus and not his disciples, who were actually the ones picking the grain (Matt. 12:2). It appears that Matthew intentionally focuses on Jesus' position.

Matthew then continues by telling the readers that the disciples were hungry (οἱ δὲ μαθηταὶ αὐτοῦ ἐπείνασαν) when they began to pluck grain to eat (Matt. 12:1). Mark 2:23 and Luk. 6:1 do not speak of their hunger. Matthew apparently refers to the hunger of the disciples to demonstrate the correlation between situation of the disciples with that of David and his companions later in the argument (Matt. 12:3-4) (Hill, 1978:114; Lohmeyer, 1967:184).

However, scholars have suggested more reasons for Matthew's reference to their hunger. Matthew's version is often regarded as a softening of the Markan text as to make the actions of the disciples acceptable according to *halakhic* regulations (Hagner, 1993:328). *Mishnah* Sabbath, 14.3; 22.6 makes provision that work on the Sabbath is acceptable to prevent the loss of human life. However, there surely was no threat of life in this case, which makes such a *halakhic* exception irrelevant (Deines, 2008:67). Schlatter (1959:308) has proposed that Matthew's reference to the disciples' hunger proves that needs take precedence over commandments. However, it is very unlikely that Matthew would argue that God's commandments could be set aside in times of need. Carter (2000a:264) has argued that this scene concerns fundamental issues of access to food resources and the alleviation of human need. While the dispute is about interpreting the divine will for the Sabbath, Carter has argued that criticism is levelled against systems that hinder access to resources. It is indeed possible that some kind of counter-narrative can be involved in this scene. Doing good, especially for the needy, appears to be an important matter for Matthew's Gospel. However, the denial of access to the grain is not mentioned in the narrative and is not likely to have been the issue[206], but rather the fact that the plucking took place on the Sabbath. Work on the Sabbath was not permitted in the Hebrew Bible (Exod. 20:8-11; 31:14; 34:21; Deut. 5:12-15), yet this controversy presupposes not only the Law of the Sabbath rest as laid down in the Hebrew Bible, but also the regulations (e.g. as described in the *Mishnah Sabbath*) that were developed by the scribes (Beare, 1981:269).

Matthew omits the Markan more casual ἤρξαντο ὁδὸν ποιεῖν (as they made their way) (Mark 2:23) and replaces it with the more formal ἤρξαντο τίλλειν στάχυας

---

[206] There is little reason to doubt the Pharisees acceptance of the law that the hungry were entitled to food as a gift (Lev. 25:35-37) and that they could glean after harvest (Lev. 19:9-10; 23:22; Deut. 23:25)

(they began to pick grain) (Matt. 12:1), which sounds more like work (Oliver, 2013:87). The Pharisees' accusations must have been based on their assumption that the disciples were engaged in the work of reaping. The rubbing of the grain between the hands and blowing to remove the husks (as in Luk. 6.1) could be understood as threshing and winnowing (Morris, 1992:300). Reaping, threshing and winnowing were all listed under the 39 categories of work that were prohibited by *Mishnah Sabbath*, 73B. The point at issue is therefore rather whether the slightest form of gleaning is permitted on the Sabbath.

7.4.3.2   *Objection by the Pharisees (Matt. 12:2)*

The Pharisees confront Jesus and it sounds as if they are asserting their conviction rather than questioning Him. As discussed before, throughout his gospel, Matthew portrays the Pharisees as opponents of Jesus. Once again they are depicted as critical of Jesus' behaviour and malicious in their intent. In their accusation they explicitly refer to the Law: Ἰδοὺ οἱ μαθηταί σου ποιοῦσιν ὃ οὐκ ἔξεστιν ποιεῖν ἐν σαββάτῳ ("your disciples are doing what is unlawful on the Sabbath) (Matt. 12:2), an accusation that Matthew retains from Mark's account[207].

7.4.3.3   *Jesus' response with questions and statements (Matt. 12:3-8)*

Jesus does not dispute what the disciples have done, but challenges the Pharisees on their evaluation of the disciples' conduct. Kilpatrick (1950:116) has proposed that the disciples accidently broke the law, which should explain Jesus' defence of the disciples' actions. However, Jesus does not admit this in the narrative. Furthermore, it is very unlikely that Matthew would entertain a conviction that Jesus would find the accidental breaking of the Law acceptable. Matthew's argument rather lies in Jesus' response in the rhetorical questions and statements that follow.

7.4.3.3.1   *Two rhetorical questions: "Haven't you read" (Matt. 12:3b-5)*

Jesus begins by responding with two rhetorical questions, each time introduced by οὐκ ἀνέγνωτε (haven't you read?). In the honour and shame dominated

---

[207] Harvesting on the Sabbath must have been a contentious issue in Jesus' time. The Midrash Ps. 73:4 reads: "Said Rabbi Shimon in the name of Rabbi Simeon Hasida: 'In this world a person goes to pick figs [on the Sabbath], the fig doesn't say anything; but in the world to come a person goes to pick a fig on the Sabbath, and she cries and says: It is the Sabbath!'".

society Jesus responds to their challenge and defeats them with a strong insult against those who claim to be experts of the Scriptures (Keener, 1997:225).

7.4.3.3.1.1 Reference to David and the bread of presence (Matt. 12:3b-4)

In the first question Jesus refers to the Nob incident about David and the bread of presence in 1 Sam. 21 (Matt. 12:3b-4 // Mark 2:25b-26 // Luk. 6:3b-4). In that story David and his men were hungry and were therefore permitted to eat the shrine's holy bread, though the Law stipulated that only the priests were allowed to do that (Lev. 24:5-9)[208]. David was not punished by God. He seems to approve the deed and it strengthens David to continue his task. Likewise, Jesus supports his disciples. Jesus argues that Sabbath praxis should be shaped by mercy. However, this appeal of Jesus raises several questions. One could assume that Jesus argued that if a righteous man like David could break the Law, the disciples could do so too. This, however, is unlikely. Jesus never accepted that his disciples actually broke the Sabbath law. The fundamental reason for Jesus' appeal to 1 Sam. 21:1-6 should rather be related to the statement on the authority of Jesus. As David the king had the authority to interpret the Law, Jesus the ultimate King and Messiah has the authority to a higher degree (France, 1971:47). It is important to recognise this implicit David-typology that follows in Matt. 12:6, ὅτι τοῦ ἱεροῦ μεῖζόν ἐστιν ὧδε (someone greater than the temple is here) to understand the explicit claim in the temple-typology in the following response (Yang, 1997:176).

7.4.3.3.1.2 Reference to Sabbath offering (Matt. 12:5)

Matthew requires more than reference to the actions of David to justify the conduct of the disciples (Hill, 1978:114) and makes an addition to Mark's (and Luke's) version with a second question. In Matt. 12:5-6 Jesus makes a second biblical allusion by referring to the commands on Sabbath offering (Num. 28:9f). The priests were permitted to perform certain duties on the Sabbath in the temple. One only has to consider the work involved in dismembering and burning the Sabbath sacrifices (Num. 28:1-10). This response of Jesus seems to appeal to one of the well-known rabbinic exceptions. According to Tannaitic literature the rabbis allowed the "violation" of the Sabbath law for at least six

---

[208] According to some Rabbinic traditions (b. Menah. 95b; Yalq. 130 on 1 Sam. 21:5) David did so on a Sabbath, as the Sabbath was the day that the bread was changed according to Lev. 24:8 (France, 2008:206; Strack-Billerbeck, 1965:618). Though this is not explicitly mentioned in Matthew's narrative, it might be implied.

occasions, namely circumcision, Passover, saving Scriptures or food from a fire, self-defensive war, saving a life, and temple service (Weren, 1994:120; Yang, 1997:84)[209]. It is, however, highly unlikely that Jesus would deal with rabbinic casuistry. The actual argument probably once again lies in verse 6 where Jesus proclaims his own authority: ὅτι τοῦ ἱεροῦ μεῖζόν ἐστιν ὧδε (someone greater than the temple is here). If the temple service requires the suspension of some Sabbath Laws, how much more does the presence of someone that is greater than the temple?

7.4.3.3.2 Two statements (Matt. 12:6-7)

Following the two rhetorical questions, Jesus continues his response with two statements.

7.4.3.3.2.1 Jesus is greater than the temple (Matt. 12:6)

It is remarkable that Matthew (like Luke) omits Jesus' statement, τὸ σάββατον διὰ τὸν ἄνθρωπον ἐγένετο, καὶ οὐχ ὁ ἄνθρωπος διὰ τὸ σάββατον (the Sabbath was made for man, not man for the Sabbath), which is found in Mark's version (Mark 2:27). Mark's version implies that the Sabbath should be regarded as a gift from God to man. This statement has rabbinic parallels (Melkitha Exod. 31:13, 14) and could have dismantled much of the Pharisees' criticism (Strack-Billerbeck, 1965: 5).

Matthew, however, replaces this statement with a different Christological statement that would rather incite further Pharisaic criticism: ὅτι τοῦ ἱεροῦ μεῖζόν[210] ἐστιν ὧδε (I tell you that one greater than the temple is here) (Matt.

---

[209] The author of Jubilees would certainly not have agreed with Matthew's argument: "On the Sabbath day do not do any work which you have not prepared for yourself on the sixth day so that you may eat, drink and rest. Keep the Sabbath on this day from all work ... and do rest on it from any work that belongs to the work of mankind except to burn incense and to bring before the Lord offerings and sacrifices for the days and the Sabbaths. Only this kind of work is to be done on the Sabbath days in the sanctuary or the Lord" (Jub. 50:9-11).

[210] It should be considered that the comparative μεῖζόν is in the neuter form. It could therefore be argued that it could better be translated with "something" and not with "someone". However, similar neuter uses of μεῖζόν appear in Matt. 12:41-42 that undoubtedly refer to the persons of Jonah and Solomon in contrast to Jesus Himself. Turner (1965:21) has remarked that grammatically the neuter can be used to refer to persons provided that the emphasis is less on the individual than on some outstanding general quality. Gundry (1994:223) has explained this specific occurrence accordingly as he has remarked that the neuter gender stresses the quality of Jesus' superior greatness rather than his personal identity.

12:6). This argument roughly resembles the rabbinic *qal vahomer* style of argumentation (Oliver, 2013:97). As the temple has been the focus of God's presence amongst his people, the Matthean statement implies that God can be found much better in Jesus than in the temple (France, 2008:207; Gnilka, 1986:443). This claim of Matthew must have resounded strongly in the aftermath of 70 C.E. when the people were confronted with the cultic vacuum left by the destruction of the temple. Rabbinic sages referred to Hos. 6:6 to develop the study of the *Torah* and practices of charity to fill this gap (Avot R. Nat. A4; B 8-9; Pirqe R. El. 11, 16) (Oliver, 2013:97). In Matthew a Christological argument is presented as Jesus presents Himself as God's agent and the one through whom God carries out functions previously associated with the temple (Carter, 2000a:266). What God does in his sending of Jesus by far surpasses what He did when setting up the temple worship (Morris, 1992:303; Senior, 1998:137). The point is that temple service took precedence over the Sabbath, and Jesus' ministry and messianic office supersedes the temple service (Osborne, 2010:453). Jesus therefore has even greater authority over the Sabbath.

Jesus explicitly makes use of temple-typology, latching on to the implicit David-typology in his first rhetorical question (Matt. 12:3b-4). As the presence of God could be experienced in the temple, it can now be experienced in the company of Jesus. Jesus is greater than the temple. This was a very strong claim to make, as the temple was seen as the centre of Israel's religious and political tradition. The temple was much more than a religious building. It was the focus of national identity and the visible symbol that Israel was the chosen people of Yahweh. Jesus supersedes what was before as the role of the temple is transferred to and fulfilled in Him (France, 2008:109).

The fulfilment of God's presence is a central motif in Matthew's Gospel (cf. Menken, 2004:12). He begins his Gospel with Ἐμμανουήλ ... μεθ' ἡμῶν ὁ Θεός (Immanuel ... God with us) (Matt. 1:23) and concludes with ἐγὼ μεθ' ὑμῶν εἰμι πάσας τὰς ἡμέρας ... (I am with you always ...) (Matt. 28:20). This motif is asserted with Jesus' words: οὗ γάρ εἰσιν δύο ἢ τρεῖς συνηγμένοι εἰς τὸ ἐμὸν ὄνομα, ἐκεῖ εἰμι ἐν μέσῳ αὐτῶν (for where two or three come together in my name, there I am with them) (Matt. 18:20.) If the temple has more authority than the Sabbath because it manifests the presence of God, then Jesus (who is the replacement and fulfilment of the role of the temple) has even more authority than the Sabbath (Matt. 12:8). As the priests were guiltless while working in the temple on the Sabbath (as the temple had authority over the Sabbath), so much more are the disciples of Jesus as they are in his presence.

Thus the authority and presence of Jesus create new attitudes and new ways of observance of the Sabbath (McIver, 1995:242).

7.4.3.3.2.2 Mercy rather than sacrifice (Matt. 12:7)

Jesus' second statement also only appears in Matthew. Jesus appeals to Hos. 6:6: εἰ δὲ ἐγνώκειτε τί ἐστιν, Ἔλεος θέλω καὶ οὐ θυσίαν (If you had known what these words mean, "I desire mercy not sacrifice"). By its insertion into the Markan *Vorlage* Matthew typifies the character of God as the merciful rather than the demanding one. He wants loving-kindness rather than blind sacrifice. In Matthew it is "the compassionate attitude and merciful action which give concrete expression to one's faithful adherence to and love for God" (Hill, 1978:110) rather than blind sacrifice is required. "Es legitimiert die Freigabe des Sabbats für die Liebestat gegenüber dem Pharisäismus" (Hummel, 1966:45). This citation explains what Jesus meant by his previous statement about someone that is greater than the temple. The character of the fulfiller of this will of God is being demonstrated in the Person of Jesus. Ἔλεος (mercy) is presented as the guiding principle of the ministry of Jesus (Lybaek, 1997:493). Therefore Jesus declares that mercy is more important than temple sacrifice, or sacrifice without mercy is missing the point. The antagonistic and unmerciful character of the Pharisees stands in stark contrast with this mercy.

France (2008:207) has remarked that Matt. 12:7 has the same effect as the pronouncement in Mark 2:27, τὸ σάββατον διὰ τὸν ἄνθρωπον ἐγένετο, καὶ οὐχ ὁ ἄνθρωπος διὰ τὸ σάββατον (the Sabbath was made for man, not man for the Sabbath). The outward sacrificial service is contrasted to the spiritual sacrifice offered by Jesus and his disciples. Their sacrifice is characterized by mercy and "doing good on the Sabbath" (τοῖς σάββασιν καλῶς ποιεῖν) (Matt. 12:12). Gerhardsson (1974:28) has remarked: "The comparison here is between two kinds of worship: the *latreia* which the priests perform in the temple, and the *latreia* in which Jesus and his disciples are engaged".

The question remains as to what Jesus meant by this quotation. Scholars have suggested a variety of explanations:

- Strecker (1971:32) has proposed that Jesus contrasted ritual law with moral law, but the plucking of the grain can hardly be regarded as the implementation of a moral law (Banks, 1975:117).
- Hagner (1993:330) has suggested that "mercy" should be regarded as tolerance towards the disciples for their behaviour. A similar interpretation is made by Hare (1993:132), according to which Jesus

wishes the Pharisees to have mercy on the disciples. Yet, interpretations such as of Hagner and Hare have implied that the disciples indeed had broken the Law. Weren (1994:119) has aptly warned: "Barmhartigheid staat hier niet gelijk met vergeving". This would not fit into Jesus' argument in the pericope as He states that if the Pharisees had understood the meaning of Hos. 6:6, οὐκ ἂν κατεδικάσατε τοὺς ἀναιτίους (you would not have condemned the innocent) (Matt. 12:7). It rather seems that Jesus do not merely tolerate his disciples or ask the Pharisees to do the same. He argues that they did nothing wrong in terms of the true intention of the Law. He furthermore criticises the Pharisees for their attitude, not because of their lack of tolerance, but because of their misunderstanding of the will of God (Yang, 1997:184).

- Another explanation would be to regard acts of mercy as superior to sacrifices. Rabbis recognized the importance of mercy. Already in the third century B.C.E. Simon the Just had said: "By three things is the world sustained: by the Law, the (temple-) service, and by deeds of loving kindness" (*Mishnah Abot* 1.2) and a teaching attributed to Johanan ben Zakkai after the destruction of the temple reads that the practice of loving kindness replaces the temple worship (*Abot R. Nat.* 4). Accordingly, Jesus did not argue that the disciples' actions should mercifully be accepted, but that they themselves behaved according to the principle of mercy (Saldarini, 1994:130). Being merciful towards themselves, the disciples would therefore be permitted to alleviate their own hunger. However, this interpretation of Matt. 12:8 also does not really satisfy. The only need that could override Sabbath regulations was the threat of death (France, 2008:206). There is no indication that the hunger of the disciples was life-threatening and this interpretation still implies that the disciples had broken the Law, which Jesus does not admit.
- A more satisfactory explanation is that the quotation primarily relates to the character of God (France, 2008:168; Hill, 1978:118-119). In a loving covenantal relationship God shows mercy towards people and He expects a response of loving kindness rather than heartless sacrifice from people. Davies and Allison (2004b:105) has subsequently remarked: "cultic observance without inner faith and heart-felt covenant loyalty is vain".

This last explanation seems to be the most plausible. Jesus argues that there is a relation between God's merciful character and the Sabbath (Yang, 1997:186). The Hebrew Bible taught that the Sabbath should not be regarded as a burden, but as an expression of God's mercy and grace. Practicing mercy is the divine will for the Sabbath (Carter, 2000a:266). If piety hinders practicing mercy, that kind of piety is wrong. Green (1975:125) has remarked: "the Pharisees were so anxious to study what Scripture said that they could not hear what Scripture meant". The Lord expects Israel to call the Sabbath a "delight" (Isa. 58:13), and He regards Sabbath assemblies as vain if they are conducted by people who behave unmercifully (Isa. 1:15-17). This seems to be the Matthean Jesus' intention with his reference to Hos. 6:6. If one legalistically keeps the Sabbath without understanding that the expression of mercy and grace is the intention of the Sabbath, God would not be pleased with such a person.

It is significant that Jesus in Matt. 12:7 for the second time quotes from Hos. 6:6. As mentioned before, this is the only quotation to be repeated in the Gospel and clearly is of special importance to Matthew (Hill, 1978:107). It seems that Matthew found this quotation particularly applicable to his community who struggled because of the strenuous separation from their Jewish mother-religion and community. With this double occurrence Matthew connects the material of Matt. 12:7 with Matt. 9:13. In both cases Jesus is represented as in dispute with the Pharisees and passing judgement on their conduct. The quotation is introduced in similar ways, πορευθέντες δὲ μάθετε τί ἐστιν (go and learn what this means) (Matt. 9:13) and εἰ δὲ ἐγνώκειτε τί ἐστιν (if you had known what the words mean) (Matt. 12:7). On both occasions these words are directed at the antagonistic Pharisees. Furthermore, both passages are preceded and followed by Christological pronouncements (Lybaek, 1997:496). In Matt. 9 Jesus' practical compassion is described as He forgives sins (Matt. 9:6) and has fellowship with τελῶναι καὶ ἁμαρτωλοί (tax collectors and sinners), whom He calls to become disciples (Matt. 9:1-13). Christologically interpreted, the quotation in both contexts illustrates the praxis of Matt. 5:17.

As mentioned before, in the original context of the citation in Hosea, ἔλεος (mercy) refers to the faithfulness and covenantal loyalty of God. Hosea repeatedly warns Israel against its disloyalty and calls God's people to repent. With his repeated use of this quotation Matthew alluded to this Hosean context of an urge to repentance and covenantal loyalty to God. Matthew implies an urge for an on-going fellowship with God and a prophetic judgement against those who would not recognise the mercy of God in the ministry of Jesus. It is therefore clear that in quoting Hos. 6:6 there is more at stake than the mere defence of the disciples' behaviour. By not ministering mercy, one can put oneself outside the covenantal community. With this reference Matthew obtains a theological confirmation of the authority of Jesus.

7.4.3.3.3 Concluding pronouncement (Matt. 12:8)

Matthew presents Jesus as the fulfilment of the Sabbath with the concluding Christological assertion κύριος γάρ ἐστιν τοῦ σαββάτου ὁ υἱὸς τοῦ ἀνθρώπου (the Son of Man is the Lord of the Sabbath) (Matt. 12:8, paralleled in Mark 2:28 and Luk. 6:5). The fundamental question is who has the authority to interpret the Sabbath law. This forms part of Matthew's broader argument that Jesus is the authoritative and definitive interpreter of the *Torah* (Hagner, 1993:330). Jesus declares his Lordship over the Sabbath outright. In the First Testament God's Lordship over the Sabbath is repeatedly expressed (e.g. Exod. 16:23, 25; 20:10; 31:15; 35:2). This Lordship that was in the First Testament repeatedly claimed by God, is now claimed by Jesus as the Son of Man[211]. He has come to fulfil the Sabbath and therefore has the right to claim Lordship. The Law came under the authority of Jesus. Once Jesus' authority over the Sabbath is established, Jesus should be considered as the authoritative Lord of all.

As the Son of man, Jesus does not break the Sabbath law, but claims to have the authority to interpret it in a way that undercuts the legalism of the Pharisees (France, 2008:208; Oliver, 2013:99). His teaching legitimizes a merciful life-giving praxis as the divine will (Carter, 2000a:266). While the disciples' action was acceptable in terms of who Jesus was (McIver, 1995:240), the Pharisees' regulations to observe the Sabbath paradoxically fought God's purpose with the Sabbath, while they rejected God's authoritative envoy.

7.4.4 Jesus healing a man with a withered hand on the Sabbath (Matt. 12:9-14)

Directly after the discussion of the meaning of the Sabbath, Matthew describes Jesus performing an act of mercy; He heals a man with a withered hand. Jesus here does something that is repeatedly asked from Him in the first Gospel "Son of David, have mercy ..." (Matt. 9:27; 20:30[212]; 15:22[213]; 17:15, etc.). Jesus

---

[211] The background for Matthew's "Son of Man" most probably should be seen in Daniel 7:13-14. The majority of Matthew's uses of the term relates to the vindication and glory of the Son of Man with references to clouds, heaven, coming, glory, kingdom and judgement (France, 1998:291).

[212] The blind men (or in Mark and Luke's case, blind man) ask for mercy in all three the Synoptic Gospels (Matt. 9:27; 20:30; Mark 10:47; Luk. 18:38).

[213] Matthew adds a request for mercy to the story of the woman asking Jesus to heal her daughter (Matt. 15:22; Mark 7:24ff).

becomes the presence and source of mercy. Five of the seven occurrences of the verb ἐλεέω in Matthew occur within the context of healing stories. Before being healed, people ask for mercy (Matt. 9:27; 15:22; 17:15). In the case of the healing of the man with the withered hand, Jesus does not respond to such a request from the man, but as an answer to the question whether it is lawful to heal on the Sabbath. Legitimate adherence to the Law is expressed in merciful actions to a person in need (Hinkle Edin, 1998:357; Weren, 1994:119). Jesus demonstrates the difference between adhering to God's intention with the Law and the Pharisees' rule-bound approach.

The story is paralleled in all three the Synoptic Gospels. All three gospels describe the setting, the controversy between Jesus and the Pharisees, and a conclusion consisting of an ironic contrast. Matthew, however, has recognizable uniquenesses.

Matt. 12:9-14	Mark 3:1-6	Luk. 6:6-11
Setting in the synagogue (Matt. 12:9-10a): 9. **Καὶ μεταβὰς ἐκεῖθεν** ἦλθεν εἰς τὴν συναγωγὴν αὐτῶν: 10a. καὶ ἰδοὺ ἄνθρωπος χεῖρα ἔχων ξηράν. Going on from that place, he went into their synagogue, and a man with a shrivelled hand was there.	Setting in the synagogue (Mark 3:1) 1. Καὶ εἰσῆλθεν πάλιν εἰς συναγωγήν, καὶ ἦν ἐκεῖ ἄνθρωπος ἐξηραμμένην ἔχων τὴν χεῖρα. Another time Jesus went into the synagogue, and a man with a shrivelled hand was there.	Setting in the synagogue (Luk. 6:6) 6. Ἐγένετο δὲ ἐν ἑτέρῳ σαββάτῳ εἰσελθεῖν αὐτὸν εἰς τὴν συναγωγὴν καὶ διδάσκειν· καὶ ἦν ἄνθρωπος ἐκεῖ καὶ ἡ χεὶρ αὐτοῦ ἡ δεξιὰ ἦν ξηρά· On another Sabbath he went into the synagogue and was teaching, and a man was there whose right hand was shrivelled
Sabbath controversy between Jesus and the Pharisees (Matt. 12:10b-12): Looking for reasons to charge Jesus (Matt. 12:10b) καὶ ἐπηρώτησαν **αὐτὸν λέγοντες, Εἰ ἔξεστιν τοῖς σάββασιν θεραπεῦσαι**; ἵνα κατηγορήσωσιν αὐτοῦ. Looking for a reason to bring charges against Jesus, they asked him,	Sabbath controversy between Jesus and the Pharisees (Mark 3:2-4 Looking for reasons to charge Jesus (Mark 3:2) καὶ παρετήρουν αὐτὸν εἰ τοῖς σάββασιν θεραπεύσει αὐτόν, ἵνα κατηγορήσωσιν αὐτοῦ. Some of them were looking for a reason to accuse Jesus, so they watched him closely to see if he would heal him on the Sabbath,	Sabbath controversy between Jesus and the Pharisees (Luk. 6:7-10a) Looking for reasons to charge Jesus (Luk. 6:7) παρετηροῦντο δὲ αὐτὸν οἱ γραμματεῖς καὶ οἱ Φαρισαῖοι εἰ ἐν τῷ σαββάτῳ θεραπεύει, ἵνα εὕρωσιν κατηγορεῖν αὐτοῦ. The Pharisees and the teachers of the Law were looking for a reason to

"Is it lawful to heal on the Sabbath?"		accuse Jesus, so they watched him closely to see if he would heal on the Sabbath.
Response of Jesus (Matt. 12:11-12)	Response of Jesus (Mark 3:3-4)	Response of Jesus (Luk.6:8-9)
11. ὁ δὲ εἶπεν αὐτοῖς, Τίς ἔσται ἐξ ὑμῶν ἄνθρωπος ὃς ἕξει πρόβατον ἕν, καὶ ἐὰν ἐμπέσῃ τοῦτο τοῖς σάββασιν εἰς βόθυνον, οὐχὶ κρατήσει αὐτὸ καὶ ἐγερεῖ; 12. πόσῳ οὖν διαφέρει ἄνθρωπος προβάτου. ὥστε ἔξεστιν τοῖς σάββασιν καλῶς ποιεῖν. 11. He said to them, "If any of you has a sheep and it falls into a pit on the Sabbath, will you not take hold of it and lift it out? 12. How much more valuable is a person than a sheep! Therefore it is lawful to do good on the Sabbath."	3. καὶ λέγει τῷ ἀνθρώπῳ τῷ τὴν χεῖρα ἔχοντι ξηράν Ἔγειρε εἰς τὸ μέσον. 4. καὶ λέγει αὐτοῖς Ἔξεστιν τοῖς σάββασιν ἀγαθὸν ποιῆσαι ἢ κακοποιῆσαι, ψυχὴν σῶσαι ἢ ἀποκτεῖναι; οἱ δὲ ἐσιώπων. 3. Jesus said to the man with the shrivelled hand, "Stand up in front of everyone." 4. Then Jesus asked them, "Which is lawful on the Sabbath: to do good or to do evil, to save life or to kill?" But they remained silent.	8. αὐτὸς δὲ ᾔδει τοὺς διαλογισμοὺς αὐτῶν, εἶπεν δὲ τῷ ἀνδρὶ τῷ ξηρὰν ἔχοντι τὴν χεῖρα Ἔγειρε καὶ στῆθι εἰς τὸ μέσον· καὶ ἀναστὰς ἔστη 9. εἶπεν δὲ ὁ Ἰησοῦς πρὸς αὐτούς Ἐπερωτῶ ὑμᾶς εἰ ἔξεστιν τῷ σαββάτῳ ἀγαθοποιῆσαι ἢ κακοποιῆσαι, ψυχὴν σῶσαι ἢ ἀπολέσαι; 8. But Jesus knew what they were thinking and said to the man with the shrivelled hand, "Get up and stand in front of everyone." So he got up and stood there. 9. Then Jesus said to them, "I ask you, which is lawful on the Sabbath: to do good or to do evil, to save life or to destroy it?"
Outcome with an ironic contrast (Matt. 12:13-14)	Outcome with an ironic contrast (Mark 3:5-6)	Outcome with an ironic contrast (Luk. 6:10)
13. τότε λέγει τῷ ἀνθρώπῳ, Ἔκτεινόν σου τὴν χεῖρα. καὶ ἐξέτεινεν, καὶ ἀπεκατεστάθη ὑγιὴς ὡς ἡ ἄλλη. 14. ἐξελθόντες δὲ οἱ Φαρισαῖοι συμβούλιον ἔλαβον κατ' αὐτοῦ ὅπως αὐτὸν ἀπολέσωσιν. 13. Then he said to the man, "Stretch out your hand." So he stretched it out and it was completely restored, just	5. καὶ περιβλεψάμενος αὐτοὺς μετ' ὀργῆς, συνλυπούμενος ἐπὶ τῇ πωρώσει τῆς καρδίας αὐτῶν, λέγει τῷ ἀνθρώπῳ Ἔκτεινον τὴν χεῖρα. καὶ ἐξέτεινεν, καὶ ἀπεκατεστάθη ἡ χεὶρ αὐτοῦ. 6. καὶ ἐξελθόντες οἱ Φαρισαῖοι εὐθὺς μετὰ τῶν Ἡρῳδιανῶν συμβούλιον ἐδίδουν κατ' αὐτοῦ, ὅπως αὐτὸν ἀπολέσωσιν. 5. He looked around at them	καὶ περιβλεψάμενος πάντας αὐτοὺς εἶπεν αὐτῷ Ἔκτεινον τὴν χεῖρά σου. ὁ δὲ ἐποίησεν, καὶ ἀπεκατεστάθη ἡ χεὶρ αὐτοῦ. αὐτοὶ δὲ ἐπλήσθησαν ἀνοίας, καὶ διελάλουν πρὸς ἀλλήλους τί ἂν ποιήσαιεν τῷ Ἰησοῦ. He looked around at them all, and then said to the man, "Stretch out your hand." He did so, and his hand was completely restored.

as sound as the other. 14. But the Pharisees went out and plotted how they might kill Jesus.	in anger and, deeply distressed at their stubborn hearts, said to the man, "Stretch out your hand." He stretched it out, and his hand was completely restored. 6. Then the Pharisees went out and began to plot with the Herodians how they might kill Jesus.	But the Pharisees and the teachers of the Law were furious and began to discuss with one another what they might do to Jesus.

Table 41: The parallel of the story in Matt. 12:9-14 with Mark 3:1-6 and Luk. 6:6-11 on Jesus healing a man with a withered hand on the Sabbath

7.4.4.1 Setting of the scene (Matt. 12:9-10a)

With the opening words καὶ μεταβὰς ἐκεῖθεν (going out from that place) Matthew, unlike Mark and Luke, directly links the healing of the man with the shrivelled hand with the previous controversy about the disciples plucking grain on the Sabbath. He thus uses this second story to demonstrate Jesus' argument in the previous story that the intention of the Law is to show mercy and to do good.

7.4.4.2 Controversy between Jesus and the Pharisees (Matt. 12:10b-12)

Matthew adds the provocative question of the Pharisees, αὐτὸν λέγοντες, Εἰ ἔξεστιν τοῖς σάββασιν θεραπεῦσαι (they asked him, "is it lawful to heal on the Sabbath?"). Jewish teachers disagreed amongst each other on whether physicians were permitted to work on a Sabbath when the patient's life was not in danger (Keener, 1997:227). The strict school of the Shammaites even prohibited prayer for the sick on the Sabbath (T. Sabbat 16:22[214]). Notably, Matthew leaves out the Markan phrase ψυχὴν σῶσαι (to save a life) (Mark 3:4 // Luk. 6:9) as he does not view the disability of the man as life-threatening. Matthew's intention is therefore not to construct a life-threatening argument (Oliver, 2013:119), just as he does not equate the life-threatening position of David who ran for his life with that of the disciples (Matt. 12:3b-4).

---

[214] "The House of Shammai says that one does not provide charity to the poor on the Sabbath in the synagogue even to marry an orphan boy and an orphan girl, and one does not negotiate a marriage between a husband and a wife, and one does not pray for the sick on the Sabbath" (T. Shabb. 16:22).

Matthew adds a "how much more" (πόσῳ οὖν διαφέρει ἄνθρωπος προβάτου) argument (*a fortiori*-argument) by way of an analogy between a sheep and a human being to his narrative. In contrast to the stricter Essenes (CD 11:13-14), the Pharisees accepted the necessity to rescue an animal on the Sabbath (Keener, 1997:226). Jesus concludes with a summative principle: ὥστε ἔξεστιν τοῖς σάββασιν καλῶς ποιεῖν (therefore it is lawful to do good on the Sabbath) (Matt. 12:12). Matthew seeks to justify in broad terms the right of Jesus to do good on the Sabbath and not to confine doing good only in life-threatening situations.

7.4.4.3 Outcome of the story (Matt. 12:13-14)

The outcome of the story contains an ironic contrast. While Jesus did good to the man with the shrivelled hand, the Pharisees intended to do bad. In Jewish texts the healing of paralyzed or shrivelled hands suggests great power (1 Kings 13:6; Test. Simeon 2:12-13), which should awaken awe from the onlookers. However, the response of the Pharisees exhibits their hostile attitude towards Jesus. The Pharisees in the story are so enraged with Jesus that they resort to a breach of their own laws. No sect in early Judaism had rules that would allow putting someone to death for healing on the Sabbath (Keener, 1997:227). Plotting to kill someone who differs from you would have been considered premeditated murder (Gen. 9:5-6; Num. 35:29-34). The reaction of the Pharisees in the story demonstrates their utter misunderstanding with God's intention with the *Torah*. This forms a shameful contrast with Jesus' good deed.

Matthew sharply describes the Pharisees as people with a lack of understanding (cf. Matt. 11:25) as they fail to recognize the association between law observance and mercy (Hinkle-Edin, 1998:360; Repschinski, 2000:101). They did not understand who Jesus was and did not recognize his messianic ministry. Therefore they reacted negatively on Jesus' act of mercy and went out to conspire against Him (Matt. 12:14). The Pharisees are portrayed as involved in a misplaced mechanical and burdensome observance of the Sabbath law. Such observance contradicts God's intention (Turner, 2008:310). This conflict regarding the Sabbath illustrates two different interpretations of the Law. Jesus is presented as the embodiment of divine Wisdom whose yoke brings rest (Matt. 11:28), while the behaviour of the Pharisees illustrates that the knowledge of the Law is "hidden for the wise and the learned" (Matt. 11:25).

As with the story of Jesus who calls Matthew and has a meal with marginalized people of the Jewish society (Matt. 9:9-13), the story on the Sabbath (Matt. 12:1-14) also exhibits some elements of identity formation of the Matthean community. Seemingly this community was accused of laxity in Sabbath observance by Pharisaic Judaism. This story, however, proposes that Sabbath observance remained an important matter in their community. However, the way they observed it differed from the depicted legalistic approach of the Pharisees. For the Matthean community Sabbath observance should entail experiencing God's rest and mercy and by showing constant loyalty and love towards God and his people.

7.4.5 "Epilogue" to the Sabbath controversy stories: God's chosen One (Matt. 12:15-21)

Jesus' Christological affirmation is developed in the fulfilment quotation following the Sabbath controversy. Matthew cites from the servant song in Isa. 42:1-4. This citation forms Matthew's longest quotation. This quotation defends the position of Jesus in this highly polemical context and can be considered as an epilogue to the Sabbath controversy.

The brief report on Jesus' withdrawal (ὁ δὲ Ἰησοῦς γνοὺς ἀνεχώρησεν ἐκεῖθεν - aware of this, Jesus withdrew from that place) and healing ministry (καὶ ἠκολούθησαν αὐτῷ πολλοί, καὶ ἐθεράπευσεν αὐτοὺς πάντας - a large crowd followed him, and he healed all who were ill) (Matt. 12:15-16) functions as a bridge from the previous scene and an extended introduction formula to the quotation to follow. In this report Jesus' mercifulness is sharply contrasted with the aggressive opposition of the Pharisees in the previous scene. The quotation has several thematic points of contact that link the quotation with the preceding Sabbath narrative (Neyrey, 1982:459). Jesus' announcement that He is the Lord of the Sabbath and healing ministry comes as further witness that He is the promised One, the servant Messiah who came to fulfil the Law and the Prophets. Matthew uses Isa. 42:1-4 as a Christological portrait of Jesus to illuminate the preceding events.

By quoting the servant song, ἰδοὺ ὁ παῖς μου ὃν ᾑρέτισα, ὁ ἀγαπητός μου ὃν εὐδόκησεν ἡ ψυχή μου ... (here is my servant (child) whom I have chosen, the one I love …) in Matt. 12:18-21, Matthew affirms that Isaiah's prophecy has reached its fulfilment. Jesus is God's chosen One. According to Isa. 42:1-4 the servant (Jesus the Messiah for Matthew; cf. Matt. 12:18-21) would bring judgement (*mishpat*) and Torah (cf. Num. 24:17; Deut. 18:18-19; Isa. 52:7; 61:2-3; Dan. 9:25). John describes a similar expectation with the Samaritan woman who expressed her faith that when the Christ comes, ἀναγγελεῖ ἡμῖν ἅπαντα (He will explain everything to us) (John 4:25). These expectations clarify Matthew's presentation of Jesus as the one who brought the "messianic Torah" (Gerhardsson, 1964:327).

Matthew introduces Jesus as the bearer of the Spirit (θήσω τὸ Πνεῦμά μου ἐπ' αὐτόν - I will put my Spirit on Him) (Matt. 12:18), which attests to his authority in claiming to be the Lord of the Sabbath. His bearing of the Spirit was further demonstrated in his healing activity (Matt. 12:9-14). Thus Matthew also compares Jesus with the Pharisees whose synagogue (ἡ συναγωγὴ αὐτῶν - their synagogue) (Matt. 12:9) lacks the Spirit and who were not able to recognise the bearer of the Spirit. Matthew underscores the authority of Jesus in his continuing confrontation with the synagogue[215].

It is highly significant that Matthew used ὁ παῖς (son) rather than δοῦλος (slave/servant). He changed both the MT (*ebed*, servant) and LXX (δοῦλος, slave) to conform the quotation with the voice from heaven at two other occasions. Matthew links this quotation to the highly Christological quotation, οὗτός ἐστιν ὁ υἱός μου ὁ ἀγαπητός, ἐν ᾧ εὐδόκησα (this is my Son, whom I love; with him I am well pleased), which occurs at Jesus' baptism (Matt. 3:17) and at his transfiguration (Matt. 17:5). By assimilating this quotation into these two key Christological references, Matthew poses the Christological importance of this servant quotation on the same level as the other two. Matthew moves the focus from a "servant of God Christology" to a "Son of God Christology" (Luz, 2001a:193). By linking these quotations, Matthew implicitly claims that the Messiah's mission as inaugurated with his baptism is now being fulfilled in the Son of God (France, 1998:206). While the Pharisees condemned Jesus and his disciples and plotted how they could kill Him (Matt. 12:2, 10 and 14), God loves Him and takes delight in Him (Matt. 12:18). "God's verdict about Jesus, then, serves as an important apologetic response to the hostility of the Pharisees" (Neyrey, 1982:460). While the Pharisees are deeply displeased with Jesus, God is well pleased. This authorisation of Jesus is evidently important since Jesus claims extraordinary authority to pronounce judgements on Sabbath observance. Matthew strengthens Jesus' crucial Christological statements τοῦ ἱεροῦ μεῖζόν ἐστιν ὧδε (one greater than the temple is here) (Matt. 12:6) and κύριος γάρ ἐστιν τοῦ σαββάτου ὁ υἱὸς τοῦ ἀνθρώπου (the Son of Man is Lord of the Sabbath) (Matt. 12:8).

---

[215] The citation probably also functions as an apology for the Matthean community in its ongoing confrontation with the synagogue.

The quotation also says that κρίσιν τοῖς ἔθνεσιν ἀπαγγελεῖ (He will proclaim justice to the nations) (Matt. 12:18) and will lead justice to victory (Matt. 12:9). Κρίσις implies an imminent judgement and victory of justice, while ἀπαγγελεῖν is associated with the heralding of good news about Jesus. This is an indication of the judgement that awaits the stubborn unbelieving Pharisees against the disciples of Jesus who do accept the gospel about Jesus.

Jesus' humility and gentleness for the poor and the needy is stated: οὐκ ἐρίσει οὐδὲ κραυγάσει ... κάλαμον συντετριμμένον οὐ κατεάξει ... (He will not quarrel and cry ... a bruised reed He will not break ...) (Matt. 12:19-20). This reaffirms Jesus' declaration in Matt. 11:28-30 (the "prologue" to the Sabbath narrative) which is practically illustrated in the two Sabbath stories (Matt. 12:1-14). Once again this depiction of Jesus stands in sharp contrast with the mercilessness of the Pharisees and their lack of understanding of the meaning of the *Torah*.

7.4.6 Implications for the Matthean community

The narrative teaches that the law of love and the commandment καλῶς ποιεῖν (to do good) should be fulfilled on the Sabbath. Matthew's narrative "legitimiert die Freigabe des Sabbats für die Liebestat gegenüber dem Pharisäismus" (Hummel, 1966:45). Matthew demonstrates the implications of Jesus' words: "All the Law and the Prophets hang on these two (love) commandments" (Matt. 22:40).

The debate in Matthew is not *if* the Sabbath law should be obeyed, but *how* it should be done. God's intention with the Sabbath law must be recognised to ensure true Sabbath observance.

Jesus, the Son of Man, did not come to abolish the Sabbath as some (especially the Pharisees and likeminded people) may have suspected, but to fulfil it. The fulfilment motif of the Sabbath pericopes reiterates Matthew 5:17-20. Matthew's plot focuses on Jesus as the Messiah who fulfilled the whole Scriptural revelation of the Jewish Bible. The Law is not only preserved, but Jesus also brought freshness with his approach it. The Law requires loyalty and love to God, and mercy and kindness towards humans. Jesus lived this commandment to love, also in his observance of the Sabbath. His approach stands in strong contrast to the stubbornness of the Pharisees who heartlessly contested Jesus' authority to extend mercy on the Sabbath. They did not accept the challenge of love and thus failed to understand the Law.

Matthew argues that as Son of God, Jesus has the authority to give this fresh interpretation of the Sabbath commandment. Rest is to be found if people positively respond to his invitation to accept wise teaching. It is God's will that the Sabbath be honoured by way of doing good.

7.5 CONCLUSION

The passage "I desire mercy not sacrifice" (Hos. 6:6) forms an important hermeneutical key for Matthew. In Chapter 9 Jesus tells the Pharisees to "go and learn" the meaning of this passage. In chapter 12 their failure to learn results in Jesus stating that they do not know what this passage means. Jesus emerges as informed in understanding how the Law actually relates to social relations and Sabbath observance.

Matthew uses Hos. 6:6 in two scenes of conflict between Jesus and the Pharisees. He defines the differences between them in terms of adherence to the Law with a focus on the חֶסֶד (ἔλεος / mercy) that God desires. It implies constant covenantal loyalty and love towards God and his people. Such mercy is of fundamental importance for understanding the will of God as expressed in the Law.

Matthew depicts Jesus as one who teaches based on his own authoritative interpretation of the Law and the Prophets. His interpretations frequently differ from the tradition, though his interpretation of Hos. 6:6 reflects continuity with the original intention of that statement in its prophetic context. Jesus also teaches by example by enacting mercy towards the marginalized and people in need. He loves the way Hosea announces that God intends his people to love. Jesus Himself becomes the presence and source of mercy. Thus He fulfils the intention of this prophetic saying.

By his calling and association with the marginalized of the community, the tax collectors and sinners, Jesus offers steadfast love. By defending his disciples and healing the man with the withered hand He again demonstrates what the mercy of God entails. Mercy is found in and with Him. Matthew thus argues that if one wants to adhere to God's will, one should learn to recognize the steadfast love of God for his people as is taught and enacted by Jesus.

It seems that these narratives express certain issues in Matthew's community. The narratives demonstrate how his community interprets the Law. The experience of this community may not have been very different from that of Jesus Himself. With reference to Matt. 9: 9-13, Matthew and his community should overcome religious and social barriers to bringing outsiders into the church. The Pharisees in the narrative become some sort of theological construct for a rejecting generation in his contemporary situation. The Christian community is probably confronted with some attitudes of exclusiveness that would keep them from showing mercy to those who are considered to be the marginalized and outsiders in a Jewish society. Those who oppose the acceptance of these people should go and learn what Hos. 6:6 means by observing the teaching and behaviour of Jesus. With reference to Matt. 12:1-13, Matthew justifies what his community considered as doing good on the Sabbath. It might be that they were accused of laxity in Sabbath observance. The narrative teaches that the Law of love and the commandment "to do good" should be fulfilled on the Sabbath. The expression of mercy and steadfast love of God in attitudes and actions of consideration and kindness are promoted.

Markers of identity formation can be recognized in these stories. It is therefore probable that Matthew used these stories as part of his construction of the communal identity of his community and to legitimate their lifestyle. Focus on a central figure is a typical marker. Jesus forms the central focus and prototype of this community. Another typical marker is that a community follows its leader's teaching and example. Jesus calls his disciples to follow Him. As part of this community one should obey his teaching and imitate his covenantal steadfast love and mercy in accepting and serving others. As central figure and prototype of the community He is the authoritative interpreter of the Scriptures and the enactment of God's will and covenantal loyalty and steadfast love. In the social organization of the community each follower should realize that he or she is a sinner who needs Jesus as doctor. Members of the community should follow the prototype and act in an appropriate manner. Each member should be willing to practice inclusive mercy towards outsiders and marginalized people. Unique practices and rituals develop. Within this community, Sabbath observance is characterized by doing good and helping the needy. This mind-set fashions a lifestyle according to God's will. The community is warned against opponents. The Pharisees are regarded as the opponents of the Matthean community, since they fail to understand the meaning of the Scriptures. The community is warned not to be intimidated by the Pharisees or to act like them.

CHAPTER 8

THE LAW AND PURITY IN MATTHEW: JESUS TOUCHING A BLEEDING WOMAN AND A DEAD GIRL

8.1 INTRODUCTION

The topic of the Law and purity in the first Gospel is complex. It seems that Matthew's Jesus is not concerned about becoming impure or pure again after contracting impurity (Deines, 2008:65). Matthew does not mention any purification rites in connection with Jesus and the disciples, not even before entering the temple. He only describes actions of Jesus that apparently contravene the purity regulations of the Hebrew Bible. While Jesus in the Sermon on the Mount emphatically states that He did not come to abolish the Law (Matt. 5:17-19) (as investigated in Chapter 3), that He requires greater righteousness (Matt. 5:20) (cf. Chapter 5) and explains the true intention of the Law in six antitheses (Matt. 5:21-47) (cf. Chapter 4), one would expect Matthew to show concern for purity regulations as well. However, nothing in this regard is mentioned. It seems as if Matthew and his community developed a different understanding of purity requirements. In the Beatitudes Jesus states that those who are pure in heart are blessed and will see God (Matt. 5:8) (Viljoen, 2012b). Some other passages in Matthew also imply a development in purity interpretation, namely Jesus touching a leper (Matt. 8:1-4) (cf. Chapter 6), Jesus responding to Pharisees who question why He eats with tax collectors and sinners (Matt. 9:9-13) (cf. Chapter 7) and Jesus responding to the Pharisees and teachers of the Law who accuse Jesus' disciples of not washing their hands before they eat (Matt. 15:1-20) (cf. Chapter 9).

This chapter investigates two occasions where purity implications are at stake. Jesus was supposed to avoid or at least purify Himself after contact with a woman with abnormal menstrual discharge (Lev. 25-30), but Matthew's Jesus does not object when such a woman touches Him and no mention is made of any purification rites (Matt. 9:20-22). He should also have avoided contact with a dead body (Num. 5:2; 19:11-13) or entering the room of a dead person (Num. 19:14), but Jesus enters the room with the dead girl and touches her (Matt.

9:25). In cases where such contact with a dead or haemorrhaging person is accidental, performed as deed of compassion or as a necessity, the Hebrew Bible prescribes that the defiled person has to undergo specific purification rites (Num. 19). The neglect of such purification rites was regarded as prohibited impurity and reason to be cut off from the community (Num. 19:13, 20). Matthew, however, makes no mention of Jesus undergoing such purification rites. One could ask whether this was intentional. Considering that Matthew's readers, unlike those of Mark and Luke, were mostly Jewish Christians[216], hearing about such seeming negligence by Jesus, would have been noted as cause for concern. Though Jesus emphasises that He did not come to abolish the Law (Matt. 5:17-19), He seemingly demonstrates an alternative interpretation of the purity Law.

The intention of this chapter is to establish the relation between Matthew's Jesus and the purity Laws as demonstrated by this double story. To do this, the applicable Jewish purity regulations are first investigated and then compared with Jesus' actions when healing the bleeding woman and dead girl. The chapter ends with certain conclusions drawn from this comparison.

8.2 PURITY REGULATIONS REGARDING DEATH AND MENSTRUAL BLEEDING

Purity or the lack thereof plays a fundamental role in Ancient Israel's religion. According to the laws of Exodus, Leviticus and Numbers, purity or impurity refers to a state of physical and spiritual purity or impurity that permitted or prohibited access to God. Cultic purity implies moral purity. It has its roots in the command: "Be holy, because I, the Lord your God, am holy" (Lev. 19:2) (Vriezen & Van der Woude, 2005:244).

Similar references to purity are found in later writings of the Hebrew Bible, such as the Psalms and the Prophets. Purity is demanded by the "Holy One of Israel" (*qadosh Yisrael*) (Isa. 1:4; 5:19, 24). God is the ideal manifestation and source of holiness (Chilton, 2000:877). Only the one who has clean hands and a pure heart may ascend the mountain of the Lord and stand in his holy place (Ps 24:3-4) (cf. Pss. 18:21; 24:3-6; 26:4-7; 51:4, 8, 9, 12; 119:9).

---

[216] Whether the addressees of the first Gospel were known as Christians as such, is disputable. They were, however, followers of Jesus.

Some impurities are avoidable, and are prohibited under all circumstances. Prohibited impurities result from contamination that could have been avoided or as a result of mismanagement of unavoidable impurities or from the violation of moral norms. Others are unavoidable as they come about as a result of natural circumstances, for example death, sexual relations, disease, etc. However, for such unavoidable impurities specific methods of purification are prescribed, like washing, sacrifices, disposal or required time lapses (Wright, 1992b:736-737). Amongst all these laws prescribed for different situations, the purity laws related to death and sexual discharge are applicable to the stories of Matt. 9:18-26.

8.2.1 Purity regulations related to death

Touching a human corpse is regarded as the most serious of permitted impurities. A person becomes impure through contact with a "dead body", which includes significant parts of a body or the soil in which the body has decomposed, or by being present in a building or roofed structure containing a dead body[217]:

> "Command the Israelites to send away from the camp anyone ... who is ceremonially unclean because of a dead body" (Num. 5:2); and
> "Whoever touches a human corpse will be unclean for seven days" (Num. 19:11).

Various restrictions and purification requirements are applicable to such corpserelated impurities. Persons and objects that are polluted remain impure for seven days and have to undergo several prescribed purification rituals:

> "They must purify themselves with the water on the third day and on the seventh day; then they will be clean. But if they do not purify themselves on the third and seventh days, they will not be clean ..." (Num. 19:12-19).

Related, but less serious than the impurity contracted by touching a human corpse, is that of coming into contact with certain dead animals, including most insects and all lizards (listed in Lev. 11:29–32). Restrictions and purifications

---

[217] One can become impure by contact with a primary source of impurity or an object that has been in contact with a primary source of impurity (Lev. 15:4-27).

for such contaminations are prescribed, but they are fewer than when touching a dead person. Lev. 11:24-25 states:

> "Whoever touches their carcasses will be unclean till evening. Whoever picks up one of their carcasses must wash their clothes, and they will be unclean till evening" (also see Lev. 11:27-28, 39-40).

It is reasonable to assume that the Jews still observed purity regulations related to the touching of corpses in the time of Jesus. The parable of the Good Samaritan implies this as the priest and the Levite in the parable avoid contact with the beaten traveller (Luk. 10:25-37). Even in later rabbinic traditions (*Rashi* on *b. Pesah,* 14b, 17a; *m. Kelim,* 1:1-4; *Tohar,* 1:5) touching a corpse is called "the father of fathers of uncleanness[218]" (Hayes, 2007:747). Although scholars generally suppose that these rabbinic writings date from a late stage, namely 200 to 600 C.E. (Neusner, 1999:652), one has to keep in mind that the date of a document and the date of the ideas taken up in it may stand some distance from one another. Ideas within the rabbinic literature most probably reflect ideas of some earlier stage in history.

When reading of Jesus entering the room of a dead girl and taking her hand without hesitating, the first readers, who were mostly Jews, would expect Jesus to perform the required purity rites. Yet, nothing in this regard is mentioned (Matt. 9:25)[219]. This would have raised questions and concern.

8.2.2 Purity regulations related to sexual discharge

The five "fathers of sexual impurities" are listed as seminal emission (Lev. 15:16-18, 32), menstruation (Lev. 15:19-24; 18:19; 20:18), vaginal discharge after birth (Lev. 12), abnormal genital discharge of a male (Lev. 15:2-15; 22:4-6) and abnormal menstrual discharge (Lev. 15:25-30) (Hayes, 2007:747; Wright & Jones, 1992a:204-207; Wright, 1992b:731).

---

[218] The phrase "father of uncleanness" forms part of rabbinic terminology, which refers to impurity that can generate offspring of lesser impurities (Wright, 1992b:730).

[219] Mark 5:41 and Luk. 8:54 also don't mention Jesus performing purification rites. However these evangelists don't put the same emphasis on Jesus' claim to observe the Law in its finest detail (Matt. 5:17-20).

According to the Jewish Scriptures, semen-polluted persons cannot pollute other persons and things of the community, but are restricted from the holy sphere (Lev. 22:4-7). Impurity of menstruation is more serious as it can pollute others for seven days from the beginning of the blood flow. Persons or objects touching a woman with such bleeding become impure and persons touching something which she sat or laid on also become polluted (Lev. 15:19-24). The impurity of vaginal discharge after birth is even more severe than menstruation. By giving birth to a child the regarded time of impurity is seven days after the birth of a boy and fourteen days after the birth of a girl (Lev. 12) and such a woman should be treated as a menstruant during this period (Lev. 12:2-5). The effect of pollution of a man with abnormal sexual discharge (*zab*) is similar to that of a menstruant. Once such a man is cured, he can undergo purity rituals after seven days (Lev. 16:2-15). The female counterpart of a *zab* is that of a woman with abnormal menstrual discharge. Such a woman would pollute another person just like a man with abnormal genital discharge:

> "When a woman has a discharge of blood for many days at a time other than her monthly period or has a discharge that continues beyond her period, she will be unclean (*temeh'ah*) as long as she has the discharge, just as in the days of her period. Any bed she lies on while her discharge continues will be unclean, as is her bed during her monthly period, and anything she sits on will be unclean (*tame*), as during her period. Anyone who touches them will be unclean (*yitma*); they must wash their clothes and bathe with water, and they will be unclean (*tame*) till evening" (Lev. 15:25-30).

Based on these references to the Jewish Scriptures it becomes clear that for Jesus not to be concerned when being touched by the woman with blood flow (Mark 5:25; Matt. 9:20; Luk. 8:34)[220], would have been unusual for the readers of the first Gospel.

8.2.3 Neglect of purification rites

The delay of purification after becoming impure is prohibited. The Hebrew Bible prescribes various purification rites such as bathing, laundering, sacrifices and in some cases even punishment to rectify such impurities. If the deed of

---

[220] Once again Mark 5:25 and Luk. 8:34 also don't mention Jesus performing purification rites, but Matthew writes to a predominantly Jewish audience and shows a specific interest in the maintenance of the details of the Law.

becoming impure was avoidable and intentional it can result in the execution of the culprit (in cases of murder), cutting off (*karat*), or purification on the Day of Atonement (Wright, 1992b:737-738).

The delay of purification after being polluted by touching human corpses, animal carcasses, and impure objects is considered sinful and requires additional sacrifice and ablution (Chilton, 2000:874; Hayes, 2007:749):

> "If anyone becomes aware that they are guilty--if they unwittingly touch anything ceremonially unclean (whether the carcass of an unclean animal, wild or domestic, or of any unclean creature that moves along the ground) and they are unaware that they have become unclean, but then they come to realize their guilt; or if they touch human uncleanness (anything that would make them unclean) even though they are unaware of it, but then they learn of it and realize their guilt; ..." (Lev. 5:2-3).

Persons who advertently do not purify themselves will suffer being *karet* (cut off), or expelled:

> "...Everyone who does any of these detestable things--such persons must be cut off (*karat*) from their people ...." (Lev. 18:24-30) (see also; Num. 19:13, 20).

In Jesus' cultural context, it would have been unacceptable for Him not to undergo purification rites after his contact with the bleeding woman or the dead girl.

Considering the above-mentioned regulations regarding purity, it seems as if the Matthean Jesus did not observe these purity laws in a similar way as the Jews of his days. The question therefore arises how this described behaviour of Jesus correlates with his explicit statement that his mission was not to abolish the Law or Prophets, but to fulfil them (Matt. 5:17-19). With this narrative Matthew apparently intends to advise his readers of a specific interpretation of purity laws in terms of their relation to Jesus. With the coming of Jesus these laws got new meaning. This investigation can shed further light on what is implied by the statement by the Matthean Jesus that He came to fulfil the Law and the Prophets.

8.3 JESUS' APPARENT NEGLECT OF PURITY REGULATIONS

When observing the healings described in Matt. 9-10, it is important to recognize the textual context of the Law in which these stories are set.

8.3.1 The teacher of the Law enacts the Law

Once Matthew has ended the Sermon on the Mount, he continues to tell how Jesus came down from the mountain as Moses once did from Mount Sinai (Exod. 19:14; 32:1; 34:29)[221].

The Sermon on the Mount and healing discourse are compositionally framed by two summaries of the miracles Jesus had performed (Matt. 4:23-25 and 9:35) (Morris, 1992:186; Senior, 1998:94; Talbert, 2010:109). In both these summaries reference is made to the βασιλεία (Kingdom) of heaven. With his inaugural proclamation "Repent, for the Kingdom of Heaven is at hand" (Matt. 4:17), Jesus states that the future Kingdom of Heaven is already present (Duling, 1992:57). The coming of the Kingdom is connected to the person of Jesus. The Kingdom does not only signify the territory where God rules, but also his activity as ruler as envisioned in Deutero-Isaiah (Davies & Allison, 2004a:389). The Apocalypse of Baruch (2 Bar. 73:1-2)[222] describes this anticipation:

> "And it shall come to pass, when He has brought low everything that is in the world and has sat down in peace for the age on the throne of His kingdom. That joy shall then be revealed and rest

---

[221] As discussed in Chapter 6, Matthew thus draws a parallel between Jesus and Moses, and the Mount of Jesus' sermon and Mount Sinai (Carter, 2000a:198; Davies & Allison, 2004a:9; Luz, 2001a:5). The impressive and authoritative teacher of the Law of the discourse is presented in the subsequent narrative as going into action by demonstrating the meaning and correct practice of the Law. He confirms his authority by performing ten miracles. Grundmann has fittingly described the Sermon on the Mount as "das Wirken des Christus Jesus durch das Wort" (the work of Christ Jesus through the word) (Grundmann, 1971:111) and the miracles that follow as "das Wirken des Christus Jesus durch die Tat" (the work of Christ Jesus through the deed) (Grundmann, 1971:245).

[222] Though 2 Baruch is attributed to the Biblical Baruch, it was probably written after the destruction of the Jerusalem in 70 C.E. (Klijn, 1983:194), in the late first century or early in the second century. This document therefore reflects sentiments contemporary to Matthew. The document was most likely composed in Hebrew or Aramaic, but this original-language text did not survive. The only complete text of 2 Baruch is preserved in one Syriac manuscript (7a1).

shall appear. And then healing shall descend in dew, and disease shall withdraw, and anxiety and anguish and lamentation pass from amongst men, and gladness proceeds through the whole earth."

For Jesus the coming of the Kingdom did not comprise of one moment, but it realizes through a series of events over a period of time. When Jesus announces that the Kingdom of Heaven has come and is coming, He indicates that the process of the realisation of God's rule has started, but the completion lies in the future, when the last things will come. The coming of the Kingdom is being established by Jesus. His teaching (Sermon on the Mount) and activity (healing miracles) form part of the realization of the blessings associated with the coming of the Kingdom. He proves that He is the conqueror of illness and death (Weren, 1979:85). Purity regulations remind God's people of the devastating effect of sin and evil that destroys their relation with God, but with his miracles Jesus subdues these evil powers of sin and restores the relation between God and his people. With his purifying power He removes evil and establishes the Kingdom of Heaven (Van der Walt, 2007:196).

8.3.2 Double story of Jesus healing a woman with blood flow and resurrecting a dead girl (Matt. 9:18-26)

Matt. 9:18-34 presents the third triad of Matthew's miracle stories[223]. These three short miracle stories include four miracles in which Jesus heals five people:

- The double story of the woman with blood flow and the ruler's[224] daughter (Matt. 9:18-26);
- The story of two blind men (Matt. 9:27-31); and
- The story of a demoniac (Matt. 9:32-34).

These miracle stories demonstrate the coming of God's Kingdom in anticipation of the wholeness expected in future.

---

[223] Matthew tells a series of nine healing miracles stories (Matt. 8-9) and a nature miracle of Jesus stilling the storm (Matt. 8:23-27) in three triads (Weren, 1994:85). The nine healings are that of the leper, the centurion's servant, Peter's mother in law, the Gaderene demoniacs, the paralyzed man, the ruler's daughter, the woman with blood flow, the blind men and the dumb man (cf. Chapter 7).

[224] In Matthew the ruler is unnamed, while both Mark and Luke call him Jairus.

The double story with which this triad of miracle stories begins, describes examples of how Jesus dealt with purity matters.

8.3.2.1 Matthew's redaction of the story

Matthew (Matt. 9:18-26) tells a much shorter version than Mark (5:21-43) of the double story of Jesus healing the woman subject to bleeding for twelve years and of Him healing the dead girl aged twelve[225] years. Mark's priority is assumed. The redaction by Matthew should be considered in a comparison of these two versions.

Matt. 9:18-26	Mark 5:21-43	Luk 8:40-56
Setting of the stories (Matt. 9:18a) ¹⁸ Ταῦτα αὐτοῦ λαλοῦντος αὐτοῖς ¹⁸ While he was saying this,	Setting of the stories (Mark 5:21) ²¹ Καὶ διαπεράσαντος τοῦ Ἰησοῦ ἐν τῷ πλοίῳ πάλιν εἰς τὸ πέραν συνήχθη ὄχλος πολὺς ἐπ' αὐτόν, καὶ ἦν παρὰ τὴν θάλασσαν. ²¹ When Jesus had again crossed over by boat to the other side of the lake, a large crowd gathered around him while he was by the lake.	Setting of the stories (Luk. 8:40) ⁴⁰ Ἐν δὲ τῷ ὑποστρέφειν τὸν Ἰησοῦν ἀπεδέξατο αὐτὸν ὁ ὄχλος· ἦσαν γὰρ πάντες προσδοκῶντες αὐτόν. ⁴⁰ Now when Jesus returned, a crowd welcomed him, for they were all expecting him
Story of the dead girl: part 1, the ruler's request (Matt. 9:18-19) ἰδοὺ **ἄρχων** εἷς προσελθὼν **προσεκύνει** αὐτῷ λέγων ὅτι **Ἡ θυγάτηρ μου ἄρτι ἐτελεύτησεν**· ἀλλὰ ἐλθὼν ἐπίθες τὴν χεῖρά σου ἐπ' αὐτήν, καὶ ζήσεται. ⁹ καὶ ἐγερθεὶς ὁ Ἰησοῦς ἠκολούθει αὐτῷ καὶ **οἱ μαθηταὶ αὐτοῦ**. a leader came and knelt before him and said, "My daughter has just died. But	Story of the dead girl: part 1, the ruler's request (Mark 5:21-24) ²² καὶ ἔρχεται εἷς τῶν ἀρχισυναγώγων, ὀνόματι Ἰάειρος, καὶ ἰδὼν αὐτὸν πίπτει πρὸς τοὺς πόδας αὐτοῦ, ²³ καὶ παρακαλεῖ αὐτὸν πολλὰ λέγων ὅτι Τὸ θυγάτριόν μου ἐσχάτως ἔχει, ἵνα ἐλθὼν ἐπιθῇς τὰς χεῖρας αὐτῇ, ἵνα σωθῇ καὶ ζήσῃ. ²⁴ καὶ ἀπῆλθεν μετ' αὐτοῦ. καὶ ἠκολούθει αὐτῷ ὄχλος πολύς, καὶ συνέθλιβον αὐτόν.	Story of the dead girl: part 1, the ruler's request (Luk. 8:41-42a) ⁴¹. καὶ ἰδοὺ ἦλθεν ἀνὴρ ᾧ ὄνομα Ἰάϊρος, καὶ οὗτος ἄρχων τῆς συναγωγῆς ὑπῆρχεν, καὶ πεσὼν παρὰ τοὺς πόδας τοῦ Ἰησοῦ παρεκάλει αὐτὸν εἰσελθεῖν εἰς τὸν οἶκον αὐτοῦ, ⁴². ὅτι θυγάτηρ μονογενὴς ἦν αὐτῷ ὡς ἐτῶν δώδεκα καὶ αὐτὴ ἀπέθνῃσκεν. ⁴¹· Then a man named Jairus,

---

[225] The woman suffered bleeding over a period of twelve years, the same span of time as the age of the ruler's daughter. Menses also typically begins at the age of twelve.

come and put your hand on her, and she will live." [19] Jesus got up and went with him, and so did his disciples.	[22] Then one of the synagogue leaders, named Jairus, came, and when he saw Jesus, he fell at his feet. [23] He pleaded earnestly with him, "My little daughter is dying. Please come and put your hands on her so that she will be healed and live." [24] So Jesus went with him. A large crowd followed and pressed around him.	a synagogue leader, came and fell at Jesus' feet, pleading with him to come to his house [42] because his only daughter, a girl of about twelve, was dying.

Story of the woman with blood flow: parenthetical story

Matt. 9:20-21	Mark 5:24-34	Luk. 8:42b-48
[20] **Καὶ ἰδοὺ** γυνὴ **αἱμορροοῦσα** δώδεκα ἔτη προσελθοῦσα ὄπισθεν **ἥψατο τοῦ κρασπέδου τοῦ ἱματίου αὐτοῦ** [21] ἔλεγεν γὰρ ἐν ἑαυτῇ Ἐὰν μόνον ἅψωμαι τοῦ ἱματίου αὐτοῦ σωθήσομαι. [22] ὁ δὲ Ἰησοῦς στραφεὶς καὶ ἰδὼν αὐτὴν εἶπεν Θάρσει, θύγατερ· ἡ πίστις σου σέσωκέν σε. καὶ ἐσώθη ἡ γυνὴ ἀπὸ τῆς ὥρας ἐκείνης. [20] Just then a woman who had been subject to bleeding for twelve years came up behind him and touched the edge of his cloak. [21] She said to herself, "If I only touch his cloak, I will be healed." [22] Jesus turned and saw her. "Take heart, daughter," he said, "your faith has healed you." And the woman was healed at that moment.	[25] Καὶ γυνὴ οὖσα ἐν ῥύσει αἵματος δώδεκα ἔτη, [26] καὶ πολλὰ παθοῦσα ὑπὸ πολλῶν ἰατρῶν καὶ δαπανήσασα τὰ παρ' αὐτῆς πάντα, καὶ μηδὲν ὠφεληθεῖσα ἀλλὰ μᾶλλον εἰς τὸ χεῖρον ἐλθοῦσα, [27] ἀκούσασα τὰ περὶ τοῦ Ἰησοῦ, ἐλθοῦσα ἐν τῷ ὄχλῳ ὄπισθεν ἥψατο τοῦ ἱματίου αὐτοῦ [28] ἔλεγεν γὰρ ὅτι Ἐὰν ἅψωμαι κἂν τῶν ἱματίων αὐτοῦ σωθήσομαι. [29] καὶ εὐθὺς ἐξηράνθη ἡ πηγὴ τοῦ αἵματος αὐτῆς, καὶ ἔγνω τῷ σώματι ὅτι ἴαται ἀπὸ τῆς μάστιγος. [30] καὶ εὐθὺς ὁ Ἰησοῦς ἐπιγνοὺς ἐν ἑαυτῷ τὴν ἐξ αὐτοῦ δύναμιν ἐξελθοῦσαν ἐπιστραφεὶς ἐν τῷ ὄχλῳ ἔλεγεν Τίς μου ἥψατο τῶν ἱματίων; [31] καὶ ἔλεγον αὐτῷ οἱ μαθηταὶ αὐτοῦ Βλέπεις τὸν ὄχλον συνθλίβοντά σε, καὶ λέγεις Τίς μου ἥψατο; [32] καὶ περιεβλέπετο ἰδεῖν τὴν τοῦτο ποιήσασαν. [33] ἡ δὲ γυνὴ φοβηθεῖσα καὶ τρέμουσα, εἰδυῖα ὃ γέγονεν αὐτῇ, ἦλθεν καὶ προσέπεσεν αὐτῷ καὶ εἶπεν αὐτῷ πᾶσαν	Ἐν δὲ τῷ ὑπάγειν αὐτὸν οἱ ὄχλοι συνέπνιγον αὐτόν. [43]. καὶ γυνὴ οὖσα ἐν ῥύσει αἵματος ἀπὸ ἐτῶν δώδεκα, ἥτις ἰατροῖς προσαναλώσασα ὅλον τὸν βίον οὐκ ἴσχυσεν ἀπ' οὐδενὸς θεραπευθῆναι, [44]. προσελθοῦσα ὄπισθεν ἥψατο τοῦ κρασπέδου τοῦ ἱματίου αὐτοῦ, καὶ παραχρῆμα ἔστη ἡ ῥύσις τοῦ αἵματος αὐτῆς. [45] καὶ εἶπεν ὁ Ἰησοῦς· Τίς ὁ ἁψάμενός μου; ἀρνουμένων δὲ πάντων εἶπεν ὁ Πέτρος· Ἐπιστάτα, οἱ ὄχλοι συνέχουσίν σε καὶ ἀποθλίβουσιν. [46] ὁ δὲ Ἰησοῦς εἶπεν· Ἥψατό μού τις, ἐγὼ γὰρ ἔγνων δύναμιν ἐξεληλυθυῖαν ἀπ' ἐμοῦ. [47] ἰδοῦσα δὲ ἡ γυνὴ ὅτι οὐκ ἔλαθεν τρέμουσα ἦλθεν καὶ προσπεσοῦσα αὐτῷ δι' ἣν αἰτίαν ἥψατο αὐτοῦ ἀπήγγειλεν ἐνώπιον παντὸς τοῦ λαοῦ καὶ ὡς ἰάθη παραχρῆμα. [48] ὁ δὲ εἶπεν αὐτῇ· Θυγάτηρ, ἡ πίστις σου σέσωκέν σε· πορεύου εἰς εἰρήνην.

	τὴν ἀλήθειαν. ³⁴ ὁ δὲ εἶπεν αὐτῇ Θυγάτηρ, ἡ πίστις σου σέσωκέν σε· ὕπαγε εἰς εἰρήνην, καὶ ἴσθι ὑγιὴς ἀπὸ τῆς μάστιγός σου ²⁵ And a woman was there who had been subject to bleeding for twelve years. ²⁶ She had suffered a great deal under the care of many doctors and had spent all she had, yet instead of getting better she grew worse. ²⁷ When she heard about Jesus, she came up behind him in the crowd and touched his cloak, ²⁸ because she thought, "If I just touch his clothes, I will be healed." ²⁹ Immediately her bleeding stopped and she felt in her body that she was freed from her suffering. ³⁰ At once Jesus realized that power had gone out from him. He turned around in the crowd and asked, "Who touched my clothes?" ³¹ "You see the people crowding against you," his disciples answered, "and yet you can ask, 'Who touched me?' " ³² But Jesus kept looking around to see who had done it. ³³ Then the woman, knowing what had happened to her, came and fell at his feet and, trembling with fear, told him the whole truth. ³⁴ He said to her, "Daughter, your faith has healed you. Go in peace and be freed from your suffering."	As Jesus was on his way, the crowds almost crushed him. ⁴³ And a woman was there who had been subject to bleeding for twelve years,c but no one could heal her. ⁴⁴ She came up behind him and touched the edge of his cloak, and immediately her bleeding stopped. ⁴⁵ "Who touched me?" Jesus asked. When they all denied it, Peter said, "Master, the people are crowding and pressing against you." ⁴⁶ But Jesus said, "Someone touched me; I know that power has gone out from me." ⁴⁷ Then the woman, seeing that she could not go unnoticed, came trembling and fell at his feet. In the presence of all the people, she told why she had touched him and how she had been instantly healed. ⁴⁸ Then he said to her, "Daughter, your faith has healed you. Go in peace."
Story of the dead girl continued (Matt. 9:23-29) ²³ καὶ ἐλθὼν ὁ Ἰησοῦς εἰς τὴν	Story of the dead girl continued (Mark 5:35-43) ³⁵ Ἔτι αὐτοῦ λαλοῦντος	Story of the dead girl continued (Luk. 8:49-56) ⁴⁹ Ἔτι αὐτοῦ λαλοῦντος

οἰκίαν τοῦ ἄρχοντος **καὶ ἰδὼν τοὺς αὐλητὰς καὶ τὸν ὄχλον θορυβούμενον** ²⁴ ἔλεγεν Ἀναχωρεῖτε, οὐ γὰρ ἀπέθανεν τὸ κοράσιον ἀλλὰ καθεύδει· καὶ κατεγέλων αὐτοῦ. ²⁵ ὅτε δὲ ἐξεβλήθη ὁ ὄχλος, εἰσελθὼν ἐκράτησεν τῆς χειρὸς αὐτῆς, καὶ ἠγέρθη τὸ κοράσιον. ²⁶ καὶ ἐξῆλθεν ἡ φήμη αὕτη εἰς ὅλην τὴν γῆν ἐκείνην.

²³ When Jesus entered the synagogue leader's house and saw the noisy crowd and people playing pipes, ²⁴ he said, "Go away. The girl is not dead but asleep." But they laughed at him. ²⁵ After the crowd had been put outside, he went in and took the girl by the hand, and she got up.
²⁶ News of this spread through all that region.

ἔρχονται ἀπὸ τοῦ ἀρχισυναγώγου λέγοντες ὅτι Ἡ θυγάτηρ σου ἀπέθανεν· τί ἔτι σκύλλεις τὸν διδάσκαλον; ³⁶ ὁ δὲ Ἰησοῦς παρακούσας τὸν λόγον λαλούμενον λέγει τῷ ἀρχισυναγώγῳ Μὴ φοβοῦ, μόνον πίστευε. ³⁷ καὶ οὐκ ἀφῆκεν οὐδένα μετ' αὐτοῦ συνακολουθῆσαι εἰ μὴ τὸν Πέτρον καὶ Ἰάκωβον καὶ Ἰωάνην τὸν ἀδελφὸν Ἰακώβου. ³⁸ καὶ ἔρχονται εἰς τὸν οἶκον τοῦ ἀρχισυναγώγου, καὶ θεωρεῖ θόρυβον, καὶ κλαίοντας καὶ ἀλαλάζοντας πολλά, ³⁹ καὶ εἰσελθὼν λέγει αὐτοῖς Τί θορυβεῖσθε καὶ κλαίετε; τὸ παιδίον οὐκ ἀπέθανεν ἀλλὰ καθεύδει. ⁴⁰ καὶ κατεγέλων αὐτοῦ. αὐτὸς δὲ ἐκβαλὼν πάντας παραλαμβάνει τὸν πατέρα τοῦ παιδίου καὶ τὴν μητέρα καὶ τοὺς μετ' αὐτοῦ, καὶ εἰσπορεύεται ὅπου ἦν τὸ παιδίον. ⁴¹ καὶ κρατήσας τῆς χειρὸς τοῦ παιδίου λέγει αὐτῇ Ταλιθὰ κούμ, ὅ ἐστιν μεθερμηνευόμενον Τὸ κοράσιον, σοὶ λέγω, ἔγειρε. ⁴² καὶ εὐθὺς ἀνέστη τὸ κοράσιον καὶ περιεπάτει· ἦν γὰρ ἐτῶν δώδεκα. καὶ ἐξέστησαν εὐθὺς ἐκστάσει μεγάλῃ. ⁴³ καὶ διεστείλατο αὐτοῖς πολλὰ ἵνα μηδεὶς γνοῖ τοῦτο, καὶ εἶπεν δοθῆναι αὐτῇ φαγεῖν.

³⁵ While Jesus was still speaking, some people came from the house of Jairus, the synagogue leader. "Your daughter is dead," they said. "Why bother the teacher

ἔρχεταί τις παρὰ τοῦ ἀρχισυναγώγου λέγων ὅτι Τέθνηκεν ἡ θυγάτηρ σου, μηκέτι σκύλλε τὸν διδάσκαλον. ⁵⁰ ὁ δὲ Ἰησοῦς ἀκούσας ἀπεκρίθη αὐτῷ· Μὴ φοβοῦ, μόνον πίστευσον, καὶ σωθήσεται. ⁵¹ ἐλθὼν δὲ εἰς τὴν οἰκίαν οὐκ ἀφῆκεν εἰσελθεῖν τινα σὺν αὐτῷ εἰ μὴ Πέτρον καὶ Ἰωάννην καὶ Ἰάκωβον καὶ τὸν πατέρα τῆς παιδὸς καὶ τὴν μητέρα. ⁵² ἔκλαιον δὲ πάντες καὶ ἐκόπτοντο αὐτήν. ὁ δὲ εἶπεν· Μὴ κλαίετε, οὐ γὰρ ἀπέθανεν ἀλλὰ καθεύδει. ⁵³ καὶ κατεγέλων αὐτοῦ, εἰδότες ὅτι ἀπέθανεν. ⁵⁴ αὐτὸς δὲ κρατήσας τῆς χειρὸς αὐτῆς ἐφώνησεν λέγων· Ἡ παῖς, ἔγειρε. ⁵⁵ καὶ ἐπέστρεψεν τὸ πνεῦμα αὐτῆς, καὶ ἀνέστη παραχρῆμα, καὶ διέταξεν αὐτῇ δοθῆναι φαγεῖν. ⁵⁶ καὶ ἐξέστησαν οἱ γονεῖς αὐτῆς· ὁ δὲ παρήγγειλεν αὐτοῖς μηδενὶ εἰπεῖν τὸ γεγονός.

⁴⁹ While Jesus was still speaking, someone came from the house of Jairus, the synagogue leader. "Your daughter is dead," he said. "Don't bother the teacher anymore."
⁵⁰ Hearing this, Jesus said to Jairus, "Don't be afraid; just believe, and she will be healed."
⁵¹ When he arrived at the house of Jairus, he did not let anyone go in with him except Peter, John and James, and the child's father and mother.

| | | anymore?" ³⁶ Overhearing what they said, Jesus told him, "Don't be afraid; just believe." ³⁷ He did not let anyone follow him except Peter, James and John the brother of James. ³⁸ When they came to the home of the synagogue leader, Jesus saw a commotion, with people crying and wailing loudly. ³⁹ He went in and said to them, "Why all this commotion and wailing? The child is not dead but asleep." ⁴⁰ But they laughed at him. After he put them all out, he took the child's father and mother and the disciples who were with him, and went in where the child was. ⁴¹ He took her by the hand and said to her, "Talitha koum!" (which means "Little girl, I say to you, get up!"). ⁴² Immediately the girl stood up and began to walk around (she was twelve years old). At this they were completely astonished. ⁴³ He gave strict orders not to let anyone know about this, and told them to give her something to eat. | ⁵² Meanwhile, all the people were wailing and mourning for her. "Stop wailing," Jesus said. "She is not dead but asleep." ⁵⁴ They laughed at him, knowing that she was dead. ⁵⁴ But he took her by the hand and said, "My child, get up!" ⁵⁵ Her spirit returned, and at once she stood up. Then Jesus told them to give her something to eat. ⁵⁶ Her parents were astonished, but he ordered them not to tell anyone what had happened. |

Table 42: The parallel of Matt. 9:18-26 with Mark 5:21-43 and Luk. 8:46-50 on the stories of Jesus' healing of the woman with blood flow and the dead girl

The most obvious difference is the much shortened version by Matthew, which is a general tendency with Matthew in his miracle stories. Matthew usually shortens Mark's narratives, especially the miracle stories, while he expands and inserts discourse material. Earlier scholars of the Synoptics were of the opinion that Matthew was careless in his abbreviations and weakened the narratives (Schniewind, 1930:139; Wellhausen, 1911:50). Yet Bornkamm (1963a:52-57) has demonstrated with his article on the stilling of the storm in Matthew that the evangelist exercises great care in his version of this miracle story[226]. Scholars have become convinced that Matthew abbreviates the miracle stories for the sake of interpretation (Held, 1963:165-192). In comparison with Mark's version, Matthew cuts out a third of the first part of the story of the girl, two thirds of the woman with the blood flow and two thirds of the conclusion. Matthew makes no reference to the crossing of the lake (Mark 5:21), and it seems as if Jesus is still at table in the house (cf. Matt. 9:10). He does not mention the crowds who followed and pressed against Jesus either (Mark 5:24). He omits details on how the haemorrhaging woman suffered due to the treatment of the doctors (Mark 5:26) or about Jesus who turned around asking who had touched Him (Mark 5:30). Furthermore, he twice omits reference to the disciples (Mark 5:31 and 37). He does not describe how the healed woman fell at the feet of Jesus trembling with fear (Mark 5:33). Furthermore, he does not mention the child's father and mother whom Jesus took with Him (Mark 5:40). Similar to many other cases, "Matthew seems impatient of Mark's asides and details and gives only the bare essentials of the story" (Hagner, 1993:246). It seems that Matthew abbreviates the story so that he can focus on the message he wants to convey with it. In Matt. 5:18-26 faith in Jesus and his healing power occupies centre stage in the story.

A significant difference is that Mark 5:23 (// Luk. 8:24) mentions that the daughter was dying and only after the healing of the haemorrhaging women messengers announced her death (Mark 5:35 // Luk. 8:49), but according to Matt. 9:25 she had died before her father first approached Jesus. In Matthew the ruler believes that Jesus can raise is daughter form death, while in Mark and Luke he expects that Jesus could save her from dying. While Mark refers to the father as εἷς τῶν ἀρχισυναγώγων (one of the rulers of the synagogue) (Mark 5:22) and Luke to him as ἄρχων τῆς συναγωγῆς (leader of the synagogue) (Luk. 8:41), Matthew refers to him as ἄρχων (a ruler) (Matt. 9:18). As is typical of Matthew, he once again omits any positive reference to the synagogue. The first Gospel throughout contrasts the hostile attitude of the synagogue and its leaders with the positive attitude of the church and its believing community. Matthew emphasises the ruler's trust in Jesus. He replaces Mark's πίπτει πρὸς τοὺς πόδας αὐτοῦ (he fell before his [Jesus'] feet) (Mark 5:22) (// Luk. 8:41: πεσὼν παρὰ

---

[226] Matthew not only retells the story, but exegetes it. He applies the story of the stilling of the storm to the trials and tribulations of discipleship and the church. Jesus rescues his disciples and people who believe in Him. He provides them security. Greeven (1955:69) indicates how Matthew abbreviates the story of the healing of the paralytic to reach the essentials of the story more quickly.

τοὺς πόδας τοῦ Ἰησοῦ, he fell at Jesus' feet) with προσεκύνει (he knelt before Him) (Matt. 9:18). This verb describes the ruler prostrating before Jesus as his a superior in a gesture of worship. Matthew uses προσεκύνειν (to worship) to refer to the worship of God (Matt. 4:10) and to describe how people put their trust in Jesus and worship Him (Matt. 2:2, 8, 11; 8:2; 14:33; 15:25; 20:20 and 28:9, 17). Matthew clearly emphasises the ruler's faith in Jesus and his power to conquer death. Jesus also mentions the faith of the bleeding woman when telling her ἡ πίστις σου σέσωκέν σε (your faith has healed you) (Matt. 9:22). As with the story of the stilling of the storm (Matt. 8:23-27), the double story of Jesus healing these two women describes how Jesus rescues people from trouble and tribulation. Matthew also replaces the ὄχλος πολύς (large crowd) who followed Jesus (Mark 5:24) (// Luk. 8:42: οἱ ὄχλοι, crowds) with οἱ μαθηταὶ αὐτοῦ (his disciples) (Matt. 9:19). Matthew focuses on the faith community who witness and experience the restoring power of Jesus.

As part of his interpretation Matthew also adds some detail in his retelling of miracle stories (Held, 1963:168). A significant addition by Matthew in this double story is that he mentions that Jesus wore a garment with tassels. The woman wanted to touch the fringe of his garment (τοῦ κρασπέδου τοῦ ἱματίου αὐτοῦ). The fringe probably does not simply refer to the edge of Jesus' garment, but to the tassels (צִיצָת) required according to Num. 15:38-41 and Deut. 22:12. These tassels had to remind Jews to remain obedient to the Law (Carter, 2000a:225; Hagner, 1993:249; Luz, 2001a:42; Osborne, 2010:349). Matthew takes an interest in Jesus' faithfulness to the *Torah*, even in his clothing. Furthermore, Matthew replaces οὖσα ἐν ῥύσει αἵματος (who had been subject to bleeding) (Mark 5:25 // Luk. 8:43) with the rare compound verb and *hapax legomenon* in the New Testament, αἱμορροοῦσα (who suffered of haemorrhage) (Matt. 9:20). This verb is also used in the LXX of Lev. 15:33, a passage in which sexual impurities and contamination are explained. It seems that Matthew wants to emphasise that Jesus was pious to the *Torah*, but nevertheless was not concerned by the touch of this woman. Later He would also touch the dead girl. Wainwright (1991:199) has remarked: "... both (the woman and the girl) can be considered dead (one socially and religiously, the other physically), and both therefore have the capacity to contaminate life". Matthew emphasises that even though these two females had the capacity to contaminate Jesus, Jesus in contrast had the power to heal them.

Matthew, like the other Synoptics, places the story of the bleeding woman as intercalation within the framework of the story of the raising of the young girl. In Matthew's version the sharp intercalation is marked with καὶ ἰδοὺ (and then) (Matt. 9:20).

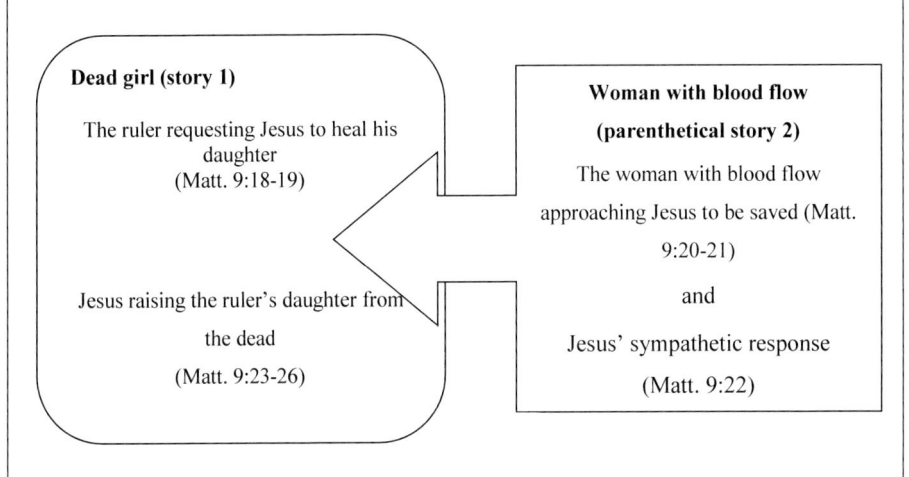

Figure 3: The intercalation of the stories of Jesus' healing the dead girl and the woman with blood flow in Matt. 9:18-26

The technique of intercalation builds suspense and highlights similarities between the stories (Carter, 2000a:224; Osborne, 2010:347). Both stories vividly tell about faith. The faith of the ruler is tested by the intervention of the bleeding woman and Jesus commends the faith of the woman. Both stories tell about females in need, one twelve years of age and the other about a woman who suffered for twelve years. The one story is about a daughter, and the other about a woman whom Jesus calls daughter. Both tell about suffering, of the father and of the bleeding woman. In both stories touching is involved, the woman touching the fringe of Jesus' garment and Jesus taking the daughter by the hand. In both cases healing takes place. Both these healings are miracles. Both stories vividly describe hope in Jesus for people otherwise in hopeless situations. In both stories the people are powerless, but experience the power of Jesus. The one story tells about a direct approach and request, and the other about an indirect touching of Jesus. In both stories the focus is on Jesus. Faith is directed at Him, He offers healing power and He brings wholeness and restoration (Weren, 1979:86).

Taking the cultural and textual context into consideration, it becomes clear that Matthew does not tell these stories for their own sake, but to tell something about the coming of the Kingdom, about faith and expectation, about the power and character of Jesus, about healing and access to Jesus. Purity regulations find new meaning through the teachings and healings of Jesus. With his healing power and care, Jesus enacts the true intention of the Law.

8.3.2.2 Jesus' reaction when touched by a woman with blood flow (Matt. 9:20-22)

While Jesus was on his way to heal the daughter of the ruler who had just died, a woman who had been subject to bleeding for twelve years came up behind Him and touched the fringe of his cloak (Matt. 5:20). The interruption of this new story is marked by καὶ ἰδοὺ (and look). According to purity regulations her bleeding made her perpetually unclean, which caused constant social and religious separation (Lev. 15:25-30) (Anderson, 1983:11; Morris, 1992:229; Wainwright, 1994:648). "She was a virtual leper who would have had to leave family and village, lest contact with her renders everyone unclean" (Osborne, 2010:348). Even a touch from her would make someone unclean (Lev. 15:19[227]). This includes a woman who's blood flow[228] continues for a longer period (Lev. 15:25[229]). Also according to the *Tannaim* (*Mishnah Zabim*, 5.1, 6)[230], the impurity of a woman with blood flow can be transmitted through touch (Davies & Allison, 2004b:128; Talbert, 2010:121). The woman in the story therefore took a risk by touching Jesus, which is probably the reason why she approached Him from behind (Luz, 2001a:42; Morris, 1992:229; Witherington, 2006:203). This touching would leave Jesus ritually impure. Yet, when He realises that He was being touched, Jesus responds positively in a very sympathetic way. He turns to the woman and says to her: "Take heart, daughter ... your faith has healed you" (Matt. 9:22).

It is noteworthy to recognize the interaction between Jesus and the woman as illustrated in the following diagram.

---

[227] "When a woman has her regular flow of blood, the impurity of her monthly period will last seven days, and anyone who touches her will be unclean till evening" (Lev. 15:19).

[228] Matthew uses the same word for blood flow as has been used in the LXX to Lev. 15:33, i.e.: αἱμορροούσῃ.

[229] "When a woman has a discharge of blood for many days at a time other than her monthly period or has a discharge that continues beyond her period, she will be unclean as long as she has the discharge, just as in the days of her period" (Lev.Ex 15:25).

[230] The *Tannaim* were Rabbinic sages who acted approximately from 10 to 220 CE. Their views were recorded in the *Mishnah*. The period of the *Tannaim* is also referred to as the *Mishna*ic period. Though the *Mishnah* was produced about 200 C.E. the ideas recorded in it, stem from an earlier period. The *Mishnah* therefore provides useful background information about the time of Jesus' ministry and the early church (Neusner, 1994:97).

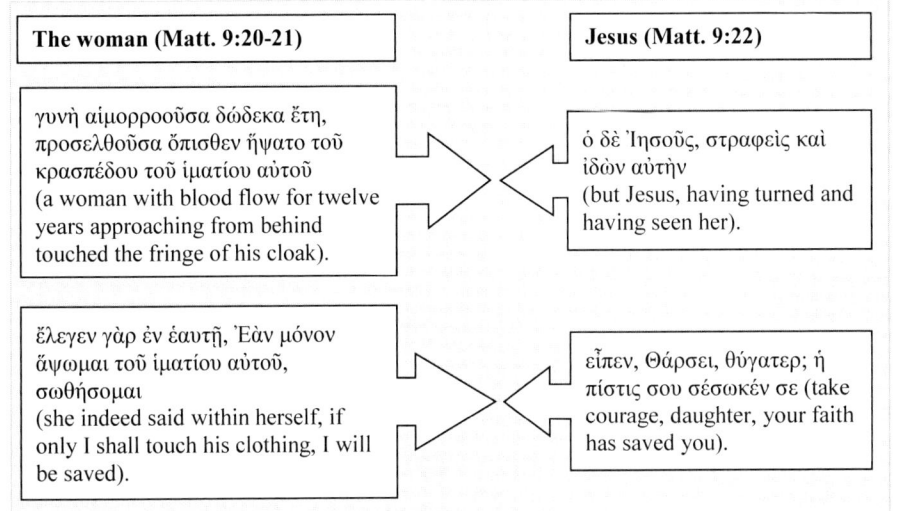

Figure 4: The interaction between the woman with blood flow and Jesus in Matt. 9:20-22

Matthew focuses on the interaction between the woman and Jesus alone. The vivid scene in Mark 5:25-26 of the seriousness of her sickness and how the woman tries to conceal herself in the crowd is omitted. Though presupposed, the crowd and the disciples disappeared from the picture. No detail is given about the place, time or circumstances. In parallel style Matthew describes the interaction between the woman and Jesus. The initiative of the woman to approach Jesus from behind and to touch the fringe of his cloak[231], is paralleled by Jesus' turning around and seeing her. Her touching draws Jesus' attention. The woman is almost caught in her act, but Jesus turns to her sympathetically. Furthermore, the prayer-like reasoning of the woman, "I will be saved" (σωθήσομαι)[232], is paralleled by Jesus' positive response "your faith has saved you" (ἡ πίστις σου σέσωκέν). Matthew frequently refers to faith in the context of miracles (Matt. 8:13; 9:28, 15:28, 17:20 and 21:21). Faith implies trust in the

---

[231] The notion that healing could take place by touching a healer's clothing was common (cf. Acts 19:12) in those times (Davies & Allison, 2004b:129).

[232] It might be argued that the woman only expected Jesus to "save" her from her illness, but Matthew places her request firmly in context of faith.

power of Jesus to perform miracles[233]. The woman's expectation that Jesus could save her is comparable with a believer's prayer to God. She approaches Jesus in much the same way as one would approach God. As the Father knows the request of his children before they ask (Matt. 6:8), Jesus knows the need of this woman (Davies & Allison, 2004b:129).

According to Jewish custom, one would expect Jesus to be upset for being defiled by the woman's action. Surprisingly, Jesus responds with kindness as He knows both her faith and her plight. He encourages her to "take courage" and addresses her tenderly as "daughter". In comparison with Mark, Matthew omits that Jesus sensed that the power streamed out from Him, that He did not know who had touched Him and that the woman reacted fearfully when coming forward to confess that she did it (cf. Mark 5:19-33).

The verbs that describe the woman's healing, both derivatives of save (σωζειν), are significant. This alludes to the task of Jesus as stated in Matt. 1:21: "He will save his people from their sins"[234]. This is a statement with programmatic significance. It declares the messianic identity of Jesus, as well as what could be expected from Him (Novakovic, 2003:63-69). Jesus adds that her faith has saved her. Her bleeding and its consequent impurity devalued her social status and she was excluded from society. To understand the impact of this desired healing, one has to consider what healing implied in the ancient Mediterranean world. Healing involved (at that time and even today) more than physical healing from a disease. Healing implied the restoration of the total well-being of a person (Malina & Rohrbauch, 2003:368; Pilch, 1988:60-66; Weren, 1994:86). This includes the restoration of meaning of life and honour. A healed person can fully participate in societal activities again. Healing, therefore, is culturally constructed. In this regard, one has to consider the difference between disease and illness. A disease causes sickness and is a pathological issue. Sickness exists irrespective of whether a culture recognizes it or not. Sickness is caused by viruses and germs. Illness, on the other hand, refers to misfortunes in well-being beyond a pathological state. An ill person is a socially devalued person. Restoring the meaning of life for an ill person implies healing. The bleeding woman had the expectation and belief that Jesus could heal her from this

---

[233] Matthew places the double story alongside the healing of two blind men (Matt. 9:27-31) where the question about faith also plays a central role. All of these stories illustrate genuine faith in miracles.

[234] Though the woman's faith could also refer to faith in God or in the Pharisaic robes, within this context is seems that she had faith in Jesus.

deprived state. Jesus heals more than her physical ailment. Her whole person is healed and she can again fully participate in society.

Matthew's version intensifies the compassionate interaction between Jesus and the woman, with no hint of Jesus being upset for being touched by the unclean woman. Compassionate interaction forms a key component of the intention of the Law (Matt. 22:34-40). Matt. 9:20-22 describes the positive story in contrast to the suffering of the woman. She suffered not only because of the illness itself, but also from the purity restrictions. She is wholly presented in a positive light, no mention is made of her impurity, nothing is said about the fact that her touch would indignify Jesus, and onlookers do not mention anything about Jesus coming into contact with this unclean woman. Surely something different is at stake: "Instead of uncleanness passing from the woman to Jesus, healing power flows from Jesus to the woman" (Davies & Allison, 2004b:130). In the ancient Mediterranean world, healers are considered to be holy men. Holy men have direct contact with the realm of God. The activity of holy men is supposed to benefit the people of society (Malina & Rohrbauch, 2003:369). Jesus is identified as the Holy One, as the Holy Spirit came upon Him and He is called the Son of God (Matt. 3:13-17). Jesus acts as Saviour and messianic Healer. He is Emmanuel, the Holy One. His healing forms part of the coming of the Kingdom of Heaven. The purity regulations found their fulfilment in this act of Jesus who can bring an end to the ungodly power of impurity. He heals the woman by restoring her to her proper place in the community. Jesus is depicted as the miracle-working Saviour (Held, 1963:260). In Matt. 8:17 Matthew applies Isa. 53:4 to Jesus. As servant of the Lord, He does away with the infirmities and sickness of this woman.

From this narrative it can be derived that the Matthew developed a new understanding of purity laws. As Jesus saves this woman from her distress, He saves his followers from their sins. He transposes purity for his followers from an external ritual to an internal ethical and moral level. This is probably intended in the sixth beatitude: "Blessed are the pure at heart" (Matt. 5:8).

8.3.2.3   *Jesus taking a dead girl by the hand (Matt. 9:25)*

This inserted story of Jesus' healing of the woman with blood flow is framed by the story of Jesus' raising the ruler's daughter from the dead.

Before this interruption, the father's request is reported. Unlike Mark, who wrote that the ruler's daughter was near dying (ἐσχάτως ἔχει) (Mark 5:23 // Luk. 8:24), Matthew wrote that the daughter has just died (ἄρτι ἐτελεύτησεν) (Matt.

9:19). This has the effect of emphasising the faith of the ruler even in the face of death. He does not only believe that Jesus can heal his sick daughter, but that He can raise her from the dead. Right through the narrative he firmly and confidently trusts Jesus. This implies that the father's request that Jesus should lay his hand on her would place Jesus in a state of impurity. Nevertheless, Jesus does not mention anything in this regard or hesitate to follow the ruler to his house.

After the interruption about the bleeding woman, the story continues with Jesus arriving at the house where the dead daughter was. Though Matthew limits the detail of the story, he does, however, add the references to the flute players and noisy crowd. These activities signify a funeral procession and emphasises the death of the girl (Hagner, 1993:250).

Matthew's version of the story is therefore, from the start right through to the end, about Jesus responding to the plea of the father to raise his daughter from the dead[235]. The flow of Matthew's carefully structured narrative can be demonstrated by the following diagram:

Ἡ θυγάτηρ μου ἄρτι ἐτελεύτησεν (my daughter has just died) (Matt. 9:18b) (A)

ἀλλὰ ἐλθών, ἐπίθες τὴν χεῖρά σου ἐπ' αὐτήν, καὶ ζήσεται (but come, lay your hand on her and she will live) (Matt. 9:18c) (B)

καὶ ἐγερθεὶς, ὁ Ἰησοῦς ἠκολούθησεν αὐτῷ, καὶ οἱ μαθηταὶ (and Jesus got up and followed him, as well as the disciples) (Matt. 9:19) (C)

(parenthetical story) (Matt. 9:20-22)

Καὶ ἐλθὼν ὁ Ἰησοῦς εἰς τὴν οἰκίαν τοῦ ἄρχοντος (and as Jesus came at the house of the ruler) (Matt. 9:23a) (C')

καὶ ἰδὼν τοὺς αὐλητὰς καὶ τὸν ὄχλον θορυβούμενον (and having seen the flute-players and the crowd making commotion) (Matt. 9:23b)

εἰσελθών, ἐκράτησεν τῆς χειρὸς αὐτῆς (having entered, He took hold of her hand (Matt. 9:25b) (B')

---

[235] Levine (1996:394-396) notes the contrast between Jesus' constructive power with the destructive power of Herod who killed children (Matt. 2:16-18) and Herod Antipas who orders a killing because of a daughter (Matt. 14:1-12).

καὶ ἠγέρθη τὸ κοράσιον (and He raised the girl) (Matt. 9:25c) (A')

Table 43: The structure of the narrative of Jesus' healing of the dead girl in Matt. 9:18-25

In this story the father states that his daughter has just died (Matt. 9:18b), which correlates with Jesus who raises her (Matt. 9:25c). This parallel accentuates the message that Jesus has the power to do much more that any human can. Similarly the father's request that Jesus should come and lay his hand on his daughter (Matt. 9:18c) is paralleled with Jesus entering the room and taking the girl by her hand (Matt. 9:25b). Matthew also refers to the hand of Jesus when healing a leper (Matt. 8:3). The hand of Jesus probably refers to the hand of Yahweh in the Hebrew Bible. The hand of Jesus can do what the powerful hand of Yahweh had done. The third parallel lies between Jesus and his disciples getting up and following the ruler (Matt. 9:19) and Jesus coming to the house of the ruler (Matt. 9:23a). Within this parallel structure Matthew's addition of the flute players and noisy crowds of the funeral procession is significant. This girl was dead indeed. Jesus does not hesitate to make contact with the dead girl, despite the fact that purity regulations state that this would leave Him impure.

The way Matthew describes Jesus' activity in the room intensifies the private and close character of this miracle. After sending out the mourners, Jesus enters the room where the daughter is laying. Different from Mark, Matthew does not mention anything about the daughter's parents or his disciples (cf. Mark 5:37, 40). Having entered the room (εἰσελθών), Jesus takes the hand of the girl (ἐκράτησεν τῆς χειρὸς αὐτῆς) (Matt. 9:25). Unlike Mark (Mark 5:41) and Luke (Luke 8:54), who records that Jesus also spoke to the girl, Matthew only mentions Him taking her hand. Matthew explicitly mentions that Jesus takes the girl by the hand to raise her up (Luz, 2001a:43; Witherington, 2006:203). Jesus' hand once again symbolizes his healing power (cf. Matt. 8:3, 15) (Hagner, 1993:250; Luz, 2001:41; Malina & Rohrbauch, 2003:368). It is also significant that Matthew uses a series of three participles leading up to the two finite verbs to describe Jesus' actions at the house: The participles ἐλθών (coming) + ἰδών (seeing) + εἰσελθών (entering) intensify the expectation leading to the climactic finite verbs, ἐκράτησεν (He touched) + ἠγέρθη (He raised).

Apparently entering the room and touching the girl would leave Jesus ritually impure. Nevertheless, Matthew makes no reference to Jesus hesitating to enter the room or to touch her. He actually intensifies the tension with a series of participles leading up to the climactic finite action words. Jesus conquers death and its defiling power. Matthew also does not make any reference to Jesus performing purification rituals after this deed. With this narrative, Matthew clearly relates a deeper message. While death is associated with impurity, Jesus does not become impure as a result of this contact. The contrary happens. Life flows from Jesus to the girl to raise her from death. Death and its associated impurity are conquered. He is the healer and Holy One. Jesus has yet again brought the Kingdom of Heaven a step closer. With his coming, the purity laws are fulfilled. Jesus enacts the intention of the Law.

8.4 CONCLUSION

The double story of Jesus healing the woman with blood flow and the daughter of the ruler describes a significant fulfilment of the purity laws of the Hebrew Bible. The Sermon on the Mount (Matt. 5-7) and the healing narrative (Matt. 8-9) are closely connected. While the Sermon on the Mount describes Jesus' teaching of the Law, the healing narrative describes his enactment of it. Thus the Law provides the background for this story of Jesus, while the story of Jesus gives new meaning to the Law. The purity laws form part of this.

Matthew's redactional intent becomes evident in the way he retells this double story. He does not merely tell it for its own sake, but for the message it contains. His descriptive parts are quite bare. He omits much of the pictorial details of Mark's narrative to concentrate on the messages he wishes to convey. His additions to Mark's version likewise show his special interests and intentions. The narrative demonstrates the nature of miracle faith in Jesus as the Servant of the Lord and Holy One who can cure these two women by touching them. Jesus is described as Emmanuel and the one who would save his people from their sins. As Saviour He purifies people who believe in Him of that which defiles them. As the Holy One, He touches people and purity flows from Him to them, while He Himself does not become impure. He conquers illness and death, seemingly not being affected by illness and death. These healings form part of the coming of the Kingdom of Heaven where eventually no impurity, sickness, illness and death will persist. Jesus thus has come to bring the purity laws to their fulfilment.

Followers of Jesus share the healing and purifying power of Jesus. Within their faith community purity regulations are transformed from an external ritual to an internal moral level. Jesus expects from them to be pure at heart (Matt. 5:8).

CHAPTER 9

EXTERNAL CULTIC TRADITION AND INTERNAL ETHICAL PURITY IN MATTHEW 15

9.1 INTRODUCTION

As discussed this far, Jesus' relation to the *Torah* forms a central motive in the first Gospel (cf. Loader, 1997:165). Perhaps the most important passage in Matthew on the *Torah* is found in Matt. 5:17-19 (cf. Chapter 3). This passage is considered as the fundamental statement of Matthew on the Law. In Matthew, Jesus is presented as the ultimate interpreter of this Law. Parallel to this, the Pharisees are described as people obsessed with observing the *Torah*, both the written as well as the oral traditions. The Gospel continuously describes Jesus and the Pharisees as being in conflict about the true interpretation of the Law. For example, Jesus calls for greater righteousness than the Pharisees and teachers of the Law do (Matt. 5:20) (Chapter 5), Jesus' *halakhic* argument on the true intention of the Law (Matt. 5:21-48) (Chapter 4), Jesus' response to the accusations of the Pharisees when He ate with tax collectors and sinners (Matt. 9:10-13) (Chapter 7) and the Sabbath controversy (Matt. 12:1-14) (Chapter 7).

In Matt. 15:1-20 the oral Law, as observed and developed by the Pharisees[236], is in dispute. Different communities of Judaism interpreted the *Torah* in various ways (Neusner, 2007:111). After the destruction of the temple in 70 C.E., the Pharisees and scribes carried forward the oral traditions that were associated with the *Torah*. They formed the community of Judaism that observed the written *Torah* in accordance with these oral traditions. This approach earned them the title and identity of "the Judaism of the Dual *Torah*" (Neusner, 1994:5-7; 2007:111). In the "Judaism of the Dual *Torah*" the *Torah* is preserved in three forms: the Hebrew Scriptures, the memorized oral tradition (first written

---

[236] The Sadducees, however, only observed the written *Torah*.

down in the *Mishnah* ca. 200 C.E.), and by the sages called rabbis[237] (Neusner, 1994:5).

In addition to the written Law, the Pharisees believed that God had also given laws to Moses that were transmitted orally (Cohen, 2006:222)[238]. These laws had to be memorized and passed on through generations (Neusner, 1971:1-11). The oral laws derived from the written Law, supplement it and interpreted it (Cohen, 2006:195). The Pharisees believed that the written *Torah* could not be understood on its own and that it had to be explicated by these oral traditions. Besides the traditions, which they believed had originated with Moses and had been passed on through generations, the Pharisees were very innovative in extending these laws to account for the needs of their own times. Flavius Josephus, the first century Romano-Jewish historian remarked: "The Pharisees have imposed on the people many laws from the tradition of the fathers not written in the Law of Moses" (*Ant.* 13. 297). One of these ideas was the development of the laws on hand-washing, which were intended to ensure the observance of purity laws (cf. *Mishnah Berkakhot*, 8:12-4)[239].

In Matt. 15:1-20 Jesus responds to the accusation made by the Pharisees and the scribes that his disciples do not observe the tradition of hand-washing. In this dispute story two ideas are interwoven, namely the locus of impurity (external or internal) and the tradition of the elders (ἡ παράδοσις τῶν πρεσβυτέρων) versus the Word of God (ὁ λόγος τοῦ Θεοῦ). The fact that Matthew's Jesus

---

[237] A rabbi was considered as equivalent to a scroll of the *Torah* (Neusner, 1994:6) as presented in the following statements from the Babylonian Talmud: "He who sees a disciple of a sage who has died is as if he sees a scroll of the *Torah* that has burned" (Y. Moed Qatan 3:7.X) and "An elder who forgot his learning because of some accident which happened to him – they treat him with the sanctity owed to an ark [of the *Torah*]" (Y. Moed Qatan 3:1.XI).

[238] Rabbinic terminology distinguished between oral and written *Torah*, as the "Torah in writing" and the "Torah by word of mouth" (*b. Git.* 60b; *Midr.* Tanhuma, *Ki. Tassa* 17).

[239] The *Mishnah Berakhot* (completed around the year 200 C.E) states:

8.2   The House of Shammai say: "They wash the hands and afterward mix the cup." And he House of Hillel say: "They mix the cup and afterward wash the hands".

8.3   The House of Shammai say: "He dries his hands on the cloth and lays it on the table" and the House of Hillel say: "On the pillow".

8.4   The House of Shammai say: "They clean the house, and afterward they wash the hands" and the House of Hillel say: "They wash the hands, and afterward they clean the house.

contrasts the tradition of the elders with the Word of God implies that He doesn't regard these traditions as coming from God. They are man-made. The Pharisees are depicted as obsessed with external man-made rules to ensure purity, while Jesus is concerned with inner purity based on God's Word. Earlier in this Gospel the Pharisees' concern about purity is also emphasised when some Pharisees objected to Jesus' association with "sinners and tax collectors" (Matt. 9:11). The story of hand-washing reflects debates about purity as well as the status of oral Law in comparison to the written Law, a debate that emerged during the first century C.E. (Evans, 2012:299).

In this chapter, the story is once again interpreted on two levels. The first level describes the dispute between Jesus and the Pharisees. The second level explores the tension that the Matthean community experienced in their encounter with the Pharisean Judaism[240] of their day. The Matthean community[241] was in the process of forming their own identity alongside that of Pharisean Judaism and other main Jewish sects of their time (Overman, 1990:41). However, an attempt to reconstruct the social and religious setting of the first audience should be done with caution. Unlike the letters, the Gospels don't directly provide such information of their first readers.

The aim of this chapter is to explain how the dispute as described in Matt. 15:1-20 fits into Matthew's overall teaching of Jesus and the *Torah*. The question is which aspect of the *Torah* is challenged by Matthew's Jesus, and what He considers to be the true meaning of the Law. It seems that Matthew uses this story to define and maintain the identity of his community over and against the views of the dominant Pharisean Judaism that they encountered. To reach this aim, the three scenes of this story each receive attention. In the first scene the objection of the Pharisees and the scribes regarding their traditions and Jesus' response is investigated to establish the opposing views on the oral Law. In the second scene where Jesus addresses the crowds, Jesus' central philosophical

---

[240] As discussed in Chapter 2, Matthew identifies the Pharisees as chief opponents, though a variety of Jewish groups existed throughout the period from the Maccabean revolt to the end of the first century. Judaism was quite fragmented and fluid with various groups exercising influence at one stage or another (Cohen, 2006:12; Stanton, 2013:125; Repschinski, 2000:346). It seems as if the Pharisees were the dominant group in Matthew's situation. See Neusner (1973) on the evolution of Pharisean Judaism.

[241] The "Matthean community" should not be seen as one small localized group of people who would be able to gather at one house church, but rather as a linked set of communities sharing similar convictions about Jesus (Stanton, 2013:125) (cf. Chapter 2).

view regarding purity is identified. In the third scene, where Jesus responds to questions of his disciples, Jesus' explanation of his central view on purity is investigated. From this, the investigative devices[242] that Matthew uses to define the identity and required morality for his community are identified.

9.2. THE COMPOSITION OF THE NARRATIVE

Matt. 15:1-20 contains a parallel to the hand-washing dispute described in Mark 7:1-23[243], but with significant changes. For the sake of comparison, significant passages that only appear in one of the versions, are underlined.

Matt. 15:1-20	Mark 7:1-23
Scene 1: Jesus and the Pharisees: Streitgespräch with a challenge and riposte	
Pharisees' challenge	
¹ Τότε προσέρχονται τῷ Ἰησοῦ ἀπὸ Ἱεροσολύμων Φαρισαῖοι καὶ γραμματεῖς ... ¹ Then some Pharisees and teachers of the Law came to Jesus from Jerusalem ...	¹ Καὶ συνάγονται πρὸς αὐτὸν οἱ Φαρισαῖοι καί τινες τῶν γραμματέων ἐλθόντες ἀπὸ Ἱεροσολύμων. ¹ The Pharisees and some of the teachers of the Law who had come from Jerusalem gathered around Jesus
	² καὶ ἰδόντες τινὰς τῶν μαθητῶν αὐτοῦ ὅτι κοιναῖς χερσίν, τοῦτ' ἔστιν ἀνίπτοις, ἐσθίουσιν τοὺς ἄρτους, ³ οἱ γὰρ Φαρισαῖοι καὶ πάντες οἱ Ἰουδαῖοι ἐὰν μὴ πυγμῇ νίψωνται τὰς χεῖρας οὐκ ἐσθίουσιν, κρατοῦντες τὴν παράδοσιν τῶν πρεσβυτέρων, ⁴ καὶ ἀπ' ἀγορᾶς ἐὰν μὴ ῥαντίσωνται οὐκ ἐσθίουσιν, καὶ ἄλλα πολλά ἐστιν ἃ παρέλαβον κρατεῖν, βαπτισμοὺς

---

[242] In Chapter 4 I discussed the devices the ancient authors used to mark the identity of their communities, e.g. commitment to a central figure, the naming of groups, claims of ultimate revelation and interpretation, critique of opponents, eschatological expectations, and appropriate conduct for their communities.

[243] Luke does not have a direct parallel to this story, though an indirect parallel can be found in Luk. 11:37-41: "When Jesus had finished speaking, a Pharisee invited him to eat with him; so he went in and reclined at the table. But the Pharisee was surprised when he noticed that Jesus did not first wash before the meal. Then the Lord said to him, "Now then, you Pharisees clean the outside of the cup and dish, but inside you are full of greed and wickedness. You foolish people! Did not the one who made the outside make the inside also? But now as for what is inside you—be generous to the poor, and everything will be clean for you. Luke's Jesus also condemns an external ceremony of washing while ones internal being is filled with evil.

	ποτηρίων καὶ ξεστῶν καὶ χαλκίων.
	² and saw some of his disciples eating food with hands that were defiled, that is, unwashed. ³ (The Pharisees and all the Jews do not eat unless they give their hands a ceremonial washing, holding to the tradition of the elders. ⁴ When they come from the marketplace they do not eat unless they wash. And they observe many other traditions, such as the washing of cups, pitchers and kettles.)
Λέγοντες ² Διὰ τί οἱ μαθηταί σου παραβαίνουσιν τὴν παράδοσιν τῶν πρεσβυτέρων; οὐ γὰρ νίπτονται τὰς χεῖρας ὅταν ἄρτον ἐσθίωσιν. ... and asked, ² "Why do your disciples break the tradition of the elders, because they don't wash their hands whenever they eat bread!"	⁵ καὶ ἐπερωτῶσιν αὐτὸν οἱ Φαρισαῖοι καὶ οἱ γραμματεῖς Διὰ τί οὐ περιπατοῦσιν οἱ μαθηταί σου κατὰ τὴν παράδοσιν τῶν πρεσβυτέρων, ἀλλὰ κοιναῖς χερσὶν ἐσθίουσιν τὸν ἄρτον; ⁵ So the Pharisees and teachers of the Law asked Jesus, "Why don't your disciples live according to the tradition of the elders instead of eating their food with defiled hands?"

Jesus' riposte

| ³ ὁ δὲ ἀποκριθεὶς εἶπεν αὐτοῖς· Διὰ τί καὶ ὑμεῖς παραβαίνετε τὴν ἐντολὴν τοῦ θεοῦ διὰ τὴν παράδοσιν ὑμῶν; ⁴ ὁ γὰρ θεὸς εἶπεν· Τίμα τὸν πατέρα καὶ τὴν μητέρα, καί· Ὁ κακολογῶν πατέρα ἢ μητέρα θανάτῳ τελευτάτω· ⁵ ὑμεῖς δὲ λέγετε· Ὃς ἂν εἴπῃ τῷ πατρὶ ἢ τῇ μητρί· Δῶρον ὃ ἐὰν ἐξ ἐμοῦ ὠφεληθῇς, ⁶ οὐ μὴ τιμήσει τὸν πατέρα αὐτοῦ· καὶ ἠκυρώσατε τὸν λόγον τοῦ θεοῦ διὰ τὴν παράδοσιν ὑμῶν. ⁷ ὑποκριταί, καλῶς ἐπροφήτευσεν περὶ ὑμῶν Ἡσαΐας λέγων· ⁸ Ὁ λαὸς οὗτος τοῖς χείλεσίν με τιμᾷ, ἡ δὲ καρδία αὐτῶν πόρρω ἀπέχει ἀπ' ἐμοῦ· ⁹ μάτην δὲ σέβονταί με, διδάσκοντες διδασκαλίας ἐντάλματα ἀνθρώπων. ³ Jesus replied, "And why do you break the command of God for the sake of your tradition? ⁴ For God said, 'Honour your father and mother' and 'Anyone who curses their father or mother is to be put to death.' ⁵ But you say that if anyone declares that what might have been used to help their father or mother is 'devoted to God,' ⁶ they are not to 'honour their father or mother' with it. Thus you nullify the word of God for the sake of | ⁶ ὁ δὲ εἶπεν αὐτοῖς· Καλῶς ἐπροφήτευσεν Ἡσαΐας περὶ ὑμῶν τῶν ὑποκριτῶν, ὡς γέγραπται ὅτι Οὗτος ὁ λαὸς τοῖς χείλεσίν με τιμᾷ, ἡ δὲ καρδία αὐτῶν πόρρω ἀπέχει ἀπ' ἐμοῦ·⁷ μάτην δὲ σέβονταί με, διδάσκοντες διδασκαλίας ἐντάλματα ἀνθρώπων· ⁸ ἀφέντες τὴν ἐντολὴν τοῦ θεοῦ κρατεῖτε τὴν παράδοσιν τῶν ἀνθρώπων. ⁹ Καὶ ἔλεγεν αὐτοῖς· Καλῶς ἀθετεῖτε τὴν ἐντολὴν τοῦ θεοῦ, ἵνα τὴν παράδοσιν ὑμῶν τηρήσητε·¹⁰ Μωϋσῆς γὰρ εἶπεν· Τίμα τὸν πατέρα σου καὶ τὴν μητέρα σου, καί· Ὁ κακολογῶν πατέρα ἢ μητέρα θανάτῳ τελευτάτω·¹¹ ὑμεῖς δὲ λέγετε· Ἐὰν εἴπῃ ἄνθρωπος τῷ πατρὶ ἢ τῇ μητρί· Κορβᾶν, ὅ ἐστιν Δῶρον, ὃ ἐὰν ἐξ ἐμοῦ ὠφεληθῇς, ¹² οὐκέτι ἀφίετε αὐτὸν οὐδὲν ποιῆσαι τῷ πατρὶ ἢ τῇ μητρί, ¹³ ἀκυροῦντες τὸν λόγον τοῦ θεοῦ τῇ παραδόσει ὑμῶν ᾗ παρεδώκατε· καὶ παρόμοια τοιαῦτα πολλὰ ποιεῖτε. ⁶ He replied, "Isaiah was right when he prophesied about you hypocrites; as it is written: |

your tradition. ⁷You hypocrites! Isaiah was right when he prophesied about you: ⁸" 'These people honour me with their lips, but their hearts are far from me. ⁹They worship me in vain; their teachings are merely human rules.' "	" 'These people honour me with their lips, but their hearts are far from me. ⁷ They worship me in vain; their teachings are merely human rules.' ⁸ You have let go of the commands of God and are holding on to human traditions." ⁹ And he continued, "You have a fine way of setting aside the commands of God in order to observeᶜ your own traditions! ¹⁰ For Moses said, 'Honour your father and mother,' and, 'Anyone who curses their father or mother is to be put to death.' ¹¹ But you say that if anyone declares that what might have been used to help their father or mother is Corban (that is, devoted to God)— ¹² then you no longer let them do anything for their father or mother. ¹³ Thus you nullify the word of God by your tradition that you have handed down. And you do many things like that."
Scene 2: Jesus and the crowds: Midpoint axiom	
¹⁰ Καὶ προσκαλεσάμενος τὸν ὄχλον εἶπεν αὐτοῖς· Ἀκούετε καὶ συνίετε·¹¹ οὐ τὸ εἰσερχόμενον εἰς τὸ στόμα κοινοῖ τὸν ἄνθρωπον, ἀλλὰ τὸ ἐκπορευόμενον ἐκ τοῦ στόματος τοῦτο κοινοῖ τὸν ἄνθρωπον. ¹⁰ He called the crowd to him and said, "Listen and understand. ¹¹ What goes into someone's mouth does not defile them, but what comes out of their mouth, that is what defiles them."	¹⁴ Καὶ προσκαλεσάμενος πάλιν τὸν ὄχλον ἔλεγεν αὐτοῖς· Ἀκούσατέ μου πάντες καὶ σύνετε. ¹⁵ οὐδέν ἐστιν ἔξωθεν τοῦ ἀνθρώπου εἰσπορευόμενον εἰς αὐτὸν ὃ δύναται κοινῶσαι αὐτόν· ἀλλὰ τὰ ἐκ τοῦ ἀνθρώπου ἐκπορευόμενά ἐστιν τὰ κοινοῦντα τὸν ἄνθρωπον. ¹⁴ Again Jesus called the crowd to him and said, "Listen to me, everyone, and understand this. ¹⁵ Nothing outside a person can defile them by going into them. Rather, it is what comes out of a person that defiles them." [¹⁶]
Scene 3: Jesus and his disciples: teaching	
¹² Τότε προσελθόντες οἱ μαθηταὶ λέγουσιν αὐτῷ· Οἶδας ὅτι οἱ Φαρισαῖοι ἀκούσαντες τὸν λόγον ἐσκανδαλίσθησαν; ¹³ ὁ δὲ ἀποκριθεὶς εἶπεν· **Πᾶσα φυτεία ἣν οὐκ ἐφύτευσεν ὁ πατήρ μου ὁ οὐράνιος ἐκριζωθήσεται.** ¹⁴ ἄφετε αὐτούς· τυφλοί εἰσιν ὁδηγοί τυφλῶν· τυφλὸς δὲ τυφλὸν ἐὰν ὁδηγῇ, ἀμφότεροι εἰς βόθυνον πεσοῦνται. ¹⁵ Ἀποκριθεὶς δὲ ὁ Πέτρος εἶπεν αὐτῷ· Φράσον ἡμῖν τὴν παραβολὴν ταύτην.	¹⁷ Καὶ ὅτε εἰσῆλθεν εἰς οἶκον ἀπὸ τοῦ ὄχλου, ἐπηρώτων αὐτὸν οἱ μαθηταὶ αὐτοῦ τὴν παραβολήν. ¹⁸ καὶ λέγει αὐτοῖς· Οὕτως καὶ ὑμεῖς ἀσύνετοί ἐστε; οὐ νοεῖτε ὅτι πᾶν τὸ ἔξωθεν εἰσπορευόμενον εἰς τὸν ἄνθρωπον οὐ δύναται αὐτὸν κοινῶσαι, ¹⁹ ὅτι οὐκ εἰσπορεύεται αὐτοῦ εἰς τὴν καρδίαν ἀλλ' εἰς τὴν κοιλίαν, καὶ εἰς τὸν ἀφεδρῶνα ἐκπορεύεται; — καθαρίζων πάντα τὰ βρώματα. ²⁰ ἔλεγεν δὲ ὅτι Τὸ ἐκ τοῦ ἀνθρώπου ἐκπορευόμενον ἐκεῖνο κοινοῖ τὸν

¹⁶ ὁ δὲ εἶπεν· Ἀκμὴν καὶ ὑμεῖς ἀσύνετοί ἐστε; ¹⁷ οὐ νοεῖτε ὅτι πᾶν τὸ εἰσπορευόμενον εἰς τὸ στόμα εἰς τὴν κοιλίαν χωρεῖ καὶ εἰς ἀφεδρῶνα ἐκβάλλεται; ¹⁸ τὰ δὲ ἐκπορευόμενα ἐκ τοῦ στόματος ἐκ τῆς καρδίας ἐξέρχεται, κἀκεῖνα κοινοῖ τὸν ἄνθρωπον. ¹⁹ ἐκ γὰρ τῆς καρδίας ἐξέρχονται διαλογισμοὶ πονηροί, φόνοι, μοιχεῖαι, πορνεῖαι, κλοπαί, ψευδομαρτυρίαι, βλασφημίαι. ²⁰ **ταῦτά ἐστιν τὰ κοινοῦντα τὸν ἄνθρωπον, τὸ δὲ ἀνίπτοις χερσὶν φαγεῖν οὐ κοινοῖ τὸν ἄνθρωπον.**

¹² Then the disciples came to him and asked, "Do you know that the Pharisees were offended when they heard this?"
¹³ He replied, "Every plant that my heavenly Father has not planted will be pulled up by the roots. ¹⁴ Leave them; they are blind guides. If the blind lead the blind, both will fall into a pit."
¹⁵ Peter said, "Explain the parable to us."
¹⁶ "Are you still so dull?" Jesus asked them. ¹⁷ "Don't you see that whatever enters the mouth goes into the stomach and then out of the body? ¹⁸ But the things that come out of a person's mouth come from the heart, and these defile them. ¹⁹ For out of the heart come evil thoughts—murder, adultery, sexual immorality, theft, false testimony, slander. ²⁰ These are what defile a person; but eating with unwashed hands does not defile them."

ἄνθρωπον· ²¹ ἔσωθεν γὰρ ἐκ τῆς καρδίας τῶν ἀνθρώπων οἱ διαλογισμοὶ οἱ κακοὶ ἐκπορεύονται, πορνεῖαι, κλοπαί, φόνοι, ²² μοιχεῖαι, πλεονεξίαι, πονηρίαι, δόλος, ἀσέλγεια, ὀφθαλμὸς πονηρός, βλασφημία, ὑπερηφανία, ἀφροσύνη· ²³ πάντα ταῦτα τὰ πονηρὰ ἔσωθεν ἐκπορεύεται καὶ κοινοῖ τὸν ἄνθρωπον.

¹⁷ After he had left the crowd and entered the house, his disciples asked him about this parable. ¹⁸ "Are you so dull?" he asked. "Don't you see that nothing that enters a person from the outside can defile them? ¹⁹ For it doesn't go into their heart but into their stomach, and then out of the body." (In saying this, Jesus declared all foods clean.)
²⁰ He went on: "What comes out of a person is what defiles them. ²¹ For it is from within, out of a person's heart, that evil thoughts come—sexual immorality, theft, murder, ²² adultery, greed, malice, deceit, lewdness, envy, slander, arrogance and folly. ²³ All these evils come from inside and defile a person."

Table 44: The composition of the narrative on the hand-washing dispute in Matt. 15:1-20 and its parallel Mark 7:1-23

Matthew's redaction of the story is quite extensive. He truncates the story by almost half. He omits the section explaining the ceremony of hand-washing (Mark 7:2-4) (indicated by underlining in the table). Matthew commonly omits explanations of Jewish traditions and practices, probably because he, unlike Mark, wrote to a community that was familiar with Jewish traditions (Oliver, 2013:266). Furthermore, Matthew omits the statement that Jesus made all the food clean, which would imply *kashrut* (food) laws (Mark 7:19). He thus limits his discussion to the ritual of hand-washing based on oral tradition, without attending to food laws in general. This is quite significant, as it indicates that Matthew had some sensitivity for these Jewish laws. It is significant that in

Matthew the disciples, unlike Mark, express their concern about the offence Jesus' remarks could have caused amongst the Pharisees (Matt. 12:12). This may point to friction that the author sensed within his circles with contemporary Pharisees (Oliver, 2013:273). On the other hand, he adds a parable and a condemnation of the leaders as "blind guides" (Matt. 15:13-14) (indicated in bold). Such a sharpening of the conflict between Jesus and the Pharisees is typical of Matthew, and it signifies a bitter separation between the Pharisean Judaism and the Matthean community. Another addition is the conclusion of Matthew's Jesus with a reference to the washing of hands (Matt. 15:20b). He thus refers back to initial challenge to tighten the overall structure of the three scenes of the narrative and to emphasise the key issue of the narrative. Matthew also transposes the quotation of Isa. 29:13 to the end of Jesus' riposte[244], probably as his "punch line" since their contents derive from Scripture (Oliver, 2013:269). In such a way he tightens the structure of the *Streitgespräch*. In this narrative, themes of external tradition and purity are intertwined with the Law and internal purity. Scribal regulations are explicitly set aside (Matt. 15:20). While Matthew sharpens the conflict with the Pharisees, he softens Mark's comments on dietary laws. This redaction probably reflects Matthew's and his community's struggle with the Jewish leadership about the value of the Pharisees' tradition, while he makes the passage more acceptable for Jewish Christians who probably were inclined to observing dietary laws.

Like in Mark, Matt. 15:1-20 gives an outdrawn objection narrative in three scenes (Davies & Allison, 2004b 516). The narrative has a close-knit structure as can be demonstrated with the following table.

---

[244] In Matt. 9:10-13 and 12:1-8 the Scripture quotation also concludes the controversy stories.

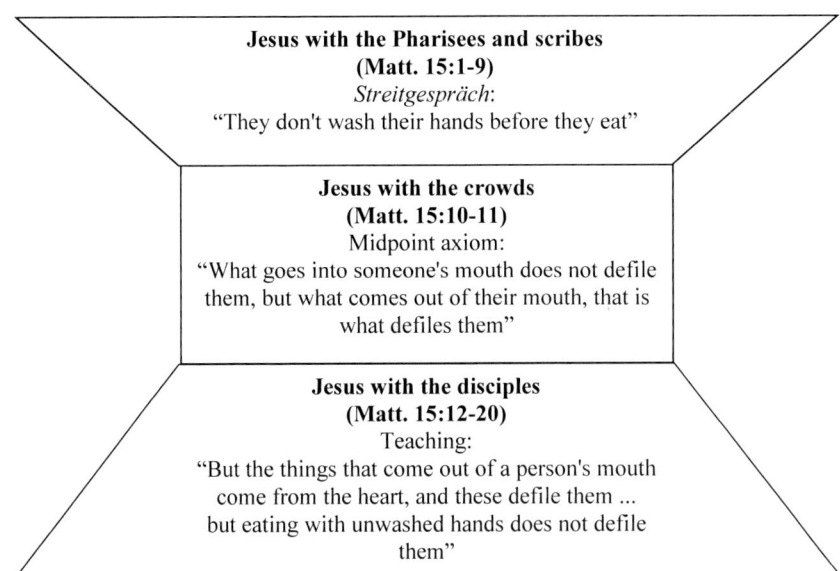

Table 45: The structure of the narrative on hand-washing in Matt. 15:1-9

The first scene depicts Jesus with the Pharisees and scribes[245] (Matt. 15:1-9), the second, Jesus with the crowds (Matt. 15:10-11) and the third, Jesus with the disciples (Matt. 15:12-20)[246]. Scenes one and three each begins with a question directed at Jesus, in the first scene with a question by the Pharisees and scribes (Matt. 15:2-3) and in the third scene with a question by the disciples (Matt. 15:12). Verse 11 ("what goes into someone's mouth does not defile them, but what comes out of their mouth, that is what defiles them") forms the midpoint of the story (Davies & Allison, 2004b:516). It forms a response to the first scene, while the third scene provides an explanation of the second scene. Verse

---

[245] It is noteworthy that in the seven times that Matthew links the scribes and Pharisees, this is the only occurrence where the Pharisees are mentioned first, "Pharisees and scribes". In the other six occurrences the order is "scribes and Pharisees". This can be because of Matthew's dependence on Mark here, but what is more probable is that Matthew wants to emphasise that the "παράδοσις" (traditions) at stake here are specifically those of the Pharisees (Hagner, 1995:430). Notably, the reference to the scribes is dropped later in this story (Matt. 15:12).

[246] In Matthew the Pharisees are usually depicted as disbelieving and hostile, the crowds as potential believers and neutral, and the disciples as believers and loyal.

18 elaborates on the response of the midpoint ("but the things that come out of a person's mouth come from the heart, and these defile them") and verse 20 concludes the response ("these are what defile a person; but eating with unwashed hands does not defile them") and refers back to the accusation of verse 2 ("they don't wash their hands before they eat!"). Thus the third scene creates a sense of unity between the first and second scenes, while confirming the main issue in the narrative.

The significant reference to the "mouth" in the mid-point of the story should be recognized. In terms of zones of interaction with the world around, the ancient Mediterranean people considered one's mouth to function in the zone of self-expressive speech (Malina & Rohrbauch, 1992:56). As centre of his argument Matthew's Jesus contrasts the effect of food entering the mouth (which doesn't defile a person), with self-expressive speech that exits the mouth (which indeed defiles a person).

9.3 FIRST SCENE: *STREITGESPRÄCH* BETWEEN THE PHARISEES AND THE SCRIBES AND JESUS (MATT. 15:1-9)

The first scene forms a typical *Streitgespräch* with the elements of challenge and riposte (Repschinski, 2000:254). In honour and shame societies it was a common phenomenon to challenge the honour of an opponent and a response with an equal challenge in return (Malina & Rohrbauch, 1992:42; Witherington, 2013:47). Such a challenge had to be played in public to reach its aim. The challenge of the Pharisees and scribes (Matt. 15:1-2) is countered by Jesus' twofold charge, namely that the Pharisees transgress God's command with their tradition (Matt. 15:3-6) and the claim that Isaiah prophesied against them (Matt. 15:7-9).

9.3.1 Challenge

The challenge of the Pharisees and scribes consists of a setting, a charge and a reason for the charge, as depicted in the following table:

> **Challenge of the Pharisees and the scribes (Matt. 15:1-2)**
>
> Setting (Matt. 15:1):
> Τότε προσέρχονται τῷ Ἰησοῦ ἀπὸ Ἱεροσολύμων Φαρισαῖοι καὶ γραμματεῖς λέγοντες
> (Then some Pharisees and teachers of the law came to Jesus from Jerusalem and asked)
>
>> Charge (Matt. 15:2a):
>> Διὰ τί οἱ μαθηταί σου παραβαίνουσιν τὴν παράδοσιν τῶν πρεσβυτέρων;
>> (Why do your disciples break the tradition of the elders?)
>>
>> Reason (Matt. 15:2b):
>> οὐ γὰρ νίπτονται τὰς χεῖρας ὅταν ἄρτον ἐσθίωσιν.
>> They don't wash their hands whenever they eat bread!"

Table 46: The challenge of the Pharisees and the scribes in Matt. 15:1-2

In the setting (Matt. 15:1), the hostility of the challenge is highlighted by the reference to the fact that the Pharisees and scribes came from Jerusalem. Jerusalem, not mentioned in the previous ten chapters[247], is associated with the home town of Jesus' opponents (Elliot, 1977:462-469). Matthew mentions Pharisees and scribes as a united front opposing Jesus[248]. The sketching of this coalition is highly significant (Weren, 1979:143). It is highly unusual that these two parties would form such an alliance as their doctrinal differences were significant and the tradition of hand-washing was unique to the Pharisees. Matthew thus forms a dramatic climax in his narrative, expressing the tension between the Jewish leaders and Jesus. The Matthean community probably would recognize some of the tension as it possibly reflects the worsening relationship between the community and the Jewish society (Weren, 1979:143).

---

[247] In Matthew Jerusalem is usually used in a hostile context: Herod and Jerusalem are disturbed when hearing of the new born King (Matt. 2:1 and 3); Jerusalem is the place where Jesus suffers and is killed (Matt. 16:21; 20:17, 18) and Jerusalem kills the prophets and stones those sent to them (Matt. 23:37). Though Jesus had a triumphal entrance into Jerusalem (Matt. 21:1) the whole city is stirred and asks: "Who is this?"(Matt. 21:10). Matthew nevertheless mentions that people from Jerusalem and all Judea and the whole region of the Jordan came out to be baptized by John (Matt. 3:5) and that large crowds, including people from Jerusalem, followed Jesus (Matt. 4:25). In the Sermon on the Mount, Jerusalem is also mentioned as a place by which the Jews swear their oaths (Matt. 5:33).

[248] In Mark 7:1 the Pharisees seem to be already in place, while certain scribes came from Jerusalem.

The historic present form of the verb "προσέρχονται" (come) makes the coming particularly dramatic so that it probably refers to a semi-official delegation sent to test Jesus' faithfulness to the *Torah*, both written and oral (Osborne, 2010:585; Turner, 2008:378; Witherington, 2006:295). France (2007:575) has described this as "a foretaste of the confrontation to come".

In the charge of the Pharisees and the scribes, the status of "ἡ παράδοσις τῶν πρεσβυτέρων" (the tradition of the elders)[249] (Matt. 15:2a) is at stake. The "παράδοσις" (tradition) was a technical term referring to the collection of Jewish traditions. These traditions went beyond what was written in the *Torah* (Baumgarten, 1987:66). These traditions probably refer to *massoret* (Davies & Allison, 2004b:520). Initially they were transmitted orally and were then formalized in the *Mishnah*, around the beginning of 200 C.E. (Baumgarten, 1987:64; Davies & Allison, 2004b:520; Neusner, 1994:5). In the time of Jesus, the tradition was still quite fluid and the use of such tradition to apply the *Torah* was regarded as quite innovative[250] (Senior, 1998:176). Schiffman (1994:280-281) has remarked that during the late Second Temple Judaism "sectarian law was a living, developing phenomenon constantly giving rise to new compilations of lists of laws". After the destruction of the temple, the Pharisees and scribes felt themselves obliged to preserve these oral traditions (Neusner, 2007:111).

The reason for the charge refers to the transgressing (παραβαίνουσιν[251], they transgress) of the tradition of hand-washing (Matt. 15:2b)[252]. The tradition of hand-washing was more than a hygienic custom. It formed part of ceremonial and ritual cleansing. There is no commandment in the Hebrew Bible concerning the washing of hands for ordinary meals. It seems that the Pharisees adopted the

---

[249] In the Gospels only Mark and Matthew use this word, and only in the context of this story.

[250] Some rabbinic traditions indicate that the tradition was valued more than the written *Torah*: "Greater stringency applies to the observance of the words of the scribes than to the observance of the works of the written Law" (m. Sanh. 11:3) and "My son, be more careful in the observance of the words of the scribes than in the words of the *Torah* ... whoever transgresses any of the enactments of the Scribes incurs the penalty of death" (b. Eruv. 21b) (Talbert, 2010:188).

[251] The verb παραβαίνω (transgress) is only used three times. Twice in this context (Matt. 15:2 and 3) and once to describe the act of Judas "to go where he belongs" (Acts 1:25).

[252] This is now the third occurrence in Matthew where the Pharisees object against Jesus and his disciples' eating customs. Previously the objected when Jesus ate with tax collectors and sinners (Matt. 9:11) and when the disciples plucked grain on the Sabbath to eat (Matt. 12:2) (cf. Chapter 7).

requirement set for priests before they ate consecrated food. The Pharisees also applied these requirements to themselves and all Jews, even when eating ordinary food[253] (Booth, 1986:173; Carter, 2000a:316; Finklestein, 1966:278; Hagner, 1995:430; Neusner, 1973:83; Witherington, 2006:296). This tradition goes back as far as regulations imposed by the rabbi schools of Hillel and Shammai early in the first century C.E. (Hauck, 1964:946-948). Neusner has attested that the practice of hand-washing prevailed amongst Pharisees in the time of Jesus. He has written: "What was the dominant trait of Pharisees before 70 C.E.? It was ... concern for the matters of rite, in particular, eating one's meals in a state of ritual purity as if one were a temple priest" (Neusner, 1977:670). The tradition of hand-washing thus developed as an identity marker of the Pharisees. The Pharisees reasoned that there were many unclean objects that one would touch during a day. This would lead to unclean hands and when touching food with unclean hands, it would result in unclean food. When eating such unclean food, one would become unclean. The tradition therefore evolved that all Jews had to perform a ritual of hand-washing along with the blessing that preceded the eating of meals (*Mishnah*. Ber. 8:2-4). The *Yadayim*[254] is a treatise of the *Mishnah* (c.a. 200 C.E.) and the *Tosefta* (c.a. 300 C.E.), dealing with the laws of hand-washing and their ritual impurity. The issue of hand-washing became so important that a whole tractate in the Babylonian Talmud (c.a. 600 C.E.), the *Yadayim* (the Hands), was devoted to this. Though it is clear that the Pharisees observed traditions of hand-washing in the time of Jesus and when Matthew wrote his Gospel, it is difficult to determine to what extent this developed legislation of *Yadayim* as described in Rabbinic literature was observed in the times of Jesus.

---

[253] Mark 7:3 explains this habit: "The Pharisees and all the Jews do not eat unless they give their hands a ceremonial washing, holding to the tradition of the elders". John 2:6 also implies such a custom: "Nearby stood six stone water jars, the kind used by the Jews for ceremonial washing". It seems that this habit was widespread.

[254] The treatise on the *Yadayim* is eleventh in the order of *Tohorot* in most editions of the *Mishnah*, and is divided into four chapters, containing twenty-two paragraphs in all (Herr, 2007:264). The first chapter deals with the quantity of water that is needed to wash hands when pouring it over them; the vessels from which the water may be poured over the hands; the kinds of water which may not be used to cleanse the hands, and persons who may perform the act of manual ablution. The second chapter deals with how the water should be poured over the hands, the first and second washing and doubtful cases, which include whether the ablution was properly performed. Chapters three and four discuss the objects which make hands unclean with specific reference to the canonical books. According to this tractate everyone, therefore, had to eat everyday meals in a state of ritual purity as if one where a temple priest (Davies & Allison, 2004b:521). The Qumran-community required total immersion before a meal (1 QS3.8-9; 5:13; CD 10:10-13) (Newton, 1985:26).

In Matt. 15:2 ὅταν (whenever) is inserted to describe the practice of Jesus' disciples[255]. This indicates that eating with unwashed hands was not a single incident, but a customary procedure with his disciples. This probably reflects a custom of the Matthean community that was in conflict with the traditions of the elders (Repscinski, 2000:156). This issue about washing of hands before meals might be an example of the Matthean community breaking with Pharisaic traditions.

9.3.2 Riposte

In Matthew's narrative, Jesus responds to the accusation of the Pharisees and Sadducees in a twofold manner. First He charges them with the fact that their tradition causes them to violate God's commandments (Matt. 15:3-6) and secondly that Isaiah prophesied against their way of worship (Matt. 15:7-9).

Unlike in Mark 7:8-9, Matthew does not open Jesus' riposte with reference to Isa. 29:13, but with a counter-argument that parallels the question posed by the Pharisees and the scribes (Repschinski, 2000:159). As the Pharisees accused the disciples with the words, "Why do your disciples break (παραβαίνουσιν) the tradition of the elders?" (Matt. 15:2), Jesus begins his response with "And why do you break (παραβαίνετε) the command of God (τὴν ἐντολὴν τοῦ θεοῦ) for the sake of your tradition (διὰ τὴν παράδοσιν ὑμῶν)?" (Matt. 15:3), using the same verb. It is significant that Jesus refers to "your traditions" (τὴν παράδοσιν ὑμῶν) (Matt. 15:3), while the Pharisees spoke of the tradition of the elders (τὴν παράδοσιν τῶν πρεσβυτέρων) (Matt. 5:2) (Weren, 1994:141). Jesus thus seemingly does not regard all tradition of the fathers as negative, but now focuses on this tradition of the Pharisees themselves.

In the first part of the counter-charge, the tradition (παράδοσις) of the Pharisees is contrasted in parallel form with the command of God (ἐντολή)[256] and the Word of God (λόγος). This juxtaposition intensifies the contrast between God's commandments and man-made legislation:

---

[255] It is now the third time that Jesus and his disciples are criticized for their eating habits. Earlier in the Gospel Jesus was accused of eating with tax collectors and sinners (Matt. 9:11) and the disciples of picking grain to eat on the Sabbath (Matt. 12:2).

[256] As in Mark 7:8 Matthew here uses the word ἐντολή (command). This noun occurs 6 times in Matthew (5:19; 15:3; 19:17; 22:36. 38 and 40) referring to the commandments of the Law. Matthew uses νόμος to refer to refer to the Law which consists of different commandments (Matt. 5:17, 18; 7:12; 11:13; 12:5; 22:36 and 40).

> διὰ τί καὶ ὑμεῖς (and why do you)
>
>> **παραβαίνετε** τὴν ἐντολὴν τοῦ θεοῦ διὰ τὴν παράδοσιν ὑμῶν
>> (break the command of God for the sake (because) of your tradition?) (Matt. 15:3)
>>
>>> ὁ γὰρ θεὸς εἶπεν (for God said)
>>> τίμα τὸν πατέρα καὶ τὴν μητέρα (honour your father and mother)
>>> καὶ ὁ κακολογῶν πατέρα ἢ μητέρα θανάτῳ τελευτάτω (and anyone who curses their father or mother is to be put to death) (Matt. 15:4)
>>
>> **ἠκυρώσατε** τὸν λόγον τοῦ θεοῦ διὰ τὴν παράδοσιν ὑμῶν
>> (thus you nullify the word of God for the sake of your tradition) (Matt. 15:6b)

Table 47: **The juxtaposition between God's commandment and man-made rules in Matt. 15:3 and 15:6**

Matt. 15:3 and 6 have parallel phrases:

- "παραβαίνετε" (verse 3) parallels "ἠκυρώσατε" (verse 6b);
- "τὴν ἐντολὴν τοῦ θεοῦ" (verse 3) parallels "τὸν λόγον τοῦ θεοῦ[257]" (verse 6b) ; and
- the precise wording is repeated in both verses "διὰ τὴν παράδοσιν ὑμῶν" (for the sake (because[258]) of your tradition) (verse 3 and 6b).

These parallel phrases make the same point. Jesus charges the Pharisees with the accusation that they break and nullify the command and Word of God not "despite your[their] tradition", but much harsher, "for the sake (because) of your[their] tradition". While Mark 7:8 speaks of the tradition of people (τὴν

---

[257] Within this context "of God" (τοῦ θεοῦ) in verses 3 and 6b is a subjective genitive referring to what God commanded and said.

[258] The proposition διά is here used with the accusative (τὴν παράδοσιν). When used with the accusative its meaning can be defined as "through, on account of, by reason of, for the sake of, because of". If used with the genitive the meaning can be "through, throughout, by the instrumentality of" (Blass & DeBrunner, 1961:119).

παράδοσιν τῶν ἀνθρώπων), Matthew emphasises that it is "your" tradition (παράδοσιν ὑμῶν). Implicitly the juxtaposition is not only between the Law and the tradition, but (more personal) also between God and the Pharisees and the scribes. Matthew's Jesus thus argues that his disciples do not follow the tradition of the Pharisees, because the Pharisees do not follow the commandment of God (Repschinski, 2000:159). It seems that Matthew's Jesus is opposed to "Dual *Torah*", an identity marker of the Pharisean Judaism, as portrayed here. This signifies a separation of the Matthean community from the observance of rabbinic traditions.

The parallel phrases form an *inclusio* of verses 4b-6a in which Jesus gives an example of how the tradition is used to break the command of God. The command of God is referred to as something that God said: "ὁ γὰρ θεὸς εἶπεν" (for God said) (Matt. 15:4a and 6b). The divine origin of the commandment is emphasized and contrasted with the man-made tradition. What God said cannot be compared to the tradition of people. Man-made commandments cannot substitute divine commandments. Morris (1992:394) comments on this Pharisean tradition: "Their motives may possibly have been excellent, but the result was deplorable".

This counter-challenge probably reveals the rivalry between the Matthean community and Pharisean Judaism of their day about being the real keepers of God's Law. In their desire to meet the specific obligations of the Law, they engaged in competitive disputes as to what the obligations meant. Each group claimed to be living according to the principles of the *Torah*, but thus implied that others were not doing so (Dunn, 2003:292).

In Matt. 15:5 Jesus elaborates on his previous statement and continues to contrast the commandment of God with the behaviour of the Pharisees. He refers to the fifth commandment ("honour your father and your mother" (Exod. 29:12)) and a regulation ("let the one be put to death who speaks evil of their father and mother" (Exod. 21:17)), which enforces the seriousness of breaking the fifth commandment. Τίμα (honour) is an emphatic present meaning that one has to honour one's parents at all times, which includes caring for them financially (Derret, 1977:112-117). From the Gospel accounts it seems as if the Pharisees introduced the tradition that children could dedicate the money with which they were supposed to support their parents as a gift to God. The *Mishnah Ned.* 9.1 refers to such Corban vows and the honour one owes to ones father and mother[259]. While performing this cultic activity, they neglect their moral duty to care for their parents. Matthew's objection is that the Pharisees have a misplaced prioritization of values (Oliver, 2013:267). Bailey (2000:193-209) has explained the Jewish backgrounds to this misuse of the Corban and how this led to a growing antagonism against the Pharisees.

Jesus, however, regards the written Law of Moses as the commandment of God. Several phrases are therefore used to refer to these stipulations of the *Torah*: the command of God (ἐντολὴ), the word of God (λόγος) and what God said (ὁ γὰρ θεὸς εἶπεν). In contrast to these, the tradition (παράδοσις) of the Pharisees is considered an infringement (Oliver, 2013:270). As a result of their tradition, they legally invalidate the Word of God (ἠκυρώσατε τὸν λόγον τοῦ θεοῦ).

Ironically the παράδοσις (tradition) was intended to form a fence around the written *Torah* (Hagner, 1995:430; Osborne, 2010:585), but Jesus accuses the Pharisees of the fact that this very fence causes them (διὰ τὴν παράδοσιν ὑμῶν, for the sake of your tradition) to break God's commandments. There was much dispute in ancient times about the status of this tradition, even beyond the New Testament. There was a variety of viewpoints amongst the Pharisees, Sadducees and the Qumran community on purity issues (Bowley, 2000:873). The more conservative Sadducees opposed these traditions, arguing that "the Pharisees had passed down to the people certain regulations handed down by former generations and not recorded in the Law of Moses[260] [and] for [this] reason they are rejected by the Sadducean group" (Josephus, *Ant.*, 13.10.6)[261]. According to some of the Sadducees, the παράδοσις (tradition) led to unnecessary self-denial (*Ps. Clem. Recog.*, 1. 53-54). As the Sadducees did not believe in an afterlife, they regarded this burden and loss of pleasure as useless and a Pharisaic pursuit of an illusion (Baumgarten, 1987:70). The composers of the Dead Sea Scrolls also criticized these traditions "Teachers of lies ... have schemed a devilish scheme ... to exchange the Law engraved on my heart by Thee for the smooth

---

[259] Though Corban vows were performed in the time of Jesus and when Matthew wrote his Gospel, it is difficult to determine to what extent it was done at that stage.

[260] Baumgarten (1987:70-71) points out that modern scholarship increasingly observes that the laws in the *Mishnah* often bears little relation to the written *Torah*.

[261] When they were in power under Hyrcanus, the Sadducees even punished the Jews who followed the παράδοσις (tradition) of the Pharisees (Josephus, *Ant.*, 13.10.6), but when the Pharisees came back into power under Alexandra, they reinstated the tradition (Josephus, *Ant.*, 13.6.2) (see Baumgarten, 1987:69).

things (which they speak[262])" (1QH 4.14-15). The Pharisees were sensitive to such criticism as they often referred to the "tradition of the fathers[263]" or the "tradition of the elders[264]" (Josephus, *Ant.* 10.51 and 13.408). They attempted to give their traditions a reliable pedigree, as the fathers and elders were regarded as the leaders of the nation. As family traditions were widely respected in antiquity, the Pharisees indicated that the tradition of the fathers and elders was more than just that of a school[265]. It therefore seems that the critique on the tradition in Matt. 15:1-20, at least in part, reflects conventional criticism[266] against the Pharisean tradition (Carter, 2000a:315).

Jesus enforces his criticism of the tradition with a second charge (Matt. 15:7-9). He addresses the Pharisees with the negative label of hypocrites (ὑποκριταί) (Matt. 15:7). Such negative labelling referring to stereotypes was common practice in a challenge and riposte setting (Malina & Rohrbauch, 1992:98). Persons were not known for their individual personalities, but by social categories and groups they belonged to. Stereotypes could be either positive or negative. When Matthew's Jesus uses the negative stereotype of "hypocrites" to label the Pharisees, He seriously challenges their credibility in the community. Jesus states that they pretend to be different from who they really are. They pretend to worship God, but they fail in this regard. Jesus claims that Isaiah actually prophesied about their attitude, as the prophet of old raised a similar complaint against the religious authorities of his (Isaiah's) day. The addressees of Matt. 15 would all agree that the people Isaiah denounces were hypocrites. Based on what He previously argued (Matt. 15:3-6) about the Pharisees, Matthew's Jesus now states that the Pharisees are just like the people in Isaiah's days – hypocrites too. Jesus refers to Isa. 29:13 providing two reasons as to why the Pharisees should be considered as hypocrites:

---

[262] In the Dead Sea Scrolls the speakers of smooth things are identified as the Pharisees (Davies & Allison, 2004b:520.)

[263] In Gal. 1:14 Paul also refers to the extreme zeal for "the tradition of the fathers" which he earlier had.

[264] Matt. 15:3 and Mark 7:3 use the term "tradition of the elders".

[265] By making their tradition priestly, they took it further than what is plausible, as there was competition between the Pharisees and the priests as well (Baumgarten, 1987:73).

[266] As could be expected, the Church Fathers followed the Gospels in criticising the traditions of the Pharisees (e.g. Just, *Dial.* 38; Clem. Al. *Strom.* 6.7.58.2; Iren. Adv. Haer. 4.12.1) (Klijn & Reinink, 1973:220-223).

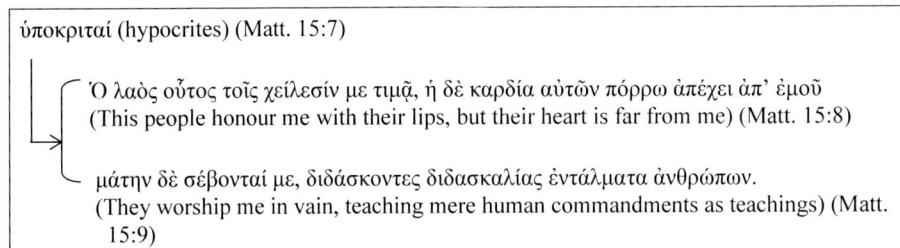

Table 48: Two reasons for the Pharisees being called hypocrites in Matt. 15:7

The first reason is that they pretend to worship God, but they do so with their lips and not with their hearts (15:8). Osborne (2010:587) has interpreted this statement by saying "a detailed *Torah* tradition without heart commitment is irrelevant before God". According to the traditional Mediterranean thought, this implies that they were behaving with the zone of speech, but without the zone of emotion-fused thought. Mediterraneans thought of a person in terms of zones of interaction with the world around them, namely the zones of emotion-fused thought, which involves the activity of the eyes and heart (sight, insight, loving, valuing, etc.), the zone of self-expressive speech, which involves the activity of the mouth[267] and ears (speaking, hearing, etc.) and the zone of purposeful action, which involves the hands, fingers and legs (touching, walking, accomplishing, etc.) (Malina & Rohrbauch, 1992:56). Human activity could be described in terms of a particular zone of activity or a combination of these zones. Jesus charges the Pharisees that only one zone of activity is involved when they honour God, while the heart is not involved. One's heart was considered as one's religious centre that forms the root of religious life and ethical conduct (Walker, 2000:563). It refers to the affective centre or desire producer of one's being, and the seat of thought and understanding (Behm, 1978:611-613). The Pharisees' hearts were lacking in their honour to God.

The second reason why Jesus regards their honour of God as superficial is that they adhere to precepts of human origin and not of the Law God has given. They worship God by teaching mere human commandments as teachings (Matt. 15:9). In this prophecy, Isaiah warns his people against the vanity of their worship if it is based on the teachings of people. They try to do this with their

---

[267] The Isaiah quotation refers to "lips" and Jesus' argument in Matt. 15:8 is that the "lip-zone" when speaking is detached from the "heart-zone" of their personalities. Significantly in Matt. 15:10 and 18 He indeed links what exits the "mouth" with the heart, but not food that enters through the mouth, as it goes to the stomach and then exits the body (Matt. 15:10).

own man-made tradition by which they replace the commandments of God. The alliteration of διδάσκοντες διδασκαλίας emphasizes the importance of "teaching teachings". Matthew's Jesus defines the "tradition of the elders" (ἡ παράδοσις τῶν πρεσβυτέρων) (Matt. 15:2 and 3) as human "teaching of teachings". Teaching must be based on God's truth, not on human ideas. Matthew's Jesus clearly rejects this oral tradition.

The Pharisees and scribes do not respond to Jesus. The *Streitgespräch* ends with Jesus victoriously having the final say.

From the first scene the following conclusions can be drawn regarding the Law. This scene clearly pronounces the Pharisees' concern for purity and the observance of their tradition. According to them, the ritual of hand-washing was necessary to ensure purity. Jesus opposes their view by contrasting man-made traditions with the Word and commandments of God. With biting irony He charges them with the fact that their tradition causes people to nullify God's Law. They are hypocrites as they pretend to be honouring God by observing their tradition, but by doing this, they are actually doing the opposite.

This *Streitgespräch* probably reveals the rivalry between the Judaism of the "Dual *Torah*" and the Matthean community. The Pharisees in the story represent the Judaists who valued the oral Law as just as important as the written Law. The story describes the oral Law as man-made traditions, in contrast to the written Law as the Word of God. Based on Jesus' performance, He, and thus Matthew and his community, distance themselves from these oral traditions and regard themselves as faithful to the real *Torah*.

9.4 SECOND SCENE: AXIOM OF JESUS BEFORE THE CROWDS (MATT. 15:10-11)

The next scene of the narrative is introduced with Jesus turning to the crowds (Matt. 15:10). Having rebuked the Pharisees, He continues by stating an axiom to the crowd. For Matthew's Jesus, the Pharisees with the scribes and the Jewish crowds are different types of groups who are treated differently. Pharisees and scribes are usually depicted as hostile and disbelieving (cf. Matt. 9:34; 12:2, 14), while the crowds are considered as neutral. They are potential believers, but who also can be easily convinced by the Jewish leaders to reject Jesus[268].

---

[268] Matthew at several occasions mentions that Jesus saw and addressed the crowd (Matt. 5:1; 13:2, 34), that He felt compassion to them (Matt. 9:36; 14:14, 19), how the crowds followed Jesus (Matt.

In this second scene Jesus addresses the crowds on the issue of defilement (Matt. 15:10-11). The crowd being potential believers, He urges them "Ἀκούετε καὶ συνίετε" (listen and understand) (Matt. 15:10). If they would only listen, they would remain the crowd, but if they would understand, they would become disciples. In Matthew "understanding" is the distinctive response of disciples (Matt. 13:13-15, 19, 23, and 51) (cf. France, 2007:582). What Jesus then tells them in a contrasting parallel axiomatic statement (Matt. 15:11) forms the midpoint of the narrative. He postulates this principle as the basis for his further argument against the viewpoint of the Pharisees:

> οὐ τὸ εἰσερχόμενον εἰς τὸ στόμα κοινοῖ τὸν ἄνθρωπον,
> (What goes into someone's mouth does not defile him)
> ἀλλὰ τὸ ἐκπορευόμενον ἐκ τοῦ στόματος τοῦτο κοινοῖ τὸν ἄνθρωπον
> (but what comes out of his mouth, that is what defiles him).

Table 49: The basis of Jesus' argument in Matt. 15:10-11

The contrast on the one hand lies between what is entering and exiting a person's mouth ("εἰς τὸ στόμα" versus "ἐκ τοῦ στόματος") and on the other hand, between material and spiritual references[269]. Matthew omits Mark's statement that Jesus made all food clean (Mark 7:19). It seems as if Matthew intentionally refrains from making a statement about the overthrowing of food laws as such (e.g. Booth, 1986:221; Davies & Allison, 2004b:527; Hagner, 1995:437; Luz, 2001a:332; Oliver, 2013:273). Matthew, with his mainly Jewish-Christian audience, might have been more hesitant to explicitly include Mark's comment. Matthew's argument focuses on the contamination of food as a result of unwashed hands (Oliver, 2013:272). Osborne (2010:588) and Witherington (2006:296) have conversely argued that Mark's comment is surely implied in Matthew's text. According to them, Matthew merely shortened the text, as he often does. Whatever the case, the dispute in the narrative is not about food laws as such, but about the oral traditions of the Pharisees versus the written *Torah*. The oral tradition of hand-washing was intended to prevent

---

4:25; 8:1; 14:13) and that they were deeply impressed and amazed by his teaching (Matt. 7:28; 9:33). However, the crowd were also persuaded by the chief priests and the elders to ask Jesus to be crucified (Matt. 27:20).

[269] Using tradition historical and legal historical arguments Booth (1986:214) has suggested the *logion* of the historical Jesus to be: "There is nothing outside a man which cultically defiles him as much as the things coming from a man ethically defile him". According to Booth it is credible that Jesus would depreciate external cultic purity in favour of internal ethical purity.

impurity from entering the body, and Matthew's Jesus distances Himself from this tradition.

However, a second dimension is added to Jesus' understanding of the Law by this statement of his. The argument is that what people eat, even if their food is contaminated with unwashed hands, cannot defile (κοινοῖ)[270] them. To the contrary, defilement is caused by the moral intention of a person. Jesus argues that true defilement does not come about as a result of consuming possibly contaminated food, as defilement is a moral issue (Carlston, 1968/69:75)[271]. Words that come out of the mouth results from the self-expressive zone of a person and is self-revealing (Malina & Rohrbauch, 1992:56). Words reveal the inner morality of a person, and thus shows that the whole person is unclean. This relates to a remark Jesus makes earlier in the text: "For the mouth speaks what the heart is full of" (Matt. 12:34). Morris (1992:395) has made a fitting comment: "Words that go out of the mouth are more likely to indicate defilement than food that goes in." Matt. 15:11 can somehow be regarded as a *crux interpretum* for the understanding of the Law in Matthew. Jesus uses irony to expose untrue human piety and external purity by comparing it with true piety and internal purity[272].

According to rabbinic writings, there was also an opinion amongst rabbis that God would once again permit the eating of all flesh in the Messianic age (*Midr, Teh.* on Ps. 146:7). Based on passages like Num. 14:21: "all the earth shall be filled with the glory of the Lord", and Zech. 14:21: "Every pot in Jerusalem and Judah will be holy to the Lord Almighty, and all who come to sacrifice will take some of the pots and cook in them", they assumed that complete purity and total sanctification will once again exist according to these Biblical references

---

[270] The use of the verb "κοινοῖ", is significant. The word usually means "make common" or "share", but the meaning is transferred to "defile". The explanation of this seems to lie in the distinction between "holy" and "general" in ritual terms. What is holy, is suitable for ritual use, and should be distinguished from what is only useful for general use. To "defile" something, is to make it ceremonially unclean (Davies & Allison, 2004b: 527; Morris, 1992:395).

[271] In Matt. 23:23-6 Jesus emphasises the importance of internal rather than external purity.

[272] Similar sentiments about defilement, namely in a moral rather than physical sense, are found in extra-biblical literature. Manader (*frag.* 540) wrote: "All that brings defilement comes from within", Philo (*Spec. Leg.* 3:209) remarked: "For the unjust and impious man is in the truest sense unclean", and Sextus (*Sent.* 110): "a person is not defiled by the food and drink he consumes, but by those acts which result form an evil character" (cf. Davies & Allison, 2004b:526-527). Jesus was therefore not the only one in this time to utter such critique.

(Davies & Allison, 2004b:527; Talbert, 2010:188). However, as Matthew omits Mark's reference that Jesus declared all foods clean (Mark 7:19b), he limits the issue to the tradition of hand-washing. Matthew's Jesus explicitly rejects the ritual of hand-washing without making any particular remark on food laws. In the Matthean community's conflict with the Pharisean Judaism, the status of the oral traditions apparently was the main issue. Food laws as such did not form part of the debate.

9.5 THIRD SCENE: JESUS TEACHING HIS DISCIPLES (MATT. 15:12-20)

In the third scene, Jesus turns to his disciples, his own group. Jesus responds to their question about Him having upset the Pharisees[273]: "Do you know that the Pharisees were offended when they heard this?" (Matt. 15:12)[274]. Jesus responds to the group of people who are regarded as believers and people who are supposed to understand. Jesus provides two explanations (Matt. 15:13-14 and 16-19) and a conclusion (Matt. 15:20) which ties the narrative together. In this performative speech[275], Jesus not only passively describes the position of the Pharisees and purity, but changes the way his disciples perceive their religious and social reality.

In the first explanation (Matt. 15:13-14) does not occur in Mark. This addition is noteworthy as Matthew usually shortens Mark's narratives. Once Matthew adds to Mark's version, it signifies an issue the evangelist wants to emphasise. Matthew's Jesus uses two metaphors about plants planted by God and about blind guides. These two metaphors are separated by an exhortation to leave the Pharisees (ἄφετε αὐτούς, leave them) (Matt. 15:14). Matthew's Jesus orders his disciples, and Matthew also his community, to part from the Pharisees and their teaching. Jesus tells his disciples that the Pharisees are like plants not of his

---

[273] The scribes, as referred to in Matt. 15:1, are not mentioned here. Matthew's remark that the disciples were concerned about offending the Pharisees is unique to Matthew and somewhat odd, as the Pharisees are usually portrayed as the opponents of Jesus and his disciples. In Mark the disciples merely ask for an explanation. This is the only occurrence of such concern for Pharisees in the Matthean Gospel.

[274] The Pharisees' honour was impaired and the disciples, living in an honour and shame society, realized this (cf. Malina & Rohrbauch, 1992:42).

[275] Performative utterances are defined in the S*peech acts theory,* which refers to statements that change the (social) reality they are describing. The contemporary use of the term goes back to Austin's definition of performative language (Austin, 2005 [1962]).

"heavenly Father" that will be weeded in judgement (Matt. 15:13)[276]. When Jesus refers to God as "my Father", He not only indicates his special relationship with God, but also his authority to criticize the Pharisees (Witherington, 2006:298). Furthermore, Jesus denotes the Pharisees as blind guides misleading other blind people (Matt. 15:14). With irony and word play Jesus remarks that the Pharisees regard themselves as guides for the blind[277], but they are actually blind themselves. There is no use in arguing with them, as they are not able to see and discern the truth, in other words they are not able to understand. Jesus argues that while the Pharisees regard themselves as teachers of the Law, they are blind for God's true law (Osborne, 2010:590). Even worse, they increase the blindness of the people they guide. The ancient Mediterranean people believed that people could see because light proceeded from their hearts through their eyes (Malina & Rohrbauch, 1992:64; Viljoen, 2009a). On the other hand, with blind people darkness proceeded from their hearts through their eyes, indicating that there was something wrong in their hearts. Darkness was not considered as the absence of light, but as an objective evil reality. This criticism anticipates the diatribe of Matt. 23:16 and 24 where the scribes and Pharisees are also denoted as "blind guides" (Evans, 2012:301).

This interpolated explanation probably reflects the tension between the Matthean community and the Pharisaic Judaism of their time. The remark that the disciples should leave the Pharisees could refer to the separation between church and synagogue (Gundry, 1994:307). The issue at stake is not limited to the tradition of hand-washing, but it is about the status of the Pharisees and their teachings in general. The community is warned not to be misled by the Pharisees and rather to go their own way.

---

[276] The comparison of the plants reminds the reader of the parable of the wheat and the weeds (Matt. 13:24-30). In Matt. 15:16 Jesus warns that the Pharisees and the scribes run the risk of being identified as bad seeds, as plants not planted by God and that will be rooted up on judgement day (Evans, 2012:301). Evidently Isa. 60:21 ("Your people shall all be righteous ... the shoot that I planted, the work of my hands") resonates in these comparisons. Jesus' warning stands in contrast to rabbinic interpretation of Isaiah 60 that finds in it the assurance of the salvation of every Israelite: "All Israelites have a share in the world to come, as is said: 'Then all your people will be righteous ... the branch of my planting'" (*m. Sanh.*, 10.1).

[277] In Isa. 42:6-7 Israel is called to be a light for the Gentiles and to open the eyes of the blind (cf. Wis. 18:4). According to Paul the Jewish people considered themselves to be a "guide for the blind, a light for those who are in the dark" (Rom. 2:19).

In his second explanation (Matt. 15:16-19), Jesus responds to the request of Peter to explain the parable (τὴν παραβολήν[278]) to them (Matt. 15:15). Jesus' response includes all the material from Matt. 15:11-14, but the argument about what goes into the mouth and what exits it is mainly intended. Jesus responds with two questions: "Are you also still without understanding"? (Matt. 15:16) and "Don't you see that whatever enters the mouth goes into the stomach and then out of the body? (Matt. 5:17). With these two questions the ignorance (ἀσύνετοί) and lack of understanding (οὐ νοεῖτε) of the disciples are expressed.

In the first question (Matt. 15:16), Jesus expresses his disappointment that the disciples, after all He taught and showed them, are still ignorant (ἀσύνετοί). Earlier in the text Jesus implies that his disciples are "teachers of the Law" (Matt. 13:52), but now they fail to comprehend his charge that the Pharisees teach the Law incorrectly. This remark by Matthew's Jesus is probably intended as a warning to the Matthean community about their lack of discernment about the role of the Pharisees and their traditions in their community.

In the second question Jesus elaborates on the statement He made to the crowds. Jesus' response is once again given in parallel form with contrasting phrases:

> **πᾶν τὸ εἰσπορευόμενον** εἰς τὸ στόμα εἰς τὴν κοιλίαν χωρεῖ καὶ εἰς ἀφεδρῶνα ἐκβάλλεται
> (Whatever enters the mouth goes into the stomach and then out of the body) (Matt. 15:17).

> **τὰ δὲ ἐκπορευόμενα** ἐκ τοῦ στόματος ἐκ τῆς καρδίας ἐξέρχεται κἀκεῖνα κοινοῖ τὸν ἄνθρωπον
> (But the things that come out of a person's mouth come from the heart, and these defile them) (Matt. 15:18).

Table 50: Jesus' response in Matt. 15:17-18 on the charge of the Pharisees' and teachers of the Law

The first part of the parallelism explains what does not defile a person (referring to the first half of verse 11), while the second explains what does (referring to the second half of verse 11). The contrast lies between what goes into the mouth

---

[278] On the surface level it seems as if the παραβολή would refer to the parables of the planting of blind guides of Matt. 15:13-14. However, the word should rather be interpreted as an analogy with a broader reference referring to all the material in verses 11-14.

(εἰς) and what comes out of it (ἐκ). Things entering the mouth do not defile a person. What enters the stomach is expelled again, it does not enter the heart (only the stomach) and therefore cannot defile a person (Luz, 2001a:333). However, the inner thoughts of the heart define a person's integrity. Similar sentiments are found in Philo's writings, which state that impurity is primarily injustice and godlessness (Spec. leg. 3.208-9). The true character of a hypocrite (Matt. 15:7) is that such a person pretends to be religious by performing outward ceremonies, but whose inner person is defiled. This explanation by Jesus must be interpreted according to biological and anthropological views of the first century Mediterranean people (Malina & Rohrbauch, 1992:56, 110). They considered that things that one put in one's mouth, will eventually be expelled. However, one's heart and mouth, when speaking, represent two zones of interaction with the outside world. The speaking mouth forms part of self-expression and is self-revealing. The heart forms the centre of the emotion-fused zone that involves understanding, choosing, loving, thinking and valuing. Jesus argues that what one speaks, reveals the centre of one's emotion-fused zone.

In contrast to external food (food that may be contaminated with unwashed hands), which does not defile a person, Jesus continues to talk about things that come out of the mouth, which indeed defile a person or exhibit the inner defilement of a person.

The evils from the heart are then listed[279]. Lists of vices and virtues are common in Hellenistic Judaism (e.g. Wisdom of Solomon, 14:25-26; Philo, *Sacr.* 32; 4 Macc. 1:26-27; 1QS 4.8-11) and in the New Testament (e.g. in Rom. 1:29-31; 1 Cor. 6:9-10; 2 Cor. 12:20) (Charles, 2000:1252-1257). Matthew starts with evil thoughts that can lead to all kinds of evil deeds (ἐκ γὰρ τῆς καρδίας ἐξέρχονται διαλογισμοὶ πονηροί (for from the heart comes all evil thoughts)). What is pure or impure extends from the person, what he or she says or does[280]. Matthew's Jesus thus links cleanness with integrity. Integrity is revealed in a person's deeds. Jesus describes these deeds based on the second table of the Decalogue (as the lists in 1 Cor. 5:9-10 and 1 Tim. 9-10). These commandments follow immediately after the fifth commandment which was under discussion when

---

[279] Didache 5.1 contains a part of Matthew's vice list and hence is probably dependent on Matthew.

[280] This remark probably harks back to Matt. 12:34: "You brood of vipers! How can you speak good things, when you are evil? For out of the abundance of the heart the mouth speaks" (Evans, 2012:302). What comes out of one's mouth is what defiles a person.

Jesus responded to the Pharisees and scribes (Matt. 15:4): murders[281] (sixth), adulteries and fornications (seventh), thefts (eighth), false testimonies and blasphemies[282] (ninth). Jesus points out that impurity does not come from overlooking some ceremonial physical regulation, but from one's innermost being (Loader, 1997:220; Morris, 1992:389). Personal sin, and not eating with unwashed hands, is what defiles a person. This signifies a shift from cultic purity (hand-washing ceremonies and the Corban) towards moral purity[283].

In his conclusion, Jesus refers back to the issue of eating with unwashed hands stated in Matt. 15:2 and gives the final verdict. He specifically applies the principle stated in Matt. 15:11 to the issue of hand-washing. The ritual of hand-washing does not ensure true purity. Jesus challenges the traditions of the Pharisees and focuses on a person's attitude. Jesus' teaching discards the idea that human beings are pure in themselves, and that they only have to keep away from the impurities from outside to remain pure. Evil is in the innermost part of a human from where it proceeds to the outside.

What, therefore, matters above all is the purity of one's heart. Purity of heart was a fundamental teaching of the prophets (e.g. Isa. 1:12-17) (Senior, 1998:178). This correlates to the moral instruction of Matt. 5:8 ("Blessed are the pure at heart").

9.6 CONCLUSION

The narrative of Matt. 15:1-20 provides yet another scene in the overall picture of Matthew's Jesus and the *Torah*. It provides and explanation of the relationship between Matthew's Jesus and the tradition of the Pharisees and the Law of Moses. The basic matter in this narrative is that Jesus contrasts the tradition of the Pharisees with the written *Torah*. While Matthew's Jesus makes

---

[281] Matthew states all the vices in plural form (φόνοι, μοιχεῖαι, πορνεῖαι, κλοπαί, ψευδομαρτυρίαι, βλασφημίαι), referring to the multiplicity of evil deeds that can be associated with such terms.

[282] It is significant that Matthew adds blasphemy (βλασφημίαι), which is not found in Mark's list. Its inclusion was most probably prompted by the experience of slander and blasphemy that the Matthean community had to endure from the other Jewish communities.

[283] This shift is also recognizable in Matthew's reference to Hos. 6:6, "I desire mercy, not sacrifice" in his Gospel. As discussed in Chapter 7, this reference doesn't occur in one of the other Gospels. Matthew uses this quotation twice: when the Pharisees object that Jesus eats with tax collectors and sinners (Matt. 9:13) and when the Pharisees object that his disciples pick some heads of grain to eat on the Sabbath (Matt. 12:2).

no explicit remark on food laws (as in Mark's version), He rejects the tradition of the Pharisees on the hand-washing ritual. He does not oppose the Mosaic Law, but the Pharisaic oral tradition.

In this narrative two issues regarding the observance of the Law are accentuated. Firstly, the Law given by God is contrasted with the regulations made by the Pharisees. Several words and phrases are used to refer to the Law as given by God: the command of God (ἐντολή), the Word of God (λόγος) and what God said (ὁ γὰρ θεὸς εἶπεν). In contrast to these, the tradition (παράδοσις) of the Pharisees is mentioned as regulations made by humans. The Pharisees are teaching the teachings on human rules (διδάσκοντες διδασκαλίας ἐντάλματα ἀνθρώπων). Though the tradition was intended to prevent that infringement of the Law of God takes place, Jesus accuses the Pharisees of letting the opposite happen. Jesus expresses it very frankly: Not despite adding their tradition to the *Torah*, but because of this addition (διὰ τὴν παράδοσιν), they break the Law of God.

The second issue relates to the locus and origin of impurity and this is illustrated with reference to the tradition of hand-washing. The idea behind the hand-washing ritual is that the locus of impurity lies outside a person. Accordingly, impurity can enter a person from outside through the mouth. A person should avoid taking in impurities by observing cultic practices such as hand-washing before eating. Jesus dismisses this kind of thinking. The locus of impurity lies in the heart, the innermost part of a person. One's heart is considered as the affective centre or desire producer of one's being. From an evil heart, all kinds of evil deeds emerge, but Jesus urges his disciples to seek a pure heart. Earlier in the Gospel Jesus told his disciples: "Blessed are the pure in heart, for they will see God" (Matt. 5:8). Jesus replaces the Pharisean emphasis on cultic purity with moral purity. Followers of Jesus should be concerned about keeping their hearts clean and not about the threat of impurity from the outside world. From an impure heart all kinds of evil deeds emerge. A human being is not controlled by external codes of conduct, but by what emerges from his/her inner heart.

Matthew tells this story to inform his audience of this dispute between Jesus and the Pharisees (and the scribes) (on the first level of the story), but also to form their identity (on the second level). Several devices can be recognized that Matthew employs to define his community and distinguish them from outsiders:

The Matthean community should identify themselves with the disciples in the story. Commitment to Jesus and his teachings form the central focus of their identity. Jesus, as the Son of God, should be revered as having the authority to interpret the Law and to criticize the Pharisees. As his disciples, the community is not supposed to be ignorant or lack understanding of Jesus' teaching. Jesus' performative teaching is intended to convince his disciples and per implication the Matthean community. They should comprehend the teachings of Jesus as the ultimate interpretation of the *Torah* and adhere to it. They should reject the oral tradition of the Pharisees and their traditional interpretation of the *Torah*, as it poses a threat to the observance of the written Law of God. This story implies an estrangement between the Matthean community and Judaism of the "Dual *Torah*" that considered the memorized tradition as equally important compared to the written *Torah*. The community should expect to be confronted because of their loyalty towards Jesus and their negation of the oral tradition. While the oral tradition attends to external purity, the moral behaviour of Matthew's community should be governed by inner purity. The community should realize that religious activities, performed without heartfelt commitment towards God, are worthless.

In the narrative the two outsider groups are named as the Pharisees (with the scribes) and the crowds.

The Pharisees (with the scribes) are portrayed as the opponents of Jesus. This outsider group somehow reflects the people who challenge the Matthean community because of their loyalty towards Jesus. These outsiders interpret the *Torah* according to the tradition of the Pharisees. They could also be identified with those who confront the community for their rejection of the duality of the *Torah*. These outsiders are labelled as people unable to understand the teachings of Jesus. They strictly perform formal religious rituals, but without heartfelt commitment to God. They are also labelled as hypocrites who pretend to honour God, but who ultimately fail to do so. They perform cultic ceremonies, but neglect moral duties. They are depicted as blind guides who mislead others with their teachings. Although they attempt to improve their observance of the Law by way of the tradition, they actually nullify the Word of God in this way. For this delusion they will be judged on judgement day.

The other outsider group is the crowds. The crowds probably reflect Jewish people or gentiles who stand neutral and who do not yet have convictions about Jesus. For Matthew the mission to Israel and the gentiles has to continue. They are potential believers. Jesus and his teachings can be proclaimed to them. If they listen, they can be brought to understanding. While the Matthean community proclaimed Jesus to neutral outsiders, they are reminded that these people should have the opportunity to listen and be brought to the understanding of Jesus' teachings rather than that of the Judaism of the Dual *Torah* as presented by the Pharisees.

From this narrative it seems that both the Matthean community as the Pharisean movement with whom they interacted in their time were much concerned about the correct interpretation of the *Torah*. It seems that the Pharisaic movement held some attraction for and influence on members of the society. This story warns the society against the Pharisaic movement. They are labelled as hypocrites and blind guides that would lead the blind into a pit. The story proposes that Jesus' teaching is the true interpretation of the *Torah*. People with insight and understanding should realize this. It seems as if the objection of the opponents was directed against customary practices of the Matthean community. Matthew counters their objection by arguing that his community is more faithful to the commandments of God. He argues that the traditions of the Pharisees and the scribes are opposed to the Word of God. He claims that the greater faithfulness of his community is based on the authority of Jesus. He describes Jesus as the superior interpreter of the *Torah*.

CHAPTER 10

THE DOUBLE LOVE COMMANDMENT

10.1 INTRODUCTION

Matt. 22:34-40 describes yet another scene where the Jewish leaders confront Jesus about the *Torah*[284]. This scene concludes a series of hostile interrogations (*Streitgesprächen*): the first on whether one should pay tax to the Caesar (Matt. 22:15-22), the second on who the husband would be after the resurrection of a woman who had seven husbands on earth (Matt. 22:23-33) and thirdly on which commandment of the *Torah* should be regarded as the greatest. The questions of these challenges are posed in such a manner that whatever Jesus answers, his answer would be embarrassing and damaging to his credibility. However, Jesus time and again overcomes these challenges with his unexpected answers. This series of challenges ends with Jesus taking the lead by posing a question to the Pharisees about the Christ, whose son He is (Matt. 22:42). After their expected response Jesus poses two more questions (Matt. 22:43-45). The narrative concludes with the comment that Jesus' opponents were unable to respond and they no longer dared to interrogate Jesus (Matt. 22:46) (Meier, 2009:482, 486)[285]. Matt. 23 then follows, where Jesus warns his disciples and the crowds against the hypocrisy of the scribes and the Pharisees. Jesus is depicted as the undisputed victor in these conflict settings.

In this chapter, the conflict story about the greatest commandment is once again read on two levels. The first level relates the conflict between an expert of the Law and Jesus and functions within the story world internal to the text, and the second level reflects the external world in which the text came into existence.

---

[284] In Matt. 9:10 the Pharisees blame Jesus for eating with tax collectors and sinners, in Matt. 12:2 for the fact that his disciples do what is forbidden on the Sabbath (Chapter 7), and in Matt. 15:2 the Pharisees and the scribes confront Jesus as his disciples do not observe the tradition of hand washing (Chapter 9).

[285] Jesus possesses all authority (πᾶσα ἐξουσία), and Matthew once again presents Jesus as the victor in this case (cf. Matt. 7:29, 23:23-27; 28:18).

The formation of the Matthean community is investigated by considering the Mediterranean perspectives of group-oriented societies that were prevalent in the first century. In such societies meaningful human existence relied on being embedded in a group (Malina & Rohrbaugh, 1992:57). Such a group provided a sense of self and an interactive support system, where love functioned to bind the group together. The subordinates showed their undivided loyalty towards their superiors because of the favours they received from them, while they supported and cared for other members of the group as themselves. Reading the double love commandment of Matt. 22:34-40 from this perspective reveals significant aspects of the community's identity, which I explore in this essay.

10.2 COMPOSITION OF THE NARRATIVE

The composition of this short narrative is straightforward. It consists of a narrative introduction that describes the setting of the challenge (Matt. 22:34-35), the short challenging question of the expert of the Law (Matt. 22:36) and the longer answer of Jesus as riposte. This riposte consists of two components (Matt. 22:37-40) in which Jesus overcomes the challenge by quoting and linking two passages from the *Torah,* the first about the vertical dimension of love (quoting from Deut. 6:5) and the second on the horizontal dimension (quoting from Lev. 19:18). The narrative concludes with a comment about the significance of the commandments as quoted.

> **The narrative introduction: setting of the challenge (Matt. 22:24-35)**
> ... καὶ ἐπηρώτησεν εἷς ἐξ αὐτῶν νομικὸς πειράζων αὐτόν
> (... and one of them, an expert of the Law, tested Him asking)
> **The question to test Jesus: challenge (Matt. 22:36)**
> Διδάσκαλε, ποία ἐντολὴ μεγάλη ἐν τῷ νόμῳ;
> (Teacher, which is the great(est) commandment in the Law?)
> **Jesus' twofold response: riposte (Matt. 22:37-40)**
> ┌ ... Ἀγαπήσεις κύριον τὸν Θεόν σου ἐν ὅλῃ τῇ καρδίᾳ σου καὶ ἐν ὅλῃ
> │ τῇ ψυχῇ σου καὶ ἐν ὅλῃ τῇ διανοίᾳ σου ....
> │ (... Love the Lord your God with all your heart and with all your
> │ soul and with all your mind ...)
> └ ... Ἀγαπήσεις τὸν πλησίον σου ὡς σεαυτόν ...
>   (... Love your neighbour as yourself ...).

Table 51: Composition of the narrative on the greatest commandment in Matt. 22:24-40

The catchword νόμος (law) brackets the whole conversation. The Law is the contents and real focus of the discussion. The word connects the concluding statement in Matt. 22:40, ἐν ταύταις ταῖς δυσὶν ἐντολαῖς ὅλος ὁ νόμος κρέμαται καὶ οἱ προφῆται (on these two commandments hang all the Law and the Prophets) with the person who asks the question in the opening verse, καὶ ἐπηρώτησεν ... νομικὸς πειράζων αὐτόν (an expert of the Law, tested Him asking) (Matt. 22:35) (Luz, 2005:75).

Matthew follows Mark's version (Mark 12:28-34) of the event, but with significant differences (see Hultgren, 1974:374), which demonstrates some of the intentions and concerns of Matthew[286]. The two passages are presented in parallel form to indicate omissions and additions by Matthew on Mark's version. Significant changes are indicated in bold.

Matt. 22:34-40	Mark 12:28-34
Setting of the challenge	
34. **Οἱ δὲ Φαρισαῖοι ἀκούσαντες ὅτι ἐφίμωσεν τοὺς Σαδδουκαίους, συνήχθησαν ἐπὶ τὸ αὐτό,** (³⁴ Hearing that Jesus had silenced the Sadducees, the Pharisees got together)	
³⁵ καὶ ἐπηρώτησεν **εἷς ἐξ αὐτῶν νομικὸς** πειράζων αὐτόν ³⁵ One of them, an expert of the Law, tested him with this question:	²⁸ Καὶ προσελθὼν εἷς τῶν γραμματέων, ἀκούσας αὐτῶν συζητούντων, (²⁸ One of the scribes came and heard them debating ... [he asked him].)
	εἰδὼς ὅτι καλῶς ἀπεκρίθη αὐτοῖς, (noticing that Jesus had given them a good answer)
Challenging question of the expert of the Law	
³⁶ Διδάσκαλε, ποία ἐντολὴ μεγάλη ἐν τῷ νόμῳ; (³⁶ "Teacher, which is the greatest commandment in the Law?")	ἐπηρώτησεν αὐτόν Ποία ἐστὶν ἐντολὴ πρώτη πάντων; (he asked him, "Of all the commandments, which is the most important?")
Response of Jesus	

---

[286] Luk 10:25-28 has an indirect parallel: "On one occasion an expert in the law stood up to test Jesus. "Teacher," he asked, "what must I do to inherit eternal life?" "What is written in the Law?" he replied. "How do you read it?" He answered, " 'Love the Lord your God with all your heart and with all your soul and with all your strength and with all your mind'; and, 'Love your neighbour as yourself.'" "You have answered correctly," Jesus replied. "Do this and you will live."

	... Ἄκουε, Ἰσραήλ, Κύριος ὁ Θεὸς ἡμῶν Κύριος εἷς ἐστιν, ... (... 'Hear, O Israel: The Lord our God, the Lord is one ...)
[37] ὁ δὲ ἔφη αὐτῷ Ἀγαπήσεις κύριον τὸν Θεόν σου ἐν ὅλῃ τῇ καρδίᾳ σου καὶ ἐν ὅλῃ τῇ ψυχῇ σου καὶ ἐν ὅλῃ τῇ διανοίᾳ σου. 38 **αὕτη ἐστὶν ἡ μεγάλη καὶ πρώτη ἐντολή.** ([37] Jesus replied: " 'Love the Lord your God with all your heart and with all your soul and with all your mind. [38] This is the first and greatest commandment)	[29] ἀπεκρίθη ὁ Ἰησοῦς ὅτι Πρώτη ἐστίν ... 30 καὶ ἀγαπήσεις Κύριον τὸν Θεόν σου ἐξ ὅλης τῆς καρδίας σου καὶ ἐξ ὅλης τῆς ψυχῆς σου καὶ ἐξ ὅλης τῆς διανοίας σου καὶ ἐξ ὅλης τῆς ἰσχύος σου. ([29] "The most important one," answered Jesus, "is this: .... [30] Love the Lord your God with all your heart and with all your soul and with all your mind and with all your strength.')
[39] δευτέρα **ὁμοία αὐτῇ** Ἀγαπήσεις τὸν πλησίον σου ὡς σεαυτόν. ([39] And the second is like it: 'Love your neighbour as yourself.')	[31]δευτέρα αὕτη Ἀγαπήσεις τὸν πλησίον σου ὡς σεαυτόν. ([31] The second is this: 'Love your neighbour as yourself.')
40 **ἐν ταύταις ταῖς δυσὶν ἐντολαῖς ὅλος ὁ νόμος κρέμαται καὶ οἱ προφῆται.** ([40] All the Law and the Prophets hang on these two commandments.")	μείζων τούτων ἄλλη ἐντολὴ οὐκ ἔστιν (There is no commandment greater than these.")
	32 καὶ εἶπεν αὐτῷ ὁ γραμματεύς Καλῶς, Διδάσκαλε, ἐπ' ἀληθείας εἶπες ὅτι εἷς ἐστιν καὶ οὐκ ἔστιν ἄλλος πλὴν αὐτοῦ. 33 καὶ τὸ ἀγαπᾶν αὐτὸν ἐξ ὅλης καρδίας καὶ ἐξ ὅλης τῆς συνέσεως καὶ ἐξ ὅλης τῆς ἰσχύος καὶ τὸ ἀγαπᾶν τὸν πλησίον ὡς ἑαυτὸν περισσότερόν ἐστιν πάντων τῶν ὁλοκαυτωμάτων καὶ θυσιῶν. 34 καὶ ὁ Ἰησοῦς ἰδὼν αὐτὸν ὅτι νουνεχῶς ἀπεκρίθη εἶπεν αὐτῷ Οὐ μακρὰν εἶ ἀπὸ τῆς βασιλείας τοῦ θεοῦ. Καὶ οὐδεὶς οὐκέτι ἐτόλμα αὐτὸν ἐπερωτῆσαι. (32 "Well said, teacher," the man replied. "You are right in saying that God is one and there is no other but him. 33 To love him with all your heart, with all your understanding and with all your strength, and to love your neighbour as yourself is more important than all burnt offerings and sacrifices." 34 When Jesus saw that he had answered wisely, he said to him, "You are not far from the kingdom of God." And from then on no one dared ask him any more questions.)

Table 52: The parallel between Matt. 22:34-40 and Mark 12:28-34 on the greatest commandment

Matthew omits a number of sections from Mark's text. The first omission is "noticing that Jesus had given them a good answer" (Mark 12:28). The reason for this omission is most probably that such an amicable remark would not form a fitting setting for a challenge by this very same person, Jesus. The second, somewhat surprising omission is that of the quotation of the *Shema*: "Hear, o Israel, the Lord our God, the Lord is one" (Mark 12:29). It is a redactional tendency of Matthew to shorten Mark so that he can focus on the essence of his argument. The *Shema* seemingly does not form an essential part of Matthew's argument and he probably assumes that his mainly Jewish readers would associate the first commandment, as quoted, with the *Shema*[287]. Matthew also omits one of the four faculties Mark mentions, "with all your strength" (Mark 12:33), reducing the number of qualifications to three faculties as in Deut. 6:5. However, the phrase he drops "with all your strength" is found in Deut. 6:5, while he maintains "with all your mind", which is an addition to Deut. 6:5. This probably reflects a certain understanding of the character of love. The longest omission is where the scribe admits that Jesus is right and Jesus commends him by stating that he is not far from the kingdom of God (Mark 12:32-34). Such an amicable remark obviously would not fit well into the *Streitgespräch* and the increasing hostility that Matthew describes in his narrative (Hagner, 1995:645; Loader, 1997:235). Matthew rather continues with a conflict setting where the opposition deepens to reach its climax in the denunciation of the Pharisees in Matt. 23.

On the other hand, Matthew makes a number of additions to the text. The entirety of Matt. 22:34 is added, which indicates that this is yet another attempt of the Pharisees to tempt Jesus. Matthew replaces "one of the scribes" (Mark 12:28) with "an expert of the Law" (Matt. 22:35) to indicate how formidable this challenger as spokesperson of the Pharisees is. Matthew replaces the positive attitude of the scribe who asks Jesus a question (Mark 12:28) with a challenge of testing Jesus (Matt. 22:35). Furthermore, Matthew adds "teacher" as the addressee (Matt. 22:36), a term that only Jesus' adversaries use to address him in Matthew and never his adherents. In Matt. 22:38 a remark about the first commandment is added: "this is the first and greatest commandment" and about the second commandment "similar to it" (Matt. 22:39) is added. Furthermore, Matthew replaces Mark's "there is no commandment greater than these" (Mark

---

[287] Though omitting the opening confession of faith of the *Shema*, Matthew's Jesus responds with the love of Yahweh, taken from Deut. 6:4-5. In later rabbinic period, the *Shema* had become to be defined as containing three texts joined together: Deut. 6:4-9; 11:13-21 and Num. 15:37-41 (Meier, 2009:490).

12:31) with "all the Law and the Prophets hang on these two commandments" (Matt. 22:40), which indicates the significance of these two commandments for the interpretation of all the Jewish Scriptures.

The general tendency of Matthew to shorten Mark's narrative is once again evident in this story. What is more, Matthew amends Mark's version to create a better parallel between the two commandments as the first and second commandments respectively. With this shortened story in which he presents the issue of the Law in parallel form, Matthew succeeds in creating a sharp focus on the Law.

10.3 READING THE NARRATIVE AS *STREITGESPRÄCH*

Back in 1954 Bornkamm (1954:85-93) expounded how Matthew turns the didactic narrative (*Schulgespräch*) of Mark[288] on the greatest commandment (which has an amiable tone) into a conflict narrative (*Streitgespräch*)[289] (which has a controversial tone). Matthew's story forms a continuation of two previous conflict narratives, namely the narrative on the payment of taxes (Matt. 22:15-22) and about the resurrection (Matt. 22:23-33) (Repschinski, 2000:262). Despite their agreement with Jesus in the dispute on the resurrection, the Pharisees in the narrative side with the Sadducees in a continuing conflict setting. One would expect the Pharisees to rejoice in the Sadducees' defeat as they were usually rivalling Jewish factions, but in this instance they conspire together against Jesus, as is also the case in Matt. 16:1-2. The Pharisees are determined to challenge Jesus and use the expert of the Law as their spokesperson. Matthew concludes the narrative on the greatest commandment by depicting Jesus as the victor. The expert of the Law and the Pharisees are silenced. Jesus then continues by asking a question of his own: "What do you think of the Messiah?" (Matt. 22:42). Matthew's Jesus continues with a Christological revelation about David calling his son Lord (Matt. 22:41-46). Matthew creates tension with a climactic ending by delaying the last statement of Mark 12:34, "no one dared ask him any more questions" to end this passage. In this *Streitgespräch* Jesus is the clear victor.

---

[288] Though Mark 12:28-34 is usually described as a *Schulgespräch*, an irenic dialogue does not really fit into the series of preceding conflict stories and Jesus' attack on the scribes that follows. Meier (2009:499) has been of the opinion that Mark 12:28-34 probably circulated originally as an independent oral tradition.

[289] Notably Luke 10:25 also presents the story as a *Streitgespräch*: "ἐκπειράζων αὐτὸν" (testing Him).

A central phenomenon to a *Streitgespräch* is the interaction of challenge and riposte (Malina & Rohrbaugh, 1992:42; Repshinski, 2000:262-272). It consists of a challenge with the intention to undermine another person's reputation and a response that measures up to the challenge. Honour and shame were pivotal values in ancient Mediterranean societies (Malina & Rohrbaugh, 1992:76; Witherington, 2013:47). Honour is acquired by the conduct of a person, but also by other people's recognition of it. In this culture one would do anything to achieve honour and to avoid shame[290]. In this *Streitgespräch* the intention of the expert of the Law and the Pharisees is to shame Jesus. However, Jesus acquires honour by his skilful riposte to this challenge. The Pharisees witness Jesus' victory in this *Streitgespräch*. Instead of recognizing Jesus' honour, their jealousy apparently increases. In Matt. 23 Jesus continues by addressing the crowds and his disciples by warning them against the scribes and the Pharisees. They witness how Jesus maintains his honour while He exposes the shame of the Jewish leaders. Jesus emerges as the clear victor and the respect the disciples and crowds have for Jesus, increases.

By presenting this event in the form of a *Streitgespräch,* Matthew expresses his and his community's opposition to the Pharisaic Rabbinate of their society regarding the understanding of the Law (Barth, 1963:76). The evangelist pronounces the conflicting hermeneutical approaches to the Law and Prophets by the Pharisees of their day and of his own community (Hultgren, 1974:378).

10.4 THE POLEMICAL CHALLENGE BY THE EXPERT OF THE LAW (MATT. 22:24-36)

This scene opens with a remark that refers back to the previous *Streitgespräch* where Jesus put the Sadducees to silence. Their inability to respond is implied, ἐφίμωσεν τοὺς Σαδδουκαίους (He silenced the Sadducees). It is not merely that the Sadducees did not say anything, but they could not say anything. Jesus was the clear victor in the previous dispute. The dispute then continues with the challenge from the teacher of the Law.

---

[290] In the Ancient Mediterranean culture the most important value was the honour of one's name and one's family name. Life and truth were regarded further down the hierarchy of values (Witherington, 2013:47).

While Mark only mentions one scribe questioning Jesus (Mark 12:28)[291], Matthew adds the presence of the Pharisees to this hostile debate. Matthew writes that the "Pharisees were gathered together" (συνήχθησαν), which could be an intended echo of Ps. 2:2[292] (Carter, 2000a:444; Osborne, 2010:822; Turner, 2008:535). The scene suggests a full scale assembly for a concerted and malicious effort by the Pharisees[293]. They use the expert of the Law as their spokesperson in this *Streitgespräch*.

While Mark uses γραμματεύς (Mark 12:28) and Matthew usually also uses γραμματεύς to refer to a scribe (e.g. Matt. 2:4; 5:20; 7:29), Matthew here uses the word νομικός (expert of the Law). As a matter of fact, this is the only time Matthew uses the word νομικός. Obviously Matthew wants to emphasise that the questioner should be regarded as a daunting interlocutor about this crucial legal issue (regarding the νομός) at stake (Gerhardsson, 1976:133; Osborne, 2010:822). The terms used to describe the conduct of the expert of the Law underline the nature of the interlocution. He questions (ἐπηρώτησεν) Jesus (using the intensified form of ἐρωτάω, ask), while trying to test (πειράζων) Him. Matthew uses πειράζω significantly. This word is also used in other malicious debates and temptations in Matthew (Matt. 16:1; 19:3; 21:45 and 22:15-18) where Pharisees are also involved. Furthermore, the supreme tempter, the devil, is called ὁ πειράζων (the tempter) (Matt. 4:1). Surely the intention of the νομικός (expert of the Law) is not to ascertain the truth, but to shame Jesus by tricking Him to give a disputable answer on legal matters.

The expert of the Law addresses Jesus as teacher (διδάσκαλος). At first this form of address does not indicate hostility. In Matthew, only Jesus' adversaries address Him as teacher, namely the scribes, Pharisees, collectors of temple tax

---

[291] As indicated above, Matthew omits the positive and amicable attitude of the teacher of the Law reflected in Mark 12:28: "Noticing that Jesus had given them a good answer" and adds that he tried to test Jesus.

[292] The identical phrase, συνήχθησαν ἐπὶ τὸ αὐτό (they got together) occurs in Ps 2:2 LXX. Within the context of opposition against the Lord' anointed, Ps 2:2 reads: "The kings of the earth rise up and the rulers band together against the Lord and against his anointed". Reference to Ps. 2:2 is also made in Acts 4:26. Neh. 6:2 describes a similar malicious gathering.

[293] As mentioned before, in Matthew Jewish religious leaders, in particular the scribes and the Pharisees, are consistently described in a negative light. While Mark only once refers to Pharisees as hypocrites (Mark 7:6) and Luke not at all, Matthew makes twelve such references, of which six are in Matt. 23 (see Stanton, 2013:108-112).

and the rich young man who goes away disappointed with Jesus' answer[294]. People who respect and honour Jesus address Him as Lord (κύριος)[295] (Repschinski, 2000:274). It seems that the expert of the Law uses "teacher" in an ironic or even sarcastic manner. If Jesus pretends to be a teacher (rabbi) who has adherents, let He then prove Himself really to be a teacher. By addressing Jesus as teacher, the expert of the Law expresses his sinister intention to challenge Jesus' honour. His intention is clearly not to gain new insight into the Law, but to challenge Jesus to give a disputable or wrong answer. Thus he would get an opportunity to shame and ridicule Jesus. With this challenge he wants to demonstrate Jesus' ignorance and unworthiness of being regarded as a credible rabbi. The teacher of the Law asks Jesus about the great(est) command (ἐντολὴ μεγάλη)[296] of the Law. He wants Jesus to single out one commandment that stands qualitatively above the rest. This was a typical point of debate amongst the rabbis (Hagner, 1995:646; Keener, 2009:530; Luz, 2001b:82). They counted 248 commandments and 365 prohibitions, adding up to 613 *mitzvot*. To underline the seriousness of the Law, they often warned that the violation of even the smallest commandment of the Law is extremely serious, as some have remarked: "Violating even a light commandment is the result of pride" (4 Macc. 5:20-21) and commended even the smallest commandments: "Scriptures credit both light and weighty" (*b. Hag.* 5a). James poses a similar warning: "For whoever keeps the whole law and yet stumbles at just one point is guilty of breaking all of it" (James 2:10). The question of the expert of the Law is therefore an excellent challenge posed to Jesus. Whichever commandment Jesus singles out, it would be disputable.

While the rabbis accepted all commandments as given by God so that none could therefore be neglected, they did distinguish between "heavy" and "light"

---

[294] Jesus is addressed as teacher (διδάσκαλος) by a scribe who tells Jesus that he would follow Him, but he receives a disappointing answer from Jesus (Matt. 8:18); by scribes and Pharisees asking a sign from Jesus (Matt. 12:38); by the rich young man who asks what good deed he must do to get eternal life (Matt. 19:16), by the Pharisees who challenge Jesus on the payment of taxes (Matt. 22:16) and the Sadducees who challenge Him on the resurrection (Matt. 22:24).

[295] Jesus is addressed as Lord (κύριος) by his disciples when they call for help during the storm at sea (Matt. 8:25); by the two blind men who Jesus heals (Matt. 9:28), by Peter when he loses faith while walking on the sea (Matt. 14:30) etc.

[296] Matthew here probably uses the Semitic style of the superlative, which also became common in Koine Greek (cf. Keener, 2007:530; Turner, 2008:535).

commandments[297] (cf. Hillel's *middoth*, rules 1 and 5) (Gerhardsson, 1976:137). Montefiore and Loewe (1974:199-201) have indicated several rabbinic passages[298] in which commandments are prioritised. The Babylonian Talmud, *b. Sanh.* 74a, for example, refers to martyrdom when Jews are forced into committing sins. The Talmud identifies some specific sins that were absolutely prohibited during such martyrdom, namely idolatry, unchastity and murder. Neighbourly love has long been regarded as fundamental in Jewish ethics (*m. Abot.* 1:12; Jub. 36:4, 8). Late in the first century Rabbi Akiba regarded neighbourly love as the greatest commandment of the Law (*Sifra Qed.* pq. 4.200.3.7). Other rabbis again stressed the prohibition of idolatry (*b. Qidd.* 40a; *p. Ned.* 3:9). Similar discussions on which of the laws should be regarded as the "greatest" are found in *m. Hag.*, 1:8; *b. Mak.*, 24a; *b. Ber.*, 63a; and *b. Sabb.*, 31a) (cf. Hultgren, 1974:376; Keener, 2009:530).

The teacher of the Law is therefore initiating a discussion that would provide an opportunity to trap Jesus into giving a disputable answer and thus damage Jesus' reputation.

10.5 THE NON-POLEMICAL RIPOSTE GIVEN BY JESUS (MATT. 22:37-40)

In this *Streitgespräch* Jesus responds with a twofold answer, the first focusing on one's relationship with God (Matt. 22:37-38) and the second on one's relationship with one's neighbour (Matt. 22:39) and a concluding remark about the centrality of these two commandments (Matt. 22:40)[299]. There is nothing polemical in Jesus' answer, but according to Matthew, this answer leaves the expert of the Law speechless. Jesus is portrayed as the honourable figure in this scene.

---

[297] In Matt. 23:23 Jesus charges the Pharisees that they regarded some commandments so important that they neglected others: "You give a tenth of your spices—mint, dill and cumin. But you have neglected the more important matters of the law—justice, mercy and faithfulness. You should have practiced the latter, without neglecting the former".

[298] Though such rabbinic writings are dated later, it can be assumed that they reflect earlier Jewish thinking that was prevalent in the times of Jesus and the Matthean community.

[299] From the text itself it is not clear whether this concluding remark is made by Matthews' Jesus or whether it is a direct comment by the author himself.

10.5.1 Love of God

In the first part of his response Jesus focuses on the first table of the Decalogue and describes the vertical dimension between a human and God[300]. This response is uncontroversial and not polemical, but defuses much of the challenge. While Matthew used words like ἐπηρώτησεν (he interrogated), the intensified form of questioning, and πειράζων (testing) to describe the challenge put by the expert of the Law, he uses a non-polemical neutral word, ἔφη (He stated) to describe Jesus' response. Though without the opening words of the *Shema* as in Mark[301], Matthew's Jesus cites the part of the *Shema* dealing with the commandment (Deut. 6:5), ἀγαπήσεις Κύριον τὸν θεόν σου ἐν ὅλῃ καρδίᾳ σου καὶ ἐν ὅλῃ τῇ ψυχῇ σου καὶ ἐν ὅλῃ τῇ διανοίᾳ σου ("love the Lord your God with all your heart and with all your soul and with all your mind"). The citation of the *Shema* is significant as it was a central and well-known text in Judaism (Meier, 2009:490). Pious Jews recited it twice daily. The Israelites had to memorize these words, instruct their children, write out the *Torah*, and wear fringes (*tzitzit*) to remind themselves of these words. Judaism stressed the importance of loving God with one's whole being (Jub. 1:15-16; 16:25; 1 QS. 1.2). By stating the importance of this commandment, Jesus asserts that He firmly stands within this tradition, and thus avoids the embarrassment the teacher of the Law might have expected.

Interpreting the meaning of the love of God, one must consider the group orientation of the first-century Mediterranean world. Love formed part of a positive reciprocity within the group (Malina & Rohrbaugh, 1992:56). People did not have last names, so their identity was formed by who they were related to and to which group they belonged (Witherington, 2013:49). Balanced reciprocity implied that one should return in equal measure to the favour one receives[302]. The love of God functions in the vertical dimension. The people of

---

[300] This commandment from Deut. 6:5 can easily be identified with the first commandment of the Decalogue: "I am the Lord your God ...You shall have no other gods before me" (Exod. 20:2-3).

[301] Matthew, writing to a mainly Jewish-Christian audience, probably assumes his audience would relate the commandment to the *Shema*, ("Hear, o Israel, the Lord our God, the Lord is one").

[302] The requirement to return of favours becomes clearer when considering the context of treaties (covenants) in the Ancient Near East. In some of these treaties, the vassal, often after being defeated in battle, promised to "love" the suzerain. "Love" implies the fulfilment of the obligations the suzerain imposes on the vassal in the treaty, above all maintaining the exclusive relationship with the suzerain (Meier, 2009:490).

God considered themselves as receiving their whole existence and well-being from God (from top to bottom). Matthew depicts God as merciful, gracious and loving (Matt. 9:13 and 12:7). Such privileged people should therefore respond with honour, loyalty and devotion (from bottom to top). God formed the ultimate personage of their group[303]. Loving God implied attachment to God and behaviour that would honour Him within this reciprocal relationship (cf. Witherington, 2013:50). Love implied the fulfilment of obligations that are required within such a relationship (Meier, 2009:490).

As in the *Shema*, (Hear, O Israel: The Lord our God, The Lord is one ...) (Deut. 6:4-6), Jesus continues to describe the way one should love God with a trisected series of nouns describing a person's faculties. These faculties were regarded as the different constituents of a human being that influence his/her behaviour. The faculties differ in the Synoptic versions as indicated in the following table.

MT Deut. 6:5	LXX Deut. 6:5	Mark 12:30	Matt. 22:37	Luk 10:27
Lēbab	Καρδία	καρδία	καρδία	Καρδία
Nepeš	Ψυχή	ψυχή	ψυχή	Ψυχή
		Διανοία	διανοία	διανοία[304]
Mě'ōd	Δύναμις	ἰσχύς		ἰσχύς

Table 53: Synoptic comparison of the faculties involved when loving according God's commandment

The *Shema* in the Masoretic Text and the LXX refers to three faculties (with all your heart, and with all your soul and with all your strength) (Deut. 6:5)[305]. Mark adds a fourth faculty, ἐξ ὅλης τῆς καρδίας σου καὶ ἐξ ὅλης τῆς ψυχῆς σου καὶ ἐξ ὅλης τῆς διανοίας σου καὶ ἐξ ὅλης τῆς ἰσχύος σου (with all your heart and with all your soul and with all your mind and with all your strength) (Mark 12:30). As in the *Shema*, Matt. 22:37 only mentions three faculties, ἐν ὅλῃ τῇ καρδίᾳ σου καὶ ἐν ὅλῃ τῇ ψυχῇ σου καὶ ἐν ὅλῃ τῇ διανοίᾳ σου (with all your heart and with all your soul and with all your mind)[306], though the last, "all your

---

[303] In the patriarchal and hierarchical culture of the ancient Mediterranean world, one needed a patron. The better the status of the patron, the better for the client (Witherington, 2013:50).

[304] For some reason Luke mentions ἰσχύς and διανοία in inverted order.

[305] The combination of "heart and soul" signifying loving in entirety is found in Jewish writings (Jub. 1:15-16; 16:25 and 1 QS 1.2).

[306] Matthew is closer to the Masoretic text and LXX by introducing the faculties with ἐν plus the dative, instead of ἐξ plus the genitive as in Mark.

mind", is similar to the fourth faculty in Mark and differs from the third faculty, of the *Shema,* "all your strength"[307]. Luk. 10:27 followed Mark by mentioning all four faculties, but inverts the last two faculties, ἐξ ὅλης καρδίας σου καὶ ἐν ὅλῃ τῇ ψυχῇ σου καὶ ἐν ὅλῃ τῇ ἰσχύι σου καὶ ἐν ὅλῃ τῇ διανοίᾳ σου, καὶ τὸν πλησίον σου ὡς σεαυτόν (with all your heart and with all your soul and with all your strength and with all your mind).

The faculties as mentioned represent the entire person. One cannot love God with some of one's faculties while excluding others. Nevertheless, in Jewish tradition each faculty gathered interpretation to itself as it referred to a functional composite part of a human being (Davies & Allison, 2004c:241; Gerhardsson, 1976:140).

The first faculty Jesus refers to, "all your heart", is found in all the versions, as indicated in the table above. Heart is mentioned over 800 times in the Bible, but never to refer to the literal physical pump that drives the blood. One's heart was regarded as the centre of one's thoughts, will, knowledge, decisions and actions (Jacob, 1974:626; Walker, 2000:563). It refers to the affective centre or desire producer of one's being. The following two verses from the Jewish Bible illustrate the point. In Jer. 32:41 *lēbab* (heart) refers to the place of willing and planning and in 1 Sam. 12:20 to the source of religious and ethical conduct (Baumgartel, 1978:606-607). In the New Testament καρδία (heart) is used with a similar meaning. It refers to one's religious centre, which forms the root of religious life and determines ethical conduct (Luk. 16:15; Rom. 5:5; 8:27; Eph. 3:17), it is the seat of thought and understanding (Matt. 7:21; John 12:40; Acts 8:22) (Behm, 1978:611-613). Jesus therefore states that one should be totally devoted to God with one's innermost religious centre (Piper, 1979:205).

The second faculty "all your soul" is also found in all the versions. Ψυχή (soul) is etymologically related to ψύχω (blow). In the Jewish Bible the soul is regarded as the direct result of God breathing (blowing) his gift of life into a person (Gen. 2:7). This would make a person an "ensouled" being. One's ψυχή (soul) is the vital force which comes to expression especially in breathing. At the moment of death the ψυχή (soul) leaves a person (Dihle, 1974:609). In Hebrew Bible *nepeš* (soul) is regarded as the decisive mark of a living creature (Ps. 16:10) (Jacob, 1974:618). In the New Testament ψυχή (soul) is used with similar meaning. In Matt. 2:20 the Herod seeks the ψυχή (soul) of Jesus. Jesus

---

[307] Interesting enough, Plautus also combined these faculties: "I'll work my hardest for, and follow up with *corde et animo atque viribus* (with heart and soul and strengths)" (Captivi, 2.3.27).

announces that He would give his ψυχή (soul) as ransom for many (Mark 10:45) and in Acts 15:26, Paul is willing to give his ψυχή (soul) for the sake of the name of the Lord Jesus Christ (Schweizer, 1974:637-656). The word "soul" thus frequently designates the life force of a living creature (Carrigan, 2000:1245). Reference to "all your soul" therefore signifies that one should totally surrender one's life to God. Loving God with all your soul implies that one should be devoted to God and his commandments even to the point of martyrdom.

The third faculty, "with all your mind" (ἐν ὅλῃ τῇ διανοίᾳ σου), does not occur in Deut. 6:5, but Matthew probably took it over from Mark's addition of the faculty, while he drops "with all your strength" (ἐξ ὅλης τῆς ἰσχύος σου (LXX) and mĕ'ōd (MT)). One's mind (διανοία) was regarded as the seat of one's intellectual capacity, of reason, apprehension and insight (Spencer, 2000:901; Würthwein, 1978:963). It represents the faculty of thorough reasoning (Mark 12:30; Heb. 8:10; 10:16). It incorporates both sides of a matter to reach meaningful and personal conclusions. Col. 1:21 refers to the pre-Christian mode of thinking, being alienated and hostile in mind (ὄντας ἀπηλλοτριωμένους καὶ ἐχθροὺς τῇ διανοίᾳ). In Eph. 4:17-18 the defect of the νοῦς (mind) is traced back to a defect of διανοία (reasoning faculty). Διανοία is also used for reasoning and speech between characters in ancient Greek dramas (Aristotle, *Ars Rhetorica*, 1.404). Matthew's Jesus states that such "full-breadth reasoning" is essential to loving the Lord God. Matthew's omission of "strength" while maintaining "mind" suggests an intellectual approach to the love of God[308]. "Mind" (διάνοια) is used only here in Matthew. This fits in with some Jewish interpretations of the "love of God" in Deut. 6:5, referring mainly to faithfulness to the *Torah* (see *b. Ber.* 61b and *Philo, Decal.* 64). Luz (2001b:82) has proposed that a Hellenistic Jewish tradition lies behind this choice. According to this tradition loving God does not entail a mere feeling or mystical flight out of this world. Instead, for Hellenistic Jews it implied knowing God and obeying his commandments, carefully considering all reasoning. Once again Matthew's Jesus defuses the challenge of the teacher of the Law. A person who loves God with his/her entire mind, would also obey all the commandments He has given. One's whole reasoning should be orientated towards God and obeying his commandments (Carter, 2000a:445). Thus the love of God becomes the fundamental and first commandment that would incorporate the other commandments.

---

[308] Strength (ἰσχύς) refers to one's energy and power. Mark uses this term to describe the power of God (Mark 9:1; 12:24; 14:62) and of Jesus (Mark 5:30; 6:2, 5, 14) (Stein, 2008:561).

Jesus therefore concludes this first part of his response by stating that this commandment is the most important, αὕτη ἐστὶν ἡ μεγάλη καὶ πρώτη ἐντολή (this is the great and first commandment) (Matt. 22:38). This statement in Matthew is unparalleled in Mark and Luke, though Josephus also uses πρώτη to refer to the first commandment (*Contra Apionem,* 2.190)[309]. Jesus confirms that this commandment forms the beginning of all obedience and ethics.

10.5.2 Love of neighbours

Being loyal towards God and his commandments provides a logical link with the second commandment Jesus adds. In the ancient Mediterranean world the identity of the group was dependent on the honour and status of personages (patrons) of the group and members of the group considered themselves embedded in these personages (Malina & Neyrey, 1996:167; Witherington, 2013:50). Love implied faithfulness and loyalty towards personages in whom one was embedded. This required obedience to prescribed duties towards the one in whom one is embedded. A religious person is embedded in God. Love of God therefore requires loyalty to his will and commandments, which entails loving the other members of the group. The obligation to show love towards one's neighbours is motivated by the love one receives from God (cf. Matt. 18:21-35) (Barth, 1963:85).

Without waiting for a reaction from the expert of the Law, Jesus continues: ἀγαπήσεις τὸν πλησίον σου ὡς σεαυτόν (love your neighbour as yourself) (Matt. 22:39). Philo (*Decal.* 109-110) similarly remarked that the two halves of the Decalogue, the love of God and the love of one's neighbour, are incomplete without one another. This second part focuses on the second table of the Decalogue, the horizontal dimension[310]. This wording follows that of Lev. 19:18. It is significant that Matthew's Jesus has cited Lev. 19:18 twice before (Matt. 5:42 and 19:19) (Piper, 1979:152). Both of these references are unique to Matthew. Lev. 19:18 is also the most cited Old Testament text in Matthew's Gospel. In Matt. 5:43 Jesus broadens the meaning of one's neighbour to even include loving enemies (Piper, 1979:141). In Matt. 19:19 Jesus cites Lev. 19:18

---

[309] "What are the things then that we are commanded or forbidden?—They are simply and easily known. The first command is concerning God, and affirms that God contains all things, and is a being every way perfect and happy, self-sufficient, and supplying all other beings; the beginning, the middle, and the end of all things ..." (Contra Apionem, 2.190).

[310] In Rom. 13:8-11 Paul also states that loving one's neighbour is the fulfilment of the Law.

as the fundamental summary of the moral demands of the Decalogue, namely "You shall not murder, you shall not commit adultery, you shall not steal, you shall not give false testimony, honour your father and mother". In Matt. 22:39 this commandment is brought into close connection with loving God (ὁμοία αὐτῇ, similar to it). It is clear that this commandment forms an important part in Matthew's ethics. Davies and Allison (2004c: 241) have remarked that Matthew thus fuses religion and ethics. This fits well with the connection of religion and group identity in the ancient Mediterranean world (Malina & Neyrey, 1996:167). Performing one's duties towards one's neighbours was regarded as part of one's piety directed at God.

The question arises why Jesus calls this the second (δευτέρα) commandment. Does it refer to the second in number or second in importance? In answer to this question one should consider the use of ὁμοία αὐτῇ (similar to it), by which the importance of the second commandment is emphasised. In Jewish interpretation the love for God and the love for one's neighbour are closely related, as it is also found elsewhere in Jewish sources. *Test. Benj.* 3.3-4 states: "fear of God and honouring the brothers ... [are] the essence of the Law" (see also *Test Issachar* 5:2; 7:5; *Test. Dan* 5:3). In some cases they are even identified with one another. *Ep. Arist.* 229 speaks of the pious person who will be helped by the love of the Lord that he has for his neighbour. In Matt. 10:40 Jesus also emphasises the close link between the love of God and the love of people, stating that a person who welcomes a disciple actually also welcomes Jesus and God. Jesus confirms this link once again in Matt. 25:31-46. Love of God is demonstrated in feeding the poor, housing the homeless, clothing the naked, etc. (Carter, 2000a:445). Though this command is second in number, it remains equally important. As a matter of fact, it forms part and is the logical result of executing the first commandment. According to the Jewish interpretive principle of *gezerah shewah* (equal category), it was common to link two commandments together based on their opening words. In Matt. 22 the opening words, "you shall love" are the same, but the objects of love differ, love of God and love of neighbours (Keener, 2009:531; Meier, 2009:493; Turner, 2008:536). Matthew presents the double love commandment in a chiastic structure, which gives each of the quoted commandments equal weight (Repschinski, 2000:263). In order to create a better parallel between the two commandments, he amends Mark's version.

> Ἀγαπήσεις Κύριον τὸν θεόν σου ...
> (Love the Lord your God ...)
>> αὕτη ἐστὶν ἡ μεγάλη καὶ πρώτη ἐντολή
>> (this is the great and first commandment)
>> δευτέρα ὁμοία αὐτῇ
>> (the second similar to it)
> Ἀγαπήσεις
> τὸν πλησίον σου ...
> (Love your neighbour)

Table 54: The parallel between the love commandments in Matt. 22:37-38

The second commandment can be seen as the result of the first, while these two commandments are interconnected. Turner (2008:537) has remarked: "Fallen humans cannot love their neighbours as themselves if they have not first acknowledged their obligation to love the only true God" and "the theocentric vertical obligation is the basis of the anthropocentric horizontal obligation". Without loving one's neighbour, one cannot love God, since one expresses one's love of God by obeying his commandments and many of these commandments are about human relationships.

Also, in this second commandment the meaning of "love" is determined by the interpretation of Lev. 19:18 in its contemporary Jewish interpretation (Luz, 2001b:83). Lev. 19:11-18 deals with God's ethical commandments about the neighbour, the socially weak and the opponent in a court of Law. Loving is defined as not stealing from, lying to, deceiving, swearing falsely against, defrauding or robbing one's neighbour, etc. Lev. 19:34 also includes aliens living in ones land. Though some Jewish interpreters regarded foreigners as neighbours (Test. Iss. 7:6), and others included aliens and proselytes (Jub. 7:20; 20:2; 36:4), they mostly regarded Israelites only as "neighbours" (CD 6.20-21; Jos. War. 2.119; Test. Sim. 4:6-7) and as people deserving of Israel's love.

Malina and Neyrey (1996:153-201) have provided a helpful perspective to define neighbourly love in the ancient Mediterranean world. They have pointed out that the Mediterranean people lived in collectivist societies that were group-orientated and non-individualistic. The individual person was always a group-embedded person connected with a social unit that forms around a notable person. The individual shares the group's loyalty towards the notable person and forms a virtual identity with the group as a whole and with other members in the group. Loyalty and solidarity keep the group together. The love of neighbours entails such group connection. Love is considered as faithfulness and loyalty towards the group in whom one is embedded. The welfare of the group was the concern of each member of the group. Loving one's neighbour implies promoting, protecting and if needed, restoring a person's honour and status within the community (Meier, 2009:492).

Reading the Matthean Gospel it seems that Jesus, and for that matter the Matthean community, had a broader view of the group that should be loved than what the Jews commonly thought. From Matthew's text, it seems that the Jews[311] limited neighbourly love to Israelites or fellow members of the cultic community (Meier, 2009:492). In the Matthean tradition, however, the notion of a neighbour (ὁ πλησίος) is broadened to include people that the Jews usually would regard as outsiders. This is clear from Jesus' command in the sixth antithesis to love one's enemy "... for the Father in heaven causes his sun to rise on the evil and the good, and sends rain on the righteous and the unrighteous" (Matt. 5:43-48) and the Golden Rule, "do to others what you would have them do to you" (Matt. 7:12). In light of the Great Commission in Matt. 28:18-20, it seems that the Matthean community advocated gentile mission. This must have been controversial in Jewish communities. In a Hellenistic culture within the Roman Empire the Jews struggled to maintain their unique identity, there was a strong tendency towards exclusiveness by drawing strict lines between their communities and outsiders. This must have created much tension between the Jews and the Matthean community, who crossed these lines because of their mission-mindedness.

In Deut. 19:18 LXX ὡς σεαυτόν (as yourself) is interpreted as direct object: love your neighbour as you love yourself (Luz, 2001b:83). According to some traditional Jewish understanding loving oneself was commendable (Wis. 19:8). According to the *Targum Yerushalmi* 1, reference to "as yourself" does not imply surrendering yourself, but is intended to overcome inequalities and injustices in the community. However, *Baba Mesia* 62a records the words of Rabbi Akiba taking self-love even a step further: "Your own life takes precedence over the life of your neighbour".

The research of Malina and Neyrey (1996:153-201) on the embeddedness of each individual into a society has added perspective to the love of oneself. As group-orientated persons the main concern of the individual was that of his/her group. The welfare of the group assures the welfare of each member of the group. Self-love is therefore incorporated in love for one's group. Meier

---

[311] At least those Jews with whom Matthew's community interacted.

(2009:492) provides further light on the implication of ὡς σεαυτόν (as yourself). Since the neighbour should be regarded as a fellow-member of the cultic community, the fellow member should enjoy similar rights, privileges, support and honour that the person that is addressed in the command expects from his/her community.

Reading self-love in Matthew from this perspective shows that Jesus' teachings must have been quite controversial. Jesus broadens the boundaries of love and therefore also the exposure of the self. In the Sermon on the Mount Jesus teaches that one should love one's enemy (Matt. 5:43-47). Such love crosses the traditional boundaries of love. Jesus also commands his followers not to resist an evil person, but to turn the other cheek (Matt. 5:38-42). But there is a good reason for this. It is for the sake of the new community that gathers around Jesus as the leading personage of this group. Matthew describes how Jesus was willing to lay down his life to give it as ransom to many (Matt. 20:26-28) so that this new community could be established. Jesus expects his followers to be willing to sacrifice themselves if needed to follow Him and for the sake of this community (Matt. 10:37-39 and 16:24-26). On the other hand Jesus teaches "do to others what you would have them to do to you" (Matt. 7:12). Though Matthew's Jesus does not propagate an unconditional self-denial, He proposes a willingness to do so for the sake of the broadening of the community of his followers in whom the individual is embedded. While Matthew's Jesus accuses the teachers of the Law and Pharisees of being hypocrites in their attempt to win a single convert (Matt. 23:15), He defines neighbourly love in such a way that it enhances his missional drive (cf. Matt. 28:19).

The following figure illustrates the double love commandment within Matthew's Gospel. The "self" expresses his/her love to God in a vertical dimension and to the neighbour in a horizontal dimension. The commandment to horizontal love, however, crosses the boundaries of the community to reach even the enemies, people considered to be bad, and the gentiles.

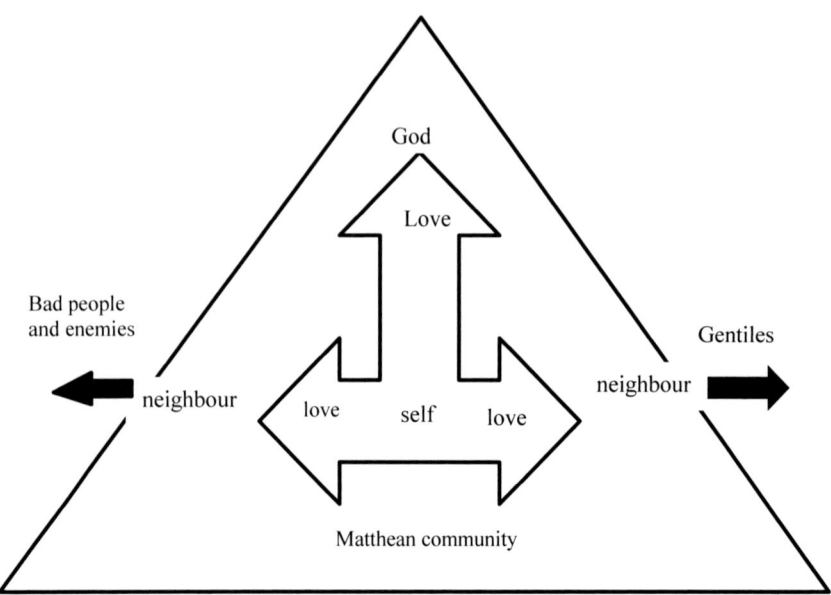

Figure 5: The double love commandment for the Matthean community

10.5.3 All the Law and the Prophets hang on the double love commandment

Matthew's Jesus concludes[312] his response with "ἐν ταύταις ταῖς δυσὶν ἐντολαῖς ὅλος ὁ νόμος κρέμαται καὶ οἱ προφῆται" (all the Law and the Prophets hang on these two commandments) (Matt. 22:40). This reference to the Law and the Prophets closely links this double love commandment to two other passages in which this reference is also made, namely Jesus' foundational statement on the Law (Matt. 5:17[313]) and his admonishment that one should do to others what one wants others to do to oneself (Matt. 7:12[314]) in the Sermon on the Mount. Jesus confirms that these two commandments are nothing new when compared to Israel's Bible. As a matter of fact, they are its fulfilment.

---

[312] As indicated before, verse 40 could probably also be a comment made by Matthew on the great commandments.

[313] Matt. 5:15 reads: "'Do not think that I have come to abolish the Law or the Prophets; I have not come to abolish them but to fulfil them".

[314] Matt. 7:12 reads: "So in everything, do to others what you would have them do to you, for this sums up the Law and the Prophets".

The direct combination of Deut. 6:5 and Lev. 19:18 does not appear in Jewish writings, though it is suggested in some of them (Gerhardsson, 1976:146; Luz, 2001b:84). In the Letter to Aristeas 131, Philo places the two tablets of the Decalogue respectively under two headings, the first being εὐσέβεια (piety) and ὁσιότης (devoutness), and the second φιλανθρωπία (kindness) and δικαιοσύνη (righteousness). Philo (*Spec. Leg.* 2.63) regarded εὐσέβεια (piety) / ὁσιότης (devoutness) and φιλανθρωπία (kindness) / δικαιοσύνη (righteousness) as the two κεφάλαια (headings) of the divine δόγματα (teachings). The *Sipre Deut.* 32.29 regarded the fear of God and the works of love as the centre of the *Torah*.

"Hang" (κρεμάννυμι) refers to a rabbinic formulation (Donaldson, 1995:689-709). This expression refers to the image of something depending on an overarching principle, like a door hanging on its hinges[315] (Luz, 2001b:85). Lohmeyer (1967:329) has fittingly called the double love commandment the "double peg" on which the entire *Torah* and Prophets depend. Osborne (2010:824) has argued that this is fulfilment language, similar to Paul's words in Rom. 13:10: "Therefore love is the fulfilment of the law". All Scripture is an exposition of the ideals expressed in Deut. 6:5 and Lev. 19:18 (Turner, 2008:536). All the commandments of the *Torah* and Prophets are somehow related to the commandment to love God and to love one's neighbour. While keeping this big commandment, one also has to keep the small commandments (cf. Matt. 5:17-19 and 23:23). These two commandments form the basis for all relationships and ethics. Hagner (1995:647) has fittingly remarked: "This is a way of saying that the commandments of the Law and the teaching of the prophets cannot be fulfilled apart from the twofold love commandment" and Barth (1963:77) has written: "The whole law and the prophets can be exegetically deduced from the command to love God and the neighbour, they 'hang' exegetically on these". This statement probably reflects the reaction of the Matthean community against what they experienced as the casuistry of the Pharisees (cf. Matt. 23:23ff) (Hultgren, 1974:377).

These two commandments form the "hermeneutic programme" for the understanding and application of the *Torah* and Prophets in the Matthean gospel (Gerhardsson, 1976:129-150). According to Matthew, the interpretation and application of the books of the Bible of Israel should be guided by the two commandments of love. It forms the "canon of interpretation" (Bornkamm,

---

[315] *B. Ber.* 63a uses the same expression, stating that Prov. 3:6 forms the text on which all *Torah* principles depend and *Ex. Rab.* on Exod. 21:1 states that the whole *Torah* "hangs" on justice.

1954:93) which should steer all the exegesis of *Torah* and the Prophets. This is probably also the guiding principle Matthew proposes and expects from his community when interpreting those documents.

The similarity between Jesus' teaching on the *Torah* in Matt. 22:34-40 and the Sermon on the Mount (Matt. 5-7) is significant. Both of these teachings describe the close connection between the love of God and the love of one's neighbour. Furthermore, both these passages refer to the "Law and the Prophets". The phrase, the Law and the Prophets, forms an *inclusio* of Matt. 5:17-7:12 and the *conclusio* of Matt. 22:34-40.

10.6. CONCLUSION

The double love commandment can be regarded as fundamental to Matthew's Jesus' teaching on the *Torah* as the Matthean Jesus states that all the Law and the Prophets hang on these two commandments. This statement probably parallels the *Shema* (Deut. 6:4-9) in importance in the Gospel. McKnight (2004:viii) has called it "the Jesus creed", and the vision of Jesus. McKnight (2004:viii) has summarized this vision of Jesus as: "A spiritually formed person loves God by following Jesus and loves others". While the expert of the Law challenges Jesus to distinguish between or rank the commandments, Jesus explains in his riposte the coherence and centre of God's will. The double love commandment epitomizes the *Torah* and forms the overarching principle to which all the commandments are connected and should be interpreted. It can be assumed that the double love commandment also stands central to Matthean ethics. As group-oriented people, the ancient Mediterranean people saw love towards God as implying faithfulness and loyalty towards his people. Piety towards God manifests in faithfulness and loyalty towards the group in which one is embedded. In this embedded group, love has both a vertical dimension, focusing on God as the basic personage in whom all are embedded, and a horizontal dimension, focusing on fellow members of the embedded community. These two dimensions are closely related. One cannot love God without loving one's neighbour, or the other way around. One's love of God motivates one's love for neighbours. Loving community-directed ethical behaviour is rooted in a loving relationship with God. Love of God or love of one's neighbour cannot be absorbed in one another. Though they are inseparable, they are different. Loving God is not the same as loving one's neighbour and love is more than human ethics.

Interpreting the double love commandments in both the original and the Matthean contexts, it becomes clear that love does not imply a mere feeling or mystical flight into union with God. It implies knowledge and obedience of God and his commandments. In its vertical dimension love implies reverence, obedience and commitment to God. In its horizontal dimension love implies unselfish acting towards others with their well-being as goal.

The double commandment on love is no new principle given by Jesus. Both these commandments find their roots in the Bible of Israel. Though the direct combination of these two commandments does not appear in Jewish interpretation, Jewish writers did associate them with one another and with the two tablets of the Decalogue respectively.

In Matthew Jesus' teaching about loving one's neighbour differs from traditional Jewish teachings. While the Jews predominantly limited neighbourly love to fellow Jews, proselytes or aliens within their borders, Jesus taught love beyond such borders. Jesus instructed his disciples to go out and make disciples of all nations (Matt. 28:19). People of all nations had to be baptized in the name of the Father and the Son and the Holy Spirit. Thus they would be embedded in the community in which the Father, Son and Holy Spirit form the basic personages. Love even had to be extended towards enemies (Matt. 5:43). Loving enemies has implications for self-loving. Jesus takes self-love for granted as model for the way one should love one's neighbour, but extends neighbourhood to include people who the Jews regarded as outsiders. The specific connotation that self-love had in a group-orientated society implied that one had to be willing to sacrifice oneself for the benefit of the group, as Jesus did (Matt. 20:28). One should be willing to turn the other cheek for the sake of the Kingdom of God (Matt. 5:39). In a group-orientated community, one unselfishly had to seek the good of other members for the sake of the group.

Jesus' answer to the expert of the Law about the greatest commandment is closely related to his teaching about the Law in the Sermon on the Mount. In both cases Jesus confirms that He upholds the Law and the Prophets and that He ensures their fulfilment. Jesus has no intention of abolishing the Law.

It is clear that the double love commandment is central to Matthean ethics. It seems as if the Matthean Pharisees had a casuistic approach to the Law and the Prophets, while the Matthean community viewed the double love commandment as the basis for understanding the Law and the Prophets and from which particularities proceed.

With this short narrative Matthew obviously wants to define the lifestyle of his community. They were not to retreat from this world. Love of God should be demonstrated in faithful obedience to God's will and active compassion with people. The Gospel concludes with the assurance that Jesus had received all authority and had thus become an important personage in the community. People of the Matthean community were expected to obey everything Jesus has commanded them (Matt. 28:20), which includes his teaching on love.

CHAPTER 11

TO OBEY THE WORDS OF TEACHERS OF THE LAW AND PHARISEES, BUT NOT TO DO WHAT THEY DO (MATT. 23:3)

11.1 INTRODUCTION

The instruction of Jesus to the crowds in Matt. 23:3 to obey and do everything the teachers of the law and the Pharisees tell them (πάντα οὖν ὅσα ἐὰν εἴπωσιν ὑμῖν ποιήσατε καὶ τηρεῖτε) is the only case in Matthew where the words of the Jewish leaders are seemingly portrayed in a positive light. If this portrayal indeed is positive, it seems to stand in tension with how Matthew construes these leaders and their teachings in the rest of the gospel (e.g. Matt. 5:20[316]; 15:3–6[317], 15:14[318]; 16:11–12[319]). Jesus' positive remark furthermore seemingly stands in contrast to Matt. 28:20[320], where Jesus claims all authority to himself and instructs his disciples to teach all the nations to obey everything he has commanded them. The wording in Matt. 23:3 and Matt. 28:20 is so similar that some kind of relationship between these verses seems probable. Furthermore, the Jewish leaders receive very harsh criticism in the verses that follow in Matt.

---

[316] Matt. 5:20: "For I tell you that unless your righteousness surpasses that of the Pharisees and the teachers of the law, you will certainly not enter the kingdom of heaven."

[317] Matt 15:3-6: "Jesus replied, 'And why do you break the command of God for the sake of your tradition? …. Thus you nullify the word of God for the sake of your tradition."

[318] Matt. 15:14: "They are blind guides. If the blind lead the blind, both will fall into a pit."

[319] Matt. 16:11-12: "Be on your guard against the yeast of the Pharisees and Sadducees. Then they understood that he was not telling them to guard against the yeast used in bread, but against the teaching of the Pharisees and Sadducees."

[320] Matt. 28:18-20: "Then Jesus came to them and said, 'All authority in heaven and on earth has been given to me. Therefore go and make disciples of all nations, baptizing them in the name of the Father and of the Son and of the Holy Spirit, and teaching them to obey everything I have commanded you."

23:3. How is it then possible that Jesus encourages the crowds and his disciples to adhere and do everything they tell them?

Does Jesus at this stage endorse their teachings of the *Torah* and their *halakha*, and by doing so contradict himself? Should this statement in the gospel be regarded as a remnant of the pre-Matthean tradition that the author inattentively incorporated into the text, though it is out of keeping with the rest of the gospel? Does it belong to a pre-Easter sentiment within the Jesus-movement before the development of their critical view on Pharisaic Judaism? Is the phrase, "all their teachings" an exaggeration so that Jesus is actually only referring to part of their teachings? Does Jesus make an ironic pronouncement? Does Jesus insinuate that the Jewish teachers of the Law are inconsistent with their teachings, that their teachings are confusing? Does it demonstrate that the Jewish teachers are ignorant of their own teachings, which are indeed correct? Do the teachers teach the correct stuff, though their conduct contradicts their teachings? Does Jesus illustrate that their own teachings condemn them? Does Jesus differentiate between their words directly from the *Torah* and from their *halakha*? Or should we accept that the *halakhic* traditions laid down by the Pharisees remained valid and provided the Matthean community with practical ways to obey the *Torah*, and that Jesus only criticizes their neglect of the "weightier matters" of the Law?

To choose between these suggestions is not simple, and there may even be more options for interpreting these words of Jesus. This investigation follows an intra-textual approach to reach an informed conclusion on the meaning of this statement. The intra-textual approach implies that this statement would be read with consideration of the context provided by similar statements in the same document and its setting within the immediate development of the plot of this gospel. Such an intra-textual setting clarifies the development of Matthew's argument. The interpretation is thus constructed by making use of cues from in the text itself.

The broader context is first examined (Matt. 21–25), after which the context is narrowed down to the immediate (Matt. 23).

11.2 INCREASING CONFRONTATION DURING FIRST FOUR DAYS OF THE PASSION WEEK (MATT. 21:1–25:46)

11.2.1 Intensifying confrontation

It is significant that this pronouncement is embedded in a narrative[321] where Jesus is in constant confrontation with the religious leaders in Jerusalem (Talbert, 2010:245). Jesus' journey to Jerusalem is described in Matt. 19–20 and the beginning of Matt. 21 describes how he enters the place of his destiny. The powers of darkness are set to erupt as the passion narrative commences (Osborne, 2010:751). Matt. 21:1–22:46 describes the intense disputes during the first four days of the Passion week, followed by the final period of Jesus' passion in Matt. 26:1–27:56.

Matt. 21:1–25:46 forms a literary unit (Garland, 1979) and forms the context for Matt. 23. Wilson (2004:69) demonstrates how the theme of the coming King, first humbly (Matt. 21:1–17) and then in glory (Matt. 25:31–46), forms an *inclusio* around Matt. 21–25. This unit is further defined by the citation of Ps. 118:26 in Matt. 21:9 and again in 23:39 to form a bracket denoting these chapters (Viviano, 1990:7). The central message seems to be that the Pharisees, who put themselves on a legal and moral high ground and who constantly challenge the authority Jesus as teacher, are on trial themselves. Their hypocrisy and unrighteousness will be exposed and they will be judged for it.

It seems that this major literary unit is composed of two rhetorical units (Scholtz, 2015:1). The first unit comprises of Matt. 21:1–23:39, with the Messianic greeting as its *inclusio* (Matt. 21:9; 23:39). The second unit comprises Matt. 24:1–25:46, with its *inclusio* being Jesus exiting from the temple and subsequently sitting on the Mount of Olives, juxtaposed with his return to the Mount of Olives and his sitting on the throne of his glory as King and Judge (Matt. 24:1–3; 25:31–46; cf. Zech 14:4; Ac 1:9–12). Although part of a larger rhetorical unit (21:1–25:46), the change in setting from the temple to the Mount of Olives, the change in audience to only Christ's disciples, and the distinct (but related) themes separate Matt. 24:1–25:46 as rhetorical unit (cf. Carson 1995:469; France 2007:768; Turner 2008:543–544). Matt. 21:1–23:39 describes the judgement of the religious leaders and ἡ γενεὰ αὕτη (this generation) in Israel who rejected the Messiahship of Jesus at his first coming. In Matt. 24:1–25:46 the scope moves to a worldwide judgement of all nations who reject the coming King at the end of the age (cf. Blomberg 1992:351; Wilson 2004:254–255).

---

[321] This narrative is kept together with two inclusions: a reference to "Mount of Olives" (21:1 and 24:3) and the statement: "Blessed is he who comes in the name of the Lord!" (Matt. 21:9 and 23:39).

The current investigation is limited to the first of these two rhetorical units. The sections of this unit can broadly be identified as follows:

Commencement of the Passion week (Matt. 21:1–22)
Jesus' humble entry and enthusiastic acclaim (Matt. 21:1–11)
Judgement of the temple (Matt. 21:12–17)
Cursing of the fig tree (Matt. 21:18–22)
Controversies in the temple court (Matt. 21:23–22:46)
Introduction to the controversies (Matt. 21:23–27)
Challenge of Jesus' authority (Matt. 21:23–27)
Three judgement parables (Matt. 21:28–22:14)
1. Parable of two sons (Matt. 21:28–32)
2. Parable of the wicked tenants (Matt. 21:33–46)
3. Parable of the wedding banquet (Matt. 22:1–14)
Three challenging questions posed by religious leaders (Matt. 22:15–40)
1. Question on paying taxes to the Caesar (Matt. 22:15–22)
2. Question on marriage after resurrection (Matt. 22:23–33)
3. Question on the greatest commandment (Matt. 22:34–40)
Decisive question posed by Jesus (Matt. 22:41–46)
Whose son is the Christ (Matt. 22:41–46)
Guilt and judgement of Israel (Matt. 23:1–25:46)
Seven woes upon the teachers of the Law and the Pharisees (Matt. 23:1–39)

Table 55: Broad outline of Matt. 21-25

11.2.2 Commencement of the Passion Week (Matt. 21:1–22)

The description of the Passion Week commences with Jesus' humble entry into Jerusalem, where he is met with enthusiastic acclaim (Matt. 21:1–11). This entry illuminates his lowliness, but also his authority (Bruner, 1990:353; Gundry, 1994:409). Jesus' entry parodies the Roman triumphal entries (Carter, 2000b:67) and echoes the entry of Solomon[322] as Jewish royal figure and all wise king, riding on a donkey into town to be anointed as David's successor (1 Kings 1:32–40). Reference is made to Zech. 9:9, a text that was generally acknowledged as Messianic (Keener, 2002:97). Jesus enters the city triumphal as Zechariah's king of peace. This Solomonic tradition in 1 Kings 1 and the message of the Messiah in Zech. 9:9–10 guide the way Matthew portrays Jesus

---

[322] The name Solomon has symbolic meaning, as it is derived from *shalom*. Solomon was David's peace child and royal figure who was the wise king of peace (Witherington, 2006:388).

(Witherington, 2006:387–389). Jesus is the wise King and Messiah, and his wisdom exceeds that of Solomon, but his wisdom is increasingly challenged by the Jewish religious leaders.

Jesus' entry is immediately followed by his cleansing of the temple (Matt. 21:12–17). Jesus is depicted in the form of an enacted parable as the righteous and mighty judge who accuses the practices of religious leadership in the temple courts[323]. He brings wholeness and new life as He heals the blind and lame who were excluded from the temple (Carter, 2000b:67). Obviously this cleansing was a public insult to the religious elite who exercised control over the temple. Jesus challenged their honour, which obviously would evoke revenge from them (Keener, 2002:98).

The scene to follow is that of the cursing of the fig tree[324] (Matt. 21:18–22), the only negative miracle in the gospel, which pictures the coming judgement of Israel. The link between the cleansing of the temple and the cursing of the fig tree makes the incidents most dramatic symbols of God's rejection of the Jewish religious leaders (Gundry, 1994:415). The cursed fig tree represents "this wicked and adulterous generation" in Israel (Toussaint 1980:245) on whom "all these things" of Matt. 23:34−36 come because they have rejected the true Christ. The suddenness of the withering of the fig tree leaves the disciples amazed.

Jesus's actions set the table for the controversy dialogues to follow. Jesus is the wise prophet and teacher, similar to, but greater than Solomon the temple builder, for this is Jesus who is offended by temple practices and announces the end of the corrupt temple and religious leaders (Witherington, 2006:389).

11.2.3 Controversies in the temple court (Matt. 21:23–22:46)

Following Jesus' entry into Jerusalem, the events of two days are narrated with Jesus entering and leaving the temple (Matt. 21:12–22 and 21:23–24:2). As Jesus is about to exit the temple, he does not refer to it as ὁ οἶκός μου (my house) anymore like in Matt. 21:13, but as ὁ οἶκος ὑμῶν (your house), which

---

[323] According to Matt. 26:61, two chief priests or members of the Sanhedrin mention Jesus' words of the temple being destroyed and rebuilt. 2 Sam. 7:13 promised that the Davidic messiah would one day build the eschatological temple as Solomon had done before (Witherington, 2006:396).

[324] In Micah 7:1 a fruitless and barren fig tree symbolizes morally and spiritually barren people of God.

will be left desolate. Every time Jesus leaves the temple, he makes a severe pronouncement of judgement (Matt. 21:19[325] and 24:1, 2[326]). The theme of judgement then continues in following passages that deal with the final judgement (Matt. 24:3–25:46). Matt. 23 forms the conclusion to Jesus' second day at the temple (Matt. 21:23–24:2), but like a Janus-like hinge, also forms the introduction to the Olivet discourse on the end time judgement (Matt. 24–25) (Viviano, 1990:8). The theme of judgement on the religious establishment (Matt. 23:12–33) and the demise of the temple (Matt. 23:35–38) continues in Matt. 24:24–25:30 and 24:1–3, 15 respectively (Keener, 1999:535).

The religious leaders who were publically dishonoured tried to recover their honour by publicly challenging Jesus (Keener, 2002:99). As was typical of debate in antiquity, challenging questions are met with clever responses. Matt. 21:23–22:46 deals with various challenges by the religious leaders to dishonour Jesus and to contest his authority to teach. With challenging questions the religious leaders attempt to expose Jesus as an unworthy teacher, though without success. The rivals Jesus battled against became increasingly more skilled; it began with the chief priests and elders (Matt. 21:23), the disciples of the Pharisees and Herodians (Matt. 22:15), Sadducees (Matt. 22:23) and an expert of the Law (Matt. 22:35) (Simmonds, 2009:338).

The challenge of Jesus' authority opens with the question of the chief priests and elders of the people on the basis of Jesus' authority to teach, that is to act as a rabbi (Matt. 21:23), while the question in Mark revolves around Jesus' authority to cleanse the temple (Mark 11:28). Jesus responds by arguing that his authority has the same origin as that of John, namely from God (Matt. 21:24–25). The chief priests and elders of the people are unable to respond, and in such a way Matthew emphasizes the superior authority and knowledge of Jesus.

Jesus proceeds by telling three judgement parables; of the two sons (Matt. 21:28–32), the wicked tenants (Matt. 21:33–46) and of the wedding banquet (Matt. 22:1–14). The parable of the two sons (Matt. 21:28–32) is unique to Matthew and opens a series of this three parables. Though the second and third

---

[325] Matt. 21:19: "Seeing a fig tree by the road, he went up to it but found nothing on it except leaves. Then he said to it, "May you never bear fruit again!" Immediately the tree withered."

[326] Matt. 24:1-2: "Jesus left the temple and was walking away when his disciples came up to him to call his attention to its buildings. 'Do you see all these things?' he asked. 'Truly I tell you, not one stone here will be left on another; every one will be thrown down.'"

parables have parallels, they are not side-by-side as in Matthew. All three of these parables deal with the way Jesus is rejected (Gundry, 1994:421). By arranging these parable consecutively, Matthew emphasizes the controversy and rejection that took place.

The parable of the two sons (Matt. 21:28–32) falls out in two parts, the polemical parable (Matt. 21:28–30) and its allegorical application (Matt. 21:31–32) (Davies & Allison, 2004c:164). The first son represents the tax collectors and sinners who repented and came to obey God through the ministry of John. The second son represents the chief priests and elders, who despite their religious profession, disobeyed God by not believing John. The second halve opens with Jesus' polemic question on which of the two did the will of the father. The priests and the elders approve behaviour that is unlike their own. The parable concludes with the question of why the chief priests and elders do not repent as the first son, and why they did not believe John.

The parable of wicked tenants (Matt. 21:33–46) divides into the parable as such (Matt. 21:33–39), followed by the application (Matt. 21:40–46). Jesus reminds the religious leaders that they are mere custodians of God. This parable combines the motif of God being the benevolent landowner with that of the religious leaders who challenge his honour and test his patience. The murder of the prophets finds its climax in the rebellion and killing of God's Son. The conclusion of the parable is filled with irony (Matt. 21:45–46) (Davies & Allison, 2004c:187). Shortly after answering Jesus on what would happen with those who killed the owner's son, they realize that Jesus is referring to them. Their response is to scheme how they could get rid of Jesus, in that way inviting the same fate over themselves as that of the wicked tenants.

The parable of the wedding banquet (Matt. 22:1–14), which has a parallel in Luke, carries the polemic with the Jewish leaders further. The parable falls out in the parable (Matt. 22:1–13b) and the application (Matt. 22:13c–14). The parable contains two parallel sequences (Matt. 22:2–7 and 8–13), each opening with invitations, and closes with punishment. The whole parable is dominated by the speech of the king, indicating his authority (Davies & Allison, 2004c:194). The reader automatically identifies the king as God, and his son, the bridegroom, as Jesus. The royal wedding represents the eschatological banquet, and the murder of the servants, an absurdly inexplicable response to the king's repetitive kind invitations, represents the murder of the prophets and of Jesus.

The Jewish religious leaders respond to these three parables by posing three hostile questions to Jesus: on paying taxes to the Caesar (Matt. 22:15–22), on marriage after the resurrection (Matt. 22:23–33), and on the greatest commandment (Matt. 22:34–40). All three of these scenes portray the negative character of these leaders.

Firstly, the Pharisees and Herodians challenge Jesus (Matt. 22:15–22). They hypocritically address Him as διδάσκαλε (teacher) and ironically speak the truth about Jesus οἴδαμεν ὅτι ἀληθὴς εἶ καὶ τὴν ὁδὸν τοῦ Θεοῦ ἐν ἀληθείᾳ διδάσκεις (we know that you are a man of integrity and that you teach the way of God in accordance with the truth) (Matt. 22:16). Jesus gives no simple "yes" or "no" to their question, but instructs them to weigh the demands of God and the Caesar; they should render to the Caesar what belongs to him, and to God what belongs to him. Jesus does not only avoid a well-conceived trap, but also advances his teaching. Instead of trapping Jesus, the Pharisees and Herodians are trapped by him (Davies & Allison, 2004c:216). They are unable to offer any rebuttal. They simply have to accept their defeat. The reader realizes that Jesus teaches with unmatched authority.

Following the political question posed by the Pharisees and Herodians, the Sadducees follow with a theological riddle (Matt. 22:23–33). While these parties oppose each other regarding the resurrection, they are united in opposing Jesus. The Sadducees address Jesus as διδάσκαλε (teacher), but they surely do not seek instruction, but maliciously and sarcastically set a trap for Jesus. Their question clearly implies that they reject the resurrection and find polyandry unacceptable. Jesus treats their question as the shameful ignorance and bad theology, πλανᾶσθε μὴ εἰδότες τὰς γραφὰς μηδὲ τὴν δύναμιν τοῦ Θεοῦ (you are in error because you do not know the Scriptures or the power of God) (Matt. 22:29) (Davies & Allison, 2004c:226). This challenging scene is concluded by emphasizing the authority of Jesus as teacher, as the crowds were astonished with his teaching καὶ ἀκούσαντες οἱ ὄχλοι ἐξεπλήσσοντο ἐπὶ τῇ διδαχῇ αὐτοῦ (when the crowds heard this, they were astonished at his teaching) (Matt. 22:33).

As representative of the Pharisees, one of them, an expert in the Law (νομικὸς), continues the series of hostile challenges with his question on the most important commandment (Matt. 22:34–40). Again Jesus responds in such a manner as not to be trapped. He uses two summaries of the Law, the commandment to love God and to love one's neighbour.

Concluding the three challenges, Jesus ends his defensive approach in which he shows that he can answer the most difficult questions by posing a question to his opponents about his identity, David's Son or David's Lord (Matt. 22:41–46). His question is a riddle based on Ps 110:1. The opponents are speechless as they are unable to answer Jesus, which forms a climax of the crescendo of the previous challenges. The result is that the debate with presumed learned opponents is ended and the table is set for the series of woe-sayings to follow.

The teaching authority of Jesus is clearly contrasted with the impotence of his opponents, who regard themselves as learned. By describing these disputes, Matthew confirms the authority and trustworthiness of Jesus in contrast with the lack of authority and deceitfulness of the Jewish religious leaders. Jesus clearly emerges as the victor in these disputes. Jesus' successful refutation of the challenges is mentioned repeatedly:

- καὶ ἀκούσαντες ἐθαύμασαν, καὶ ἀφέντες αὐτὸν ἀπῆλθαν (when they [the disciples of the Pharisees and Herodians] heard this, they were amazed. So they left him and went away.) (Matt 22:22);
- καὶ ἀκούσαντες οἱ ὄχλοι ἐξεπλήσσοντο ἐπὶ τῇ διδαχῇ αὐτοῦ (when the crowds heard this, they were astonished at his teaching" (Matt. 22:33);
- Οἱ δὲ Φαρισαῖοι ἀκούσαντες ὅτι ἐφίμωσεν τοὺς Σαδδουκαίους συνήχθησαν ἐπὶ τὸ αὐτό (hearing that He had silenced the Sadducees, the Pharisees got together) (Matt. 22:34); and
- καὶ οὐδεὶς ἐδύνατο ἀποκριθῆναι αὐτῷ λόγον, οὐδὲ ἐτόλμησέν τις ἀπ' ἐκείνης τῆς ἡμέρας ἐπερωτῆσαι αὐτὸν οὐκέτι (no one could say a word in reply, and from that day on no one dared to ask him any more questions) (Matt. 22:46).

Matthew emphasizes Jesus' superiority by depicting the reactions of the disciples of the Pharisees and Herodians (Matt. 22:22), the crowds (Matt. 22:23) and the Pharisees (Matt. 22:34) with emotive wording. The challenging Sadducees are silenced (Matt. 22:34) and no one can say a word in reply or dares to ask him any more questions (Matt. 22:46).

These disputes where Jesus emerge as the honourable victor set the table for Jesus' teaching in the temple about the Pharisees' bad teaching, hypocrisy and lack of righteousness, which would lead towards the judgement of the Pharisees and Jerusalem (Matt. 23:1–24:2) (Talbert, 2010:250).

11.3 CRITICISM ON THE TEACHERS OF THE LAW AND PHARISEES (MATT. 23)

Jesus's pronouncement on the teachings of the religious leaders opens the last of Matthew's five great discourses in the gospel[327]. The symmetry between the first and last discourses is noteworthy and they frame Jesus's public ministry Matthew. While the first great discourse opens with blessings (μακάριοι οἱ – Matt. 5:3–12), the last contains a series of seven woes (οὐαὶ δὲ ὑμῖν – Matt. 23:13–32). These two discourses are of similar length. Both of these sermons are associated with a mountain and Jesus takes the seated position of a teacher (Matt. 5:2 and 24:3) (Gundry, 1994:453; Osborne, 2010:831). Jesus is presented as the new Moses. As Moses came down the mountain to present the Law, Jesus went up the mountain to teach the Law authoritatively (Sermon on the Mount), and to expose false and hypocritical practices regarding the Law on Mount Olives (Matt. 23–25).

While conflict between Jesus and the religious leaders is central throughout Matthew's plot[328], the conflict intensifies significantly in the final discourse (Keener, 1999:536; Repschinski, 2000). In this way Matt. 23 prepares the reader for the passion narrative where Jesus is cruelly rejected by the Jewish leaders (Davies & Allison, 2004c:262).

Luz (1968:96) goes as far as remarking: "With its woes and its unjust wholesale judgement about scribes and Pharisees, Matthew 23 is the unloveliest chapter in the gospel," a sentiment Viviano (1990:3) shares. Carter (2000b:66) describes it as "the bleakest spot" in Matthew's gospel. Esler (2015:39–59) is of the opinion that this challenging text is best understood in terms of intergroup conflict

---

[327] The five great discourses in the gospel are: the Sermon on the Mount (Matt. 5-7), the missionary charge (Matt. 10:5-42), the parables discourse (Matt. 13:3-52), instructions to the community (Matt. 18:3-35), and the woes and eschatological discourse (Matt. 23-25) (Riesner, 1978:177-178). Combrink (1983:61-90) identifies a chiastic structure between these discourses: the Sermon on the Mount (Matt. 5-7) is parallel to the woes and the eschatological discourse (Matt. 23-25). The missionary charge (Matt. 10) is parallel to the community discourse (Matt. 18). The parables discourse (Matt. 13) is framed by the above-mentioned parallels. The woes and the eschatological discourse (Matt. 23-25) approximately balances the first discourse, the Sermon on the Mount (Matt. 5-7) (Keener, 1999:535; Osborne, 2010:831; Viviano, 1990:9).

[328] Kingsbury (1995:169) regards the religious leaders more central to Matthew's plot than the disciples, as this conflict forms the focus of the plot. Keener (2002:103) concurs and opines that this may be because the successors of the teachers of the Law and the Pharisees were the main Jewish opposition that the addressees faced in Syria-Palestine.

between a branch of the Christ-movement and a Judean outsider group. He investigates the passage in terms of social identity theory and describes Matt. 23 as one of the most extreme forms of intergroup conflict. He opines that this passage is the product of the evangelist and not of the historical Jesus, as he regards the polemic as untypical of the historical Jesus (Esler, 2015:56). Kümmel (1967:146–147) remarks that the zealous polemic in Matt. 23 distorts the reality and spirit of Jesus.

The continuous theme of judgement is significant and particularly intense in this final discourse. Obviously this should therefore be taken into account with the interpretation of Matt. 23:3.

In honour and shame societies, as in New Testament times, it was a common phenomenon to challenge the honour of an opponent and to respond with an equal challenge in return (de Silva, 2004:128–130; Malina & Rohrbauch, 1992:42; Witherington, 2013:47). Such a challenge had to be played in public to be effective in gaining honour or imposing shame. In the Matthean text the religious leaders' public challenges of Jesus's authority to teach (Matt. 21:23–22:46) are balanced by Jesus's public response with his pronouncements of judgement on the Pharisees and Jerusalem (Matt. 23:1–24:2).

The intensity of the Matthean controversy becomes apparent when considering the probable source material for Matt. 23:1–39. It seems that Mark 12:38–40 formed the impetus for Matt. 23:1–39 (Davies & Allison, 2004c:266). If this is the case, Matthew developed a lengthy polemic of thirty-nine verses based on a mere three verses in Mark.

Mark 12:38–40	Matt. 23:1–39
As he taught, Jesus said (Mark 12:38a)	Then Jesus said to the crowds and to his disciples (Matt. 23:1)
Watch out for the teachers of the law (Mark 12:38b)	So you must be careful to do everything they tell you. But do not do what they do, for they do not practice what they preach (Matt. 23:3)
They like to walk around in flowing robes (Mark 12:38c)	Everything they do is done for people to see: They make their phylacteries wide and the tassels on their garments long (Matt. 23:5)
and be greeted with respect in the marketplaces (Mark 12:38d)	they love to be greeted with respect in the marketplaces and to be called 'Rabbi' by others (Matt. 23:7)

and have the most important seats in the synagogues (Mark 12:39a)	they love the most important seats in the synagogues (Matt. 23:6b)[329]
and the places of honour at banquets (Mark 12:39b).	the place of honour at banquets (Matt. 23:6a)
They devour widows' houses (Mark 12:40a)	
and for a show make lengthy prayers (Mark 12:40b).	Cf. Matt. 23:5
These men will be punished most severely ((Mark 12:40c)	Series of seven "Woe to you …" pronouncements (Matt. 23:13–14, 15, 16–22, 23–24, 25–26, 27–28, 29–32) "You snakes! You brood of vipers! How will you escape being condemned to hell? (Matt. 23:33)

Table 56: Matthew's elaboration on Mark's polemic

From this comparison it is clear that Jesus' criticism in Matthew (Matt. 23:1–24:2[330]) is much more extensive and intense than in Mark.

Jesus's seemingly positive pronouncement on the words of the religious leaders (Matt. 23:3) falls in the first of three sections of Matt. 23, each addressing a different audience (Osborne, 2010:832):

- in Matt. 23:1–12, Jesus warns the crowds and the disciples against the teachers of the Law and the Pharisees;
- in Matt. 23:13–36, he addresses the teachers of the Law and the Pharisees directly in his criticism; and
- in Matt. 23:37–39, he addresses Jerusalem with sorrow lamenting its immanent judgement.

The section is concluded with the pronouncement of a distressing judgement over the temple (Matt. 24:1–2)[331].

---

[329] In Luke's version, this accusation of the Jewish leaders form part of his "woe sayings": (Woe to you Pharisees, because you love the most important seats in the synagogues and respectful greetings in the marketplaces) (Luk. 11:43).

[330] This extended polemical discourse is unique to Matthew, with only a few parallels: Matt. 23:4 // Luk. 11:46; Matt. 23:6-7a // Mark 12:38-39 and Luk. 20:46-47) and Matt. 23:12 // Luk. 14:11 and 19:14.

11.3.1 Addressing the crowds on the hypocrisy of the teachers of the Law and the Pharisees (Matt. 23:1–12)

In his criticism of the teachers of the Law and the Pharisees in Matt. 23:1–12, Jesus addresses the crowds who have heard how these Jewish religious leaders had challenged Jesus, and how he time and again refuted these challenges and wisely emerged as victor (Matt 22:22, 33, 34, 46). Jesus's profile is that of a wise and superior teacher.

Jesus tells the crowds what the teachers of the Law and the Pharisees do (Matt. 23:1–7) and then proceeds to talk about what his disciples should do instead (Matt. 23:8–12). It seems that the main idea is to contrast the pride and hypocrisy of the religious leaders with the humility and servanthood required from Jesus' followers (Osborne, 2010:833).

11.3.1.1 The hypocritical conduct of the teachers of the Law and Pharisees (Matt. 23:1–7)

In the first part of his criticism of the teachers of the Law and the Pharisees, Jesus addresses the crowds and his disciples, τότε ὁ Ἰησοῦς ἐλάλησεν τοῖς ὄχλοις καὶ τοῖς μαθηταῖς αὐτοῦ λέγων (then Jesus said to the crowds and to his disciples) (Matt. 23:1), as in the Sermon on the Mount (Matt. 5:1–2). In contrast to the Sermon on the Mount where these words open the blessings and wise instruction of Jesus, the opening words in Matt. 23 form the introduction of the woes and stern polemic to follow.

The criticism is twofold (Davies & Allison, 2004c:264; Talbert, 2010:256). Firstly, Jesus depicts the hypocritical teaching and conduct of the religious leaders (Matt. 23:2–4) and secondly, their desire for public acclaim (Matt. 23:5–7).

---

[331] Newport (1995:76-79) proposes that the source for Matt. 23:2-31 is a pre-70 CE Jewish-Christian tract, and that Matt. 23:32-39 is a later redaction. He argues that Matt. 23:2-31 exhibits an *intra muros* setting, while he assumes that Matthew writes from an *extra muros* position. He argues that Matt. 23:2-31 describes customs and practices of first-century Jews, which indicates an intra-Jewish debate. He regards the *Sitz im Leben* of this section similar to that of the Sermon on the Mount and as being different to the rest of the gospel (Newport, 1995:157). In such a way Newport escapes the difficulty to fit this troublesome passage within the gospel as a whole. However, as difficult it is to explain, this passage does form part of the text and needs interpretation.

Matt. 23:2–4: Hypocritical teaching and conduct	
Ἐπὶ τῆς Μωϋσέως καθέδρας ἐκάθισαν οἱ γραμματεῖς καὶ οἱ Φαρισαῖοι.	The teachers of the law and the Pharisees sit in Moses' seat.
πάντα οὖν ὅσα ἐὰν εἴπωσιν ὑμῖν ποιήσατε καὶ τηρεῖτε,	So you must be careful to do everything they tell you.
κατὰ δὲ τὰ ἔργα αὐτῶν μὴ ποιεῖτε, λέγουσιν γὰρ καὶ οὐ ποιοῦσιν.	But do not do what they do, for they do not practice what they preach.
δεσμεύουσιν δὲ φορτία βαρέα καὶ ἐπιτιθέασιν ἐπὶ τοὺς ὤμους τῶν ἀνθρώπων, αὐτοὶ δὲ τῷ δακτύλῳ αὐτῶν οὐ θέλουσιν κινῆσαι αὐτά.	They tie up heavy, cumbersome loads and put them on other people's shoulders, but they themselves are not willing to lift a finger to move them.
Matt. 23:5–7: Desire for public acclaim	
πάντα δὲ τὰ ἔργα αὐτῶν ποιοῦσιν πρὸς τὸ θεαθῆναι τοῖς ἀνθρώποις·	Everything they do is done for people to see:
πλατύνουσι γὰρ τὰ φυλακτήρια αὐτῶν καὶ μεγαλύνουσι τὰ κράσπεδα	for they make their phylacteries wide and the tassels on their garments long;
φιλοῦσι δὲ τὴν πρωτοκλισίαν ἐν τοῖς δείπνοις	they love the place of honour at banquets
καὶ τὰς πρωτοκαθεδρίας ἐν ταῖς συναγωγαῖς,	and the most important seats in the synagogues;
καὶ τοὺς ἀσπασμοὺς ἐν ταῖς ἀγοραῖς	and to be greeted with respect in the marketplaces
καὶ καλεῖσθαι ὑπὸ τῶν ἀνθρώπων· Ῥαββί.	and to be called 'Rabbi' by the people.

Table 57: Jesus' twofold criticism of the religious leaders

Jesus remarks that the teachers of the law and the Pharisees are sitting on Moses's seat (ἐπὶ τῆς Μωϋσέως καθέδρας ἐκάθισαν οἱ γραμματεῖς καὶ οἱ Φαρισαῖοι). Though Moses's seat may refer to a physical chair, it is most probably used metaphorically to refer to persons who are considered to have teaching authority[332]. Powell (1995:419–435) lists ten options of what the phrase may refer to, and concludes that it most probably refers to the authority of those who controlled access to the *Torah* scrolls and who could read and interpret them for the people. They occupied a powerful social and religious position in a world where most people were illiterate and copies of the *Torah* were limited. The verb, ἐκάθισαν, is used in the aorist, which most probably

---

[332] Not all Pharisees were authoritative teachers of the Law. Matthew frequently lumps them together. It seems that in Matthew's experience they formed a unified Jewish front of confrontation (Davies & Allison, 2004c:267).

should be read as gnomic, referring to the general claim for authority as made by the religious leaders (Osborne, 2010:835). The Pharisees claimed to be Moses' successors and therefore had the presumption that they were the official interpreters of the *Torah* who could speak with ultimate authority (Davies & Allison, 2004c:268; Gundry, 1994:454; Keener, 2002:103; Viviano, 1990:11). Yet it can also simply mean that they were the only ones who had access the the written *Torah*, as they were sitting on the seat of Moses (Powell, 1995:435)

It seems obvious that this remark should be read against the previous set of challenges set by these religious leaders who were trying to expose Jesus' lack of authority to teach (Matt. 21:23–22:46). The religious leaders presume to have the ultimate authority to read and interpret the *Torah*.

Jesus' instruction to obey the words of the teachers of the Law and the Pharisees, can be interpreted in two differing ways. The one way would be that Jesus ironically refers to their own presumption of being authoritative instructors of the Law[333] (Mason, 1990:363–381). Based on their presumption, Jesus then proceeds to criticize them. If they are as authoritative as they presume to be, the crowds and his disciples should carefully do whatever the religious leaders tell them to do (πάντα οὖν ὅσα ἐὰν εἴπωσιν ὑμῖν ποιήσατε καὶ τηρεῖτε) (Matt. 23:3a)[334]. However, Jesus then immediately continues by warning the crowds and disciples not to do what the religious leaders do, because they do not practice what they say (κατὰ δὲ τὰ ἔργα αὐτῶν μὴ ποιεῖτε, λέγουσιν γὰρ καὶ οὐ ποιοῦσιν) (Matt. 23:3b). This could imply a stern irony by Jesus. The words κατὰ δὲ emphasizes the paradox and irony.

This verse exhibits Matthew's love for parallelisms and his emphasis on the fact that there should be consistency between words and actions (Gundry, 1994:454), which is lacking in the case of these Jewish leaders. In parallel form, Matthean Jesus states the paradox between their presumed positive teachings and their negative conduct.

---

[333] Josephus mentioned that the general populace regarded the Pharisees as the most skilful in interpreting the Jewish laws (Ant. 17:41; Jewish Wars. 1.110; 2.162; Life 191). However, he lamented this fact, as he accused them of not always doing this with pure motives (Talbert, 2010:257).

[334] This command of Jesus echoes the wording of Deut. 17:11 where Moses instructs the Jewish people to adhere to the legal rulings of the priests of the judges of their generations (Rabbinowitz, 2003:432).

Presumed positive teaching:
> πάντα οὖν ὅσα ἐὰν **εἴπωσιν** ὑμῖν
> ποιήσατε καὶ τηρεῖτε,

Negative conduct:
> κατὰ δὲ τὰ ἔργα αὐτῶν μὴ ποιεῖτε,
> **λέγουσιν** γὰρ καὶ οὐ ποιοῦσιν.

This parallel seems to be a reflection on the parable of the disobedient son in Matt. 21:28–32. Therefore it seems as if the imperative of Matt. 23:3a is meant ironically. Though the religious leaders claim to have the authority to interpret the *Torah* accurately, their lives testify to the opposite. Their teachings are insincere and untrustworthy. This results in a harsh accusation of the inconsistency of these teachers. The Matthean Jesus continues to criticize the distorted teachings of the teachers of the Law and their inability to keep the Law correctly, as they neglect the Law for the sake of their traditions (e.g. Matt. 15:3). Jesus criticizes their claim to be the most skilful interpreters of the Law by pointing out that their conduct reveals the opposite.

However, Gundry (1994) and Powell (1995) offer an alternative interpretation of the verse, which should be considered. Gundry (1994:455) argues that Jesus' pronouncement means that as long as the teachers of the Law are sitting on the seat of Moses, they are purely reading the Law of Moses (the written *Torah*) and not their interpretive traditions (*halakha*). In such circumstances people should obey them. However, one should not follow their conduct, as their conduct do not correlate with their reading. Powell (1995:431-433) proposes a similar argument. He argues that when Jesus mentions that the Pharisees speak (εἴπωσιν and λέγουσιν), He refers to their reading of the *Torah* only. This action of the Pharisees Jesus commends. However, when Jesus mentions what they do (ποιοῦσιν), he refers to their interpretation of the Torah as revealed in their *halakha*. Their interpretations reveal a skewed understanding of the Torah. They do not understand the Torah they so correctly cite. Jesus therefor warns his disciples not to follow their *halakha*.

This string of thought continues in the next verse which supports the argument of Gundry and Powell in a sense. The Matthean Jesus continues his argument by illustrating verses 2–3. In Matt. 23:4 Jesus criticizes the teachers of the Law and the Pharisees for compiling multiple obligations to the Law with their interpretations, making it extremely difficult to bear, and Jesus accuses them of not adhering to their own obligations: δεσμεύουσιν δὲ φορτία βαρέα καὶ ἐπιτιθέασιν ἐπὶ τοὺς ὤμους τῶν ἀνθρώπων, αὐτοὶ δὲ τῷ δακτύλῳ αὐτῶν οὐ θέλουσιν κινῆσαι αὐτά (they tie up heavy, cumbersome loads and put them on other people's shoulders, but they themselves are not willing to lift a finger to move them). The Matthean Jesus once again uses δὲ to stress the antithesis. The image implies a heavy and burdensome yoke[335] being laid on the shoulders of the people who they teach. This imagery recalls the light yoke and the easy commandments of Jesus in Matt. 11:30 in stark contrast with the burden implied by the teachings of the Jewish teachers of the Law (Esler, 2015:44; Gundry, 1994:455). The Jewish teachers are guilty of making the Law a crushing and unbearable burden..

In Matt. 23:5–7, Jesus proceeds to depict the teachers of the Law and Pharisees as people who do things because of wrong motives (Talbert, 2010:257). In this depiction Jesus does not only refer to their interpretation of the *Torah*, but indeed to their insincere overall conduct. Matthew's Jesus starts off with a general indictment, followed by a series of examples.

General indictment πάντα δὲ τὰ ἔργα αὐτῶν ποιοῦσιν πρὸς τὸ θεαθῆναι τοῖς ἀνθρώποις	Everything they do is done for people to see:
Example 1 πλατύνουσι γὰρ τὰ φυλακτήρια αὐτῶν καὶ μεγαλύνουσι τὰ κράσπεδα,	They make their phylacteries wide and the tassels on their garments long;
Example 2a&b φιλοῦσι δὲ 1. *τὴν πρωτοκλισίαν ἐν τοῖς δείπνοις* 2. *καὶ τὰς πρωτοκαθεδρίας ἐν ταῖς συναγωγαῖς*	they love 1. *the place of honour* at banquets 2. and *the most important seats* in the synagogues;
Example 3a&b 1. *καὶ τοὺς ἀσπασμοὺς ἐν ταῖς ἀγοραῖς* 2. *καὶ καλεῖσθαι ὑπὸ τῶν ἀνθρώπων·* Ῥαββί.	3. and *to be greeted* with respect in the marketplaces 4. and *to be called* 'Rabbi' by others.

Table 58: Jesus' indictment of the religious leaders illustrated with examples

---

[335] In the First Testament, "yoke" is often used as a symbol for foreign and harsh rule (e.g. Gen. 27:40; 1 Kings. 12:4-14). The release of the foreign yoke implies freedom and forgiveness (Isa. 9:3; 10:27). During the Second Temple Period, the term yoke was commonly used for the instruction of the Torah (e.g. 2 En. 34:1-2; 2 Apoc. Bar. 4:13; cf. Acts 15:10 and Gal. 5:1; cf. Deines, 2008:67; Hagner, 1993:324; Oliver, 2013:85). In Sir. 6:18-31 and 51:23-27 the terms "wisdom", "law" and "yoke" are linked together. The yoke of wisdom is the instruction of the law.

The general indictment is similar to what the Jewish leaders are accused of in Matt. 6:1–6)[336]. It also echoes what is written in b. Sotah 22b in a section labelled as "The Plagues of the Pharisees." In the rubric "There are seven types of Pharisees," one of the types are described as people who perform religious duties with unworthy and pretentious motives (Talbert, 2010:257). Within their honour and shame society, they sought honour through affirmation by society (cf. de Silva, 2004:125; Keener, 2002:104). Jesus radically rejects this prevailing mode of conduct that was typical of this ancient Mediterranean society.

Jesus' accusation is followed by a series of examples of what they do (Matt. 23:5–7):

- they make their phylacteries wide and the tassels on their garments long;
- they love the place of honour at banquets and the most important seats[337] in the synagogues; and
- they love to be greeted in the market places and to have men call them 'Rabbi'.

From this text it seems that much of the conflict between the Matthean community and the religious leaders was about the conduct of seeking honour along with public recognition, not just about the teaching (*halakha*) of the religious leaders (Davies & Allison, 2004c:275; Keener, 2002:104). Matt. 23:1–7 provides a vigorous polemic portrait of the vanity of the Pharisees and the teachers of the Law. Yet, criticism of their teaching role is pertinent, as Jesus accuses them of their fixation on attracting honour in their teaching roles as they strive towards being called "Rabbi" (Esler, 2015:46). They taught with wrong motives in mind.

11.3.1.2 What the disciples should do instead (Matt. 23:8–12)

In contrast to the vanity of the Pharisees and teachers of the Law in Matt. 23:1–7, Jesus proceeds to set out the antithetical behaviour required of discipleship, with an emphasis on "but you" (ὑμεῖς δὲ) in Matt. 23:8–12, which reads as a

---

[336] Matt. 6:1-4: "Be careful not to do your acts of righteousness before men, to be seen by them ... do not announce it with trumpets ... to be honoured by men ...".

[337] The seat of honour in the synagogue could refer to the seat of Moses (Matt. 23:2) (Viviano, 1990:11).

small community rule on humility (Davies & Allison, 2004c:265). Wiefel (1998:397) opines that this passage is probably based on a *kleine Gemeinderegel* from tradition. This rule signifies a contrast in community values between that of the Pharisees and teachers of the Law, and that of the followers of Jesus.

ὑμεῖς δὲ μὴ κληθῆτε Ῥαββεί· *εἷς γάρ* ἐστιν ὑμῶν ὁ διδάσκαλος, πάντες δὲ ὑμεῖς ἀδελφοί ἐστε.	*But you* are not to be called 'Rabbi,' **for** you have **one** Teacher, and you are all brothers.
καὶ *πατέρα μὴ καλέσητε* ὑμῶν ἐπὶ τῆς γῆς· *εἷς γάρ* ἐστιν ὑμῶν ὁ Πατὴρ ὁ οὐράνιος.	And *do not call* anyone on earth 'father,' **for** you have **one** Father, and he is in heaven.
μηδὲ *κληθῆτε* καθηγηταί, ὅτι καθηγητὴς ὑμῶν ἐστιν εἷς ὁ Χριστός.	Nor *are you to be called* instructors, **for** you have one Instructor, the Messiah.
ὁ δὲ **μείζων** ὑμῶν ἔσται ὑμῶν **διάκονος**.	The **greatest** among you will be your **servant**.
Ὅστις δὲ *ὑψώσει* ἑαυτὸν *ταπεινωθήσεται*, καὶ ὅστις *ταπεινώσει* ἑαυτὸν *ὑψωθήσεται*.	For those who exalt themselves *will be humbled*, and those who **humble** themselves *will be exalted*.

Table 59: Contrast in community values of the Pharisees and teachers of the Law, and that of the followers of Jesus

These guidelines remind of Matt. 18:1–4[338] and 20:25–28[339], where humility is mentioned as the basic premise of being a disciple. The contrast between εἷς (one) and πάντες (all) is striking. The Matthean Jesus emphasizes equality of "all" and subjection to "one," meaning Jesus with his teaching authority (Gundry, 1994:457). The disciples are warned not to claim being called "Rabbi," "father" or "teacher," which would signify superior ranking among inferiors (Keener, 2002:104). They are all equal ἀδελφοί (brothers). This warning is summed up with the saying: "For whoever exalts himself will be humbled, and whoever humbles himself, will be exalted" (Matt. 23:12). The passive voice implies divine action and the future, probably the last judgement (Gundry, 1994:459). Clearly, the Matthean Jesus challenges the teachings,

---

[338] Matt. 18:1-4: "Who is the greatest in the kingdom of heaven? ... Therefore, whoever humbles himself like this child is the greatest in the kingdom of heaven."

[339] Matt. 20:25-28: "... whoever want to become great among you, must be your servant, and whoever wants to be first must be your slave – just as the Son of Man did not come to be served, but to serve, and to give his life as ransom to many."

positions and conduct of the teachers of the Law and the Pharisees and prescribes alternative community values (Esler, 2015:48). The injunction in verse 8 not to be called "Rabbi" follows directly after the accusation of the teachers of the Law and Pharisees who desire to be called "Rabbi's," which would imply holding authoritative teaching roles. Again Jesus denounces their self-acclaimed teaching positions.

The Matthean Jesus then states that in his community, members should not strive to be called καθηγηταί (instructors) as they have but one καθηγητὴς (instructor) (Matt. 23:10), which is Christ. Matthew's use of καθηγητὴς is noteworthy (Esler, 2015:49). These two appearances of the word are unique to the New Testament and do not occur in the Septuagint. France (2007:864) and Viviano (1990:12) demonstrate that this word is used for teachers in the sense that they show the way intellectually and spiritually. A καθηγητὴς (instructor) was regarded of a higher rank than an ordinary διδάσκαλος (teacher). With his final commission in Matt. 28:18–20, Jesus instructs the eleven to teach his commandments, strongly emphasizing that he is their καθηγητὴς (instructor) with ultimate authority.

11.3.2 Addressing the teachers of the Law and the Pharisees (Matt. 23:13–36)

In Matt. 23:13–36 Jesus addresses the teachers of the Law and Pharisees, which forms the second part of Matt. 23 (Talbert, 2010:258). This address consists of a series of seven "woe–sayings"[340] (οὐαὶ δὲ ὑμῖν) against the teachers of the Law and the Pharisees (γραμματεῖς καὶ Φαρισαῖοι) and serve as a reverse of the blessings (μακάριοι) spoken to his disciples (οἱ μαθηταὶ αὐτοῦ) in Matt. 5:3–12.

This contrast between judgements and blessings resembles the similar contrast found in the repetitive recital of the Levites in Deut. 27–28. The Levites should warn Israel not to transgress the commands and decrees given to them: "Cursed is anyone who …" (Deut. 27:15–26). In contrast, blessings are recited for obedience to the commands of the Lord (if you fully obey the Lord your God and carefully follow all his commands I give you today …" (Deut 28:1) and the result would be "you will be blessed …" (Deut. 28:3–14). However, "if you do not obey the Lord your God and do not carefully follow all his commands and decrees I am giving you today, all these curses will come on you and overtake you …" (Deut. 28:15). This warning is confirmed by the Levites' repetitive

---

[340] Cf. Isa. 5:8-23 and Luke 11:42-52 each with its series of six woe-sayings.

recital of "you will be cursed ..." (Deut. 28:16–68) (Keener, 2002:104). Jesus' addressees most likely would interpret Jesus' cursing of the Pharisees and teachers of the Law in terms of the curses in Deuteronomy. The conduct and teachings of the Pharisees and teachers of the Law would be understood as being untrue to the commands and decrees of the Lord.

The outcry, οὐαὶ (woe), combines the ideas of wrath and pain, and anger and sorrow (Bruner, 2007:443; Esler, 2015:50). While Jesus communicates salvation to his disciples with his blessed-sayings (μακάριοι), he communicates judgement to the teachers of the Law and the Pharisees with these woe-sayings (οὐαί). As in Matt. 11:21[341] these woe-sayings express proleptic condemnation, anticipating the downfall of the Jewish religious leaders. Some parallels can be recognized between the seven "woe-sayings" of Matt. 23:13–36 and the six of Luk. 11:42–52[342].

Judgement for closing the kingdom for others (Matt. 23:13)	Judgement for closing the kingdom for others – Luke's sixth woe saying
Οὐαὶ δὲ ὑμῖν, γραμματεῖς καὶ Φαρισαῖοι ὑποκριταί, ὅτι κλείετε τὴν βασιλείαν τῶν οὐρανῶν ἔμπροσθεν τῶν ἀνθρώπων· ὑμεῖς γὰρ οὐκ εἰσέρχεσθε, οὐδὲ τοὺς εἰσερχομένους ἀφίετε εἰσελθεῖν. (Woe to you, teachers of the law and Pharisees, you hypocrites! You shut the door of the kingdom of heaven in people's faces. You yourselves do not enter, nor will you let those enter who are trying to)	(Luk. 11:52) οὐαὶ ὑμῖν τοῖς νομικοῖς, ὅτι ἤρατε τὴν κλεῖδα τῆς γνώσεως· αὐτοὶ οὐκ εἰσήλθατε καὶ τοὺς εἰσερχομένους ἐκωλύσατε. (Woe to you experts in the law, because you have taken away the key to knowledge. You yourselves have not entered, and you have hindered those who were entering.)
1. Judgement for leading proselytes to hell (Matt. 23:15) Οὐαὶ ὑμῖν, γραμματεῖς καὶ Φαρισαῖοι ὑποκριταί,	

---

[341] Matt. 11:21: "Woe to you, Korazin! Woe to you, Bethsaida! ..."

[342] Luke's second and fourth "woe-sayings" to the Pharisees (Luk. 11:43, "Woe to you Pharisees, because you love the most important seats in the synagogues and respectful greetings in the marketplaces" and Luk. 11:46, "And you experts in the law, woe to you, because you load people down with burdens they can hardly carry, and you yourselves will not lift one finger to help them") respectively runs parallel to Jesus' address to the crowds (Matt. 23:6-7 and Matt. 23:4). Luke's third "woe-saying" (Luk. 11:44) has no direct parallel in Matthew.

ὅτι περιάγετε τὴν θάλασσαν καὶ τὴν ξηρὰν ποιῆσαι ἕνα προσήλυτον, καὶ ὅταν γένηται ποιεῖτε αὐτὸν υἱὸν γεέννης διπλότερον ὑμῶν. (Woe to you, teachers of the law and Pharisees, you hypocrites! You travel over land and sea to win a single convert, and when you have succeeded, you make them twice as much a child of hell as you are)	
2. Judgement for false teaching on swearing (Matt. 23:16–22) Οὐαὶ ὑμῖν, ὁδηγοὶ τυφλοὶ οἱ λέγοντες· Ὃς ἂν ὀμόσῃ ἐν τῷ ναῷ, οὐδέν ἐστιν, ὃς δ' ἂν ὀμόσῃ ἐν τῷ χρυσῷ τοῦ ναοῦ ὀφείλει. **μωροὶ καὶ τυφλοί**, τίς γὰρ μείζων ἐστίν, ὁ χρυσὸς ἢ ὁ ναὸς ὁ ἁγιάσας τὸν χρυσόν;… **τυφλοί**, τί γὰρ μεῖζον, τὸ δῶρον ἢ τὸ θυσιαστήριον τὸ ἁγιάζον τὸ δῶρον;… (Woe to you, **blind** guides! You say, 'If anyone swears by the temple, it means nothing; but anyone who swears by the gold of the temple is bound by that oath.' **You blind fools!** Which is greater: the gold, or the temple that makes the gold sacred? … **You blind** men! Which is greater: the gift, or the altar that makes the gift sacred? ...)	
3. Judgement for meticulous tithing while being merciless (Matt. 23:23–24) Οὐαὶ ὑμῖν, γραμματεῖς καὶ Φαρισαῖοι **ὑποκριταί**, ὅτι ἀποδεκατοῦτε τὸ ἡδύοσμον καὶ τὸ ἄνηθον καὶ τὸ κύμινον, καὶ ἀφήκατε τὰ βαρύτερα τοῦ νόμου, τὴν κρίσιν καὶ τὸ ἔλεος καὶ τὴν πίστιν· ταῦτα ἔδει ποιῆσαι κἀκεῖνα μὴ ἀφιέναι ὁδηγοὶ **τυφλοί**, οἱ διϋλίζοντες τὸν κώνωπα τὴν δὲ κάμηλον καταπίνοντες. (Woe to you, teachers of the law and Pharisees, **you hypocrites**! You give a tenth of your spices—mint, dill and cumin. But you have neglected the more important matters of the law—justice, mercy and faithfulness. You should have practiced the latter, without	**Judgement for meticulous tithing while being merciless – Luke's first woe saying (Luk. 11:42)** οὐαὶ ὑμῖν τοῖς Φαρισαίοις, ὅτι ἀποδεκατοῦτε τὸ ἡδύοσμον καὶ τὸ πήγανον καὶ πᾶν λάχανον, καὶ παρέρχεσθε τὴν κρίσιν καὶ τὴν ἀγάπην τοῦ Θεοῦ· ταῦτα δὲ ἔδει ποιῆσαι κἀκεῖνα μὴ παρεῖναι Woe to you Pharisees, because you give God a tenth of your mint, rue and all other kinds of garden herbs, but you neglect justice and the love of God. You should have practiced the latter without leaving the former undone.

neglecting the former. You blind guides! You strain out a gnat but swallow a camel)	
4. **Judgement for ritual cleanness yet unclean hearts (Matt. 23:25–26)** Οὐαὶ ὑμῖν, γραμματεῖς καὶ Φαρισαῖοι **ὑποκριταί**, *ὅτι καθαρίζετε τὸ ἔξωθεν τοῦ ποτηρίου καὶ τῆς παροψίδος, ἔσωθεν δὲ γέμουσιν ἐξ ἁρπαγῆς καὶ ἀκρασίας.* Φαρισαῖε τυφλέ, καθάρισον πρῶτον τὸ ἐντὸς τοῦ ποτηρίου καὶ τῆς παροψίδος, ἵνα γένηται καὶ τὸ ἐκτὸς αὐτοῦ καθαρόν. (Woe to you, teachers of the law and Pharisees, **you hypocrites**! You clean the outside of the cup and dish, but inside they are full of greed and self-indulgence. Blind Pharisee! First clean the inside of the cup and dish, and then the outside also will be clean)	**Judgement for ritual cleanness yet unclean hearts; though without the use of οὐαὶ ὑμῖν of a formal woe saying (Luk. 11:39–40)** εἶπεν δὲ ὁ Κύριος πρὸς αὐτόν Νῦν ὑμεῖς οἱ Φαρισαῖοι τὸ ἔξωθεν τοῦ ποτηρίου καὶ τοῦ πίνακος καθαρίζετε, τὸ δὲ ἔσωθεν ὑμῶν γέμει ἁρπαγῆς καὶ πονηρίας. ἄφρονες, οὐχ ὁ ποιήσας τὸ ἔξωθεν καὶ τὸ ἔσωθεν ἐποίησεν; πλὴν τὰ ἐνόντα δότε ἐλεημοσύνην, καὶ ἰδοὺ πάντα καθαρὰ ὑμῖν ἐστιν. "Now then, you Pharisees clean the outside of the cup and dish, but inside you are full of greed and wickedness. You foolish people! Did not the one who made the outside make the inside also? But now as for what is inside you—be generous to the poor, and everything will be clean for you.
5. **Judgement for external self-righteousness yet wicked interior (Matt. 23:27–28)** Οὐαὶ ὑμῖν, γραμματεῖς καὶ Φαρισαῖοι **ὑποκριταί**, *ὅτι παρομοιάζετε τάφοις κεκονιαμένοις, οἵτινες ἔξωθεν μὲν φαίνονται ὡραῖοι ἔσωθεν δὲ γέμουσιν ὀστέων νεκρῶν καὶ πάσης ἀκαθαρσίας· οὕτως καὶ ὑμεῖς ἔξωθεν μὲν φαίνεσθε τοῖς ἀνθρώποις δίκαιοι, ἔσωθεν δέ ἐστε μεστοὶ ὑποκρίσεως καὶ ἀνομίας.* ("Woe to you, teachers of the law and Pharisees, **you hypocrites**! You are like whitewashed tombs, which look beautiful on the outside but on the inside are full of the bones of the dead and everything unclean. In the same way, on the outside you appear to people as righteous but on the inside you are full of hypocrisy and wickedness)	
6. **Judgement for participating in the sins of their ancestors (Matt. 23:29–32)**	**Judgement for participating in the sins of their ancestors – Luke's fifth**

	woe saying (Luk. 11:47–48)
Οὐαὶ ὑμῖν, γραμματεῖς καὶ Φαρισαῖοι ὑποκριταί, ὅτι οἰκοδομεῖτε τοὺς τάφους τῶν προφητῶν καὶ κοσμεῖτε τὰ μνημεῖα τῶν δικαίων, … ὥστε μαρτυρεῖτε ἑαυτοῖς ὅτι υἱοί ἐστε τῶν φονευσάντων τοὺς προφήτας. (Woe to you, teachers of the law and Pharisees[343], you hypocrites! You build tombs for the prophets and decorate the graves of the righteous, … So you testify against yourselves that you are the descendants of those who murdered the prophets …)	οὐαὶ ὑμῖν, ὅτι οἰκοδομεῖτε τὰ μνημεῖα τῶν προφητῶν, οἱ δὲ πατέρες ὑμῶν ἀπέκτειναν αὐτούς. ἄρα μάρτυρές ἐστε καὶ συνευδοκεῖτε τοῖς ἔργοις τῶν πατέρων ὑμῶν, ὅτι αὐτοὶ μὲν ἀπέκτειναν αὐτούς, ὑμεῖς δὲ οἰκοδομεῖτε … (Woe to you, because you build tombs for the prophets, and it was your ancestors who killed them. So you testify that you approve of what your ancestors did; they killed the prophets, and you build their tombs …)

Table 60: Parallels between the seven "woe-sayings" of Luke and Matthew

The woe sayings are composed of two parts: the addressees and their wrongs, while the judgements are heaped up at the end of the address (Matt. 23:32–39) (Bruner, 2007:442).

11.3.2.1   Addressees of the woe-sayings

Jesus' rejection of the teachers of the Law and the Pharisees is expressed in the manner he addresses them. The accusations in the Matthean version are much sharper and more extensive than in Luke. The Matthean Jesus repetitively charges them of being hypocrites (ὑποκριταί) in six of the sayings (Matt. 23:13, 15, 23, 25, 27 and 29), and of being blind guides (ὁδηγοὶ τυφλοὶ) three times in the third saying (Matt. 23:16), a charge that is repeated in the fourth (Matt. 23:24) and fifth saying (Matt. 23:26).

The Matthean Jesus in quite a number of instances does not hesitate call the teachers of the Law and Pharisees hypocrites (e.g. Matt. 6:2, 16; 15:7; 23:13, 15, 25, 29). In his address to the crowds, Jesus had already exposed the hypocritical conduct of these religious leaders. He criticized them for being hypocritical as they boast about their righteous accomplishments (cf. Matt. 6:1–2). They act with ethical pretence by making people into spectators and trying to impress them to sustain their own status, as Jesus warns in Matt. 23:5–

---

[343] With the exception of Matt. 27:62, this is the last mention of the Pharisees in Matthew. They leave the stage in disgrace under looming judgement (Davies & Allison, 2004c:304).

7 with respect to them parading their pious acts in public to gain praise. Such conduct was typical of the honour and shame society in which Jesus and his disciples lived, as one's good reputation was sustained by the esteem of others (Carter, 2000a:158; de Silva, 2004:125; Malina & Rohrbauch, 2003:370; Witherington, 2013:49). Jesus therefore opposes a fundamental societal pattern in which they participated.

As in Matt. 15:14, Jesus labels the teachers of the Law and Pharisees as blind guides (ὁδηγοὶ τυφλοί). Jesus' fulmination against blindness refers to their inability to distinguish between the important and unimportant emphases of the Scriptures (cf. Matt. 23:17[344], 19[345]) (Bruner, 2007:446). He therefore accuses them of false interpretation of the Law, their *halakha*, as they are blind guides who mislead their followers (Matt. 23:24) (Powell, 1995:432).

11.3.2.2   Wrongs of the addressees

The second part of each woe-saying expresses the wrong of the teachers of the Law and the Pharisees. The extent of Matthew's woe-sayings expresses the strong disapproval of the Matthean Jesus, not only of the conduct of the teachers of the Law and Pharisees, but also of their teachings. The first three woe-sayings focus on the false teaching of the leaders (Matt. 23:13–22), the next three mainly on their false practice (Matt. 23:23–28), while the last saying accuses their false security as if they were not guilty of killing the prophets (Matt. 23:29–36) (Bruner, 2007:442).

Woes for wrong teachings	Woes for wrong conduct
Shutting the door of the kingdom of heaven in people's faces (Matt. 23:13)[346].	Meticulous tithing while being merciless (Matt. 23:23–24)[347]
Proselyting using false teaching (Matt. 23:15)	Ritual cleanness yet unclean hearts (Matt. 23:25–26)
False teachings on swearing (Matt. 23:22)	External self-righteousness yet with wicked interior (Matt. 23:27–28)

Table 61: Woes for wrong teaching and conduct

---

[344] Matt. 23:17: You blind fools! Which is greater: the gold, or the temple that makes the gold sacred?

[345] Matt. 23:19: You blind men! Which is greater: the gift, or the altar that makes the gift sacred?

[346] The Lukan parallel reads: "you have taken away the key to knowledge" (Luk. 11:52)

[347] The Lukan parallel woes the neglect of justice and the love of God (Luk. 11:42)

- Woes for wrong teaching

The first three woe-sayings mainly denounce the wrong teachings (*halakha*) of the religious leaders.

The first saying (Matt. 23:13–14) accuses them of shutting the door of the kingdom in people's faces. How they shut it is not explicitly mentioned, but it probably refers to the laying of heavy burdens on people's shoulders (Matt. 23:4). Earlier in the text, Jesus reflected on the heavy yoke of complicated *halakhic* teachings and traditions (Matt. 11:28–30). The parallel in Luk. 11:52 mentions that they have taken away the keys of knowledge. This interpretation correlates with the assumed authority of the teachers of the Law and Pharisees, who sit on the seat of Moses (Matt. 23:2). They were regarded as the custodians of the *Torah*, of God's will (Davies & Allison, 2004c:267). In contrast with this accusation, Jesus has given Peter the keys of the kingdom (Matt. 16:18), the one who has confessed Jesus to be the Christ, the Son of the living God (Matt. 16:16).

The second saying (Matt. 23:15), which does not have a parallel in Luke, continues the accusation of the first saying by describing the devastating effect of the teachers of the law and the Pharisees on others. They who shut the kingdom of heaven in people's faces (Matt. 23:13), are those who travel all around to make proselytes[348], but by doing so they prepare people for hell (Matt. 23:15). The proselytes were convinced by the teachings of the teachers of the law and the Pharisees, and thus became severe opponents of the teachings of Jesus (Bruner, 2007:444).

The third saying (Matt. 23:16–22), which also lacks a parallel in Luke, accuses the complicated teachings of the Jewish religious leaders on swearing. This woe resembles Matt. 5:33–37 with its critique on *halakha,* which proposes a distinction between binding and non-binding oaths (Davies & Allison, 2004c:290). The Matthean Jesus lists a series of variant forms of swearing as proposed by the Pharisees in parallel statements (Gundry, 1994:462). By

---

[348] Rabbi Eleazar of Modiim says: "God scattered Israel among the nations for the sole purpose that proselytes would be numerous among them" (b. Pesach. 87b). Though Pharisees did not have missionaries as such, Jewish people outside Palestine were eager to make converts of the Gentiles. It was said that Hillel was especially open to converting non-Jews to Judaism (Keener, 2002:104). Nevertheless, the emphasis does not lie in the missionary activity of the Pharisees, but on the irony of the fact that their efforts result in disastrous results (Gundry, 1994:461).

replacing the divine name with lesser and ranking substitutes, they regard the oaths as less serious (Keener, 2002:104).

- Woes for wrong conduct

The next three woes mainly focus on the wrong conduct of the teachers of the Law and the Pharisees.

The third (Matt. 23:16–22), fourth (Matt. 23:23–24) and the fifth woes (Matt. 23:25–26) are bound together with reference to "ὁδηγοὶ τυφλοὶ" (blind guides), which forms an *inclusio* in (Matt. 23:16 and 24). In the fourth woe, Jesus accuses his addressees of meticulous attention to ceremonial cleanliness and external devotions of piety, but then neglecting more important issues. Though Jesus primarily refers to their wrong conduct, he accuses them of misleading others with their *halakha* as they are "ὁδηγοὶ τυφλοὶ" (blind guides) (Davies & Allison, 2004c:293). France (2007:870) remarks: "The basis of Jesus' criticism is that the scribal approach is superficial, and fails to think through the principles underlying the details on which their debate is focussed". Once again, Jesus criticizes their presumed teaching authority. Jesus uses the humorous hyperbole of "straining out a gnat, but then swallowing a camel[349]" (Matt. 23:24) to drive the point. While the tithing of mint, dill and cumin was not required by the Law, they neglected justice, mercy and faithfulness. The Matthean Jesus more than once emphasizes the importance of justice, mercy and covenantal faithfulness (Matt. 9:13; 12:7) (Keener, 2002:105). This accusation against the Pharisees and teachers of the Law continues Jesus' argument of Matt. 15:3–9[350].

The fifth saying (Matt. 23:25–26) adds to the charge of the fourth saying of doing the less important things, while neglecting the more important ones. The teachers of the Law and the Pharisees clean the outside of their cups and dishes, but not their insides. Jesus uses this as a figurative statement about the inside of the hearts (Davies & Allison, 2004c:296; Keener, 2002:105). On the outside, the addressees propose to be righteous, but in the inside they are full of greed and indulgence. Jesus carries forward the theme of the Sermon on the Mount where he states that one's inner attitude determines one's external behaviour

---

[349] Camels were the largest animals in Palestine and also ritually unclean (Lev. 11:4).

[350] "And why do you break the command of God for the sake of your tradition? ..." (Matt. 15:3-9)

(Matt. 5:8 and 6:22–23[351]). The focus of morality should be one's heart, which is not the case with his addressees (Gundry, 1994:465).

In the sixth saying (Matt. 23:27–28), the topic continues. The fifth and sixth woes are bound together by the common contrast between inside and outside (Matt. 23:25–28). Jesus figuratively refers to white washed tombs full of dead men's bones and everything unclean. Nothing spread ritual impurity as severely as a corpse[352], as one who touched a corpse was unclean for a week (Num. 19:11) (Keener, 2002:105). Matthew's emphasis lies on the hiding of inward corruption, as the washing symbolizes the hypocrisy of the Pharisees (Gundry, 1994:466). While teachers of the Law and Pharisees are pretentiously preoccupied with matters of external purity and outer appearance, their inner beings are accused of being sources of severe impurity (Davies & Allison, 2004c:302).

- Woe for false security

In the seventh saying (Matt. 23:29–32), the Matthean Jesus exposes the contrast between their confession and conduct, which provides a clear illustration of their hypocrisy. Jesus accuses them of a gulf between their words and deeds, being the essence of hypocrisy (Gundry, 1994:468). While they are descendants of those forefathers who abhorred the prophets, they now honour the same prophets by erecting tombs and elaborate monuments for them. Jer. 26:20–23 and 2 Chron. 36:15–16 describe how Israel had martyred its prophets and Jesus argues that corporate guilt continued among descendants. Jesus closes with an ironic challenge to proceed with their sin, πληρώσατε τὸ μέτρον τῶν πατέρων ὑμῶν (fill up, then, the measure of the sin of your forefathers) (Matt. 23:32), but God will judge them (Keener, 2002:105). Filling up the measure of the sin probably not only refers to the building of the tombs, but like their forefathers, they were about to murder yet another prophet, this time Jesus and his followers (Gundry, 1994:468).

---

[351] "Blessed are the pure in heart ..." (Matt. 5:8) and "... If then the light within you is darkness, how great is that darkness!" (Matt. 6:22-23).

[352] Pharisees presumably believed that even if one's shadow touched a corpse or a grave, one would become impure (Keener, 2002:105).

11.3.2.3 Judgement (Matt. 23:33–36)

The sinful conduct of the addressees leads toward eschatological judgement. The teachers of the Law and Pharisees are labelled as snakes and the charge is doubled, as they are also labelled as offspring of vipers (ὄφεις, γεννήματα ἐχιδνῶν) (Matt. 23:33)[353] (Gundry, 1994:469)[354].

According to the Matthean Jesus, the conduct of the teachers of the Law and the Pharisees resemble the rejection of the prophets in the days of Zechariah. This passage seems to be based on 2 Chron. 24:17–22, 25 using the historical language of the Chronicles and applying it to the time of Jesus. The analogy lies in what had happened in the days of Zechariah, would again happen in the days of Jesus (Davies & Allison, 2004c:318). The prophets were rejected in the times of Zechariah and so again Jesus and his disciples would be rejected as the prophets of God. The teachers of the Law and Pharisees would deliver Jesus and his disciples to be crucified and would flog them in their synagogues (Matt. 23:34). Crucifixion was the most severe punishment, reserved for non-Romans. Jews who would deliver fellow Jews for crucifixion obviously were despised by fellow Jews. Flogging in synagogues was a form of discipline for errant members (Keener, 2002:106).

The result is that all the righteous blood that has been shed on earth would come upon them (ὅπως ἔλθη ἐφ' ὑμᾶς πᾶν αἷμα δίκαιον ἐκχυννόμενον) (Matt. 23:35), and they would be punished for all their wrongdoings (ἥξει ταῦτα πάντα ἐπὶ τὴν γενεὰν ταύτην) (Matt. 23:36). The shedding the blood of Abel, whom the Jews regarded as the first martyr (Gen. 4:8), and that of Zechariah, whom the Jews regarded as the last martyr (2 Chron. 24:22) are mentioned (Gundry, 1994:471; Keener, 2002:106; Simmonds, 2009:346). Zechariah explicitly prayed for judgement. According to Jesus, the judgement from the first to the last martyr is saved for this wicked generation.

---

[353] A similar train of thought appears earlier in the gospel when John the Baptist also calls the Pharisees and Sadducees offspring of vipers, though they claim to have Abraham as their father (Matt. 3:7b-9).

[354] According to Keener (2002:105), to be labelled a venomous snake is bad, but it is even worse to be labelled offspring of vipers, as vipers presumably were notorious for eating its way out of their pregnant mother's bellies.

11.3.3 Addressing Jerusalem with sorrow and lament (Matt. 23:37–39)

The chapter is concluded with a lament addressing Jerusalem. Jesus uses the well-known image of God's love for his people, namely of protecting them under his wings (Ps. 17:8; 46:7; 57:1; 61:4; 63:7; 91:4). Converted gentiles were also brought under the protecting wings of God's presence (Ruth 2:12). Jesus applies this image to demonstrate his efforts to take care of Jerusalem: ποσάκις ἠθέλησα ἐπισυναγαγεῖν τὰ τέκνα σου, ὃν τρόπον ὄρνις ἐπισυνάγει τὰ νοσσία αὐτῆς ὑπὸ τὰς πτέρυγας (Keener, 2002:106). However, Jerusalem rejected his loving care (καὶ οὐκ ἠθελήσατε) (Matt. 23:17). In the past, Jerusalem forsook the Lord, and He therefore forsook the city. He withdrew his divine presence. Now Jerusalem forsakes Jesus, and the city and the temple will therefore be forsaken.

11.4 CONCLUSION

Considering the intra-textual setting of Matt. 23:3, it is clear that the Matthean Jesus is critical of the conduct and the teaching of the teachers of the Law and the Pharisees. While the sentiment towards these leaders is negative throughout the gospel, the conflict clearly intensifies during the week of the Passion, forming a crescendo of this conflict. Following Jesus' humble entry into Jerusalem, he cleanses and judges the temple. This judgement is symbolized by his cursing of the fig tree. This conduct of Jesus entices the antagonism of the Jewish religious leaders, who challenge Jesus' authority of Jesus. The Matthean Jesus proceeds by telling three parables in which the unreliability of these leaders are exposed. A series of three challenges follow in which Jesus takes on increasingly skilled teachers of his day, but he proceeds victorious. The challenges are concluded by the question of Jesus about his authority, which leaves his opponents dumb and without any answer. This culminates in Jesus's extensive criticism in Matt. 23. First, Jesus addresses the crowds, warning them of the insincerity of these Jewish leaders. Their conduct is hypocritical and their teachings are misleading. He pronounces a series of woes in which He accuses them of being hypocritical and spiritually blind. He bemoans the destiny of Jerusalem, which as in the days of Zechariah, will be desolate as this city has opposed and killed the true prophets of God.

When Jesus instructs the crowds to obey the teachers of the Law and the Pharisees in everything they tell them (Matt. 23:3a), He does this in context of accusing them of doing something wrong. The suggestion of Gundry and Powell makes sense that Jesus only refers positively to their precise citing of the written *Torah*, but criticizes their interpretation (*halakha*) of it. When Jesus proceeds to illustrate his statement later on, it is clear that He accuses the teachers of the Law and the Pharisees both of wrong teachings and hypocritical conduct. However, it is also possible that Jesus makes this instruction in an ironic way to sternly expose the hypocrisy of the Jewish leaders, as saying the one, but paradocically doing the other. The overall sentiment towards them remains negative.

In Matt. 21–23, Jesus battles and defeats his rivals. Jesus is highly vocal and assertive. These scenes are followed by scenes where He is meek and silent in his trial and execution, a lamb to be slaughtered. He is seemingly defeated, but is finally victorious in his resurrection.

CHAPTER 12

CONCLUSION

12.1 INTRODUCTION

The goal of this final chapter is to provide a theological reflection on the *Torah* in the first Gospel based the investigation done on the religious world of Matthew and the different passages on the *Torah* in this Gospel. Though this reflection does not intend to provide a comprehensive view of the *Torah* in Matthew, it does illuminate some of the most significant traits.

12.2 FINAL THEOLOGICAL REFLECTION ON MATTHEW'S UNDERSTANDING OF THE *TORAH*

This study demonstrates the significant role of the *Torah* in the first Gospel. From the study it can be deducted that:

- the *Torah* holds a central position in Matthew;
- the *Torah* continues to remain valid;
- Jesus teaches and enacts an alternative interpretation of the *Torah*;
- Jesus has the authority to interpret the *Torah*;
- with Jesus the *Torah* forms part of God's plan of salvation;
- love and mercy form the hermeneutical keys to *Torah* interpretation and practice;
- Jesus advocates a different range of the *Torah*;
- Jesus' teaching and enactment of the *Torah* is met with sharp opposition;
- the teachings and enactment of the *Torah* by the Pharisees and teachers of the Law is strongly criticised; and
- an alternative *Torah*-abiding community came into existence.

This role is apparent from Matthew's use of *Torah*-related material and his editorial activity with this material.

12.2.1 The *Torah* holds a central position

The central position of the *Torah* is especially notable in the way Jesus teaches the Torah and proceeds to enact the intention of the *Torah*.

12.2.1.1 Jesus teaches the Torah

The Sermon on the Mount especially signifies the importance of the *Torah* in Matthew. This Sermon holds a prominent position in the Gospel as the first of five great discourses in the Gospel, these being the Sermon on the Mount (Matt. 5-7), the missionary charge (Matt. 10:5-42), the parables discourse (Matt. 13:3-52), instructions to the community (Matt. 18:3-35), and the woes and eschatological discourse (Matt. 23-25). Each of these discourses is followed by a narrative on the actions or sayings of Jesus that are related to the preceding discourses. It seems that this fivefold structure could be a deliberate imitation by Matthew of the Pentateuch to indicate the relation between his Gospel and Pentateuchal material.

In the Sermon on the Mount, Matthew alludes to Moses when presenting Jesus. Right from the beginning of this carefully composed sermon, the Sinai typology is significant as Jesus went up the mountain to teach (Matt. 5:1-2). This opening creates an anticipation of a new revelation to be delivered by a new Lawgiver. This expectation is met when Jesus declares the purpose of his coming with his "I have come"-sayings with regard to the Law in Matt. 5:17 and his repeated reference to the meaning and intention of the Law in the Sermon *inter alia* with his sixfold elaboration on stipulations of the Law (Matt. 5:21-47) and his disapproval of hypocritical righteousness in charity, praying and fasting (Matt. 6:1-18). As indicated in the study, it was a well-known idea in Judaism that the Mosaic character could transmigrate to later legislators and teachers (e.g. in Ezekiel and 4 Ezra 14). Within this convention, Jesus is portrayed as teacher and revealer comparable to Moses.

Beyond the Sermon on the Mount, Jesus teaching on the *Torah* echoes in several other passages as well, e.g. Matt. 15:1-20 and 22:34-40. Significantly, the Gospel concludes with Jesus' Great Commandment that his disciples should go and make disciples by teaching them to obey everything He has commanded them (Matt. 28:18-20). Jesus is depicted as the one who taught the Law and commands His disciples to teach others the contents of what He taught.

12.2.1.2 The teacher of the Torah, enacts the Torah

Once Jesus ended the Sermon on the Mount, with its strong emphasis on the meaning of the *Torah*, Matthew tells that Jesus came down from the mountain (Matt. 8:1) as Moses once did from Mount Sinai (Exod. 19:14; 32:1; 34:29). Matthew thus apparently draws a parallel between Jesus and Moses, and the Mount of Jesus' Sermon and Mount Sinai. The impressive and authoritative teacher of the Law found in the discourse is subsequently presented in the narrative as going into action with a series of ten miracles (Matt. 8-9) to demonstrate how the Law should be practiced. Matthew links the Sermon on the Mount and the narrative describing Jesus' ten miracles with two summaries of the teaching and miracles Jesus performed (Matt. 4:23-25 and Matt. 9:35) forming some sort of compositional frame around them. As Moses performed signs and miracles, so did Jesus. Jesus can therefore be regarded as the new Moses. However, these healing and saving miracles of Jesus significantly contrast with the plagues in Egypt, which signifies God's plan of salvation in and through Jesus.

12.2.2 The *Torah* continues to remain valid

Matthew frequently affirms that the *Torah* continues to remain valid. It seems that Matthew intends to refute accusations that Jesus abrogated the *Torah*.

12.2.2.1 The importance of the Torah in Jewish society

From the investigation into the religious world of the Matthean community, it seems that a reconsideration of the correct interpretation of the *Torah* was an important and contentious issue in those times. In a fragmented post-70 C.E. Jewish society newly formed communities used the *Torah* to define their own norms of existence and to fend themselves from others who were not like-minded. The Sabbath observance, circumcision, dietary and purity laws functioned as identity markers to separate Jews from gentiles. In the first Gospel it appears that the author likewise defines his and his community's position in terms of specific *Torah* observance, yet with alternative interpretation of such identity markers. While Judaism(s) started to use the *Torah* as means to fend themselves off from foreign influences, the Matthean community propagated Gentile mission. This decision apparently intensified their conflict with the synagogue, who accused them of not adhering to the *Torah*. While it could be that Matthew defends their stance against some form of antinomian Christian libertinism, it rather seems that his main concern was with non-Christian Jewish allegations that his community neglected the *Torah*. Matthew firmly enters the debate on the importance of the *Torah* and its correct interpretation in terms of meaning and praxis.

12.2.2.2 Jesus' foundational statement on the continuing validity of the Torah

A very significant statement is made by Jesus in Matt. 5:17-20. He starts off with an emphatic statement about his mission. In Matt. 5:17 Jesus uses ἦλθον–sayings in parallel form to firmly state that He did not come to abolish (καταλῦσαι) the *Torah*, but to fulfil (πληρῶσαι) it. The Gospel teaches that Jesus brought and taught the intended meaning of the Law. This statement is reinforced in Matt. 5:18 with a solemn declaration (ἀμὴν γὰρ λέγω ὑμῖν) about Jesus' respect for even the seemingly insignificant parts of the Law (ἰῶτα ἓν ἢ μία κεραία). Matt. 5:19 presents a double *Satz heiligen Rechtes* with a warning about the negative implication of setting the *Torah* aside and teaching others the same (ἐλάχιστος κληθήσεται ἐν τῇ βασιλείᾳ τῶν οὐρανῶν). The warning is contrasted with the positive implication of practicing the commands and teaching others accordingly (οὗτος μέγας κληθήσεται ἐν τῇ βασιλείᾳ τῶν οὐρανῶν). The statement concludes with yet another solemn declaration in Matt. 5:20 with a *Satz heiligen Rechtes*, explaining the kind of righteousness that surpasses that of that of the Pharisees and teachers of the Law (ἡ δικαιοσύνη πλεῖον τῶν γραμματέων καὶ Φαρισαίων) required from disciples of Jesus. The greater righteousness can be considered as an identity marker of the followers of Jesus.

12.2.2.3 The requirement of righteousness

The requirement of greater righteousness (ἡ δικαιοσύνη πλεῖον) (Matt. 5:20) confirms the continuing validity of the *Torah*. As argued before, the word δικαιοσύνη fulfils an important role in the first Gospel, and Matthew uses this word primarily with an ethical meaning.

Jesus is depicted as the righteous one who is committed to fulfilling all righteousness (δικαιοσύνη). Matt. 3:13-17 describes how John tried to dissuade Jesus from being baptized, but that Jesus demonstrated his determination to fulfil all righteousness (γὰρ πρέπον ἐστὶν ἡμῖν πληρῶσαι πᾶσαν δικαιοσύνην) (Matt. 3:15). Jesus forms the prototype *par excellance* of one that is totally committed towards enacting God's will.

The character of John also demonstrates commitment to enacting God's will. John is described as the prototype of a loyal follower of Jesus and δικαιοσύνη is identified as his distinctive attribute (Matt. 21:32). John came in the way of righteousness (ἐν ὁδῷ δικαιοσύνης), an idiom that implies the full spectrum of proper response to God's will.

As John has acted faithfully according God's will, Jesus' other disciples are required to do the same. This is apparent from the use of δικαιοσύνη in the Sermon on the Mount. This word plays an important role in this Sermon and could be considered to express the essence of this Sermon. In the fourth beatitude Matthew's Jesus mentions the intense longing for righteousness (μακάριοι οἱ πεινῶντες καὶ διψῶντες τὴν δικαιοσύνην) as attribute of blessed ones (Matt. 5:6). This implies a passionate and persistent longing for the ideal conduct in adherence to God's ordinances. Δικαιοσύνη is mentioned again in the eighth beatitude, where the blessed ones' adherence to δικαιοσύνη is the cause of persecution (Matt. 5:10). Matthew's Jesus speaks of those who are committed to conduct that is appropriate for people under God's rule. In Matt. 6:1 Jesus urges his followers to practice their acts of δικαιοσύνη in a sincere manner, not as to impress people as the hypocrites do, but to adhere to the will of the heavenly Father. Three examples that were central to Jewish piety are mentioned: doing charity (Matt. 6:2-4), praying (Matt. 6:5-15) and fasting (Matt. 6:16-18). These acts must continue, but not in a hypocritical manner. The fact that sincere acts of piety are required while hypocritical acts are denounced demonstrates that Matthew's Jesus still regards such acts as important.

In Matt. 6:33 Jesus urges his disciples to put themselves under the rule of God and constantly seek to do his will (ζητεῖτε δὲ πρῶτον τὴν βασιλείαν [τοῦ θεοῦ] καὶ τὴν δικαιοσύνην αὐτοῦ). This implies thoroughgoing determination to continuously obey the deepest intent of the Law.

12.2.2.4 Jesus' halakhic argument and the continuing validity of the Torah

With an inattentive reading of Jesus' sixfold antithetical argument in Matt. 5:21-48, the conclusion can be drawn that Jesus disregarded at least some of the stipulations of the *Torah*. While it is clear that Jesus sharpens the meaning of the *Torah* in the first antithetical argument (on murder, Matt. 5:21-26) and in the second (on adultery, Matt. 5:27-30) there is some scholarly concern (e.g. Bornkamm, 2009:16; Strecker, 1971:146) that Jesus in other arguments replaces at least some of the stipulations of the *Torah*. However, as argued in this study, upon careful consideration of the contextual setting of these arguments, this does not seem to be the case.

Following his foundational statement on the continuing validity of the Law and its fulfilment (Matt. 5:17-19), and his call for a higher form of righteousness (Matt. 5:20), Jesus proceeds by arguing how the *Torah* continues to be valid and what this higher form of righteousness means in practice. It rather seems that Jesus objects to a literal and narrow interpretation of the *Torah*, by which the true intention of some stipulations of the Law have lost their meaning. The argument is rather that Jesus with his antithetical statements reinforces the actual and original intention of the *Torah*.

Though it might seem that Jesus with his third argument (Matt. 5:31-32) objects to the order of Moses to a formal certificate in case of a divorce, Jesus rather argues that the certificate was intended to protect women within the harsh reality of men who abused them, and not as a means to easily dissolve a marriage. He restricts this permission to cases where divorce *de facto* already has occurred.

Though it might seem that Jesus in the fourth argument (Matt. 5:33-37) objects against Moses' rules for the taking of oaths, it rather seems that Jesus argues that the taking of oaths is only necessary in unjust societies. In the ideal and truthful society the taking of oaths should not be necessary.

Though it might seem as if Jesus in the fifth argument (Matt. 5:38-42) objects against Moses' regulation on fair (the restriction of excessive) retaliation, Jesus argues that retaliation should rather be avoided and be replaced by benevolence.

In the sixth argument (Matt. 5:43-47) Jesus objects to an interpretation of the commandment of neighbourly love, which was understood in such a way that enemies could be hated. Jesus argues that such an understanding proves a misinterpretation of this commandment. Love even to enemies is required.

The antitheses are concluded with an admonishment to be perfect as the heavenly Father is perfect (Ἔσεσθε οὖν ὑμεῖς τέλειοι ὡς ὁ πατὴρ ὑμῶν ὁ οὐράνιος τέλειός ἐστιν) (Matt. 5:48). By this concluding statement Jesus shows that his explication of the *Torah*, as described in the preceding six *halakhic* arguments, illustrates perfect adherence to the *Torah*. Thus He argues that the true meaning of the *Torah* should perfectly be adhered to.

12.2.2.5 *"Go and learn" and "if you knew" what the Torah means*

Jesus' response to the Pharisees' objection that He ate with tax collectors and sinners (Matt. 9:13) remarkably demonstrates his regard for God's will. As discussed before, the introductory words, πορευθέντες δὲ μάθετε τί ἐστιν (but go and learn what it means), represent a rabbinic formula to urge pupils for careful *Torah* study. This means that they should "go and discern the sense of Scripture" or "go and make a valid inference from the scriptural statement". Jesus argues that the fact that the Pharisees accuse Him of eating with the marginalized proves that they do not understand the true meaning of the *Torah*. In contrast, He argues that what He is doing, demonstrates the praxis of true adherence to God's will.

Jesus makes a similar remark about the ignorance of the Pharisees in Matt. 12:7, εἰ δὲ ἐγνώκειτε τί ἐστιν (if you had known what this means). Jesus expresses his disappointment with the fact that the Pharisees do not understand the meaning of Scripture. He declares that He actually demonstrates the true intention of the *Torah* in the way He observes that Sabbath in contrast to the ignorant interpretation of the *Torah* by the Pharisees that causes a burdensome yoke on people (cf. Matt. 11:25-3).

12.2.2.6 *Jesus' accusation that the Pharisees break the command of God*

Jesus' response to the Pharisees and the teachers of the Law after they have accused the disciples for breaking the tradition of the elders (Matt. 15:2) once again demonstrates reverence to the commands of God. Jesus begins his response with "and why do you break (παραβαίνετε) the command of God (τὴν ἐντολὴν τοῦ Θεοῦ)?" (Matt. 15:3). Jesus contrasts the tradition (παράδοσις) of the Pharisees with the command of God (ἐντολὴ) and the Word of God (λόγος). This juxtaposition intensifies the contrast between God's commandments and man-made legislation. Matthew's Jesus therefore argues that his disciples do not follow the tradition of the Pharisees, because the Pharisees do not follow the commandment of God. The command of God is referred to as something that God said (ὁ γὰρ Θεὸς εἶπεν) (Matt. 15:4a and 6b). The divine origin of the commandment is emphasized and contrasted with the man-made tradition. Jesus argues that man-made commandments cannot substitute divine commandments. God's commandments should be respected.

It therefore seems that Matthew is firmly committed to the adherence of the *Torah* in its true meaning. He does not intend to present a Jesus who brought a new or a differing Law, but one for whom the *Torah* remains valid and important.

12.2.3 Jesus teaches and enacts an alternative interpretation of the *Torah*

While Matthew argues that the *Torah* remains valid, the meaning and practise of the *Torah* is understood differently from other Jewish traditions.

12.2.3.1 An alternative interpretation for an alternative community

From the investigation in this study it seems that in the post-70 C.E. period newly formed Jewish groups used the *Torah* to justify their parting from other groups and to define their alternative norms of existence. Their rivalry very much centred on claims to the correct interpretation of the *Torah*. Because of the importance of the *Torah* in Judaism, the interpretation of the *Torah* became a feature of the division. The different groups studied the Law in minute thoroughness. Yet, this desire to meet the specific obligations of the Law resulted in competitive disputes as to what the commandments meant in practice. Obviously this implied that other groups were doing it wrongly.

In Matthew the evangelist similarly developed a subtle dialectic with his opponents. Matthew describes Jesus as the one who brought the definitive interpretation of God's will. Jesus superseded current understandings of the Law with his reinterpretation. Matthew narrates the story of Jesus and his disciples seemingly to defend and establish the respectability of the seemingly "deviant" behaviour of his community. The Gospel challenges the conventional standards and delegitimizes the religious leaders who controlled the definitions of what is considered to be normal and deviant.

12.2.3.2 Jesus teaches an alternative interpretation of the Torah

Jesus' alternative teaching of the *Torah* is particularly noticeable in his pronouncements on righteousness and his *halakhic* argument in the Sermon on the Mount.

12.2.3.2.1 Jesus teaches an alternative form of righteousness

The alternative teaching and praxis of the *Torah* is demonstrated in the use of δικαιοσύνη (righteousness) in Matt. 5:20 and 6:1. Δικαιοσύνη is used in an ethical sense. The righteousness that Jesus required should in quality transcend what the scribes and Pharisees considered as righteous.

In Matt. 5:21-47 this transcending form of righteousness (ἡ δικαιοσύνη πλεῖον) as required in Matt. 5:20 is explicated in Jesus' six antithetical *halakhic* arguments.

In Matt. 6:1 the alternative form of δικαιοσύνη is again explained. While Matt. 5:20 deals with the nature of true δικαιοσύνη as demonstrated with six examples (Matt. 5:21-47), Matt. 6:1 warns against practising insincere δικαιοσύνη. In a polemical context Jesus denounces the demonstrative religious performances of the Pharisees when fasting (Matt. 6:2-4), when praying (Matt. 6:5-15) and when fasting (Matt. 6:16-18) to impress people in a theatrical manner. He contrasts this with the righteousness that He considers to be pleasing to the Father in heaven. The contrast does not lie in what is done, but in how it is done. The Pharisees also gave alms, prayed and fasted, but according to Matthew they did it hypocritically in order to promote their personal reputation. These deeds are only regarded as truly righteous if they are done with sincerity to honour God.

12.2.3.2.2 Jesus argues six alternative interpretations of Law stipulations

Jesus *halakhic* argument in Matt. 5:21-47 strongly demonstrates that Jesus teaches an alternative interpretation of the *Torah*. Matthew presents a series of six paragraphs, each stating a thesis followed by Jesus' interpretation of that thesis in contrast to the popular understanding of his day.

Each of these arguments opens with a common understanding of a stipulation of the Law, introduced by a repetitive formula, either the full formula ἠκούσατε ὅτι ἐρρέθη τοῖς ἀρχαίοις (you have heard that it was said to/by the people long ago) (Matt. 5:21 and 33), or the medium formula ἠκούσατε ὅτι ἐρρέθη (you have heard that it was said) (Matt. 5:27, 38 and 43) or the short formula ἐρρέθη δέ (it was said) (only in Matt. 5:31). Each of these statements is then followed by an antithetical response with the definite alternative interpretation of Jesus. Jesus time and again declares ἐγὼ δὲ λέγω ὑμῖν (but I say to you), implying that there are deeper principles to the Law as commonly assumed. The dominant note, hinted at by the emphatic "but I tell you", is the independent, authoritative teaching of Jesus.

The antitheses are concluded with an admonishment to be perfect as the heavenly Father is perfect (Ἔσεσθε οὖν ὑμεῖς τέλειοι ὡς ὁ πατὴρ ὑμῶν ὁ οὐράνιος τέλειός ἐστιν) (Matt. 5:48). By this concluding statement Jesus shows that his alternative explication of the *Torah,* as described in the preceding six *halakhic* arguments, illustrates perfect adherence to the *Torah*.

Beyond the Sermon on the Mount, alternative interpretation of the *Torah* echoes in arguments such as Matt. 15:1-16 (as will be argued below about Jesus' enactment of alternative interpretations of the *Torah*) on what makes a person unclean.

12.2.3.3 Jesus enacts alternative interpretations of the Torah

Besides his alternative teaching of the *Torah*, the Matthean Jesus also enacts the *Torah* differently. The following two short narratives investigated in this study serve as significant examples of this.

12.2.3.3.1 Jesus calls a tax collector and eats with tax collectors and sinners

Matt. 9:9-12 describes Jesus calling a "tax collector" as a disciple and having dinner with Matthew's fellow tax collectors and "sinners". Tax collectors were associated with sinners, people who in those days were regarded as shameful and impure figures in the Jewish society. Jesus breaks a social and religious convention not to associate with tax collectors. He calls Matthew, the tax collector, into a close relationship with Him. To emphasise the point, Jesus proceeds by eating with these tax collectors and sinners, presumably in Matthew's house (Matt. 9:10), a place Pharisees would avoid for the sake of purity and righteousness. The way in which they eat together demonstrates fellowship with these people. The description of Jesus reclining (αὐτοῦ ἀνακειμένου) and many tax collectors reclining (συνανέκειντο) with Him depicts closeness of the participants (Matt. 9:10). Through his behaviour Jesus expresses full acceptance of tax collectors and sinners. Jesus cuts the Pharisaic religious understanding and practice of who should be regarded as righteous and worthy of fellowship. The Pharisees in the narrative strongly object to this conduct of Jesus (διὰ τί μετὰ τῶν τελωνῶν καὶ ἁμαρτωλῶν ἐσθίει ὁ διδάσκαλος ὑμῶν (Matt. 9:11)). Table fellowship with tax collectors and sinners is depicted as objectionable to Pharisaic observance of the *Torah*. In contrast to the Pharisees' religious and social pre-occupations about people whom they regard to be fit only for the judgement of God, Jesus fully accepts them. He even depicts the reason for his coming as to call such people to be healed (Matt. 9:12-13). He accuses the Pharisees of ignorance of the meaning of the Scriptures for objecting his conduct by instructing them to "Go and learn what it means: 'I desire mercy, not sacrifice'" (Matt. 9:13a).

12.2.3.3.2 Jesus defends the conduct of his disciples on the Sabbath

Another clear example of Jesus' alternative enactment of the *Torah* is demonstrated in the controversy story about the Sabbath (Matt. 12:1-13).

The Pharisees object to the conduct of Jesus' disciples of picking grain on the Sabbath. In their accusation they explicitly refer to the Law: Ἰδοὺ οἱ μαθηταί σου ποιοῦσιν ὃ οὐκ ἔξεστιν ποιεῖν ἐν σαββάτῳ ("your disciples are doing what is unlawful on the Sabbath) (Matt. 12:2). Jesus does not dispute what the disciples have done, but challenges the Pharisees on their evaluation of the disciples' conduct. Jesus argues that God wants the expression of loving-kindness on the Sabbath, rather than blind religious practice.

Matthew argues this point in several ways. The Sabbath controversy is preceded by the invitation of Jesus that all who are weary and burdened should come and take his yoke upon them (Matt. 11:28-30). Implicitly his "easy" and "light" yoke (religious practices intended to ensure adherence to the *Torah*) is contrasted with the burdensome practices of the Pharisees. With his citation of Hos. 6:6 ("I desire mercy and not sacrifice") in Matt. 12:7, mercy is presented as the guiding principle in religious practices. To demonstrate the point, Jesus proceeds on the Sabbath to heal the man with the shrivelled hand (Matt. 12:9-13).

Matthew narrates that this conduct enflames the Pharisees, as they went out to plot against Jesus to kill Him (Matt. 12:17). Their dismay accentuates the alternative enactment of Jesus of the *Torah*.

12.2.3.3.3   Jesus defends his disciples for eating with unwashed hands

Jesus's response to the accusation made by the Pharisees and the scribes that his disciples do not observe the tradition of hand-washing in Matt. 15:1-20 is another example of how Jesus practices the *Torah* differently. While the Pharisees are depicted as obsessed with external man-made rules to ensure purity, Jesus is depicted as being concerned with inner purity based on God's Word.

While the Pharisees supplemented the written *Torah* with oral traditions of the elders to ensure total adherence to the *Torah*, Jesus rejects these traditions. With the tradition of the handwashing the Pharisees adopted the requirement set for priests before they ate consecrated food and applied these requirements to themselves and all Jews, even when eating ordinary food. Thus they intended to ensure adherence to purity requirements of the *Torah*. Jesus, however, has no problem when ordinary people eat food with unwashed hands. Jesus transposes these external purity rituals to a requirement of internal purity. He regards internal purity as decisive. It is not what enters one's mouth that makes a person unclean, but what exits one's mouth, as it reveals the intentions of one's inner being.

12.2.4 Jesus has the authority to interpret the *Torah*

Jesus is depicted as the one who has the authority to provide the interpretation of the *Torah* as God intended it to be. The following examples from the first Gospel serve to demonstrate this argument.

12.2.4.1   Jesus is the representative of God

Matthew describes Jesus as the representative of God amongst people. At the beginning of his Gospel Matthew writes about the name of Jesus: "'... they will call him Immanuel', which means 'God with us' (Μεθ' ἡμῶν ὁ Θεός)" (Matt. 1:26). He likewise ends his Gospel with the promise of Jesus: "And surely I am with you always (ἐγὼ μεθ' ὑμῶν εἰμι πάσας τὰς ἡμέρας), to the very end of the age." (Matt. 28:20). Jesus is described as the Risen One ruling and commanding in the congregation (Matt. 28:16-20). Furthermore, Matthew describes the presence of Jesus in the church "For where two or three gather in my name, there am I with them (οὗ γάρ εἰσιν δύο ἢ τρεῖς συνηγμένοι εἰς τὸ ἐμὸν ὄνομα, ἐκεῖ εἰμι ἐν μέσῳ αὐτῶν")" (Matt. 18:20).

Jesus is also identified as the beloved Son of God. Matthew uses the highly Christological quotation, οὗτός ἐστιν ὁ υἱός μου ὁ ἀγαπητός, ἐν ᾧ εὐδόκησα (this is my Son, whom I love; with him I am well pleased) which occurs at Jesus' baptism (Matt. 3:17) and at his transfiguration (Matt. 17:5).

In the Sabbath controversy, Matthew is unique in introducing the Christological statement: τοῦ ἱεροῦ μεῖζόν ἐστιν ὧδε (one greater than the temple is here) (Matt. 12:6). As the temple has been the focus of God's presence amongst his people, the Matthean statement implies that in Jesus God is to be found much better than in the temple. In the aftermath of 70 C.E., with the cultic vacuum left by the destruction of the temple, this claim of Matthew must have resounded strongly. The Matthean Jesus presents Himself as God's agent and the one through whom God authoritatively carries out functions previously associated with the temple.

Jesus is depicted as the present deity (*deus praesens*), which equals Roman claims that the Caesar was the agent of Jupiter and the present deity (*deus praesens*) (Statius, *Silvae* 5.2.170). Jesus is the representative of the one true God, the God of Israel, the original giver of the *Torah*, amongst his people. Matthew thus argues that Jesus is the one who has the authority to provide the correct interpretation of the *Torah* as God intended it to be is.

12.2.4.2 Jesus is a Moses-like figure who teaches with authority

In the Sermon on the Mount Matthew alludes to Moses when presenting Jesus. The setting of the Sermon is stated at the beginning when Jesus goes up the mountain to teach (Matt. 5:1-2). The Sinai typology is noticeable from this setting. This opening leads to an anticipation of a teaching to be delivered by a Lawgiver. This expectation is met when Jesus confirms the continuing validity of the Law (Matt. 5:17-20), repeatedly refers to the meaning and intention of the Law, and elaborates on the Decalogue as such (Matt. 5:21-47). Matthew links with a well-known Jewish concept that the Mosaic character could transmigrate to later legislators and teachers. This comparison between Jesus and Moses echoes expectations found in Jewish literature. Baruch emerges as God's agent who truly instructs the righteous community (2 Bar. 38:1-4). Baruch is paralleled with Moses as Baruch left his people and ascended Mount Zion to receive God's instructions. Like Moses, Baruch is portrayed as God's lawgiver. In 4 Ezra 14, Ezra appears as Moses *redivivus*: "I revealed myself in the bush, and spoke to Moses, ... So too I now give this order to you" (4 Ezra 14: 3-7). Within this convention, Jesus is portrayed as teacher and revealer comparable to Moses. Matthew draws a parallel between Jesus and Moses, both as mediators of the commandments of God.

The authority of Jesus' teaching is explicitly mentioned as Matthew concludes the Sermon with its Sinai typology with a postscript: "the crowds were amazed at his teaching, because He taught as one who had authority (ἦν γὰρ διδάσκων αὐτοὺς ὡς ἐξουσίαν ἔχων), and not as their teachers of the law" (Matt. 7:28-29).

Matthew then proceeds with the narrative by telling that Jesus came down from the mountain. Matthew inserts the transition from the Sermon on the Mount to the miracle story (καταβάντος δὲ αὐτοῦ ἀπὸ τοῦ ὄρους, Matt. 8:1), which almost identically parallels the LXX version of Moses' descent from Sinai (καταβαίνοντος δὲ αὐτοῦ ἀπὸ τοῦ ὄρους) (Exod. 34:29). As mentioned before, the impressive and authoritative teacher of the Law found in the discourse is subsequently presented in the narrative as going into action to demonstrate how the Law should be practiced. As Moses in Exodus did ten miracles and gave the Law, Jesus authoritatively interprets the Law in the Sermon on the Mount (Matt. 5-7) and then authoritatively performs his interpretation of the Law in the miracle narratives (Matt. 8-9). The contrast between the plagues by Moses and the healing of Jesus is significant. The miracle narratives in Matthew depict the authority (ἐξουσία) of Jesus over illness, nature, demons, paralysis, disabilities and death. The early Christian writing, Pseudo-Clementine, expresses this similarity and contrast: "As Moses did signs and miracles, so also did Jesus.

And there is no doubt but that the likeness of the signs proves him (Jesus) to be that prophet of whom he (Moses) said that he should come 'like myself'" (Pseudo-Clementine, *Recognitiones*, 1.57).

12.2.4.3 Jesus emerges as the victor in conflict scenes

Matthew depicts Jesus in several conflict scenes with the Pharisees about the meaning of the *Torah* (e.g. Matt. 12:1-14; 15:1-20 and 22:24-40). It is significant the Jesus time and again emerges as the victor from these scenes.

Most significant is the scene where Jesus is challenged by an expert of the *Torah* (νομικὸς) in a *Streitgespräch* on the greatest commandment (Matt. 22:34-45). In response to the challenge of this expert, Jesus victoriously defuses the challenge. A central pattern of such a *Streitgespräch* is the interaction of challenge and riposte. The intention of the expert of the *Torah* is depicted as to undermine Jesus' reputation, to expose his ignorance and thus to ridicule Him. However, Jesus rather acquires honour by his skilful riposte to this challenge. The Pharisees witness Jesus' victory in this *Streitgespräch*. This expert of the Law and his fellow Pharisees are silenced. Jesus then continues by asking a question of his own: "What do you think of the Messiah?" (Matt. 22:42). Matthew concludes with a climactic ending "no one dared ask him any more questions". Jesus emerges as the clear victor and the respect the disciples and crowds have for Jesus, increases.

When entering the synagogue on the Sabbath Jesus' opponents were looking for a reason to accuse Him and asked Him whether it is lawful to heal on the Sabbath. Jesus responds and heals the man with the shrivelled hand (Matt. 12:9-13). Matthew mentions no direct counter-response to Jesus, but that the Pharisees left the synagogue and plotted how they might kill Him (Matt. 12:14). As we have no evidence that any sect in early Judaism had rules that would allow putting someone to death for healing on the Sabbath, such plotting to kill would have been considered premeditated murder (Gen. 9:5-6; Num. 35:29-34). The reaction of the Pharisees in the story demonstrates their utter misunderstanding with God's intention with the *Torah* and forms a shameful contrast with Jesus' good deed. Matthew sharply describes the Pharisees as people with a lack of understanding (Matt. 11:25) as they proceed to break the Law in their fervour to get rid of Jesus. The evangelist proceeds to tell how many followed Jesus and that He continued to heal all their sick (Matt. 12:15). Matthew then uses a fulfilment quotation to state that Jesus is the promised One, the servant Messiah, who came to fulfil the Law and the Prophets (Isa. 42:1-4).

With this portrait of Jesus, the Christological authority of Jesus is illuminated in contrast to the devious conduct of the Pharisees.

In response to the objection of the Pharisees and the scribes that Jesus' disciples ate with unwashed hands (Matt. 15:1), Jesus responds by defining the "tradition of the elders" (ἡ παράδοσις τῶν πρεσβυτέρων) (Matt. 15:2 and 3) as human "teaching of teachings". He rejects the teachings based on their human ideas. Jesus argues that his disciples do not follow the tradition of the Pharisees, because the Pharisees do not follow the commandment of God ("τὴν ἐντολὴν τοῦ θεοῦ) (Matt. 15:3) or the Word of God (τὸν λόγον τοῦ θεοῦ) (Matt. 15:6). Despite this strong riposte, the Pharisees and scribes do not respond to Jesus. Jesus proceeds to address the crowd and his disciples respectively (Matt. 15:10-20). The *Streitgespräch* ends with Jesus victoriously making the final statement: "Eating with unwashed hands, does not make one clean (Matt. 15:19).

12.2.4.4 Jesus who has all authority commands that His interpretation be taught

The authority of Jesus is clearly stated in the climactic conclusion of the Gospel: "All authority has been given to me" (Ἐδόθη μοι πᾶσα ἐξουσία ἐν οὐρανῷ καὶ ἐπὶ τῆς γῆς). Therefore go and make disciples ... teaching them to obey everything I have commanded you (διδάσκοντες αὐτοὺς τηρεῖν πάντα ὅσα ἐνετειλάμην ὑμῖν)" (Matt. 28:18-20). Matthew claims that Jesus has the authority to interpret the Scriptures. His interpretation provides the answer to the correct way of understanding the Scriptures, in contradiction with the teaching of the Pharisees that are proven wrong throughout the Gospel. The disciples of Jesus are commanded to teach others the contents of what Jesus taught them. In this climatic ending Matthew describes Jesus as the authoritative interpreter and teacher of the Scriptures. His teaching serves the salvation of all people.

12.2.5 With Jesus the *Torah* forms part of God's plan of salvation

Matthew interprets the *Torah* by integrating it into God's plan of salvation history and linking it to Christology. Jesus is depicted is the one who reveals and establishes the true intention of the *Torah*.

12.2.5.1 Jesus fulfils the Torah

In Matthew Jesus fulfils all righteousness for his people in his teaching, living and dying.

12.2.5.1.1 Jesus fulfils the righteousness with his baptism

The theme of Jesus who came to fulfilment God's righteousness is introduced with his baptism (Matt. 3:13-16). Only Matthew describes how John tried to dissuade Jesus from baptising Him and of how Jesus responded that He had to be baptised by John so that all righteousness could be fulfilled for them: "οὕτως γὰρ πρέπον ἐστὶν ἡμῖν πληρῶσαι πᾶσαν δικαιοσύνην" (it is proper for us to do this to fulfil all righteousness) (indicated in bold and underlining) (Matt. 3:15). Significantly Matthew adds two key Matthean themes, namely "fulfilment" (πληρῶσαι) and "righteousness" (δικαιοσύνη). Jesus and John needed to do what God wanted in eschatological context, and thus fulfilled God's plans set forth for each of them respectively in the predictions of the Jewish Scriptures. Matthew confirms that Jesus' baptism was intended to fulfil the requirements set in the Jewish Scriptures and to establish righteousness in with his mission. However, this act to fulfil all righteousness is not meant to be exhaustive, as indicated by the ingressive aorist of the verb πληρῶσαι. This act is rather the beginning of more to follow, namely God's salvific activity through Jesus who came to save his people from their sins (Matt. 1:21). He would salvivicly fulfil the requirements of the *Torah* so that his people can be saved. A voice from heaven confirms this role of Jesus: "This is my Son, whom I love; with whom I am pleased" (Matt. 3:17). A similar voice confirms this mission of Jesus on the Mount of Transfigurations shortly after Jesus predicted his salvific death: "This is my Son, whom I love; with him I am well pleased. Listen to him" (Matt. 17:5).

12.2.5.1.2 Jesus' mission is to fulfil the Torah and the Prophets

In a mission statement, Matthew's Jesus affirms that his coming forms part of God's salvific plan. After assuring that He did not come to abolish the *Torah* and the Prophets (οὐκ ἦλθον καταλῦσαι), He positively affirms that He came to fulfil them (πληρῶσαι) (Matt. 5:17). The operative word, πληρῶσαι, is significant. The word used as contrary to "abolish", is not to "confirm" or to "enforce" the Law, but to "fulfil" it. The proper way to keep any commandment was to fulfil the purpose for which it was intended. The fulfilment of the Jewish Scriptures in Jesus is the basic orientation of Matthew's Gospel. Jesus describes his mission as bringing the *Torah* and Prophets to their full intent. The intention of the *Torah* is to express the covenantal relationship between Him and his people. Jesus' intention is to completely fulfil the requirements of the Law to restore this relationship. Thus He brought the *Torah* to its fruition.

12.2.5.1.3 Jesus fulfils the servant song

By quoting the servant song, ἰδοὺ ὁ παῖς μου ὃν ᾑρέτισα, ὁ ἀγαπητός μου ὃν εὐδόκησεν ἡ ψυχή μου ... (here is my servant (child) whom I have chosen, the one I love ...) in Matt. 12:18-21, Matthew affirms that Isaiah's prophecy has reached its fulfilment in Jesus. Jesus is God's chosen One. According to Isa. 42:1-4 the servant (Jesus the Messiah for Matthew; cf. Matt. 12:18-21) would bring judgement (*mishpat*) and *Torah* (cf. Num. 24:17; Deut. 18:18-19; Isa. 52:7; 61:2-3; Dan. 9:25). It is highly significant that Matthew uses ὁ παῖς (son) rather than δοῦλος (slave/servant). He changes both the MT (*ebed*, servant) and LXX (δοῦλος, slave) to bring the quotation in conformity with the voice from heaven at two other occasions. He thus links this quotation to the highly Christological quotation, οὗτός ἐστιν ὁ υἱός μου ὁ ἀγαπητός, ἐν ᾧ εὐδόκησα (this is my Son, whom I love; with him I am well pleased) which occurs at Jesus' baptism (Matt. 3:17) and at his transfiguration (Matt. 17:5). Matthew moves the focus from a "servant of God Christology" to a "Son of God Christology". By linking these quotations, Matthew implicitly claims that the Messiah's mission as inaugurated with his baptism is fulfilled in the Son of God. While the Pharisees condemned Jesus and his disciples and plotted how they could kill Him (Matt. 12:2, 10 and 14), God loves Him and takes delight in Him (Matt. 12:18).

Fulfilment can be seen as the key to understanding Jesus' relation to the Law. This implies that the practical functioning of the Law probably would not remain the same as it was before his coming. Even though the Law remains permanently important, it should function differently in a pre- and post-fulfilment situation. The argument is that Jesus completed the Law by extending its demands and bringing it to which it pointed. Jesus' teaching and ministry would demonstrate this fulfilment. Matthew is therefore saying to his adversaries, who accuse the Jesus followers of their way of observing the *Torah*, that the *Torah* is fulfilled. Matthew poses two strongly divergent options to his readers: Either you continue with the traditional way of Law observance, thereby ignoring the fulfilment of the Law and the prophets, or you accept the authority of Jesus who divinely interpreted the true intention of the Law.

12.2.5.2 With Jesus God's Kingdom comes

Matthew links the coming of the Kingdom (βασιλεία) of Heaven with the teaching and miracles of Jesus. The Sermon on the Mount and the narrative describing Jesus' ten miracles are connected by two summaries of the teaching and miracles Jesus performed ("Jesus went through all the towns and villages, teaching in their synagogues, proclaiming the good news of the kingdom (τὸ εὐαγγέλιον τῆς βασιλείας) and healing every disease and sickness" (Matt. 4:23-25 and Matt. 9:35)) to form some sort of compositional frame around them. For Jesus the coming of the Kingdom did not comprise one moment, but realizes through a series of events over a period of time. In the Sermon on the Mount (Matt. 5-7) Jesus is depicted as the Teacher of this Kingdom. With the series of miracles that follows (Matt. 8-9) He demonstrates his Kingship. In the Sermon on the Mount the King declares the rules for the Kingdom and with his healing miracles and stilling the storm He demonstrates the character of the Kingdom. When Jesus announces that the Kingdom of Heaven has come and is coming, He proclaims that He initiated the process of the realisation of God's rule, but that the completion lies in the future, when the last things will come. His teaching in the Sermon on the Mount, and healing and stilling activities step-by-step realize the blessings associated with the coming of the Kingdom.

12.2.5.3 Jesus is the Holy One who purifies

The scenes where Jesus touches unclean persons or is being touched is noteworthy. In Biblical times one was to avoid touching unclean persons as that would lead to being contaminated. However, when Jesus touches a leper (Matt. 8:3), the leprosy and impurity does not spread to Jesus. To the contrary, the leper is healed. When the bleeding woman touches Jesus, she is healed (Matt. 9:20-22). Similarly, the dead girl is raised from death when He takes her by the hand (Matt. 9:25). Jesus is not regarded as an ordinary person who can be defiled be impure people. The reverse happens. Purity flows from Jesus over to the impure people. This relates to the connotation of touching in ancient healing stories. It was assumed that power and energy would flow from the holy person or healer to the ill one.

In the Biblical text death is regarded as the ultimate consequence of sin. Sickness lies on the continuum between sin and death. Sickness is the sequel to sin and the predecessor of death. Underlying this connection is also the social implication of both illness and healing. Jesus overturns this sequel. The power to heal and cleanse flows from Jesus to the leper, the bleeding woman and the dead girl. Jesus is depicted as the mighty conqueror of illness and death.

Jesus, the Holy One, is the Saviour who has the authority to heal and to cleanse. In Jesus the intention of the purity laws is realized. God, the "Holy One of Israel" (Isa. 1:4; 5:19, 24), is the ideal manifestation and source of holiness. As God is holy, He requires of his people to be holy too. Holiness for his people is the intention of the *Torah*. Jesus restores the holiness of his people. Through

Jesus God establishes messianic times of life. Such times are characterized by health and the absence of illness and death.

12.2.6 Love and mercy form the hermeneutical keys to *Torah* interpretation and practice

It subsequently seems that love and mercy epitomize the *Torah* and forms the overarching principle to which all the commandments are connected. The *Torah* and should be interpreted in terms of love and practiced with mercy.

12.2.6.1 Double love commandment

While the Rabbinate developed an elaborate series of hermeneutical rules and formal criteria to guarantee the observance or the *Torah*, Matthew deduces the keeping of the Law from the central point of the double love commandment (Matt. 22:34-40). This commandment forms the hermeneutical key for the keeping of the *Torah*. Jesus states: "ἐν ταύταις ταῖς δυσὶν ἐντολαῖς ὅλος ὁ νόμος κρέμαται καὶ οἱ προφῆται" (all the Law and the Prophets hang on these two commandments) (Matt. 22:40). All the commandments of the *Torah* and Prophets thus are dependent on the commandment to love God and to love one's neighbour. These two commandments form the basis for all relationships and ethics. None of the commandments of the Law and the teaching of the prophets can be fulfilled apart from love. The whole Law and the prophets can be exegetically deduced from the command to love God and the neighbour. Obedience to the *Torah* is apparent by the showing of love.

12.2.6.2 Jesus enacts love and mercy

The double love commandment in the first Gospel is underscored by depicting Jesus as the one who shows love and mercy. Matthew's Jesus heals the miserables and associates Himself with the despised and outsiders to the community. Jesus heals sick people and raises the dead (Matt. 8:1-9:35).

In two cases Jesus' enactment of mercy is described in terms of the quotation from Hos. 6:6: "I desire mercy, not sacrifice". As demonstration of his mercy (ἔλεος), Jesus calls a tax collector to become his disciple and He feasts with tax collectors who were regarded as outsiders (Matt. 9:9-13). Matthew contrasts inadequate responses to Jesus' ministry (of the Pharisees) with what should be the proper response (of the tax collectors and sinners) (Matt. 9:11-13). This quotation is also used when Jesus defends his disciples' conduct on the Sabbath (Matt. 12:1-8) and proceeds to demonstrate his mercy by healing the man with the shrivelled hand on the Sabbath (Matt. 12:9-13).

12.2.7 A different range of the *Torah*

While Matthew makes a strong statement on the retention of the *Torah*, the range of the Law differs from that of the Rabbinate. Matthew's Jesus rejects "the Judaism of the Dual *Torah*". Matthew does not retain the status of the oral law, nor the detailed regulations developed in Jewish tradition. He opposes traditional interpretations of stipulations of the *Torah* with the antitheses in the Sermon on the Mount (Matt. 5:21-47). He eats with marginalized people (Matt. 9:11). He criticizes the traditions of the Pharisees as burdensome (Matt. 11:28-30). He sharply reacts to the ceremonial washing of hands (Matt. 15:3).

It seems that Matthew does not reject ceremonial law as such, though it has undergone a reassessment under Christian motives. Matthew's Jesus still refers to the offering of a gift at the altar (Matt. 5:23-24). Though He urges the Pharisees to go and learn what the words of Hos. 6:6 (I desire mercy not sacrifice) means (Matt. 9:13; 12:7) He uses this reference congruent to its original setting. Sacrifice without loyalty and true devotion to God is meaningless. The Sabbath is still observed, but in a different way from how the Rabbinate does so. Mercy becomes determinative (Matt. 12:1-13).

Nevertheless, it should be noted that he Gospel does not mention circumcision, not of the baby Jesus, nor as practice for the disciples of Jesus. On the other hand, the baptism of converted Gentiles is prescribed (Matt. 28:19). Whether Matthew proposes baptism to replace the ritual of circumcision, is unsure, though it seems like it could be.

12.2.8 Sharp opposition to Jesus' *Torah* interpretation

Sharp opposition to Pharisaic and the Rabbinic interpretation of the *Torah* runs throughout the Gospel. The Pharisees are depicted not to be the pious people they claim to be (Matt. 5:21; 6:1; 23) and the teachers of the Law not that authoritative (Matt. 7:48) or knowledgeable (Matt. 9:13; 11:25; 12:7).

In the Gospel the Pharisees and teachers of the Law act as the main opponents (antagonists*)* of Jesus (the protagonist of the narrative)*.* They question his and his disciples' conduct (Matt. 9:11; 12:1; 15:2) and challenges Him about the greatest commandment (Matt. 22:36).

Matthew's polemic with the Pharisees is particularly harsh. Heightened conflict against the Pharisees is strongly reflected in Matthew's controversy stories. Especially the discourse of the woes (Matt. 23) and the parables on the tenants and wedding banquet (Matt. 21:33-22:14) express this conflict. This conflict is also expressed as Matthew intensifies the conflict in the narratives he took over from Mark (e.g. Matt. 22:34-40).

This conflict probably reflects the hostile environment in which Matthew and his community practised their understanding of the *Torah*. Though Matthew's Gospel holds an indirect warning against antinomians who appeal to faith and discounts good works, his main defence is against the Pharisees and the teachers of Law. It seems that anti-Pharisaic arguments played an important role in the self-definition of the Matthean community in the crises of separation and transition. It seems that the first Gospel forms a "counter-narrative" against synagogual control by the Pharisees.

12.2.9 Strong criticism of the Pharisees and teachers of the Law

The criticism of the teachings and enactment of the *Torah* by the Pharisees and teachers of the Law, is particularly harsh in the Matthew.

In Matt. 9:13 and 9:13 Jesus passes judgement on the conduct of the Pharisees by referring them to Hos. 6:6. In both cases the quotation is introduced in similar ways, πορευθέντες δὲ μάθετε τί ἐστιν (go and learn what this means) (Matt. 9:13) and εἰ δὲ ἐγνώκειτε τί ἐστιν (if you had known what the words mean) (Matt. 12:7). The introductory words πορευθέντες δὲ μάθετε τί ἐστιν (but go and learn what it means) represents a rabbinic formula to encourage pupils for *Torah* study, which means "go and discern the sense of Scripture" or "go and make a valid inference from the scriptural statement". This is extremely ironic as the Pharisees regarded themselves the true keepers of the Scriptures. Jesus argues that the fact that the Pharisees accuse Him misconduct proves that they in fact do not understand the true meaning of the *Torah*.

In Matt. 15 the Matthean Jesus uses several words and phrases to refer to the Law as given by God: the command of God (ἐντολὴ), the Word of God (λόγος) and what God said (ὁ γὰρ θεὸς εἶπεν). In contrast to these, the tradition (παράδοσις) of the Pharisees is mentioned as regulations made by humans. The Pharisees are teaching the teachings on human rules (διδάσκοντες διδασκαλίας ἐντάλματα ἀνθρώπων). Though the tradition was intended to prevent that infringement of the Law of God takes place, Jesus accuses the Pharisees of letting the opposite happen. Jesus expresses it very frankly: Not despite adding their tradition to the *Torah*, but because of this addition (διὰ τὴν παράδοσιν), they break the Law of God.

While the sentiment towards the Jewish religious leaders is negative throughout the gospel, the conflict clearly intensifies during the week of the Passion (Matt.

21-23), forming a crescendo of this conflict. This conflict is introduced with Jesus' cleansing and judgement of the temple (Matt. 21:12-17). This judgement is further symbolized by his cursing of the fig tree (Matt. 21:18-22). The Matthean Jesus proceeds by telling three parables in which the unreliability of these leaders are exposed (Matt. 21:28-22:14). This culminates in Jesus's extensive criticism in Matt. 23. First, Jesus addresses the crowds, warning them of the insincerity of these Jewish leaders. He uses irony when instructing the crowds to obey the words of the teachers of the Law and the Pharisees, and then continuing to describe their hypocritical conduct which includes their skewed *halakha*. He thus exposes their teachings as misleading and their conduct insincere. He pronounces a series of woes in which He accuses them of being hypocritical and spiritually blind. He concludes by bemoaning the destiny of Jerusalem under the leadership of these leaders.

12.2.10 An alternative *Torah*-abiding community

It seems that an alternative community was formed with an alternative interpretation of the *Torah* as foundation.

12.2.10.1 An alternative community

People who have benefitted from the righteousness (δικαιοσύνη) of Jesus and are honestly committed to his teaching form a new community in the Kingdom of Heaven, separate from the Jewish synagogue. It seems that the Matthean community was dislodged from its synagogues. This distance between Matthew and the synagogue is reflected in Matthew's references to the synagogue. Matthew uses the phrase "their synagogue" five times (Matt. 4:23, 9:35; 10:17; 12:9; 13:54) and "your synagogue" once (Matt. 23:34) to underline the distance between Jesus and the synagogue community. It seems that Matthew distances his group from the synagogues and establishes a separate structure that stands independent from the synagogues. Matthew's Jesus refers to this new community as the ἐκκλησία (church) (Matt. 16:18 and 18:17). Being a general LXX translation for *qahal*, the congregation of the people of God (e.g. Deut. 31:30), Jesus uses the term to describe the group of restored Israelites that He was gathering around Himself. In the usage of this emotive concept from the Jewish Bible, and translating it distinctively as ἐκκλησία (church), Matthew indicates that his group took over the role of the congregation of the people of God and distinguishes them from the synagogue (συναγωγή) and its leaders. Matt. 8:11-15 even speaks of transference of the kingdom of God to a new people. While the Jewish leaders claimed to lead the synagogue, the church was led by leaders who confessed Jesus as the Christ, the Son of the living God (Matt. 16:16).

From the Gospel it seems that the ἐκκλησία was met with sharp criticism and rejection. Matthew seemingly applies the story of the stilling of the storm to the trials and tribulations of discipleship and the church (Matt. 8:27-27). Yet, Jesus rescues his disciples and people who believe in Him. He provides them with security. Matthew describes the presence of Jesus as representative of God in the church "For where two or three gather in my name, there am I with them (οὗ γάρ εἰσιν δύο ἢ τρεῖς συνηγμένοι εἰς τὸ ἐμὸν ὄνομα, ἐκεῖ εἰμι ἐν μέσῳ αὐτῶν" (Matt. 18:20).

12.2.10.2 A community with a higher level of righteousness

Matthew describes the differentiating virtues and righteousness required of the followers of Jesus. Matthew requires a different level of morality. Followers of Jesus must entertain a higher level of righteousness (δικαιοσύνη) (Matt. 5:20) and should be perfect (τέλειος) (Matt. 5:20). This higher level of morality distinguishes the followers of Jesus from others and forms an identity mark of the congregation. This higher level of morality is based on the different interpretation of the *Torah*, as being taught by the Matthean Jesus. This morality must result from an honest and heartfelt devotion to God. True morality flows from a pure heart (Matt. 5:8; 15:12-20). Matthew contrasts this kind of morality with a superficial keeping of God's commandments by the Jewish leaders who propose to be pious (Matt. 6:1-18).

12.2.10.3 A community that incorporates outsiders

While it seems that the way the Pharisees interpreted the *Torah* caused them to exclude some people from their community, the Matthean community incorporated such people into their community. Jesus urges his disciples to also love their enemies (Matt. 5:44). Jesus demonstrates this by associating Himself with tax collectors and sinners (Matt. 9:9-12). He commands his disciples to go make disciples of all nations (Matt. 28:19). Jesus establishes a new community of believers. It seems that this community was met with rejection by other *Torah*-abiding Jews.

12.2.10.4 A community signified by humility

In his final discourse the Matthean Jesus tells the crowds what the teachers of the Law and the Pharisees do (Matt. 23:1–7) and then proceeds to talk about what his disciples should do instead (Matt. 23:8–12). It seems that the main idea is to contrast the pride and hypocrisy of the religious leaders with the humility and servanthood required from Jesus' followers. Matt. 23:1–7 provides a vigorous polemic portrait of the vanity of the Pharisees and the teachers of the Law. Jesus accuses them of their fixation on attracting honour in their teaching roles as they strive towards being called "Rabbi". In contrast to the vanity of the Pharisees and teachers of the Law in Matt. 23:1–7, Jesus proceeds to set out the antithetical behaviour required of discipleship, with an emphasis on "but you" (ὑμεῖς δὲ) in Matt. 23:8–12, which reads as a small community rule on humility. This rule signifies a contrast in community values between that of the Pharisees and teachers of the Law, and that of the followers of Jesus. Humility is mentioned as the basic premise of being a disciple of Jesus.

LIST OF REFERENCES

Aejmelaeus, A., 2007, *On the trail of the Septuagint translators*, Peeters, Leuven.

Allison, D.C., 1993, *The new Moses. A Matthean typology*, T. & T. Clark, Edinburgh.

Anderson, J.C., 1983, 'Matthew: Gender and reading', *Semeia*, 28, 3-27.

Ascough, R.S., 2001, 'Matthew and community formation', in D.E. Aune (ed.), *The Gospel of Matthew in current study*, pp.96-126, Eerdmans, Grand Rapids.

Aune, D. 1988. *The New Testament in Its Literary Environment*, James Clark, Cambridge.

Austin, J.L., 2005, *How to do things with words*, Cambridge University Press, Cambridge.

Avi-yonah, M., 2007, 'Second Temple', in F. Skoling & M. Berenbaum (eds.), *Encyclopaedia Judaica*, 2nd. edn., vol. 19, pp. 608-611, Thompson Gale, Detroit, New York, San Francisco, New Haven, Waterville, Maine & London.

Bacchiocchi, S., 1986, 'Sabbatical typologies of messianic redemption', *Journal for the Study of Judaism*, 17, 153-176.

Bacon, B.W., 1930, *Studies in Matthew*, Holt, New York.

Bailey, J., 2000, 'Vowing away the fifth commandment: Matthew 15:3-6 / Mark 7:9-13', *Restoration Quarterly*, 42, 193-209.

Banks, R., 1974a, *Jesus and the Law in the synoptic tradition*, Cambridge University Press, Cambridge.

Banks, R., 1974b, 'Matthew's understanding of the Law: authenticity and interpretation in Matthew 5:17-20', *Journal of Biblical Literature*, 93, 226-242.

Banks, R.J., 1975, *Jesus and the Law in the Synoptic tradition*, Cambridge University Press, Cambridge. (SNTS Monograph Series, 28).

Barth, G., 1963, 'Matthew's understanding of the Law', in G. Bornkamm, G. Barth, & H.J. Held (eds.), *Tradition and interpretation in Matthew*, pp. 58-164, Westminster Press, Philadelphia.

Barton, J., 1999, 'Historical-critical approaches', in J. Barton (ed.), *The Cambridge companion to Biblical Interpretation*, pp.9-20, Cambridge University Press, Cambridge.

Batey, R., 1971, 'Jesus and the theatre', *New Testament Studies* 30, 563–574.

Bauckham, R.J., 1998, *The Gospels for all Christians: Rethinking the Gospel audiences*, Eerdmans, Grand Rapids.

Baumgartel, F., 1978, 'Καρδία', in G. Kittel (ed.), *Theological Dictionary of the New Testament*, vol III, pp. 605-607, William Eerdmans Publishing Company, Grand Rapids.

Baumgarten, A.I., 1987, 'The Pharisaic Paradosis', *Harvard Theological Review*, 80(1), 63-77.

Baur, F.C., 1847, *Kritische Untersuchungen über die kanonischen Evangelien, ihr Verhältniss zu einander, ihren Charakter und Ursprung*, Fues, Tübingen.

BDAG, *see* Greek-English lexicon of the New Testament and other Christian literature.

Beare, F.W., 1981, *The Gospel according to St. Matthew. A commentary*, Basil Blackwell, Oxford.

Behm, J., 1978, 'Heart', in G. Kittel (ed.), *Theological Dictionary of the New Testament*, vol III, pp. 608-617, William Eerdmans Publishing Company, Grand Rapids.

Berger, K., 1972, *Die Gesetzesauslegung Jesu. Ihr historischer Hintergrund im Judentum und im Alten Testament. Teil 1: Markus und Parallelen*, Neukirchen-Vluyn, Neukirchener.

Betz, H.D., 1985, *Essays on the Sermon on the Mount*, Fortress Press, Philadelphia.

Betz, H.D., 1992, *The Greek magical papyri in translation including the demonic spells*, University Press, Chicago.

Betz, H.D., 1995, *The Sermon on the Mount including the Sermon on the Plain (Matthew 5:3-7:27 and Luke 6:20-49)*, Fortress Press, Minneapolis. (Hermeneia – a critical and historical commentary on the Bible).

Bickerman. E.J., 1947, *The Maccabees*, Shocken, New York.

Blass, F. & Debrunner, A., 1961, *A Greek grammar of the New Testament and other early Christian literature*, University Press, Chicago.

Blenkinsopp, J., 1981, 'Interpretation and sectarian tendencies: an aspect of second temple history', in E.P. Sanders (ed.), *Jewish and Christian self-definition*, pp.1-26, Fortress Press, Philadelphia.

Blomberg, C.L., 1992, *Matthew. The New American commentary*, vol. 22, Broadman, Nashville.

Blomberg, C.L., 2005, *Contagious holiness: Jesus` meals with sinners*, Downers Grove, Ill: InterVarsity Press; Apollos: Leicester, U.K. (New Studies in Biblical Theology (NSBT)).

Blomberg, C.L. & Markley, J.F., 2010, *A handbook of New Testament exegesis*, Baker Academic, Grand Rapids.

Booth, R.P., 1986, *Jesus and the laws of purity. Tradition History and Legal History in Mark 7*, JSOT Press, Sheffield. (Journal for the Study of the New Testament, Supplement Series, 13).

Bornkamm, G., 1954, 'Das Doppelgebot der Liebe', in R. Bultmann (ed.), *Neutestamentliche Studien: Beihefte zur Zeitschrift für die neutestamentliche Wissenschaft*, pp. 85-93, Alfred Töpelmann, Berlin.

Bornkamm, G., 1963a, 'The stilling of the storm in Matthew', in G. Bornkamm, G. Barth & H.J. Held (eds.), *Tradition and interpretation in Matthew*, pp. 52-57, SCM, London.

Bornkamm, G., 1963b, 'End-expectations and church in Matthew', in G. Bornkamm, G. Barth & H.J. Held (eds.), *Tradition and interpretation in Matthew*, pp.15-51, SCM, London.

Bornkamm, G., 2009, *Studien zum Matthäus-Evangelium*. Neukirchener Verlag, Neukirchen-Vluyn. (Wissenschaftliche Monographien zum Alten und Neuen).

Bowley, J.E., 2000, 'Purification texts', in C.A. Evans & S.E. Porter (eds.), *Dictionary of New Testament Background*, pp.873-874, Intervarsity Press, Downers Grove & Leicester.

Braaten, C.E., 1968, *History and Hermeneutics. New directions in Theology today*, Lutterworth, London.

Bratcher, R.G., 1989, '"Righteousness" in Matthew', *Bible Translator*, 40, 228-235.

Broer, I., 1994. Das Ius Talionis im Neuen Testament, *New Testament Studies*, 40(1):1-21.

Brooks, S.H., 1987, 'Matthew's community, the evidence of his special sayings material', *Journal for the Study of the Old Testament Press*, Sheffield.

Brown, C., 1975, *The New International dictionary of New Testament Theology, vol. 1*, Zondervan, Grand Rapids.

Brown, F., Driver, S.R. & Briggs, C.A., 1952, *A Hebrew and English lexicon of the Old Testament*, Clarendon Press, Oxford.

Brown, R.E., 1966, *The Gospel according to John*, Doubleday, New York. (Anchor Bible).

Brown, R.E., 1997, *An introduction to the New Testament*, Doubleday, New York.

Bruce F.F., 1983, *Hard sayings of Jesus*, Intervarsity Press, Downers Grove.

Brueggemann, W., 1997, *Cadences of home: preaching among exiles*, Westminster John Knox, Louisville.

Bruner, F.D., 1990, *Matthew, a commentary, volume 2: The Churchbook Matthew 13-28*, William Eerdmans, Grand Rapids & Cambridge.

Bultmann, R., 1951, *Theology of the New Testament*, vol. 1, University Press, Oxford.

Bultmann, R., 1963, *The history of the synoptic Tradition*, Blackwell, Oxford.

Burridge, R.A., 1992, *What are the gospels? A comparison with Greco-Roman Biography*, University Press, Cambridge.

Carlston, C.E., 1968/69, 'The things that defile (Mark vii. 14) and the law in Matthew and Mark', *New Testament Studies* 15, 75-96.

Carrigan, H.L., 2000, 'Soul', in D.N. Freedman, A.C. Myers & A.B. Beck (eds.), *Eerdmans Dictionary of the Bible*, p. 901, William Eerdmans Publishing Company, Grand Rapids & Cambridge.

Carson, D.A., 1982, 'Jesus and the Sabbath in the four Gospels', in Carson, D.A. (ed.), *From Sabbath to the Lord's Day*, pp. 57-97, Zondervan, Grand Rapids.

Carson, D.A., 1984, *Matthew. The expositor's Bible commentary*, Zondervan, Grand Rapids.

Carson, D.A., 1995, The expositor's Bible commentary with the New International Version of the Holy Bible: Matthew chapters 13 through 28, Zondervan, Grand Rapids.

Carter, W., 1994, *Household and discipleship: a study of Matthew 19-20*, Academic Press, Sheffield. (Journal for the Study of the New Testament, Supplement Series, 103).

Carter, W., 2000a, *Matthew and the margins. A socio-political reading*, Academic Press, Sheffield. (Journal for the Study of the New Testament, Supplement Series 204).

Carter, W., 2000b, 'Matthew 23:37-39', *Interpretation*, 66-68.

Carter, W., 2001, *Matthew and empire: initial explorations*, Trinity Press International, Harrisburg.

Carter, W., 2004, *Matthew, storyteller, interpreter, evangelist*, Hendrickson, Massachusetts.

Catchpole, D.R., 1997, 'Source, form and redaction criticism of the New Testament', in S.E. Porter (ed.), *Handbook of exegesis of the New Testament*, pp. 167-188, Brill, Leiden, New York & Köln.

Charles, J.D., 2000, 'Vice and virtue lists', in C.A. Evans & S.E. Porter (eds.), *Dictionary of New Testament Background*, pp. 1252-1257, InterVarsity Press, Downers Grove & Leicester.

Chatman, S., 1978, *Story and discourse: Narrative structure in fiction and film,* Cornell University Press, Ithaca.

Childs, B.S., 1984, *The New Testament as canon: an introduction*, SCM, London.

Chilton, B.D., 2000, 'Purity', in C.A. Evans & S.E. Porter (eds.), *Dictionary of New Testament Background*, pp. 874-882, Intervarsity Press, Downers Grove & Leicester.

Clines, D.J.A., 2011. *The dictionary of classical Hebrew.* Sheffield Academic Press, Sheffield.

Cohen, A. 1975. 'Gemara and Midrash', A. Corré (ed.), *Understanding the Talmud.* Ktav Publishing House, New York.

Cohen, S.J.D., 2006, *From the Maccabees to the Mishnah.* Westminster John Knox Press, Louisville & London.

Combrink, H.J.B., 1983, 'The structure of the Gospel of Matthew as narrative', *Tyndale Bulletin*, 34, 61-90.

Combrink, H.J.B., 2006, 'The challenge of overflowing righteousness; to learn to live the story of the gospel of Matthew', in Van der Watt, J.G. (ed.), *Identity, ethics, and ethos in the New Testament*, pp. 23-48, Walter de Gruyter, Berlin & New York.

Conzelmann, H., 1960, *The Theology of St. Luke*, Harper & Row, New York.

Cope, O.L., 1976, *Matthew: A scribe trained for the Kingdom of Heaven*, Catholic Biblical Association of America, Washington. (The Catholic Biblical quarterly monograph series).

Coser, L.A., 1998, *The functions of social conflict*, Routley, London.

Cruse, D., 1986, *Lexical Semantics*, University Press, Cambridge.

Cullmann, O., 1950, *Baptism in the New Testament*, SCM, London.

Daube, D., 1956, *The New Testament and Rabbinic Judaism. Jordan Lectures in Comparative Religion*, Athlone Press, London.

Davies, P.R., 1983, *The Damascus covenant: An interpretation of the 'Damascus document'*, JSOT Press, Sheffield. (Journal for the Study of the Old Testament Supplementum).

Davies, W.D., 1966, *The setting of the Sermon on the Mount*, University Press, Cambridge.

Davies, W.D. & Allison, D.C., 2004a, *Matthew 1-7*, T. & T. Clark, London & New York. (International Critical Commentary, vol. 1).

Davies, W.D. & Allison, D.C., 2004b, *Matthew 8-18*, T. & T. Clark, London & New York. (International Critical Commentary, vol. 2).

Davies, W.D. & Allison, D.C., 2004c, *Matthew 19-28*, T. & T. Clark, London & New York. (International Critical Commentary, vol. 3).

De Saussure, F., 1966, *Kursus in die Algemene Taalkunde (Cours de Linguistique Generale)*, transl. A. Lee, Van Schaik, Pretoria.

De Saussure, F., 1972 [1916], *Cours de linguistique générale,* Payot, Paris.

De Silva, D.A., 2004, *An Introduction to the New Testament. Contexts, Methods and Ministry Formation*, Intervarsity Press, Downers Grove & Leicester.

Dearman, J.A., 2010, *The Book of Hosea*, Eerdmans, Grand Rapids & Cambridge. (The New International commentary on the Old Testament).

Deines, R., 2004, *Die Gerechtigkeit der Tora im Reich des Messias: Mt 5,13–20 als Schlüsseltext der matthäischen Theologie*, Mohr Siebeck, Tübingen. (Wissenschaftliche Untersuchungen zum Neuen Testament 177).

Deines, R., 2008, 'Not the Law but the Messiah: Law and Righteousness in the Gospel of Matthew – an ongoing debate', in D.M. Gurtner & J. Nolland (eds.), *Built upon the Rock. Studies in the Gospel of Matthew*, pp.53-84, Eerdmans, Grand Rapids & Cambridge.

Derret, J.D.M., 1977, *Studies in the New Testament*, Brill, Leiden.

Descamps, A., 1995, 'Essai d'interprétation de Mt 5, 17-48: Formgeschichte ou Redactionsgeschichte?', *Studia evangelica*, 1, 156-173.

Dihle, A., 1974, 'Ψυχή in the Greek world', in G. Friedrich (ed.), *Theological Dictionary of the New Testament*, vol IX, pp.608-617, William Eerdmans Publishing Company, Grand Rapids.

Domeris, W.R., 1990, '"Blessed are you ..." (Matthew 5:1-12)', *Journal of Theology for Southern Africa*, 73(1), 67-76.

Donaldson, T.L., 1995, 'The Law that hangs (Matthew 22:40): Rabbinic formulation and Matthean social world', *Catholic Biblical Quarterly* 57, 689-709.

Du Toit, A. (ed.), 2009a, *Focussing on the message. New Testament hermeneutics,. exegesis and methods*, Protea, Pretoria.

Du Toit, A., 2009b, 'New Testament exegesis in theory and practice', in A. du Toit (ed.), *Focussing on the message. New Testament hermeneutics, exegesis and methods*, pp.107-152, Protea, Pretoria.

Du Toit, A., 2009c, 'Exploring textual structure: discourse analysis', in A. du Toit (ed.), *Focussing on the message. New Testament hermeneutics, exegesis and methods*, pp.217-265, Protea, Pretoria.

Duling, D.C., 1992, 'Kingdom of God, Kingdom of Heaven', in D.N. Freedman (ed.), *The Anchor Bible Dictionary*, vol. 4, pp.56-69, Doubleday, New York, London, Toronto, Sydney & Auckland.

Dunn, J.D.G., 1990, *Jesus, Paul, and the Law: studies in Mark and Galatians*, Westminster/John Knox Press, Louisville,.

Dunn, J.D.G., 2003, *Jesus remembered. Christianity in the making*, vol. 1, Eerdmans, Grand Rapids & Cambridge.

Dunn, J.D.G., 2008, *The new perspective on Paul*, Eerdmans, Grand Rapids.

Dupont, J., 1973, *Les Béatitudes: Les Évangelistes*, vol. 3, Gabalda, Paris.

Dupont-Sommer, A., 1961, *The Essene writings from Qumran*, Basil Blackwell, Oxford.

Edwards, J.R., 1987, 'The use of προσέρχεσθαι in the Gospel of Matthew', *Journal for Biblical Literature*, 106, 65-74.

Egger, W., 1996, *How to read the New Testament: an introduction to linguistic and historical-critical methodology*, Hendrickson Publishers, Peabody.

Eisen, Y., 2004, *Miraculous journey: A complete history of the Jewish people from creation to the present*, Targum Press, Brooklyn.

Eissfeldt, O., 1970, 'Πληρωσαι πασαν δικαιοσυνην in Matthäus 3:15', *Zeitschrift für die neutestamentliche Wissenschaft* 61, 209-215.

Ellingworth, P., 1992, 'Leprosy', in J.B. Green & S. McKnight (eds.), *Dictionary of Jesus and the Gospels*, pp.463-464, Intervarsity Press, Downers Grove & Leicester.

Elliot, J.H., 1995, *Social-Scientific Criticism of the New Testament. An introduction*, SPCK, London.

Elliot, J.K., 1977, 'Jerusalem in Acts and the Gospels', *New Testament Studies*, 23, 462-469.

Esler, P.F., 1998, 'Community and Gospel in early Chritianity: A response to Richard Bauckham's Gospel for all nations', *Scottish Journal of Theology*, 51, 235-248.

Esler, P.F., 2015. 'Intergroup conflict and Matthew 23: Towards responsible historical interpretation of a challenging text', *Biblical Theology Bulletin*, 45(1), 38-95.

Evans, C.A., 2012, *Matthew,* Cambridge University Press, Cambridge. (New Cambridge Bible Commentary).

Fiedler, M.J., 1977, 'Gerechtigkeit im Matthäus-Evangelium', *Theologische Versuche* 8, 63–75.

Finklestein, I., 1966, *The Pharisees*, Jewish Publication Society, Philadelphia.

Fitzmyer, J.A., 1970, 'The languages of Palestine in the first century ad.', *Catholic Biblical Quarterly*, 32, 501-531.

Floor, L., 1969, *De nieuwe exodus: representatie en inkorporatie in het Nieuwe Testament,* Ph.D. thesis , PU for CHE, Potchefstroom.

Fokkelman, J.P., 2000. *Reading Biblical narrative: and introductory*. John Knox Press, Westminster.

Foster, P., 2004, *Community, law and mission in Matthew's Gospel*, Mohr Siebeck, Tübingen. (WUNT, 2, Reihe 177).

France, R.T., 1971, *Jesus and the Old Testament: his application of Old Testament passages to Himself and His Mission*, Tyndale, London.

France, R.T., 1985, *Matthew*, Intervarsity Press, Nottingham. (Tyndale New Testament Commentaries).

France, R.T., 1998, *Matthew evangelist and teacher. New Testament profiles*, Intervarsity Press, Downers Grove.

France, R.T., 2007, *The Gospel of Matthew*, Eerdmans, Grand Rapids. (The New International Commentary of the New Testament).

France, R.T., 2008, *The Gospel according to Matthew: an introduction and commentary*, Intervarsity Press, Leicester.

Frankemölle, H., 1997, *Matthäuskommentar*, Patmos, Dusseldorf.

Friedman, R.E., 1992, 'Torah (Pentateuch)', in Freedman, D.N. (ed.), *The Anchor Bible Dictionary, vol. 6*, pp. 605-622, Doubleday: New York, London, Toronto, Auckland.

Garland, D.E., 1979, *The intention of Matthew 23*, Brill, Leiden.

Garland, D.E., 2001, *Reading Matthew: A literary and theological commentary on the first Gospel*, Smyth & Helwys, Macon.

Garrett, D.A., 1997, *Hosea and Joel. The American commentary*, vol. 19A, Broadman & Holman, Nashville.

Genette, G., 1980, *Narrative discourse: An essay in method*, Cornell University, Ithaca.

Gerhardsson, B., 1964. *Memory and manuscript: oral tradition and written transmission in Rabbinic Judaism and Early Christianity*. Uppsala: Gleerup.

Gerhardsson, B., 1974, 'Sacrificial service and atonement in the Gospel of Matthew', in Banks, R. (ed.), *Reconciliation and hope: New Testament essays on atonement and eschatology; presented to L.L. Morris on his 60th birthday*, pp.25-35, University Press, Exeter.

Gerhardsson, B., 1976, 'The hermeneutic program in Matthew 22:37-40', in R. Hammerton-Kelly & R. Scroggs (eds.), *Jews, Greeks and Christians. Religious cultures in late antiquity*, pp.129-150, Brill, Leiden.

Giesen, H., 1982, *Chrisliches Handeln: Eine redaktionskritische Untersuchung zum δικαιοσυνη – Begriff im Matthäus-Evangelium*, Peter Lang, Frankfurt.

Gnilka, J., 1986, *Das Matthäusevangelium Bd. I, Herders theologischer Kommentar zum Neuen Testament*, Herder, Freiburg.

Gnilka, J., 1988, *Das Matthäusevangelium Bd. II, Herders theologischer Kommentar zum Neuen Testament*, Herder, Freiburg

Greek-english lexicon of the New Testament and other Christian literature, 2000, 3rd edn., University of Chicago Press, Chicago.

Green, H.B., 1975, *The Gospel according to Matthew in the Revised Standard Version, The New Clarendon Bible*, Oxford University Press, London.

Green, H.B., 2001, 'Matthew, poet of the Beatitudes', *Journal for the Study of the New Testament*, Supplement Series 203.

Greeven, H., 1955, 'Die Heilung des Gelähmten nach Matthäus', in *Wort und Dienst, Jahrbuch der Theologische Schule Bethel*, pp. 61-75, Theologische Schule, Bethel.

Greidanus, S., 1988, *The modern preacher and the ancient text: Interpreting and preaching Biblical literature*, Eerdmans, Grand Rapids.

Greimas, A.J., 1970, *Sign, language, culture*, Mouton, The Hague, Paris.

Grintz, Y.M., 2007, 'First Temple', in F. Skoling & M. Berenbaum (eds.), *Encyclopaedia Judaica*, second edn., vol. 19, pp.601-603, Thompson Gale, Detroit, New York, San Francisco, New Haven, Waterville, Maine & London.

Grundmann, W., 1971, *Das Evangelium nach Matthäus. Theologischer Handkommentar zum Neuen Testament 1*, Evangelische Verlagsanstalt, Berlin.

Guelich, R.A., 1982, *The Sermon on the Mount: a Foundation for understanding*, Word, Waco.

Gundry, R.H., 1967, *The use of the Old Testament in St. Matthew's Gospel, with special reference to the Messianic hope*, Brill, Leiden.

Gundry, R.H., 1982, *Matthew: A Commentary on his Literary and Theological Art*, Eerdmans, Grand Rapids.

Gundry, R.H., 1994, *Matthew – a commentary on his handbook for a mixed church under persecution*, Eerdmans, Grand Rapids.

Hagner, D.A., 1992, 'Righteousness in Matthew's Theology', in M.J. Wilkens & T. Paige (eds.), *Worship, theology and ministry in the early church*, pp. 101–120, JSOT Press, Sheffield. (Journal for the Study of the New Testament, Supplement Series 87).

Hagner, D.A., 1993, *Matthew 1-13*, Word Books, Dallas. (Word Biblical Commentary 33A).

Hagner, D.A., 1995, *Matthew 14-28*, Word Books, Dallas. (Word Biblical Commentary. 33B).

Hagner, D.A., 1997, 'Balancing the Old and the New. The Law in Moses in Matthew and Paul', *Interpretation*, 51(1), 20-30.

Hands, A.R., 1968, *Charities and social aid in Greece and Rome*, Cornell University Press, New York.

Hanson, K.C., 1994, 'How honourable! How shameful! A cultural analysis of Matthew's makarisms and reproaches', *Semeia* 68, 81-111.

Hare, D.R.A., 1967, *The theme of persecution of Christians in the Gospel according to Matthew*, University Press, Cambridge. (SNTSMS, 6).

Hare, D.R.A., 1993, *Matthew*, John Knox Press, Louisville.

Harlow, D.C., 2012, 'Early Judaism and early Christianity', in J.J. Collins & D.C. Harlow (eds.), *Early Judaism. A comprehensive overview*, pp. 391-419, Eerdmans, Grand Rapids.

Harper, W.R., 1979, *A Critical and exegetical commentary on Amos and Hosea*, T. & T. Clark, Edinburgh.

Harrington, D.J., 1991, *Gospel of Matthew*, Liturgical, Collegeville.

Hauck, F., 1964, 'Νίπτω, ἄνιπτος', in G. Kittel (ed.), *Theological Dictionary of the New Testament*, vol. 4, pp. 946-948, Eerdmans, Michigan.

Hayes, C., 2007, 'Purity and impurity, ritual', in F. Skoling & M. Berenbaum (eds.), *Encyclopaedia Judaica*, 2nd. edn., vol. 16, pp. 746-756, Thompson Gale, Detroit, New York, San Francisco, New Haven, Waterville, Maine & London.

Hayes, J. H. & Holladay, C. R., 2007, *Biblical exegesis: A beginner's handbook*, Westminster John Knox Press, Louisville & London.

Held, H.J., 1963 'Matthew as interpreter of the miracle stories', in G Bornkamm, G Barth & H.J. Held (eds.), *Traditions and interpretation in Matthew*, pp. 165-300, SCM Press, London.

Herr, M.D., 2007, 'Yadayim', in F. Skolnik & M. Berenbaum (eds.), *Encyclopaedia Judaica*, 2nd. edn., vol. 21, p. 264, Thompson Gale, Detroit, New York, San Francisco, New Haven, Waterville, Maine & London.

Hill, D., 1967, *Greek words with Hebrew meanings*, University Press, Cambridge.

Hill, D., 1972, *The Gospel of Matthew*, Marshall, Morgan & Scott, London.

Hill, D., 1978, 'On the use and meaning of Hosea 6:6 in Matthew's gospel', *New Testament Studies*, 24(1), 107-119.

Hinkle E., M., 1998, 'Learning what righteousness means: Hosea 6:6 and the ethic mercy in Matthew's gospel', *Word and World*, 18(4), 355-363.

Holtzmann, H., 1911, *Lehrbuch der neutestamentlichen Theologie*, Tübingen: Mohr (Paul Siebeck).

Horbury, W., 1982, 'The Benediction of the Minim and early Jewish Christian controversy', *Journal of Theological Studies*, 33, 19-61.

Hübner, H., 1986, *Das Gesetz in der synoptischen Tradition*, Vandenhoeck & Ruprecht, Göttingen.

Hübner, H., 1992, 'Unclean and clean (New Testament)', in D.N. Freedman (ed.), *The Anchor Bible Dictionary*, pp. 741-745, Doubleday, New York, London, Toronto, Sydney & Auckland.

Hultgren, A.J., 1974, 'The double commandment of love in Matt. 22:34-40; its and sources and compositions', *Catholic Biblical Quarterly*, 36, 373-378.

Hummel, R., 1966, *Die Auseinandersetzung zwischen Kirche und Judentum im Matthäusevangelium*, Kaisar, München.

Jacob, E., 1974, 'The anthropology of the Old Testament', in G. Friedrich (ed.), *Theological Dictionary of the New Testament*, vol IX, pp. 617-631, William Eerdmans Publishing Company, Grand Rapids.

Jaffee, M.S., 2001, *Torah in the mouth. Writing and oral tradition in Palestinian Judaism 200B.C.E – 400 C.E*, University Press, Oxford.

Janzen, D, 2000, 'The meaning of porneia in Matthew 5:32 and 19:9: an approach form the study of Ancient Near East culture', *Journal for the Study of the New Testament*, 80, 66-80.

Jeremias, J., 1963, *The Sermon on the Mount*, Athlone Press, University of London.

Jeremias, J., 1966, *Eucharistic words of Jesus*, Fortress Press, Philadelphia.

Johnson, S.E., 1951, *The Gospel according to St. Matthew*, Broadman & Holman, Nashville.

Joosten, J., 2004, 'Aramaic or Hebrew behind the Greek Gospels', *Analecta Bruxellensia*, 9, 88-102.

Jordaan, G.J.C., 2014, *Die binnewerk van Antieke Grieks. Handleiding vir eksegete en ander studente van Klassieke en Nuwe Testamentiese Grieks*, Potchefstroom Teologiese Publikasies, Potchefstroom.

Käsemann, E., 1955, 'Sätze Heiligen Rechtes im Neuen Testament', *New Testament Studies*, 1, 248-260.

Käsemann, E., 1969, 'The beginnings of Christian theology', *Journal for Theology and the Church*, 6, 17-46.

Kee, H.C., 1990, 'The transformation of the synagogue after 70CE: Its import for Early Christianity', *New Testament Studies*, 36, 1-24.

Keener, G.S., 1997, *Matthew*, Intervarsity Press, Downers Grove & Leicester.

Keener, G.S., 1999, *A commentary on the Gospel of Matthew*, Eerdmans, Michigan & Cambridge.

Keener, G.S., 2002, *The IVP Bible Background Commentary; New Testament*, IVP Academic, Downers Grove.

Keener,G.S., 2009, *The Gospel of Matthew. A Socio-rhetorical Commentary*, Eerdmans, Grand Rapids & Cambridge.

Keil, C.F., 1980, *Commentary on the Old Testament in ten volumes; volume X – Minor Prophets*, Eerdmans, Michigan.

Kennedy, W., 1966, *How to analyze fiction*, Monarch, New York.

Kennedy, G.A., 1980, *Classical rhetoric and its Christian and secular tradition from ancient to modern times*, University of North Carolina, Chapel Hill.

Kennedy, P., 2006, *A modern introduction to Theology: New Questions for old beliefs*, I.B. Tauris, London & New York.

Kertelge, K., 1971, *Rechtfertigung bei Paulus*, Aschendorff, Münster.

Kilpatrick, G.D., 1950, *The origins of the Gospel according to Matthew*, Clarendon Press, Oxford.

Kingsbury, J.D., 1988, *Matthew as story*, Fortress Press, Philadelphia.

Kingsbury, J.D., 1995. 'The developing conflict between Jesus and the Jewish leaders in Matthew's Gospel: A Literary-Critical study'. In Stanton, G. (ed.), The interpretation of Matthew. T & T Clark, Edinburgh, p. 179-197.

Klijn, A.F.J., 1968, *De wordingsgeschiedenis van het Nieuwe Testament,* Het Spectrum NV, Utrecht & Antwerpen.

Klijn, A.F.J., 1983, '(Syriac Apocalypse of) Baruch, a new translation and introduction', in J. Charlesworth (ed.), *The Old Testament Pseudepigrapha*, vol. 1, pp. 193-199, Double Day, New York.

Klijn, F.J. & Reinink, G.J., 1973, *Patristic evidence for Jewish-Christian sects*, Brill, Leiden.

Klinghardt, M., 1988, *Gesetz und Volk Gottes. Das lukanische Verständnis des Gesetzes*, Mohr Siebeck, Tübingen.

Klostermann, E., 1927, *Das Matthäusevangelium. Handbuch zum Neuen Testament*, Mohr Siebeck, Tübingen.

Knight, J., 2004, *Jesus; an Historical and Theological investigation*, T. & T. Clark, London & New York.

Koch, K., 1974, *Was ist Formgeschichte? Neue Wege der Bibelexegese*, Neukirchener Verlag, Neukirchen-Vluyn.

Koester, H., 1982, *Introduction to the New Testament*, De Gruyter, Berlin & New York.

Kooyman, A.C., 1992, *De joodse konteks van Mattheüs 5:31-32: een bijdrage aan het debat over het gebruik van rabbijnse teksten voor de bestudering van het Nieuwe Testament*, Rijksuniversiteit, Utrecht.

Kotila, M., 1988, *Umstrittende Zeuge. Studien zur Stellung de Gesetzes in der johannseischen Theologiegeschichte*, Suomalainen Tiedeakatemia, Helsinki.

Kraft, R.A. & Nickelsburg, G.W.E. (eds.), 1986, *Early Judaism and its Modern Interpreters*, Scholars, Atlanta.

Kümmel, W.G., 1934, 'Jesus und der jüdische Traditionsgedanke', *Zeitschrift für die neuetestamentliche Wissenschaft*, 33, 121-127.

Kümmel, W.G., 1967, 'Die Weherufe über die Schriftgelehrten un Pharisäer (Matthäus 23,13-36). In Eckert, W.P. (ed.), Antijudaismus in Neuen Testament? Kaiser Verlag, München, p. 135-147.

Kümmel, W.G., 1975, *Introduction to the New Testament*, SCM Press, London.

Ladd, G.E., 1971, 'The search for perspective', *Interpretation*, 25, 41-62.

Ladd, G.E., 1993, *A theology of the New Testament*, Eerdmans, Michigan.

Lapide, P.E., 1984, *De Bergrede, utopie of program?*, Matthias-Grünewald-Verlag, Mainz.

Lategan, B., 2009, 'New Testament hermeneutics (part 1). Defining moments in the developement of biblical hermeneutics', in A. du Toit (ed.), *Focussing on the message. New Testament hermeneutics, exegesis and methods*, pp. 13-63, Protea, Pretoria.

Levine, A.J., 1996, 'Discharging responsibility: Matthean Jesus, Biblical law and haemorrhaging woman', in D.R. Bauer & M.A. Powell (eds.), *Treasures new and old: Contributions to Matthean studies,* SBL Symposium Series 1, pp. 379-397, Scholars Press, Atlanta.

Lightfoot, R.H., 1935, *History and interpretation in the Gospels*, Hodder & Stoughton, London.

Limburg, J., 1988, *Hosea – Micah. Interpretation*, John Knox Press, Atlanta.

Lindars, B., 1988, *Law and religion. Essays on the place of the Law in Israel and early Christianity*, Clarke, Cambridge.

Lioy, D., 2004, *The Decalogue in the Sermon on the Mount*, Peter Lang, New York. (Studies in Biblical Literature, 66).

Lloyd-Jones, D.M., 1976, *Studies in the Sermon on the Mount*, Eerdmans, Grand Rapids.

Loader, W.R.G., 1997, *Jesus' attitude towards the Law. A study of the Gospels,* Mohr Siebeck, Tübingen. (Wissenschaftliche Untersuchungen zum Neuen Testament 2. Reihe).

Lohmeyer, E., 1967, *Das Evangelium des Matthäus*, Vandenhoeck & Ruprecht, Göttingen.

Louw, J.P., 1982, *Semantics of New Testament Greek*, Fortress Press, Philadelphia.

Louw, J.P. & Nida, E.A., 1989, *Greek-English lexicon of the New Testament based on semantic domains*, 2 volumes, United Bible Societies, New York.

Love, S.L., 2009, *Jesus and marginal Women: The Gospel of Matthew in social-scientific perspective*, James Clarke & Co., Cambridge.

Luz, U., 1968, *The Synoptic Gospels*, Ktav, New York.

Luz, U., 1990, *Matthew 1-7. A commentary*, T. & T. Clark, Edinburgh.

Luz, U., 2001a, *Matthew 8-20, a commentary*, Fortress Press, Minneapolis.

Luz, U., 2001b, *Matthew 21-28*, Fortress Press, Minneapolis.

Luz, U., 2005, *Studies in Matthew,* Eerdmans, Grand Rapids & Cambridge.

Lybaek, L., 1997. 'Matthew's Use of Hosea 6.6 in the Context of the Sabbath Controversies', *The Scriptures in the Gospels*, 491-499.

Macintosh, A.A., 1997, *Hosea. A critical and exegetical commentary*, T. & T. Clark, Edinburgh.

Mack, B.L., 1990, *Rhetoric and the New Testament: Guides to biblical scholarship*, Fortress Press, Minneapolis.

Malina, B.J., 2009, 'Social-scientific approaches and the gospel of Matthew', in Powell, M. A. (ed.), *Methods for Matthew*, pp. 154-193, Cambridge University Press, Cambridge & New York.

Malina, B.J. & Neyrey, J.H., 1996, *Portraits of Paul. An archaeology of ancient personality*, Westminster John Knox Press, Louisville.

Malina, B.J. & Rohrbauch, R.L., 1992, *Social-science commentary on the Synoptic Gospels*, Fortress Press, Minneapolis.

Malina, B.J. & Rohrbauch, R.L., 2003, *Social-science commentary on the Synoptic Gospels*, Fortress Press, Minneapolis.

Marcus, J., 1988, 'Entering into the kingly power of God', *Journal of Biblical Literature* 107, 663–675.

Marshall, I.H., 1978, *Commentary on Luke*, Eerdmans, Grand Rapids. (The New international Greek Testament commentary).

Marxsen, W., 1969, *Mark the evangelist*, Abingdon, Nashville.

Mason, S., 1990. 'Pharisaic dominance before 70 CE and the Gospels' hypocrisy charge (Matt. 23:2-3), *Harvard Theological Review*, 83, 363-381.

Matera, F.J., 1987, *What are they saying about Mark?*, Paulist, New York.

McConnell, R.S., 1969, *Law and prophecy in Matthew's Gospel: The authority and use of the Old Testament in the Gospel of Matthew*, Friedrich Reinhardt Kommissionsverlag, Basel.

McIver, R.K. 1995., The Sabbath in the Gospel of Matthew: a paradigm for understanding the law in Matthew? Andrews University Seminary Studies, 2:231-243.

McKnight, S., 2004, *The Jesus Creed: Loving God, loving others*, Paraclete, Brewster.

McNeile, A.H., 1980[1915], *The Gospel according to Matthew*, Baker, Grand Rapids.

Meeks, W.A., 1983, *The first urban Christians*, Yale University Press, New Haven & London.

Meier, J.P., 1976, *Law and history in Matthew's Gospel*, Biblical Institute Press, Rome.

Meier, J.P., 1980, *Matthew, New Testament message*, Veritas, Dublin.

Meier, J.P., 2009, *A marginal Jew; rethinking the historical Jesus*, vol. 4, Love and Law, Yale University Press, New Haven & London.

Menken, M.J.J., 2003, 'Fulfilment of Scripture as a propaganda tool in early Christianity', in Van der Horst, P.W., Menken, M.J.J., Smit, J.F.M. & Van Vijen, G. (eds.), *Persuasion and discussion in early Christianity, Ancient Judaism and Hellenism*, pp.179-198, Peeters, Leuven.

Menken, M.J.J., 2004, *Matthew's Bible. The Old Testament text of the Evangelist*, University Press, Leuven.

Mohrlang, R., 1984, *Matthew and Paul: A comparison of ethical perspectives*, University Press, Cambridge. (Society for New Testament Studies Monograph Series, 48)

Montefiore, C.C. & Loewe, H.M.J., 1974, *A rabbinic anthology*, Cambridge University Press, Cambridge.

Moo, D.J., 1992, 'Law', in J.B. Green, S. McKnight & I.H. Marshall (eds.), *Dictionary of Jesus and the Gospels*, IVP, Downers Grove.

Moo, J.M., 1984, 'Jesus and the authority of the Mosaic Law', *Journal for the Study of the New Testament*, 20, 3-49.

Moore, G.F., 1970, *Judaism in the first centuries of the Christian Era. The age of the Tannaim*, University Press, Harvard.

Morris, L., 1981, *Testaments of love: A study of love in the Bible*, Eerdmans, Grand Rapids.

Morris, L., 1992, *The Gospel according to Matthew*, Grand Rapids, Eerdmans.

Moule, C.F.D., 1967/8, 'Fulfilment words in the New Testament: use and abuse', *New Testament studies*, 14, 293-320.

Moule, C.F.D., 1977, *The origin of Christology*, University Press, Cambridge.

Moule, C.F.D., 1982, *Essays in New Testament interpretation*, University Press, Cambridge.

Mounce, R.H., 1991, *Matthew. New International Biblical commentary*, Hendrickson Publishers, Massachusetts.

Mueller, J.R., 1980, 'The Temple Scroll and the Gospel Divorce Texts', *Revue de Qumran*, 10, 247-256.

Müller, M., 1999, 'The Theological interpretation of the figure of Jesus in the Gospel of Matthew: Some principle features in Mattean Christology', *New Testament Studies*, 44, 157-173.

Müller, M., 2001, 'The reception of the Old Testament in Matthew and Luke-Acts: From interpretation to proof from Scripture', *Novum Testamentum*, 43(4), 315-330.

Neisser, U., 1967, *Cognitive psychology*, Meredith, New York.

Nel, M., 2014, 'Of that day and hour no one knows: Mark 13', PhD thesis, Radboud University, Nijmegen.

Neusner, J., 1971, *The rabbinic traditions about the Pharisees before 70*, Brill, Leiden.

Neusner, J., 1972, 'Judaism in a time of crisis: Four responses to the destruction of the second temple', *Judaism*, 21, 313-327.

Neusner, J., 1973, *From politics to piety: The emergence of Pharisaic Judaism*, Prentice Hall, Englewood Cliffs.

Neusner, J., 1977, 'Judaism after the destruction of the temple', in J.H. Hayes & J.M. Miller (eds.), *Israelite and Judaean History*, p. 670, SCM Press, London.

Neusner, J., 1979, 'The formation of Rabbinic Judaism: Yavneh form 70-100', in H. Temporini & W. Haase (eds.), *Aufstieg und Niedergang der Römischen Welt: Geschichte und Kultur Roms im Spiegel der Neueren Forshung*, pp.3-42, Walter de Gruyter, Berlin & New York.

Neusner, J., 1994, *Introduction to rabbinic literature*, Doubleday, New York, London, Toronto, Sydney & Auckland.

Neusner, J., 1999, *Introduction to rabbinic literature*, Doubleday, New York.

Neusner, J., 2007, *Judaism*, Routledge, London & New York.

Neusner, J. & Frerichs, E.S. (eds.), 1985, *'To see ourselves as others see us': Christians, Jews, 'Others' in late Antiquity*, Scholars Press, Chicago & California.

Neyrey, J.H.,1982. The thematic use of Isaiah 42:1-4 in Matthew 12. Biblica, 63:457-473.

Newport, K.G.C., 1995, *The sources and Sitz im Leben of Matthew 23*, JSNTSup 117, Academic Press, Sheffield.

Newton, M., 1985, *The concept of purity at Qumran and in the Letters of Paul*, University Press, Cambridge.

Nida, E.A., 1983, *Style and discourse: with special reference to the text of the Greek New Testament*, Bible Society, Cape Town.

Nida, E.A. & Taber, C.R., 1974, *The theory and practice of translation*, Brill, Leiden.

Novakovic, L., 2003, *Messiah, the healer of the sick*, Mohr Siebeck, Tübingen. (WUNT 2 Reihe 170).

Oliver, I.W., 2013, *Torah praxis after 70CE; reading Matthew and Luke-Acts as Jewish texts*, Mohr Siebeck, Tübingen.

Orton, D.E., 1989, *The understanding scribe: Matthew and the apocalyptical ideal*, JSOT Press, Sheffield. (Journal for the Study of the New Testament Supplement Series 25).

Osborne, G.R., 2010, *Matthew*, Zondervan, Grand Rapids. (Zondervan exegetical commentary on the New Testament).

Overman, J.A., 1990, *Matthew's Gospel and Formative Judaism. The social world of the Matthean community*, Fortress Press, Minneapolis.

Overman. J.A., 1996, *Church and community in crisis. The Gospel according to Matthew*, Trinity Press International, Pennsylvania.

Pakaluk, M., 2005, *Aristotle's Nicomachean ethics: An introduction*, University Press, Cambridge. (Cambridge Introduction of key philosophical texts).

Pancaro, 1975., *The Law in the Fourth Gospel. The Torah and the Gospel, Moses and Jesus, Judaism and Christianity according to Johan*, Brill, Leiden. (SuppNovT 42).

Patte, D., 1987, *The Gospel according to Matthew: a structural commentary on Matthew's faith*, Fortress Press, Philadelphia.

Pennington, J.T., 2012. *Reading the Gospels wisely: A narrative and theological introduction*, Baker academic, Grand Rapids.

Perrin, N., 1972, 'The evangelist as author: Reflections on method in study and interpretation of Synoptic Gospels and Acts', *Biblical Research*, 17, 5-18.

Pilch, J.J., 1981, 'Biblical leprosy and body symbolism', *Biblical Theology Bulletin,* 11, 108-113.

Pilch, J.J., 1988, 'Understanding Biblical healing: selecting the appropriate model', *Biblical Theology Bulletin*, 18, 60-66.

Pilch, J.J. & Malina, B.J., 1998, *Handbook of Biblical social values*, Hendrickson Publishers, Peabody.

Piper, J., 1979, *"Love your enemies"; Jesus' love command in the Synoptic Gospels and the early Christian paraenesis*, University Press, Cambridge. (Society for New Testament Studies monograph series, 38).

Plummer, A. 1982[1909], *An exegetical commentary of the Gospel according to st. Matthew*, Baker, Grand Rapids.

Porton, G.G. 1992a. 'Haggadah', in Freedman, D.N. (ed.), *The Anchor Bible Dictionary, vol. 3*, pp. 19-20, Doubleday: New York, London, Toronto, Auckland.

Porton, G.G. 1992b. 'Halakah', in Freedman, D.N. (ed.), *The Anchor Bible Dictionary, vol. 3*, pp. 26-27, Doubleday: New York, London, Toronto, Auckland.

Porter, S.E., 1995, 'Literary approaches to the New Testament: From formalism to deconstruction and back', in S.E. Porter & D. Tombs (eds.), *Approaches to New Testament study*, pp.321-337, Academic Press, Sheffield. (*Journal for the Study of the New Testament,* Supplement Series 120).

Powell, M.A., 1995, 'Do and keep what Moses says (Matthew 23:2-7)', *Journal of Biblical Literature*, 419-435.

Prince, G., 2003, *A Dictionary of Narratology*. Nebraska, University of Nebraska Press.

Przybylski, B., 1980, *Righteousness in Matthew and his world of thought*, Cambridge University Press, Cambridge. (Monograph Series).

Qimron, E. & Strugnell, J., 1994, *Qumran cave 4: Discoveries in the Judaean desert*, Clarendon, Oxford.

Quell, G., 1964, 'The concept of Law in the Old Testament', in G. Kittel & F. Gerhard (eds.), *Theological dictionary of the New Testament*, vol. 2, p. 175, Eerdmans, Grand Rapids.

Rabbinowitz, N.S., 2003, 'Matthew 23:2-4: Does Jesus recognize the authority of the Pharisees and does He endorse their *halakhah*?', *Journal of the Evangelical Theological Society*, 46(3), 423-447.

Rackham, H. (ed.), 1934, *Aristotle: The Nicomachean ethics*, Harvard University Press, Cambridge & Massachusetts. (Loeb Classical Library).

Radford Ruether, R., 1974, *Faith and fratricide. The theological roots of Anti-Semitism*, Seabury, New York.

RepschinskI, B., 2000, *The controversy stories in the Gospel of Matthew: Their redaction, form and relevance for the relationship between the Matthean community and formative Judaism*, Vandenhoeck & Ruprecht, Göttingen.

Reumann, J., 1982, *Righteousness in the New Testament: Justification in the United States Lutheran-Roman Catholic dialogue*, Fortress Press, Philadelphia.

Reumann, J., 1992, 'Righteousness: Early Judaism', in D.L. Freedman (ed.), *The Anchor Bible Dictionary*, vol. 5, pp. 736–742, Doubleday, New York.

Ridderbos, H.N., 1971, *Paulus. Ontwerp van zijn Theologie*, Kok, Kampen.

Ridderbos, H.N., 1987, *Matthew*, Zondervan, Grand Rapids.

Riesner, R., 1978, 'Der Aufbau der Reden im Matthäus-Evangelium' *Theologische Beiträge*, 9, 177-178.

Roitto, R., 2011, *Behaving as a Christ-believer: A cognitive perspective on identity and behaviour norms in Ephesians*, Eisenbrauns, Winona Lakes.

Rordorf, W., 1968, *Sunday*, SCM, London.

Roth, S.J., 1994, *The blind, the lame and the poor: Character types in Luke-Acts*, Academic Press, Sheffield. (Journal for the Study of the New Testament Supplement Series 144).

Saldarini, A.J., 1991, 'The Gospel of Matthew and Jewish-Christian conflict', in Balch, D.L. (ed.), *Social History of the Matthean community. Cross-disciplinary approaches*, pp.38-61, Fortress Press, Minneapolis.

Saldarini, A.J., 1994, *Matthew's Christian-Jewish Community*, University of Chicago, Chicago & London.

Salo, K., 1991, *Luke's treatment of the Law. A redaction-chritical investigation*, Suomalainen Tiedeakatemia, Helsinki.

Sanders, E.P., 1983a, 'Jesus and the sinners', *Journal for the Study of the New Testament*, 19, 5-36.

Sanders, E.P., 1983b, *Paul, the Law, and the Jewish People*, Augsburg, Fortress.

Sanders, E.P., 1990, *Jewish Law from Jesus to the Mishnah*, SCM Press, London.

Sanders, E.P., Baumgarten, A.I, Mendelsohn, A. & Meyer, B.F. (eds.), 1980–1982, *Jewish and Christian self definition*, vol. 1–3, Fortress, Philadelphia.

Sariola, H., 1990, *Markus und das Gesetz. Eine redaktionsgeschichtliche Untersuchung*, Suomalainen Tiedeaketemia, Helsinki.

Schiffman, L., 1994, *Reclaiming the Dead Sea Scrolls*, Jewish Publication Society of America, Philadelphia.

Schiffman, L.H., 2012, 'Early Judaism and Rabbinic Judaism', in J.J. Collins and D.C. Harlow (eds.), *Early Judaism. A comprehensive overview*, pp. 420-434, Eerdmans, Grand Rapids.

Schlatter, A., 1959, *Der Evangelist Matthäus: seine Sprache, sein Ziel, siene Selbstandigkeit; ein Kommentar zum ersten Evangelium*, Calwer, Stuttgart.

Schniewind, J., 1930, 'Zur Synoptikerexegese', *Theologische Rundschau*, 2, 135-149.

Schoeps, H.J., 1949. *Theologie und Geschichte des Judenchristentums*. Mohr (Siebeck), Tübingen.

Scholtz, J.J., 2015, 'Behold the glory of the King: The chiastic structures of Matthew 21−25', *In die Skriflig*, 49(1), Art. #1856, 8 pages. http://dx.doi. org/10.4102/ids.v49i1.1856.

Schrenk, G., 1978, 'Δίκη, δίκαιος, διακοσύνη, δικαιόω, δικαίωμα, δικαίωσις, δικαιοκρισία', in G. Kittel (ed.), *Theological Dictionary of the New Testament*. pp. 178-225, Eerdmans, Michigan.

Schweizer, E., 1963, 'Matthaus 5.17-20: Anmerkungen zum Gesetzverständnis des Matthäus', *Neotestamentica*, 399-406.

Schweizer, E., 1974, 'Ψυχή in the New Testament', in G. Friedrich (ed.), *Theological Dictionary of the New Testament*, vol IX, pp. 637-656, William Eerdmans Publishing Company, Grand Rapids.

Schweizer, E., 1976, *The Good News according to Matthew*, SPCK, London.

Scullion, J.J., 1992, 'Righteousness, Old Testament', in D.L. Freedman (ed.), *The Anchor Bible Dictionary*, vol. 5, pp. 724–736, Doubleday, New York.

Segal, A.F., 1991, 'Matthew's Jewish voice', in Balch, D.L. (ed.), *Social history of the Matthean community: cross-disciplinary approaches*, pp.3-37, Fortress, Minneapolis.

Senior, D., 1998, *Matthew, Abingdon New Testament Commentaries*, Abingdon Press, Nashville.

Shanks, H., 1963, 'Is the title "Rabbi" anachronistic in the Gospels?', *Jewish Quarterly Review*, 53(4), 337-345.

Shields, M.E., 2006, 'Adultery', in K.D. Sakenfeld (ed.), *The new interpreter's dictionary of the Bible*, A-C, vol. 1, p., Abingdon Press, Nashville.

Sigal, P., 2007, *The halakhah of Jesus of Nazareth according to the gospel of Matthew*, Brill, Leiden. (Studies in Biblical Literature, 18).

Sim, D.C., 1999, *The Gospel of Matthew and Christian Judaism: The history and social setting of the Matthean Community*, T. & T. Clark, Edinburg.

Sim. D.C., 2001, 'The Gospels for all Christians? A response to Richard Bauckham', *Journal for the Study of the New Testament*, 84, 3-27.

Simmonds, A.R., 2009, '"Woe to you ... hypocrites!" Re-reading Matthew 23:13-36', *Bibliotheca Sacra*, 166, 336-349.

Smith, D.C., 1980, 'Social obligation in the context of communal meals', Th.D thesis, Harvard University.

Snodgrass, K., 1996, 'Matthew and the Law', in D.R. Bauer & M.A. Powell (eds.), *Treasures new and old: Contributions to Matthean studies,* pp. 99−127, Scholars Press, Atlanta.

Soares Prabhu, G.M., 1976, *The Formula Quotations in the infancy narrative of Matthew*, Biblical Institute Press, Rome.

Spencer, R.A., 2000, 'Mind', in D.N. Freedman, A.C. Myers & A.B. Beck (eds.), *Eerdmans Dictionary of the Bible*, p. 901, William Eerdmans Publishing Company, Grand Rapids & Cambridge.

Spicq, C., 2012, *Theological lexicon of the New Testament*, vol. 1, Hendrikson, Massachusetts.

Stanton, G.N., 1992, The communities of Matthew, *Interpretation*, 46(4), 379-391.

Stanton, G.N., 1993, *A gospel for a new people: Studies in Matthew*, T. & T. Clark, Edinburgh.

Stanton, G.N., 2013, *Studies in Matthew and early Christianity*, Mohr Siebeck, Tübingen. (WUNT 309).

Stein, R.H., 2008, *Mark. Baker exegetical commentary on the New Testament*, Baker Academic, Grand Rapids.

Stendahl, K., 1968, *The school of St. Matthew and its use of the Old Testament*, Fortress, Philadelphia.

Stonehouse, N.B., 1944, *The witness of Matthew and Mark to Christ*, Tyndale Press, London.

Stott, J.R.W., 1978, *The message of the Sermon on the Mount (Matthew 5−7): Christian counter culture*, Inter-Varsity Press, Downers Grove.

Strack, H.L. & Billerbeck, P., 1965, *Kommentar zum Neuen Testament aus Talmud und Midrasch*, Beck, München.

Strecker, G., 1971, *Der Weg der Gerechtigkeit: Untersuchung zur Theologie des Matthäus*, Vandenhoeck & Ruprecht, Göttingen.

Streeter, B.H., 1924, *The Four Gospels, a study of origins treating of the manuscript tradition, sources, authorship, & dates*, Macmillan, London.

Stuart, S., 1987, *Hosea-Jonah. Word Biblical commentary*, vol. 31, Word Books, Waco.

Stuhlmacher, P., 1966, *Gerechtigkeit Gottes Bei Paulus, Forschungen zur Religion und Literatur des Alten u*, Vandenhoeck & Ruprecht, Göttingen.

Stuhlmacher, P., 1986, *Reconciliation, law, and righteousness*, Fortress, Philadelphia.

Tagawa, K., 1970, 'People and community in the gospel of Matthew', *New Testament Studies* 16, 149-162.

Talbert, C.H., 1992, 'Biography, Ancient', in Friedman, D.N. (ed.), *The Anchor Bible Dictionary*, pp. 745-749, Doubleday, New York.

Talbert, C.H., 2010, *Matthew*, Baker Academic, Grand Rapids. (Paideia commentaries on the New Testament).

Theissen, G., 1983, *The miracle stories of the early Christian tradition*, Fortress Press, Philadelphia.

Theissen, G., 2007, *Erleben und Verhalten der Ersten Christen: Eine Psychologie des Urchristentums*, Gütersloh Verlags-Haus, Gütersloh.

Thiselton, A.C., 1979, 'Semantics in New Testament interpretation', in I.H. Marshall (ed.), *New Testament interpretation. Essays on principles and methods*, pp. 75-104, Paternoster, Exeter.

Thom, J.C., 2009, 'Justice in the Sermon on the Mount', *Novum Testamentum* 51, 314-338.

Toussaint, S.D., 1980, Behold the King: A study of Matthew, Kregel Publications, Grand Rapids.

Trilling, W., 1964, *Das wahre Israel. Studien zur Theologie des Matthäuse-Evangeliums*, Kösel-Verlag, München.

Tuckett, C., 1987, *Reading the New Testament. Methods of interpretation*, SPCK, London.

Turner, D.L., 2008, *Matthew. Baker exegetical commentary of the New Testament*, Baker academic, Michigan.

Turner, N., 1965, *Grammatical insights into the New Testament*, T. & T. Clark, Edinburgh.

Van Aarde, A., 1994, 'God-with-us: The dominant perspective in Matthew's story', *HTS Teologiese Studies/Theological Studies*, supplement 5.

Van Aarde, A., 2009, 'Narrative criticism', in A. du Toit (ed.), *Focussing on the message. New Testament hermeneutics, exegesis and methods*, pp.381-417, Protea, Pretoria.

Van Aarde, A., 2011, '"On earth as is in heaven" – Matthew's eschatology as the Kingdom of Heavens that has come', in J.G. van der Watt (ed.), *Eschatology of the New Testament and some related documents*, pp. 35-63, Mohr Siebeck, Tübingen. (WUNT (2) 315).

Van Bruggen, J., 1990, *Matteüs: het evangelie voor Israël*, Kok, Kampen. (Commentaar op het Nieuwe Testament).

Van der Walt, T., 2006, *Die Messias het gekom!*, Potchefstroomse Teologiese Publikasies, Potchefstroom.

Van der Walt, T., 2007, *The Messiah has come*, Potchefstroom Theological Publications, Potchefstroom.

Van Leeuwen, C., 1978, *De prediking van het Oude Testament; Hosea*, Callenbach, Nijkerk.

VanderKam, J.C., 2009, *The Dead Sea Scrolls today*, Eerdmans, Grand Rapids.

Vermes, G., 1975, *The Dead Sea Scrolls in English*, Penguin, New York.

Versteeg, J., 1992, *Evangelie in viervoud. Een karakteristiek van de vier evangeliën*, Kok, Kampen.

Viljoen, F.P., 2003, 'Luke, the Gospel of the Saviour of the world', *Nederduits Gereformeerde Teologiese Tydskrif*, 44(1&2), 199-209.

Viljoen, F.P., 2007, 'Fulfilment in Matthew', *Verbum et Ecclesia*, 28(1), 301-324.

Viljoen, F.P., 2008, 'The double call for joy, "Rejoice and be glad" (Matt. 5:12), as conclusion of the Matthean macarisms', *Acta Theologica*, 28(1), 205-221.

Viljoen, F.P., 2009a, 'A contextualised reading of Matthew 6:22–23: "Your eye is the lamp of your body"', *HTS Theological Studies*, 65(1), 1-5.

Viljoen, F.P., 2009b, 'Die kerk en geregtigheid in die Matteus-evangelie', *In die Skriflig (In Luce Verbi)*, 43(3), 649-667.

Viljoen, F.P., 2012a, 'Die gesag waarmee Jesus geleer het volgens Matteus 7:29', *Hervormde Teologiese Studies*, 68(1), 1-7.

Viljoen, F.P., 2012b, 'Interpreting the visio Dei in Matthew 5:8', *Hervormde Teologiese Studies*, 68(1), 1-7.

Viviano, B.T., 1990, 'Social word and community leadership: The case of Matthew 23:1-12, 34', *JSNT*, 39, 3-21.

Von Harnack, A., 1912, '"Ich bin gekommen": die ausdrücklichen Selbstzeugnisse Jesu über den Zweck seiner Sendung und seines Kommes', *Zeitschrift für Theologie und Kirche*, 22, 1-30.

Vorster, J., 2009, 'Rhetorical criticism', in A. du Toit (ed.), *Focussing on the message. New Testament hermeneutics, exegesis and methods*, pp.505-578, Protea, Pretoria.

Vouga, F., 1988, *Jésus et la Loi selon la Tradition synoptique*, Labor et Fides, Geneve.

Vriezen, T.C. & Van der Woude, A.S., 2005, *Ancient Israelite and early Jewish literature*, Brill, Leiden & Boston.

Wainwright, E.M., 1991, *Towards a critical reading or the Gospel according to Matthew*, De Gruyter, New York.

Wainwright, E.M., 1994, 'The Gospel of Matthew', in E.S. Fiorenza (ed.), *Searching the Scriptures. A Feminist commentary*, vol. 2, pp. 645-655, Cross Road, New York.

Walker, L.L., 2000, 'Heart', in D.N. Freedman, A.C. Myers & A.B. Beck (eds.), *Eerdmans Dictionary of the Bible*, p. 901, William Eerdmans Publishing Company, Grand Rapids & Cambridge.

Weiss, H., 1990, 'The Sabbath in the Synoptic Gospels', *Journal for the Study of the New Testament*, 38, 13-27.

Wellhausen, J., 1911, *Einleitung in die drei ersten Evangelien*, De Gruyter, Berlin.

Weren, W.J.C., 1979. *De broeders van de Mensenzoon: Mt 25, 31–46 als toegang tot de eschatologie van Matteus*. Bolland, Amsterdam.

Weren, W.J.C., 1994, *Belichting van het Bijbelboek; Matteüs*, Katholieke Bijbelstichting, 's-Hertogenbosch.

Weren, W.J.C., 2014, Studies in Matthew's Gospel, *Literary Design, Intertextuality, and Social Setting*, Brill, Leiden & Boston.

Westerholm, S., 1992, 'Clean and unclean', in J.B. Green & S. McKnight (eds.), *Dictionary of Jesus and the Gospels*, pp. 125-132, InterVarsity Press, Downers Grove & Leicester.

Westermann, C., 1982, *Elements of Old Testament Theology*, John Knox, Atlanta.

Wiefel, W., 1998, *Das Evangelium nach Matthäus*, Theologischer HandKommentar zum Neuen Testament, I, Evangelische Verlagsanstalt, Leipzig.

Wilkins, M.J., 1988, *The concept of disciple in Matthew's gospel as reflected in the use of the term μαθητής*, Brill, Leiden.

Wilson, B.R., 1973, *Magic and the millennium: A sociological study of religious movements of protest among tribal and Third-World peoples*, Heinemann, London.

Wilson, S.G., 1983, *Luke and the Law*, Cambridge University Press, Cambridge. (SNTSMS 50).

Wilson, A.I., 2004, *When will these things happen? A study of Jesus as judge in Matthew 21–25*, Paternoster, Milton Keynes.

Witherington, B., 2006, *Matthew, Smyth & Helwys Bible commentary*, vol. 19, Smyth & Helwys Publishing, Macon.

Witherington, B., 2013, *Invitation to the New Testament; First things*, University Press, Oxford.

Wright, A.T., 2013, 'Jewish identity, beliefs, and practices', in J.B. Green & L.M. McDonald (eds.), *The World of the New Testament. Cultural, social and historical contexts*, pp. 310-423, Baker, Michigan.

Wright, D.P., 1992a, 'Holiness (Old Testament)', in D.N. Freedman (ed.), *The Anchor Bible Dictionary*, vol. 3, pp. 237-249, Doubleday, New York, London, Toronto, Sydney & Auckland.

Wright, D.P., 1992b, 'Unclean and clean (Old Testament)', in D.N. Freedman (ed.), *The Anchor Bible Dictionary*, vol. 5, pp. 729-741, Doubleday, New York, London, Toronto, Sydney & Auckland.

Wright, D.P. & Jones, R.N., 1992a, 'Discharge', in D.N. Freedman (ed.), *The Anchor Bible Dictionary*, vol. 2, pp. 204-207, Doubleday, New York, London, Toronto, Sydney & Auckland.

Wright, D.P. & Jones, R.N., 1992b, 'Leprosy', in D.N. Freedman (ed.), *The Anchor Bible Dictionary*, vol. 4, pp. 277-282, Doubleday, New York, London, Toronto, Sydney & Auckland.

Wright, N.T., 2014. *Paul and his recent interpreters*, Ausburg, Fortress

Würthwein, E., 1978, 'Διανοία', in G. Kittel (ed.), *Theological Dictionary of the New Testament*, vol IV, pp. 963-968, William Eerdmans Publishing Company, Grand Rapids.

Yang, Y.E., 1997, *Jesus and the Sabbath in Matthew's Gospel*, Academic Press, Sheffield. (Journal for the Study of the New Testament Supplement Series 139).

Ziesler, J.A., 1972, *The meaning of righteousness in Paul*, University Press, Cambridge. (SNTS monograph series 20).

Zimmepli, W., 1985, 'Χαρις', in G. Friedrich (ed.), *Theological Dictionary of the New Testament*, vol. 9, pp. 376-402, Eerdmans, Michigan.

Theology in Africa
edited by Prof. Dr. Jan van der Watt Radboud Universieit, Nijmegen)

Marius Nel
"He Changes Times and Seasons"
Narratological-historical investigation of Daniel 1 and 2
Pentecostal interpretation of biblical texts starts with the reader experiencing the revelation of the Spirit in the biblical narrative, and leading to the reader witnessing about the spiritual experience in terms that remind of the biblical narrative. Their experience is formed by the expectation that what people in biblical times experienced is to be repeated today. Pentecostals engage in narrative theology based on and described in terms of the narrative texts in the Bible. This book suggests that in their exegetical labors, Pentecostals should consider utilizing the results of a historical analysis combined with a functional and semiotic analysis to interpret narrative texts. The methods are described before it is demonstrated at the hand of Daniel 1 and 2.
vol. 8, 2017, 450 pp., 49,90 €, br., ISBN-CH 978-3-643-90881-0

Johannes Wessels
Paul's Approach to the Cultural Conflict in Corinth
A socio-historical study
The problem of cultural conflict in congregations have been a serious challenge to the church throughout its history. Many approaches to tackling the problem of cultural intolerance and tensions have often been quite pragmatic in nature, without the presence of a solid biblical foundation or pastoral model. In this book Paul's approach as a slave-leader, emptying himself in analogy of Christ's own kenosis is thoroughly discussed, and posed as a biblical approach and solution to handling this very complex and contentious issue in churches, especially in the context of Botswana.
vol. 7, 2017, 188 pp., 34,90 €, br., ISBN-CH 978-3-643-90742-4

LIT Verlag Berlin – Münster – Wien – Zürich – London
Auslieferung Deutschland / Österreich / Schweiz: siehe Impressumsseite

Gys Loubser
Paul Cries Freedom in Galatia!
On Ethics in the New Creation
This study emphasises Paul's urgency in conveying the radical newness of life since the advent of Christ and his Spirit. Just as the Spirit introduces believers to the life in Christ, he equally leads them to live life in the faithfulness of Christ, producing the fruit of the Spirit. Paul describes this as a life of freedom from flesh and its secondi: law and the elements of the world.
Guiding believers ethically from inside and empowering them to do God's will, the Spirit has no need of law, making the christologicalpneumatological ethic of the new creation wholly anomistic.
vol. 6, 2017, 356 pp., 39,90 €, br., ISBN-CH 978-3-643-90725-7

Marius Nel
Aspects of Pentecostal Theology
Recent Developments in Africa
At the current rate of growth, some researchers predict there will be one billion Pentecostals by 2025, with most of them located in Asia, Africa, and Latin America. In this volume professor Marius Nel speaks his mind from an African perspective on what is distinctive about Pentecostal Theology in contradistinction to other theological paradigms. What makes a Pentecostal spirituality and hermeneutic different? Africa has much to contribute to the discussion of Pentecostal Theology, and this voice of Nel will not only stimulate this discussion, but will co-determine the progress and outcome.
vol. 5, 2015, 296 pp., 39,90 €, br., ISBN-CH 978-3-643-90706-6

LIT Verlag Berlin – Münster – Wien – Zürich – London
Auslieferung Deutschland / Österreich / Schweiz: siehe Impressumsseite

Marius Nel; Jan G. van der Watt; Fika J. van Rensburg (Eds.)
The New Testament in the Graeco-Roman World
Articles in Honour of Abe Malherbe
Abraham J. Malherbe (1930–2012), taught Theology of New Testament and Early Christianity at the Abilene Christian University, Dartmout, and was Buckingham Professor of New Testament Criticism and Literature Emeritus at Yale Divinity School. A member of The Society of Biblical Literature for over fifty years, Abe was a highly productive scholar who made major contributions in several areas. This book in honor of Prof. Abe Malherbe is the product of South African and international scholars honoring the memory of a great New Testament scholar working in the USA and influencing especially the country of his birth South Africa
vol. 4, 2015, 322 pp., 39,90 €, br., ISBN-CH 978-3-643-90632-8

Marius Nel
Of that Day and Hour no one knows: Mark 13 as an Apocalypse?
Many researchers accept that Mark 13 functions as an apocalypse. But does this assumption reflect the purpose of the eschatological discourse that the evangelist places in Jesus' mouth? The present work investigates Mark 13 in order to answer the question whether the evangelist also utilizes Jewish apocalypticism as the matrix to answer the four disciples' question, When will the Temple be destroyed, and what sign will there be that it is all about to take place? The study concludes that the Markan Jesus employs apocalyptic language but turns his discourse into anti-apocalyptic to address the overheated eschatological expectations of disciples at the time of the destruction of the Temple in 70 CE.
vol. 3, 2014, 456 pp., 49,90 €, br., ISBN-CH 978-3-643-90570-3

Stephan J. Joubert
Echoes of Charis
Paul's Contextual Reflections on Salvation
This study focuses on Paul's theological understanding of grace within the framework of benefaction in ancient Mediterranean world. Amidst various forms of asymmetrical reciprocal exchange, which permeated social relationships in these societies, Paul deliberately chose another path. His theological reflections on *charis*, as well as his leadership and social interactions with his churches, reflect an intentional shift away from reciprocity to *charis*, as well as from *euergetism* to selfless service. Paul's theology of *charis* introduces a fresh understanding of God who freely extends his goodness to all in Christ since all his actions are exclusively motivated by grace, not reciprocity.
vol. 2, 2014, 232 pp., 29,90 €, br., ISBN-CH 978-3-643-90547-5

Nkosinathi Ndwandwe; Elijah Mahlangu; Jan van der Watt (Eds.)
Reading the Bible in Africa
Experimenting with a hermeneutic of contextual relevance
vol. 1, 2018, ca. 200 pp., ca. 29,90 €, br., ISBN-CH 978-3-643-90482-9

LIT Verlag Berlin – Münster – Wien – Zürich – London
Auslieferung Deutschland / Österreich / Schweiz: siehe Impressumsseite